MCAT®
PHYSICS
REVIEW

Related Titles

Kaplan MCAT Biology Review*

Kaplan MCAT General Chemistry Review*

Kaplan MCAT Organic Chemistry Review*

Kaplan MCAT Physics Review*

Kaplan MCAT Verbal Reasoning Review*

Kaplan MCAT Premier

Kaplan MCAT 45

MCAT Flashcards

Get into Medical School*

Med School Rx*

Applications for iPhone

MCAT Comprehensive Flashcards

MCAT Review Notes

*Also available in eBook format

MCAT® PHYSICS REVIEW

THIRD EDITION

The Staff of Kaplan

KAPLAN PUBLISHING

New York

© 2012 by Kaplan, Inc.

Published by Kaplan Publishing, a division of Kaplan, Inc.
395 Hudson Street
New York, NY 10014

Printed in the United States of America

10 9 8 7 6 5 4 3 2

ISBN: 978-1-60978-626-7

Kaplan Publishing books are available at special quantity discounts to use for sales promotions, employee premiums, or educational purposes. For more information or to purchase books, please call the Simon & Schuster special sales department at 866-506-1949.

Contents

KAPLAN'S EXPERT MCAT TEAM

Kaplan has been preparing premeds for the MCAT for more than 40 years. In the past 15 years alone, we've helped more than 400,000 students prepare for this important exam and improve their chances for medical school admission.

Marilyn Engle

MCAT Master Teacher; Teacher Trainer; Kaplan National Teacher of the Year, 2006; Westwood Teacher of the Year, 2007; Westwood Trainer of the Year, 2007; Encino Trainer of the Year, 2005

John Michael Linick

MCAT Teacher; Boulder Teacher of the Year, 2007; Summer Intensive Program Faculty Member and Academic Director

Dr. Glen Pearlstein

MCAT Master Teacher; Teacher Trainer; Westwood Teacher of the Year, 2006

Matthew B. Wilkinson

MCAT Teacher; Teacher Trainer; Lone Star Trainer of the Year, 2007

Thanks to Jason Baserman, Jessica Brookman, Da Chang, John Cummins, David Elson, Jeff Koetje, Alex Macnow, Andrew Molloy, David Nagle, Deeangelee Pooran-Kublall, Josh Rohrig and Amjed Saffarini.

ABOUT SCIENTIFIC AMERICAN

As the world's premier science and technology magazine, and the oldest continuously published magazine in the United States, *Scientific American* is committed to bringing the most important developments in modern science, medicine, and technology to 3.5 million readers worldwide in an understandable, credible, and provocative format.

Founded in 1845 and on the "cutting edge" ever since, *Scientific American* boasts over 140 Nobel laureate authors, including Albert Einstein, Francis Crick, Stanley Prusiner, and Richard Axel. *Scientific American* is a forum where scientific theories, and discoveries are explained to a broader audience.

Scientific American published its first foreign edition in 1890 and, in 1979, was the first Western magazine published in the People's Republic of China. Today, *Scientific American* is published in 17 foreign language editions with a total circulation of more than 1 million worldwide. *Scientific American* is also a leading online destination (www.ScientificAmerican.com), providing the latest science news and exclusive features to more than 2 million unique visitors monthly.

The knowledge that fills our pages has the power to inspire, to spark new ideas, paradigms, and visions for the future. As science races forward, *Scientific American* continues to cover the promising strides, inevitable setbacks and challenges, and new medical discoveries as they unfold.

How to Use this Book

Kaplan MCAT Physics, along with the other four books in our MCAT Subject series, brings the Kaplan classroom experience to you—right in your home, at your convenience. This book offers the same Kaplan content review, strategies, and practice that make Kaplan the #1 choice for MCAT prep. All that's missing is the teacher.

To guide you through this complex content, we've consulted our best MCAT instructors to call out **Key Concepts** and **Key Equations**, to offer **Bridges** to better understanding of the material, and **Mnemonic** devices to assist in learning retention. When you see these sidebars, you will know you're getting the same insight and knowledge that classroom students receive in person. Look for these as well as references to the **Real World** and **MCAT Expertise** callouts throughout the book.

HIGH-YIELD MCAT REVIEW

Following the content section, you will find a **High-Yield Problems** section. These questions tackle the most frequently tested topics found on the MCAT. For each type of problem, you will be provided with a stepwise technique for solving the question, as well as important directional points on how to solve it—specifically for the MCAT.

Our experts have again called out the **Key Concepts**, which show you which terms to review. Next, the **Takeaways** box offers a concise summary of the problem-solving approach best used. **Things to Watch Out For** points out any caveats to the approach discussed, which can lead to wrong answer choices. Finally, **Similar Questions** allows you to practice the stepwise technique on analogous, open-ended questions. Please note that answers to the Similar Questions follow the High-Yield Problems section of your book.

STAR RATING

The star rating is a Kaplan-exclusive system to help you focus your studies, using a 6-star scale. Two factors are considered when determining the rating for each topic: the "learnability" of the topic—or how easy it is to master—and the frequency with which it appears on the MCAT exam. For example, a topic that presents relatively little difficulty to master and appears with relatively high frequency on the MCAT would receive a higher star rating (e.g., 5 or 6 stars) than a topic that is very difficult to master and appears less frequently on the test. The combination of these two factors represented by the star rating will help you prioritize and direct your MCAT studies.

We're confident that this guide and our award-winning instructors can help you achieve your goals of MCAT success and admission to med school. Good luck!

Introduction to the MCAT

The Medical College Admission Test (MCAT) is different from any other test you've encountered in your academic career. The knowledge-based exams you took in high school and college placed an emphasis on memorizing and regurgitating information. However, medical schools can assess your academic prowess by looking at your transcript. The MCAT isn't like other standardized tests you may have taken, where the focus was on assessing your general skills.

Medical schools use MCAT scores to assess whether you possess the foundation upon which to build a successful medical career. Though you certainly need to master the content to do well, the stress is on the thought process, because the MCAT is, above all else, a critical thinking test. That's why it emphasizes reasoning, analytical thinking, reading comprehension, data analysis, and problem-solving skills.

The MCAT places more weight on your thought process, but you must have a strong grasp of the required core material. The MCAT is not a perfect gauge of your abilities, but it is a relatively objective way to compare you with students from different backgrounds and undergraduate institutions.

The MCAT's power comes from its use as an indicator of your abilities. Strong scores can open doors. Your advantage comes from sound preparation and a focused mindset, as the key to MCAT success is knowing what you're up against. That's where this section of this book comes in. We'll explain the philosophy behind the test, review the sections one by one, show you sample questions, share some of Kaplan's proven methods, and clue you in to what the test makers are really after. You'll get a handle on the process, find a confident new perspective, and achieve your highest possible scores by MCAT Test Day. Let's get started.

ABOUT THE MCAT

Information about the MCAT CBT (Computer-Based Test) is included below. For the latest information about the MCAT, visit **www.kaptest.com/mcat**.

MCAT CBT

Format	U.S.—All administrations on computer
	International—Most on computer with limited paper and pencil in a few isolated areas
Breaks	Optional break between each section
Length of MCAT Day	Approximately 5.5 hours
Test Dates	Multiple dates in January, April, May, June, July, August, and September
	About 24 administrations each year.
Delivery of Results	Within 30 days. If scores are delayed notification will be posted online at www.aamc.org/mcat
	Electronic and paper
Security	Government-issued ID
	Electronic thumbprint
	Electronic signature verification
Testing Centers	Small computer testing sites

PLANNING FOR THE TEST

As you look toward your preparation for the MCAT, consider the following advice:

Complete your core course requirements as soon as possible. Take a strategic eye to your schedule, consult with your pre-health advisor, and get core requirements out of the way earlier rather than later.

Take the MCAT once. The MCAT is a notoriously grueling standardized exam that requires extensive preparation. It is longer than the graduate admissions exams for business school (GMAT) law school (LSAT), and graduate school (GRE), which are all about 3.5 hours long. You want to do well the first time–so that it's your last MCAT administration. Plan and prepare accordingly.

THE ROLE OF THE MCAT IN ADMISSIONS

More people are applying to medical school, so that means more people are taking the MCAT. It's important for you to recognize that while a high MCAT score is a critical component of gaining admission to a top-ranked medical school, it's not the only factor. Medical school admission officers weigh your grades, interviews, MCAT scores, level of involvement in extracurricular activities, as well as personal essays.

In a Kaplan survey of 130 pre-med advisors, 84 percent called the interview a "very important" part of the admissions process, followed closely by college grades (83%) and MCAT scores (76%). Kaplan's college admissions consulting practice works with students on all of these issues so that they can position themselves as strongly as possible. In addition, the AAMC has made it clear that scores will continue to be valid for a three year time period.

REGISTRATION

The only way to register for the MCAT is online. The registration site is: www.aamc.org/mcat.

You should access the site approximately six months before your test date. Payment must be made by MasterCard or Visa.

Go to www.aamc.org/mcat/registration.htm and download *MCAT Essentials* for information about registration, fees, test administration, and preparation. For other questions, contact:

MCAT Care Team
Association of American Medical Colleges
Section for Applicant Assessment Services
2450 N. St., NW
Washington, DC 20037
www.aamc.org/mcat
Email: mcat@aamc.org

Keep in mind that you will need to take the MCAT the year prior to your planned medical school start date. For example, if you are on a four-year plan at your institution, you would take your MCAT during your junior year, in preparation for applications and interviews during your senior year. Don't drag your feet gathering information. You'll need time not only to prepare and practice for the test, but also to get all of your registration work completed.

The MCAT should be viewed just like any other part of your application: This is an opportunity to show the medical schools who you are and what you can do. Take control of your MCAT experience.

ANATOMY OF THE MCAT

Before mastering strategies, you need to know exactly what you're dealing with on the MCAT. Let's start with the basics: The MCAT is, among other things, an endurance test.

Approach it with confidence and stamina, so that you don't lose your composure. To succeed, you need to be in control of the test.

The MCAT consists of four separately timed sections, three of which include Physical Sciences, Verbal Reasoning, and Biological Sciences. Starting in January 2013 and continuing through 2014, the Writing Sample will no longer be a part of the MCAT administration. If you do take the test in 2012, your Writing Sample score will be valid for the next 3 years. In its place, a voluntary, unscored trial section will be added. What does this mean for you? This experimental section won't affect your overall score, but it's something to be prepared for before Test Day. Topics including psychology, sociology, and biochemistry will be trial-tested, and starting in 2015, they will count as a score-qualifying section. All of the testing times will remain the same in 2013 and 2014. Later in this section we'll take an in-depth look at each MCAT section, including sample question types and specific test-smart hints, but here's a general overview, reflecting the order of the test sections and number of questions in each.

Physical Sciences

Time	70 minutes
Format	• 52 multiple-choice questions: approximately 7–9 passages with 4–8 questions each • approximately 10 stand-alone questions (not passage-based)
What it tests	basic general chemistry concepts, basic physics concepts, analytical reasoning, data interpretation

Verbal Reasoning

Time	60 minutes
Format	• 40 multiple-choice questions: approximately 7 passages with 5–7 questions each
What it tests	critical reading

Biological Sciences

Time	70 minutes
Format	• 52 multiple-choice questions: approximately 7–9 passages with 4–8 questions each • approximately 10 stand-alone questions (not passage-based)
What it tests	basic biology concepts, basic organic chemistry concepts, analytical reasoning, data interpretation

Experimental Section

Time	60 minutes
Format	• Trial multiple choice questions (UNSCORED) • What it tests
	psychology, sociology, and biochemistry

KAPLAN

The sections of the test always appear in the same order:

Physical Sciences
[optional 10-minute break]
Verbal Reasoning
[optional 10-minute break]
Biological Sciences
[optional 10-minute break]
Experimental Section

SCORING

Each MCAT section receives its own score. Physical Sciences, Verbal Reasoning, and Biological Sciences are each scored on a scale ranging from 1–15, with 15 as the highest. In 2013 or 2014, the Writing Sample will be replaced by an experimental, unscored section. Starting in 2015, topics such as psychology, sociology, and biochemistry will be tested in a new scored section, once again on a scale of 1–15.

The number of multiple-choice questions that you answer correctly per section is your "raw score." Your raw score will then be converted to yield the "scaled score"—one that will fall in the 1–15 range. These scaled scores are reported to medical schools as your official MCAT scores. All multiple-choice questions are worth the same amount—one raw point—and ***there's no penalty for guessing***. That means that *you should always select an answer for every question, whether you get to that question or not!* This is an important piece of advice that you shouldn't forget. Never let time run out on any section without selecting an answer for every question.

The raw score of each administration is converted to a scaled score. The conversion varies with administrations. Hence, the same raw score will not always give you the same scaled score.

Your score report will tell you and your potential medical schools not only your scaled scores, but also the national mean score for each section, standard deviation, national scoring profile for each section, and your percentile ranking.

WHAT'S A GOOD SCORE?

There's no such thing as a cut-and-dry "good score." Much depends on the strength of the rest of your application (if your college GPA is near a 4.0, the pressure to score high on the MCAT is less intense) and on where you want to go to school (different schools have different score expectations). Here are a few interesting statistics:

For each MCAT administration, the average scaled scores are approximately 8s for Physical Sciences, Verbal Reasoning, and Biological Sciences. You need scores of at least 10–11s to be considered competitive by most medical schools, and if you're aiming for a top-tier medical school (Harvard, Yale, Johns Hopkins, etc.), you need to perform at a higher level, with scores of 12s and above in each of the sections. However, you will also need strong recommendation letters, volunteer/research experience, and a good GPA as well.

Here's the bottom line: you don't have to be perfect to do well. For instance, on the AAMC's Practice Test 5R, you can get as many as 10 questions wrong in Verbal Reasoning, 17 in Physical Sciences, and 16 in Biological Sciences and still score in the 80th percentile. To score in the 90th percentile, you can get as many as 7 wrong in Verbal Reasoning, 12 in Physical Sciences, and 12 in Biological Sciences. Even students who receive "perfect" (raw score: 45) scaled scores get a handful of questions wrong.

With that being said, it's important to maximize your performance on every question. Just a few questions one way or the other can make a big difference in your scaled score. Here's a look at recent score profiles so you can get an idea of the shape of a typical score distribution.

Physical Sciences		
Scaled Score	Percent Achieving Score	Percentile Rank Range
15	0.1	99.9–99.9
14	1.2	98.7–99.8
13	2.5	96.2–98.6
12	5.1	91.1–96.1
11	7.2	83.9–91.0
10	12.1	71.8–83.8
9	12.9	58.9–71.1
8	16.5	42.4–58.5
7	16.7	25.7–42.3
6	13.0	12.7–25.6
5	7.9	04.8–12.6
4	3.3	01.5–04.7
3	1.3	00.2–01.4
2	0.1	00.1–00.1
1	0.0	00.0–00.0
Scaled Score Mean = 8.1 Standard Deviation = 2.32		

Verbal Reasoning		
Scaled Score	Percent Achieving Score	Percentile Rank Range
15	0.1	99.9–99.9
14	0.2	99.7–99.8
13	1.8	97.9–99.6
12	3.6	94.3–97.8
11	10.5	83.8–94.2
10	15.6	68.2–83.7
9	17.2	51.0–68.1
8	15.4	35.6–50.9
7	10.3	25.3–35.5
6	10.9	14.4–25.2
5	6.9	07.5–14.3
4	3.9	03.6–07.4
3	2.0	01.6–03.5
2	0.5	00.1–01.5
1	0.0	00.0–00.0
Scaled Score Mean = 8.0 Standard Deviation = 2.43		

KAPLAN

Biological Sciences		
Scaled Score	Percent Achieving Score	Percentile Rank Range
15	0.1	99.9–99.9
14	1.2	98.7–99.8
13	2.5	96.2–98.6
12	5.1	91.1–96.1
11	7.2	83.9–91.0
10	12.1	71.8–83.8
9	12.9	58.9–71.1
8	16.5	42.4–58.5
7	16.7	25.7–42.3
6	13.0	12.7–25.6
5	7.9	04.8–12.6
4	3.3	01.5–04.7
3	1.3	00.2–01.4
2	0.1	00.1–00.1
1	0.0	00.0–00.0
Scaled Score Mean = 8.2 Standard Deviation = 2.39		

WHAT THE MCAT REALLY TESTS

It's important to grasp not only the nuts and bolts of the MCAT, so you'll know *what* to do on Test Day, but also the underlying principles of the test so you'll know *why* you're doing what you're doing on Test Day. We'll cover the straightforward MCAT facts later. Now it's time to examine the heart and soul of the MCAT, to see what it's really about.

THE MYTH

Most people preparing for the MCAT fall prey to the myth that the MCAT is a straightforward science test. They think something like this:

> *"It covers the four years of science I had to take in school: biology, chemistry, physics, and organic chemistry. It even has equations. OK, so it has Verbal Reasoning but that is just to see if we're literate, right? The important stuff is the science. After all, we're going to be doctors."*

Well, here's the little secret no one seems to want you to know: The MCAT is not just a science test; it's more importantly a critical thinking test. This means that the test is designed to let you demonstrate your thought process in addition to your thought content.

The implications are vast. Once you shift your test-taking paradigm to match the MCAT modus operandi, you'll find a new level of confidence and control over the test. You'll begin to work symbiotically with the MCAT rather than against it. You'll be more efficient and insightful as you prepare for the test, and as a result, you'll be more relaxed on Test Day. In fact, you'll be able to see the MCAT for what it is rather than for what it's dressed up to be. We want your Test Day to feel like a visit with a familiar friend instead of an awkward blind date.

THE ZEN OF MCAT

Medical schools do not need to rely on the MCAT to see what you already know. Admission committees can measure your subject-area proficiency using your undergraduate coursework and grades. Schools are most interested in the potential of your mind.

In recent years, many medical schools have shifted pedagogic focus away from an information-heavy curriculum to a concept-based curriculum. There is currently more emphasis placed on problem solving, holistic thinking, and cross-disciplinary study. Be careful not to dismiss this important point, figuring you'll wait to worry about academic trends until you're actually in medical school. This trend affects you right now, because it's reflected in the MCAT. Every good tool matches its task. In this case the tool is the test, used to measure you and other candidates, and the task is to quantify how likely it is that you'll succeed in medical school.

Your intellectual potential—how skillfully you annex new territory into your mental boundaries, how quickly you build "thought highways" between ideas, how confidently and creatively you solve problems—is far more important to admission committees than your ability to recite Young's modulus for every material known to humankind. The schools assume they can expand your knowledge base. They choose applicants carefully because expansive knowledge is not enough to succeed in medical school or in the profession. There's something more. It's this "something more" that the MCAT is trying to measure.

Every section on the MCAT essentially tests the same higher-order thinking skills: analytical reasoning, abstract thinking, and problem solving. Most test takers get trapped into thinking they are being tested strictly on biology, chemistry, and so on. Thus, they approach each section with a new outlook on what's expected. This constant mental gear-shifting can be exhausting, not to mention counterproductive. Instead of perceiving the test as parsed into radically different sections, you need to maintain your focus on the underlying nature of the test: It's designed to test your thinking skills, rather than your information-recall skills. Each test section presents a variation on the same theme.

WHAT ABOUT THE SCIENCE?

With this perspective, you may be left asking these questions: "What about the science? What about the content? Don't I need to know the basics?" The answer is a resounding "Yes!" You must be fluent in the different languages of the test. You cannot do well on the MCAT if you don't know the basics of physics, general chemistry, biology, and organic chemistry. We recommend that you take at least one year each of biology, general chemistry, organic chemistry, and physics before taking the MCAT, and that you review the content in this book thoroughly. Also, starting in 2015, the MCAT will test the basic principles of biochemistry, so we also recommend at least one semester of biochemistry or its equivalent. Knowing these basics is just the beginning of doing well on the MCAT. That's a shock to most test takers. Often, students presume that once they recall or relearn their undergraduate science, they are ready to do battle against the MCAT, but that is wrong! They merely have directions to the battlefield. They lack what they need to beat the test: a copy of the test maker's battle plan!

You won't be drilled on facts and formulas on the MCAT. You'll need to demonstrate ability to reason based on ideas and concepts. The science questions are painted with a broad brush, testing your general understanding.

TAKE CONTROL: THE MCAT MINDSET

In addition to being a thinking test, as we've stressed, the MCAT is a standardized test. As such, it has its own consistent patterns and idiosyncrasies that can actually work in your favor. This is the key to why test preparation works. You have the opportunity to familiarize yourself with those consistent peculiarities, to adopt the proper test-taking mindset.

The following are some overriding principles of the MCAT mindset that will be covered in depth in the chapters to come:

- Read actively and critically.
- Translate prose into your own words.
- Save the toughest questions for last.
- Know the test and its components inside and out.
- Do MCAT-style problems in each topic area after you've reviewed it.
- Allow your confidence to build on itself.
- Take full-length practice tests a week or two before the test to break down the mystique of the real experience.
- Review and learn from your mistakes—get the most out of your practice tests.
- Look at the MCAT as a challenge, the first step in your medical career, rather than as an arbitrary obstacle.

That's what the MCAT mindset boils down to: taking control. Being proactive. Being on top of the testing experience so that you can get as many points as you can as quickly and as easily as possible. Keep this in mind as you read and work through the material in this book and, of course, as you face the challenge on Test Day.

Now that you have a better idea of what the MCAT is all about, let's take a tour of the individual test sections. Although the underlying skills being tested are similar, each MCAT section requires that you call into play a different domain of knowledge. So, although we encourage you to think of the MCAT as a holistic and unified test, we also recognize that the test is segmented by discipline and that there are characteristics unique to each section. In the overviews, we'll review sample questions and answers and discuss section-specific strategies. For each of the sections—Verbal Reasoning, Physical/Biological Sciences—we'll present you with the following:

- **The Big Picture**
  You'll get a clear view of the section and familiarize yourself with what it's really evaluating.
- **A Closer Look**
  You'll explore the types of questions that will appear and master the strategies you'll need to deal with them successfully.
- **Highlights**
  The key approaches to each section are outlined, for reinforcement and quick review.

TEST EXPERTISE

The first year of medical school is a frenzied experience for most students. In order to meet the requirements of a rigorous work schedule, students either learn to prioritize and budget their time or else fall hopelessly behind. It's no surprise, then, that the MCAT, the test specifically designed to predict success in the first year of medical school, is a high-speed, time-intensive test. It demands excellent time-management skills as well as that sine qua non of the successful physician—grace under pressure.

It's one thing to answer a Verbal Reasoning question correctly; it's quite another to answer several correctly in a limited time frame. The same goes for Physical and Biological Sciences—it's a whole new ballgame once you move from doing an individual passage at your leisure to handling a full section under actual timed conditions. When it comes to the multiple-choice sections, time pressure is a factor that affects virtually every test taker.

So when you're comfortable with the content of the test, your next challenge will be to take it to the next level—test expertise—which will enable you to manage the all-important time element of the test.

THE FIVE BASIC PRINCIPLES OF TEST EXPERTISE

On some tests, if a question seems particularly difficult you'll spend significantly more time on it, as you'll probably be given more points for correctly answering a hard question. This isn't true for the MCAT. Remember, every MCAT question, no matter how easy or hard, is worth a single point. There's no partial credit or "A" for effort, and because there are many questions to do in a timed-section, it would be foolish to spend 10 minutes on one question and miss an opportunity for easy points later on.

Given this combination—limited time, all questions equal in weight—you must develop a game plan to attack each of the test sections to make sure you get as many points as quickly and easily as you can. Here are the principles that will help you do that.

1. FEEL FREE TO SKIP AROUND

One of the most valuable strategies to help you finish the sections in time is to learn to recognize and deal first with the questions that are easier and more familiar to you. That means you must temporarily skip those that promise to be more challenging and time-consuming, if you feel comfortable doing so. You can always come back to these at the end, and if you run out of time, you're much better off not getting to questions you may have had difficulty with, rather than missing out on quick points on Test Day. Of course, because there's no guessing penalty, always click on an answer to every question on the test, whether you get to it or not.

This strategy is difficult for most test takers; we're conditioned to do things in order. Nevertheless, give it a try when you practice. If you take the test in the exact order given, you're letting the test makers control you. YOU control how you take this test. On the other hand, if skipping around goes against your moral fiber and makes you a nervous wreck—don't do it. Just be mindful of the clock, and don't get bogged down with the tough questions.

2. LEARN TO RECOGNIZE AND SEEK OUT QUESTIONS YOU CAN DO

Another thing to remember about managing the test sections is that MCAT questions and passages are not presented in order of difficulty, unlike items on the SAT and other standardized tests. There's no rule that says you have to work through the sections in any particular order; in fact, the test makers scatter the easy and difficult questions throughout the section, in effect rewarding those who actually get to the end. Don't lose sight of what you're being tested on along with your reading and thinking skills: efficiency and cleverness.

Don't waste time on questions you can't complete with the time constraints. We know that skipping a tough question is easier said than done; we all have the natural instinct to plow through test sections in their given order, but this strategy doesn't pay off on the MCAT. The computer won't be impressed if you get the toughest question right. If you dig in your heels on a tough question, refusing to move on until you've cracked it, well, you're letting your ego get in the way of your test score. A test section (not to mention life itself) is too short to waste on lost causes.

3. USE A PROCESS OF ANSWER ELIMINATION

Using a process of elimination is another way to answer questions both quickly and effectively. There are two ways to get all the answers right on the MCAT. You either know all the right answers, or you know all the wrong answers. Because there are three times as many wrong answers, you should be able to eliminate some if not all of them. By doing so you either get to the correct response or increase your chances of guessing the correct response. You start out with a 25 percent chance of picking the right answer, and with each eliminated answer, your odds go up. Eliminate one, and you'll have a $33\frac{1}{3}$ percent chance of picking the right one; eliminate two, and you'll have a 50 percent chance; and, of course, eliminate three, and you'll have a 100 percent chance. Increase your efficiency by crossing out the wrong choices on the screen with the strike-through feature, using the right-click button on the mouse. Look for wrong-answer traps when you're eliminating. Some answers are designed to seduce you by distorting the correct answer.

4. REMAIN CALM

It's imperative that you remain calm and composed while working through a section. You can't allow yourself to become so rattled by one challenging passage that it throws off your performance on the rest of the section. Expect to find at least one passage like this in every section, but bear in mind that you won't be the only one to have trouble with it. The test is curved, taking this tough material into account. A difficult question isn't going to ruin your score—but getting upset about it and letting it throw you off track will. When you understand that part of the test maker's goal is to reward those who keep their composure, you'll recognize the importance of not panicking when you run into challenging material.

5. KEEP TRACK OF TIME

Of course, the last thing you want to happen is to have time called on a particular section before you've gotten to half the questions. Therefore, it's essential that you pace yourself, keeping in mind the general guidelines for how long to spend on any individual question or passage. Have a sense of how long you have to do each question, so you know when you're exceeding the limit and should start to move faster.

Always keep track of time. We'll talk more about strategies for this in your MCAT course. You don't want to fall into the trap of spending a disproportionate amount of time on any one question or group of questions. Also, give yourself about a minute or so at the end of each section to fill in answers for any questions you haven't gotten to.

SECTION-SPECIFIC PACING

Now, let's look at the section-specific timing requirements and some tips for meeting them. Keep in mind that the times per question or passage are only averages; there will be questions that take less time, and others that take more. Try to stay balanced. Since every question is weighed equally, don't spend more than a minute on any one.

VERBAL REASONING

Allow yourself approximately eight to ten minutes per passage and corresponding questions. It may sound like a lot of time, but it goes by quickly. Also, keep in mind that some passages are longer than others. On average, give yourself about three or four minutes to read and then four to six minutes for the questions.

PHYSICAL AND BIOLOGICAL SCIENCES

Averaging over each section, you'll have about one minute and 20 seconds per question. Some questions, of course, will take more time, and some less. A science passage plus accompanying questions should take about eight to nine minutes, depending on how many questions there are. Stand-alone questions can take anywhere from a few seconds to a minute. Again, the rule is to do your best work first. Also, don't feel that you have to understand everything word-for-word in a passage before you move on to the questions. You may not need a deep understanding to answer the questions because some information in the passage can be extraneous. Overcome your perfectionism and use your time wisely.

COMPUTER-BASED TESTING STRATEGIES

ARRIVE AT THE TESTING CENTER EARLY

Get to the testing center early to jump-start your brain. However, if they allow you to begin your test early, decline.

USE THE MOUSE TO YOUR ADVANTAGE

If you are right-handed, practice using the mouse with your left hand for Test Day. This way, you'll increase speed by keeping the pencil in your right hand to write on your scratch paper. If you are left-handed, use your right hand for the mouse.

KNOW THE TUTORIAL BEFORE TEST DAY

You will save time on Test Day by knowing exactly how the test will work. Click through any tutorial pages on practice tests and familiarize yourself with them, and on Test Day you will save time.

PRACTICE WITH SCRATCH PAPER

Going forward, always practice using scratch paper when solving questions because this is how you will do it on Test Day. Never write directly on a written test.

REMEMBER YOU CAN ALWAYS GO BACK

Just because you finish a passage or move on, remember you can come back to questions about which you are uncertain. You have the "marking" option to your advantage. However, as a general rule try not to mark up more than one question per passage.

MARK INCOMPLETE WORK

If you need to go back to a question, clearly mark the work you've done on the scratch paper with the question number. This way, you will be able to find your work easily when you come back to tackle the question.

LOOK AWAY AT TIMES

Taking the test on computer leads to faster eye-muscle fatigue. Use the Kaplan strategy of looking at a distant object at regular intervals. This will keep your mind alert throughout the test.

PRACTICE ON THE COMPUTER

This is the *most critical* aspect of adapting to computer-based testing. Like anything else, in order to perform well on computer-based tests, you must practice. Spend time reading passages and answering questions on the computer. You often will have to scroll when reading passages.

Part I
Review

Units and Kinematics

In this chapter:

Introduction

A professor once said, "Biology is chemistry. Chemistry is physics. Physics is life." Not surprisingly, this was the claim of a physics professor.

Then I went to medical school, and I grew up—and I came to understand what, exactly, that professor meant. I learned that when we treat patients at the rehab hospital, we often talk about motion, forces, and bone strength. An ophthalmologist had me draw ray diagrams to help me better understand myopia and presbyopia. When we talk about mitochondria functioning as the "batteries" of the cell, we mean that literally.

Physics is all around us. The first order of business is to make sure that you begin your preparation for the MCAT with the right attitude. Kaplan's integrated focus on science content, critical-thinking skills, and Test Day strategies is the key to building confidence. That confidence leads to Test Day success.

This first chapter reviews the three systems of units encountered on the MCAT, namely, MKS (meter-kilogram-second), CGS (centimeter-gram-second), and SI (International System of Units). Then we'll review the fundamental mathematics necessary for the study of MCAT Physics, such as scientific notation, trigonometric functions, and vectors. Finally, we consider an important branch of Newtonian mechanics (Chapter 2) that deals with the motion of objects: kinematics.

10^{26} meter:
Observable
universe

10^{21} meter:
Milky Way galaxy

10^{13} meter:
Solar system

10^7 meter:
Earth

10^{-2} meter:
Insect

10^{-10} meter:
Atom

10^{-15} meter:
Atomic nucleus

10^{-18} meter:
Smallest distance
probed by particle
accelerators

10^{-18} to 10^{-35} meter:
Typical size of
fundamental strings
and of extra dimensions

10^{-35} meter:
Minimum meaningful
length in nature

**Figure 1.1. Size In Meters
of Natural Phenomena**

1.1 Units

Physics relies on the language of mathematics to convey important descriptions and explanations of the world around us. Yet those numbers would themselves be meaningless, or confusing at best, without the labels of units. **Units** give context to numbers, and from that context comes meaning.

FUNDAMENTAL MEASUREMENTS AND DIMENSIONS

Over the years, various systems of units have been developed. Some of these systems are used commonly in everyday life but rarely in science. The **British system** (foot-pound-second) is used commonly in the United States but virtually nowhere else—not even in Britain. Basic units for length, weight, and time are the foot (ft), the pound (lb), and the second (s), respectively. The MCAT does not utilize FPS in passages or questions.

The most common system of units is the metric system, which is the basis for the SI units that you will encounter on the MCAT. In the **metric system,** the unit for length is either the centimeter (cm) or the meter (m), the unit for mass (rather than weight) is the gram (g) or kilogram (kg), and the unit for time is the second (s). The **SI system** (which is also sometimes called the MKS system) uses the base units of meter, kilogram, and second, as well as ampere (A) for current, kelvin (K) for temperature, joule (J) for energy, candela (c) for luminosity, and mole (mol) for amount of substance.

Table 1.1 lists some important units in the systems described. Please note that the MCAT will provide conversion factors as needed, except for the most basic units (e.g., meters to centimeters or hours to seconds).

Table 1.1. Important Units in Various Systems of Measurement

Quantity	CGS	SI	FPS
Length	centimeter (cm)	meter (m)	foot (ft)
Mass	gram (g)	kilogram (kg)	slug (sl)
Force	dyne (dyn)	newton (N)	pound (lb)
Time	second (s)	second (s)	second (s)
Work & Energy	erg	joule (J)	foot-pound (ft • lb)
Power	erg/second	watt (W)	foot-pound/sec

At the molecular, atomic, or subatomic level, the extremely small scale of size and interactions can be expressed using different units that are easier to work with. Useful length units on the atomic scale include the angstrom ($1\text{Å} = 10^{-10}$ m) and the nanometer (1 nm = 10^{-9} m). Energy on the atomic scale can be expressed in the unit of the electron-volt (1 eV = 1.6×10^{-19} J). One electron-volt is the amount of energy gained by an electron accelerating through a potential difference of one volt. This may not make intuitive sense, but think of it as analogous to defining a unit of energy as the amount of kinetic energy associated with a unit of mass falling through a unit of displacement.

Converting from kilometers to meters to centimeters requires only knowing the power of 10 that separates them. Prefixes are added to the base units in the metric system to make very big and very small numbers easier to handle. Tables 1.2 and 1.3 list prefixes commonly encountered on the MCAT.

MCAT Expertise

While the various systems of measurement are good to be aware of, the only system that you are required to know for the MCAT is the SI system.

Table 1.2. Multiples

factor	prefix	prefix abbreviation
10^9	giga	G (or B)
10^6	mega	M
10^3	kilo	k

Table 1.3. Submultiples

factor	prefix	prefix abbreviation
10^{-2}	centi	c
10^{-3}	milli	m
10^{-6}	micro	μ
10^{-9}	nano	n
10^{-12}	pico	p

One challenge that some U.S.-educated students encounter is difficulty in developing an intuitive sense of the metric system. Although the MCAT will not require you to work with or convert to or from FPS, you may find it beneficial to practice some conversions from FPS to metric so that on Test Day you will be more confident in your ability to assess the reasonability of numbers in metric units. (Often you will be able to eliminate numerical answer choices because they are either too big or too small to be reasonable.) For the kind of practice that we are suggesting, see the Real World sidebar on this page.

Real World

At the time of this writing, the cost of gas in the United States is about $3/gallon. A lot of people complain about the price of gas, yet few raise an eyebrow when paying $2 for a two-liter bottle of cola at the grocery store. *What's the big deal?* you say. *Doesn't that work out to about the same as that gallon of gas, maybe even less?* Well, how many liters are there in one gallon? One-and-a-half? Two? Two-and-a-half? Actually, there are almost four liters in one gallon. The conversion is 3.785 liters per gallon! That two-liter bottle of cola that you just bought for $2 is costing you $3.79 per gallon (plus the bottle deposit)!

MCAT Concept Check 1.1

Before moving on, ensure that you are able to:

✓ Define the common SI units

✓ Convert between common multiples and submultiples of units

1.2 Scientific Notation

Scientific notation is a convention for expressing numbers that simplifies calculations and standardizes the results. Very large or very small numbers can become unwieldy. To express any number in scientific notation, convert it into a number between 1 and 10 by moving the decimal to the right or left, then multiply it by 10 raised to the appropriate power. The value of the power is determined by the number of places the decimal was moved. The number before the power of 10 is called the *significand*.

$$0.0000000004 = 4 \times 10^{-10}$$
$$500,000,000,000,000 = 5 \times 10^{14}$$

Expressed in scientific notion, numbers can easily be multiplied or divided. When multiplying, simply multiply the significands and then add the exponents.

> **Example:** $(4 \times 10^{-10})(5 \times 10^{14}) = ?$
>
> **Process:** Multiply 4 by 5 and add the exponents.
>
> **Answer:** $20 \times 10^4 = 2 \times 10^5$

To divide numbers in scientific notation, divide the significand in the numerator by the significand in the denominator. Then, subtract the exponent in the denominator from the exponent in the numerator.

> **Example:** $\dfrac{4 \times 10^{-10}}{5 \times 10^{14}} = ?$
>
> **Process:** Divide 4 by 5 and subtract 14 from −10.
> Note: $(-10) - (14) = (-10) + (-14) = -24$
>
> **Answer:** $0.8 \times 10^{-24} = 8 \times 10^{-25}$

When a number expressed in scientific notation is raised to a power, the significand is raised to that power and the exponent is multiplied by that number.

Example: $(6.0 \times 10^4)^2$

Solution: Square the 6.0 and multiply the exponent by 2.

$$(6.0)^2 \times 10^{4 \times 2} = 36.0 \times 10^8 = 3.6 \times 10^9$$

(Note that when we move the decimal point one place to the left, we must increase the power of 10 by one, from 8 to 9.)

When numbers expressed in scientific notation are added or subtracted, they must have the same exponent. If they do not, you must first convert one of the numbers so that both are to the same power of 10.

Example: $3.7 \times 10^4 + 1.5 \times 10^3 = ?$

Solution: First convert 1.5×10^3 to 0.15×10^4 so both numbers have the same exponent. Then $3.7 \times 10^4 + 0.15 \times 10^4 = 3.85 \times 10^4$, which is rounded to 3.9×10^4.

> **MCAT Expertise**
>
> The MCAT is a timed test without a calculator; being able to do math quickly by hand is an essential skill. As said before, this is often aided by rounding, though we can often manipulate the numbers to make the math easier without rounding.

Let us take a moment to encourage you to appreciate the value of practicing scientific notation. You will without a doubt perform more strongly on the Physical Science section of the MCAT if you are proficient in its use. Many calculations that you would normally do with a calculator must be done by hand on Test Day. Remember, no calculators are allowed into the testing room, so you must become adept at working out calculations by hand on your scratch paper.

MCAT Concept Check 1.2

Before moving on, ensure that you are able to:

✓ Multiply, divide, add, subtract, and calculate exponents and roots using scientific notation

---

1.3 Trigonometric Relations ★★☆☆☆☆

Another mathematical concept essential for strong performance in the Physical Science section is the ratio relationship between the sides of right triangles. Knowing these ratios will save you a lot of time on Test Day; expect to use them often. There are several "classic angles" that the MCAT tends to use in the setup of a problem.

Mnemonic

Remember learning SOH("so"), CAH("ca"), TOA("toe-a") in high school? SOH = Sine is Opposite over Hypotenuse; CAH = Cosine is Adjacent over Hypotenuse; TOA = Tangent is Opposite over Adjacent.

Table 1.4 lists some important angles and the values of their trigonometric functions.

θ	$\sin \theta$	$\cos \theta$
0°	0	1
30°	$\dfrac{1}{2}$	$\dfrac{\sqrt{3}}{2}$
45°	$\dfrac{\sqrt{2}}{2}$	$\dfrac{\sqrt{2}}{2}$
60°	$\dfrac{\sqrt{3}}{2}$	$\dfrac{1}{2}$
90°	1	0
180°	0	−1

Table 1.4. Trigonometric Functions

MCAT Concept Check 1.3

Before moving on, ensure that you are able to:

✓ Quickly identify the cosine and sine of the common angles used on Test Day

1.4 Logarithms

MCAT Expertise

Because you don't have calculators on the MCAT, you will be able to solve any of the problems on Test Day by using either the Pythagorean theorem or the values of sine and cosine shown in Table 1.4. It will also be to your advantage to remember a few of the most common Pythagorean triples, such as 3:4:5 or 5:12:13.

All the math necessary for any calculation problem will have to be done by hand, using your scratch paper. (Avoid doing math "in your head" to minimize the risk of introducing errors into your calculations.) On the other hand, the MCAT is not a math test. The MCAT test writers aren't interested in testing you on difficult mathematical manipulations simply for the sake of testing your ability "to do the math." What they want to find out is if you know *how* and *when* to use the math. You can rest assured that the numbers used on Test Day will have been chosen for their manageability, allowing for evaluation of your understanding of the concepts and principles themselves, not simply your ability to work with difficult numbers or calculations.

What you need to know about logarithms are the basics and a few helpful rules. The **logarithm** of a number for a given base is simply the power to which that base must be raised to equal that number. In other words, a base raised by some power will equal a number, and that power is the logarithm of that number for that particular base. The base can be any positive number, but the two most common bases are 10 and *e*.

The base of 10 is so common that it is called the "common log" and any time you see *log* you should assume the base-10 log. When you see *ln*, which stands for "natural log" and is pronounced "ell-enn," you will need to use the value of *e*.

Example: Calculate the log and ln of 45.

Process: Log is base-10, and ln is base-*e*. By what power must 10 and *e* be raised to equal 45?

Solution:

$$\log 45 = x$$
$$10^x = 45$$
$$x = 1.6532$$

$$\ln 45 = y$$
$$e^y = 45$$
$$y = 3.8067$$

MCAT Expertise

This example is provided only to demonstrate the algebra used in calculating common and natural logarithms. Remember, on Test Day, you will *not* be expected to calculate these values so precisely!

When we examine the common log (that is, the base-10 log), we begin to see its utility as a way of expressing very small and very big numbers, or very large ranges of numerical values, in a more manageable way. Think, for example, of the difficulty you would have if you were instructed to record on a graph the number of grains of sand along the shores of Miami Beach. If each unit along the *x*-axis of your graph were to represent one grain of sand, the final point along that axis might extend out into the billions and maybe even the trillions. Imagine what that graph might look like if, rather than counting the individual grains and marking them along the *x*-axis, you count the sand grains and at the end ask yourself how many powers of 10 are represented by that final number. Let's say that there are 1 trillion (1,000,000,000,000) grains of sand. In scientific notation, this is 1×10^{12}. In other words, 1 trillion is 10 raised to the power of 12 (or 10 multiplied by itself 12 times). If, on the graph, each unit of the *x*-axis stood for a power of 10 (e.g., $x = 1 = 10^1$, $x = 2 = 10^2$, etc.), then the point along the *x*-axis representing 1 trillion would be at $x = 12$. That's a graph all of us can work with and understand, as long as we remember that the real difference in value between each unit on the *x*-axis is a power of 10.

There are many scales with which we work and are familiar that are logarithmic: pH and pOH, decibel, and Richter scales are base-10 logarithmic scales; radioactive decay scales are base-*e* logarithmic. Now we can better appreciate the ease by which we can express, say, the range of hydrogen ion concentrations in different solutions through the pH scale. The difference of five units on the pH scale between the acidity of your stomach juices (pH = 2) and that of distilled water (pH = 7) may not seem like much, but remember that this really means that your stomach juices have a hydrogen ion concentration that is 10^5 (100,000) times greater than the hydrogen ion concentration in the distilled water.

Real World

If you've ever wondered why vomiting is such a particularly unpleasant experience, this high acid concentration has a lot to do with it. This also explains why one of the clinical signs of bulimia nervosa is significant tooth decay: The repeated exposure of the teeth to highly acidic stomach fluids causes demineralization and dissolution of the tooth enamel.

Key Equations

$\log(mn) = \log m + \log n$

$\log\left(\dfrac{m}{n}\right) = \log m - \log n$

$\log(m^n) = (n)\log m$

Knowing a few rules about logarithms, shown below, will allow you to make approximations that will help you arrive at the correct answer to any problem involving logarithms.

$$\log(mn) = \log m + \log n$$
$$\log\left(\frac{m}{n}\right) = \log m - \log n$$
$$\log(m^n) = (n)\log m$$

Example: Calculate $\log(8.5 \times 10^5)$.

Process: Recognize that you are asked to calculate the log of the product of two numbers. Use the first rule of logarithms to solve the problem.

Solution:

$\log(8.5 \times 10^5) = \log 8.5 + \log 10^5$
$\log 10^5 = 5$, so
$\log(8.5 \times 10^5) = \log 8.5 + 5$
$\log 1 < \log 8.5 < \log 10$, so
$0 < \log 8.5 < 1$
Therefore, $(0 + 5) < (\log 8.5 + 5) < (1 + 5)$
$5 < (\log 8.5 + 5) < 6$
Thus, $\log(8.5 \times 10^5)$ is between 5 and 6. The true answer is closer to 6 than to 5 because $\log 8.5$ is closer to 1 than to 0. Actual value of $\log(8.5 \times 10^5)$ is 5.929.

MCAT Concept Check 1.4

Before moving on, ensure that you are able to:

✓ Calculate logarithms using logarithmic rules

✓ Graph values using a log scale

✓ Approximate the value of common logs

1.5 Vectors and Scalars ★★★☆☆

Vectors are numbers that have magnitude and direction. Vector quantities include displacement, velocity, acceleration, and force. **Scalars** are numbers that have magnitude only. They do not have a direction. Scalar quantities include distance, speed, energy, pressure, and mass. Pacing back and forth across the lobby of the MCAT testing center may help you burn off a few kilocalories of nervous energy, but aside

from that, you're not actually going to accomplish much. You may clock in several hundred steps before making your way into the testing room, and we could calculate the cumulative linear distance that you paced during your wait. Nevertheless, your displacement—or change in position—was zero. The difference between distance and displacement can be further illustrated with vector representations.

VECTOR REPRESENTATION

An arrow can represent a vector. The direction of the arrow indicates the direction of the vector. The length of the arrow may or may not be proportional to the magnitude of the vector quantity. Common notations for a vector quantity are either an arrow or boldface. For example, the straight-line path from "here" to "there" might be represented by a vector identified as $\vec{A}$ or **A**. The magnitude of the displacement between the two positions can be represented as $|\vec{A}|$ or $|\mathbf{A}|$, or A.

VECTOR ADDITION

The sum or difference of two or more vectors is called the **resultant** of the vectors. One way to find the sum or resultant of two vectors, **A** and **B,** is to place the tail of **B** at the tip of **A** without changing either the length or the direction of either arrow. In this head-to-tail method, the lengths of the arrows must be proportional to the magnitudes of the vectors. The vector sum **A** + **B** is the vector joining the tail of **A** to the tip of **B** and pointing toward the tip of **B.** For three or more vectors, proceed similarly. Figures 1.2a and b illustrate the addition of two and three vectors, respectively.

Real World

The difference between vectors and scalars is a very important concept. Anything that can exist without a direction is a scalar. For example, when you climb a mountain and you reach 14,000 feet, it doesn't matter which direction you approached from or which direction you are going, you're at 14,000. This means that elevation is a scalar quantity.

Key Concept

Remember when adding vectors: Add tip to tail!

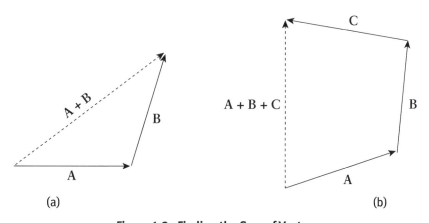

Figure 1.2. Finding the Sum of Vectors
(a) Vectors A and B with resultant A + B
(b) Vectors A, B, and C with resultant A + B + C

Another method more commonly used for finding the resultant of several vectors involves breaking each vector into perpendicular (**X** and **Y**) components. These components are often, but not always, horizontal and vertical.

Given any vector **V**, we can find the **X** component and the **Y** component by drawing a right triangle with **V** as the hypotenuse (see Figure 1.3). If θ is the angle between **V** and the **X** direction, then $\cos \theta = \dfrac{\mathbf{X}}{\mathbf{V}}$ and $\sin \theta = \dfrac{\mathbf{Y}}{\mathbf{V}}$. In other words:

$$\mathbf{X} = \mathbf{V} \cos \theta$$

$$\mathbf{Y} = \mathbf{V} \sin \theta$$

Key Equations

$\mathbf{X} = \mathbf{V} \cos \theta$

$\mathbf{Y} = \mathbf{V} \sin \theta$

$\mathbf{X}^2 + \mathbf{Y}^2 = \mathbf{V}^2$

Example: $\mathbf{V} = 10 \text{ m/s}$
$\theta = 30°$
$\mathbf{X} = 10 \cos 30° = \dfrac{10\sqrt{3}}{2}$
$\quad = 5\sqrt{3} \text{ m/s}$
$\mathbf{Y} = 10 \sin 30° = \dfrac{10}{2} = 5 \text{ m/s}$

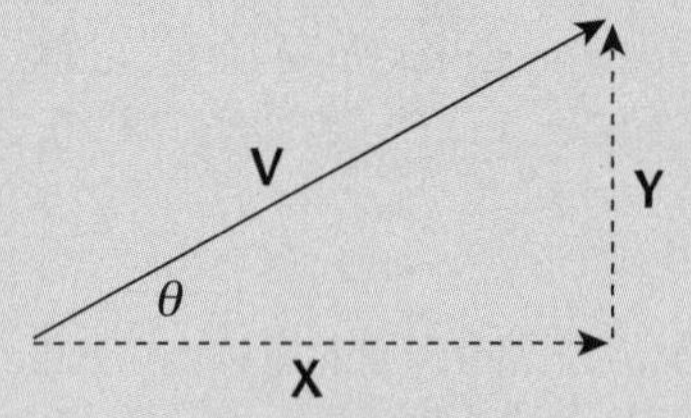

Figure 1.3

Conversely, if we know **X** and **Y**, we can find **V** by using the Pythagorean theorem: $\mathbf{X}^2 + \mathbf{Y}^2 = \mathbf{V}^2$, or $\mathbf{V} = \sqrt{\mathbf{X}^2 + \mathbf{Y}^2}$.

Example: $\mathbf{X} = 3 \text{ m/s}$
$\mathbf{Y} = 4 \text{ m/s}$
$\mathbf{V} = \sqrt{3^2 + 4^2} = \sqrt{25}$

$\quad = 5 \text{ m/s}$

(Also note that we can find θ from $\tan \theta = \dfrac{\mathbf{Y}}{\mathbf{X}}$. In this example, $\tan \theta = \dfrac{4}{3}$, so a calculator would tell us that $\theta = 53°$.)

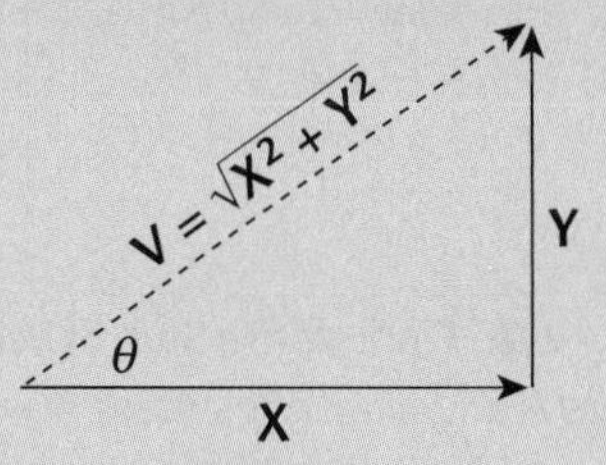

Figure 1.4

The **X** component of the resultant vector is the sum of the **X** components of the vectors being added. Similarly, the **Y** component of the resultant vector is the sum of the **Y** components of the vectors being added.

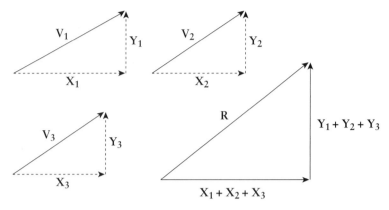

Figure 1.5. Finding the Resultant (R) of V₁ + V₂ + V₃

To find the resultant **(R)** using the components method, follow these steps:

1. Resolve the vectors to be summed into their **X** and **Y** components.
2. Add together the **X** components to get the **X** component of the resultant (**Rₓ**). In the same way, add the **Y** components to get the **Y** component of the resultant (**R_y**).
3. Find the magnitude of the resultant by using the Pythagorean theorem. If **Rₓ** and **R_y** are the components of the resultant, then

$$\mathbf{R} = \sqrt{\mathbf{R}_x^2 + \mathbf{R}_y^2}$$

4. Find the direction (θ) of the resultant by using the relation $\tan \theta = \dfrac{\mathbf{R}_y}{\mathbf{R}_x}$. From the value of $\tan \theta$ you can find θ, the angle **R** makes with the *x*-direction.

Example: Find the horizontal and vertical components of **V**.

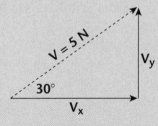

Figure 1.6

Solution: Let *x* be the horizontal direction and *y* be the vertical direction. Then

$$\mathbf{V}_x = \mathbf{V} \cos \theta = 5 \cos 30° = \frac{5\sqrt{3}}{2} = 2.5\sqrt{3} \text{ N} \approx 4.3 \text{ N}$$

$$\mathbf{V}_y = \mathbf{V} \sin \theta = 5 \sin 30° = \frac{5}{2} = 2.5 \text{ N}$$

Example: Find the resultant of **A**, **B**, **C**, and **D**.

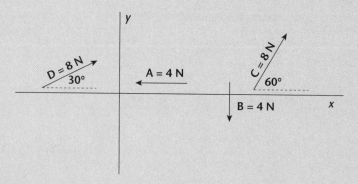

Figure 1.7

Solution: Resolve the vectors into their horizontal (x) and vertical (y) components. Note that we have x-components going both left and right and y-components going both up and down. **In each case, choose one direction as the positive direction. The other direction is then automatically the negative direction.** In this example, we chose going to the right as the positive x-direction (so to the left is negative) and up as the positive y-direction (so down is negative). **A component in the positive direction is then positive, and a component in the negative direction is then negative.**

a. $\mathbf{A}_x = -4$ N

$\mathbf{B}_x = 0$

$\mathbf{C}_x = 8\cos 60° = \dfrac{8}{2} = 4$ N

$\mathbf{D}_x = 8\cos 30° = \dfrac{8\sqrt{3}}{2} = 4\sqrt{3}$ N

b. $\mathbf{A}_y = 0$

$\mathbf{B}_y = -4$ N

$\mathbf{C}_y = 8\sin 60° = \dfrac{8\sqrt{3}}{2} = 4\sqrt{3}$ N

$\mathbf{D}_y = 8\sin 30° = \dfrac{8}{2} = 4$ N

Add together the components of **A**, **B**, **C**, and **D** to get the components of the resultant **R**:

a. $\mathbf{R}_x = (-4) + 0 + 4 + 4\sqrt{3} = 4\sqrt{3}$ N

b. $\mathbf{R}_y = 0 + (-4) + 4\sqrt{3} + 4 = 4\sqrt{3}$ N

Find the magnitude of the resultant:

$$\mathbf{R} = \sqrt{\mathbf{R}_x^2 + \mathbf{R}_y^2}$$

$$\mathbf{R} = \sqrt{(4\sqrt{3})^2 + (4\sqrt{3})^2} = \sqrt{96} = 4\sqrt{6} \text{ N}$$

Find the angle the resultant makes with the horizontal:

$$\tan\theta = \frac{4\sqrt{3}}{4\sqrt{3}} = 1; \ \theta = 45°$$

Thus, we have found that **R** is a vector of magnitude of $4\sqrt{6}$ N, making an angle of 45° with the horizontal. (In general, $\tan\theta = \dfrac{|\mathbf{R}_y|}{|\mathbf{R}_x|}$, where θ is the smallest angle with the x-axis.)

VECTOR SUBTRACTION

Subtracting two vectors can be accomplished by adding the opposite of the vector that is being subtracted. Expressed mathematically, this looks very familiar:

$$\mathbf{A} - \mathbf{B} = \mathbf{A} + (-\mathbf{B})$$

By "$-\mathbf{B}$," we mean a vector with the same magnitude of $\mathbf{B}$ but pointing in the opposite direction.

Example: What is the resultant of $\mathbf{A} - \mathbf{B}$ as pictured below?

Figure 1.8

> **Key Concept**
>
> Notice that when you subtract vectors, you are simply flipping the direction of the vector being subtracted and then following the same rules as normal: adding tip to tail.

Solution: The first thing to do is make the vector $-\mathbf{B}$. This is done by erasing the arrow head at the tip of $\mathbf{B}$ and redrawing it where the tail used to be (see Figure 1.9a). Now, add this to $\mathbf{A}$. To do this, move the tip of $\mathbf{A}$ to the tail of $-\mathbf{B}$, and join the tail of $\mathbf{A}$ to the tip of $-\mathbf{B}$ (see Figure 1.9b).

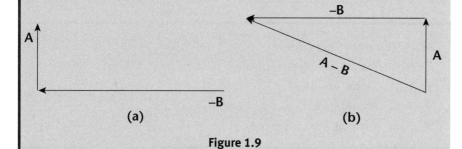

(a)   (b)

Figure 1.9

To find $-\mathbf{B}$ using the method whereby the vectors are broken up into their horizontal and vertical components, each vector component is multiplied by -1 before adding.

Example: If $\mathbf{A}$ has components $\mathbf{A}_x = 3$ and $\mathbf{A}_y = 4$ and $\mathbf{B}$ has components $\mathbf{B}_x = 2$ and $\mathbf{B}_y = 1$, then what is $\mathbf{A} - \mathbf{B}$?

Solution: First, remember $\mathbf{A} - \mathbf{B} = \mathbf{A} + (-\mathbf{B})$. Since $\mathbf{B}$ has components $\mathbf{B}_x$ and $\mathbf{B}_y$, $-\mathbf{B}$ has components $-\mathbf{B}_x$ and $-\mathbf{B}_y$.

$$R_x = A_x - B_x = 3 - 2 = 1$$
$$R_y = A_y - B_y = 4 - 1 = 3$$

Get the magnitude of the final resultant vector **R**:

$$\mathbf{R} = \sqrt{(3^2 + 1^2)}$$

$$= \sqrt{(9 + 1)} = \sqrt{10}$$

Get the direction:

$$\tan \theta = \frac{\mathbf{R}_y}{\mathbf{R}_x} = 3$$

$$\theta = 72°$$

MULTIPLYING A VECTOR BY A SCALAR

Vectors can be multiplied by a scalar to change either or both the length and the direction. If we multiply vector **A** by the scalar value n, we produce a new vector, **B**, such that $\mathbf{B} = n\mathbf{A}$. To find the magnitude of the new vector, **B**, simply multiply the magnitude of **A** by the absolute value of n. To determine the direction of the vector **B**, we must look at the sign on n. If n is a positive number, then **B** and **A** are in the same direction. However, if n is a negative number, then **B** and **A** point in opposite directions. For example, if vector **A** is multiplied by the scalar +3, then the new vector **B** is three times as long as **A**, and **A** and **B** point in the same direction. If vector **A** is multiplied by the scalar −3, then **B** would still be three times as long as **A** but would now point in the opposite direction.

MCAT Concept Check 1.5

Before moving on, ensure that you are able to:

✓ Add and subtract vectors

✓ Break vectors into their x- and y-components

✓ Multiply vectors by scalar quantities

1.6 Kinematics   ★★★★☆

This is the first of many important topics in physics that will prove to be high yield for the MCAT. Pay attention to this discussion because a strong understanding of kinematics will pay off in points on Test Day! **Kinematics** is the branch of Newtonian mechanics that deals with the description of motion. In physics, the position of an object or particle is defined on a three-dimensional coordinate axis. However, most kinematics problems on the MCAT will describe motion in only one dimension (e.g., dropping objects) or two (e.g., projectile motion).

DISPLACEMENT

An object in motion may experience a change in its position in space, known as **displacement.** This is a vector quantity and, as such, has both magnitude and direction. The displacement vector connects (in a straight line) the object's initial position and its final position. Understand that displacement does not account for the actual pathway taken between the initial and the final positions.

> **Example:** A man walks 2 km east, then 2 km north, then 2 km west, and then 2 km south. His actual total distance traveled is 8 km, since distance is a scalar. But his displacement is a vector quantity that is the change in position. In this case, his displacement is zero, since the man ends up the same place he started (see Figure 1.10).

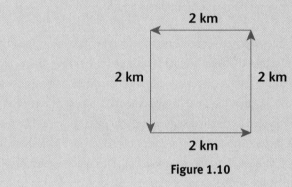

Figure 1.10

VELOCITY

As was mentioned earlier, **velocity** is a vector. Its magnitude is measured as the rate of change of displacement in a given unit of time. The direction of the velocity vector is the same as the direction of the displacement vector. The SI units for velocity are meters/second. **Speed,** you will recall, is the rate of actual distance traveled in a given unit of time. The distinction is subtle, so let's look at this a little more carefully. The **instantaneous speed** of an object will always be equal to the magnitude of the object's **instantaneous velocity**, which is a measure of the average velocity as the change in time (Δt) approaches 0.

$$v = \lim_{\Delta t \to 0} \frac{\Delta x}{\Delta t}$$

As a measure of speed, instantaneous speed is also a scalar number. Average speed will not necessarily always be equal to the magnitude of the average velocity. This is because average velocity is the ratio of the displacement vector over the change in time (and is a vector), whereas average speed (which is scalar) is the ratio of the total

MCAT Expertise

When dealing with kinematics questions, always draw a quick picture of what is happening in the problem; this will keep everything in its proper relative position and help prevent you from making easy mistakes.

distance traveled over the change in time. Average speed accounts for actual distance traveled, whereas average velocity does not.

$$\bar{\mathbf{v}} = \frac{\Delta x}{\Delta t}$$

Consider the following example. Let's say your younger brother recently acquired his driver's license. Without asking for permission, he takes your mother's convertible out and with the top down, stereo up, he speeds along a winding stretch of road. Hitting 90, then 100, then 110 miles per hour, he throws up his hands and opens his mouth to scream when all of a sudden—splat! He gasps, chokes, and then begins to taste the bitter juices of the obliterated bug carcass mashed up against his front teeth. The car screeches to a halt. Defeated, deflated, and a little nauseous, your brother slowly heads home, top up, stereo down, obeying all speed limits, and parks the convertible in the garage hoping that your mom doesn't notice.

Your brother's joyride provides the perfect scenario in which to make clear the differences between velocities and speeds. Your brother took a path from the garage, along a winding road, and back to the garage. Because the starting and ending positions of the car are the same, we can say that the total displacement of the car is zero. But we know that the car actually traveled a certain distance, and that distance would be measured on the dashboard odometer. Another measurement displayed on the dashboard is the instantaneous speed, as indicated by the speedometer. The speedometer displays the instantaneous measure of the actual distance that the car would travel in an hour: 90 mph, 100 mph, and so on. Instantaneous speed is simply the magnitude of the instantaneous velocity. How do the magnitude of the average velocity and the average speed relate and compare to each other? Average velocity is calculated as the ratio of the displacement vector over the change in time. As a velocity, it is a vector. Average speed is calculated as the ratio of the actual distance traveled over the change in time. As a speed, it is a scalar. Because actual distance traveled is not always the same as the magnitude of the displacement vector, average speed and the magnitude of the average velocity will not always be the same. In the example, your little brother may have driven the convertible at an impressive average speed of 60 mph, but his average velocity—given his displacement of 0 miles—is a totally unimpressive 0 mph.

ACCELERATION

Acceleration is the rate of change of velocity over time. It is a vector quantity. As we will learn in Chapter 2, acceleration results from application of force(s). **Average acceleration,** a, is the change in instantaneous velocity over the change in time.

$$\bar{a} = \frac{\Delta v}{\Delta t}$$

Instantaneous acceleration is defined as the average acceleration as Δt approaches 0.

$$a = \lim_{\Delta t \to 0} \frac{\Delta v}{\Delta t}$$

On a graph of velocity versus time, the tangent to the graph at any time t, which corresponds to the slope of the graph at that time, would indicate the instantaneous acceleration. If the slope is positive, the acceleration is positive and is in the direction of the velocity. If the slope is negative, the acceleration is negative and is in the direction opposite of the velocity, and it may be called deceleration.

MCAT Concept Check 1.6

Before moving on, ensure that you are able to:

✓ Define displacement, velocity, average velocity, speed, acceleration, and average acceleration

✓ Calculate displacement, velocity, and acceleration

1.7 Motion with Constant Acceleration

Objects can basically undergo only two "kinds" of motion—that which is constant (no acceleration) or that which is changing (with acceleration). An object accelerates when a force is applied to it, and the acceleration that results from the force is proportional to it. Chapter 2 highlights the special case of objects experiencing translational or rotational equilibrium, in which the motional behavior of the object is constant. If an object's motion is changing, as indicated by a change in velocity, then the object is experiencing acceleration, and that acceleration may be constant or itself changing. A moving object that experiences constant acceleration presents a relatively simple case for analysis. The MCAT limits the presentation of kinematics problems to those that involve motion with constant acceleration.

LINEAR MOTION

In linear motion, the object's velocity and acceleration are along the line of motion. The pathway of the moving object is a straight line. Linear motion does not need to be limited to vertical or horizontal paths; the inclined surface of a ramp will provide a path for linear motion at some angle. On the MCAT, the most common presentations of linear motion problems involve objects, such as balls, being dropped to the ground from some starting height.

Key Concept

This is known as Newton's Second Law and is represented by $F = ma$; this is one of the most important physics concepts on the MCAT. If you see force, think acceleration; if you see acceleration, think force.

Key Equations

$$v = v_0 + at$$

$$\Delta x = v_0 t + \frac{at^2}{2}$$

$$v^2 = v_0^2 + 2a\Delta x$$

$$\bar{v} = \frac{v_0 + v}{2}$$

$$\Delta x = \bar{v}t$$

v is velocity in m/s, a is acceleration in m/s², x is displacement in m, t is time in s

Falling objects exhibit linear motion with constant acceleration. This one-dimensional motion can be fully described by the following equations.

$$v = v_0 + at$$

$$x - x_0 = v_0 t + \frac{at^2}{2}$$

$$v^2 = v_0^2 + 2a(x - x_0)$$

$$\bar{v} = \frac{(v_0 + v)}{2}$$

$$\Delta x = \bar{v}t = \left(\frac{v_0 + v}{2}\right)t$$

Notes:

1. v_0 and x_0 are v and x at $t = 0$.

2. When the motion is vertical, we use y instead of x.

3. As illustrated below, when using these equations, we must remember that velocity and acceleration are vector quantities

Anyone who has ever had a cat as a pet knows that cats love to perch on windowsills. They will occasionally leap through an open window to catch their prey only to find themselves plummeting one, two, ten, or more stories to the ground below. Interestingly, veterinarians noticed that, paradoxically, cats that fell from higher floors typically had fewer and less severe injuries than those that fell from lower floors. The key to this mystery was discovered in high-speed video footage of a cat actually falling. What became clear is that a fall from a greater height provided sufficient time for the cat not only to right itself but also to flatten and spread out to maximize air resistance and reduce terminal velocity. The cat then relaxes its muscles prior to impact, which reduces the stress load to the limb bones, decreasing the risk of injury or breakage. Falling from lower heights does not provide sufficient time to accomplish all of these bodily preparations for the landing.

To demonstrate the typical setup of a kinematics problem on the MCAT, we will make use of Seymour, whose lack of fur makes him so streamlined that, if he were to take a fall, we could discount air resistance. This means that the only force acting on a falling Seymour would be the gravitational force causing him to fall. Consequently, he would fall with a constant acceleration (the **acceleration due to gravity** (**g**), 9.8 m/s²) and would not reach **terminal velocity.** This is called **free fall.** Under these conditions, typical for Test Day, we could analyze the fall, using the relevant kinematics equations.

Example: Seymour the cat leaps vertically up into the air from a window ledge 30 meters above the ground with an initial velocity of 10 m/s.
a. Find the position and velocity of Seymour after two seconds.
b. Find the distance and time at which Seymour reaches his maximum height above the window ledge.

Solution:
a. Remember that velocity and acceleration are vector quantities. Taking the initial position of the cat $y_0 = 0$, and taking "up" as positive, the initial velocity is $v_0 = +10$ m/s, and the acceleration is $g = -9.8$ m/s^2. Notice g is negative because its direction is down and we are taking up to be the positive direction. Velocity after two seconds can be found using the equation:

$$\begin{aligned} v &= v_0 + at \\ &= (+10) + (-9.8)(2) \\ &= -9.6 \text{ m/s} \end{aligned}$$
(Minus sign for a means that the cat is coming down.)

After two seconds, the position of the cat is found using the equation:

$$y = v_0 t + \frac{at^2}{2} \qquad (y_0 = 0)$$
$$= 10(2) + \frac{(-9.8)(2)^2}{2}$$
$$= 20 - 19.6$$
$$= +0.4 \text{ m (above the window ledge)}$$

b. When the cat is at its maximum height, the velocity, v, which has been decreasing on the way up, is zero. Using the following equation and plugging in values, we can find the maximum height the cat reaches above the window ledge:

$$v^2 = v_0^2 + 2ay$$
$$0 = (10)^2 + 2(-9.8)y$$
$$y = 5.1 \text{ m}$$

The time at which the cat reaches its maximum height can be found from the equation:

$$v = v_0 + at$$
$$0 = 10 + (-9.8)t$$
$$t = 1.0 \text{ s}$$

Key Concept

Terminal velocity is due to the upward force of air resistance equaling the downward force of gravity. As the net force on the object at this point becomes zero, the acceleration is also zero. The object remains at a constant velocity until it is acted upon by another force.

MCAT Expertise

When dealing with free fall problems, you can make "down" either positive or negative, thus making the force of gravity either positive or negative. As long as you keep all forces upward with the opposite sign of all forces downward, you will get the correct answer. Though, for the sake of simplicity, ALWAYS make "up" positive and "down" negative.

PROJECTILE MOTION

Projectile motion is motion that follows a path along two dimensions. The velocities and accelerations in the two directions (usually horizontal and vertical) are independent of each other and must, accordingly, be analyzed separately. Objects in projectile motion on Earth, such as cannonballs, baseballs, or bullets, experience the force and acceleration of gravity only in the vertical direction ("along the y-axis"). This means that v_y will change at the rate of g but v_x will not. In fact, on the MCAT, you will be able to assume that the horizontal velocity, v_x, will be constant, because we assume that air resistance is negligible and, therefore, no measurable force is acting along the x-axis.

To demonstrate projectile motion and apply the kinematics equations to motion in two dimensions, we can turn our attention to cannonballs from a cannon. Projectiles display motion that can be analyzed with relatively simple mathematics. The following problem demonstrates a classic MCAT presentation of projectile motion.

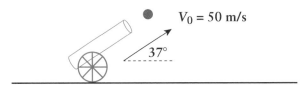

Figure 1.11. Projectile Motion
Cannonball with initial velocity of 50 m/s, 37° above
the horizontal

Key Concept

Whenever an object reaches its maximum height, its vertical velocity will be zero for the brief instant that it stops going up and starts falling down. As soon as an object is "in flight," the only force acting on it will be gravity; thus an object's *acceleration* will be −9.8 m/s² the *entire* time it is in flight.

Example: A projectile is fired from ground level with an initial velocity of 50 m/s and an initial angle of elevation of 37° (see Figure 1.11). Assuming $g = 10$ m/s², find the following:
a. The projectile's total time in flight
b. The maximum height attained
c. The total horizontal distance traveled
d. The final horizontal and vertical velocities just before it hits the ground

Solution:

a. Let y equal the vertical height; let up be the positive direction.

$$a = -10 \text{ m/s}^2$$

$$y = v_{0y}t + \frac{1}{2}at^2 \qquad (y_0 = 0)$$

$$v_{0y} = v_0 \sin 37°$$

$$v_{0y} = 50(0.6) = 30 \text{ m/s}$$

$$y = 30t - 5t^2$$

$y = 0$ both when the projectile is first fired and when it hits the ground later. Its time in flight will be the difference between the values of t at the two points when $y = 0$.

$$30t - 5t^2 = 0$$

$$5t(6 - t) = 0$$

$$t = 0 \text{ (first fired)}, \ t = 6 \text{ (hits the ground)}$$

Time in flight $= 6 - 0 = 6$ s

b. Find the maximum height attained:

$$v_y^2 = v_{0y}^2 + 2ay$$

$$0 = 30^2 + 2(-10)(y) \qquad (v_y = 0 \text{ at highest point})$$

$$y = \frac{900}{20}$$

$$y = 45 \text{ m}$$

c. Find the horizontal distance traveled:

$$x = v_x t \qquad (a_x = 0)$$

$$v_x = 50 \cos 37° = 40 \text{ m/s}$$

$$x = 40(6) = 240 \text{ m}$$

d. The horizontal velocity remains constant, so $v_x = 40$ m/s. Find the vertical velocity at impact:

$$v_y = v_{0y} + at$$

$$v_y = 30 - 10(6)$$

$$v_y = 30 - 60$$

$$v_y = -30 \text{ m/s}$$

Because we chose up as positive, the minus sign means the vertical component of the velocity is directed down.

MCAT Expertise

The amount of time that an object takes to get to its maximum height is the same time it takes for the object to fall back down; this fact makes solving these problems much easier. Because you can solve for the time to reach maximum height by setting your final velocity to zero, you can then multiply your answer by two, getting total time in flight. Because the only force acting on the object after it is launched is gravity, the velocity it has in the x-direction will remain constant throughout its time in flight. By multiplying the time by the x-velocity, you can find the horizontal distance traveled.

Pay attention to the equations that can be applied to objects in motion with constant acceleration. You must know them for Test Day. Do more than simply memorize them, however. Spend the time that you need to really understand these—and all the other—equations. Learn them through application. The best way to understand any equation is to see how it can and will be useful on Test Day. Take advantage of the practice resources available to you in this review book and throughout your Kaplan program.

> **MCAT Concept Check 1.7**
>
> Before moving on, ensure that you are able to:
>
> ✓ Define linear motion, free fall, acceleration due to gravity, terminal velocity, and projectile motion
> ✓ Use the kinematics equations to solve problems with constant acceleration, such as free fall and projectile motion

Conclusion

All right! One chapter down! We have reviewed the most important principles of mathematics relevant to the MCAT, including units, scientific notation, trigonometry, logarithms, and vectors. With this basic review, we've equipped you with the math—the language of physics—necessary to understand our first important topic for the MCAT Physical Science section, kinematics. This study of objects in motion allows us to describe an object's velocity, speed, acceleration, and position with respect to time. We now understand how to use the five kinematics equations when objects experience constant acceleration, a relatively simple scenario presented on Test Day.

Our goal in this chapter and throughout all of our review of the basic sciences is to demystify the concepts that have far too often been viewed by students as incomprehensible or irrelevant. We believe that every student who commits herself or himself to consistent and thoughtful preparation can understand the mathematical and scientific concepts presented here and elsewhere in the Kaplan MCAT program. Furthermore, we hope that you will come to appreciate the relevance that these concepts and principles have for your performance not only on the MCAT but also in medical school, residency training, and your career as a physician.

CONCEPT SUMMARY

SI Units (p. 4)

- ☐ International system of units for length (m), mass (kg), volume (L), temperature (K), force (N), time (s), velocity (m/s), acceleration (m/s^2), energy (J), current (A), electric potential (V) and resistance (ohm)

Scientific Notation (p. 6)

- ☐ Allows for easy expression and manipulation of very large and small numbers

Trigonometric Functions (p. 7)

- ☐ Knowing **cosine and sine** for the classic angles (0°, 30°, 45°, 60°, 90°, 180°, and 270°) of right triangles is essential for adding and subtracting vectors, working with inclined planes, and solving for projectile motion

Logarithms (p. 8)

- ☐ The two logarithmic bases you need to know are **base-10** and **base-*e***
- ☐ Logs will be important for **pH, pOH**, the **decibel scale**, and **nuclear decay**

Vectors (p. 10)

- ☐ Have both a magnitude and direction
- ☐ Include **velocity, acceleration, displacement, force**, and **electric** and **magnetic fields**

Scalars (p. 10)

- ☐ Have only magnitude
- ☐ Include **distance, speed, mass, pressure, energy**, and **work**

Average Velocity (p. 18)

- ☐ Is the total displacement divided by the total time

Average Speed (p. 17)

- ☐ Is total distance divided by the total time
- ☐ Average velocity may be less than or equal to the average speed in magnitude, but never greater
- ☐ **Instantaneous velocity** and **instantaneous speed** are always equal

Deceleration (p. 19)

- ☐ Is acceleration in the direction opposite to the initial velocity
- ☐ **"Negative" acceleration** causes the object in motion to slow down as well as possibly stop and reverse directions

Constant Acceleration (p. 19)

- ☐ Implies a constant force

Free Fall (p. 20)

- ☐ **Objects in free fall** experience acceleration equal to that of gravity (9.8 m/s^2), neglecting air resistance
- ☐ **Objects in terminal velocity** experience a net force of 0 N and therefore an acceleration of 0 m/s^2 because the upward force of air resistance equals the downward force due to gravity

Projectile Motion (p. 22)

☐ The **initial velocity** must be broken into its x- and y-components

☐ The **y-component velocity vector** ($\mathbf{v}_y$) will change at the rate of g if subjected to gravity

☐ The **x-component velocity vector** ($\mathbf{v}_x$) remains constant, neglecting the force of air resistance

EQUATIONS TO REMEMBER

Notes:

☐ $v = v_0 + at$

☐ $x - x_0 = v_0 t + \dfrac{at^2}{2}$

☐ $v^2 = v_0^2 + 2a(x - x_0)$

☐ $\bar{v} = \dfrac{(v_0 + v)}{2}$

☐ $\Delta x = \bar{v}t = \left(\dfrac{v_0 + v}{2}\right)t$

1. v_0 and x_0 are v and x at $t = 0$.

2. When the motion is vertical, we use y instead of x.

3. As illustrated below, in using these equations, we must remember that velocity and acceleration are vector quantities.

SHARED CONCEPTS

HIGH-YIELD PRACTICE PROBLEMS

Practice Questions

1. A man walks three blocks (30 m) east and then another five blocks (50 m) north to the drugstore (point B). What is the magnitude of his final displacement from his original location (point A)?

   A. 20 m
   B. 40 m
   C. 60 m
   D. 3,400 m

2. A submarine sends out a sonar signal (sound wave) in a direction directly downward. It takes 2.3 s for the sound wave to travel from the submarine to the ocean bottom and back to the submarine. How high up from the ocean floor is the submarine? (The speed of sound in water is 1,489 m/s.)

   A. 1,700 m
   B. 3,000 m
   C. 5,000 m
   D. Cannot be determined.

3. A car is traveling at 40 km/hr and the driver puts on the brakes, bringing the car to rest in a time of 6 s. What is the magnitude of the average acceleration of the car in units of km/hr²?

   A. 240 km/hr²
   B. 12,000 km/hr²
   C. 24,000 km/hr²
   D. 30,000 km/hr²

4. If an object is released 19.6 m above the ground, how long does it take the object to reach the ground?

   A. 1 s
   B. 2 s
   C. 4 s
   D. 10 s

5. At a place where g is 9.8 m/s², an object is thrown vertically downward with a speed of 10 m/s while a different object is thrown vertically upward with a speed of 20 m/s. Which object undergoes a greater change in speed in a time of 2 s?

   A. The first object, because the speed vector points in the same direction as the acceleration due to gravity
   B. The second object, because it has a higher velocity
   C. Both objects undergo the same change in speed
   D. Cannot be determined from the information given

6. A firefighter jumps horizontally from a burning building with an initial speed of 1.5 m/s. At what time is the angle between his velocity and acceleration the greatest?

   A. The instant he jumps
   B. When he reaches terminal velocity
   C. Halfway through his fall
   D. Right before he hits the ground

7. A circus clown is catapulted straight up in the air (the catapult is 1.5 m off the ground level). If her velocity as she leaves the catapult is 4 m/s, what is the maximum height that she reaches, as measured from the ground?

  A. 0.4 m

  B. 0.8 m

  C. 1.9 m

  D. 2.3 m

8. Which of the following expressions correctly illustrates the SI units of each one of the variables in the formula?

$$m\Delta v = F\Delta t$$

  A. lb × mph = ft × lb × s

  B. lb × km = N × s

  C. kg × m/s = N × s

  D. g × m/s = N × s

9. If a toy magnet is able to generate one centitesla, how many teslas would 10^8 magnets be able to generate?

  A. 1 kT

  B. 1 MT

  C. 1 GT

  D. 1 TT

10. Which of the following quantities is NOT a vector?

  A. Velocity

  B. Force

  C. Displacement

  D. Distance

11. A rifle is held by a man whose arms are 1.5 m above the ground. He fires a bullet at 100 m/s at an angle of 30° with the horizontal. After 2 s, how far has the object traveled in the horizontal direction?

  A. 87 m

  B. 140 m

  C. 174 m

  D. 175.5 m

12. A BASE jumper runs off a cliff with a speed of 3 m/s. What is his overall velocity after 0.5 seconds?

  A. 3 m/s

  B. 6 m/s

  C. 8 m/s

  D. 10 m/s

13. A rock ($m = 2$ kg) is shot up vertically at the same time that a ball ($m = 0.5$ kg) is projected horizontally. If both start from the same height,

  A. the rock and ball will reach the ground at the same time.

  B. the rock will reach the ground first.

  C. the ball will reach the ground first.

  D. More information is needed to answer this question.

Small Group Questions

1. Two men, holding identical bullets, stand side by side in a large field. One uses a gun to shoot his bullet across the field while the other simultaneously drops his bullet from the same height as the gun. Which bullet will hit the ground first, assuming that air resistance is negligible and the field is flat?

2. The Richter scale uses a logarithmic function to rate the intensity of earthquakes. How does the intensity of a 3.0 earthquake compare to a 5.0 earthquake on the Richter scale?

Explanations to Practice Questions

1. C

Using the Pythagorean theorem, calculate the magnitude of his displacement, x, from point A to point B:

$$x^2 = (30)^2 + (50)^2$$
$$= 900 + 2,500$$
$$= 3,400$$

Therefore, $x = \sqrt{3,400} = 10\sqrt{34}$ m $\approx 10 \times 6$ m ≈ 60 m. Choice (C) matches our prediction and is thus the correct answer.

2. A

This is a straightforward mechanics question. To calculate the distance traveled, we need to multiply the speed by the time.

$$d = st$$
$$d = (1,490 \text{ m/s})(2.3 \text{ s})$$
$$d \approx (1,500 \text{ m/s})(2 \text{ s})$$
$$d \approx 3,000 \text{ m}$$

However, this distance represents the distance from the submarine to the ocean floor and back to the submarine, or in other words, twice the distance from the submarine to the ocean floor. It follows, therefore, that the submarine is 3,000/2, or about 1,500 m from the bottom of the ocean. Choice (A) best matches our prediction and is thus the correct answer.

3. C

The magnitude of the average acceleration is the change in speed divided by the time. The speed changes by 40 km/hr because the car comes to rest. The time, in hours, is

$$(6 \text{ s}) \times (1 \text{ hr}/3,600 \text{ s}) = \frac{1}{600} \text{ hr}$$

The average acceleration is then

$$a = \frac{v}{t}$$
$$a = \frac{40 \text{ km/hr}}{\frac{1}{600} \text{ hr}} = (40 \text{ km})(600)$$
$$a = 24,000 \text{ km/hr}^2$$

Choice (C) is therefore the correct answer.

4. B

We are given the distance above the ground, the initial velocity, and the acceleration due to gravity, and our task is to solve for time. Let's assume the downward direction to be "positive." We can use one of the kinematics equations to calculate t.

$$d = v_o t + \frac{1}{2} at^2$$

Since $v_o = 0$ m/s, we can say that

$$d = \frac{1}{2} at^2$$

Notice that while we usually approximate the acceleration due to gravity as 10 m/s^2, in this problem, it is actually more convenient to use the real value of 9.8 m/s^2 because this number is exactly half of the distance, 19.6 m, so our calculations will simplify more easily. Solving for t, we obtain

$$t^2 = \frac{2d}{a}$$
$$t^2 = \frac{2 \times 19.6 \text{m}}{9.8 \text{m}/\text{s}^2}$$
$$t^2 = 4$$
$$t = 2 \text{ s}$$

Choice (B) is therefore the correct answer.

5. C

Each object experiences an acceleration of 9.8 m/s², which means that each object's speed changes by 9.8 m/s each second. Therefore, both objects experience the same change in speed over the 2-second period (i.e., 19.6 m/s). Choice (C) best matches our prediction and is thus the correct answer.

6. A

The firefighter's acceleration is always directed downward, whereas his velocity starts out horizontal and gradually rotates downwards as his downward velocity increases. Therefore, as time progresses, the angle between his velocity and acceleration decreases, which means that the maximum angle occurs at the instant he jumps. Choice (A) is the correct answer.

7. D

At the instant the clown reaches her maximum height, her vertical velocity is zero. Taking "up" as positive and the final speed, v_f, at the maximum height as zero, we can solve for h using the following kinematics equation:

$$v_f^2 = v_0^2 + 2\,a\Delta h$$
$$0 = v_0^2 + 2\,a\Delta h$$
$$-v_0^2 = -2g\Delta h$$
$$\Delta h = \frac{v_0^2}{2g}$$
$$\Delta h = \frac{(4\,\mathrm{m/s})^2}{2 \times 10\,\mathrm{m/s}^2}$$
$$\Delta h = \frac{16}{20}\,\mathrm{m}$$
$$\Delta h = \frac{4}{5}\,\mathrm{m} = 0.8\ \mathrm{m}$$

Because the catapult is 1.5 m above the ground, the maximum height is thus $1.5 + 0.8 = 2.3$ m, making (D) the correct answer.

8. C

In SI units, mass is measured in kilograms (kg), velocity in meters per second (m/s), force in newtons (N), and time in seconds (s). Choice (C) is therefore the correct answer.

9. B

If one magnet generates one centitesla (10^{-2} T), then 10^8 magnets would generate $10^{-2} \times 10^8 = 10^6$ teslas, or one megatesla (1 MT). Choice (B) matches our result and is thus the correct answer.

10. D

A vector is characterized by both magnitude and direction. From the given answer choices, all are vectors except for distance, (D), which is a scalar because it has only a numerical value and lacks direction.

11. C

Though this question may seem complicated, it is relatively straightforward. The fact that the rifle is 1.5 m above the ground is unimportant because the question asks about horizontal distance. Use the linear motion equations to answer this question. Since $a_x = 0$,

$$x - x_0 = v_0 t$$

But how can you determine v_0? Because you're concerned with the horizontal component of velocity, you know to use cosine.

$$v_0 = v_{ix} = v_i \cos \theta$$
$$= (100\ \mathrm{m/s})(\cos 30°)$$
$$= (100)(0.87)$$
$$= 87\ \mathrm{m/s}$$

The final step is

$$x - x_0 = v_0 t$$
$$= (87\ \mathrm{m/s})(2\ \mathrm{s}) = 174\ \mathrm{m}$$

Therefore, (C) is the correct answer.

12. B

This is a projectile motion question, and making matters easier, you can take the starting velocity to be the given velocity, 3 m/s. However, there are two components to velocity. Horizontal velocity remains the same (recall that $a_x = 0$), but for vertical velocity:

$$v = v_{0y} + at$$
$$v = 0 + at$$
$$v = (10 \text{ m/s}^2)(0.5 \text{ s}) = 5 \text{ m/s}$$

To get the overall velocity, consider the horizontal and vertical velocities using vector analysis and find the resultant. Doing so gives $v = \sqrt{3^2 + 5^2} = \sqrt{34}$. The answer is around 5.8 m/s, which, when rounded to the correct number of significant figures, matches with (B), 6 m/s.

13. C

Using the basic principles of projectile motion and one-dimensional motion, this question shouldn't be too difficult to answer. The rock has to rise higher than the ball. At the apex of its movement, it will be falling freely; think of the ball as doing the same, at least in its horizontal sense. However, at the point where the rock starts falling freely, the ball has already begun doing so, so it will reach the ground before the rock. Choice (A) would be correct if the rock were dropped straight down at the same time that the ball was projected. Choice (B) would be tempting if you allowed yourself to be swayed by the inclusion of masses. Choices (A) and (B) are included as distractors—mass has nothing to do with the time required to reach the ground.

Explanations to Small Group Questions

1. Since the two bullets are the same height above the ground and will experience the same gravitational force in the downward direction, both bullets will hit the ground at the same time. The bullet shot from the gun will also have a horizontal velocity. However, there is no force acting on the bullet in the horizontal direction, so the horizontal motion has no effect on the acceleration of the bullet toward the ground, in the vertical direction.

2. The logarithmic scale means that when an earthquake increases ten-fold in intensity, or amplitude, its Richter magnitude will increase by 1 point on the Richter scale. Therefore, a 3.0 earthquake has an amplitude only one-hundredth that of a 5.0 earthquake.

Newtonian Mechanics

In this chapter:

Introduction

The dozen eggs you dropped yesterday morning on the kitchen floor, the mailbox mangled by bat-wielding neighborhood bullies, the squeaking sound as you slid bare-legged down the metal slide: all Newtonian mechanics acted out in real life. The ways in which objects move from one place to another are described by Newton's laws of motion. While the results of these laws will not always be so tragic, it is impossible to take even one step in the real world without being subjected to them. The related concepts of force, mass, and acceleration are fundamental not only to an understanding of mechanics but also to your success on the Physical Sciences section of the MCAT. In fact, these concepts will account for the largest aggregate of physics-related points on test day! Learn them well now and then apply them over and over again in your online practice for MCAT proficiency.

This chapter looks at each of Newton's three laws and marvels that a world as complex as ours can really be quite well understood by three relatively simple laws. Far more interesting than the laws themselves will be the use of the laws to make sense of the kinds of motion that we observe every day: falling, sliding, and rotating.

Because we've already learned how to divide forces into their geometric components, also known as resolving forces (Chapter 1), we can understand how to hang pictures so that they are level, make predictions about who will win a tug-of-war contest, and even calculate the speed at which your friend will smash into the snow bank at the bottom of the double black diamond ski slope. Considering the application of forces to objects that are free to rotate around a fixed point will tell us why wrenches and bolts are better than screwdrivers and screws, and why sometimes chubby and skinny kids have difficulty finding balance on a seesaw. Lastly, we will think about centripetal motion, which will help explain why race cars tend to crash on the curves and why your puppy on his leash keeps running around you in a perfect circle.

2.1 Newton's Three Laws

Any discussion of Newtonian mechanics must start with the basic concepts of mass, force, and acceleration. The three laws, then, just describe the relationships among these three concepts.

FORCE

Force (F) is a vector quantity (remember from Chapter 1: vectors have magnitude and direction) that is experienced as pushing or pulling on objects. The amazing thing about forces is that they can exist between objects that aren't even touching. While it is common in our experience for forces to be exerted by one object touching another, there are even more instances in which forces exist between objects nowhere near each other. On a grand scale, the oceanic tides are the result of the attractive gravitational force of the Moon on the water. On an even grander scale, the gravitational pull of planets orbiting a sun causes the sun to "wobble" on its axis. On a more human scale, we can feel the repulsive force that exists between the north ends (or the south ends) of two bar magnets. The SI unit for force is the newton (N) and is equivalent to one kilogram • meter/second^2.

MASS AND WEIGHT

Pay attention to this: Mass and weight are not the same things! **Mass (m)** is a measure of a body's inertia—the amount of matter in something, the amount of "stuff." Mass is a scalar quantity. (Remember, scalar numbers have magnitude only.) The SI unit for mass is the kilogram. Measurement of mass is independent of gravity. One kilogram of chocolate on Earth will have the same mass as one kilogram of chocolate on the Moon (and will be equally delicious). **Weight (W)** is a measure of gravitational force, usually that of the Earth, on an object's mass. Weight is sometimes represented as F_g, or the force due to gravity. Because weight is a force, it is a vector quantity and has the same SI unit as any other force, the newton (N). Mass and weight are not the same things, but they are related by this equation:

$$W = m\mathbf{g},$$

where W = weight = acceleration due to gravity, $\mathbf{g}$, exerted on the mass, m.

The weight of an object can be thought of as being applied at a single point in that object, called the center of gravity. Only for a homogeneous body (symmetrical shape and uniform density) can the center of gravity be located at its geometric center. For example, we can approximate the center of gravity for a metal shot-put ball as the geometric center of the sphere. The same cannot be said, however, for a human body, complex automobile, or any asymmetrical, non-uniform object.

ACCELERATION

Acceleration (a) is the rate of change of velocity that an object experiences as a result of some applied force. Acceleration, like velocity, is a vector quantity and is measured in SI units of meters/seconds². Acceleration in the direction opposite the initial velocity may be called deceleration. Failure to notice your untied shoelace may cause rapid acceleration of your face toward the pavement. The meeting of your face with said pavement will cause rapid, destructive, and painful deceleration of facial and dental tissues.

NEWTON'S LAWS OF MOTION

Now that we have a clear understanding of force, mass, and acceleration, let's examine how they relate to each other. While it is unlikely that an apple actually fell onto Newton's head, he recorded that he was indeed inspired by observing apples falling from trees. Of course, Newton did not "discover" gravity. He merely thought a little bit longer and a little bit harder about things that everyone, everywhere, in every time had observed. His observations about objects in motion and at rest are the basis for the branch of physics that we now know as mechanics. Newton's laws, which are expressed as equations, do a nice job of describing the effect forces have on objects that have mass.

1. $\mathbf{F} = m\mathbf{a} = 0$.

   A body either at rest or in motion with constant velocity will remain that way unless a net force acts upon it. This is also known as the law of inertia: "A body in motion will stay in motion, and a body at rest will stay at rest, unless acted upon by an external force." Newton's first law ought to be thought of as a special case of his second law, which is described next.

Key Equation

Weight
$W = mg$
$N = (kg)(m/s^2)$

MCAT Expertise

Gravity, g, decreases with height above the Earth and increases the closer you get to the Earth's center of mass. Near the Earth's surface, use $g = 10$ m/s².

Key Concept

If there is no acceleration, then there is no net force on the object. This means that any object with a constant velocity has no net force acting on it.

---

2. $\sum \mathbf{F} = m\mathbf{a}$ or, in terms of the component force vectors,

$\sum \mathbf{F}_x = m\mathbf{a}_x$ and

$\sum \mathbf{F}_y = m\mathbf{a}_y$.

The symbol in front of the $\mathbf{F}$ stands for "sum of" and, in this case, means the "vector sum of." What Newton's second law states is actually the corollary of the first: No acceleration of an object with mass m will occur when the vector sum of the forces results in a cancellation of those forces (vector sum equals zero). An object of mass m will accelerate when the vector sum of the forces results in some nonzero resultant force vector. In a game of tug-of-war, one team will eventually end up in the mud pit because the uneven application of forces to the rope will cause an acceleration of the (losing) team toward the center.

3. $\mathbf{F}_B = -\mathbf{F}_A$

This law is also known as the law of action and reaction: "To every action, there is always an opposed but equal reaction." More formally, the law states that for every force exerted by object B on object A, there is an equal but opposite force exerted by object A on object B. For example, when you hit your hand against your desk, your hand may have exerted quite the force against your desk, but it is an unavoidable law of Newtonian mechanics that your desk exerted the same force back against your hand. It is most likely your hand, not the desk, that is worse for the wear, but don't be fooled by this example. Physical contact is not necessary for Newton's third law. The mutual gravitational pull between the Earth and the Moon traverses hundreds of thousands of kilometers of space.

MCAT Concept Check 2.1

Before moving on, ensure that you are able to:

✓ Break down the SI units of force

✓ Explain the relationship between mass and weight

✓ Describe and explain Newton's three laws

2.2 Drawing Free-Body Diagrams

While we all have an intuitive sense of forces (and their effects) in everyday life, more of us struggle to represent them diagrammatically. Drawing free-body diagrams takes some practice but will be an invaluable tool on the MCAT. On test day, make sure that you draw a free-body diagram for every problem involving forces. The following examples demonstrate the use of this technique.

Example: Three people are pulling on ropes tied to a tire with forces of 100 N, 150 N, and 200 N, as shown in Figure 2.1. Find the magnitude and direction of the resultant force.

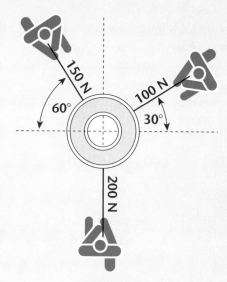

Figure 2.1

Solution: First we draw a free-body diagram (Figure 2.1) that shows the forces acting on the tire. Its purpose is to identify and visualize the acting forces.

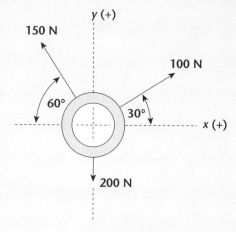

Figure 2.2

The resultant force is simply the sum of the forces. To find the resultant force vector, first we need the sum of the force components:

$$\mathbf{R}_x = \Sigma\mathbf{F}_x = 100\cos 30° - 150\cos 60°$$
$$= 86.6 - 75$$
$$= 11.6 \text{ N (positive } x\text{-direction, to the right)}$$
$$\mathbf{R}_y = \Sigma\mathbf{F}_y = 100\sin 30° + 150\sin 60° - 200$$
$$= 50 + 129.9 - 200$$
$$= -20.1 \text{ N (negative } y\text{-direction, down)}$$

Figure 2.3a shows the x- and y- components of each force, and Figure 2.3b shows the vector sums of the x and y force components, $\mathbf{R}_x$ and $\mathbf{R}_y$, respectively.

$$\mathbf{R} = \sqrt{(11.6)^2 + (-20.1)^2}$$
$$= 23.2 \text{ N}$$
$$\tan\theta = \frac{-20.1}{11.6}$$
$$\theta = -60° \text{ (R is in the 4th quadrant; see Figure 2.3c)}$$

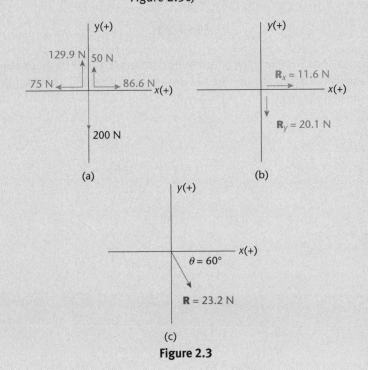

(a)

(b)

(c)

Figure 2.3

Example: Starting from rest, a 5 kg block takes 4 s to slide down a frictionless incline. Find the normal force, the acceleration of the block, and the vertical height h the block starts from, if the plane is at an angle of 30°.

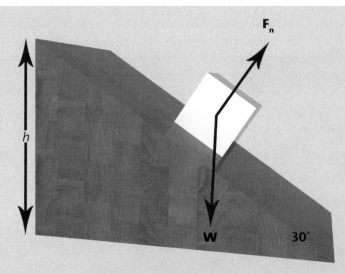

Figure 2.4

Solution: It is usually best to choose the x- and y-axes such that one of the axes is parallel to the surface, even when the surface is not horizontal. That is what we will do here. The force that the surface exerts on the block is broken up into two components, one perpendicular to the surface, called the **normal force (F$_n$),** and the other parallel to the surface, called the **friction force (f).** In this problem, the incline is frictionless (i.e., no **f**), so we have only the normal force **F$_n$**. The block's weight **W** is, of course, vertically down. We need to find the components of **W** parallel and perpendicular to the inclined surface (i.e., the components of **W** in the x- and y-directions, **W$_x$** and **W$_y$**).

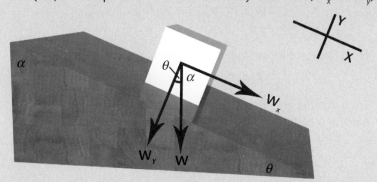

Figure 2.5

Note that in Figure 2.5, the angle **W** makes with the x-axis is α, and we would normally use this angle in expressing the components of **W**: **W$_x$** = **W** cos α and **W$_y$** = **W** sin α. However, it is more useful to express the components of **W** in terms of the angle θ that the inclined surface makes with the horizontal. In terms of θ, the components of **W** are these:

$$\mathbf{W}_x = \mathbf{W} \sin \theta = mg \sin \theta \quad (\mathbf{W} = mg)$$
$$\mathbf{W}_y = \mathbf{W} \cos \theta = mg \cos \theta$$

So let the x-axis be parallel to the inclined surface and the y-axis perpendicular (see Figure 2.6). The motion is along the inclined surface; in other words, along the x-axis. Therefore, any acceleration is only in the x-direction, and $\mathbf{a}_y$ is automatically zero.

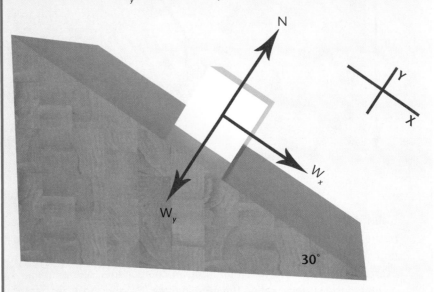

Figure 2.6

Only the forces in the x-direction affect the motion of the block. Because there is no acceleration in the y-direction, the sum of those forces equals zero.

$$\sum \mathbf{F}_x = \mathbf{W}_x = (5)(9.8)\sin 30° = 24.5 \text{ N} = m\mathbf{a}_x$$
$$\sum \mathbf{F}_y = m\mathbf{a}_y = \mathbf{F}_n - \mathbf{W}_y = 0$$

From the second equation, we can solve for $\mathbf{F}_n$:

$$\mathbf{F}_n = (5)(9.8)\cos 30° = 42.4 \text{ N}$$

From the first equation, we can solve for $\mathbf{a}_x$ (note that $\mathbf{a}_x = \mathbf{a}$ since $\mathbf{a}_y = 0$):

$$\mathbf{a} = \frac{\mathbf{F}}{m}$$
$$= \frac{24.5}{5}$$
$$= 4.9 \text{ m/s}^2$$

The length d of the incline from where the block started can now be found using:

$$d = \frac{at^2}{2} \qquad (\mathbf{V}_0 = 0)$$
$$= \frac{(4.9)(4)^2}{2}$$
$$= 39.2 \text{ m}$$

From trigonometry, the vertical height h is readily available:

$$\sin 30° = \frac{h}{d}$$

$$h = 39.2 \sin 30°$$
$$= 19.6 \text{ m}$$

MCAT Concept Check 2.2

Before moving on, ensure that you are able to:

✓ Draw an accurate free body diagram based on a written description of an object

✓ Solve for a resultant force using vector addition and trigonometry

---

2.3 Gravity ★★★★☆☆

When Newton watched apples falling out of trees, he was struck by the fact that they always fell perpendicularly to the ground, rather than sideways or even away from the ground. Furthermore, Newton began to wonder about the farthest reaches of gravity: If the apple feels this attractive pull toward the Earth, then what about the Moon? Indeed, what Newton came to understand he called "universal gravitation."

Gravity is an attractive force that is felt by all forms of matter. We usually think of gravity as acting on us to keep us from floating off of the Earth's surface, and of course, the planets of our solar system are kept in their orbits by the gravitational pull of the Sun. However, did you know that the book you are reading at this very moment is exerting a gravitational pull on you, and you on it? The same can be said for your cell phone, the couch in your living room, and all objects around you. Moreover, if all this matter is exerting this attractive force called gravity, why don't we all end up in one big messy ball of people, couches, and cell phones? Well, it's because gravity is only one kind of force and it just happens to be the weakest of the four forces known to us. There are a lot of other forces that are working to oppose gravity (for example, friction, which is an electromagnetic force), and so it is that we do not usually find ourselves tangled up in the world's largest ball of stuff.

The magnitude of the **gravitational force (F)** between two objects is

$$F = \frac{Gm_1m_2}{r^2}$$

Real World

Newton's third law states that the force of gravity on m_1 from m_2 is equal and opposite of the force of gravity on m_2 from m_1. This means that the force of gravity on you from the Earth is equal and opposite of the force of gravity from you on the Earth. This may sound strange, but with Newton's second law, you can make sense of it. Because the forces are equal but the masses are very different, you know that the accelerations must also be very different, from $\mathbf{F} = m\mathbf{a}$. Because your mass compared to that of the Earth is very small, you experience a large acceleration from it. In contrast, because the Earth is very massive and it feels the same force, it only experiences a tiny acceleration from you.

where G is the universal gravitational constant (6.67×10^{-11} N·m²/kg²), m_1 and m_2 are the masses of the two objects, and r is the distance between their centers. This is an equation you should know and understand for the MCAT. Don't just memorize it, though. Understanding, for instance, that the magnitude of the gravitational force is inverse to the square of the distance (that is, if r is halved, then F will quadruple) will help you predict the answer to a gravity problem on Test Day. The following example will demonstrate the use of the gravitational force equation.

Example: Find the gravitational attraction between an electron and a proton at a distance of 10^{-11} m. (Proton mass = 10^{-27} kg; electron mass = 10^{-30} kg.)

Solution: Use Newton's law of gravitation:

$$F = \frac{Gm_1 m_2}{r^2}$$
$$= \frac{(6.67 \times 10^{-11})(10^{-27})(10^{-30})}{(10^{-11})^2}$$
$$= 6.67 \times 10^{-46} \text{ N}$$

MCAT Concept Check 2.3

Before moving on, ensure that you are able to:

✓ Utilize and understand the equation for gravitational force

---

2.4 Different Kinds of Motion ★★★☆☆

Newton noticed that the apple fell in a straight line from the tree branch to the ground. This kind of motion, in which there is no rotation of the object, is called translational motion. Other kinds of motion that can be observed include rotational, circular, and periodic, and these will be the types covered on the MCAT. We will deal with the first three here in this chapter. Periodic motion will be covered in Chapter 9.

TRANSLATIONAL MOTION

Translational motion occurs when forces cause an object to move without any rotation about a fixed point in the object. The simplest pathways may be linear, such as when a child slides down a snowy hill on a sled, or parabolic, as in the case of a clown shot out of a cannon. Translational motion problems are pretty common on the MCAT, so be sure to practice them. Armed with your free-body diagram skills and your understanding of Newton's three laws, you'll be able to solve any problem that comes your way on the Physical Sciences section.

ROTATIONAL MOTION

Rotational motion occurs when forces are applied against an object in such a way as to cause the object to rotate around a fixed pivot point, also known as the fulcrum. Application of force at some distance from the fulcrum, along the lever arm, generates **torque, τ,** or the **moment of force**. It is the torque that generates the rotational motion, not the mere application of the force itself. This is because torque depends not only on the magnitude of the force but also on the angle at which the force is applied against the lever arm as well as the distance between the fulcrum and the point of force application. The equation that describes rotational motion is

$$\tau = rF \sin \theta$$

where F is the magnitude of the force, r is the distance between the fulcrum and the point of force application, and θ is the angle between F and the lever arm.

Once again, we encounter a physical phenomenon for which we all have an intuitive understanding, even if the mathematics seem, initially at least, at little scary. We've all seen someone (or been the one) pushing on a door when the sign says "Pull." We've seen the skinny kid being catapulted through the air by the chubby kid straddling the opposite end of the seesaw. The next section examines the special case of rotational motion in which the vector sum of the torques is zero.

CIRCULAR MOTION

Circular motion occurs when forces cause an object to move in a circular pathway. Upon completion of one cycle, the displacement of the object is zero. Although the MCAT focuses on uniform circular motion, in which case the speed of the object is constant, you ought to know that there is also nonuniform circular motion. Nonuniform circular motion is covered briefly after we discuss uniform circular motion.

For circular motion that demonstrates a constant speed at all points along the pathway (see Figure 2.7), the instantaneous velocity vector is always tangent to the circular path. What this means is that the object moving in the circular motion has a tendency (inertia) to "break out" of its circular pathway and move in a linear direction along the tangent. So why doesn't it just do that? Well, we need to talk about the forces that are acting on the object. In all circular motion, we can resolve the forces into radial (center-seeking) and tangential components. In uniform circular motion, the tangential force is zero (because there is no change in the speed of the object).

Key Equation

Torque
$t = rF \sin\theta$
$N \cdot m = (m)(N)(\textit{unitless})$

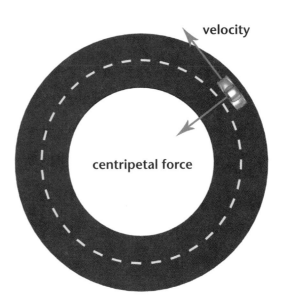

Figure 2.7. Circular Motion
A car traveling at a constant speed in a circle in uniform circular motion

Key Equation

Centripetal Force

$$F = \frac{mv^2}{r}$$

$$N = \frac{(kg)(m/s)^2}{m}$$

Thus, the resultant force is the radial force. This is known as the **centripetal force,** and according to Newton's second law, this generates **centripetal acceleration.** Remember, also, from our discussion of Newton's laws that both force and acceleration are vectors and the acceleration is always in the same direction as the resultant force. Thus it is this acceleration generated by the centripetal force that keeps an object in its circular pathway. When the centripetal force is no longer acting on the object, it will simply exit the circular pathway and assume a path tangential to the circle at that point. The equation that describes circular motion is

$$F = \frac{mv^2}{r}$$

where v^2/r is the centripetal acceleration and F is the force necessary to keep an object of mass m in orbit with radius r.

Real World

Examples of centripetal force in action are the force of gravity in maintaining a satellite's orbit and the tension in a rope attached to an object that is being spun around. This is the force that keeps the object from flying off tangentially.

Think about a puppy running around you and getting you all tangled up in his leash. Standing still, you are the center of a circle whose radius is defined by the length of the leash. As the puppy attempts to run off to chase a shadow, he finds that he is restricted in his movement by the leash. In fact, the tension in the leash keeps him running in a circle. The tension, in this case, provides the centripetal force necessary for the centripetal acceleration. Of course, every time the puppy runs a complete circle around you, the leash gets shorter, creating a smaller radius.

The puppy on the leash more likely presents the situation of nonuniform circular motion, in which the speed of the moving object changes over the course of the path. This means, then, that there is a tangential force acting to create a tangential acceleration. This force vector adds to the radial force vector to produce a resultant force (and resultant acceleration) that is not directed toward the center of the circle. On the MCAT, you will encounter nonuniform circular motion in the context of planetary and satellite orbits, but rest assured that the passage will provide you with all the information you need about the orbit to answer the more basic questions about the fundamental Newtonian mechanics discussed here.

> **MCAT Concept Check 2.4**
>
> Before moving on, ensure you that are able to:
>
> ✓ Describe the relationship between torque and applied force
> ✓ Utilize and understand the relationship between centripetal force and circular motion

2.5 Forces of Friction

Friction is a kind of force—electromagnetic, actually (more on that in Chapter 3)—that works to oppose the movement of objects. Unlike other kinds of forces, such as gravity or electromagnetic force, which can cause objects either to speed up or slow down, friction forces almost always oppose an object's motion and cause it to slow down or become stationary. Actually, there are two kinds of friction, static and kinetic. **Static friction (F_s)** exists between a stationary object and the surface upon which it rests. The equation that describes static friction is

$$0 \le f_s \le \mu_s F_n$$

where μ_s is the **coefficient of static friction** and F_n is the normal force. Don't forget that the normal force is the component of the contact force that is perpendicular to the plane of contact between the object and the surface upon which it rests.

What is really interesting, and what some students find difficult to understand about this equation, is its use of the less-than-or-equal-to signs. These signify that there is a range of possible values for static friction. The minimum, of course, is zero, and on the MCAT, you will sometimes be presented with the ideal frictionless surface. However, the MCAT also tends to deal with real-world situations in which friction is present. The maximum value of static friction can be calculated from the right side of the previous equation. Objects that are stationary ought not

to be assumed to be experiencing that maximum value. In fact, one can demonstrate quite easily that the static friction between an object and a surface is not at its maximal value.

Consider standing in the long security lines at a major U.S. airport. To avoid paying baggage overweight charges, you have stuffed your carry-on bag nearly to the bursting point. Throwing your bag down to the floor, you decide that it will be easier to kick it along rather than lift it every time the line moves. The first time, you kick it gently—you're exhausted after all—and the bag doesn't even budge. You kick it a little harder, but it still doesn't move. Now you're getting mad. This time you give it a good swift kick, and it slides a couple of feet and then comes to a rest. What happened? Why didn't the first couple of kicks work? The difference is that the first two kicks were matched by an increase in the static friction between the bag and the floor. Remember, friction always works to oppose motion. The third kick (the hard one) was so strong that not even the maximum static friction could withstand the force applied through your foot. As a result, the bag, now experiencing a vector sum of forces in the desired direction of movement, actually moves.

Kinetic friction (F_k) exists between a sliding object and the surface over which the object slides. Sometimes, students misidentify the presence of kinetic friction. A wheel, for example, that is rolling along a road does not experience kinetic friction because the tire is not actually sliding against the pavement. The tire maintains an instantaneous point of static contact with the road and, therefore, experiences static friction! Only when the tire begins to slide on, say, an icy patch during the winter will kinetic friction come into play. To be sure, any time two surfaces slide against each other, kinetic friction will be present and can be measured according to this equation:

$$f_k = \mu_k F_n$$

where μ_k is the **coefficient of kinetic friction** and F_n is the normal force. There's an important distinction between this equation for kinetic friction and the previous equation for static friction. The kinetic friction equation has an equals sign, not the less-than-or-equals sign. This means that kinetic friction will have a constant value for any given combination of a coefficient of kinetic friction and normal force. It does not matter how much surface area is in contact or even the velocity of the sliding object. Furthermore, the maximum value for static friction will always be greater than the constant value for kinetic friction. If that doesn't make sense, think about this: The carry-on bag that you're kicking around in the airport security line requires more force to get it sliding than to keep it sliding.

Example: Two blocks are in static equilibrium, as shown in Figure 2.8.

a. If block A has a mass of 15 kg and the coefficient of static friction μ_s equals 0.20, then find the maximum mass of block B.

b. If an extra 5 kg are added to B, find the acceleration of A and the tension T in the rope. (μ_k equals 0.14.)

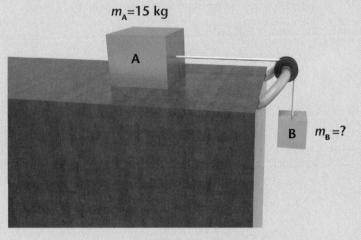

$m_A = 15$ kg

A

B $m_B = ?$

Figure 2.8

Solution:

a.

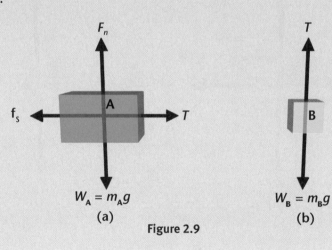

F_n

f_s A T

$W_A = m_A g$

(a)

T

B

$W_B = m_B g$

(b)

Figure 2.9

For block B (Figure 2.9b):

$$\Sigma F_y = 0 = T - W_B$$

$$T = W_B = m_B g$$

For block A (Figure 2.9a):

Asking for the maximum mass of block B means that the coefficient of static friction holding block A is at its maximum, $f_s = \mu_s F_n$.

$$\Sigma F_y = 0 = F_n - W_A$$

$$F_n = W_A = m_A g$$

$$\Sigma F_x = 0 = T - \mu_s F_n$$

$$T = \mu_s m_A g$$

$$T = (0.2)(15)(9.8)$$

$$T = 29.4 \text{ N}$$

Since block B is in static equilibrium, the tension in the rope must equal the weight of the block, so we have

$$m_B g = 29.4$$

$$m_B = 3 \text{ kg}$$

b.

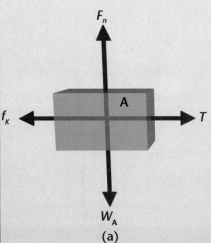

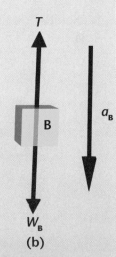

(a)

(b)

Figure 2.10

We found the maximum mass of B for the system to be in static equilibrium. Adding an extra 5 kg to B means that the system is now in motion.

For block B (Figure 2.10b):

$$\Sigma F_y = m_B g - T = m_B a_B$$

For block A (Figure 2.10a):

$$\Sigma F_x = T - \mu_k F_n$$
$$= T - \mu_k m_A g$$
$$= m_A a_A$$

Since the blocks are connected by the string, the magnitude of the acceleration for both of them is the same:

$$a_A = a_B = a$$

and

$$m_B g - T = m_B a$$
$$T - \mu_k m_A g = m_A a$$

Adding the two equations gives this:

$$m_B g - T + T - \mu_k m_A g = (m_A + m_B)a$$

Solving for a:

$$a = \frac{(m_B - \mu_k m_A)g}{(m_A + m_B)}$$

$$= \frac{\left[(8 - (0.14)(15))\right]9.8}{(15 + 8)}$$

$$= 2.5 \text{ m/s}^2$$

Substituting this value into the equation $m_A a = T - \mu_k m_A g$ and solving for the tension gives this:

$$T = m_A(\mu_k g + a)$$
$$= 15[(0.14(9.8) + 2.5)]$$
$$= 58.1 \text{ N}$$

As previously mentioned in the discussion of static friction, you must pay close attention to the conditions set in the MCAT passage or question. Does it tell you that friction can be assumed to be negligible, or does it provide the coefficient values, which will most likely need to be used in a calculation of friction values? The sample problem in this section will help you get ready for the MCAT practice problems in your online resources.

MCAT Concept Check 2.5

Before moving on, ensure that you are able to:

✓ Compare and contrast static and kinetic friction

✓ Calculate the force of friction exerted on stationary and moving objects

2.6 Mechanical Equilibria

We will spend a lot of time discussing and applying the concept of equilibrium to many different situations, as it is one of the dominant concepts tested on the MCAT. Here we will examine mechanical equilibrium, which occurs when the vector sum of the forces or torques acting on an object is zero; that is, when all of the force or all of the torque vectors cancel out.

TRANSLATIONAL EQUILIBRIUM

Translational equilibrium exists only when the vector sum of all of the forces acting on an object is zero. This is called the first condition of equilibrium. It's merely an instance of Newton's first law, which, remember, is only a special case of the second. When the resultant force upon an object is zero, the object will not accelerate. Its motional behavior will be constant. That may mean that the object is stationary, but it could just as well mean that the object is moving with a constant nonzero velocity. What is important to remember is that an object experiencing translational equilibrium will have a constant speed (which could be a zero or nonzero value) and a constant direction.

$$\sum F = 0$$
$$\sum F_x = 0 \text{ and } \sum F_y = 0$$

Translational equilibrium is necessary for a surprising array of scenarios. Undoubtedly, reading this book would be difficult if it weren't stationary in your lap or resting on a desktop. Even hanging a sign or a picture is an exercise in achieving translational equilibrium. The following problem demonstrates the steps necessary to determine the appropriate tension in a system of wires used to hang a 20 kg block.

> ### Key Concept
> Just because the net force equal zero does not mean the velocity equals zero; this is an extremely important concept.

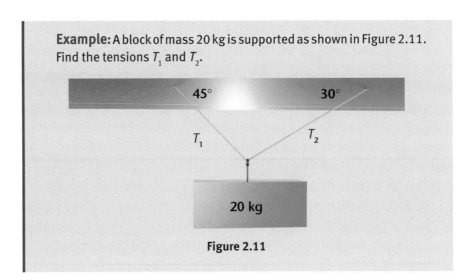

Example: A block of mass 20 kg is supported as shown in Figure 2.11. Find the tensions T_1 and T_2.

45° 30°

T_1 T_2

20 kg

Figure 2.11

Solution: A free-body diagram at the point of intersection of the three cords will help solve this problem (see Figure 2.12). Cords, strings, and the like can only exert pulling forces, and these are in the direction of each cord. Note also that the tension in the vertical cord is equal to the weight of the 20 kg mass, as shown in the other free-body diagram on the right.

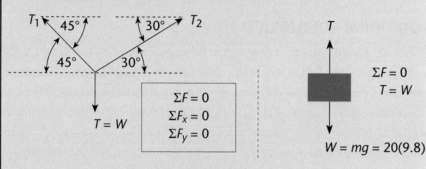

Figure 2.12

The force components are as follows:

$$\sum F_x = 0 = T_2 \cos 30° - T_1 \cos 45°$$
$$\sum F_y = 0 = T_1 \sin 45° + T_2 \sin 30° - 20(9.8)$$

Solve the second equation for T_1:

$$T_1 = \frac{20(9.8) - T_2 \sin 30°}{\sin 45°}$$

$$= \frac{20(9.8) - T_2/2}{\sqrt{2}/2}$$

$$= \frac{196(2) - (T_2/2)2}{\sqrt{2}}$$

$$= \frac{392 - T_2}{\sqrt{2}}$$

Substitute this into the first equation:

$$\frac{T_2\sqrt{3}}{2} - \frac{\sqrt{2}}{2}\left(\frac{392 - T_2}{\sqrt{2}}\right) = 0$$

$$T_2(\sqrt{3} + 1) = 392$$

$$T_2 = \frac{392}{\sqrt{3} + 1}$$

$$= 143.5\,\text{N}$$

And now T_1 follows from this:

$$T_1 = \frac{392 - 143.5}{\sqrt{2}}$$

$$= 175.7 \text{ N}$$

ROTATIONAL EQUILIBRIUM

Rotational equilibrium exists only when the vector sum of all the torques acting on an object is zero. This is called the second condition of equilibrium. Torques that generate clockwise rotation are conventionally negative, while torques that generate counterclockwise rotation are positive. Thus, in rotational equilibrium, it must be that all of the positive torques exactly cancel out all of the negative torques. Similar to the motional behavior defined by translational equilibrium, there are two possibilities of motion in the case of rotational equilibrium. Either the lever arm is not rotating at all (that is, it is stationary), or it is rotating with a constant angular frequency (analogous to a constant velocity). The MCAT usually, and more simply, takes rotational equilibrium to mean that the lever arm is not rotating at all.

$$\tau = rF \sin \theta$$

Key Concept

Remember that sin 90° equals 1. This means that torque is greatest when the force applied is 90 degrees (perpendicular) to the length of the lever arm. Knowing that sin 0° equals 0 tells us that there is no torque when the force applied is parallel to the lever arm.

MCAT Expertise

Before jumping to the math on any of these problems, use your knowledge to get a general idea of what the mass should approximately be. This way, you can eliminate some of the answer choices first. Because the second block is much closer to the fulcrum, you know that it must be more massive. Always make these predictions before moving on to the math.

Example: A seesaw with a mass of 5 kg has one block of mass 10 kg two meters to the left of the fulcrum and another block 0.5 m to the right of the fulcrum (see Figure 2.13). If the seesaw is in equilibrium,

a. find the mass of the second block.
b. find the force exerted by the fulcrum.

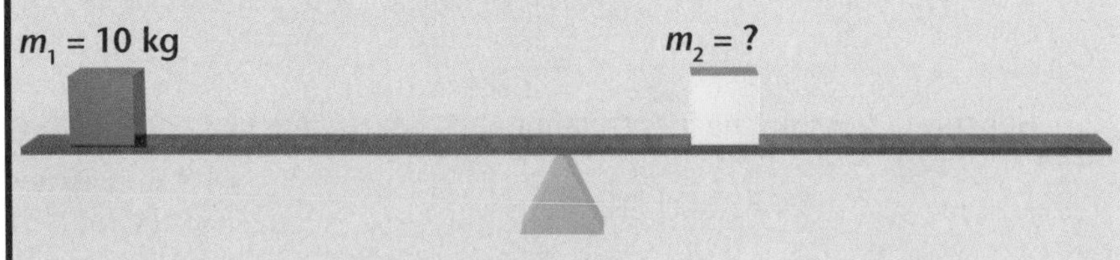

$m_1 = 10$ kg $m_2 = ?$

Figure 2.13

Solution:

a. To find τ, take the point of the fulcrum as the pivot point. This way, both the normal force and the weight of the seesaw will be eliminated from the equation ($r = 0$). Let's call the 10 kg mass object 1 and the block whose mass we are trying to find object 2.

$\tau = mgd \sin \theta$ (Note: $\theta = 90°$, therefore, $\sin \theta = 1$)

$\sum \tau = 0 = m_1 g d_1 - m_2 g d_2$

$m_2 = \dfrac{m_1 d_1}{d_2}$

$= \dfrac{10(2)}{0.5}$

$= 40 \text{ kg}$

b. To find the normal force, F_n, exerted by the fulcrum, use $\sum F_y = 0$. There are the upward forces exerted by the fulcrum and the downward weights of the seesaw and the two masses. Don't forget that $W = mg$. Taking up as positive,

$$F_n - 5(9.8) - 10(9.8) - 40(9.8) = 0$$
$$F_n = 49 + 98 + 392 = 539 \text{ N}$$

MCAT Concept Check 2.6

Before moving on, ensure that you are able to:

✓ Define translational equilibrium

✓ Define rotational equilibrium

✓ Determine the magnitudes of forces acting on objects at equilibrium

Conclusion

In this chapter, we learned that different kinds of forces act on objects to cause them to move in certain ways. Application of forces may cause objects to accelerate or decelerate, according to Newton's second law. If the vector sum of all the forces acting on an object is equal to zero, the forces cancel out, and the object experiences no acceleration, a condition known as translational equilibrium. This is expressed in Newton's first law. Even when objects aren't touching, they can still exert forces between them, as described by Newton's third law. Forces can cause objects to translate (move with linear motion), and centripetal forces cause objects to move in a circle. Applying forces to objects that have pivot points can generate torques, which cause the objects to rotate. Sometimes those torques cancel out to produce rotational equilibrium. Newtonian mechanics is an MCAT favorite. Your careful consideration of the discussion topics in this chapter and your practice with the kinds of problems demonstrated here will pay off in many points on Test Day.

CONCEPT SUMMARY

Newton's Laws (p. 36)

- ☐ **Mass and Weight**
  - ○ Weight = force due to gravity, g, exerted on the mass, m
- ☐ **Newton's three laws**
  - ○ Newton's First Law
    - ■ A body in motion will stay in motion, and a body at rest will stay at rest, unless acted upon by a net force
  - ○ Newton's Second Law
    - ■ $\Sigma \mathbf{F} = m\mathbf{a}$
  - ○ Newton's Third Law
    - ■ To every action there is an opposed but equal reaction
    - ■ Objects do not need to be in direct physical contact
      - ● e.g., gravitational or electrostatic force
    - ■ Normal force: a reactive force between objects in direct physical contact

Free-Body Diagrams (p. 38)

- ☐ Always draw a free-body diagram when solving problems involving Newtonian mechanics
- ☐ Practice drawing free-body diagrams of objects on inclined planes
  - ○ To resolve the forces into their x-and y-components, you must know the trigonometric functions of sine and cosine for the classic right triangle angles

Gravitational Force (p. 43)

- ☐ The magnitude of gravitational force between two objects is inversely proportional to the square of the distance separating their respective centers of gravity
  - ○ This equation is in the same form as the electrostatic force equation, but the force due to mass is much smaller than the force due to charge
- ☐ "Little g" is an approximation of the acceleration due to gravity on an object close to the surface of the earth
  - ○ Although g is given as a constant, 9.8 m/s^2, in reality, the true acceleration due to gravity depends on r and can be determined with the gravitational force equation

Types of Motion (p. 44)

- ☐ Translational
  - ○ Forces cause an object to move without any rotation
- ☐ Rotational
  - ○ Forces are applied perpendicularly to a fulcrum, generating torque and causing rotation around the fulcrum

☐ Circular

    ○ In uniform circular motion, the centripetal force vector and the centripetal acceleration vector point directly to the center of the circular pathway

    ○ The instantaneous velocity vector is tangential to the circular pathway at any given point

Frictional Forces (p. 47)

☐ Frictional forces act in the direction opposite or opposing intended or actual motion.

☐ On the MCAT you will be told when you can ignore friction and when you must account for it

    ○ The forces of air resistance, static friction, and kinetic friction are commonly encountered on the test

☐ For an object in contact with a surface, the maximum value of static friction will always be greater than the (constant) value of kinetic friction

Equilibrium

☐ **Translational equilibrium** (p. 52): occurs when the vector sum of forces acting on an object is equal to 0

    ○ No net acceleration, and the object's motional behavior continues unchanged

    ○ Does not require than an object be stationary, only that its motional behavior (stationary or moving) be constant

☐ **Rotational equilibrium** (p. 54): occurs when the vector sum of torques acting on an object is equal to 0

    ○ No net rotational acceleration, object's motional behavior continues unchanged

    ○ No requirement that the object be stationary, only that its motional behavior (stationary or rotating) be constant

EQUATIONS TO REMEMBER

☐ $\sum F = ma$

☐ $W = mg = F_g$

☐ $F_B = -F_A$

☐ $F = \dfrac{Gm_1 m_2}{r^2}$

☐ $\tau = rF \sin \theta$

☐ $F = \dfrac{mv^2}{r}$

☐ $0 \le f_s \le \mu_s F_n$ (for static friction)

☐ $f_k = \mu_k F_n$ (for kinetic friction)

SHARED CONCEPTS

HIGH YIELD PRACTICE PROBLEMS

Practice Questions

1. A 1,000 kg rocket ship, traveling at 100 m/s, is acted on by an average force of 20 kN applied in the direction of its motion for 8 s. What is the change in velocity of the rocket?

   A. 100 m/s
   B. 160 m/s
   C. 1,600 m/s
   D. 2,000 m/s

2. An elevator is designed to carry a maximum weight of 9,800 N (including its own weight) and to move upward at a speed of 5 m/s after an initial period of acceleration. What is the relationship between the maximum tension in the elevator cable and the maximum weight of 9,800 N when the elevator is accelerating upward?

   A. The tension is greater than 9,800 N.
   B. The tension is less than 9,800 N.
   C. The tension equals 9,800 N.
   D. It cannot be determined from the information given.

3. A 10 kg wagon rests on a frictionless inclined plane. The plane makes an angle of 30° with the horizontal. What is the force, F, required to keep the wagon from sliding down the plane?

   A. 10 N
   B. 30 N
   C. 49 N
   D. 98 N

4. A 20 kg wagon is released from rest from the top of a 15 m long plane, which is angled at 30° with the horizontal. Assuming there is friction between the ramp and the wagon, how is this frictional force affected if the angle of the incline is increased?

   A. The frictional force increases.
   B. The frictional force decreases.
   C. The frictional force remains the same.
   D. It cannot be determined from the information given.

5. An astronaut weighs 700 N on Earth. What is the best approximation of her new weight on a planet with a radius that is two times that of Earth, and a mass three times that of Earth?

   A. 200 N
   B. 500 N
   C. 700 N
   D. 900 N

6. A 30 kg girl sits on a seesaw at a distance of 2 m from the fulcrum. Where must her father sit to balance the seesaw if he has a mass of 90 kg?

   A. 67 cm from the girl
   B. 67 cm from the fulcrum
   C. 133 cm from the girl
   D. 267 cm from the fulcrum

7. An object is moving uniformly in a circle whose diameter is 200 m. If the centripetal acceleration of the object is 4 m/s², then what is the time for one revolution of the circle?

A. 10π s
B. 20π s
C. 100 s
D. 200 s

8. A distant solar system is made up one small planet of mass 1.48×10^{24} kg revolving in a circular orbit about a large, stationary star of mass 7.3×10^{30} kg. The distance between their centers is 5×10^{11} m. What happens to the speed of the planet if the distance between the star and the planet increases (assume the new orbit is also circular)?

A. The speed of the planet increases.
B. The speed of the planet decreases.
C. The speed of the planet remains the same.
D. It cannot be determined from the information given.

9. An elevator is accelerating down at 4 m/s². How much does a 10 kg fish weigh if measured inside the elevator?

A. 140 N
B. 100 N
C. 60 N
D. 50 N

10. A 1 kg ball with a radius of 20 cm rolls down a 5 m high inclined plane. Its speed at the bottom is 8 m/s. How many revolutions per second is the ball making when at the bottom of the plane?

A. 6 revolutions/s
B. 12 revolutions/s
C. 20 revolutions/s
D. 23 revolutions/s

11. A 1,000 kg satellite traveling at speed v maintains an orbit of radius R around the Earth. What should be its speed if it is to develop a new orbit of radius $4R$?

A. $\frac{1}{4} v$
B. $\frac{1}{2} v$
C. $2 v$
D. $4 v$

12. A 100 kg elevator initially at rest accelerates up at rate $\bar{a}$. What is the average force acting on the elevator if it covers a distance x over a period of 10 s?

A. $2x + 1,000$
B. $100(\bar{a} + 1)$
C. $2\bar{a} + 1,000$
D. $2\bar{a} x$

Small Group Questions

1. Consider Figure 2.14 below, in which a brick placed on a level board is connected to a second block that hangs off the edge of the board by a rope and pulley system. Weight is added to the hanging block until the brick begins to slide. Describe in general terms how the velocity and displacement of the brick change with respect to time once the brick begins to slide.

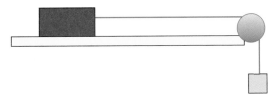

Figure 2.14

2. Suppose a car is traveling with velocity v around a circle. Using Newton's third law, describe the pair of opposing forces that are responsible for the circular motion of the car.

3. Can any force produce a torque? If not, which kinds of forces cannot generate torque? What are the conditions required to produce torque?

Explanations to Practice Questions

1. B

The average force on the rocket equals its mass times the average acceleration; the average acceleration equals the change in velocity divided by the time over which the change occurs. So the change in velocity equals the average force times the time divided by the mass:

$$F = ma, \text{ so } a = \frac{F}{m}$$

$$a = \frac{\Delta v}{\Delta t}$$

$$\Delta v = a\Delta t = \frac{F\Delta t}{m}$$

$$\Delta v = \frac{(20{,}000 \text{ N} \times 8\,s)}{1{,}000 \text{ kg}}$$

$$\Delta v = 160 \text{ m/s}$$

Choice (B) is therefore the correct answer.

2. A

The forces on the elevator are the tension upward and the weight downward, so the net force on the elevator is the difference between the two. When the elevator is accelerating upward, the tension in the cable must be greater than the maximum weight so that the difference produces a nonzero acceleration. Choice (A) is therefore the correct answer. In contrast, when the elevator is moving at a constant speed, its acceleration is zero, so the net force on the elevator is also zero, which means that the tension and the weight are equal. Similarly, when the elevator is accelerating downward, the tension is less than 9,800 N so that there is a nonzero acceleration.

3. C

The weight of the wagon ($W = mg$) acts in a direction straight down. This force can be separated into x-and y-components, with the x-axis parallel to and the y-axis perpendicular to the plane of the incline.

$$W_x = W \sin 30°$$
$$W_y = W \cos 30°$$

To keep the wagon from moving (i.e., to keep it in equilibrium), the sum of the forces must equal zero. In terms of the components,

$$\Sigma F_x = 0 \text{ and } \Sigma F_y = 0$$

From a free-body diagram, it can be seen that the y-component of the weight is counteracted by an equal and opposite force from the surface of the plane (the normal force, $\mathbf{F}_n$). Similarly, the x–component of the weight, which tends to cause the wagon to roll down the plane, must be counteracted by an equal and opposite force parallel to the plane. This is the unknown force, $\mathbf{F}$. (Remember, the plane is frictionless.) The magnitude of the required force can be determined by recognizing that the sum of the forces in the x-direction must equal zero:

$$\Sigma F_x = F - W \sin 30° = 0$$
$$F = W \sin 30°$$
$$F = mg \sin 30°$$
$$F = 10 \text{ kg } (10 \text{ m/s}^2)\,(0.5)$$
$$F \approx 50 \text{ N (or kg} \times \text{m/s}^2)$$

Choice (C) best matches our result and is thus the correct answer.

Note: We let "up the plane" be the positive x-direction. We could have also taken "down the plane" to be the positive x-direction as long as we use the correct signs when we calculate the components. The choice of positive direction is arbitrary.

4. B

The force of friction on an object sliding down an incline equals the coefficient of friction times the normal force. The normal force, which is given by $mg \cos \theta$, decreases as the angle of the incline, θ, increases. Therefore, the frictional force decreases as the angle of the incline increases. Choice (B) best reflects this and is thus the correct answer.

5. B

The weight of an object on a planet can be found by using Newton's law of gravitation with one minor simplification. Because the planet is much larger than the person, r, which is the distance between the centers of the two objects (the planet and person), can be taken simply as the radius of the planet; the additional few meters to the center of the astronaut can be ignored. The astronaut's weight on earth equals

$$F = \frac{GmM_E}{r_E^2} = 700 \text{ N}$$

On a planet that is three times as massive as earth ($M_P = 3M_E$), and has twice the radius ($r_P = 2r_E$), the force would be equal to

$$F = \frac{GmM_P}{r_P^2}$$

$$F = \frac{Gm(3M_E)}{(2r_E)^2}$$

$$F = \frac{3GmM_E}{(4r_E^2)}$$

$$F = \frac{3}{4}\left(\frac{GmM_E}{r_E^2}\right)$$

$$F = \frac{3}{4} \text{ (the astronaut's weight on earth)}$$

$$F = \frac{3}{4} \times 700 \text{ N}$$

$$F \approx 500 \text{ N}$$

Choice (B) is therefore the correct answer.

6. B

For the seesaw to be balanced, the torque due to the girl must be exactly counteracted by the torque due to her father. More generally stated, the sum of the torques about any point must be equal to zero. Taking the torques about the fulcrum for the girl and the father, obtain the following (note, the "f" subscript represents the father and the "g" subscript represents the girl):

$$\Sigma \sigma_{\text{fulcrum}} = m_f g x - m_g g x_g = 0$$
$$m_f g x = m_g g x_g$$
$$x = \frac{m_g x_g}{m_f}$$
$$x = \frac{(30 \times 2)}{90}$$
$$x = \frac{2}{3} \text{ m}$$
$$x = 67 \text{ cm from the fulcrum}$$

Choice (B) is therefore the correct answer. You can also solve this problem by finding the torques about any point, not just the fulcrum. Doing so, however, is usually more complicated because the force of the fulcrum on the seesaw first has to be determined. Because both the weight of the girl and the weight of the father act in a downward direction, the fulcrum must exert a force of $(30g) + (90g) = 120g$ N in an upward direction on the seesaw. Calculating the torques about the girl's location, we obtain the following:

$$\Sigma \tau = 90gx - (120g)(2) = 0$$
$$x = \frac{240}{90}$$
$$x = 2.67 \text{ m from the girl}$$

This equals 2.67 m – 2 m = 0.67 m from the fulcrum. Once again, choice (B) matches your result.

7. A

This question is testing your knowledge of circular motion. To calculate the time for one revolution of the circle, start with the centripetal acceleration: $a = \frac{v^2}{r}$. Given $r = 100$ m and $a = 4$ m/s^2, we have $v = 20$ m/s. Speed, v, and time of revolution (period), T, are related by $v = \frac{2\pi r}{T}$ (i.e., in a time equal to one revolution, the distance covered is the circumference). Therefore,

$$T = \frac{2\pi (100 \text{ m})}{(20 \text{ m/s})} = 10\pi \text{ s}$$

Choice (A) matches your result and is therefore the correct answer.

8.   B

The force on the planet due to the star is equal to

$$F = \frac{Gm_{star}m_{planet}}{r^2}$$

Because this force provides the centripetal force, it's also true that F is equal to

$$F = \frac{m_{planet}v^2}{r}$$

Equating the two expressions for F gives the following:

$$\frac{Gm_{star}m_{planet}}{r^2} = \frac{m_{planet}v^2}{r}$$

$$v^2 = \frac{Gm_{star}}{r}$$

Increasing the distance between the planet and the star, r, means that the speed, v, decreases. This means that choice (B) is the correct answer.

9.   C

You may imagine that the fish is attached to a string and the tension in the string is given by $ma = mg - T$ (because a and g point in the same direction). Then $T = m \times (g - a) = 10 \times (10 - 4) = 60$ N. A quicker way to solve this problem is to notice that when the elevator accelerates down with magnitude g, the fish is in free fall and weighs 0 N. Alternatively, when the elevator goes up, one usually feels heavier. Choice (C) is therefore the correct answer.

10.   A

In 1 second, the ball travels 8 m. One revolution is $2\pi r = 1.3$ m, so 8 m/s divided by 1.3 m/revolution is 6 revolutions/s. Therefore, choice (A) is the correct answer.

11.   B

Because of the opposing forces acting on the satellite, use this equation to solve the problem:

$$\frac{GM_E M_s}{R^2} = \frac{M_s v^2}{R}$$

Beyond this, the question is rather straightforward: $\frac{GM_E}{R} = v^2$ implies that the velocity is inversely proportional to the square root of the radius. Choice (B) is therefore the correct answer.

12.   A

This question mixes symbols with numbers. The best approach is to solve it and then look at the answers:

$$m\bar{a} = F - mg \text{ implies } F = m(\bar{a} + g)$$
$$x = \frac{1}{2}at^2 \text{ implies } \bar{a} = \frac{2x}{t^2}$$

Now you can find that

$$F = 100 \times \left(10 + \frac{2x}{t^2}\right)$$
$$= 1000 + 100\left(\frac{2x}{t^2}\right)$$
$$= 1000 + 100\left(\frac{2x}{10^2}\right)$$
$$= 1000 + \frac{200x}{100}$$
$$= 1000 + 2x.$$

This matches with choice (A), the correct answer.

Explanations to Small Group Questions

1. Once the block is attached, the only force keeping the brick in place is the force due to static friction. Thus, before the brick begins to move we can describe the net force in the x-direction as follows: $F_{net}x = m_2g - F_s = 0$, where m_2 represents the mass of the block. As weight is added to the block, the force due to static friction will rise to meet the growing force from the weight of the block until the force due to the weight of the block is greater than the maximum force of static friction. At that point, the net force equation changes as follows: $F_{net}x = m_2g - F_s = m_1a$, where m_1 represents the mass of the brick. If no more weight is added to the block once the brick begins to move, the acceleration, a, will be constant. When acceleration is constant, the change in velocity with respect to time is linear and the change in displacement with respect to time is quadratic, as shown in the graphs below.

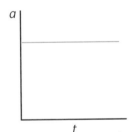

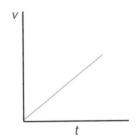

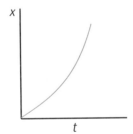

2. The car, if left on its own, would travel in a straight line. The force that is deflecting the car from this straight-line path is the friction between the tires and the road. Newton's third law states that for every force exerted by object B on object A, there is an equal but opposite force exerted by object A on object B. Thus, the force of friction the tires exert on the road is equal and opposite in direction to the force of friction that the road exerts on the tires. Specifically, the net frictional force points toward the center of the circle with a magnitude equal to $\dfrac{mv^2}{r}$, where m is the mass of the car and r is the radius of the circle.

3. Any force can produce a torque if it acts at a distance from the pivot point. This distance is also called the lever arm. A torque is produced any time a force acts on an object at a distance from a pivot point, causing rotation about an axis. If the torques are balanced by counter-forces, a condition called rotational equilibrium is achieved in which no rotational motion occurs.

Work, Energy, and Momentum

In this chapter:

Introduction

The Greek myth of Sisyphus is a tale of unending, pointless work. For eternity, Sisyphus was sentenced to roll a large, heavy rock up a steep hill as penance for his crimes. Just as Sisyphus would nearly reach the top of the hill, the rock would roll back again to the bottom. Quite literally, this is a story of work and energy. Pushing that boulder up the hill, Sisyphus exerted forces that worked on the rock, resulting in an increase in the rock's energy. When the rock escaped from his grasp and rolled backwards, its energy changed from potential (gravitational) energy into kinetic energy and other forms of energy such as thermal and sound. Though Sisyphus's punishment was an excrutiatingly futile task for him, it illustrates for us the fact that energy can be transformed. We hope to convince you throughout the Kaplan MCAT program that your preparation for Test Day is in no way a Sisyphean task.

This chapter reviews the fundamental concepts of energy and work. The work-energy theorem is a powerful expression of the relationship between energy and work which will assist you in your approach to many problems on the MCAT. Furthermore, this chapter covers the related topics of impulse and momentum. On the MCAT, momentum and impulse are most commonly tested through the presentation of collision incidents. We will discuss the different types of collisions that may be presented on Test Day, and through some examples, we'll show how best to approach them. Finally we'll discuss the topic of mechanical advantage, and we'll examine how a pulley or ramp might be helpful in raising heavy objects .

3.1 Energy

Energy is a property or characteristic of a system to do work or more broadly, to make something happen. This broad definition helps us understand that different forms of energy have the capacities to do different things. For example, mechanical energy, such as that which Sisyphus transferred to the large rock, can cause things to move or accelerate through the process of work. An ice cube sitting on the kitchen counter at room temperature will eventually melt into water, undergoing the phase transformation from solid to liquid. Internal energy, or what a few textbooks call thermal energy (and what most of us sloppily call "heat," even though heat is actually a process of energy transfer, not energy itself), can make the ice cube on the counter melt.

Let's turn our attention to the different forms that energy can take. After that, we will discuss the two ways in which energy can be transferred from one system to another.

KINETIC ENERGY

Kinetic energy is the energy of motion. Objects that have mass and are moving with some velocity will contain an amount of kinetic energy, calculated as follows:

$$K = \frac{1}{2} mv^2$$

where K is kinetic energy, m is mass in kg, and v is velocity in m/s. The SI unit for kinetic energy, as with all forms of energy, is the joule (J), which is equal to $kg \cdot m^2/s^2$.

Recall the falling objects in Chapter 1. Such objects have kinetic energy as they fall. The faster they fall, the more kinetic energy they have. We ought to be mindful of the fact that the MCAT is interested in testing students' comprehension of the relationship between kinetic energy and velocity. From the equation, we can see that the kinetic energy is a function of the square of the velocity. So if the velocity doubles, the kinetic energy will quadruple, assuming the mass is constant.

Falling objects have kinetic energy, but so do objects that are moving in all kinds of ways. For example, the kinetic energy of a fluid flowing at some velocity can be measured indirectly as the dynamic pressure, which is one of the terms in Bernoulli's equation (see Chapter 5). Objects that slide down inclined planes, such as children playing on a waterslide, gain kinetic energy as their velocities increase down the ramps.

Key Concept

Kinetic energy is incredibly important on the MCAT; any time an object has a velocity, you should think about kinetic energy and the related concepts of work and conservation of mechanical energy (we will discuss these concepts soon).

Key Equation

Kinetic Energy

$$K = \frac{1}{2} mv^2$$

$$J = kg \cdot m^2/s^2 = (kg)(m/s)^2$$

$$kg \cdot m^2/s^2 = kg \cdot m^2/s^2$$

Example:

A 15 kg block, initially at rest, slides down a frictionless incline and comes to the bottom with a velocity of 7 m/s, as shown in Figure 3.1. What is the kinetic energy at the top and at the bottom?

$v = 0$

$K = ?$

$v = 7$ m/s

$K = ?$

Figure 3.1

Solution: At the top, $v = 0$, so kinetic energy is

$$K = \frac{mv^2}{2}$$

$$= \frac{15(0)}{2}$$

$$= 0$$

At the bottom,

$$K = \frac{15(7)^2}{2}$$

$$= 367.5 \text{ J}$$

POTENTIAL ENERGY

An object with mass is said to have **potential energy** when it has the potential to do something. Potential energy is another form of energy, and it can come in different types. One type of potential energy is gravitational potential energy, and that will be our focus in this chapter. Later, in Chapter 6, we will talk about another type of potential energy called electrical potential energy. There's also mechanical potential energy, which can be found in, say, a compressed spring, and chemical potential energy (or just chemical energy), which is found in the covalent and ionic bonds holding atoms together in molecules.

Gravitational potential energy depends on a body's position with respect to some level identified as "ground," or the zero potential energy position. That level is chosen in an arbitrary way, usually for convenience. For example, you may find it convenient to identify the potential energy of the pencil in your hand with respect to the floor if you are holding the pencil over the floor or with respect to the desktop if you

Real World

The next time you are enjoying chocolate ice cream, take a look at the nutritional information printed on the side of the carton. Read the caloric content per serving and think about the energy content. There's about 1,000,000 calories in that whole pint (one food Calorie equals 1,000 calories)! One calorie equals 4.184 J.

MCAT Expertise

The height used in the potential energy equation is relative to whatever the problem states is the "ground level." It will often be simply the distance to the ground, but it doesn't need to be. The zero potential energy position may be a ledge, a desktop, or a platform. Just pay attention to the question stem and use the height that is discussed.

are holding the pencil over the desk. The equation that we use to calculate gravitational potential energy is

$$U = mgh$$

where U is the potential energy, m is the mass in kg, g is the acceleration due to gravity, and h is the height of the object above the reference level.

Once again, keeping in mind what the MCAT will test, let's examine the relationship between the potential energy and the variables. We see the potential energy is in a direct, linear relationship with all three of the variables, so changing any one of them by some given factor will result in a change in the potential energy by the same factor. Tripling the height of the pencil held in your hand above the floor would increase the pencil's potential energy by a factor of three, and it would most likely require you to stand on the desk in order to do so (thereby also increasing your own potential energy and potential for injury should you lose your balance). It's this mathematical relationship between potential energy and position that makes leaning out of the fifth-floor window of a building more dangerous than leaning out of a first-floor window.

Example:
An 80 kg diver leaps from a 10 m cliff into the sea, as shown in Figure 3.2. Find the diver's potential energy at the top of the cliff and just as he hits the water (set height equal to zero at sea level).

Figure 3.2

Solution: At the top of the cliff:
$$U = mgh$$
$$= 80(9.8)(10)$$
$$= 7,840 \, J$$

At the water's surface:
$$U = 80(9.8)(0)$$
$$= 0 \, J$$

TOTAL MECHANICAL ENERGY

The sum of an object's potential and kinetic energies is its **total mechanical energy.** The equation is

$$E = U + K$$

where E is total mechanical energy, U is potential energy, and K is kinetic energy. The **first law of thermodynamics** states that energy is never created or destroyed. It is merely transferred from one system to another. Yet this does not mean that the total mechanical energy will always remain constant. You'll notice that the total mechanical energy equation accounts for potential and kinetic energies but not for other energies like thermal energy ("heat") that is transferred as a result of friction. If frictional forces are present, some of the mechanical energy will be transformed into thermal energy and will be "lost"—or, more accurately, not accounted for by the equation. Note that there is no violation of the first law of thermodynamics, as a full accounting of all the energies (kinetic, potential, thermal, sound, light, etc.) would reveal no net gain or loss of total energy, merely the transformation of some energy from one form to another.

CONSERVATION OF MECHANICAL ENERGY

In the absence of nonconservative forces, such as frictional forces, the sum of the kinetic and potential energies will be constant. Conservative forces are those that have potential energies associated with them. On the MCAT, the two most commonly encountered conservative forces are gravitational and electrostatic. The spring system, which is mechanical, can also be approximated to be conservative, although the MCAT may include spring problems in which frictional forces are not ignored (in actuality, springs heat up when they "spring" back and forth due to the friction between the molecules of the spring material). There are two equivalent ways to determine whether a force is conservative (see Figure 3.3).

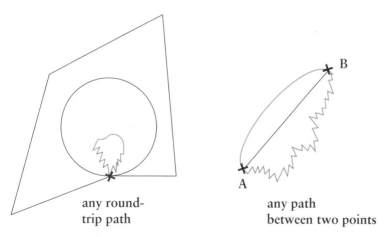

any round-
trip path

any path
between two points

Figure 3.3. Possible Paths of a Particle

a. If the net work done to move a particle in any round-trip path is zero, the force is conservative.

b. If the net work needed to move a particle between two points is the same regardless of the path taken, the force is conservative.

Basically, what this means is that a system that is experiencing only conservative forces will be "given back" an amount of usable energy equal to the amount that had been "taken away" from it in the course of a closed path. For example, an object that falls through a certain displacement in a vacuum will lose some measurable amount of potential energy but will gain exactly that same amount of potential energy when it is lifted back to its original height, regardless of whether the return pathway is the same as that of the initial descent. Furthermore, at all points during the fall through the vacuum, there will be a perfect conversion of potential energy into kinetic energy, with no energy lost to nonconservative forces (e.g., friction). Of course, in real life, outside of theoretical situations, nonconservative forces like friction and air resistance are impossible to avoid, and the balls that we throw know all too well the energy impact of nonconservative forces.

When the work done by nonconservative forces is zero, or when there are no nonconservative forces acting on the system, the total mechanical energy of the system remains constant. The conservation of mechanical energy can be expressed as

$$E = U + K = \text{Constant}$$

or equivalently,

$$\Delta E = \Delta U + \Delta K = 0$$

When nonconservative forces, such as friction or air resistance, are present, total mechanical energy is not conserved. The equation is

$$W' = \Delta E = \Delta K + \Delta U$$

where W' is the work done by the nonconservative forces only. The work done by the nonconservative forces will be exactly equal to the amount of energy "lost" from the system. Where did this energy go? The first law of thermodynamics tells us that the energy wasn't really lost. It simply was transformed into a form of energy, such as thermal energy, that isn't accounted for in the mechanical energy equation.

Real World

To visualize conservation of mechanical energy, imagine a skateboarder in a half-pipe. When she is at the top of the pipe, all of her energy is potential. As she careens down the wall, her energy is being converted to kinetic energy. When she reaches the bottom of the pipe, all of her potential energy is gone and has been converted into kinetic energy, meaning that at this point her velocity is the greatest.

Real World

If the half-pipe track mentioned here is frictionless, meaning there are no nonconservative forces, then we have a good example of the conservation of mechanical energy. When the skateboarder gets back to the top of the half-pipe, she would have the exact same potential energy that she started with. Her total mechanical energy remains constant throughout the trip; it is simply converted from potential into kinetic and back into potential again.

Example:
A baseball of mass 0.25 kg is thrown in the air with an initial speed of 30 m/s, but because of air resistance, the ball returns to the ground with a speed of 27 m/s. Find the work done by air resistance.

Solution:

Air resistance is a nonconservative force. To do this problem, the energy equation for a nonconservative system is needed. The work done by air resistance is W'.

$$W' = \Delta E = \Delta K + \Delta U$$

Since $\Delta U = 0$ (final height = initial height),

$$W' = \Delta K$$
$$= \frac{mv_f^2}{2} - \frac{mv_i^2}{2}$$
$$= \frac{1}{2}(0.25)[(27)^2 - (30)^2]$$
$$= -21.4\ J$$

Key Equation

Conservation of Mechanical Energy
$E = U + K = Constant$
Mechanical energy is conserved when no dissipative forces (e.g., friction, air resistance) are present.

MCAT Concept Check 3.1

Before moving on, ensure that you are able to:

✓ Calculate kinetic energy and potential energy (when close to the Earth's surface)

✓ Understand the path independence of work in a gravitational field

✓ Identify when mechanical energy is conserved

✓ Differentiate between conservative and nonconservative forces

---

3.2 Work

In our everyday conversations, we talk a lot about work. We talk about our jobs, our school assignments, and our volunteer activities. Premeds are certainly no strangers to hard work! However, what do physicists mean when they talk about work? Often, the term *work* is used to mean another form of energy. After all, the SI unit for work is the joule (J), which is the same SI unit for all forms of energy. Nevertheless, to say that work is just another form of energy is to miss something important, something that will be helpful for you on the MCAT. **Work** is not actually a form of energy, but a process by which energy is transferred from one system to another. In fact, it's one of only two ways in which energy can be transferred. The other transfer of energy is called heat, which we will focus on quite a bit in Chapter 4: Thermodynamics.

The transfer of energy, by work or heat, is the only way in which anything can be done. We are familiar with both processes, each being something we experience every day of our lives, although, arguably, it's easier to "see" work than it is to "see" heat. For example, every time King Sisyphus pushed the rock up the hill, the rock gained kinetic and potential energy. However, that energy didn't just come from nowhere. As we've seen, the First Law of Thermodynamics requires us to account for all energies coming into or leaving a system. Within Sisyphys's muscles, the potential energy contained in the high-energy phosphate bonds of ATP molecules was converted to the mechanical energy of the contracting muscles, which exerted forces against the rock, causing it to accelerate and move up the hill. A lot of work was done, which means a lot of energy was transferred.

The chemical potential energy in the ATP was harnessed in the "form" of heat. In fact, at the molecular level, this is no different from work, because it involves the movement of molecules and atoms, and each of them exert forces that do work on other molecules and atoms. Like any transfer of energy, it's not a perfectly efficient process, and some of that energy is "lost" as thermal energy. Our muscles quite literally "warm up" when we contract them repeatedly.

CALCULATING WORK AND POWER

Energy is transferred through the process of work when something exerts forces on or against something else. This is expressed mathematically in this equation:

$$W = Fd \cos \theta$$

where W is work, F is the force applied (on the MCAT, assumed to be constant), d is displacement through which the force is applied, and θ is the angle between the applied force vector and the displacement vector. You'll notice that work is a function of the cosine of the angle, which means that only forces (or components of forces) parallel or antiparallel to the displacement vector will do work (i.e., transfer energy). We've already said that the SI unit for work is the joule, a fact suggesting that work and energy are the same thing, but remember they are not: Work is the process by which a quantity of energy is moved from one system to another. (Don't overthink this distinction, though; most physicists—and certainly the MCAT—won't mind if you use the terms *work* and *energy* interchangeably!)

We have an intuitive understanding of work. We know what it takes to kick a box across the floor, lift a puppy into our arms, and push people out of the way to get the best seat. It takes force. Not just any force but force in the direction that we want the object to move. We wouldn't push down on a desk if we wanted to slide it from one side of the room to the other. Every time we push, pull, tug, kick, or drag an object for the purpose of moving it from one place to another, we do work, and it's not just humans that do work. Any machine designed to apply a force to generate movement is doing work.

Key Equation

Work

$W = Fd \cos \theta$

$J = N \cdot m = (N)(m)(\text{dimensionless})$

$N \cdot m = N \cdot m$

Remember, θ is the angle between the force and displacement vectors.

Real World

One way that you can conceptualize the work formula is to think of pushing a large box. By pushing straight into the side of the box, meaning pushing parallel to the ground and thus parallel to its *displacement*, you get the best results. Remembering your trig, the cosine of 0 degrees is 1, meaning that all of the force is going into the work. If you were to change the angle at which you are pushing to 60 degrees (cosine of 60 is 0.5), then only half of your force would be going into the work. In summary, if in both situations you want the box to accelerate a certain distance, it will take double the *force* to move the box the same distance if the angle is 60 degrees instead of zero, though the same amount of *work* will be done.

Example:

A block weighing 100 N is pushed up a frictionless incline over a distance of 20 m to a height of 10 m as shown in Figure 3.4. Find

a. the minimum force required to push the block.
b. the work done by the force.
c. the force required and the work done by the force if the block were simply lifted vertically 10 m.

Solution:

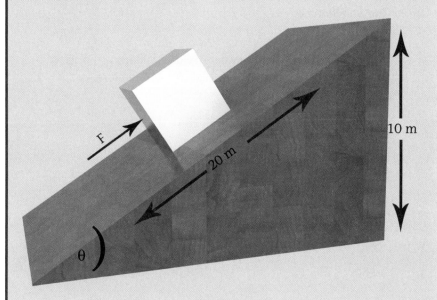

Figure 3.4

a. Figure 3.5 shows a free-body diagram of the forces acting on the block:

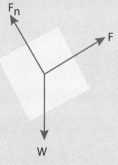

Figure 3.5

The minimum force needed is a force that will push the block with no acceleration parallel to the surface of the incline. Since $a = 0$, $\sum F = 0$:

$$\sum F = 0 = F - mg \sin \theta$$
$$F = mg \sin \theta$$

$mg = 100$ N; $\sin \theta = \dfrac{10}{20}$. Therefore,

$$F = 100 \left(\frac{10}{20} \right)$$
$$= 50 \text{ N}$$

b. The work done by F is

$$W = Fd \cos \theta$$

In this case, θ is the angle between the force vector and the displacement vector. Since they are parallel, $\theta = 0$; therefore, $\cos \theta = 1$. Substitute the numbers into the equation:

$$W = 50(20)(1)$$
$$= 1{,}000 \text{ J}$$

c. To raise the block vertically, the force should also be vertical and equal to the object's weight.

$$F = mg$$
$$= 100 \text{ N}$$

The work done by the lifting force is

$$W = Fd \cos \theta$$
$$= 100(10)(1)$$
$$= 1{,}000 \text{ J}$$

The same amount of work is required in both cases, but twice the force is needed to raise the block vertically compared with pushing it up the incline.

Key Equation

Power

$$P = \frac{W}{t}$$

$$W = J/s = \frac{J}{s}$$

$$J/s = J/s$$

Be careful not to confuse the Ws! Note that in the equation, W represents work (measured in joules). The unit for power, the watt, is also abbreviated using the letter W.

Bridge

Power is calculated in many different situations, especially those involving circuits, resistors, and capacitors. Power is always a measure of the rate of energy consumption, transfer, or transformation per unit time.

The rate at which energy is transferred from one system to another is measured as **power** and expressed by this equation:

$$P = \frac{W}{t}$$

where P is power, W is work, and t is the time over which the work is done. The SI unit for power is the watt (W), which as you can see from the equation is equal to J/s. We will identify the various ways in which power can be calculated in Chapter 8 on circuitry. Suffice it to say at this point, we encounter this measurement every day. The power of the toaster oven in your kitchen or the hair dryer in your bathroom is a measure of the rate at which these appliances transform electrical potential energy into other forms, such as thermal, light, sound, and kinetic energy. The lightbulb that just blinked on over your head is probably operating at 60 watts, unless it's an energy-efficient compact fluorescent that transforms ("consumes") energy at a much lower rate.

Example: Find the power required to raise the block (of the previous example) in four seconds in each case.

Solution: When lifted up the incline, power is

$$P = \frac{W}{t}$$

$$= \frac{1,000}{4}$$

$$= 250\ \text{W}$$

When lifted straight up, the power equals

$$P = \frac{1,000}{4}$$

$$= 250\ \text{W}$$

WORK-ENERGY THEOREM

Throughout this discussion of work and energy you have been using your own energy reserves. After all, with our expanded definition of *energy* (the capacity to do something or make something happen), we now can understand that mental exertion is as much an energy-consuming process of "work" as heavy lifting. Keep that mental energy up for just a little longer, because we're about to talk about some important concepts that will be vital for your performance on Test Day!

The **work-energy theorem** is a powerful expression of the relationship between work and kinetic energy. In particular, it offers a direct relationship between the work done by all the forces acting on an object and the change in kinetic energy of that object. The net work done on or by an object will result in an equal change in the object's kinetic energy. In other words,

$$W_{\text{net}} = \Delta K = K_{\text{f}} - K_{\text{i}}$$

> **Key Equation**
>
> **Work-Energy Theorem**
> $W_{\text{net}} = \Delta K = K_{\text{f}} - K_{\text{i}}$
> $\text{J} = \text{J}$

This relationship is really important to understand, as it will allow you to solve many problems involving work, even when you don't know the magnitude of the forces acting on an object or the displacement through which the forces act. If you can calculate the change in kinetic energy experienced by an object, then by definition you can determine the net work done on or by an object. Once again, there is no lack of real-life experiences on which to reflect to understand this principle. Every time you press the brake pedal to bring your car to a stop at a red light, you are putting the work-energy theorem into practice. The brake pads exert frictional forces against the rotors, which are attached to the wheels. These frictional forces do work against the wheels, causing them to decelerate and bringing the car to a halt. The net work done by all these forces is equal to the change in kinetic energy of the car. Even the celebratory act of college graduates throwing their caps into the air is a physical phenomenon governed by the work-energy theorem.

Example: A graduation cap of mass 0.125 kg is thrown straight up in the air with an initial velocity of 30 m/s. Assuming no air resistance, find the work done by the force of gravity when the cap is at its maximum height.

Process: We don't know the magnitude of the net force acting on the cap, nor do we know the displacement of the cap from its starting position to its maximum height. We do know that the only force acting on the cap is gravity (ignoring air resistance). We also know that the cap's velocity at its maximum height is 0 m/s. We can use the work-energy theorem to solve for the work done by the force of gravity.

Solution:

$$W = \Delta K = K_f - K_i$$
$$= 0 - \frac{1}{2}mv^2$$
$$= 0 - \frac{1}{2}(0.125)(30)^2$$
$$= 0 - \left(\frac{1}{2}\right)\left(\frac{1}{8}\right)(900)$$
$$= 0 - 56.25$$
$$= -56.25 \text{ J} = \text{work done by gravity}$$

MCAT Concept Check 3.2

Before moving on, ensure that you are able to:

✓ Derive the units of work

✓ Calculate power, which is energy transferred over time, and derive its units

✓ Relate the change in an object's kinetic energy to the net work done on it

---

3.3 Momentum

Momentum (*p*) is a quality of objects in motion. In classical mechanics, it is defined as the product of an object's mass and velocity. Because it has magnitude and direction, it is a vector quantity, like velocity and acceleration. The equation for momentum is

$$\mathbf{p} = m\mathbf{v}$$

where **p** is momentum, *m* is mass, and **v** is velocity. For two or more objects, the total momentum is the vector sum of the individual momenta.

The quality of moving objects that we've come to call momentum was observed by the Romans, who made a distinction between this and mere speed. A boxer's fist

Key Equation

Momentum

$p = mv$

$\text{kg·m/s} = (\text{kg})(\text{m/s})$

hurtling toward his opponent, a bowling ball gliding down the lane, and a horse galloping toward the finish line all have a measurable quantity of momentum. All of these objects and all objects that have mass also have inertia. **Inertia** is the tendency of objects to resist changes in their motion and momentum. We can observe the sometimes disastrous results when objects encounter forces that cause them to change their motion: a broken nose from impact with the boxer's clenched fist, a broken toe if the bowling ball happens to fall on someone's foot, and the equine pileup on the stretch turn.

IMPULSE

As we have seen over and over again, the only manner by which an object's motion can change is when there is net force acting on it to cause it to accelerate. When net force acts on an object, causing it to change its motion, this also results in change to the object's momentum. This change in momentum is called **impulse (I)** and is a vector quantity.

For a constant force applied through a period of time, impulse and momentum are related by the equation

$$\mathbf{I} = \mathbf{F}\Delta t = \Delta \mathbf{p} = m\mathbf{v}_f - m\mathbf{v}_i$$

where $\mathbf{I}$ is impulse, $\mathbf{F}$ is force, Δt is time, $\mathbf{p}$ is momentum, m is mass, and $\mathbf{v}$ is velocity.

On the MCAT, the setup of a typical momentum problem will involve changes to momentum in only one dimension, which allows us to treat the vectors as scalars along the number line. The variables are assigned positive or negative signs depending on whether the corresponding vectors are in the positive or the negative direction.

> **Example:** A 7 kg bowling ball initially at rest is acted on by a 110 N force for 3.5 s. Find the final speed of the ball.
>
> **Solution:** From the equation for impulse,
>
> $$Ft = mv - mv_0$$
> $$v = v_0 + \frac{Ft}{m}$$
> $$= 0 + \frac{110(3.5)}{7}$$
> $$= 55 \text{ m/s}$$

Look closely at the equation for impulse; you should notice an inverse relationship between force magnitude and time if impulse is constant. In other words, given a particular change in momentum, the longer the period of time through which this impulse is achieved, the smaller the force necessary to achieve the impulse. Automobile

---

Key Equation

Impulse

$I = F\Delta t = \Delta p = mv_f - mv_i$

$\text{kg·m/s} = (\text{N})(\text{s}) = (\text{kg·m/s}^2)(\text{s}) = (\text{kg})(\text{m/s})$

manufacturers take advantage of this fact in their car designs. Modern safety designs found in most cars today, such as front and side airbags and crumple zones in the front and rear of the car, are designed to increase the time through which the change in momentum associated with a collision will occur. Prolonging the duration of the collision allows the change in momentum to occur over a longer period of time, and this reduces the magnitude of the forces necessary to achieve the change in momentum. Reducing the forces exerted on the car and its occupants reduces the risk of severe injury or death.

CONSERVATION OF MOMENTUM

This is the second occurrence of the phrase "conservation of…" in this chapter. By now, you know and understand that any time we talk about conservation (of mechanical energy, of momentum, etc.), we are necessarily describing a situation in which there are no external forces acting on a system, or if external forces are present, the vector sum of the external forces acting on that system is zero. In the absence of (nonzero) external forces, or in the case of the external forces canceling each other, the total (vector sum) momentum of a system will be constant. On the MCAT, conservation of momentum will be tested in the context of three special cases of collisions between objects.

COLLISIONS

When two or more objects collide in an idealized collision (instantaneous and in a specific location), we can say that momentum is conserved as long as no (net) external forces act on the objects. Conservation of momentum means that the vector sum of the momenta is constant: The total momentum after the collision is equal to the total momentum before the collision. This does not mean that the individual momenta will necessarily be constant. Objects that collide can sometimes experience dramatic changes in their momenta, even as the total momentum of the system is constant. Individual changes in momentum may occur (e.g., objects may experience changes in velocity as a result of the collision), but total momentum is conserved as long as no external forces, such as friction, are present. For a collision between two objects, a and b, this can be expressed as follows:

$$p_{ai} + p_{bi} = p_{af} + p_{bf}$$

where p_{ai} and p_{bi} are the momenta before the collision and p_{af} and p_{bf} are the momenta after the collision. Since we've already defined momentum as the product of mass and velocity, we can rewrite the conservation of momentum equation as this:

$$m_a v_{ai} + m_b v_{bi} = m_a v_{af} + m_b v_{bf}$$

where v_{ai} and v_{bi} are the velocities before the collision and v_{af} and v_{bf} are the velocities after the collision. As is often the case on the MCAT, one-dimensional problems of collision can be treated as if the vectors were scalars along the number

MCAT Expertise

On the MCAT, momentum will almost always be tested with a collision.

Key Equation

Conservation of Momentum (Elastic and Inelastic Collisions)

$m_a v_{ai} + m_b v_{bi} = m_a v_{af} + m_b v_{bf}$

Use this equation for collisions after which the two objects, a and b, bounce apart and do not stick together.

line. The signs on the velocities (and hence on the momenta) will be determined by the direction of the velocity and momentum vectors. You will decide, for each problem, which direction is given the positive sign.

Bridge

If the momentum problem is two-dimensional, then we will have to re-solve the momentum vectors into their **X** and **Y** components using trigonometry, as we discussed in Chapter 1.

Example: Figure 3.6 shows two bodies moving toward each other on a frictionless air track. Body A has a mass of 2 kg and a speed of 4 m/s; body B has a mass of 3 kg and has a speed of 1 m/s. After the bodies collide, body A moves away with a velocity of 2 m/s to the left. What is the final velocity of body B?

Figure 3.6

Solution: This problem can be solved by equating the total momentum before the collision with the total momentum after the collision. Let the final velocity of body B be v_{bf}. Taking the right as positive (and therefore the left as negative),

$$m_a v_{ai} + m_b v_{bi} = m_a v_{af} + m_b v_{bf}$$
$$2(4) + 3(-1) = 2(-2) + 3(v_{bf})$$
$$v_{bf} = \frac{8 - 3 + 4}{3}$$
$$v_{bf} = 3 \text{ m/s}$$

The fact that the solution is positive means that body B is moving to the right after the collision.

In a crowded world such as ours, it's inevitable that things are going to bump against each other. From cars to beams of high-energy particles directed onto thin sheets of gold foil, collisions are inevitable and frequent. The MCAT will test your understanding of three types of collisions for which total momentum is conserved:

- **Completely elastic collisions**
- **Inelastic collisions**
- **Completely inelastic collisions**

MCAT Expertise

There are three types of collisions. In all collisions on the MCAT, momentum is conserved. In completely elastic collisions (objects don't stick together), we have a perfect collision in which both momentum and kinetic energy are conserved. In both inelastic colli-sions (objects don't stick together) and completely inelastic collisions (objects stick together), kinetic energy is *not* conserved, but momentum is.

Completely Elastic Collisions

Completely elastic collisions occur when two or more objects collide in such a way that both total momentum and total kinetic energy are conserved. This means that no energy of motion was transformed in the instance of the collision into another form, such as thermal, light, or sound. Nor was any energy used to change the shapes of the colliding objects. Now, from our everyday experiences, we know that rarely do collisions occur without sound, light, or heat production or deformation of objects. However, in the more theoretical world of the MCAT, this type of collision is a common occurrence. On approximation, the collision of billiard balls on a pool table or hockey pucks on ice (or on a cushion of air on an air hockey table) can be analyzed as an instance of conservation of momentum and kinetic energy. Be careful not to assume that the velocities of the colliding objects remain constant. In fact, it is almost certain that the objects will experience changes in their velocities (magnitude and/or direction) upon impact. In completely elastic collisions, it is the total kinetic energy, not the individual velocities or even the individual kinetic energies of the objects, that remains constant. In equation form, the conservation of momentum can be expressed, as we've already seen, as follows:

$$m_a v_{ai} + m_b v_{bi} = m_a v_{af} + m_b v_{bf}$$

The conservation of kinetic energy in a completely elastic collision can be expressed as

$$\frac{1}{2} m_a v_{ai}^{\,2} + \frac{1}{2} m_b v_{bi}^{\,2} = \frac{1}{2} m_a v_{af}^{\,2} + \frac{1}{2} m_b v_{bf}^{\,2}$$

> **Example:** Using the results obtained from the example accompanying Figure 3.6, establish whether the collision was completely elastic.
>
> **Solution:** For the collision to be completely elastic, both the kinetic energy and the momentum must be conserved. The second condition has already been satisfied. Now the kinetic energy before the collision and the kinetic energy after the collision must be calculated, and only if these values are equal can it be said that the collision was completely elastic.
>
> The kinetic energy before the collision is
>
> $$\frac{1}{2} m_a v_{ai}^{\,2} + \frac{1}{2} m_b v_{bi}^{\,2}$$
> $$= \frac{1}{2}(2)(4)^2 + \frac{1}{2}(3)(-1)^2$$
> $$= 17.5 \text{ J}$$

Key Equation

Conservation of Kinetic Energy (Completely Elastic Collisions)

$$\frac{1}{2} m_a v_a^2 + \frac{1}{2} m_b v_{bi}^2 = \frac{1}{2} m_a v_{af}^2 + \frac{1}{2} m_b v_{bf}^2$$

Of the three types of collisions tested on the MCAT, completely elastic collisions are the only type for which kinetic energy is conserved.

MCAT Expertise

The equations for momentum and kinetic energy as applied to collisions are immensely important for Test Day. REMEMBER THEM!

The kinetic energy after the collision is

$$\frac{1}{2}m_a v_{af}^2 + \frac{1}{2}m_b v_{bf}^2$$
$$= \frac{1}{2}(2)(-2)^2 + \frac{1}{2}(3)(3)^2$$
$$= 17.5 \text{ J}$$

Because the kinetic energy is not changed by the collision, it can be said that the collision was completely elastic.

Inelastic Collisions

Collisions can fascinate us and capture our attention with the release of a tremendous amount of energy in the form of loud noises, blindingly bright explosions, ferociously hot fires, and/or bone-rattling vibrations. When a collision results in the production of light, heat, sound, or object deformation, there is necessarily a decrease in the total kinetic energy of the system. This type of collision is an **inelastic collision** and is closer to what we typically observe in everyday life. Momentum is conserved as long as no external forces are present (as in the case of totally elastic collisions) even as kinetic energy is transformed ("lost").

The conservation of momentum equation is identical to that displayed in the discussion of completely elastic collisions. However, the final kinetic energy will be less than the initial kinetic energy.

$$\frac{1}{2}m_a v_{ai}^2 + \frac{1}{2}m_b v_{bi}^2 > \frac{1}{2}m_a v_{af}^2 + \frac{1}{2}m_b v_{bf}^2$$

Notice that the change in kinetic energy will be equal to the amount of energy released from the system in the form of heat, light, or sound.

Completely Inelastic Collisions

Of course, we know that not every collision results in mangled metal or mass extinction. Furthermore, we recognize that many collisions are necessary, even for the continuation of life. In fact, if it weren't for completely inelastic collisions, the molecules that make up the matter of our universe would never have formed. In completely **inelastic collisions,** the objects that collide stick together rather than bouncing off each other and moving apart. When atoms are moving around and colliding with each other, they sometimes stick together to become compounds as the result of formation of covalent or ionic bonds. This is not that much different than the formation of a "link" between two balls covered in Velcro that are rolled toward each other: Upon collision, they stick together and move as one object.

As with the prior two types of collisions, totally inelastic collisions result in conservation of momentum as long as the vector sum of any external forces, such as

Key Equation

Conservation of Momentum (Completely Inelastic Collisions)

$m_a v_{ai} + m_b v_{bi} = (m_a + m_b) v_f$

Use this equation for collisions after which the two objects, a and b, stick together and move as one.

frictional forces, is equal to zero. This is a variant of the inelastic collision, so total kinetic energy is not conserved. Because the objects stick together upon collision, the conservation of momentum can be expressed as

$$m_a v_{ai} + m_b v_{bi} = (m_a + m_b) v_f$$

You'll notice in this equation that the right side adds the masses of the two objects together and calculates a single final velocity, which is appropriate given that the objects move as a single mass after the collision.

Example: Two rail freight cars are being hitched together. The first car has a mass of 15,750 kg and is moving at a speed of 4 m/s toward the second car, which is stationary and has a mass of 19,250 kg. Calculate the final velocity of the two cars.

Solution: Use the modified equation above for the conservation of momentum:

$$m_a v_{ai} + m_b v_{bi} = (m_a + m_b) v_f$$

$$v_f = \frac{m_a v_{ai} + m_b v_{bi}}{m_a + m_b}$$

Take the direction of the initial velocity of the car as the positive direction:

$$v_f = \frac{15,750(4) + 19,250(0)}{(15,750 + 19,250)}$$

$$v_f = 1.8 \text{ m/s}$$

The fact that v_f is positive means that after the collision, the two cars together are moving in the direction that the first car was moving initially.

MCAT Concept Check 3.3

Before moving on, ensure that you are able to:

✓ Calculate the momentum of an object

✓ Calculate the impulse, or change in momentum, of an object

✓ Apply the conservation of momentum equation to completely elastic, inelastic, and completely inelastic collisions

✓ Differentiate between completely elastic collisions, inelastic, and completely inelastic collisions

3.4 Mechanical Advantage

Does it make a difference whether Sisyphus lifted the rock vertically to its final position or rolled it there along an incline? The difference is mechanical advantage. Sloping inclines, such as hillsides and ramps, make it easier for work to be accomplished. For a given quantity of work, any device (such as an inclined plane) that allows for work to be accomplished through a reduced applied force is said to provide **mechanical advantage**. In addition to the inclined plane, five other devices are considered the classic simple machines designed to provide mechanical advantage: wedge, axle and wheel, lever, pulley, and screw. Of these, the inclined plane, lever, and pulley are often tested on the MCAT.

$$\text{Mechanical advantage} = \frac{F_{out}}{F_{in}}$$

Mechanical advantage is the ratio of the force exerted on object *by* a simple machine (F_{out}) to the force actually applied on the simple machine (F_{in}). The mechanical advantage, because it is a ratio, is dimensionless.

This reduction in necessary force for the purpose of accomplishing a given amount of work does have a "cost" associated with it, however, and that is the distance through which the smaller force must be applied in order to do the work. Simple machines may provide mechanical advantage, but they do not violate the fundamental laws of physics! We know that energy can be neither created nor destroyed, merely changed from one form to another: energy "in" (in one form) must equal energy "out" (in another form). Inclined planes, levers, and pulleys do not "magically" change the amount of work necessary to move an object from one place to another. In mechanical terms, that work is defined as the product of the object's displacement and the magnitude of the force vector that is along the displacement vector. As we've already discussed in Chapter 1, displacement is pathway-independent, and for conservative systems, work doesn't depend upon the actual distance traveled between the final position and the initial position. An inclined plane, as we will see in the following discussion, allows for masses to be displaced through the application of lower force over a greater distance to achieve the change in position. Pulleys and levers "work," in principle, in exactly the same way. We've already considered levers in Chapter 2, in our discussion of torque and rotational equilibrium. Let's now consider, inclined planes and pulleys.

INCLINED PLANES

Every high school in the United States has at least one ramp that winds back and forth on itself, leading eventually to a main entrance. The slope allows relatively easy access from the street to the building door for those who rely on wheelchairs for mobility. In spite of what might be only a slight elevation of the main entrance above the street level, the access ramp may be quite long. The ramp allows those using it to change their position (that is, achieve a displacement) from the street level to the elevated front door in a gradual manner. This displacement requires a given quantity of work defined, as we've seen, as the product of displacement and the force vector along the displacement. If we ignore friction forces, we can say that it makes no difference whether that displacement occurs in a straight-line pathway or in the back-and-forth pathway of the entrance ramp: The work required is the same.

The difference, however, becomes apparent when we look at the work equation in terms of the relationship between force and distance. We see in the work equation an inverse relationship between applied force and distance for a constant value of work. Because the ramp is longer than a straight-line path from the street to the building door, the distance through which the ultimate displacement will be achieved is greater, and the force necessary to achieve that displacement is reduced. This is the mechanical advantage offered by an inclined plane to anyone using a wheelchair, pushing a baby carriage, or rolling a heavy object.

PULLEYS

Pulleys provide mechanical advantage in the same manner as the ramp does: a reduction of necessary force at the "cost" of increased distance to achieve a given value of work or energy transference. In practical terms, pulleys allow heavy objects to be lifted using a much-reduced force. Simply lifting a heavy object of mass m to a height of h will require an amount of work equal to mgh. If the displacement occurs over a distance equal to the displacement, then the force required to lift the object will equal mg. If, however, the distance through which the displacement is achieved is greater than the displacement, then setting $W = Fd = mgh$ shows us that the applied force will be less than mg. In other words, we've been able to lift this heavy object to the desired height by using a lower force, but we've had to apply that lower force through a greater distance in order to lift this heavy object to its final height.

Before examining how pulleys create this mechanical advantage, let's consider first the heavy block in Figure 3.7, suspended from two ropes. Because the block is not accelerating, it is in translational equilibrium, and the force that the block exerts downward (its weight) is equaled by the sum of the tensions in the two ropes. For a symmetrical system, the tensions in the two ropes are the same and are each equal to half the weight of the block.

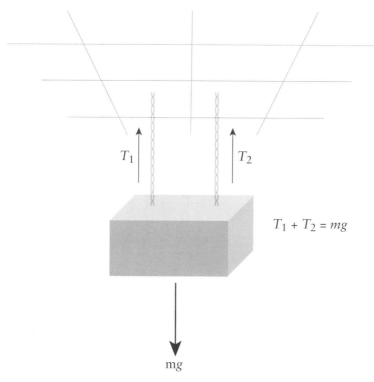

Figure 3.7. Hanging Block
A block suspended by two ropes is in translational equilibrium

Now let's imagine the heavy block in Figure 3.8 represents a heavy crate that must be lifted by a worker in a warehouse. Assuming that the crate is being held momentarily stationary, in midair, we again have a system in translational equilibrium: the weight (the *load*) is in balance with the total tension in the ropes. The tensions in the two vertical ropes are equal to each other (if they were unequal, the pulleys would turn until the tensions were equal on both sides) and each rope supports one-half of the crate's total weight. Fortunately for the warehouse employee holding onto the free end of the rope, only half the force (the *effort*) is required to lift the crate to a high shelf. This is the mechanical advantage provided by the pulley, but as we've already discussed, mechanical advantage comes at the expense of distance. To lift an object to a certain height in the air (the *load distance*), one must pull through a length of rope (the *effort distance*) equal to twice that displacement. If, for example, the crate must be lifted to a shelf 3 meters above the ground, then both sides of the supporting rope must shorten by 3 meters, and the only way to accomplish this is by pulling through 6 meters of rope.

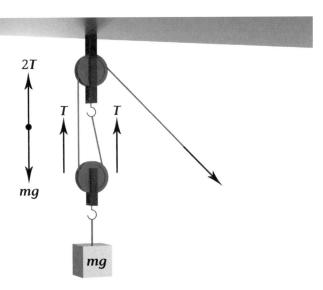

Figure 3.8. Two-Pulley System
The block is suspended from two ropes, each of which bears half the block's weight

MCAT Expertise

On the MCAT you will almost always be given a massless and frictionless pulley system.

All simple machines can be approximated as conservative systems if we ignore the usually small amount of energy that would be "lost" due to external forces, such as friction. The idealized pulley is massless and frictionless, and under these theoretical conditions, the work put into the system (the exertion of force through a distance of rope) will exactly equal the work that comes out of the system (the displacement of the mass to some height). Real pulleys (and all real machines, for that matter) fail to conform to these idealized conditions to one degree or another and, therefore, do not achieve 100 percent efficiency in conserving energy output to input. We can define work input as the product of effort and effort distance; likewise, we can define work output as the product of load and load distance. Comparing the two, as a ratio of work output to work input, defines the efficiency of the simple machine.

$$\text{Efficiency} = \frac{W_{\text{out}}}{W_{\text{in}}} = \frac{(\text{load})(\text{load distance})}{(\text{effort})(\text{effort distance})}$$

Key Equation

Efficiency of a Simple Machine

$$\text{Efficiency} = \frac{W_{\text{in}}}{W_{\text{out}}} = \frac{(\text{load})(\text{load distance})}{(\text{effort})(\text{effort distance})}$$

dimensionless = (J)/(J)
Efficiency is usually expressed as a percentage.

Efficiencies are often expressed as percentages by multiplying the efficiency ratio by 100 percent. The efficiency of a machine gives a measure of the amount of work you put into the system that "comes out" as useful work. The corollary of efficiency is the percentage of the work that you put into the system that becomes unusable due to external forces.

The old adage that if a little is good then more must be even better is true to a certain degree for all simple machines. The pulley system in Figure 3.9 illustrates the increased mechanical advantage provided by adding more pulleys: For every additional pair of pulleys, we can reduce the effort further still. In this case, the load has been divided among six lengths of rope, so the effort required is now only one-sixth the total load. Remember that we would need to pull through a length of rope that is six times the desired displacement, and too much of a good thing has its price.

For pulleys, that price is lowered efficiency due to the added weight of each pulley and the additional friction forces.

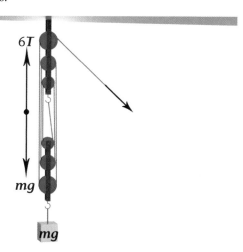

Figure 3.9. System of Six Pulleys
Increasing the number of pulleys decreases the tension in each segment of rope; this leads to an increase in the mechanical advantage of the machine

Example:
The pulley system of Figure 3.9 has an efficiency of 80 percent. A person is required to lift 200 kg using the pulley. Find
a. the distance through which the effort must move to raise the load a distance of 4 m.
b. the effort required to lift the load.
c. the work done by the person lifting the load through a height of 4 m.

Solution:

a. For the load to move through a vertical distance of 4 m, all six of the supporting ropes must shorten 4 m also. This may only be accomplished by pulling $6 \times 4 = 24$ m of rope through. So the effort must move through a distance of 24 m.

b. To calculate the effort required, the equation for efficiency must be used. The load is the weight of the object being lifted and is equal to the mass times the acceleration due to gravity g. Since g is approximately 10 m/s^2 and all the other parameters except the effort are known, it is possible to substitute into this equation to calculate the effort:

$$\text{Efficiency} = \frac{\text{Load} \times \text{Load distance}}{\text{Effort} \times \text{Effort distance}}$$

$$0.80 = \frac{(200)(10)(4)}{(\text{Effort})(24)}$$

$$\text{Effort} = \frac{(2,000)(4)}{(0.80)(24)}$$

$$= 417 \text{ N}$$

c. The work done is given by

$$\text{Work done} = \text{Effort} \times \text{Effort distance}$$

$$= 417 \times 24$$

$$= 10{,}008 \text{ J}$$

MCAT Concept Check 3.4

Before moving on, ensure that you are able to:

✓ Analyze a system of pulleys and calculate the tension in the ropes

✓ Calculate the mechanical advantage and efficiency of a simple machine

---

3.5 Center of Mass

There's one last topic to discuss before closing out this chapter on energy, work, and momentum, and that is an object's **center of mass.** This point, which can be calculated using coordinate geometry, is the point within any two- or three-dimensional object at which the entire object's mass could be represented as a single particle. The MCAT will not directly test your ability to determine center of mass; however, such a calculation may be an important step in a problem whose larger focus is Newtonian mechanics, as in the case of determining the change in gravitational potential energy of a tree that is felled in a forest.

To illustrate this concept and calculation, let's consider a tennis racket that has been thrown into the air. Each part of the racket moves in its own way, so it's not possible to represent the motion of the whole racket as a single particle. However, one point within the racket moves in a simple parabolic path, very similar to the flight of a ball. It is this point within the racket that is known as the center of mass. This is clearly shown in Figure 3.10.

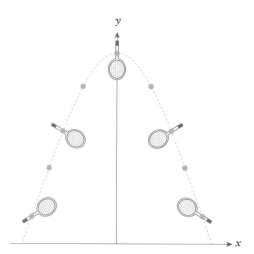

Figure 3.10. Center of Mass of a Racket
The center of mass of a racket thrown into the air travels along a parabolic pathway

For a system of two masses, m_1 and m_2, lying along the x-axis at points x_1 and x_2, respectively, the center of mass is

$$X = \frac{m_1 x_1 + m_2 x_2}{m_1 + m_2}$$

For a system with several masses strung out along the x-axis, the center of mass is given by

$$X = \frac{m_1 x_1 + m_2 x_2 + m_3 x_3 + \cdots}{m_1 + m_2 + m_3 + \cdots}$$

For a system in which the particles are distributed in all three dimensions, the center of mass is defined by the three coordinates:

$$X = \frac{m_1 x_1 + m_2 x_2 + m_3 x_3 + \cdots}{m_1 + m_2 + m_3 + \cdots}$$

$$Y = \frac{m_1 y_1 + m_2 y_2 + m_3 y_3 + \cdots}{m_1 + m_2 + m_3 + \cdots}$$

$$Z = \frac{m_1 z_1 + m_2 z_2 + m_3 z_3 + \cdots}{m_1 + m_2 + m_3 + \cdots}$$

The **center of gravity** is the point at which the entire force due to gravity can be thought of as acting. It is found from similar formulas:

$$X = \frac{w_1 x_1 + w_2 x_2 + w_3 x_3 + \cdots}{w_1 + w_2 + w_3 + \cdots}$$

$$Y = \frac{w_1 y_1 + w_2 y_2 + w_3 y_3 + \cdots}{w_1 + w_2 + w_3 + \cdots}$$

$$Z = \frac{w_1 z_1 + w_2 z_2 + w_3 z_3 + \cdots}{w_1 + w_2 + w_3 + \cdots}$$

Key Equation

Center of Mass

$$X = \frac{m_1 x_1 + m_2 x_2 + m_3 x_3 + \cdots}{m_1 + m_2 + m_3 + \cdots}$$

$$m = \frac{(kg)(m)}{kg}$$

$$m = m$$

Since $W = mg$, the center of gravity and the center of mass will be the same point as long as g is constant.

Example: Find the center of mass with respect to the x- and y-axes of two uniform metal cubes that are attached to each other as shown in Figure 3.11. One cube has a mass of 2 kg and is 0.4 m on each side, the other has a mass of 0.5 kg and is 0.2 m on each side.

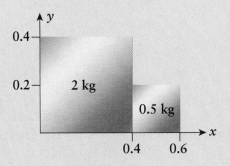

Figure 3.11

Solution: The fact that the cubes are uniform implies that the center of mass for each cube is located at the center of that cube. Therefore, the problem becomes finding the center of mass of two point masses; one is a 2 kg mass located at 0.2 m along the x-axis and 0.2 m along the y-axis, and the other is a 0.5 kg mass located at 0.5 m along the x-axis and 0.1 m along the y-axis.

Let's consider the x-coordinate first. The x-component of the center of mass can be determined by the following formula:

$$X = \frac{m_1 x_1 + m_2 x_2 + m_3 x_3 + \cdots}{m_1 + m_2 + m_3 + \cdots}$$

Take m_1 as 2 kg, x_1 as 0.2 m, m_2 as 0.5 kg, and x_2 as 0.5 m:

$$X = \frac{m_1 x_1 + m_2 x_2}{m_1 + m_2}$$
$$= \frac{2(0.2) + 0.5(0.5)}{2 + 0.5}$$
$$= \frac{0.65}{2.5}$$
$$= 0.26\,\text{m}$$

The y-component of the center of mass can be determined by the following formula:

$$Y = \frac{m_1 y_1 + m_2 y_2 + m_3 y_3 + \cdots}{m_1 + m_2 + m_3 + \cdots}$$

Take m_1 as 2 kg, y_1 as 0.2 m, m_2 as 0.5 kg, and y_2 as 0.1 m:

$$\begin{aligned} Y &= \frac{m_1 y_1 + m_2 y_2}{m_1 + m_2} \\ &= \frac{2(0.2) + 0.5(0.1)}{2 + 0.5} \\ &= \frac{0.45}{2.5} \\ &= 0.18\,\text{m} \end{aligned}$$

MCAT Concept Check 3.5

Before moving on, ensure that you are able to:

✓ Solve for the position of the center of a mass of an object or objects

✓ Understand where on an object forces are said to be applied

---

Conclusion

The conceptualization of energy as the capacity to do something or make something happen is broad enough to allow us to understand everything from pushing a rock up a hill to melting an ice cube, and from stopping a car at an intersection to raising a heavy object. Inextricably tied to this notion of energy is the understanding that none of these events or phenomena could ever happen without the transference of energy, either through work or heat. The work-energy theorem is a powerful expression that will guide our approach to many problems in the Physical Science section. A topic that you can expect to see on Test Day is momentum. Completely elastic, inelastic, and completely inelastic collisions are different instances in which momentum is conserved as objects collide and interact. Another topic of Newtonian mechanics that is often tested on the MCAT is the application of the principles of energy and work to simple machines, such as levers, inclined planes, and pulleys. These devices assist us in accomplishing work by reducing the forces necessary for displacing objects. Finally, we discussed the method for determining centers of mass and gravity, a calculation which will be helpful to you for certain problems involving gravitational potential energy.

Preparing for the MCAT is hard work. No one is denying that; nevertheless, hard work has its rewards. You are well on your way to achieving success on Test Day if you continue to pay attention to the lessons that are provided in your Kaplan MCAT materials. This MCAT Physics Review book (and all the other Kaplan materials provided in your Kaplan program) is part of a set of tools—your simple machines, if you will—that will provide you with the mechanical advantage to ease your efforts toward a higher score. Analogous to our discussion of energy, work, and momentum, there's much potential for accomplishing your goals of earning a higher MCAT score, gaining entrance into the medical school that's best for you, and becoming a great doctor. You just need to keep moving; the forces of your commitment and tenacity are more than sufficient to bring you to a place of personal and professional accomplishment.

CONCEPT SUMMARY

Energy (p. 68)

- ☐ Is the property of a system that enables it to do something or make something happen, including the capacity to do work
- ☐ **Kinetic energy** (p. 68) is energy of motion
- ☐ **Potential energy** (p. 69) is energy stored within a system and exists in forms such as gravitational, electric, and mechanical energy
- ☐ The **total mechanical energy** (p. 71) of a system will be conserved in the absence of friction forces; the sum of a system's potential energy and kinetic energy will be constant

Work (p. 73)

- ☐ Is a process by which energy is transferred from one system to another
- ☐ **Power** (p. 76) is the rate at which work is done or energy is transferred
- ☐ The **work-energy theorem** (p. 77) states that when net work is done on or by a system, the system's kinetic energy will change by the same amount

Momentum (p. 78)

- ☐ Is a quality of objects in motion and is the product of mass and velocity
- ☐ **Inertia** (p. 79) is the tendency of an object to resist changes in its motion
- ☐ **Impulse** (p. 79) is a change in momentum achieved by the application of force through some period of time
- ☐ There are three types of collisions for which the system's total momentum is conserved: **completely elastic** (p. 82), **inelastic** (p. 83), and **completely inelastic** (p. 83) collisions
  - ○ Only in a completely elastic collision is the system's total kinetic energy also conserved
  - ○ In inelastic and completely inelastic collisions, kinetic energy is transformed into another form, such as heat, light, or sound

Mechanical Advantage (p. 85)

- ☐ Is the factor by which a machine multiplies the input force or torque
- ☐ Simple machines, such as inclined planes, levers, and pulleys, provide the benefit of mechanical advantage
- ☐ Mechanical advantage makes it easier to accomplish a given amount of work since the input force necessary to accomplish the work is reduced; the distance through which the reduced input force must be applied, however, is increased by the same factor
- ☐ **Efficiency** (p. 88) is the ratio of the machine's output work to input work when friction is taken into account

Center of Mass (p. 90)

- ☐ Is the point within a two- or three-dimensional object at which all the object's mass could be represented as a single particle

- ☐ The center of mass and the **center of gravity** (p. 92) are at the same point within an object as long as g is constant

EQUATIONS TO REMEMBER

- ☐ $K = \frac{1}{2}mv^2$

- ☐ $U = mgh$ (gravitational potential energy)

- ☐ $E = U + K$

- ☐ $E = U + K =$ Constant (for conservative systems)

- ☐ $W = Fd \cos\theta$

- ☐ $P = \dfrac{W}{t}$

- ☐ $W_{net} = \Delta K = K_f - K_i$

- ☐ $p = mv$

- ☐ $I = Ft = \Delta p = mv_f - mv_i$

- ☐ $m_a v_{ai} + m_b v_{bi} = m_a v_{af} + m_b v_{bf}$ (for completely elastic and inelastic collisions)

- ☐ $\frac{1}{2}m_a v_{ai}^2 + \frac{1}{2}m_b v_{bi}^2 = \frac{1}{2}m_a v_{af}^2 + \frac{1}{2}m_b v_{bf}^2$ (for completely elastic collisions only)

- ☐ $m_a v_{ai} + m_b v_{bi} = (m_a + m_b)v_f$ (for completely inelastic collisions only)

- ☐ Mechanical advantage $= \dfrac{\text{force}_{out}}{\text{force}_{in}}$

- ☐ Efficiency $= \dfrac{W_{out}}{W_{in}} = \dfrac{(\text{load})(\text{load distance})}{(\text{effort})(\text{effort distance})}$

- ☐ $x = \dfrac{(m_1 x_1 + m_2 x_2 + m_3 x_3 + \cdots)}{(m_1 + m_2 + m_3 + \cdots)} =$ center of mass

SHARED CONCEPTS

HIGH-YIELD PRACTICE PROBLEMS

Practice Questions

1. A weight lifter lifts a 275 kg barbell from the ground to a height of 2.4 m. How much work has he done, and how much work is required to hold the weight at that height?

   A. 3,234 J and 0 J, respectively
   B. 3,234 J and 3,234 J, respectively
   C. 6,468 J and 0 J, respectively
   D. 6,468 J and 6,468 J, respectively

2. A tractor pulls a log with a mass of 500 kg along the ground for 100 m. The rope (between the tractor and the log) makes an angle of 30° with the ground and is acted on by a tensile force of 5,000 N. How much work does the tractor do? (sin 30° = 0.5, cos 30° = 0.866, tan 30° = 0.57)

   A. 250 kJ
   B. 290 kJ
   C. 433 kJ
   D. 500 kJ

3. A 2,000 kg experimental car can accelerate from 0 to 30 m/s in 6.3 s. What is the average power of the engine needed to achieve this acceleration?

   A. 143 W
   B. 143 kW
   C. 900 J
   D. 900 kJ

4. A 40 kg block is resting at a height of 5 m off the ground. If the block is released and falls to the ground, what is its total energy at a height of 2 m?

   A. 0 J
   B. 400 J
   C. 2 kJ
   D. It cannot be determined from the information given.

5. If a human is lying on a flat surface and the weights of the head, thorax, and hips and legs are determined to be 8 lbs, 20 lbs, and 20 lbs, respectively, what is the center of mass of this person? (Assume that the centers of mass of the head, thorax, and hips and legs are 5 inches, 25 inches, and 50 inches from the top of the head.)

   A. 10 inches away from the top of the head
   B. 20 inches away from the top of the head
   C. 30 inches away from the top of the head
   D. 40 inches away from the top of the head

6.

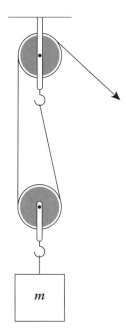

In the pulley system shown, if the mass of the object is 10 kg and the object is accelerating upwards at 2 m/s², what is the tension force in each rope?

A. 50 N
B. 60 N
C. 100 N
D. 120 N

7. Two billiard balls, one moving at 0.5 m/s, the other at rest, undergo a perfectly elastic collision. If the masses of the billiard balls are equal and the speed of the stationary one after the collision is 0.5 m/s, then what is the speed of the other ball after the collision?

A. 0 m/s
B. 0.5 m/s
C. 1 m/s
D. 1.5 m/s

8. A 2,500 kg car traveling at 20 m/s crashes into a 6,000 kg truck that is originally at rest. What is the speed of the truck after the collision, if the car comes to rest at the point of impact? (Neglect the effects of friction.)

A. 0 m/s
B. 8.33 m/s
C. 16.7 m/s
D. 83 m/s

9. Which of the following are elastic collisions?

   I. A planet breaks into several fragments.

   II. Two balls collide and then move away from each other with the same speed but reverse directionality.

   III. A volleyball hits the net, slows down, and then bounces back with one-half its initial speed.

A. I only
B. II only
C. II and III only
D. I, II, and III

10. A 1 kg cart travels down an inclined plane at 5 m/s and strikes two billiard balls, which start moving in opposite directions perpendicular to the initial direction of the cart. Ball A has a mass of 2 kg and moves away at 2 m/s, while ball B has a mass of 1 kg and moves away at 4 m/s. Which of the following statements is true?

A. The cart will come to a halt in order to conserve momentum.
B. The cart will slow down.
C. The cart will continue moving as before, while balls A and B will convert the gravitational potential energy of the cart into their own kinetic energies.
D. These conditions are impossible because they violate either the law of conservation of momentum or conservation of energy.

11. Tom, who has a mass of 80 kg, and Mary, who has a mass of 50 kg, jump off a 20 m tall building and land on a fire net. The net compresses, and they bounce back up at the same time. Which of the following statements is NOT true?

    A. Mary will bounce higher than Tom.

    B. The magnitude of the change in momentum for Tom is 1,600 kg m/s.

    C. Tom will experience a greater force upon impact than Mary.

    D. The energy in this event is converted from potential to kinetic to elastic to kinetic.

12. Two identical molecules, A and B, move with the same horizontal velocities but opposite vertical velocities. Which of the following statements MUST be true after the two molecules collide?

    A. The sum of the kinetic energies of the molecules before the collision is at least as large as the sum of the kinetic energies of the molecules after the collision.

    B. Molecule A will have a greater momentum after the collision than molecule B will.

    C. The sum of the kinetic energies of the molecules after the collision is greater than the sum of the kinetic energies of the molecules before the collision.

    D. Molecule A will have a greater vertical velocity than molecule B will.

Small Group Questions

1. The gravitational potential energy of an asteroid in a distant galaxy, traveling away from the Earth, approaches zero. However, when we roll a boulder down a hill, moving it closer to the Earth's center, we say that the gravitational potential energy of the boulder decreases, eventually becoming zero when it reaches the bottom of the hill. How can the boulder and asteroid both have potential energies of zero when they are traveling in opposite directions?

2. When a tennis ball is bounced off of a brick wall, the wall does not move. The ball experiences a change in its momentum when it bounces back, while the wall appears to have a momentum of zero. Why isn't momentum conserved?

Explanations to Practice Questions

1. C

Because the weight of the barbell (force acting downward) is $mg = 275 \text{ kg} \times 10 \text{ m/s}^2$, or about 2,750 N, it follows that the weightlifter must exert an equal and opposite force of 2,750 N on the barbell. The work done in lifting the barbell is defined as follows:

$$W = Fd$$
$$W = 2{,}750 \text{ N} \times 2.4 \text{ m}$$
$$W \approx 2{,}800 \text{ N} \times \frac{5}{2} \text{ m}$$
$$W \approx 7{,}000 \text{ J} \ (1 \text{ J} = 1 \text{ N} \times \text{m})$$

Using the same equation, it follows that the work done to hold the barbell in place is

$$W = Fd$$
$$W = 2{,}750 \text{ N} \times 0 \text{ J}$$
$$W = 0 \text{ J}$$

Because the barbell is held in place and there is no displacement, the work done is zero. Choice (C) best matches our response and is therefore the correct answer.

2. C

The total force on the rope is 5,000 N. However, the force in the direction of motion (the horizontal direction) is only $5{,}000 \text{ N} \times \cos 30° = 5{,}000 \text{ N} \times 0.866 \approx 4{,}500 \text{ N}$. Therefore, the work done by the tractor is

$$W = Fd \cos \theta$$
$$W = 5{,}000 \times 100 \times 0.866$$
$$W = 4{,}500 \times 100$$
$$W = 4.5 \times 10^5$$

This is the same as saying that the work done is 450 kJ, which best matches (C), the correct answer.

3. B

The work done by the engine is equal to the change in kinetic energy of the car:

$$W = \Delta K = \frac{1}{2} \, mv_f^2 - \frac{1}{2} \, mv_i^2$$
$$v_f = 30 \text{ m/s}$$
$$v_i = 0 \text{ m/s}$$
$$W = \Delta K = \frac{1}{2} \, mv_f^2$$
$$W = \frac{1}{2} (2{,}000 \text{ kg})(30 \text{ m/s})^2$$
$$W = 900{,}000 \text{ J}$$

The average power supplied is therefore equal to

$$P = \frac{W}{t}$$
$$P = \frac{900{,}000 \text{ J}}{6.3 \text{ s}}$$
$$P \approx 150{,}000 \text{ W}$$
$$P \approx 150 \text{ kW}$$

Choice (B) is closest to our result and is thus the correct answer.

4. C

Conservation of energy states that the total mechanical energy of the block is constant as it falls (neglecting air resistance). To calculate the total energy at any height, it is sufficient to know the total energy at a different height, say 5 m. At the maximum height of 5 m, the block only has potential energy equal to $U = mgh = 40 \text{ kg} \times 10 \text{ m/s}^2 \times 5 \text{ m} = 2{,}000 \text{ J}$. This means that if the total initial energy is 2,000 J, the total energy at any other time during the object's fall is also 2,000 J, or 2 kJ. Choice (C) is therefore the correct answer.

5. C

To calculate the center of mass of the person, we have to use the center of mass formula:

$$X = \frac{(m_1 x_1 + m_2 x_2 + m_3 x_3)}{(m_1 + m_2 + m_3)}$$

where m is mass and x is the position along the x-axis (in our case, the distance from the top of the head to the center of mass of each body part). Plugging in the numbers, we obtain the following:

$$X = \frac{(8 \text{ lb})(5 \text{ in}) + (20 \text{ lb})(25 \text{ in}) + (20 \text{ lb})(50 \text{ in})}{8 \text{ lb} + 20 \text{ lb} + 20 \text{ lb}}$$

$$X = \frac{40 \text{ lb·in} + 500 \text{ lb·in} + 1,000 \text{ lb·in}}{48 \text{ lb}}$$

$$X \approx \frac{1,500 \text{ lb·in}}{50 \text{ lb}}$$

$$X \approx 30 \text{ inches from the top of the head}$$

Choice (C) best matches our result and is thus the correct answer.

6. B

To calculate the tension force in each rope, first draw a force diagram:

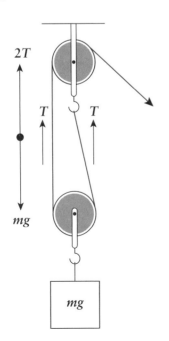

From the force diagram, notice that there are two tension forces pulling the mass up. The net force for this system is equal to $F_{net} = 2T - mg = ma$. From this equation, solve for T:

$$2T = m(a + g)$$
$$2T = 10 \text{ kg} (2 \text{ m/s}^2 + 10 \text{ m/s}^2)$$
$$2T = 10 \text{ kg} \times 12 \text{ m/s}^2$$
$$2T = 120 \text{ N}$$
$$T = 60 \text{ N}$$

Choice (B) best matches the result and is therefore the correct answer.

7. A

Because we are working with an elastic collision, either conservation of momentum or conservation of kinetic energy can be applied here. The momentum and kinetic energy of the stationary ball after the collision equal, respectively, the momentum and kinetic energy of the moving ball before the collision. Because the two balls have the same mass and the initial and final speeds are the same, 0.5 m/s, the momentum is conserved. Therefore, one of the balls must be stationary after the collision. Its speed is thus 0 m/s, making (A) the correct answer. A mathematical analysis reveals the same result:

$$mv_{1i} + mv_{2i} = mv_{1f} + mv_{2f}$$
$$v_{1i} + v_{2i} = v_{1f} + v_{2f}$$
$$0.5 \text{ m/s} + 0 \text{ m/s} = v_{1f} + 0.5 \text{ m/s}$$
$$v_{1f} = 0 \text{ m/s}$$

So, v_{1f} must be equal to zero, which confirms (A) as the correct answer.

8. B

In all collision problems, it is important to remember that the vector sum of the momentum before the collision is equal to the vector sum of the momentum after the collision; also, if the collision is elastic, the kinetic energy is conserved. Our problem deals with an inelastic collision, so it is sufficient for us to look at conservation of momentum in order to determine the speed of the truck after the impact:

$$mv_{(car)i} + mv_{(truck)i} = mv_{(car)f} + mv_{(truck)f}$$
$$2{,}500 \times 20 + 0 = 0 + 6{,}000 \, v_{(truck)f}$$
$$v_{(truck)f} = \frac{50{,}000}{6{,}000}$$
$$v_{(truck)f} \approx 8 \text{ m/s}$$

Choice (B) best matches our result and is thus the correct answer.

9. B

Only item II is correct. Elastic collisions occur when both momentum and kinetic energy are conserved. When a planet breaks into several pieces, each of them gains kinetic energy; the sum of the kinetic energies, of course, is greater than the kinetic energy of the initial object. When two balls collide and move away from each other at the same speed, kinetic energy is conserved. All collisions must conserve momentum. The volleyball lost kinetic energy to the collision, so it is partly inelastic.

10. C

The law of conservation of momentum states that both the vertical and horizontal components of momentum for a system must stay constant. If you take the initial movement of the cart as horizontal and the two balls move in perpendicular directions to the horizontal, it means that the cart must maintain its horizontal component of velocity. Therefore, (A) and (B) are incorrect . If the billiard balls move as described, then kinetic energy is not conserved; the system gains energy in this inelastic collision. Choice (C) correctly describes how this scenario is possible.

11. A

Mary will not bounce higher than Tom. Because Tom and Mary land on the net at the same time, the net does the same amount of work on both of them. The work done by the net is equal to $\frac{1}{2}kx^2$. For either person, this is converted into kinetic energy ($\frac{1}{2}m_1v^2$ and $\frac{1}{2}m_2v^2$), which is in turn converted into potential energy as m_1gh and m_2gh, respectively. The end result is that weight does not affect the height of the rebound. If the spring is perfectly efficient at converting its energy into kinetic energy, then they would both rebound back to the point from which they jumped. The change in momentum for Tom is 80 kg $\times [v_f - (-v_i)]$. v_i^2, the square of his speed at impact, is $2gh = 2 \times 10 \times 20 = 400$; therefore, his change in momentum is 80 kg $\times$ 20 = 1,600 kg $\times$ m/s. The force upon impact is equal to the change in momentum divided by the time of contact (which is the same for both individuals). Tom weighs more, which explains his greater momentum.

12. A

This question does not specify whether the collision between the two molecules is elastic or inelastic, so kinetic energy may (if the collision is elastic) or may not (if the collision is inelastic) be conserved. But either way, choice (A) is true because it allows for the initial sum of kinetic energy to be either equal to or greater than the final sum of kinetic energy. Choice (A) is therefore correct. Choices (B) and (D) are incorrect because they might be true, but they are not necessarily true, as molecule B could just as easily have the greater momentum or vertical velocity after the collision. Choice (C) is incorrect because there is no type of collision in which total kinetic energy increases.

Explanations to Small Group Questions

1. When we say that the gravitational potential energy of a boulder at the top of a hill is $U = mgh$, we are actually using an approximation of the change in potential energy of an object that only works near the Earth's surface. We use g, the acceleration due to gravity at or near the Earth's surface. We also use a height, h, which is an altitude above some arbitrarily designated zero altitude. In this instance, h is simply the height above the bottom of the hill. It would be accurate to say that we are measuring ΔU, the change in potential energy of the boulder, due to its Δh, the height above our arbitrary zero height. Therefore, $\Delta U = mg\Delta h$. So our approximation actually describes a difference in potential energy between the boulder and the bottom of the hill. This serves our purposes when discussing the relationships between potential energy, kinetic energy, and work. When the boulder reaches the bottom of the hill, Δh is zero and thus ΔU, gravitational potential energy relative to the bottom of the hill, is also zero. However, the boulder still has a *non-zero* gravitational potential energy when we consider its total distance from the center of the Earth! In fact, the measure of gravitational potential energy between any two objects is a *negative* value that increases towards zero with increasing distance. In the case of the asteroid, it is accurate to say that an object has zero gravitational potential energy when it is infinitely far away.

2. Recall that the conservation of momentum is only true for situations in which no external forces act on the system. In this case, the wall provides the external force on the ball, so momentum is not conserved. The brick wall is a solid surface of contact. Like other contact forces, such as the normal force, the wall exerts a force on the ball perpendicular to the surface of contact. In fact, all such contact forces are actually due to electrostatic interactions between molecules. In this case, the molecules of the wall are held firmly in place and repel the molecules of the tennis ball. Imagine if the bricks of the wall were not held together by mortar and were loosely laid on top of each other. Then one could throw the tennis ball hard enough to overcome the forces holding the wall together. The ball would then be able to transfer momentum to the bricks, perhaps dislodging a few and knocking down part of the wall.

4

30

20

Thermodynamics

In this chapter:

Introduction

In the attempt to help students better understand the laws of thermodynamics, some have resorted to the following three maxims:

1. The first law of thermodynamics says that you can't win the game; the best you can hope for is a tie (conservation of energy).
2. The second law of thermodynamics says that a tie is only possible at absolute zero (the entropy of the universe is always increasing except at absolute zero).
3. The third law of thermodynamics says that you'll never achieve absolute zero (a system will asymptotically approach an entropy minimum as it asymptotically approaches absolute zero).

Thermodynamics is the study of the flow of energy in the universe, as that flow relates to work, heat, the different forms of energy, and entropy. Classical thermodynamics concerns itself only with observations that can be made at the macroscopic level, such as measurements of temperature, pressure, volume, and work. Statistical mechanics, introduced in the 1870s through the work of Austrian physicist Ludwig Boltzmann, provides a molecular understanding of and predictive framework for the macroscopic observations made by classical thermodynamics. Although the MCAT will test the topic from a thermodynamic rather than statistical understanding, we will briefly discuss the statistical understanding of entropy because it clears up so much of the confusion that has arisen from the previously common (but now largely abandoned) characterization of entropy as "disorder."

This chapter reviews the laws of thermodynamics with a specific focus on the zeroth, first, and second laws. We will examine how the zeroth law leads to the formulation of temperature scales. Thermal expansion will be discussed as an example of the relationship between thermal energy and physical properties like length, volume, and conductivity. In the context of the first law, the conservation of energy, we will discuss the relationship between internal energy, heat, and work and characterize specific heat and heat of transformation. We will also review the various processes by which a system goes from one equilibrium state to another, such as isobaric, isothermal, and adiabatic processes. Finally, we will discuss the second law of thermodynamics, the concept of entropy and its measurement. The third law of thermodynamics is not directly tested on the MCAT, so we will not formally review it.

4.1 Zeroth Law of Thermodynamics

The **zeroth law** is based on a simple observation: When one object is in thermal equilibrium with another object, say a cup of warm tea and a metal stirring stick, and the second object is in thermal equilibrium with a third object, say the metal stirring stick and your hand, then the first and third object are also in thermal equilibrium and when brought into thermal contact (which doesn't necessarily imply physical contact, by the way), no net heat will flow between them.

TEMPERATURE

The formulation of the zeroth law—that no net heat flows between objects in thermal equilibrium (and the corollary that heat flows when two objects are not in thermal equilibrium)—actually came after the development of the concept and measurement of **temperature.** All substances, materials, and objects have a property called temperature. In everyday language, we use the term to describe qualitatively how hot or cold something is, but in thermodynamics, it has a more precise meaning. At the molecular level, temperature is related to the average motional (that is, kinetic) energy of the particles. At the macroscopic level, temperature, or more accurately, the difference in temperatures, determines the direction of heat flow. When allowed, heat moves spontaneously from materials that have higher temperatures to materials that have lower temperatures. *Heat (energy) flows from hot to cold.* If no net heat flows between two objects in thermal contact, then we can say that their temperatures are equal and they are in thermal equilibrium. Once we start talking about heat flowing from hotter to colder objects, we've ventured into the second law of thermodynamics, so keep that in mind for our discussion about the second law, but for the moment let's stay focused on the zeroth law.

Temperature is a physical property of matter, and one that is fundamentally related to the motional behavior of the atoms and molecules that make up matter, but we've already commented on the fact that it is something that can be observed macroscopically, so it would be helpful to have a standard way of measuring the human (macroscopic) experience of temperature. Since the 18th century, scales have been developed to quantify the temperature of matter with thermometers. Some of these systems are still in common use, including the Fahrenheit (°F), Celsius (°C), and Kelvin (K) scales. Fahrenheit and Celsius are the oldest scales still in common use and are relatively convenient because they are based on the phase changes for water. As you can see from Table 4.1, the freezing and boiling temperatures of water are assigned the 0° and 100° values, respectively, for the Celsius scale. In spite of the fact that the Fahrenheit scale is also based on the phase transformations of water, it is clearly not as straightforward.

Table 4.1. Temperature Scales

Situation	K	°C	°F
absolute zero	0	−273	−460
freezing point of water	273	0	32
boiling point of water	373	100	212

The Kelvin scale is most commonly used for scientific measurements and is one of the seven base units in SI. It defines as the zero reference point **absolute zero**, the theoretical temperature at which there is no thermal energy, and sets the freezing point of water as 273.15 K. Please note that there are no negative temperatures on the Kelvin scale because it starts from absolute zero. Although the Kelvin and Celsius scales have different zero reference points, the size of their units is the same. That is to say, a change of one degree on the Celsius scale equals a change of one unit on the Kelvin scale. Because there are 180 degrees between water's phase changes on the Fahrenheit scale, rather than 100 degrees as on both the Celsius and the Kelvin scales, the size of the Fahrenheit unit is smaller. The following formulas are used to convert from one scale to another:

$$T_C = T_K - 273$$
$$T_F = \frac{9}{5} T_C + 32$$

where T_C stands for degrees Celsius, T_K stands for degrees Kelvin, and T_F stands for degrees Fahrenheit.

Key Concept

Kelvin is a scale based around "absolute zero," which is the temperature at which all random atomic motion stops. This occurs at zero degrees Kelvin.

Key Equation

$T_C = T_K - 273$
°C = K (Even though the temperature units are different, the increments of the Celsius and Kelvin scales are equivalent.)
Use this equation to convert between Celsius and Kelvin temperature scales.

MCAT Expertise

Don't worry about Fahrenheit on the MCAT; if you need to use it, the conversions will be given.

Example: If the weatherperson says that the temperature will reach a high of 303 K today, what will be the temperature in °C and in °F?

Solution: To convert from Kelvin to Celsius, use

$$T_C = T_K - 273$$
$$= 303 - 273$$
$$= 30°C$$

Now to convert from Celsius to Fahrenheit, use

$$T_F = \frac{9}{5} T_C + 32$$
$$= \frac{9}{5}(30) + 32$$
$$= 86°F$$

THERMAL EXPANSION

It has long been noted that some physical properties of matter change when the matter gets hotter or colder. Length, volume, and even the conductivity of matter change as a function of temperature. The relationship between temperature and a physical property of some matter was used to develop the temperature scales with which we are familiar today. For example, Daniel Fahrenheit developed the temperature scale that bears his name by placing a thermometer filled with mercury into a bath of ice, water, and ammonium chloride. The cold temperature caused the mercury to contract, and when the level in the glass tube stabilized at a lower level, he marked this as the zero reference on the scale. He then placed the same mercury thermometer in a mixture of ice and water (that is, at the freezing temperature for water). The slightly warmer temperature of this mixture caused the mercury to rise in the glass column, and when it stabilized at this higher level, Fahrenheit assigned a value of 32°. When he stuck the thermometer under his (or someone else's) tongue, he marked the even higher mercury level as 96°. The details of how and why Fahrenheit came to choose these numbers (and the history of their adjustment since Fahrenheit first developed the scale) are beyond the scope of this discussion. What's important to note is that a change in some physical property on one kind of matter—in this case, the height of a column of mercury—can be correlated to certain "temperature markers," such as the phase changes for water. Once the scale has been set in reference to the decided-upon temperature markers, then the thermometer can be used to "take the temperature" of any other matter, in accordance with the zeroth law.

Because the property of **thermal expansion** was integral to the development of thermometers, let's look a little more closely at this phenomenon. A change in the temperature of most solids results in a change in their length. Rising temperatures cause an increase in length, and falling temperatures cause a decrease in length. The amount of length change is proportional to the original length of the solid and the increase in temperature according to the following equation:

$$\Delta L = \alpha L \Delta T$$

where ΔL is the change in length, L is the original length, and ΔT is the change in temperature. The coefficient of linear expansion α is a constant that characterizes how a specific material's length changes as the temperature changes. This usually has units of K^{-1}, though it may sometimes be quoted as $°C^{-1}$. This difference is ultimately inconsequential because the unit size for the Kelvin and Celsius scales is the same.

> **Example:** A metal rod of length 2 m and a coefficient of expansion of 11×10^{-6} K^{-1} is heated from 30°C to 1,080°C. By what amount does the rod expand?
>
> **Solution:** By using the information given in the problem, we can substitute directly into the thermal expansion formula:
>
> $$\Delta L = \alpha L \Delta T$$
> $$= (11 \times 10^{-6})(2)(1,080 - 30)$$
> $$= 0.023 \text{ m}$$

Liquids also experience thermal expansion, but the only meaningful parameter of expansion is **volume expansion.** The formula for volumetric thermal expansion is applicable to both liquids and solids:

$$\Delta V = \beta V \Delta T$$

where $\beta = 3\alpha$.

> **Example:** Assume that a thermometer with 1 ml of mercury is taken from a freezer with a temperature of −25°C and placed near an oven at 225°C. If the coefficient of volume expansion of mercury is 1.8×10^{-4} K^{-1}, by how much will the liquid expand?
>
> **Solution:** Use the information given:
>
> $$\Delta V = \beta V \Delta T$$
> $$= (1.8 \times 10^{-4})(1)(225 - (-25))$$
> $$= 0.045 \text{ ml}$$

Real World

It is because of this property that bridges and sidewalks have gaps between their segments; they allow for thermal expansion without damaging integrity.

Key Concept

When you see the symbol Δ, think "change in." Calculate "change in" by taking the difference between final and initial values.

Key Equation

$\Delta L = \alpha L \Delta T$

$m = (K^{-1})(m)(K)$

$m = m$

Use this equation to determine the change in length of an object subjected to a change in temperature.

Key Equation

$\Delta V = \beta V \Delta T$

$m^3 = (K^{-1})(m^3)(K)$

$m^3 = m^3$

Use this equation to determine the change in volume of a fluid or object subjected to a change in temperature.

4.2 First Law of Thermodynamics

We have already encountered the **first law of thermodynamics** in our discussion of the conservation of mechanical energy in Chapter 3. As you'll remember, we stated that in the absence of friction forces, the sum of kinetic and potential energies is constant in a system. Now, in our present discussion of thermodynamics, we will look more closely at the relationship between internal energy, heat, and work. Essentially, the first law states that the change in the total internal energy of a system is equal to the amount of energy transferred in the form of heat to the system, minus the amount of energy transferred from the system in the form of work. The internal energy of a system can be increased by adding heat, doing work on the system, or some combination of both processes. The change in internal energy ΔU is calculated from this equation:

$$\Delta U = Q - W$$

> **Key Concept**
>
> The first law of thermodynamics tells us that an increase in the total internal energy of a system is caused by transferring heat to the system or performing work on the system. The total internal energy of a system will decrease when heat is lost from the system or work is performed by the system.

where ΔU is the change in the system's internal energy, Q is the energy transferred through heat to the system, and W is the work done by the system. To use this equation properly, you must use the following **sign convention**: *work done by the system is positive, while work done on the system is negative; heat flow into the system is positive, while heat flow out of the system is negative.* By the way, don't be overly concerned with a precise definition of **system.** When physicists use the term, they only mean to identify the object or material to which they are paying attention; everything outside of the system is the **environment.** A car could be a system, and the air immediately surrounding it could be the environment. In another analysis, the system could be the earth and its total atmosphere, and the universe could be the environment. Ultimately, the entire universe can be identified as a system.

> **Key Equation**
>
> $\Delta U = Q - W$
>
> $J = J - J$
>
> Use this equation to determine the change in total internal energy of a system undergoing a thermodynamic process. Note that work done on the system and heat flow out of the system is negative.

If you're paying attention, you'll notice that the answer to the question *Is energy conserved even when friction is present?* is yes! The first law is really just a particular expression of the more universal physical law of energy conservation: Energy can be neither created nor destroyed; it can only be changed from one form to another.

Because the first law accounts for all work and all heat processes impacting the system, the presence of friction poses no problem, because the energy transfer associated with the friction will be accounted for in the first law equation. For example, when your 17-year-old brother "burns rubber" in your mom's car, all the smoke and noise coming from the front tires is a clear indication that mechanical energy is not being conserved. The strong friction forces between the tires and the street are the source of all that smoke and noise. However, if we include the energy transfers associated with the friction forces in our tally of the change in internal energy of the car, then we can confidently say that no energy has been lost at all: There may be a "loss" of energy from the car as a result of the friction, but that precise amount of energy can be "found" elsewhere, as thermal energy in the atoms and molecules of the road and air.

HEAT

We need to spend some time discussing heat and work before we look at some special cases of the first law. In Chapter 3, we defined work as the process by which energy is transferred as the result of force being applied through some distance. We noted that work and heat are the only two processes by which energy can be transferred from one object to another. Remember what the zeroth law says: Objects in thermal contact are in thermal equilibrium when their temperatures are the same. The corollary of this is the second law of thermodynamics: Objects in thermal contact and not in thermal equilibrium will exchange heat energy such that the object with a higher temperature will give off heat energy to the object with a lower temperature until both objects have the same temperature (and come to thermal equilibrium). Heat, then, is defined as the process by which a quantity of energy is transferred between two objects as a result of a difference in temperature. As we will discuss further in our examination of the second law, heat can never spontaneously transfer energy from a cooler object to a warmer one without work being done on the system.

The SI unit for heat is the joule (J), and this ought not to surprise you. Heat can also be measured in the unit of **calorie** (cal) or the **British thermal unit** (Btu). Another unit of heat that you encounter every day (if you read food labels) is the **Calorie**. The nutritional Calorie ("big C") is not the same thing as the calorie ("little c"). One Calorie is equal to 1,000 calories and, hence, is actually the kilocalorie.

The conversion factors between the units of heat are as follows:

$$1 \text{ Cal} = 10^3 \text{ cal} = 3.97 \text{ Btu} = 4,184 \text{ J}$$

Heat Transfer

For energy to be transferred between objects, they must be in thermal contact with each other. You mustn't assume that this means that the objects are

> **Key Concept**
>
> The first law of thermodynamics is that energy is neither created nor destroyed. This means the energy of a closed system (such as the universe) will always remain constant.

> **Key Concept**
>
> Heat is the process of energy transfer between two objects at different temperatures and will continue until the two objects come into thermal equilibrium (i.e., reach the same temperature).

physically touching. Like force, energy can travel tremendous distances and doesn't require a medium in order to move. There are three means by which heat can transfer energy: conduction, convection, and radiation. **Conduction** is the direct transfer of energy from molecule to molecule through molecular collisions. As this definition would suggest, there must be direct physical contact between the objects. At the molecular level, the particles of the hotter matter transfer some of their motional energy to the particles of the cooler matter through collisions between the particles of the two materials. Metals are described as the best heat conductors because the density of atoms embedded in the "sea of electrons" that characterizes the metallic bond facilitates the transfer of energy. Gases tend to be the poorest heat conductors because even though gas molecules are free to move around (in fact, the root mean square velocity of air molecules at room temperature and atmospheric pressure is around 500 m/s), there is so much space between individual molecules that energy transferming collisions occure relatively infrequently. An example of heat transfer through conduction is the heat that is rapidly, and painfully, conducted to your fingers when you touch a hot stove.

Convection is the transfer of heat by the physical motion of the heated material. Because convection involves flow, only fluids (liquids and gases) can transfer heat by this means. In convection, heated portions of the fluid rise from the heat source, while colder portions sink (because density decreases as temperature increases). Most restaurants and some home kitchens have convection ovens, which use fans to circulate hot air inside the oven. Because the heat is being transferred to the food by convection and radiation rather than only by radiation, convection ovens are more efficient and produce better results.

Radiation is the transfer of energy by electromagnetic waves. We will learn much more about electric and magnetic fields in Chapters 6 and 7 and about electromagnetic waves in Chapter 10. An important point to remember about radiation is that it can travel through a vacuum. For this reason, the energy from the sun is able to warm the earth. Most home kitchens have radiant ovens, which use either electrical coils or gas flames to heat the insulated metal box that forms the body of the oven. The hot metal box then radiates the energy through the open space of the oven, where it is absorbed by whatever food is placed inside.

Specific Heat

When heat energy is added or removed from a system, the temperature of that system will change in proportion to the amount of heat, unless the system is undergoing a phase change during which the temperature is constant. This relationship between heat and temperature for a substance is called **specific heat (c).** The specific heat of a substance is defined as the amount of heat energy required to raise 1 kg of a substance by 1°C or 1 K. For example, the specific heat of liquid water is 1,000 calories per 1 kilogram per 1°C or 1 K. Equivalently, this can be expressed as 4,184 joules per 1 kilogram per 1°C or 1 K. The specific heat for a substance changes according to its phase, and the MCAT will provide you with all the necessary specific heat values. The equation that relates the heat Q gained or lost by an object and the change in temperature of that object ΔT is

$$Q = mc\Delta T = mc(T_f - T_i)$$

where m is the mass of the object and c is the specific heat. Because the unit size for the Celsius and Kelvin scales is the same, the change in temperature will be the same for temperatures measured in Celsius or Kelvin.

If you've been sitting at a desk engaged in focused study for the MCAT for a couple of hours now, you may find yourself frequently rubbing your neck to ease the pain of the muscle cramps. Take advantage of the specific heat of water by placing a hot water bottle over your aching muscles. The warmth of a hot water heating pad can increase circulation and perfusion to the muscles, which facilitates the delivery of more oxygen and nutrients. Furthermore, the warmth increases the flexibility of the soft tissues and will stimulate other neural sensors (like heat and pressure sensors), which can help dull the perception of pain. The specific heat of water has a lot to do with the health benefits of a heating pad. First, the specific heat for liquid water is greater than that of either ice or steam. This means that more energy per unit mass must be delivered to the liquid water to raise its temperature by one degree. This is why it takes a little while to get the water in the heating pad nice and warm. However, the reverse is also true: Water can deliver a lot of energy per unit mass as it cools down by each degree. Once that heating pad is resting on your neck or back, it will be able to deliver a large quantity of heat energy for a long period of time.

Heat of Transformation

When a substance is undergoing a phase change, such as from solid to liquid or liquid to gas, the heat that is added or removed from the system does not result in a change in temperature. In other words, phase changes occur at constant temperature, and the temperature will not begin to change until all of the substance has been converted from one phase into the other. For example, water melts at 0°C. No matter how much heat is added to a mass of ice at 0°C, the temperature will not rise until all the ice has been melted into liquid water.

We've determined that adding heat raises the temperature of a system because the particles in that system now have a greater average kinetic energy, and it's true that molecules have greater degrees of freedom of movement in the liquid state than in the solid state (and even more so in the gas state). However, phase changes are related to changes in potential energy, not kinetic energy.

> **Key Concept**
>
> One calorie (little c) is the amount of heat required to raise 1 g of water one degree Celsius. One Calorie (big C) is the amount of heat required to raise 1 kg of water 1 degree Celsius.

> **Key Equation**
>
> $Q = mc\Delta T = mc(T_f - T_i)$
> $J = (kg)(J/kg \cdot K)(K)$
> $J = J$
> Use this equation to determine the heat gained or lost by a substance subjected to a change in temperature.

The molecules of water in ice, for example, aren't "frozen" in place and unable to move. Actually, there's a lot of movement. The molecules rotate, vibrate, and wiggle around. The bonds within each molecule are also free to bend and stretch. Of course, the molecules are held in relatively stable positions by the hydrogen bonds that form between them, but they still have a fairly significant amount of motional (kinetic) energy. The potential energy, however, is quite low because of the stability provided by the relative closeness of one molecule to another and by the hydrogen bonds.

Now, think about what happens when you add heat to ice that is at 0°C. The heat energy causes the water molecules to begin to break away from each other by breaking free of the hydrogen bonds between them. Not all of the hydrogen bonds and liquid water molecules still want to form hydrogen bonds, but because the water molecules are being held less rigidly in place, they now have greater degrees of freedom of movement (statistical mechanics says that these contribute to a greater number of "microstates") and their average potential energy increases. However, their average kinetic energy stays the same because they "redirect" some of their previously limited motion to other directions. Instead of only jumping up and down or swaying side to side, the molecules begin to move forward and backward. Nevertheless, to start moving forward, they have to decrease their up-and-down jumping. In this way, the average motional (kinetic) energy is constant even as the molecules begin to "enjoy" greater degrees of freedom of movement (a greater number of possible microstates).

When heat energy is added or removed from a system that is experiencing a phase change, the amount of heat that is added or removed cannot be calculated with the equation $Q = mc\Delta T$, because there is no temperature change during a phase change. Instead, the following equation is used:

$$Q = mL$$

where Q is the amount of heat gained or lost, m is the mass of the substance, and L is the **heat of transformation** of the substance.

The phase change from liquid to solid (freezing) or solid to liquid (melting or fusion) occurs at the melting point. The corresponding heat of transformation is called the **heat of fusion.** The phase change from liquid to gas (vaporization) or gas to liquid (condensation) occurs at the boiling point. The corresponding heat of transformation is called the **heat of vaporization.** The relevant heats of fusion and vaporization will be provided for you on Test Day.

Real World

It is because of the heat of transformation that sweating is such an efficient cooling mechanism. When the sweat evaporates, the heat of vaporization is lost from the surface of the body. This is why heat seems so much worse when it is very humid out. The sweat is less likely to evaporate due to the dampness of the environment, so less heat will be lost from the surface of the skin through sweating.

Key Concept

Phase changes that are good to know are sublimation (solid to gas), deposition (gas to solid), fusion (solid to liquid), freezing (liquid to solid), condensation (gas to liquid), and finally vaporization (liquid to gas).

Key Equation

$Q = mL$

J = (kg)(J/kg)

J = J

Use this equation to determine the heat gained or lost by a substance subjected to a change in phase.

> **Example:** Silver has a melting point of about 1,000°C and a heat of fusion of 1×10^5 J/kg. The specific heat of silver is roughly 250 J/kg·°C. Approximately how much heat is required to completely melt a 1 kg silver chain whose initial temperature is 20°C?
>
> **Solution:** Before melting the chain, we must first get the temperature of the chain to the melting point. To figure out how much heat is required, we use this formula:
>
> $$Q = mc(T_f - T_i)$$
> $$= 1(250)(1,000 - 20)$$
> $$= 245,000 \text{ J}$$
> $$= 245 \text{ kJ}$$
>
> This tells us we have to add 245 kJ of heat to the chain just to get its temperature to the melting point. The chain is still in the solid phase. To melt it (change its phase to liquid), we must continue to add heat in accordance with this formula:
>
> $$Q = mL$$
> $$= 1(1 \times 10^5)$$
> $$= 100,000 \text{ J}$$
> $$= 100 \text{ kJ}$$
>
> The total heat needed to melt the solid silver chain is 245 kJ + 100 kJ = 345 kJ.

WORK

We have spent a lot of time discussing work (Chapter 3) as a process of energy transfer by application of force through some distance. We will learn in our discussion of fluids (Chapter 5) that pressure can be thought of as an "energy density." Because many thermodynamic analyses are applied to gas systems, we need to concern ourselves here with a consideration of the means by which work energy is transferred to or from gas systems.

During any thermodynamic process, a system goes from some initial equilibrium state with an initial pressure, temperature, and volume to some other equilibrium state, which may be at a different final pressure, temperature, or volume. These thermodynamic processes can be represented in graphical form with volume on the *x*-axis and pressure (or temperature) on the *y*-axis.

For a gas system contained in a cylinder with a piston that is able to move up and down, we can analyze the relationship among pressure, volume, and work. When the gas expands, it pushes up against the piston, exerting a force ($F = PA$), causing the piston to move up and the volume of the system to increase. When the gas is compressed, the piston pushes down on the gas, exerting a force ($F = PA$), and the

MCAT Expertise

The units for pressure that you may encounter on the MCAT include atmosphere (atm), pascal (Pa), torr, or mm Hg: 1 atm = 1.013×10^5 Pa = 760 torr = 760 mm Hg.

 KAPLAN 117

volume of the system decreases. Because the volume of the system has changed due to an applied pressure, we can say that work has been done.

By the sign convention for the second law of thermodynamics explained previously, when a gas expands, we say that work was done by the gas and the work is positive; when a gas is compressed, we say that work was done on the gas and the work is negative. There are an infinite number of paths between an initial and final state. Different paths require different amounts of work. You can calculate the work done on or by a system by finding the area under the pressure-volume curve. Note that if volume stays constant as pressure changes (that is, $\Delta V = \Delta x = 0$), then no work is done because there is no area to calculate. On the other hand, if pressure remains constant as volume changes (that is, $\Delta P = \Delta y = 0$), then the area under the curve is a rectangle of length P and width $\Delta V (V_f - V_i)$. For processes in which pressure remains constant, the work can be calculated as follows:

$$W = P\Delta V$$

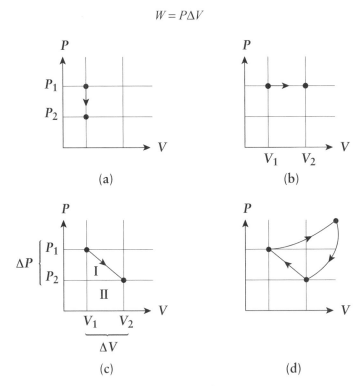

Figure 4.1. Pressure-Volume Curves
The work done on or by a system undergoing a thermodynamic process can be determined by finding the area enclosed by the corresponding pressure-volume curve

Figure 4.1a shows that the system undergoes a decrease in pressure from P_1 to P_2 at a constant volume. Because there was no change in volume, the work done in this process is zero. In Figure 4.1b, the system expands from V_1 to V_2 at a constant pressure. Whenever a system undergoes a process during which pressure is constant, the process is called isobaric. In this isobaric process, the work done is calculated according to the equation $W = P\Delta V$. Because the gas has expanded, the work was done by the gas and is positive. Figure 4.1c shows a process in which neither pressure nor volume is held constant. Calculating the work done in this situation would require calculus, but the MCAT does not test calculus-based physics, so we must tackle this problem with a graphical analysis. The total area under the graph (Regions I and II) gives the work done.

Region I is a triangle whose base is ΔV and whose height is ΔP, so the area is

$$A_\mathrm{I} = \left(\frac{1}{2}\right)\Delta V \Delta P$$

Region II is a rectangle with base ΔV and height P_2, so its area is

$$A_\mathrm{II} = P_2 \Delta V$$

The work done is the sum of the areas of regions I and II:

$$W = A_\mathrm{I} + A_\mathrm{II}$$

Figure 4.1d shows a closed cycle in which, after certain interchanges of work and heat, the system returns to its initial state. Because work is positive when the gas expands and negative when the gas is compressed, the work done is the area enclosed by the curve.

SPECIAL CASES OF THE FIRST LAW OF THERMODYNAMICS

The MCAT focuses on three particular thermodynamic processes as special cases of the first law, shown in Table 4.2. In each of these cases, some physical property is held constant through the process. These processes are **isovolumetric** (constant volume), **adiabatic** (no heat exchange), and **closed cycle** (constant internal energy). Isovolumetric processes are also known as **isochoric**; closed cycle processes are also known as **isothermal,** meaning the temperature stays constant.

Table 4.2. Some Special Cases of the First Law of Thermodynamics

Process	First Law Becomes
Adiabatic ($Q = 0$)	$\Delta U = -W$
Constant Volume ($W = 0$)	$\Delta U = Q$
Closed Cycle ($\Delta U = 0$)	$Q = W$

Example: A gas in a cylinder is kept at a constant pressure of 3.5×10^5 Pa while 300 kJ of heat are added to it, causing the gas to expand from 0.9 m³ to 1.5 m³. Find

a. the work done by the gas.
b. the change in internal energy of the gas.

Solution:

a. The pressure is held constant through the entire process so the work can be found using the equation:

$$W = P\Delta V$$
$$= (3.5 \times 10^5)(1.5 - 0.9)$$
$$= 2.1 \times 10^5 \text{ J}$$

b. The change in internal energy can be found from the first law of thermodynamics:

$$\Delta U = Q - W$$
$$= 3 \times 10^5 - 2.1 \times 10^5$$
$$= 0.9 \times 10^5$$
$$= 9 \times 10^4 \text{ J}$$

MCAT Concept Check 4.2

Before moving on, ensure that you are able to:

✓ Describe the first law of thermodynamics
✓ Recognize the equivalence of mechanical, chemical, electrical, and thermal energy units
✓ Define the modes of heat transfer (conduction, convection, radiation)
✓ Calculate heat transfer during phase changes and temperature changes
✓ Interpret *PV* diagrams (work done = area under or enclosed by curve)

4.3 Second Law of Thermodynamics and Entropy

Humans have devised ways to concentrate heat, isolate cold, chill things, heat things, hold things up, and covert one form to another—all attempts to exert control over energy. Why wouldn't we want to exert control over energy? Based on our discussion in this chapter and in Chapter 3 on work, energy, and momentum, it ought to be clear that nothing, absolutely nothing, could ever happen without the movement of energy from one place to another, either through heat or work. We seem to be doing a fairly good job in harnessing the power, so to speak, of energy to our benefit, yet one only needs to look around to see that ultimately, our grand projects of energy control fail or will fail, sometimes quietly, sometimes spectacularly, but always inevitably. Hot tea cools down, frozen drinks melt, iron rusts, buildings crumble, balloons deflate, and living things die.

In all of those examples, energy of some form or another is going from being localized or concentrated to being spread out or dispersed. The thermal energy in the hot tea is spreading out to the cooler air that surrounds it. The thermal energy in the warmer air is spreading out to the cooler frozen drink. The chemical energy in the bonds of elemental iron and oxygen is released and disperses as a result of the formation of the more stable (lower energy) bonds of iron oxide (rust). The potential energy of the building is released and dispersed in the form of light, sound, and heat (motional energy) of the ground and air as the building crumbles and falls. The motional energy of the pressurized air is released to the surrounding atmosphere as the balloon deflates. The chemical energy of all the molecules and atoms in living flesh is released into the environment during the process of death and decay.

This is the **second law of thermodynamics**: Energy spontaneously disperses from being localized to becoming spread out if it is not hindered from doing so. Pay attention to this: *The usual way of thinking about entropy as disorder must not be taken too literally, a trap that many students fall into. Be very careful in thinking about entropy as disorder*. The old analogy between a messy (disordered) room and entropy is arguably deficient and may not only hinder understanding but actually increase confusion.

Entropy, then, according to statistical mechanics, is the measure of the spontaneous dispersal of energy at a specific temperature: *how much* energy is spread out or *how widely* spread out energy becomes in a process. The equation for entropy is

$$\Delta S = \frac{Q}{T}$$

where ΔS is the change in entropy, Q is the heat that is gained or lost, and T is the temperature in Kelvin. When energy is distributed into a system at a given temperature, its entropy increases. When energy is distributed out of a system at a given temperature, its entropy decreases.

Notice that the second law states that energy will spontaneously disperse. It does not say that energy can never be localized or concentrated. However, the spontaneous concentration of energy is highly unlikely to occur (although statistically there is a finite possibility, but that is beyond the scope of the MCAT). Work must usually be done to concentrate energy. The second law has been described as "time's arrow," because there is a unidirectional limitation on the movement of energy by which we

Key Equation

$\Delta S = \frac{Q}{T}$

J/K = (J)/(K)

Use this equation to determine the change in entropy of a system at a given temperature.

Key Concept

The universe is a closed, expanding system (this will be discussed with the Doppler effect in Chapter 9), so you know that the entropy of the universe is always increasing. The more space that appears with the expansion of the universe, the more space there is for the entire universe's energy to be distributed and the total entropy of the universe to increase irreversibly.

recognize "before and after" or "new and old." Another way of understanding this is to say that energy in a closed system will spontaneously spread out and entropy will increase if it is not hindered from doing so. Remember that *system* and *closed system* can be variably defined to ultimately include the entire universe; thus, the second law ultimately claims that the entropy of the universe is increasing. That is, energy concentrations at any and all locations in the universe are in the process of becoming distributed and spread out.

When describing processes, physicists often use terms such as *natural*, *unnatural*, *reversible*, or *irreversible*. These terms confuse students but needlessly so, because these terms are descriptive of observable phenomena. For example, we expect that when a hot object is brought into thermal contact with a cold object, the hot object will transfer heat energy to the cold object until both are in thermal equilibrium (that is, at the same temperature). This is a **natural** process and also one that we would describe as **irreversible**: We are not surprised that the two objects eventually reach a common temperature, but we would be shocked (shocked!) if all of a sudden the hot object became hotter and the cold object became colder. We just wouldn't believe it because we know from experience that *cold → hot* is just not the "right direction" of spontaneous heat movement. We would call this **unnatural**.

To define a reversible reaction, let's consider a system of ice and liquid water in equilibrium at 0°C. If we place this mixture of ice and liquid water into a thermostat (device for regulating temperature) that is also at 0°C and allow infinitesimal amounts of heat to be absorbed by the ice from the thermostat so that the ice melts to liquid water at 0°C and the thermostat remains at 0°C, then the increase in the entropy ($+Q/T$) of the system (the water) will be exactly equal to the entropy decrease ($-Q/T$) of the surroundings (the thermostat). The net change in the entropy of the system and its surroundings is zero. Under these conditions, the process is **reversible**. The key to a reversible reaction is making sure that the process goes so slowly—requiring an infinite amount of time—that the system is always in equilibrium and no energy is lost or dissipated (by friction). To be frank, no real processes are reversible; we can only approximate a reversible process. Therefore, don't feel too bad if you've never actually observed one. You might be thinking that water can be "reversibly" frozen simply by putting water in the freezer, taking it out once it's frozen, and placing the ice on the countertop to melt, and repeating the process. Certainly water can be put through cycles of freezing and melting innumerable times, but that's not what physicists mean by reversible. Ice that melts on the warm countertop will not be expected to "reverse course" and freeze if it remains in the warm environment. The liquid water will need to be placed in an environment that is cold enough to cause the water to freeze, and once frozen in the cold environment, the ice would not be expected to begin melting spontaneously. The freezing and melting of water in real life is essentially an irreversible process.

For a reversible process, the entropy can be calculated as follows:

$$\Delta S = \frac{Q}{T} = L\left(\frac{m}{T}\right)$$

where L is the latent heat (either heat of fusion or heat of vaporization), m is mass, and T is the constant temperature of the system and environment in Kelvin.

Example: If, in a reversible process, 6.66×10^4 J of heat is used to change a 200 g block of ice to water at a temperature of 273 K, what is the change in the entropy of the system? (The heat of fusion of ice = 333 kJ/kg.)

Solution: We know that during a change of phase, the temperature is constant, in this case 273 K. From the information given,

$$\Delta S = \frac{Q}{T}$$
$$= \frac{6.66 \times 10^4}{273}$$
$$= 244 \text{ J/K}$$

Note that we did not need to know the mass or heat of fusion of ice in this case as we were given the amount of heat used.

MCAT Concept Check 4.3

Before moving on, ensure that you are able to:

✓ Describe the second law of thermodynamics and the concept of entropy

---

Conclusion

This chapter reviewed the zeroth law of thermodynamics, which reflects the observation that objects at the same temperature are in thermal equilibrium and the net heat exchanged between them is zero. We may consider the zeroth law to be ex post facto because it provides the thermodynamic explanation for the function of thermometers and temperature scales, which had been developed many years prior to the law's formulation. Examination of the first law of thermodynamics revealed that the energy of a closed system (up to and including the universe) is constant, such that the total internal energy of a system (the sum of all its potential and motional energies) equals the heat energy gained by the system minus the work energy done by the system. Finally, we carefully investigated the second law of thermodynamics and the concept of entropy. We understand entropy as a measure not of "disorder" but of the degree to which energy is spread out through a system, up to and including the universe. We now understand that the constant energy of the universe is progressively and irreversibly spreading out and will continue to spread out until there is an even distribution of energy throughout the universe.

That wasn't so bad now, was it? We know that few topics contribute more to the college physics student's anxiety levels than thermodynamics. This is truly unfortunate because like so many other physical principles, the laws of thermodynamics are based on observations of common phenomena and so are simply reflective of our everyday life experiences. With the exception of the third law of thermodynamics, which states that absolute zero can never be actually reached, the laws of thermodynamics are recognizable from the mundane and extraordinary occurrences of our lives. There's nothing to be anxious about; there's nothing to fear.

CONCEPT SUMMARY

Zeroth Law of Thermodynamics

- ☐ **The zeroth law of thermodynamics** (p. 108) states that objects are in thermal equilibrium when they are at the same temperature

- ☐ Objects in thermal equilibrium experience no net exchange of heat energy

- ☐ **Temperature** (p. 108) is a qualitative measure of how hot or cold an object is; quantitatively, it is related to the average kinetic (motional) energy of the particles that make up a substance

- ☐ **Thermal expansion** (p. 110) describes how a substance changes in length or volume as a function of the change in temperature

First Law of Thermodynamics

- ☐ **The first law of thermodynamics** (p. 112) is a statement of conservation of energy:

  - ○ The total energy in the universe can never decrease or increase

  - ○ For a closed system, the total internal energy is equal to the heat into or out of the system minus the work done by or on the system

- ☐ **Heat** (p. 113) is the process of energy transfer between two objects at different temperatures that occurs until the two objects come into thermal equilibrium (i.e., reach the same temperature)

- ☐ **Specific heat** (p. 114) is the amount of energy necessary to raise one kilogram of a substance by one degree Celsius or one unit Kelvin

- ☐ The specific heat of water is 1,000 cal/kg·°C

- ☐ During a **phase change** (p. 115), heat energy causes changes in the particles' potential energy, not kinetic energy, so there is no change in temperature

- ☐ There are three **special cases** (p. 119) of the first law in which one of the conditions of a gas system is held constant:

  - ○ For **isovolumetric processes**, the volume is constant, and no work is done

  - ○ For **adiabatic processes**, no heat is exchanged

  - ○ For **closed cycle processes**, the internal energy (and hence, temperature) is constant

Second Law of Thermodynamics and Entropy

- ☐ **The second law of thermodynamics** (p. 120) states that in a closed system (up to and including the entire universe), energy will **spontaneously** and **irreversibly** go from being localized to being spread out (dispersed)

- ☐ **Entropy** (p. 121) is a measure of how much energy has spread out or how spread out energy has become

- ☐ Every **natural process** (p. 122) is ultimately **irreversible**; under highly controlled conditions, certain equilibrium processes such as phase changes can be treated as **reversible**

EQUATIONS TO REMEMBER

☐ $T_C = T_K - 273$

☐ $\Delta L = \alpha L \Delta T$

☐ $\Delta V = \beta V \Delta T$

☐ $\Delta U = Q - W$

☐ $Q = mc\Delta T$

☐ $Q = mL$

☐ $W = P\Delta V$

☐ $\Delta S = \dfrac{Q}{T}$

SHARED CONCEPTS

Practice Questions

1. If an object with an initial temperature of 300 K increases its temperature by 1 K every minute, by how many degrees Celsius will its temperature have increased in 10 minutes?

   A. 10°C
   B. 27°C
   C. 100°C
   D. 270°C

2. Which of the following choices correctly identifies the following three heat transfer processes?

   1. Heat transferred from the Sun to the Earth
   2. A metal spoon heating up when placed in a pot of hot soup
   3. A rising plume of smoke from a fire

   A. 1. Radiation; 2. Conduction; 3. Convection
   B. 1. Conduction; 2. Radiation; 3. Convection
   C. 1. Radiation; 2. Convection; 3. Conduction
   D. 1. Convection; 2. Conduction; 3. Radiation

3. A 20 m steel rod at 10°C is dangling from the edge of a building and is 2.5 cm from the ground. If the rod is heated to 90°C, will it touch the ground? ($\alpha = 1.1 \times 10^{-5}$ K^{-1})

   A. Yes, because it expands by 3.2 cm.
   B. Yes, because it expands by 2.6 cm.
   C. No, because it only expands by 1.6 cm.
   D. No, because it only expands by 1.8 cm.

4. What is the final temperature of a 5 kg silver pendant that is left in front of an electric heater and absorbs heat energy at a rate of 100 W for 10 minutes? Assume the pendant is initially at 20°C and that the specific heat of silver is $c = 236$ J/kg·°C = 0.0564 cal/g·°C.

   A. 29°C
   B. 59°C
   C. 71°C
   D. 100°C

5. How much heat is required to completely melt 500g gold earrings, given that their initial temperature is 25°C? The melting point of gold is 1064.18°C, its heat of fusion is 6.45×10^4 J/kg, and its specific heat is 129 J/kg·°C.

   A. 15 kJ
   B. 32 kJ
   C. 65 kJ
   D. 99 kJ

6. Given the cycle shown, what is the total work done by the gas in the cycle?

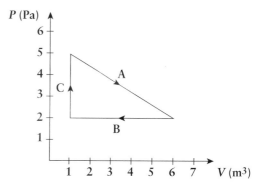

   A. −10 J
   B. 0 J
   C. 7.5 J
   D. 17.5 J

7. In an adiabatic compression process, the internal energy of the gas

    A. increases, because the work done on the gas is negative.

    B. increases, because the work done on the gas is positive.

    C. decreases, because the work done on the gas is negative.

    D. decreases, because the work done on the gas is positive.

8. The entropy of a system can

    A. never decrease.

    B. decrease when the entropy of the surroundings increases by at least as much.

    C. decrease when the system is isolated and the process is irreversible.

    D. decrease during an adiabatic reversible process.

9. The internal energy of an object increases in an adiabatic process. Which of the following must be true regarding this process?

    A. The kinetic energy of the system is changing.

    B. The potential energy of the system is changing.

    C. Work is done on the system.

    D. Heat flows into the system.

10. A certain substance has a specific heat of 1 J/mol·K and a melting point of 350 K. If one mole of the substance is currently at a temperature of 349 K, how much energy must be added in order to melt it?

    A. More than 1 J

    B. Exactly 1 J

    C. Less than 1 J but more than 0 J

    D. Less than 0 J

11. The following graphs depict the change in pressure and volume of a gas. Which graph most likely represents a process in which work is done by the gas as the process moves from point A to point B?

A.
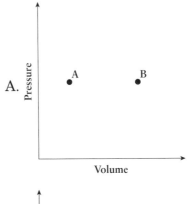

B.
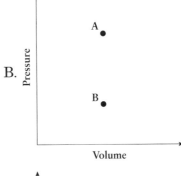

C.
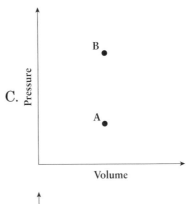

D.
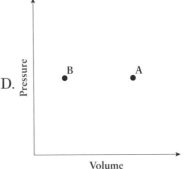

12. The figure shown depicts a thick metal container with two compartments. Compartment A is full of a hot gas, while compartment B is full of a cold gas. What is the primary mode of heat transfer in this system?

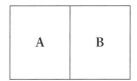

A. Radiation
B. Convection
C. Conduction
D. Enthalpy

13. Substances A and B have the same freezing and boiling points. If solid samples of both substances are heated in the exact same way, substance A boils before substance B. Which of the following would NOT explain this phenomenon?

A. Substance B has a higher specific heat.
B. Substance B has a higher heat of vaporization.
C. Substance B has a higher heat of fusion.
D. Substance B has a higher internal energy.

14. In experiment A, a student mixes ink with water and notices that the two liquids mix evenly. In experiment B, the student mixes oil with water; in this case, the liquids separate into two different layers. The entropy change is

A. positive in experiment A and negative in experiment B.
B. positive in experiment A and zero in experiment B.
C. negative in experiment A and positive in experiment B.
D. zero in experiment A and negative in experiment B.

15. Which of the following processes is LEAST likely to be accompanied by a change in temperature?

A. The kinetic energy of a gas is increased through a chemical reaction.
B. Energy is transferred to a solid via electromagnetic waves.
C. A boiling liquid is heated on a hot plate.
D. A warm gas is mixed with a cold gas.

Small Group Questions

1. If the linear thermal expansion of an object is 25% over a certain temperature range, by what percentage would the volume change over the same temperature range?

2. What would be the effect on the temperature of a running engine if the pre-existing coolant fluid (A) were replaced with another fluid (B) whose specific heat was half that of fluid A but whose density was twice as high?

3. Is it possible to design a series of thermal processes that create a closed cycle (same initial and final conditions) in which the net work done, net heat exchange, or total internal energy change is zero?

Explanations to Practice Questions

1. A

The Kelvin degree and Celsius degree are the same size; that is, a change of 1 K is equal to a change of 1°C. In other words, if the object increases in temperature by 1 K every minute, it means that in 10 minutes, its temperature will change by 10 K, which is the same as 10°C. Notice that the actual temperature of the object in degrees Kelvin and Celsius is different, but the change in the temperature is the same. Choice (A) is therefore the correct answer.

2. A

Because there is essentially only empty space between the Sun and the Earth, the only means of heat transfer is by radiation (i.e., electromagnetic waves that propagate from the sun to the earth). Therefore, the first process is radiation, allowing us to cross out (B) and (D). When a metal spoon is placed in a pot of hot soup, the molecules in the soup collide with those on the surface of the spoon, thereby transferring heat by conduction. Choice (A) must be the correct answer, but let's check that the last process corresponds indeed to convection. Fire warms the air above it, and the warmed air is less dense than the surrounding air, so it rises. A rising column of warm air means that heat is being transported in the air mass, which is simply the process of convection. The smoke particles ride along with the upward moving air mass and create a plume of smoke. Choice (A) is indeed the correct answer.

3. C

First, find the change in length due to thermal expansion:

$$\Delta L = \alpha L \Delta T$$

$$\Delta L = 1.1 \times 10^{-5} \text{ K}^{-1} \times 20 \text{ m} \times 80 \text{ K}$$

$$\Delta L \approx 10^{-5} \text{ K}^{-1} \times 20 \text{ m} \times 80 \text{ K}$$

$$\Delta L \approx 0.016 \text{ m}$$

$$\Delta L \approx 1.6 \text{ cm}$$

Because the rod is originally 2.5 cm above the ground and it increases by 1.6 cm, you can conclude that it will not touch the ground after the thermal expansion process is completed. Choice (C) correctly reflects this answer.

4. C

To answer this question, first remember that watts are equal to joules per second; in other words, power is energy over time. In 10 minutes, the pendant absorbs the following amount of energy (heat):

$$\text{energy} = \text{power} \times \text{time}$$

$$E = 100 \text{ W} \times 10 \text{ min} \times 60 \text{ s/min}$$

$$E = 6 \times 10^4 \text{ J}$$

Now that you know the heat added, $Q = 6 \times 10^4$ J, you can find the final temperature from this equation:

$$Q = mc\Delta T = mc(T_f - T_i)$$

$$6 \times 10^4 = 5 \times 236 \ (T_f - 20)$$

$$T_f \approx 70 \text{ °C}$$

Choice (C) is closest to your result and is thus the correct answer.

5. D

First determine how much heat is required to raise the temperature of the gold earrings to the melting point of gold. Then, calculate the heat required to actually melt the earrings (the latent heat). The total heat required to melt the earrings completely will be the sum of the two heats. The heat required to raise the temperature of the earrings from 25°C to 1,064.18°C is

$$Q = mc\Delta T$$

$$Q = mc(T_f - T_i)$$

$$Q \approx 0.5 \text{ kg} \times 130 \text{ J/kg·°C} \times (1,000°C - 25°C)$$

$$Q \approx 65 \text{ J/°C} \times 1,000°C$$

$$Q \approx 6.5 \times 10^4 \text{ J}$$

The result tells you to add about 65 kJ worth of heat to the earrings just to bring them to their melting point. However, at this point, the earrings are still solid. The next step is thus to calculate how much heat is needed to melt the earrings. For this, use the heat of fusion (the latent heat) of gold:

$$Q = mL$$
$$Q = (0.5 \text{ kg}) \cdot (6.45 \times 10^4 \text{ J/kg})$$
$$Q \approx 3.2 \times 10^4 \text{ J}$$
$$Q \approx 32 \text{ kJ}$$

So overall, it requires approximately 65 kJ + 32 kJ = 97 kJ of heat to melt the gold earrings. Choice (D) is therefore the correct answer. Notice how heavily approximated the numbers are because the answer choices are so spread out.

6. C

The total work done by the cycle is the sum of the work of paths A, B, and C. Knowing that the work done is equal to the pressure times the change in volume, or the area under the curve, you can calculate W_A, W_B, and W_C and then add them together. W_A is the area under the curve, which can be broken down into a triangle on top of a rectangle.

$$W_A = (1/2)(5) \times 3 + 2 \times 5$$
$$W_A = 17.5 \text{ J}$$

W_B can be calculated in the same way:

$$W_B = P\Delta V$$
$$W_B = 2 \times (-5)$$
$$W_B = -10 \text{ J}$$

Next, we know that W_C is equal to zero because the volume is constant. The total work done, therefore, is the sum of $W_A + W_B + W_C = 17.5 \text{ J} + (-10 \text{ J}) + 0 = +7.5 \text{ J}$, which matches with choice (C), the correct answer.

7. B

To answer the question, make sure you understand all the terms. An adiabatic process means that there is no exchange of heat; in other words, $Q = 0$. When a gas is compressed, positive work is being done on the gas, so the value for work done by the gas will be negative, $W < 0$. Based on this, we can determine how the internal energy of the gas changes by using the first law of thermodynamics:

$$\Delta U = Q - W$$
$$\Delta U = -W$$

Because W is negative, ΔU will end up being a positive value. Since $\Delta U = U_f - U_i$ and $\Delta U > 0$, we can inter that the internal energy of the gas will increase, which matches with correct answer (B).

8. B

The entropy of a system (not isolated) can decrease as long as the entropy of its surroundings increases by at least as much. On the other hand, the entropy of an isolated system increases for all real (irreversible) processes. Moreover, the entropy of a reversible isothermal process can be calculated using the expression $\Delta S = \dfrac{Q}{T}$, so in an adiabatic process, the entropy remains constant. Based on this, (B) is the correct answer.

9. C

In an adiabatic process, no heat enters or leaves the system, so (D) is out right away. The internal energy will increase if either kinetic or potential energy is increased, so (A) and (B) are incorrect. The first law of thermodynamics tells us that $\Delta U = Q - W$ (where ΔU is change in internal energy, Q is heat transferred into the system, and W is work done by the system); because the process is adiabatic, simplify this into $\Delta U = -W$. Because ΔU is positive, we know that W must be negative, which means that work is done on the system. This question can also be answered with simple logic. Because the total energy of a system must always be constant, the only way to increase the energy of an adiabatic system is to make the system do a negative amount of work; in other words, work must be done on the system.

10. A

To find the amount of heat needed to bring the substance to its melting point, you can use the specific heat: the product of the specific heat, the amount of the substance, and the change in temperature. This means that the heat is equal to $(1 \text{ J/mol·K})(1 \text{ mol})(1 \text{ K}) = 1$ J. After the substance reaches its melting point, additional heat (which can be determined by the formula $Q = m\Delta L$) is needed to actually induce the phase change. Therefore, the total amount of heat required is greater than 1 J.

11. A

When a gas is expanding or contracting at constant pressure, you can determine the work done in the process by finding the area under the pressure-volume curve by using the formula $W = P\Delta V$ (where P is pressure and ΔV is change in volume). In (A), ΔV is positive, meaning that the amount of work must also be positive and that work was done *by* the system. In (D), the amount of work is negative, so work was done *on* the system. In (B) and (C), ΔV is equal to zero. You can also answer this question with simple logic; if the volume of a gas is decreasing while the pressure stays constant, something must be doing work on the gas in order to overcome the pressure, which will push in the opposite direction to prevent the volume from changing. If the volume is increasing while the pressure stays constant, the gas must be doing work on the environment for the same reason.

12. C

In this situation, heat will transfer from the warm gas to the metal and then to the cold gas. Choice (B), convection, is the transfer of heat when two substances are mixed together; this cannot happen here because the gas will not naturally mix with the metal. Choice (A), heat transfer through radiation, is also implausible, not only because gases are unlikely to emit heat in the form of waves but also because the radiation would be unlikely to penetrate the thick metal container. Enthalpy, (D), is not a form of heat transfer. Conduction, (C), is the most likely option; it happens when two substances make direct contact with one another. Here, gas A makes contact with the metal container, which makes contact with gas B.

13. D

Saying that substance B has a higher internal energy, (D), cannot explain the phenomenon because the internal energy is irrelevant; the heat involved in the process is related only to the specific heat, the heat of fusion, and the heat of vaporization. All of the other choices could explain the phenomenon. The heat required to melt the solid is determined by the heat of fusion, (C). The heat required to bring the liquid to its boiling point is determined by the specific heat, (A). The heat required to boil the liquid is determined by the heat of vaporization, (B).

14. B

When the ink randomly intersperses throughout the water, the final state is more disordered than the initial state, so the entropy change of the system is positive. When the oil separates from the water, the final state is just as ordered as the initial state (because the oil and the water are still completely separate), so the entropy change is zero. You can also answer this question by noticing the reversibility of the two experiments. Experiment A has a positive entropy change because it is irreversible, while experiment B has no entropy change because the reaction is reversible. According to the second law of thermodynamics, the entropy change can never be negative in a thermodynamic process that moves from one equilibrium state to another.

15. C

If a substance is undergoing a phase change, any added heat will be used toward overcoming the heat of transformation of the phase change. During the phase change, the temperature will remain constant. Temperature is a measure of the kinetic energy of the molecules in a sample, so a change in kinetic energy, (A), is essentially the same thing as a change in temperature. The heat transfer by radiation described in (B) will definitely change the temperature of the solid as long as it is not in the process of melting. Choice (D) describes heat transfer by convection, in which the warm gas will transfer heat to the cold gas until they both reach an intermediate temperature.

Explanations to Small Group Questions

1. Before the volume expansion can be determined, an expression for the coefficient of linear expansion must be derived. In this scenario, a 25% linear thermal expansion means that $\Delta L = 0.25$ L. Thus we get 0.25 L $= \alpha L \Delta T$, and the expression simplifies to $\alpha = \dfrac{0.25}{\Delta T}$. We can plug the expression for α into the equation for β, where $\beta = 3\alpha$. Therefore, $\beta = \dfrac{0.75}{\Delta T}$ and we are ready to solve for the volume expansion.

$$\Delta V = \beta V \Delta T$$
$$\Delta V = \left(\frac{0.75}{\Delta T}\right) V \Delta T$$
$$\Delta V = 0.75V$$

2. If the specific heat of the new fluid B is one-half that of fluid A, then fluid B would only be able to absorb half as much heat over the same temperature range according to $Q = mc\Delta T$. Therefore, to absorb the standard amount of heat the engine produces, fluid B would have to reach a temperature twice that of fluid A, which would almost certainly cause the engine to overheat. However, since the density of fluid B is double that of fluid A, twice the mass of fluid B can fit into the volume of the coolant tank as fluid A. With twice the mass of fluid with half the heat capacity now in the coolant tank, there will actually be no net change in cooling capacity from the original fluid. You can do the math to confirm this; if m and c are the mass and heat capacity, respectively, of fluid A, then $2m$ and $0.5c$ are those for fluid B. $(2m)(0.5c)\Delta T = mc\Delta T$.

3. Theoretically, it is possible to design a series of processes that create a closed cycle in which the change in any one of the three key properties (work, heat, or internal energy) is zero. In order to create such a series, it is necessary to follow each compression of a given type (isothermal, adiabatic, isobaric, or isochoric) with an expansion of the exact same type to return the system to the initial conditions. In reality, however, some energy is lost to the surroundings during every process, so practically it is impossible.

Fluids and Solids

In this chapter:

Introduction

Hidden beneath the waves of the Mediterranean Sea, at depths of more than 4,000 meters, lie three lakes. The water in these "seas under the sea" is so salty—five to ten times saltier than the seawater that sits above it—that its extreme density prevents it from mixing with the ocean water above, forming a layer of separation not unlike that between the oil and water in a bottle of salad dressing. These underwater lakes behave eerily like their more common cousins found at sea level. They have tides, shore lines, beach ridges, and swash zones. When deep sea exploratory vessels set down on their surfaces, the vessels bob up and down, causing ripples to emanate outward like a stone dropped in a pond.

Suboceanic lakes and rivers present a particularly fascinating opportunity to illustrate the physics of fluids and solids. This chapter covers the important concepts and principles of fluid mechanics and elastic properties of solids as they are tested on the MCAT. We will begin with a review of some important terms and measurements, including density and pressure. Our next topic will be hydrostatics, the branch of fluid mechanics that characterizes the behavior of fluids at rest in equilibrium. We'll then turn our attention to fluid dynamics, including Bernoulli's equation and the aerodynamics of flight. Finally, the chapter concludes with a brief discussion of solids, examining the ways in which we can describe and quantify a solid object's response to applications of pressure.

5.1 Characteristics of Fluids and Solids

The half gallon of milk and the block of cheese in your refrigerator demonstrate the unique characteristics of fluids and solids. The milk (unless it has spoiled) is a **fluid** because it has the ability to flow and conform to the shape of its container. The cheese is a **solid** because it does not flow and its rigidity helps it retain a shape independent of that of any container. **Liquids** are instantly recognized as fluids, but **gases** are also fluids. The natural gas (methane) that many of us use to cook with flows through pipes to the burners on our stove and in our oven, and the air that we breathe flows in and out of our lungs, filling the spaces of our respiratory tract and the alveoli.

Fluids and solids share certain characteristics. Both can exert forces perpendicular to their surface, although only solids can withstand shear (tangential) forces. Anybody who's been hit by a fastball can attest to the strong perpendicular force and searing pain inflicted by the ball upon impact. Fluids (liquids and gases) can impose large perpendicular forces also; it doesn't take much to convince anyone that falling into water from a significant height is about as pleasant as falling onto a concrete sidewalk.

DENSITY

All fluids and solids are characterized by the ratio of their mass to their volume. This is known as **density,** which is a scalar quantity and therefore has no direction. The equation for density is

$$\rho = \frac{m}{V}$$

where ρ is the Greek letter rho (not the English letter p) and represents density. The SI units for density are kg/m^3, but you may find it convenient to use g/mL or g/cm^3, both of which may be seen on the MCAT. Remember that the milliliter and the cubic centimeter are the same volume. One mistake that students sometimes make is assuming that if the mL and the cm^3 are equivalent, then so must the liter and the m^3. This is absolutely not the case; in fact, there are 1,000 liters in a cubic meter. One way to help you remember this is that the density of water is 1,000 kg/m^3, and one liter of soda (or water) does not come close to having a mass of 1,000 kg. Actually, if you work out the conversion from kg/m^3 to kg/L, you'll find that a liter of soda has a mass of only one kilogram.

The weight of any volume of a given substance with know density can be calculated by multiplying the substance's density and volume, and the acceleration due to gravity. This is a calculation that will come in very handy when working through buoyancy problems on Test Day.

Key Equation

Density (ρ)

$$\rho = \frac{m}{v}$$

$$kg/m^3 = \frac{kg}{m^3}$$

$$g/mL = \frac{g}{mL}$$

$$W = mg$$
$$m = \rho V$$
$$W = \rho V g$$

Because the MCAT often challenges students to determine whether given objects will float or sink, we will address the topic of buoyancy momentarily. But before we do, let's look at a calculation that can be applied to buoyancy problems as a shortcut, which can save you precious seconds on Test Day. A common comparison that is generally helpful is the ratio of the density of a substance to that of pure water at 1 atm and 4°C, called **specific gravity.** Because pure water has a density of 1,000 kg/m³ or 1 g/cm³, it is a simple process to express the ratio of the two densities as a decimal. Once determined, this unitless number can be used as a tool for solving buoyancy problems.

> **Key Concept**
>
> All we need to know about specific gravity is that if an object's specific gravity is greater than 1, then it is more dense than water. If the specific gravity is less than one, then it is less dense than water.

Example: Find the specific gravity of benzene, given that the density of benzene is 879 kg/m³.

Solution: The ratio of the density of benzene to the density of water is the specific gravity.

$$\text{specific gravity} = \frac{\rho_{\text{benzene}}}{\rho_{\text{water}}}$$

$$= \frac{879}{1,000}$$

$$= 0.879$$

PRESSURE

Pressure is a ratio of normal force per unit area. The equation for pressure is

$$P = \frac{F}{A}$$

> **Key Equation**
>
> **Pressure (P)**
>
> $$P = \frac{F}{A}$$
>
> $$Pa = N/m^2 = \frac{N}{m^2}$$
>
> See text for conversion to other units of pressure (atm, torr, mm Hg).

where P is pressure, F is normal force, and A is area. The SI unit of pressure is the pascal (Pa), which is equivalent to the newton per square meter (1 Pa = 1 N/m²). Other commonly used units of pressure are the atmosphere, torr, and mm Hg. The unit of atmosphere is based on the average atmospheric pressure at sea level. The conversions between Pa, atm, torr, and mm Hg are as follows:

$$1.013 \times 10^5 \text{ Pa} = 1 \text{ atm} = 760 \text{ torr} = 760 \text{ mm Hg}$$

All substances—solids and fluids—can exert forces against other substances: Water pushes against a dam, gale-force winds hammer against windows, and spiky high-heeled shoes dig into soft pine wood floors. Pressure is a scalar quantity. It may seem surprising to learn that pressure has magnitude but not direction. The misconception probably arises because pressure is measured as the magnitude of the normal force, F, per unit area and because the normal force is the force perpendicular to the surface, the direction of the normal force is assumed to determine the direction for pressure. However, you need to remember that no matter where we position a given surface, the pressure will be the same. For example, if we placed a surface inside a closed container filled with gas, the individual molecules, which are moving randomly within the space, will exert pressure that is the same at all points within the container. Because the pressure is the same at all points along the walls of the container and within the space of the container itself, pressure applies in all directions at any point and, therefore, is scalar rather than vector. Of course, because pressure is a ratio of force to area, when unequal pressures are exerted against objects, the forces acting on the object will add in vectors, possibly resulting in acceleration. It's this difference in pressure (pressure differential) that causes air to rush into and out of the lungs during respiration, windows to burst outward during a tornado, and the plastic covering a broken car window to bubble outward when the car is moving.

MCAT Expertise

If you ever forget the units of a value, you can derive it from the equation. You know that pressure equals force over area. Because you know the units of force (N) and area (m^2), you can solve for the base units of pascal by plugging these units into the equation: N/m^2.

Example: The window of a skyscraper measures 2.0 m by 3.5 m. If a storm passes by and lowers the pressure outside the window to 0.997 atm while the pressure inside the building remains at 1 atm, what is the net force pushing the window out?

Solution: The forces acting inside and outside the building are needed. However, before the forces may be calculated, the values of the pressure both inside and outside the building must be converted from atmospheres to pascals.

$$1 \text{ atm} = 1.013 \times 10^5 \text{ Pa}$$
$$0.997 \text{ atm} = (0.997)(1.013 \times 10^5)$$
$$= 1.010 \times 10^5 \text{ Pa}$$

Using the equation for pressure, the force inside pushing out is

$$F_i = P_i A$$
$$F_i = (1.013 \times 10^5)(7.0)$$
$$= 7.091 \times 10^5 \text{ N}$$

And the force outside pushing in is

$$F_o = P_o A$$
$$F_o = (1.010 \times 10^5)(7.0)$$
$$= 7.070 \times 10^5 \text{ N}$$

The net force is the difference of these two forces:

$$F_{net} = 7.091 \times 10^5 - 7.070 \times 10^5$$
$$= 2,100 \text{ N}$$

Absolute Pressure

At this very moment, countless trillions of air molecules are exerting tremendous pressure on your body, with a total force of about 200,000 N! Of course, you don't actually feel all this pressure because your internal organs exert a pressure that perfectly balances it. Atmospheric pressure changes with altitude. Residents of Denver (altitude: 5,000 ft above sea level) experience atmospheric pressure equal to 632 mm Hg (which is equal to 0.83 atm), whereas travelers making their way through Death Valley (altitude: 282 ft below sea level) experience atmospheric pressure equal to 767 mm Hg (1.01 atm). Atmospheric pressure impacts everything from hemoglobin's affinity for oxygen to the baking time of a cake.

Absolute pressure is the total pressure that is exerted on an object that is submerged in a fluid. Remember that fluids include both liquids and gases. The equation for absolute pressure is

$$P = P_0 + \rho gh$$

where P is the absolute pressure, P_0 is the pressure at the surface, and ρgh quantifies the magnitude of pressure that is a function of the weight of the fluid sitting above the submerged object at some height h. Do not make the mistake of assuming that P_0 always stands for atmospheric pressure. In open air and most day-to-day situations P_0 is equal to 1 atm, but in other fluid systems, the surface pressure may be lower or higher than atmospheric pressure. In a closed container, such as a pressure cooker, the pressure at the surface may be much higher than atmospheric. This is, in fact, exactly the point of a pressure cooker, whose culinary benefit is that it allows food to cook at a higher temperature (to explain this, think about phase diagrams and what higher pressures do to boiling points), which reduces the cooking time and prevents loss of moisture and nutrients.

Gauge Pressure

When you check the pressure in your car or bike tires, using a device known as a gauge, you are measuring the **gauge pressure,** which is the difference between the absolute pressure inside the tire and the atmospheric pressure outside the tire. In other words, gauge pressure is the pressure in a closed space that is at a pressure above atmospheric pressure. This is a more common pressure measurement than absolute pressure, and the equation is

$$P_g = P - P_{atm} = (P_0 + \rho gh) - P_{atm}$$

Note that when $P_0 = P_{atm}$, then $P_g = P - P_0 = \rho gh$ at a depth h.

> ### Key Equation
>
> **Absolute Pressure (P)**
> $P = P_0 + \rho gh$
> $N/m^2 = N/m^2 + (g/m^3)(m/s^2)(m)$
> $= N/m^2 + g/m \cdot s^2$
> $N/m^2 = N/m^2$

> ### Real World
>
> A useful way to remember the two parts of the absolute pressure equation is by thinking of diving into a swimming pool. At the surface of the water, the absolute pressure is equal to the atmospheric pressure (P_0). But if you dive into the pool, the water exerts an extra pressure (ρgh) on you, in addition to the surface pressure. You feel this extra pressure on your eardrums.

> ### Key Equation
>
> **Gauge Pressure (P_g)**
> $P_g = P - P_{atm}$
> $Pa = Pa - Pa$

Example: A diver in the ocean is 20 m below the surface.
a. What is the absolute pressure she experiences? (density of sea water = 1,025 kg/m³)
b. What is the gauge pressure at her depth?

Solution:
a. Using the equation for absolute pressure in a liquid:

$$P = P_{atm} + \rho g h$$
$$= 1.013 \times 10^5 + (1,025)(9.8)(20)$$
$$= 3.02 \times 10^5 \text{ Pa}$$

b. Using the equation for gauge pressure:

$$P_g = P - P_{atm}$$
$$= (3.02 - 1.013) \times 10^5$$
$$= 2.01 \times 10^5 \text{ Pa}$$

MCAT Concept Check 5.1

Before moving on, ensure that you are able to:

✓ Calculate the density and specific gravity of a substance
✓ Define the concept of fluid pressure
✓ Describe the influence of depth on fluid pressure
✓ Articulate the difference between absolute pressure, atmospheric pressure, and gauge pressure

---

5.2 Hydrostatics

A fluid at rest, such as the glassy waters of a lake at dawn, is in equilibrium. This means that there is a balance of the forces acting on the fluid. When forces act on a fluid such that a pressure differential is created, that fluid will flow or change shape to restore that equilibrium. **Hydrostatics** is the study of fluids at rest and the forces and pressures associated with standing fluids. A proper understanding of hydrostatics is important for the MCAT because it will test you on the related topics of hydraulics and buoyancy.

PASCAL'S PRINCIPLE

For fluids that are incompressible—that is, fluids whose volumes cannot be reduced by any significant degree through application of pressure—when a change of pressure is applied to an enclosed fluid, that pressure change will be transmitted undiminished

Real World

When the air pressure changes above a large body of water, the water level rises or falls to re-establish pressure equilibrium between the air and the water. The surface of a water body directly below a high-pressure air pocket forms a very small but measurable "valley" of water. A low-pressure air system has the opposite effect, creating a "hill" of water.

to every portion of the fluid and to the walls of the containing vessel. This is **Pascal's principle**. For example, the milk sitting in your refrigerator is an incompressible fluid in a closed container. If you were to squeeze the container, exerting an increased pressure on the sides of the milk carton, the applied pressure would be transmitted through the entire volume of milk. If the cap were to suddenly pop off, the resulting geyser of milk would be evidence of the increased pressure.

One application of Pascal's principle has led to the development of a class of machines called hydraulic systems. These systems take advantage of the incompressibility of liquids to generate mechanical advantage, which, as we've seen in our discussion of inclined planes and pulleys (Chapter 3), allows us to accomplish a certain amount of work more easily by applying reduced forces. Many machines use hydraulics, including car brakes, bulldozers, cranes, car crushers, and lifts.

Figure 5.1 shows a simple diagram of a hydraulic car lift, so let's determine how a car lift would allow an auto mechanic to raise a heavy car with far less force than the weight of the car. We have a closed container that is filled with an incompressible liquid. On the left side of the lift, there is a piston of cross-sectional area A_1. When this piston is pushed down the column, it exerts a force equal to F_1 and generates a pressure equal to P_1. The piston displaces a volume of liquid equal to $A_1 d_1$. Because the liquid inside is incompressible, the same volume of fluid must be displaced on the right side of the hydraulic lift, where we find a second piston with a much larger surface area, A_2. The pressure generated by piston 1 is transmitted undiminished to all points within the system, including to A_2. As A_2 is larger than A_1 by some factor, the force, F_2, exerted against A_2 must be greater than F_1 by the same factor so that $P_1 = P_2$, according to Pascal's principle.

$$P = \frac{F_1}{A_1} = \frac{F_2}{A_2}$$

$$F_2 = F_1 \left(\frac{A_2}{A_1} \right)$$

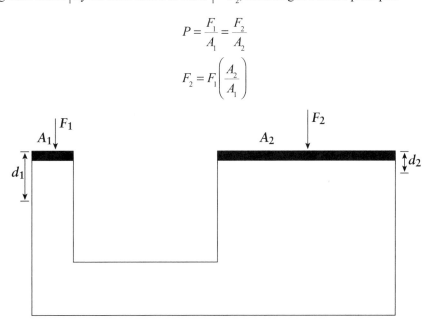

Figure 5.1. Hydraulic Lift

What this series of equations shows us is that hydraulic machines generate "output" force by magnifying an "input" force by a factor equal to the ratio of the cross-sectional area of the larger piston to that of the smaller piston. This does not violate the law of energy conservation; an analysis of the input and output work reveals that there indeed is conservation of energy (assuming the absence of frictional forces). The volume of fluid displaced by piston 1 is equal to the volume of fluid displaced at piston 2.

$$V = A_1 d_1 = A_2 d_2$$

$$d_2 = d_1 \left(\frac{A_1}{A_2} \right)$$

Key Equations

Pascal's Principle

For incompressible fluids in containers:

$$P = \frac{F_1}{A_1} = \frac{F_2}{A_2}$$

$$V = A_1 d_1 = A_2 d_2$$
$$W = F_1 d_1 = F_2 d_2$$

Combining the equations for pressure and volume, we can generate an equation for work as the product of pressure and volume change. (See Chapter 4 for a discussion of isobaric processes.)

$$W = P\Delta V = \frac{F_1}{A_1}(A_1 d_1) = \frac{F_2}{A_2}(A_2 d_2)$$

$$W = F_1 d_1 = F_2 d_2$$

The simplification of the work equation shows us the familiar form of work as the product of force and distance. Because the factor by which d_1 is larger than d_2 is equal to the factor by which F_2 is larger than F_1, we see that no additional work has been done or unaccounted for; the greater force F_2 is moving through a smaller distance d_2. Therefore, an auto mechanic needs only to exert a small force over a small area through a large distance to generate a much larger force over a larger area through a smaller distance. It's simple mechanical advantage, a concept you understand well already.

Key Concept

Remember when applying Pascal's principle, the larger the area, the larger the force, though this force will be exerted through a smaller distance.

Example: A hydraulic press has a piston of radius 5 cm, which pushes down on an enclosed fluid. A 45 kg weight rests on this piston. The other piston has a radius of 20 cm. Taking $g = 10$ m/s², what force is needed on the larger piston to keep the press in equilibrium?

Solution: Use Pascal's principle:

$$\frac{F_2}{A_2} = \frac{F_1}{A_1}$$

$$F_2 = \frac{F_1 A_2}{A_1}$$

Since $F_1 = mg$ and $A = \pi r^2$, it is possible to solve for F_2:

$$F_2 = \frac{45(10)\pi(0.2)^2}{\pi(0.05)^2}$$

$$= 7,200 \text{ N}$$

ARCHIMEDES' PRINCIPLE

You've probably heard some version of this story before: Archimedes, a physicist in ancient Greece, was tasked by his king to determine the metallic composition of a certain crown given to the king as a gift. Archimedes knew that he could do this by finding the crown's volume and mass, which would allow him to find its density and compare that density to those of known metals. Weighing the crown would be easy enough, but he was having trouble finding a way to measure its volume without melting it down and ruining its workmanship. Then one day, while getting into his bath, the water that overflowed from the tub gave him the idea to submerge the crown in water and measure the volume of the displaced liquid.

The principle that derives from the story is one of Archimedes' lasting contributions to the field of physics. Archimedes' principle deals with the buoyancy of objects when placed in a fluid. It helps us understand how ships stay afloat and why we feel lighter when we're swimming. The principle states:

> *A body wholly or partially immersed in a fluid will be buoyed up by a force equal to the weight of the fluid that it displaces.*

Just as Archimedes' body and his crown caused the water level to rise in the tub, any object placed in a fluid will cause a volume of fluid to be displaced equal to the volume of the object *that is submerged*. Since all fluids have density, the volume of fluid displaced will correspond to a certain mass of that fluid. The mass of the fluid displaced exerts a force equal to its weight against the submerged object. This force, which is always directed upward, is called the **buoyant force**.

$$F_{buoy} = (V_{fluid\ displaced})(\rho_{fluid})(g) = (V_{object\ submerged})(\rho_{fluid})(g)$$

When an object is placed in a fluid, it will sink into the fluid only to the point at which the volume of displaced fluid exerts a force that is equal to the weight of the object. If the object becomes completely submerged and the volume of displaced fluid still does not exert a buoyant force equal to the weight of the object, the object will sink and accelerate to the bottom. A gold crown will sink to the bottom of the bathtub. On the other hand, an object that is less dense than water, such as a block of wood or a cube of ice, will stop sinking (and start floating) as soon as it displaces a volume of water equal to its own mass.

Now, how can we determine how much of a floating object lies below the surface? It's not as hard as it seems, and it ties in to a principle we've already examined: comparisons of densities and calculation of specific gravity. Pay attention here, because this is a very useful principle that can be used to save time when working through buoyancy problems. An object will float, no matter what it is made of and no matter

Key Equations

Buoyant Force (F_{buoy})
For floating objects, use:
$F_{buoy} = (V_{fluid\ displaced})\ (\rho_{fluid})(g) =$ **Weight of object**

For fully submerged objects, use:
$F_{buoy} = (V_{object\ submerged})\ (\rho_{fluid})(g)$
$N = kg{\cdot}m/s^2 = (m^3)(kg/m^3)(m/s^2)$
$kg{\cdot}m/s^2 = kg{\cdot}m/s^2$

MCAT Expertise

The most common mistake students make using this equation is to use the density of the object rather than the density of the fluid. Remember always to use the density of the fluid itself.

Key Concept

One way to conceptualize the buoyant force is that it is the force of the liquid trying to return to the space from which it was displaced, thus pushing the object up and out of the water. This is an important concept because the buoyant force is due to the liquid itself, not the object. If two objects placed in a fluid displace the same volume of fluid, they will experience the same magnitude of buoyant force even if the objects themselves have different masses.

how much mass it has, if its average density is less than or equal to the density of the fluid into which it is placed. Furthermore, if we express the object's specific gravity as a percentage value, this directly indicates the percentage of the object's volume that is submerged. For instance, the density of ice is 0.92 g/cm³, and its specific gravity is 0.92. An ice cube floating in a glass of water has 92 percent of its volume submerged in the water—only 8 percent is sitting above the surface. From this principle follows something you may already know: Any object whose specific gravity is less than or equal to 1 will float in water (specific gravity of exactly 1 indicates that 100 percent of the object will be submerged but it will not sink) and any object whose specific gravity is greater than 1 will sink.

Before we look at an example of the type of calculation you can expect to perform on Test Day to solve a buoyancy problem, let's consider the physics of buoyancy in the unique marine environment of the great Dead Sea. Located between Israel and Jordan, the Dead Sea is the deepest hypersaline lake in the world. Having a salt content of about 35 percent, it is almost nine times saltier than the oceans. In fact, its salinity is so high that nothing except a few bacteria and microbial fungi can live in its waters. However, humans, protected as we are by our thick skin, are impervious to the lake's properties (the hypertonic solution is so strong that even organisms that normally thrive in salty marine environments, like bacteria, algae, and fish, die almost instantly when exposed to this highly concentrated salt solution).

Now, taking a dip in the Dead Sea is not exactly the same thing as taking a swim in any of the world's oceans. One does not swim in the Dead Sea so much as bob up and down like a human raft. All those dissolved salts make for some of the densest waters on the surface of the earth. While pure water has a density of around 1 kg/L and oceanic waters average around 1.03 kg/L, the water of the Dead Sea has a density of 1.24 kg/L! The human body has an average density of about 1.1 kg/L; our specific gravity is greater than 1 with respect to fresh and sea waters. Therefore, in most bodies of water, we have a tendency to sink. However, in the Dead Sea, the typical human has a relative density less than 1 and will thus float.

Example: A wooden block floats in the ocean with half its volume submerged. Find the density of the wood ρ_b. (The density of seawater is 1,024 kg/m³.)

Solution: The weight of the block of total volume V_b is

$$W_b = m_b g = \rho_b V_b g$$

The weight of the displaced seawater is the buoyant force and is given by

$$W_w = F_{buoy} = m_w g = \rho_w V_w g$$

where ρ_w is the density of seawater (1,024 kg/m³) and V_w is the volume of displaced water, which is also the volume of that part of the block which is submerged. Because the block is floating, the buoyant force equals the block's weight:

$$W_b = F_{buoy}$$
$$\rho_b V_b g = \rho_w V_w g$$

We are given that half the block is submerged, so $V_w = V_b/2$.

$$\rho_b V_b g = \frac{1}{2} \rho_w V_b g$$

$$\rho_b = \frac{1}{2} \rho_w$$

$$\rho_b = \frac{1}{2} (1,024)$$

$$= 512 \text{ kg/m}^3$$

MOLECULAR FORCES IN LIQUIDS

Water striders are insects in the Gerridae family that have the ability to walk on water. Water striders are able to glide across the water surface without sinking, even though they are denser than it, because of a special physical property of liquids at the interface between a liquid and a gas. **Surface tension** causes the liquid to form a thin but strong layer like a "skin" at the liquid's surface. Surface tension results from **cohesion**, which is the attractive force that a molecule of liquid feels toward other molecules of the same liquid. Imagine molecules of liquid as thousands of tiny Velcro balls that are jostling around in a container, each momentarily sticking to another. The balls in the middle of the bunch are experiencing attractive forces from all sides; these forces balance out. However, on the surface, the balls only feel an attraction to the balls below them; these attractive forces keep pulling the surface balls toward the center. There is tension in the surface due to the pulling forces. When there is an indentation on the surface (say, caused by a water strider's foot) then the cohesion can lead to a net upward force.

Another force that liquid molecules experience is **adhesion**, which is the attractive force that a molecule of the liquid feels toward the molecules of some other substance. For example, the adhesive force causes water molecules to form droplets on the windshield of a car even though gravity is pulling them downward. When liquids are placed in containers, a meniscus, or curved surface in which the liquid "crawls" up the side of the container just a little bit, will form when the adhesive forces are

> **Real World**
>
> Remember that cohesion occurs between molecules with the same properties. In a container of both water and oil, the water molecules will only be attracted to other water molecules, and the oil will only be attracted to other oil molecules.

greater than the cohesive forces. A "backwards" meniscus (with the liquid level higher in the middle than at the edges) occurs when the cohesive forces are greater than the adhesive forces. Mercury, the only metal that is liquid at room temperature, forms a "backward" meniscus when placed in a container.

MCAT Concept Check 5.2

Before moving on, ensure that you are able to:

✓ Solve questions involving Pascal's principle

✓ State Archimedes' principle and identify when it is being tested

✓ Use and apply the equation for buoyant force

✓ Explain the concepts of surface tension, cohesion, and adhesion

---

5.3 Fluid Dynamics

As the term suggests, fluid dynamics is the study of fluids in motion. This is perhaps one of the most fascinating areas of physics because its applications to real life are everywhere. Many aspects of our world, from water delivery to your bathroom sink to blood flow through your arteries and veins, can be analyzed and explained (at least in part) by the principles of fluid dynamics. The MCAT presents a relatively simplified version of the topic, so there are certain basic concepts related to fluid motion that you should understand, and with those, you will be well equipped to answer any fluid question that you encounter.

VISCOSITY

Some fluids flow very easily, while others barely flow at all. The resistance of a fluid to flow is called **viscosity**, and it can be thought of as a measure of fluid friction. "Thin" fluids, like gases, water, and dilute aqueous solutions, have low viscosity and so flow easily. Whole blood, vegetable oil, honey, cream, and molasses are "thick" fluids and flow more slowly.

All fluids (except superfluids which are not tested on the MCAT) are viscous to one degree or another; those with lower viscosities are said to behave more like **ideal fluids**, which have no viscosity and are described as inviscid. Because viscosity is a measure of a fluid's internal resistance to flow, more viscous fluids will "lose" more energy to friction. Low-viscosity fluids more closely approximate conservation of energy, and on the MCAT, you will be able to discount these small frictional forces. As we will discover momentarily, Bernoulli's equation is an expression of energy conservation for flowing fluids.

The SI unit of viscosity is the newton · second/m² (N·s/m²).

> **Key Concept**
>
> Low-viscosity fluids have low internal resistance to flow and behave like ideal fluids. Assume conservation of energy in low-viscosity fluids with laminar flow.

LAMINAR AND TURBULENT FLOW

When a fluid is moving, its flow can be **laminar** or **turbulent**. The difference between laminar flow and turbulent flow is easily illustrated by the difference between the gentle current of a "lazy river" ride at a water amusement park and the topsy-turvy rapids seen on white water rafting trips. Laminar flow is smooth and orderly. You can imagine it as concentric layers of fluid that flow parallel to each other. The layers will not necessarily have the same linear velocity. For example, the layer closest to the wall of a pipe flows more slowly than the more interior layers of fluid. Turbulent flow is rough and disorderly. Turbulence causes the formation of eddies, which are swirls of fluid of varying sizes occurring typically on the downstream side of an obstacle. In unobstructed fluid flow, turbulence can arise when the velocity of the fluid exceeds a certain critical velocity (v_c). This critical velocity depends on the physical properties of the fluid, such as its viscosity and the diameter of the tube. When the critical velocity for a fluid is exceeded, the fluid demonstrates complex flow patterns, and laminar flow occurs only in the thin layer of fluid adjacent to the wall, called the boundary layer. The flow velocity immediately at the wall is zero and increases uniformly throughout the layer. Beyond the boundary layer, however, the motion is highly irregular and turbulent. A significant amount of energy is "lost" from the system as a result of the increased frictional forces. Calculations of energy conservation, such as Bernoulli's equation, no longer can be applied. Luckily, the MCAT always assumes laminar (nonturbulent) flow. In Figure 5.2 to the left, you can see that a properly thrown frisbee encounters little turbulence, while one thrown upside down is less successful.

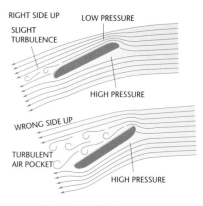

Figure 5.2. Turbulence

For a fluid flowing through a tube of diameter D, the critical velocity, v_c, can be calculated as

$$v_c = \frac{N_R \eta}{\rho D}$$

where N_R is a dimensionless constant called the Reynolds number, η is the viscosity of the fluid, ρ is the density of the fluid, and D is the diameter of the tube.

STREAMLINES

Because the movement of individual molecules of a fluid is impossible to track with the unaided eye, it is often helpful to use representations of the molecular movement called **streamlines.** Like the lines of light that are captured in a slow-shutter photograph of moving cars at night, streamlines indicate the pathway followed by tiny fluid elements (sometimes called fluid particles) as they move. The velocity vector of a fluid particle will always be tangential to the streamline at any point. Streamlines never cross each other.

> **Key Equation**
>
> **Critical Velocity (v_c)**
>
> $$v_c = \frac{N_R \eta}{\rho D}$$
>
> $$m/s = \frac{(dimensionless)(N \cdot s/m^2)}{(kg/m^3)(m)}$$
>
> If you are expected to use this equation on the MCAT, you will be given values for N_R and η.

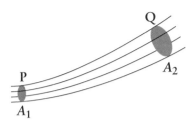

Figure 5.3. Streamlines
The stream's cross-sectional area increases from P to Q

Figure 5.3 shows a tube containing a moving fluid that passes from P to Q. The streamlines indicate some, but not all, of the pathways for the fluid along the walls of the tube. You'll notice that the tube gets wider toward Q, as indicated by the streamlines that are spreading out over the increased cross-sectional area. This leads us to consider the relationship between flow rate and the cross-sectional area of the container through which the fluid is moving. Once again, we can assume that the fluid is incompressible (which means that we are *not* considering a flowing gas). Because the fluid is incompressible, the rate at which a given volume (or mass) of fluid passes by one point must be the same for all other points in the closed system. This is essentially an expression of conservation of matter: If x liters of fluid pass a point in a given amount of time, then x liters of fluid must pass all other points in the same amount of time. Thus, we can very clearly state, without any exceptions, the volumetric rate of flow (i.e., unit of volume per unit of time) is constant for a closed system and is independent of changes in cross-sectional area.

There's another rate that we have to pay attention to, and that is the linear velocity at which the fluid flows. As with any velocity, the unit are meters per second and are a measure of the linear displacement of the fluid particle in a given amount of time. When we multiply linear velocity by cross-sectional area, we get

$$vA = \frac{V}{\text{time}}$$
$$[\text{units: } (m/s)(m^2) = m^3/s]$$

Key Equation

The Continuity Equation
$v_1 A_1 = v_2 A_2 = $ a constant (the rate of flow)
$(m/s)(m^2) = (m/s)(m^2) = m^3/s$

where v is velocity, A is cross-sectional area, and V is volume. We've already said that the volumetric rate of flow for a fluid must be constant throughout a closed system. So, at two points 1 and 2 with cross-sectional area A_1 and A_2, respectively, the product of velocity and area must be constant such that

$$v_1 A_1 = v_2 A_2 = \text{a constant}$$

This equation is known as the **continuity equation**, and it tells us that fluids will flow more quickly through narrow passages and more slowly through wider ones. This is one of the two equations of fluid dynamics that you *must* know for Test Day. The second is Bernoulli's equation.

BERNOULLI'S EQUATION

We know that students begin to panic when they encounter any discussion of Bernoulli's equation, but we want to assure you that conceptually, the equation is something with which you are already quite familiar. Furthermore, the MCAT approaches Bernoulli's equation in very recognizable ways. By practicing a few problems that require Bernoulli's calculation, you'll have the understanding and skills to tackle any fluid dynamics problem that comes your way on Test Day.

Before we cover the equation itself, let's approach flowing fluid from two perspectives that we've already discussed. The continuity equation arises from the conservation of mass of fluids. Excluding gases, we can say that all fluids (liquids) are incompressible, so the volumetric rate of flow within a closed space must be constant at all points. The continuity equation shows us that for a constant volumetric flow rate, there is an inverse relationship between the linear velocity of the fluid and the cross-sectional area of the tube: *Fluids have higher velocities through narrower tubes.*

Fluids that have low viscosity and demonstrate laminar flow can also be approximated to be conservative systems. The total mechanical energy of the system is constant if we discount the small friction forces that occur in all real liquids.

Combining these principles of conservation (of mass and energy), we arrive at the equation that has contributed to Daniel Bernoulli's infamy among college physics students:

$$P_1 + \frac{\rho v_1^2}{2} + \rho g y_1 = P_2 + \frac{\rho v_2^2}{2} + \rho g y_2 = \text{a constant}$$

where P is the absolute pressure of the fluid, $\frac{1}{2}\rho v^2$ is the dynamic pressure, and $\rho g y$ is the gauge pressure.

When you look closely at Bernoulli's equation, you'll notice that it contains terms that should look vaguely familiar to you as long as you've been paying attention to our ongoing discussion of the different forms of energy. This is an expression of equality: The sum of the three terms measured at some point within a moving fluid is equal to the sum of those same terms measured at a different point within the moving fluid. By now, this ought to raise the mental "red flag" of conservation. You ought to be thinking conservation of *something*. Let's ignore the P term for the moment; we'll talk about that shortly. For now, let's focus on the other set of terms. The term $\frac{1}{2}\rho v^2$ looks quite similar to the expression for the kinetic energy of an object. In fact, this is a measurement of what is known as the dynamic pressure—the pressure associated with the movement of the fluid. The other term, $\rho g y$, looks like the expression for the gravitational potential energy of an object. That's essentially what it is. This is the pressure associated with the mass of fluid sitting above some position of depth. In fact, you ought to recognize that this is the same expression for the gauge pressure.

Key Equation

Bernoulli's Equation

$$P_1 - \frac{\rho v_1^2}{2} + \rho g y_1 = P_2 - \frac{\rho v_2^2}{2} + \rho g y_2 = \text{a constant}$$

$\text{N/m}^2 - (\text{g/m}^3)(\text{m/s})^2 + (\text{g/m}^3)(\text{m/s}^2)(\text{m})$
$\quad = \text{N/m}^2$
$\text{N/m}^2 = \text{N/m}^2 + \text{g/m·s}^2 + \text{g/m·s}^2 = \text{N/m}^2$

So far, this ought to be all quite familiar and reassuring: an expression that involves a conservation of kinetic and potential energy of a moving fluid. How do the P terms fit into this expression of conservation, though? Pressure is a ratio of the magnitude of force exerted per unit area. It doesn't seem to have any obvious or direct connection to energy or energy conservation. Now, let's look at pressure from a slightly different perspective. If we multiply the ratio of newton/square meter by the ratio of meter/meter (which is perfectly "legal" because multiplying any value by a ratio that reduces to 1 produces the original value), we arrive at newton times meter per cubic meter. As we know well, the newton meter is the joule, the SI unit for energy. Pressure can therefore be expressed as a ratio of energy per cubic meter; that is, as an "energy density." Systems at higher pressure contain a greater density of energy than those systems at lower pressure.

The combination of P and $\rho g y$ gives us the static pressure, where P is the pressure at the surface of the fluid. Ignoring the dynamic pressure, you ought to recognize that the sum of P and $\rho g y$ is the expression that we encountered in our discussion of absolute pressure. Bernoulli's expression states, then, that for an incompressible fluid not experiencing friction forces, the sum of the static pressure and dynamic pressure will be constant within a closed container. In the end, Bernoulli's principle is nothing other than a statement of energy conservation: *More energy dedicated towards fluid movement means less energy dedicated towards fluid pressure*. The inverse of this is also true (less movement means more static pressure). One example of this principle that you may have previously encountered is how the shape of an airplane's wing helps generate lift, as shown in Figure 5.4.

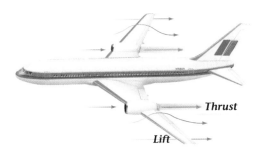

PROPELLER AND JET ENGINES generate thrust by pushing air backward. In both cases, because the wing top is curved, air streaming over it must travel farther and thus faster than air passing underneath the flat bottom. According to Bernoulli's principle, the slower air below exerts more force on the wing than the faster air above, thereby lifting the plane.

Figure 5.4. Aerodynamics of an Airplane

How does Bernoulli's expression actually work for the kinds of examples given on the MCAT? Very often, the MCAT sets up a system of fluid moving through a series of horizontal pipes so that the average height of the fluid is constant. In these cases, the $\rho g y$ terms are the same on both sides and can be cancelled out. The resulting simplified expression shows an inverse relationship between the static pressure and the dynamic pressure: When the velocity of the fluid increases (thereby leading to an increase in the dynamic pressure), the static pressure decreases. Another way to think about this is to apply Newton's second law, which relates forces and accelerations: When two points within a fluid are at different static pressures, the fluid will experience a net force from the point of higher pressure to that lower pressure and will flow (and accelerate) in that direction.

Real World

Another memorable—if somewhat juvenile—example of Bernoulli's principle is the workings of a whoopee cushion. When an unsuspecting victim sits on a full whoopee cushion, air is forced out of its rubber neck at high velocity. In accordance with Bernoulli's principle, the fast-moving air creates an area of low pressure in the cushion's neck, making it close quickly. However, the neck opens up again a fraction of a second later when more air is pushed out by the weight of the person sitting on the rubber cushion, starting the process again. This rapid, repeated opening and closing of the neck of the whoopee cushion creates sound waves in the surrounding air, creating the gag item's infamous flatulent sound.

Example: An office building with a bathroom 40 m above ground has its water enter the building through a pipe at ground level with an inner diameter of 4 cm. If the flow velocity when entering is 3 m/s and at the top is 8 m/s, find the cross-sectional area of the pipe at the top and the pressure needed at the bottom so that pressure in the bathroom is 3×10^5 Pa.

Solution: The cross-sectional area of the pipe in the bathroom is calculated using the continuity equation, where point 1 is the ground level and point 2 is the bathroom:

$$A_2 = A_1 \frac{v_1}{v_2}$$

$$= \pi (0.02)^2 \frac{3}{8}$$

$$= \pi (1.5 \times 10^{-4})$$
$$= 4.71 \times 10^{-4} \text{ m}^2$$

The pressure can be found from Bernoulli's equation:

$$P_1 + \frac{1}{2} \rho v_1^2 + \rho g y_1 = P_2 + \frac{1}{2} \rho v_2^2 + \rho g y_2$$

$$P_1 = P_2 + \frac{1}{2} \rho (v_2^2 - v_1^2) + \rho g (y_2 - y_1)$$

$$= 3 \times 10^5 + \frac{1}{2} (1 \times 10^3)[(8)^2 - (3)^2] + (1 \times 10^3)(9.8)(40)$$

$$= 7.2 \times 10^5 \text{ Pa}$$

MCAT Concept Check 5.3

Before moving on, ensure that you are able to:

✓ Contrast high-viscosity fluids with low-viscosity fluids

✓ Describe laminar and turbulent flow and when they occur

✓ Identify when the continuity equation should be used

✓ Recall and explain the various parts of Bernoulli's equation

✓ Solve questions involving fluid dynamics

5.4 Elastic Properties of Solids ★★★☆☆

We introduced solids at the beginning of this chapter, but since then we've been discussing liquids and gases exclusively, so it might be helpful to remind ourselves what characterizes the solid state of matter. Substances are solid when they are rigid enough to retain their unique shape and can withstand tangential (shearing) forces. (In reality, some solid substances—such as glass, mayonnaise, and shaving cream—classified as amorphous solids, can actually defy these principles and will flow under certain conditions. However, amorphous solids are outside the scope of this chapter because they are not tested on the MCAT.)

Of all the properties of solids, the only one the MCAT focuses on is **elasticity**, which is a measure of the response of a solid to an application of pressure. Depending on the particular way in which the pressure is exerted, the object may experience a change in length, volume, or lateral displacement known as shear. A solid's resistance to an applied pressure is measured by ratios known as moduli.

YOUNG'S MODULUS

When a stretching (tensile) or pushing (compression) force is exerted against an object, the object will experience a change in length, as shown in Figure 5.5. Because objects of the same material may require different force magnitudes to effect the same change in lengths—think, for example, of how much more difficult it is to stretch a very thick rubber band than to stretch a thin one—we quantify the relationship not between applied force and length change but between pressure and the change in length per unit length. We call the applied pressure the "stress," and the change in length per unit length is called the "strain." **Young's modulus**, Y, is defined, then, as the ratio of stress over strain and is given by:

$$Y = \frac{(F/A)}{(\Delta L/L)}$$

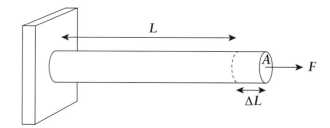

Figure 5.5. Young's Modulus
A force of *F* causes the cylinder to lengthen horizontally by a distance of Δ*L*

There's a limit to the degree to which an object can be compressed or stretched before it will be permanently deformed or ruptured. These **elastic limits** should be familiar to anyone who has seen a trash compactor in action, chopped a block of wood, or stretched a rubber band past its breaking point. **Yield strength** is the point of shape change beyond which a material will not return to its original dimensions once the applied force is removed (think of a crumpled piece of paper). If more stress is applied, eventually the **ultimate strength** will be reached, beyond which point the object will rupture (think of a broken rubber band).

SHEAR MODULUS

If a force is applied parallel to an object's surface rather than perpendicular to it, the object will experience a shape change known as **shear**. Rather than an elongation or compression, there is a lateral shift in the direction of the force. While the stress is measured, again, as the ratio of force per unit area (i.e., the pressure), the strain is measured as a ratio of the lateral movement (*x*) in the direction of the force vector per unit height (*h*). If you were to exert a shear force along the cover of this book from the free edge toward the binding, you would cause the book to shift laterally with respect to its height, just like the block in Figure 5.6. The shear modulus is given as

$$S = \frac{(F/A)}{(x/h)}$$

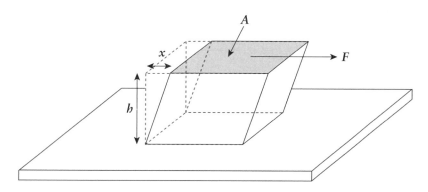

Figure 5.6. Shear Modulus
A force of *F* causes the top of the rectangular block to shift laterally by a distance of *x* while the block's base remains unmoved

Key Concept

Both Young's modulus and the shear modulus represent the same relationship: stress/strain. Both express stress in the same way as pressure (*F/A*); it is the way they represent strain that distinguishes them.

BULK MODULUS

Finally, the bulk modulus indicates the degree to which a material will experience a change in its volume in relation to an applied pressure. As with the other two moduli, the stress is the applied pressure, and the strain is a ratio of change in dimension per unit dimension. Here, the dimensional change that we are interested in is with respect to the volume, $\frac{\Delta V}{V}$. Solids and liquids have very large bulk moduli, reflective of the large amounts of pressure that must be applied to effect a change in volume. Remember, we consider liquids and solids to be essentially incompressible. Gases, on the other hand, are easily compressible and so have relatively small bulk moduli. The equation for bulk modulus is

$$B = \frac{(F/A)}{(\Delta V/V)}$$

One important connection to make for the MCAT is between this measurement and the speed of sound. The speed of sound in a material is proportional to the square root of the bulk modulus of that material. Because gases have small bulk moduli, liquids have larger bulk moduli, and solids have the largest, sound will travel fastest through solids and slowest through gases. If you were waiting for a train and you wanted to listen for its arrival, you would be able to hear the train sooner if you put your ear to the ground rather than to the wind.

Key Concept

For all three moduli, a *large* number represents a more rigid material, while a *small* number represents a more malleable material.

MCAT Concept Check 5.4

Before moving on, ensure that you are able to:

✓ State the difference between "stress" and "strain"
✓ Name the three moduli that measure elasticity
✓ Explain what an elastic limit is for a material
✓ Identify the major variables involved in measures of elasticity

---

Conclusion

The behavior of fluids and solids impacts every moment of our lives. Even if we are nowhere near an ocean or a lake, we are quite literally submerged in a vast expanse of fluid, a mix of gases known as the atmosphere, which exerts forces all over the surfaces of our bodies. Whenever we take a bath or submerge an object in water, we experience the effect of buoyant forces exerted by the displaced fluid. When we water our gardens, take a shower, or ride in a hovercraft, we experience the velocity, forces, and pressures of fluid on the move. In the world of medicine, one must consider fluids, flowing and at rest, when evaluating the function of the respiratory and circulatory systems: Conditions as varied as asthma and heart murmurs are related to the way in which the body causes fluids to flow. The balance of hydrostatic and oncotic pressures is important for maintaining the proper balance of fluid in the peripheral tissues of the body.

Now that you have the basic concepts of hydrostatics and fluid dynamics, learn to apply them to MCAT passages and questions through your Kaplan practice materials. Don't be intimidated by the seeming complexity of buoyant force problems and applications of Bernoulli's equation. Remember that all fluids, whether liquid or gas, exert buoyant forces against objects that are placed in them as a function of the mass of the fluid displaced. Remember that incompressible fluids demonstrate an inverse relationship between their dynamic pressure (as a function of velocity) and their static pressure. Congratulations on completing another chapter! Be sure to review the concepts contained here in this chapter before moving on to the next.

CONCEPT SUMMARY

Fluids (p. 138)

☐ Are substances that have the ability to flow and conform to the shape of their container

☐ Fluids can **exert perpendicular forces**, but **cannot withstand shear forces**

☐ **Liquids** and **gases** are the two phases of matter that are fluids

☐ On the MCAT, liquids are assumed to be **incompressible** and are **ideal conservative systems**

Solids (p. 138)

☐ Do not flow, and they retain their shape regardless of container

☐ Solids **exert perpendicular forces** and **can withstand shear forces**

Density (p. 138)

☐ Is the **mass per unit volume** of a substance (fluid or solid)

☐ If mass is held constant, there is an **inverse relationship between volume and density**

○ During **thermal expansion**, density decreases as volume increases

Pressure (p. 139)

☐ Defined as a measure of **force per unit area**; it is exerted by a fluid on the walls of its container and on objects placed in the fluid

☐ It is a **scalar** quantity; its value has magnitude only, and no direction

☐ The pressure exerted by a gas against the walls of its container will always be **perpendicular** (normal) to the container walls

Absolute Pressure (p. 141)

☐ Is the sum of all pressures at a certain point within a fluid; it is equal to the pressure at the surface of the fluid (usually atmospheric pressure) plus the pressure due to the fluid itself

☐ **Gauge Pressure** (p. 141) is the name for the difference between surface pressure and absolute pressure

○ In liquids, gauge pressure is caused by the weight of the liquid above the point of measurement

Pascal's Principle (p. 142)

☐ States that an applied pressure to an incompressible fluid will be distributed undiminished throughout the entire volume of the fluid

☐ **Hydraulic machines** operate based on this principle

Archimedes' Principle (p. 145)

☐ Governs the buoyant force

☐ When an object is placed in a fluid, the fluid generates a **buoyant force** (p. 145) against the object that is equal to the weight of the fluid displaced

○ The direction of the buoyant force is always opposite to the direction of **gravity**

Fluid Dynamics

- ☐ Also known as **"hydrodynamics,"** it is a set of principles regarding actively flowing fluids

- ☐ **Viscosity** (p. 148) is a measurement of a fluid's internal friction

- ☐ Fluids can move with either **laminar flow** or **turbulent flow** (p. 149)

  - ○ On the MCAT, incompressible fluids are assumed to have laminar flow and very low viscosity while flowing, allowing us to assume conservation of energy

- ☐ The **continuity equation** (p. 150) is a statement of the conservation of mass as applied to fluid dynamics

Bernoulli's Equation (p. 151)

- ☐ Is an expression of conservation of energy for a flowing fluid

- ☐ It states that the sum of the static pressure and the dynamic pressure will be constant between any two points in a closed system

  - ○ For a horizontal flow, there is an inverse relationship between pressure and velocity

Elastic Properties of Solids

- ☐ While rigid, solids have a certain degree of **elasticity** (p. 154)

- ☐ **Young's**, **shear**, and **bulk** moduli indicate three types of elasticity

- ☐ All three moduli measure the **ratio of stress to strain**

  - ○ **Stress** is a measurement of the pressure (F/A) applied to the solid

  - ○ **Strain** is the degree to which the solid deforms under pressure

    - ■ Each modulus measures a different type of strain

EQUATIONS TO REMEMBER

- ☐ $\rho = \dfrac{m}{V}$

- ☐ $P = \dfrac{F}{A}$

- ☐ $P = P_o + \rho g h$

- ☐ $P_g = P - P_{atm} = (P_o + \rho g h) - P_{atm}$

- ☐ $P = \dfrac{F_1}{A_1} = \dfrac{F_2}{A_2}$

- ☐ $F_{buoy} = (V_{fluid\ displaced})(\rho_{fluid})(g) = (V_{object\ submerged})(\rho_{fluid})(g)$

- ☐ $v_c = \dfrac{N_R \eta}{\rho D}$

- ☐ $v_1 A_1 = v_2 A_2 = \text{a constant}$

- ☐ $P_1 + \dfrac{\rho v_1^2}{2} + \rho g y_1 = P_2 + \dfrac{\rho v_2^2}{2} + \rho g y_2 = \text{a constant}$

☐ $Y = \dfrac{(F/A)}{(\Delta L/L)}$

☐ $S = \dfrac{(F/A)}{(x/h)}$

☐ $B = \dfrac{(F/A)}{(\Delta V/V)}$

SHARED CONCEPTS

HIGH-YIELD PRACTICE PROBLEMS

Practice Questions

1. Objects A and B are submerged at a depth of 1 m in a liquid with a specific gravity of 0.879. Given that the density of object B is one-third that of object A and that the gauge pressure of object A is 3 atm, what is the gauge pressure of object B? (Use the atmospheric pressure as 1 atm and $g = 9.8$ m/s^2.)

   A. 1 atm
   B. 2 atm
   C. 3 atm
   D. 9 atm

2. An anchor made of iron weighs 833 N on the deck of a ship. If the anchor is now suspended in seawater by a massless chain, what is the tension in the chain? (The density of iron is 7,800 kg/m^3, and the density of seawater is 1,024 kg/m^3.)

   A. 100 N
   B. 724 N
   C. 833 N
   D. 957 N

3. Two wooden balls of equal volume but different density are held beneath the surface of a container of water. Ball A has a density of 0.5 g/cm^3, and ball B has a density of 0.7 g/cm^3. When the balls are released, they will accelerate upward to the surface. What is the relationship between the acceleration of ball A and that of ball B? ($\rho_{water} = 1$ g/cm^3)

   A. Ball A has the greater acceleration.
   B. Ball B has the greater acceleration.
   C. Balls A and B have the same acceleration.
   D. It cannot be determined from information given.

4. Water flows from a pipe of diameter 0.15 m into one of diameter 0.2 m. If the speed in the 0.15 m pipe is 4.88 m/s, what is the speed in the 0.2 m pipe?

   A. 1.3 m/s
   B. 2.7 m/s
   C. 3.7 m/s
   D. 6.5 m/s

5. A hydraulic lever is used to lift a heavy hospital bed, requiring an amount of work W_o. When the same bed with a patient is lifted, the work required is doubled. How can the cross-sectional area of the platform on which the bed is lifted be changed so that the pressure on the hydraulic lever remains constant?

   A. The cross-sectional area must be doubled.
   B. The cross-sectional area must be halved.
   C. The cross-sectional area does not have to be changed.
   D. The cross-sectional area must be decreased.

6. The figure shown represents a section through a horizontal pipe of varying diameters into which four open vertical pipes connect. If water is allowed to flow through the pipe in the direction indicated, in which of the vertical pipes will the water level be lowest?

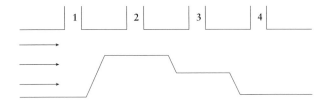

A. Pipe 1
B. Pipe 2
C. Pipe 3
D. Pipe 4

7. The speed of blood in the aorta is much higher than the speed of blood through the capillary bed. How can this fact be explained using the continuity equation?

A. The aorta is located higher than the capillary bed.
B. The pressure in the aorta is the same as the pressure in the capillary bed.
C. The cross-sectional area of all the capillaries added together is much greater than the cross-sectional area of the aorta.
D. The cross-sectional area of all the capillaries added together is much smaller than the cross-sectional area of the aorta.

8. A student wants to measure the shear modulus of gelatin. When she applies a certain amount of stress to a piece of rubber, she measures a strain of 3 (Young's modulus for rubber = 0.1 Pa). When she applies the same stress to a piece of gelatin, she measures a strain of 6. What is the shear modulus of gelatin?

A. 0.05 Pa
B. 0.1 Pa
C. 0.3 Pa
D. 0.5 Pa

9. A large cylinder is filled with an equal volume of two immiscible fluids. A balloon is submerged in the first fluid; the gauge pressure in the balloon at the deepest point in the first fluid is found to be 3 atm. Next, the balloon is lowered all the way to the bottom of the cylinder, and as it is submerged in the second fluid, the hydrostatic pressure in the balloon reads 8 atm. What is the ratio of the gauge pressure at the bottom of the first fluid to the gauge pressure at the bottom of the second fluid? (Atmospheric pressure is $P_{atm} = 1$ atm.)

A. 1:3
B. 3:4
C. 3:5
D. 3:8

10. An oddly shaped water-filled sculpture is designed to allow water levels to change depending on a force applied at the top of the tank as shown. If a force, F_1, of 4 N is applied to a square, flexible cover where $A_1 = 16$, and the area $A_2 = 64$, what force must be applied to A_2 to keep the water levels from changing?

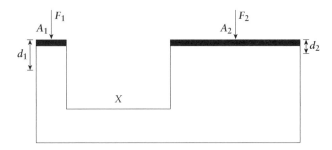

A. 4 N
B. 16 N
C. 32 N
D. No force needs to be applied.

11. Balls A and B of equal mass are floating in a swimming pool, as in the figure shown. Which will produce a greater buoyant force?

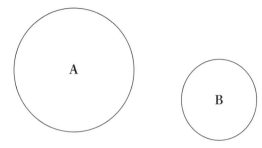

A. Ball A
B. Ball B
C. The forces will be equal.
D. It is impossible to know without knowing the volume of each ball.

12. Bernoulli's principle is the reason for the upward force that permits a lift force to cause airplane flight. What statement best summarizes the principle's relationship to flight?

A. The speed of airflow is equal on the top and bottom of a wing, resulting in nonturbulent flight.
B. The speed of airflow is greater over the curved top of the wing, resulting in less pressure on the top of the wing and the production of a net upward force on the wing, in turn resulting in flight.
C. The speed of airflow on the flat bottom of the wing is greater than over the curved top of the wing, resulting in less pressure below the wing and the production of a net upward force on the wing, in turn resulting in flight.
D. The weight of the wing is directly proportional to the weight of the air it displaces.

13. A low-pressure weather system can decrease the atmospheric pressure from 1 atm to 0.99 atm. By what percent will this decrease the force bearing on a rectangular window, 6 m by 3 m from the outside? The glass is 3 cm thick.

A. 1%
B. 10%
C. $\frac{1}{3}$%
D. 3%

14. Two fluids, A and B, have densities of x and $2x$, respectively. They are tested independently to assess absolute pressure at varying depths (see table). At what depths will the pressure below the surface of these two fluids be equal?

Depth	Density of fluid A	Density of fluid B	P_0	Absolute pressure, fluid A	Absolute pressure, fluid B
2	x	$2x$	2		
4	x	$2x$	2		
6	x	$2x$	2		
8	x	$2x$	2		

A. Whenever the depth of fluid A is 4 times that of fluid B
B. Whenever the depth of fluid A equals that of fluid B
C. Whenever the depth of fluid A is 2 times that of fluid B
D. They will never be equal.

15. A water tower operator is interested in increasing the pressure of a column of water that is applied to a piston. She hopes that increasing the pressure will increase the force being applied to the piston. The only way to increase the pressure is to alter the speed of the water as it flows through the pipe to the piston. How should the velocity of the water be changed to increase the pressure and force?

A. Increase the speed

B. Decrease the speed

C. Release water intermittently against the pipe

D. The speed of water will not change pressure at the piston.

Small Group Questions

1. When flying an airplane, it is not necessary to point the nose of the airplane up to increase the altitude of the plane. Rather, to go higher, one pushes the throttle to increase the power produced by the plane's engine, while the plane's body is kept level. How does increasing the engine power raise the altitude of the plane?

2. Imagine you live in a space station on the moon. If you take a bath on the moon, will you float higher, lower, or at the same level in the water?

Explanations to Practice Questions

1. C

The absolute and gauge pressures depend only on the density of the fluid, not that of the object.

$$P_{gauge} = \rho_{liq} gh$$
$$P_{total} = P_{atm} + P_{gauge}$$

Because the two objects are under the same atmospheric pressure, at the same depth and in the same fluid, the pressure on object A will be the same as the pressure on object B, making (C) the correct answer.

2. B

The tension in the chain is the difference between the anchor's weight and the buoyant force:

$$T = W - F_B$$

where T is the tension, W is the anchor's weight, and F_B is the buoyant force on the anchor. The object's weight is 833 N, and the buoyant force may now be found using Archimedes' principle. The buoyant force is equal to the weight of the seawater that the anchor displaces:

$$F_B = \rho_w V_w g$$

where ρ_w is the density of water, V_w is the volume of water displaced, and g is the acceleration due to gravity. Because the anchor is submerged entirely, the volume of the water displaced is equal to the volume of the anchor, $V_w = V_A$. To find the volume of the anchor, use the following equation:

$$V_A = \frac{m_A}{\rho_A}$$

Since $W_A = mg$,

$$V_A = \frac{W_A}{(g\rho_A)}$$
$$V_A = \frac{833 \text{ N}}{10 \text{ m/s}^2 \times 7{,}800 \ kg/m^3}$$
$$V_A = 1.0 \times 10^{-2} \text{ m}^3$$

This value can be then used to find the buoyant force:

$$F_B = \rho_w V_A g$$
$$F_B \approx 1{,}000 \text{ kg/m}^3 \times 1.0 \times 10^{-2} \text{ m}^3 \times 10 \text{ m/s}^2$$
$$F_B \approx 100 \text{ N}$$

Lastly, we can obtain the tension from the initial equation $T = W - F_B$:

$$T = 833 \text{ N} - 100 \text{ N}$$
$$T = 733 \text{ N}$$

Choice (B) best matches our result and is thus the correct answer.

3. A

Using Newton's second law, $F_{net} = ma$, we obtain the following equation:

$$F_{buoyant} - mg = ma$$

Thus,

$$a = \frac{F_{buoyant} - mg}{m}$$
$$a = \frac{F_{buoyant}}{m} - g$$

Both balls experience the same buoyant force because they

both have the same volume ($F_{buoyant} = \rho V g$). Thus, the ball with the smaller mass experiences the greater acceleration. In other words, since both balls have the same volume, the ball with the smaller density has the smaller mass ($m = \rho V$), which is ball A. Choice (A) is therefore the correct answer.

4. B

It is known that water flows faster through a narrower pipe. The speed is inversely proportional to the cross-sectional area of the pipe, because the same volume of water must pass by each point at each time interval. Let A be the 0.15 m pipe and B the 0.20 m pipe, and write the following expression:

$$v_A A_A = v_B A_B$$

where v is the speed and A is the cross-sectional area of the pipe. Because v is inversely proportional to the cross-sectional area, and the area is proportional to the square of the diameter $A = \pi r^2 = \dfrac{\pi d^2}{4}$, we obtain the following:

$$v_B = \frac{v_A \left(\dfrac{\pi d_A^2}{4} \right)}{\left(\dfrac{\pi d_B^2}{4} \right)} = v_A \left(\frac{d_A^2}{d_B^2} \right)$$

$$v_B = 4.88 \left(\frac{0.15^2}{0.20^2} \right)$$

$$v_B \approx 5 \left(\frac{0.0225}{0.04} \right) = 5 \left(\frac{2.25 \times 10^{-2}}{4 \times 10^{-2}} \right)$$

$$v_B \approx 2.5 \text{ m/s}$$

Choice (B) most closely matches our result and is thus the correct answer.

5. A

This question tests our understanding of Pascal's principle, which states that a change in pressure applied to an enclosed fluid is transmitted undiminished to every portion of the fluid and to the walls of the containing vessel. Given the hydraulic lever, several equations can be written:

$$\Delta P = \frac{F_1}{A_1} = \frac{F_2}{A_2}$$
$$V = A_1 d_1 = A_2 d_2$$
$$W = F_1 d_1 = F_2 d_2$$

We are told that the work required to lift the bed with the patient is double the work needed to lift just the bed. In other words, the force required doubles when both the bed and the patient have to be lifted. To maintain the same pressure, double the cross-sectional area of the platform of the hydraulic lever on which the patient and the bed are lifted. Choice (A) matches our explanation and is thus the correct answer. Notice that because (B) and (D) state almost the same thing; thus, neither could have been the correct answer.

6. B

It is not necessary to do any calculations to answer this question. The open vertical pipes are exposed to the same pressure (atmospheric) therefore, differences in the heights of the columns of water in the vertical pipes is dependent only on the differences in hydrostatic pressures in the horizontal pipe. Since the horizontal pipe has variable cross-sectional area, water will flow the fastest and the hydrostatic pressure will have its lowest value (as seen in Bernoulli's equation) where the horizontal pipe is narrowest. As a result, pipe #2 will have the lowest water level, making (B) the correct answer.

7. C

The continuity equation states that the mass flow rate of a fluid must remain constant from one cross section to another. In other words, when an ideal fluid flows from a pipe with a large cross-sectional area to one that is narrower, its speed decreases. This can be illustrated through the equation $A_1 v_1 = A_2 v_2$. In other words, the larger the cross-sectional area, the slower the fluid flows. If blood flows much more slowly through the capillaries, we can infer that the cross-sectional area is larger. This might seem surprising at a first glance, but given that each blood vessel divides into thousands of little capillaries, it is not hard to imagine that adding the cross-sectional areas of each capillary from an entire capillary bed results in an area that is larger than the cross-sectional area of the aorta. Choice (C) matches this explanation and is thus the correct answer.

8. A

To answer this question, first define Young's and the shear moduli:

$$Y = \frac{(F/A)}{(\Delta L/L)} = \frac{\text{stress}}{\text{strain}}$$
$$S = \frac{(F/A)}{(x/h)} = \frac{\text{stress}}{\text{strain}}$$

where F is the force applied, A is the cross-sectional area, L is the length, x is the horizontal change in length, and h is the height. What these two equations have in common is the idea that both Young's and the shear modulus are a measure of stress divided by strain. When the student measures a strain of 3 on the piece of rubber with a Young's modulus of 0.1 Pa, she applies a stress of

$$\text{stress} = Y \times \text{strain}$$
$$\text{stress} = 0.1 \times 3$$
$$\text{stress} = 0.3 \text{ N/m}^2$$

Because the student applies the same amount of stress to the gelatin and measures the strain, determine the shear modulus through the following equation:

$$S = \frac{\text{stress}}{\text{strain}}$$
$$S = \frac{0.3}{6} = \frac{0.1}{2}$$
$$S = 0.05 \text{ Pa}$$

Choice (A) matches our result and is thus the correct answer.

9. B

The first step in answering this question is defining the different types of pressures. Atmospheric pressure is the pressure at the top of the very first fluid, the pressure exerted by air (at sea level, it is equal to 1 atm). Gauge pressure is the pressure inside the balloon, which excludes the atmospheric pressure; gauge pressure is the total (absolute or hydrostatic) pressure inside the balloon minus the atmospheric pressure. Gauge pressure depends on the depth at which the object is submerged in the fluid, the constant of gravity, and the density of the fluid. Hydrostatic or absolute pressure is the total pressure in the balloon (i.e., the gauge pressure and the atmospheric pressure together). Because

we are given the gauge pressure at the bottom of the first fluid as 3 atm, our task now is to calculate the gauge pressure at the bottom of the second fluid. The hydrostatic pressure at the bottom of the cylinder is 8 atm. One of these atmospheres is atmospheric pressure pushing on the fluids. An other 3 atmospheres are accounted for by the first fluid that is pushing on the second fluid. Thus, the gauge pressure at the bottom of the second fluid is $8 - 1 - 3 = 4$ atm. The ratio of the gauge pressures is therefore 3:4, making (B) the correct answer.

10. B

This is a basic restatement of Pascal's principle that a force applied to an area will be transmitted through a fluid. This will result in changing fluid levels through the system. The relationship is stated as $F_2 = \frac{F_1 A_2}{A_1}$. Plugging in the numbers clearly shows the answer is 16 N, (B).

11. C

The buoyant force (F_b) is equal to the weight of water displaced, which is quantitatively expressed as

$$F_b = m_{\text{fluid displaced}}g = \rho_{\text{fluid}} V_{\text{fluid displaced}}g.$$

When an object floats in water, the gravitational force acting to pull the object towards the center of the Earth is equal in magnitude but opposite in direction to the buoyant force propping the object up, which is quantitatively expressed as

$$F_b = F_g \text{ or } m_{\text{fluid displaced}}g = m_{\text{object}}g.$$

Simplifying the quantitative expression by cancelling g indicates that the mass of a floating object is equal to the mass of water displaced. Therefore, since both balls have equal mass, both balls displace the same mass of water, and thus the buoyant force exerted on both balls is identical. As such, (C) is the correct answer.

12. B

Bernoulli's principle states that airflow over a curved surface will be faster than airflow over a flat surface. This is why wings have curved upper surfaces and flat lower surfaces. The fluid, in this case air, will move more quickly over the curved surface because it has further to travel to the end of the wing than the air at the flat bottom surface. Increased air speed will mean lower pressure within the fluid. This will result in higher pressure below the wing and an upward force. Choice (D) is an incorrect restatement of the principle of buoyancy that applies to fluids.

13. A

This question is a simple application of the following formula: pressure = force/area. The area is 18 square meters per window, and there are two windows. The thickness of the glass has no bearing on the pressure. If pressure decreases 1 percent and area does not change, and pressure is directly proportional to force, the force will be decreased 1 percent if the atmospheric pressure decreases 1 percent. Choice (B) is included to throw you off with incorrect decimal placement. Choices (C) and (D) are included to tempt you into considering the thickness of the glass, but it will not impact the pressure calculation.

14. C

The chart is a distractor. If you know the equation for absolute pressure, this will be fairly easy to figure out. $P = P_o + \rho gh$, where ρ = density. P_o, pressure at the surface, is always assumed to be atmospheric pressure, or approximately 10^5 Pa. The acceleration due to gravity, g, will be approximately 10 m/s^2, and ρ will be x or $2x$. As such, the only variable to consider is h. The pressures below the surface will be equal where the depth of fluid A is two times that of fluid B. In this case, the 2 times greater depth will cancel out the $2x$ greater density. This can be illustrated algebraically:

$$\rho_A h_A = \rho_B h_B$$
$$x h_A = 2x h_B$$
$$h_A = 2h_B$$

15. B

This is a basic interpretation of Bernoulli's equation that states, at equal heights, velocity and pressure of a fluid are inversely related. Decreasing the speed of the water, (B),

will increase its pressure. An increase in pressure over a given area will result in increased force being transmitted to the piston. Releasing water intermittently against the pipe, (D), may produce greater force at that instant, but this is unsustainable, and you have no information in the answer choice about the speed of the water to be released.

Explanations to Small Group Questions

1. The top of an airplane wing is curved (the cross-section of the wing is convex on top and flatter on the bottom). Air molecules that travel over the top of the wing actually move faster than air molecules just underneath the wing. According to Bernoulli's principle, this creates a lower pressure over the wing and a higher pressure under the wing. The plane is pushed upward by the higher pressure under the wings, a force that is more than enough to overcome the weight of the plane. Increasing the engine power increases the speed of the plane through the air, so that the air molecules must move around the wings even faster. This decreases the pressure above the wings even further, thus raising the plane up through the air. In fact, raising the nose of the plane can be counterproductive. If the nose of the plane were tipped too far upward and the plane was vertically oriented, the wings would no longer generate a pressure that opposes the force of gravity on the plane.

2. On the moon, you would float at the same level in the water that you would on Earth. On Earth and on the moon, your weight is equal to the weight of the displaced water according to Archimedes' principle. You will weigh less on the moon because the gravity is less on the moon. However, the weight of the displaced water will decrease by the same proportion because it is equally affected by the reduced gravity.

Electrostatics

6

In this chapter:

Introduction

Electrostatics is the study of stationary charges and the forces that are created by and act upon these charges. Without electrical charge, we would not be able to do many of the activities that we enjoy or consider essential to basic living. But living with electrical charge can also be dangerous and even deadly: Magnify the small shock you receive from a doorknob after walking across a carpet, and you essentially get a lightning bolt strong enough to kill you.

In this chapter, we will review the basic concepts essential to understanding charges and electrostatic forces. We will review Coulomb's law to discover that this expression of force is remarkably similar to the equation for gravitational forces. Next, we will describe the electric field that all charges set up around them, which allows them to exert forces on other charges in much the same way that fans can be set either to blow air away from or suck air toward themselves. After we've discussed how charges set up these fields of "potential forces," we'll observe the behavior of charges that are placed into these fields. In particular, we will note the motional behavior of these "test" charges inside a field in relation to the electric potential difference, or voltage, between two points in space. And in relation to the movement of a test charge, we will observe the change in electrical potential energy as the charge moves from a position of some electric potential to another. Lastly, we will describe the electric dipole and solve a problem involving one of the most important molecular dipoles known to us: the H_2O molecule.

6.1 Charges ★★★★☆☆

For the MCAT, it is sufficient to understand that charges come in two varieties. One, the **proton**, has a positive charge; the other, the **electron**, has a negative charge. While opposite charges exert attractive forces (that is, *attracting* forces), like charges, those

that have the same sign, exert repulsive forces (that is, *repelling* forces). Unlike the force of gravity, which is always an attractive force, the electrostatic force may be repulsive or attractive, depending on the signs of the charges that are interacting.

Most matter is electrically neutral: A balance of positive and negative charges ensures a relative degree of stability. When charges are out of balance, the system can become electrically unstable. From a human perspective, this can be good (as in the case of a battery that supplies energy for our use) or bad (as in the case of getting shocked when you touch a metal doorknob). Even materials that are normally electrically neutral can acquire a net charge as result of friction. When you shuffle your feet across the carpet, negatively charged particles are transferred from the carpet to your feet, and these charges spread out over the total surface of your body. The shock occurs when your hand gets close enough to the metal knob to allow that excess charge to jump from your fingers to the knob, which acts like a ground. Those who live in northern climates know full well that static charge buildup is a greater nuisance in the winter months because the lower humidity of cold air makes it easier for charge to become and remain separated. Flyaway hair, especially after the removal of a wool hat, and static cling, especially in synthetic material, result from the transfer of electrons from one material to the other, creating repulsive forces between the like charges (e.g., the flyaway hair) and attractive forces between the unlike charges (e.g., a polyester skirt sticking to a woman's legs).

The SI unit of charge is the **coulomb**, and the **fundamental unit of charge** is

$$e = 1.60 \times 10^{-19} \text{ C}$$

A proton and an electron each have this amount of charge, although as we've already stated, the proton is positively charged ($q = +e$) while the electron is negatively charged ($q = -e$). Please note that even though the proton and the electron share the same magnitude of charge, they do not share the same mass. The proton has a mass much greater than that of the electron.

> **MCAT Concept Check 6.1**
> Before moving on, ensure that you are able to:
> ✓ Recall the fundamental unit of charge
> ✓ Explain charge separation

Key Concept

The **fundamental unit of charge** is $e = 1.60 \times 10^{-19}$ coulombs. A proton and an electron each have this amount of charge; the proton is positively charged ($q = +e$), while the electron is negatively charged ($q = -e$).

Bridge

While many of the particles we discuss in electrostatics are very, very tiny, do not forget that they are still particles and they do have mass. We can still use equations such as the kinetic energy equation when solving these problems, and the MCAT will sometimes require us to do just that.

6.2 Coulomb's Law ★★★★★★

If you were to place a comb that had been rubbed with a piece of cloth next to a thin stream of water, the negatively charged comb would exert an attractive force against the polar water. The positive end of the H_2O dipole will be attracted to the electrons that had accumulated on the comb, and the stream of water would actually bend toward the comb. **Coulomb's law** gives us the magnitude of the electrostatic force F between two charges q_1 and q_2 whose centers are separated by a distance r:

$$F = k\frac{q_1 q_2}{r^2}$$

where k is called **Coulomb's constant** or the **electrostatic constant** and is a number that depends on the units used in the equation. In SI units, $k = \frac{1}{4}\pi\varepsilon_0 = 8.99 \times 10^9$ N·m²/C², where $\varepsilon_0 = 8.85 \times 10^{-12}$ C²/N·m² and is called the **permittivity of free space.**

Coulomb's law in SI units is therefore

$$F = k\frac{q_1 q_2}{r^2} = \frac{1}{(4\pi\varepsilon_0)}\frac{q_1 q_2}{r^2} = 8.99 \times 10^9 \frac{q_1 q_2}{r^2}$$

where the force F is in newtons, the charges q_1 and q_2 are in coulombs, and the distance r is in meters. The direction of the force may be obtained by remembering that unlike charges attract and like charges repel. The force always points along the line connecting the centers of the two charges.

A close examination of Coulomb's law reveals that it is remarkably similar in form to the equation for gravitational force. In the electrostatic force equation, the force magnitude is proportional to the charge magnitudes, and this is similar to the proportional relationship between gravitational force and mass. In both equations, the force magnitude is inversely proportional to the square of the distance of separation. These similarities ought to help you remember and apply both equations on Test Day.

> **Key Equation**
>
> $$F = \frac{kq_1 q_2}{r^2}$$
>
> $$N = \frac{(N \cdot m^2 \,/\, C^2)(C)(C)}{(m)^2}$$
>
> $$N = N$$
>
> Use this equation to determine the attractive or repulsive force two charges exert on one another.

> **Bridge**
>
> Notice how Coulomb's law is basically the same as the gravitational force equation, only having a different constant and using charge rather than mass. It is this fact that should remind us that this equation is dealing with electrostatic force between two charges, just as the gravitation equation is dealing with the gravitational force between two bodies of mass.

Example: A positive charge is attracted to a negative charge a certain distance away. The charges are then moved so that they are separated by twice the distance. How has the force of attraction changed between them?

Solution: Coulomb's law states that the force between two charges varies as the inverse of the square of the distance between them. Therefore, if the distance is doubled, the square of the distance is quadrupled, and the force is reduced to 1/4 of what it was originally. Note that it was not necessary to know the distance or the units being used, only the fact that the distance was doubled and that the relation was an inverse square law.

Example: Negatively charged electrons are electrostatically attracted to positively charged protons (together they form hydrogen atoms). Because electrons and protons have mass, they will be gravitationally attracted to each other as well. Compare the two forces using Coulomb's law and Newton's law of gravitation.
(Use $m_p = 1.67 \times 10^{-27}$ kg, $m_e = 9.11 \times 10^{-31}$ kg, and a Bohr radius separation between the electron and proton so that $r = 5.29 \times 10^{-11}$m.)

Solution: Both Coulomb's law and Newton's law state that the attractive forces between the electron and proton vary as the inverse of the square of the distance between them. As calculated in Chapter 2, the gravitational attractive force is

$$F_N = \frac{Gm_p m_e}{r^2}$$

$$= \frac{(6.67 \times 10^{-11})(1.67 \times 10^{-27})(9.11 \times 10^{-31})}{(5.29 \times 10^{-11})^2}$$

$$= 3.63 \times 10^{-47}\,N \approx 10^{-47}\,N$$

On the other hand, the magnitude of the electrostatic attractive force is

$$F_c = \frac{1}{4\pi\varepsilon_0}\frac{q_p q_e}{r^2}$$

$$= \frac{(8.99 \times 10^9)(1.60 \times 10^{-19})(1.60 \times 10^{-19})}{(5.29 \times 10^{-11})^2}$$

$$= 8.22 \times 10^{-8}\,N \approx 10^{-7}\,N$$

Note that the electrostatic attraction between the electron and proton is stronger than the gravitational attraction by a factor of approximately 10^{40}.

ELECTRIC FIELD

Every electric charge sets up a surrounding **electric field**. Electric fields make their presence known by exerting forces on other charges that move into the space of the field. You can think of the electric field as being like a cloud of perfume or body odor surrounding a person. The "cloud of aroma" can't be seen or felt, but it sure will be detected by another person who walks into that airspace. Whether the force exerted through the electric field is attractive or repulsive depends on whether the **stationary test charge** q_0 (i.e., the charge placed in the electric field) and the **stationary source charge** (i.e., the charge that sets up the electric field) are opposite charges (attractive) or like charges (repulsive).

Key Concept

Electric fields are produced by source charges (q). When a test charge (q_0) is placed in an electric field (E), it will experience an electrostatic force (F) equal to $q_0 E$.

The magnitude of an electric field can be calculated in one of two ways, both of which can be seen in the definitional equation for the electric field E:

$$E = \frac{F}{q_0} = \frac{kq}{r^2}$$

where E is the electric field magnitude, F is the force felt by the test charge q_0, k is the electrostatic constant, q is the source charge magnitude, and r is the distance between the charges. The electric field is a vector quantity. We will discuss the process of determining the direction of the electric field vector in a moment. Look closely: You can see that this equation for the electric field magnitude is derived simply by dividing both sides of Coulomb's law by the test charge q_0. In doing so, we arrive at two different methods for calculating the magnitude of the electric field at a particular point in space. The first method is to place a test charge q_0 at some point within the electric field, measure the force that the test charge feels, and define the electric field at that point in space as the ratio of the force magnitude to test charge magnitude. This is $\frac{F}{q_0}$.

One of the disadvantages of this method of calculation is that a test charge must actually be present in order for a force to be generated (and measured). Sometimes, however, no test charge is actually within the electric field, so we need another way to measure the magnitude of that field because charges produce electric fields whether or not other charges are present to feel them.

The second method of calculating the electric field magnitude at a point in space does not require the presence of a test charge. We only need to know the magnitude of the source charge and the distance between the source charge and point in space at which we want to measure the electric field. This is $\frac{kq}{r^2}$. Either approach, both of which will be useful on Test Day, will allow you to calculate the magnitude of the electric field, defined as the ratio of force per unit charge, at any point in space within the field.

By convention, the direction of the electric field vector is given as the direction that a positive test charge $+q_0$ would move in the presence of the source charge. If the source charge is positive, then $+q_0$ would experience a repulsive force and would accelerate away from the positive source charge. On the other hand, if the source charge is negative, then $+q_0$ would experience an attractive force and would accelerate toward the negative source charge. Therefore, positive charges have electric field vectors that radiate outward (that is, point away) from the charge, whereas negative charges have electric field vectors that radiate inward toward (that is, point to) the charge.

Since the MCAT allows you to make scratch notes, you can easily draw a representation of the electric field vectors using **field lines**, also known as **lines of force**. These are imaginary lines that represent how a positive test charge would move in the presence of the source charge. The field lines are drawn in the direction of the actual electric field vectors. Field lines also indicate the relative strength of the electric field at a given point

Key Equation

$$E = \frac{F}{q_0} = \frac{kq}{r^2}$$

$$N/C = \frac{N}{C} = \frac{(N \cdot m^2/C^2)(C)}{m^2}$$

Use this equation to determine the electric field produced by a source charge at a chosen point in space.

Key Concept

By dividing Coulomb's law by the magnitude of the test charge, we arrive at two ways of determining the magnitude of the electric field at a point in space around the source charge.

in the space of the field. When drawn on a sheet of paper, field lines look like the metal spokes of a bicycle wheel: The lines are closer together near the source charge and spread out at distances farther from the charge. Where the field lines are closer together, the field is stronger; where the lines are farther apart, the field is weaker. Since every charge exerts its own electric field, a collection of charges will exert a net electric field at a point in space that is equal to the vector sum of all the electric fields.

$$E_{total} = E_{q1} + E_{q2} + E_{q3} + \cdots$$

When a test charge is placed in an electric field, a force will be generated on the test charge by the electric field, the magnitude of which can be calculated as follows:

$$F = q_o E$$

In this vector equation, be sure to maintain the sign on the charge so that the direction of the force vector is in the direction of $q_o E$. In other words, if the charge is positive, then the force will be in the same direction as the electric field vector; if the charge is negative, then the force will be in the direction opposite to the field vector.

MCAT Concept Check 6.2

Before moving on, ensure that you are able to:

✓ Describe Coulomb's law and apply sign conventions

✓ Calculate the electric field due to one or more source charges

✓ Draw electric field lines

6.3 Electric Potential Energy ★★★★★☆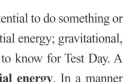

We have already defined potential energy (Chapter 3) as the potential to do something or make something happen. There are different "flavors" of potential energy; gravitational, chemical, and mechanical are three forms that you will need to know for Test Day. A fourth form, which we will examine now, is **electric potential energy**. In a manner similar to gravitational potential energy, this is a form of potential energy that is related to the relative position of one charge with respect to another charge or to a collection of charges. Just as a ball that is held high above the ground has a relatively large amount of gravitational potential energy, when one charge q is separated from another charge Q by a distance, r, the charges will have an electric potential energy equal to

$$U = \frac{kqQ}{r}$$

If the charges are like charges (both positive or both negative), then the potential energy will be positive. If the charges are unlike (one positive and the other negative), then the potential energy will be negative. Remember that work and energy have the same unit (the joule), so we can define electrical potential energy for a charge at a point in space in an electric field as the amount of work necessary to bring the charge from infinity to that point. Since $F = \dfrac{kqQ}{r^2}$ and $W = Fd$, if we define d as the distance r that separates two charges, then

$$U = W = Fd = Fr = \left(k\,\frac{qQ}{r^2} \right)(r) = k\,\frac{qQ}{r}$$

Consider two charges, a stationary negative source charge and a positive test charge that can be moved. Since these two charges are unlike, they will exert attractive forces between them in much the same way as the earth and a ball exert attractive gravitational forces toward each other. Since unlike charges attract each other, the closer they are to each other, the "happier" (that is, more stable) they will be. Opposite charges will have negative potential energy, and this energy will become increasingly negative as the charges are brought closer and closer together. Increasingly negative numbers are actually decreasing, because they are moving farther to the left of 0 on the number line.

Let's consider one more set of charges, this time two positive charges. As like charges, these will exert repulsive forces, and the potential energy of the system will be positive. Since like charges repel each other, the closer they are to each other, the "unhappier" (that is, less stable) they will be. Remember that unlike gravitational systems, the forces of electrostatics can be either attractive or repulsive. In this case, the like charges will become more stable the farther apart they move.

When like charges are moved toward each other, the electric potential energy of the system increases; when like charges move apart, the electric potential energy of the system decreases. When unlike charges move toward each other, the electrical potential energy of the system decreases; when unlike charges are moved apart, the electrical potential energy of the system increases. This is the basic concept; the equation just helps you quantify the energy! This concept also helps you predict the direction of spontaneous movement of a charge: If allowed, a charge will always move in whatever direction results in a decrease in the system's electric potential energy.

> **Key Concept**
>
> Electric potential energy is the work necessary to move a test charge from infinity to a point in space in an electric field surrounding a source charge.

> **Key Concept**
>
> The **electric potential energy** of a system will *increase* when two like charges move toward each other or when two opposite charges move apart. Conversely, the electric potential energy of a system will *decrease* when two like charges move apart or when two opposite charges move toward each other.

Example: If a charge of $+2e$ and a charge of $-3e$ are separated by a distance of 3 nm, what is the potential energy of the system? (e is the fundamental unit of charge equal to 1.6×10^{-19} C.)

Solution:

$$U = k\,\frac{qQ}{r}$$

From the question stem, we know that $q = +2e$, $Q = -3e$, and $r = 3$ nm $= 3 \times 10^{-9}$ m. So put these numbers into the equation and approximate k as 9.0×10^9:

$$U = (9 \times 10^9)\frac{(2)(1.6 \times 10^{-19})(-3)(1.6 \times 10^{-19})}{(3.0 \times 10^{-9})}$$

$$= -4.6 \times 10^{-19} \text{ J}$$

6.4 Electric Potential

Key Concept

Electric potential is the ratio of the work done to move a test charge from infinity to a point in an electric field surrounding a source charge divided by the magnitude of the test charge.

Key Equation

$$V = \frac{W}{q_0} = \frac{kQ}{r}$$

$$V = \frac{J}{C} = \frac{(N \cdot m^2 / C^2)(C)}{m}$$

$$V = J/C = N \cdot m/C$$

Use this equation to determine the electric potential due to a known source charge at a chosen point in space.

Electric potential, discussed here, and electric potential energy, discussed above, sound like the same (or nearly the same) thing. They are not, although they are very closely related. In fact, **electric potential** is defined as the ratio of the magnitude of a charge's electric potential energy to the magnitude of the charge itself. Electric potential can also be defined as the work necessary to move a charge q_0 from infinity to a point in an electric field divided by the magnitude of the charge q_0

$$V = \frac{W}{q_0}$$

where V is the electric potential measured in **volts** (V) and 1 volt = 1 joule/coulomb. Even if there is no test charge q_0, we can still calculate the electric potential of a point in space in an electric field as long as we know the magnitude of the source charge and the distance from the source charge to the point in space in the field.

$$W = \left(k\frac{qQ}{r} \right) \text{ and } V = \frac{W}{q}$$

$$V = \frac{(kqQ/r)}{q}$$

$$V = k\frac{Q}{r}$$

Electric potential is a scalar quantity whose sign is determined by the sign of the charge q_0. For a positive test charge, V is positive, but for a negative test charge, V is negative. For a collection of charges, the total electric potential at a point in space is the scalar sum of the electric potential due to each charge:

$$V_{\text{total}} = V_{q1} + V_{q2} + V_{q3} + \cdots \text{ (scalar sum)}$$

Since electric potential is inversely proportional to the distance from the source charge, a potential difference will exist between two points that are at different distances from the source charge. If V_a and V_b are the electric potentials at points a and b, respectively, then the **potential difference**, known as **voltage**, between a and b is

$V_b - V_a$. From the equation for electric potential above, we can further define potential difference as

$$V_b - V_a = \frac{W_{ab}}{q_0}$$

where W_{ab} is the work needed to move a test charge q_0 through an electric field from point a to point b. The work depends only on the potentials at the two points a and b and is independent of the actual pathway taken between a and b. Like gravitational force (Chapter 3), the electrostatic force is a conservative force.

We've already seen that charges, if allowed, will move spontaneously in whatever direction results in a decrease in electric potential energy. When a positive charge moves spontaneously though an electric field, it will move from a position of higher electric potential (higher electric potential energy divided by the positive charge) to a position of lower electric potential (lower electric potential energy divided by the positive charge). *Positive charge moves spontaneously from high voltage to low voltage.* When a negative charge moves spontaneously through an electric field, it will move from a position of lower electric potential (higher electric potential energy divided by the negative charge) to a position of higher electric potential (lower electric potential energy divided by the negative charge). *Negative charge moves spontaneously from low voltage to high voltage.*

MCAT Concept Check 6.4

Before moving on, ensure that you are able to:

✓ Define and distinguish between electric potential and voltage
✓ Calculate absolute electric potential at a point in space
✓ Calculate potential difference (voltage) between two points in space
✓ Assess charge movement based on electric potential

6.5 Equipotential Lines ★★★☆☆

An **equipotential line** is one for which the potential at every point is the same. That is, the potential difference between any two points on an equipotential line is zero. Drawn on paper, equipotential lines may look like concentric circles surrounding a source charge. In three-dimensional space, these equipotential lines would actually be spheres surrounding the source charge. From the equation for electric potential, you can see that no work is done when moving a test charge q_0 from one point to another on an equipotential line. Work will be done in moving a test charge q_0 from one line to another, but the work depends only on the potential difference of the two lines and not on the pathway taken between them. This is entirely analogous to the displacement

Bridge

Since the work to move a charge from one equipotential line to another does not depend on the path, we know that we are dealing with conservative forces.

of an object horizontally above a constant surface. Since the object's height above the surface has not changed (the object has only moved, say, to the left or to the right of its original position), its gravitational potential energy is unchanged. Furthermore, the change in the object's gravitational potential energy will not depend on the pathway taken from one height to another but only on the actual height displacement.

Example: In Figure 6.1, an electron goes from point *a* to point *b* in the vicinity of a very large positive charge. The electron could be made to follow any of the paths shown. Which path requires the least work to get the electron charge from *a* to *b*?

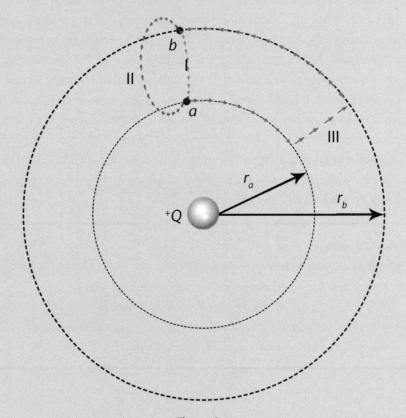

Figure 6.1

Solution: As stated, the **work depends only on the potential difference and not on the path**, so any of the paths shown would require the same amount of work in moving the electron from *a* to *b*, namely

$$W_{ab} = q_e(V_b - V_a)$$

$$= q_e\left(k\frac{Q}{r_b} - k\frac{Q}{r_a}\right)$$

So paths I, II, and III all require the same amount of work to move the electron. (Note that W_{ab} is positive in this example, since $r_a < r_b$ and $q_e = -e$).

MCAT Concept Check 6.5

Before moving on, ensure that you are able to:

✓ Define equipotential lines

✓ Utilize equipotential lines to determine voltage differences

6.6 The Electric Dipole ★★★★☆☆

Much of the reactivity of organic compounds that you will review for the Biological Sciences section of the MCAT is based on separation of charge. The **electric dipole**, which results from two equal and opposite charges being separated a small distance d from each other, can be transient (as in the case of the moment-by-moment changing distribution of electrons in the electron cloud of an atom or molecule) or permanent (as in the case of the molecular dipole of water or the carbonyl functional group).

> **Bridge**
>
> This concept of the electric dipole will be essential to understanding reactions in organic chemistry. Make sure you have the concept down solid.

The electric dipole can be thought of as a barbell: The equal weights on either end of the bar represent the equal and opposite charges separated by a small distance, represented by the length of the bar. We'll analyze the generic dipole in Figure 6.2 and then work through the specific example of one of the most important electric dipoles, the water molecule.

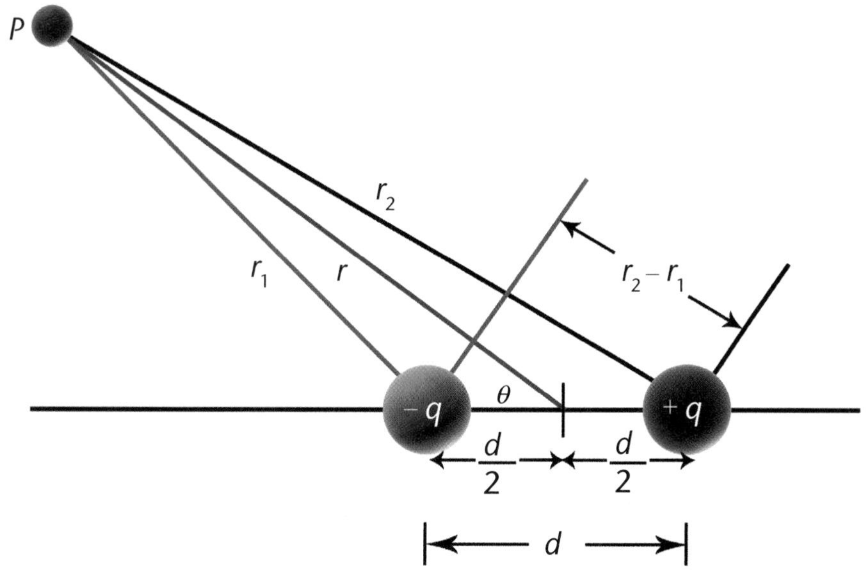

Figure 6.2. A Generic Dipole

The dipole in Figure 6.2 has charges $+q$ and $-q$ separated by a distance d. Given the dipole, we want to calculate the electric potential P at some point surrounding the dipole. The distance between the point in space and $+q$ is r_1; the distance between the point in space and $-q$ is r_2; the distance between the point in space and the midpoint of the dipole is r. We know that for a collection of charges, the electric potential P is the scalar sum of the potentials due to each charge at that point. In other words,

$$V = k\frac{q}{r_1} - k\frac{q}{r_2}$$

$$= kq\left(\frac{r_2 - r_1}{r_1 r_2}\right)$$

For points in space relatively distant from the dipole (compared to d), the product of r_1 and r_2 is approximately equal to the square of r, and the $r_2 - r_1$ is approximately equal to $d\cos\theta$. When we plug these approximations into the equation above, we get

$$V = \left(\frac{kqd}{r^2}\right)(\cos\theta)$$

The product of qd is defined as the **dipole moment p** with SI units of C·m. The dipole moment is a vector. Now, pay attention to this, because physicists and chemists have different ways of designating the direction of the dipole moment vector. Physicists define the vector along the line connecting the charges (the dipole axis), with the vector pointing from the negative charge toward the positive charge. Chemists usually reverse this convention, having p point from the positive charge toward the negative charge. Sometimes, you'll see chemists draw a crosshatch at the tail end of the dipole vector to indicate that the tail end is at the positive charge. In terms of the dipole moment p, we can rewrite the equation for calculating the potential at a point in space near a dipole as

$$V = \left(\frac{kp}{r^2}\right)(\cos\theta)$$

One very important equipotential line that you should be aware of is the plane that lies halfway between $+q$ and $-q$, called the perpendicular bisector of the dipole. Since the angle between this plane and the dipole axis is 90° (and $\cos 90° = 0$), the electric potential at any point along this plane is 0.

The electric field produced by the dipole at any point in space is the vector sum of each of the individual electric fields produced by the two charges. Along the perpendicular bisector of the dipole, the magnitude of the electric field can be approximated as

$$E = \frac{1}{4\pi\varepsilon_0}\frac{p}{r^3}$$

The electric field vectors at the points along the perpendicular bisector will point in the direction opposite to p (as defined directionally by physicists).

Key Equation

$$V = \left(\frac{kp}{r^2}\right)\cos\theta$$

$$V = \frac{(N/m^2 C^2)(C \cdot m)}{(m)^2} \quad \text{(dimensionless)}$$

$$V = N \cdot m/C = J/C$$

Use this equation to determine the electric potential at a point in space due to an electric dipole.

Key Equation

$$E = \frac{1}{4\pi\varepsilon_0}\frac{p}{r^3}$$

$$N/C = \left(\frac{1}{C^2/N \cdot m^2}\right)\left(\frac{C \cdot m}{(m)^3}\right)$$

$$N/C = N/C$$

Use this equation to determine the electric field due to an electric dipole along the perpendicular bisector of the dipole.

Example: The H_2O molecule has a dipole moment of 1.85 D, where D = debye unit = 3.34×10^{-30} C·m. Calculate the electric potential due to an H_2O molecule at a point 89 nm away along the axis of the dipole. (Use $k = 9 \times 10^9$ N·m²/C².)

Solution: Since the question asks for the potential along the axis of the dipole, the angle θ is given by 0°. Substitute the values into the equation for the dipole potential and multiply 1.85 D by 3.34×10^{-30} to convert it to C·m:

$$V = k \frac{p}{r^2} \cos \theta$$

$$= (9 \times 10^9) \frac{(1.85)(3.34 \times 10^{-30})(\cos 0°)}{([89 \times 10^{-9}])^2}$$

$$= 7 \times 10^{-6} \text{ V}$$

The diagrammatic representation of the generic electric dipole suggests that we might be able to apply a force or forces to the dipole axis, generating torque and causing the dipole axis to rotate. In the absence of an electric field, the dipole axis can assume any random orientation. However, when the electric dipole is placed in a uniform external electric field (strength of field everywhere the same), each of the equal and opposite charges of the dipole will feel a force exerted on it by the field. Since the charges are equal and opposite, the forces acting on the charges will also be equal and opposite, resulting in a situation of translational equilibrium. There will be, however, a net torque about the center of the dipole axis:

$$\tau = F \frac{d}{2} \sin \theta + F \frac{d}{2} \sin \theta$$

$$= Fd \sin \theta$$

$$= qEd \sin \theta$$

$$= (qd)E \sin \theta$$

$$= pE \sin \theta$$

where p is the magnitude of the dipole moment ($p = qd$), E is the magnitude of the uniform external electric field, and θ is the angle the dipole moment makes with the electric field. This torque will cause the dipole to reorient itself by rotating so that its dipole moment, p, aligns with the electric field E. This is shown in Figure 6.3.

Key Equation

$\tau = pE \sin\theta$

N·m = (C·m)(N/C)(dimensionless)

N·m = N·m

Use this equation to determine the net torque experienced by an electric dipole about the center of the dipole axis due to an external electric field.

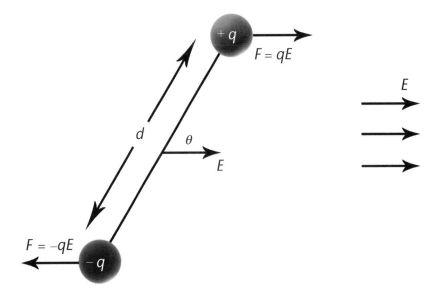

Figure 6.3. Torque on a Dipole from an External Electric Field

---

MCAT Concept Check 6.6

Before moving on, ensure that you are able to:

✓ Define an electric dipole

✓ Calculate the electric potential due to an electric dipole

✓ Describe the behavior of an electric dipole in an external electric field

---

Conclusion

In this chapter, we reviewed the very notion of charge, reminding ourselves that charge comes in two varieties, positive and negative. We learned that charges establish electric fields through which charges can exert forces on other charges. We relied on similarities between electrical and gravitational systems to better understand Coulomb's law and the nature of the forces that exist between charged particles. Don't forget that electrical forces can be repulsive as well as attractive, which is one of the differences between electrical and gravitational systems. Charges contain electric potential energy, which we defined as their energy of position with respect to other charges. Charges move within an electric field from one position of electric potential to another; they will move spontaneously through an electric potential difference, or voltage, in whichever direction results in a decrease in the charges' electric potential energy. Finally, we considered the geometry of the electric dipole and derived the equation for calculating the electric potential at any point in space around the dipole.

CONCEPT SUMMARY

Charges

☐ The SI unit of charge is the **coulomb** (p. 172)

☐ The **fundamental unit of charge** (p. 172) is $e = 1.60 \times 10^{-19}$ C

☐ **Protons** (p. 171) have a positive charge and **electrons** (p. 171) have a negative charge, each possessing the fundamental amount of charge

☐ Opposite charges exert attractive forces, like charges exert repulsive forces

Coulomb's Law

☐ **Coulomb's law** (p. 173) gives the magnitude of the electrostatic force vector between two charges, the vector always points along the line connecting the centers of the two charges

☐ Coulomb's law is analogous to the gravitational force equation, except that the constant (Coulomb's constant) is much larger and uses charge rather than mass

☐ Every stationary charge generates an **electric field** (p. 174), which exerts forces on other charges

☐ The electric field is the ratio of the force that is exerted on a test charge to the magnitude of that charge

☐ **Electric field vectors** (p. 175) can be represented as field lines that radiate outward from positive source charges and radiate inward to negative source charges

☐ Positive test charges will move in the direction of the field lines; negative test charges will move in the direction opposite of the field lines

Electric Potential Energy

☐ **Electric potential energy** (p. 176) of a charge is the amount of work required to put the charge in a given position

☐ The electric potential energy of a system will **increase** when two like charges move toward each other or when two opposite charges move apart (p. 177)

☐ The electric potential energy of a system will **decrease** when two like charges move apart or when two opposite charges move toward each other (p. 177)

Electric Potential

☐ **Electric potential** (p. 178) is the electric potential energy per unit charge

☐ Different points in the space of an electric field surrounding a source charge will have different electric potential values

☐ Test charges will move spontaneously in whichever direction results in a decrease in their electric potential energy (p. 179)

○ Positive test charges will move spontaneously from high potential to low potential

○ Negative test charges will move spontaneously from low potential to high potential

Equipotential Lines

☐ **Equipotential lines** (p. 179) are concentric lines (or concentric spheres in 3-D space) consisting of points with the same electric potential

☐ Work will be done when a charge is moved from one equipotential line to another; the work in independent of the pathway taken between the lines

☐ No work is done when a charge moves from a point on an equipotential line to another point on the same equipotential line

The Electric Dipole

☐ Two charges of opposite sign separated by a distance d generate an **electric dipole** (p. 181) of magnitude $p = qd$

☐ In an external electric field, an electric dipole will experience a net torque until it is aligned with the electric field vector

☐ An electric field will not induce any translational motion regardless of its orientation with respect to the electric field vector

EQUATIONS TO REMEMBER

☐ $F = k\dfrac{q_1 q_2}{r^2}$

☐ $E = \dfrac{F}{q_0} = k\dfrac{q}{r^2}$

☐ $F = q_0 E$

☐ $U = k\dfrac{qQ}{r}$

☐ $V = k\dfrac{Q}{r}$

☐ $V = \left(k\dfrac{qd}{r^2}\right)(\cos\theta)$

☐ $E = \dfrac{1}{4\pi\varepsilon_0}\dfrac{p}{r^3}$

☐ $\tau = (qd)E\sin\theta$

SHARED CONCEPTS

HIGH-YIELD PRACTICE PROBLEMS

Practice Questions

Questions 1–3 refer to the figure below, in which F represents the electrostatic force exerted on charged particle S by charged particle R.

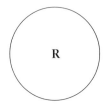 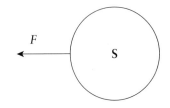

1. In the figure, the magnitude of the electric force on R due to S is

   A. $\frac{F}{2}$

   B. F

   C. $2F$

   D. $4F$

2. If the distance between the centers of the spheres is halved, the magnitude of the force on S due to R will be

   A. $\frac{F}{2}$

   B. $\frac{F}{4}$

   C. $2F$

   D. $4F$

3. Assume that the direction of F is the same direction as the electric field between R and S. If an electron were placed midway between R and S, the resultant electric force on the electron would be

   A. toward R.

   B. toward S.

   C. up.

   D. down.

4. If the electric field at a distance r away from charge Q is 36 N/C, what is the ratio of the electric fields at r, $2r$, and $3r$?

   A. 36:9:4

   B. 9:3:1

   C. 36:18:12

   D. 36:18:9

5.

A positive charge of $+Q$ is fixed at point R a distance d away from another positive charge of $+2Q$ fixed at point S. Point A is located midway between the charges, and point B is a distance $\frac{d}{2}$ from $+2Q$. In which direction will a positive charge move if placed at point A?

   A. Toward the $+Q$ charge

   B. Toward the $+2Q$ charge

   C. Upward and diagonally toward the $+2Q$ charge

   D. It will remain stationary.

6. Two parallel conducting plates, one carrying a charge $+Q$ and the other a charge $-Q$, are separated by a distance d. The voltage between the plates is 12 V. If a $+2$ μC charge is released from rest at the positive plate, how much kinetic energy does it have when it reaches the negative plate?

   A. 2.4×10^{-6} J

   B. 2.4×10^{-5} J

   C. 4.8×10^{-5} J

   D. 4.8×10^{-6} J

7. The negative charge (-1 μC) in the figure below moves from $y = -5$ to $y = +5$ and is made to follow the dashed line in the vicinity of two equal positive charges ($= +5$ C). What is the work required to move the negative charge along the dashed line?

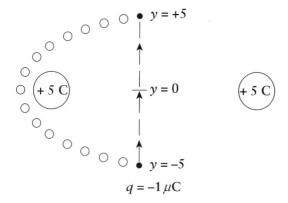

A. -5 J
B. -10 J
C. 10 J
D. No net work is done.

8. If the electric field at 3 m away from a charge is 8 N/C, what is the electric potential at a point 6 m away from the charge?

A. 2 V
B. 6 V
C. 12 V
D. 24 V

9. Given an electric dipole, the electric potential is zero

A. only at the midpoint of the dipole axis.
B. anywhere on any perpendicular bisector of the dipole axis and at infinity.
C. anywhere on the dipole axis.
D. only for points at infinity.

10. The electric potential applied to a certain electron is increased by a factor of 4. The velocity of the electron will increase by a factor of

A. 16
B. 8
C. 4
D. 2

11. Which of the following accurately depicts the field lines around a proton that is moving toward the right of this page?

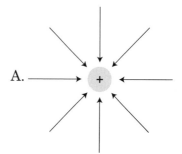

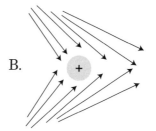

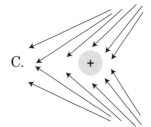

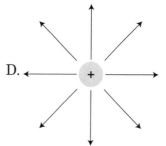

12. A certain 9-volt battery is used as a power source to move a 2 C charge. How much work is done by the battery?

A. 0 J
B. 9 J
C. 18 J
D. 36 J

13. A proton and an alpha particle (a helium nucleus) repel each other with a force of F while they are 20 nm apart. If each particle combines with three electrons, what is the new force between them?

A. $9F$
B. $3F$
C. F
D. $\dfrac{F}{9}$

14. The diagram below represents the field lines for two charges of equal magnitude. What are the signs on each charge?

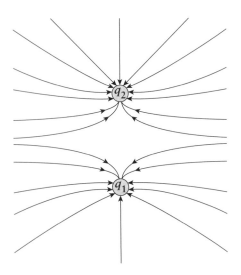

A. q_1 is positive; q_2 is negative.
B. q_1 is negative; q_2 is positive.
C. q_1 and q_2 are both positive.
D. q_1 and q_2 are both negative.

Small Group Questions

1. A sphere with a charge and mass equal to that of an electron is shot towards a fixed sphere with the exact same charge and mass on the other side of the universe. If the sphere starts with a velocity of 1,000 cm/s, at what distance from the fixed sphere will the moving sphere come to rest?

2. What is the potential energy of a dipole in a uniform electric field (E)?

Explanations to Practice Questions

1. B

According to Newton's third law, if R exerts a force on S, then S exerts an equal but oppositely directed force back on R. Therefore, the magnitude of the force on R due to S is F.

2. D

The force is inversely proportional to r^2. Thus,

$$F \propto \frac{1}{r^2}$$

If r_2 equals $\frac{r_1}{2}$, then

$$F_{old} \propto \frac{1}{r_1^2}$$

and

$$F_{new} \propto \frac{1}{r_2^2}$$

$$F_{new} \propto \frac{1}{\left(\frac{r_1}{2}\right)^2}$$

$$F_{new} \propto \frac{1}{\left(\frac{r_1^2}{4}\right)}$$

$$F_{new} \propto \frac{4}{r_1^2} = 4F_{old}$$

So, the new force is 4 times greater.

3. B

An electric field's direction at a given point is defined as the direction of the force that would be exerted on a positive test charge in that position. Since electrons are negatively charged particles, they will therefore feel a force in the opposite direction of the electric field's vector. In this case, since F points to the left (towards R), an electron would feel a force pointing to the right (towards S), so choice (B) is correct.

4. A

The first step in answering this question is to remember that the electric field is inversely proportional to the square of the radius:

$$E = \frac{kq}{r^2}$$

$$E \propto \frac{1}{r^2}$$

Therefore, if the electric field at radius r, E_r, is 36, then the electric field at radius $2r$ will be

$$E_{2r} \propto \frac{1}{(2r)^2}$$

$$E_{2r} \propto \frac{1}{4r^2}$$

$$E_{2r} = \frac{E_r}{4} = \frac{36}{4} = 9 \text{ N/C}$$

Similarly, the electric field at radius $3r$, E_{3r}, is equal to

$$E_{3r} \propto \frac{1}{(3r)^2}$$

$$E_{3r} \propto \frac{1}{9r^2}$$

$$E_{3r} = \frac{E_r}{9} = \frac{36}{9} = 4 \text{ N/C}$$

Lastly, the ratio of $E_r:E_{2r}:E_{3r}$ is 36:9:4. Choice (A) matches with our response and is therefore the correct answer.

5. A

A positive charge placed at A will experience two forces, a force to the left due to $+2Q$ and a force to the right due to $+Q$. Since point A is the same distance from $+Q$ and $+2Q$, the force due to $+2Q$ will be larger than that due to $+Q$, and there will be a net force to the left (towards $+Q$).

6. B

Recall that the change in potential energy, ΔU, and the change in potential, ΔV, are related by $\Delta U = q\Delta V$. So $\Delta U = (2 \times 10^{-6} \text{ C}) \times 12 \text{ V} = 2.4 \times 10^{-5} \text{ J}$. To move a positive charge away from negative charges and towards positive charges, we must exert a force to counteract the attractive force of the negative charges on the negative plate and the repulsive force of the positive charges on the positive plate. Thus, positive work must be done. Conservation of energy applies to charges as it does to masses; thus, the loss in electric potential energy as the charge moves from the positive plate to the negative plate must equal the gain in the kinetic energy of the charge. The loss in potential energy is just the amount of potential energy gained originally when going from the negative to the positive plate (i.e., 2.4×10^{-5} J). So the gain in kinetic energy is just 2.4×10^{-5} J, which matches with choice (B).

7. D

There will be work done in moving the negative charge from its initial position to the origin. However, in moving the negative charge from the origin to the final position, the same amount of work is done but with the opposite sign. This is because the force changes direction as the electron crosses $y = 0$. Therefore, the two quantities of work cancel each other out. This argument depends crucially on the symmetry of the initial and final positions.

8. C

Let's start by defining the relationship between the electric field and the electric potential of a charge:

$$E = \frac{kQ}{r^2}$$
$$V = \frac{kQ}{r}$$

Simply put, while the electric field is a vector that is proportional to $\frac{1}{r^2}$, the electric potential is a scalar that is proportional to $\frac{1}{r}$. Since E is 8 N/C at $r = 3$ m, then at a distance twice as far away ($r = 6$ m), E would be four times smaller; that is, 2 N/C. To determine the electric potential given the electric field, we can multiply the electric field by r:

$$E = \frac{kQ}{r^2}$$
$$\frac{kQ}{r^2} \times r = \frac{kQ}{r} = V$$

Therefore, V at $r = 6$ is 2 N/C $\times$ 6 m = 12 V. Choice (C) matches our result and is thus the correct answer.

9. B

Potential is a scalar quantity. The total potential is the sum of the potentials of the positive and negative charges. $V_+ = \frac{kq_+}{r_+}$ and $V_- = \frac{kq_-}{r_-}$. In a dipole, $-q_+ = q_-$, so the potential will be zero wherever $r_+ = r_-$. This will be at any point along any perpendicular bisector of the dipole axis. (Note the potential is also zero for all points at infinity since $\frac{kq}{\infty} = 0$, but choice (D) says **only** points at infinity. Clearly many points not infinitely far away also have zero potential.)

10. D

The electric potential (V) is equal to the amount of work done (W) divided by the test charge (q_0), according to the equation $V = \frac{W}{q_0}$. This means that the potential is directly proportional to the amount of work done, which is equal to the amount of energy exerted by the particle; therefore, the overall amount of energy increases by a factor of 4. Since energy is directly proportional to the square of the velocity (according to $E = \frac{1}{2}mv^2$), the velocity must increase by a factor of 2.

11. D

You should know that the field lines for a positively charged particle will always point away from the particle in a radial pattern, regardless of the direction in which the particle is moving. Choice (A) represents the field lines of a negatively charged particle. Choices (B) and (C) do not represent any particular scheme.

12. C

Electric potential (V) is equal to the quotient of the amount of work done (W) divided by the charge of the particle on which the work is done (q_0), according to the equation $V = \frac{W}{q_0}$. Since the potential equals 9 V and the charge equals 2 C, the work done must equal 9 V $\times$ 2 C = 18 J.

13. C

The electrostatic force is given by the equation $F = \frac{kq_1q_2}{r}$. Since the distance does not change during the interaction in the question, the value of r is irrelevant to the answer.

Currently, q_1 and q_2 are equal to $+1\ e$ and $+2\ e$, respectively; the addition of three electrons (each of which carries a charge of $-e$) will change the charges to $-2\ e$ and $-1\ e$. Therefore, the product q_1q_2 before the interaction is equal to the product q_1q_2 after the interaction ($q_1q_2 = +2\ e^2$). Because k and r remain constant in this system, the value of $\dfrac{kq_1q_2}{r}$ does not change.

14. D

A field line shows the direction of the electrostatic force that would act on a positively charged test particle. The field lines in this diagram are pointed toward q_1 and q_2, meaning that a positive particle would be accelerated in the direction of q_1 and q_2. This can only happen if both charges are negative, choice (D). The lines from q_1 can never intersect with the lines from q_2 because a positively charged test particle at any given point will always move in one specific direction; if the lines intersected, then a test particle at the intersection point would have to move in both directions at once.

Explanations to Small Group Questions

1. The moving charge only comes to rest after all its kinetic energy is transformed into potential energy, so we must first calculate the kinetic energy of the charge.

   $KE = \dfrac{1}{2}mv^2$, m = mass of electron = 9.11×10^{-31} kg,
   $v = 1{,}000$ cm/s = 10 m/s

   $KE = \dfrac{1}{2}(9.11 \times 10^{-31}\,\text{kg})(10\ \text{m/s})^2$

   $KE = 4.56 \times 10^{-29}\,\text{J}$

   All of this kinetic energy will be transformed to electric potential energy (U) such that $U = \dfrac{kqQ}{r}$, where r is the distance between the two spheres.

   $4.56 \times 10^{-29}\,\text{J} = \dfrac{kqQ}{r}$, $k = 8.99 \times 10^9$ N·m²/C²,
   $q = Q = -1.60 \times 10^{-19}$ C

   $4.56 \times 10^{-29}\,\text{J} = \dfrac{(8.99 \times 10^9\,\text{N} \cdot \text{m}^2/\text{C}^2)(-1.60 \times 10^{-19}\text{C})(-1.60 \times 10^{-19}\text{C})}{r}$,

   $r = 5.05$ m

2. The potential energy of a dipole in an electric field is equal to the work done to bring the dipole from infinity into the field. Combining the equations $U = W = q\Delta V$, $V = \left(\dfrac{kqd}{r^2}\right)\cos\theta$, and $p = qd$, we obtain the simplified expression $U = pE(\cos\theta)$. The potential energy of the dipole varies depending on the orientation of the dipole relative to the uniform electric field. We can look at two extreme cases to understand this. When the dipole is oriented in the direction of the electric field, $\theta = 0°$ and $\cos\theta = 1$, so the work required to bring the dipole from infinity into the field and the potential energy are equal to pE. When the dipole is oriented perpendicular to the direction of the electric field, $\theta = 90°$ and $\cos\theta = 0$, so the work done to bring the dipole into the field from infinity is 0. This is because the work done on the $+q$ charge of the dipole is exactly equal and opposite to the work done on the $-q$ charge of the dipole.

Magnetism

In this chapter:

Introduction

A compass, one of the simplest tools developed by humans, takes advantage of the Earth's natural magnetic field and the tendency of certain elements to be attracted to magnetic fields. The type of compass that most of us are familiar with, the magnetic compass, consists of a magnetized needle (a very small, light magnet) that is balanced on a pivot so that it is free to turn, encased within some kind of clear housing like glass or plastic. Usually there is fluid filling the housing to stabilize the needle. The magnetic needle will always be aligned with the Earth's magnetic poles. The north-seeking end of the compass needle is usually painted or colored red, and it will always point to the north magnetic pole. (The north magnetic pole, by the way, is not in exactly the same location as the geographic north pole, and to complicate things slightly, the north magnetic pole is actually the "south" pole of the imaginary bar magnet that exists inside the Earth.) Using a magnetic compass, you can be certain "where north is," and you can use the compass to guide you in whatever direction you need to go.

This chapter reviews the subject of magnetism. Unlike electrostatics, in which electric charges create electric fields that exert forces on other electric charges, magnetism has no fundamental magnetic charges. Instead, magnetic fields are created by moving charges, sometimes in the form of currents in wires, and by permanent magnets. These magnetic fields, in turn, exert magnetic forces on other moving charges, current-carrying wires, and magnets. Thus, the two necessary conditions for the generation of magnetic fields are charge and movement of that charge. Likewise, the two necessary conditions for the generation of magnetic forces are charge and movement of that charge.

The first half of this chapter will discuss the generation of magnetic fields by permanent magnets and moving charge. We will focus on the two most common configurations of current: the straight wire and the loop of wire. In the second half of the chapter, we will review the calculations involved in determining the magnetic force exerted by an external magnetic field on a moving charge or current.

Bridge

Have you heard the term *electromagnetism* before? Two words are combined into a single concept because a changing magnetic field produces an electric field and a changing electric field produces a magnetic field. It is because of this interconnectedness that both are considered part of a single fundamental force.

Figure 7.1. Drawing Magnetic Field Vectors
Use the symbol conventions depicted to indicate the desired direction of the magnetic field

7.1 Sources of Magnetic Field ★★★☆☆

Any moving charge creates a **magnetic field.** Magnetic fields may be set up by the movement of individual charges, such as an electron moving through space; by the mass movement of charge in the form of a current though a conductive material, such as a copper wire; or by the "flow" of charge in permanent magnets. We will look specifically at permanent magnets and current-carrying wires, but you ought to remember that any moving charge or collection of charges will create a magnetic field.

The SI unit of the magnetic field is the **tesla (T)** for which $1 \text{ T} = 1 \text{ N·s/m·C}$. The size of the tesla unit is quite large, so small magnetic fields are sometimes measured in **gauss**, for which $1 \text{ T} = 10^4$ gauss.

As with electric fields, we can represent magnetic field vectors by magnetic field lines drawn in the direction of the magnetic field vectors (see Figure 7.1). For magnetic field vectors that are "along the plane of the page," draw field lines as arrows with the tip of the arrow pointing in the direction of the field vector. For magnetic field vectors that are "coming out of the page," draw a dot to represent the tip of the field vector (the tip of the arrow). And for magnetic field vectors that are "going into the page," draw an X to represent the tail of the field vector (the tail of the arrow). The spacing between magnetic field lines is reflective of the strength of the field at that point in space: The farther out from the moving charge, the weaker the magnetic field, and the further apart the field lines will be spaced. At any point along a field line, the magnetic field vector itself is tangential to the line.

MAGNETIC MATERIALS

All materials can be classified as diamagnetic, paramagnetic, or ferromagnetic. (There are others, such as ferrimagnetic and antiferromagnetic, but these concepts are beyond the scope of the MCAT.) **Diamagnetic materials** are made of atoms with no unpaired electrons and that have no net magnetic field. Diamagnetic materials will be repelled by either pole of a bar magnet and so can be called weakly antimagnetic. In layperson terms, diamagnetic materials are "nonmagnetic" and include common materials that you wouldn't ever expect to get stuck to a magnet: wood, plastics, water, glass, and skin, just to name a few.

The atoms of both **paramagnetic** and **ferromagnetic materials** have unpaired electrons, so these atoms do have a net magnetic moment dipole, but the atoms in these materials are usually randomly oriented so that the material itself creates no net magnetic field (see Figure 7.2). Paramagnetic materials will become weakly magnetized in the presence of an external magnetic field, which causes the permanent magnetic dipoles of the individual atoms to align with the external field. Paramagnetic materials will be attracted toward the pole of a bar magnet, so they are sometimes called weakly magnetic. Upon removal of the external magnetic field, the thermal energy of the individual atoms will cause the individual magnetic dipoles to reorient randomly, and the material will cease to be magnetized. Some paramagnetic materials that we commonly work with include aluminum, copper, and gold.

FUNDAMENTALS OF SPIN

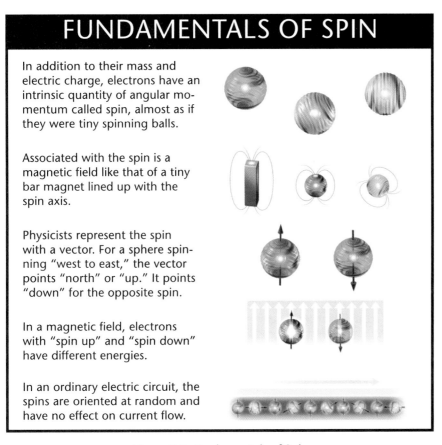

In addition to their mass and electric charge, electrons have an intrinsic quantity of angular momentum called spin, almost as if they were tiny spinning balls.

Associated with the spin is a magnetic field like that of a tiny bar magnet lined up with the spin axis.

Physicists represent the spin with a vector. For a sphere spinning "west to east," the vector points "north" or "up." It points "down" for the opposite spin.

In a magnetic field, electrons with "spin up" and "spin down" have different energies.

In an ordinary electric circuit, the spins are oriented at random and have no effect on current flow.

Figure 7.2. Fundamentals of Spin

Ferromagnetic materials, like paramagnetic materials, have unpaired electrons and permanent atomic magnetic dipoles that are normally oriented randomly so that the material has no net magnetic dipole. However, unlike paramagnetic materials, ferromagnetic materials will become strongly magnetized when exposed to a magnetic field or under certain temperatures. For all ferromagnetic materials, there is a critical temperature, called the **Curie temperature,** above which the material is paramagnetic but below which the material is magnetized as a result of a high degree of alignment of the magnetic fields of the individual atoms (which are assembled into large groups of atoms [10^{12}–10^{18}] called magnetic domains). When the ambient temperature (i.e., room temperature) is below the Curie temperature, the material is permanently magnetized. The common metal bar magnet that holds our grocery lists, photos, and holiday cards against the refrigerator door is made of permanently magnetized material, typically including iron. (Interestingly, the thin flexible magnets that have also found a home on your refrigerator are made of ground-up magnetite, a crystalline ferrimagnetic material that is weakly magnetic.) Other ferromagnetic materials are nickel and cobalt. They are sometimes called strongly magnetic because they have a large and positive susceptibility to external magnetic fields, are strongly attracted to magnetic fields, and can retain their magnetic properties for varying amounts of time after the external magnetic field has been removed. Common examples of ferromagnetic items, in addition to the ubiquitous bar magnet, include paper clips, safety pins, and sewing needles.

All bar magnets have a north and south pole. Field lines exit the north pole and enter the south pole. Because magnetic field lines are circular, it is impossible to have a monopole magnet (but it is possible for magnets to have more than two poles). If two bar magnets are allowed to interact, opposite poles will attract each other, while like poles will repel each other.

CURRENT-CARRYING WIRES

Because any moving charge creates a magnetic field, we would certainly expect that a collection of moving charge, in the form of a current through a conductive material such as a copper wire, would produce a magnetic field in its vicinity. As with the net electric field of multiple charges, the net magnetic field of a current is equal to the vector sum of the magnetic fields of all the individual moving charges that comprise the current. The configuration of the magnetic field lines surrounding a current-carrying wire will depend on the shape of the wire. Two special cases that are commonly tested on the MCAT include a long, straight wire and a circular loop of wire (with particular attention paid to the magnetic field at the center of that loop).

Chapter 8, DC and AC Circuits, discusses current and circuits more thoroughly, but for now, we will remind you that when two points at different electric potentials are connected with a conductor (such as a copper wire), charge flows between the two points. The flow of charge is called an **electric current**. The magnitude of the current i is the amount of charge Δq passing through the conductor per unit time Δt, and it can be calculated by

$$ i = \frac{\Delta q}{\Delta t} $$

The SI unit of current is the **ampere** (1 A = 1 coulomb/second). Charge is transmitted by a flow of electrons in a conductor, and because electrons are negatively charged, they move from a point of lower electric potential to a point of higher electric potential (and in doing so reduce their electrical potential energy). *By convention, however, the direction of current is the direction in which positive charge would flow from higher potential to lower potential. Thus, the direction of current is opposite to the direction of actual electron flow.*

For an infinitely long and **straight current-carrying wire,** we can calculate the magnitude of the magnetic field produced by the current i in the wire at a perpendicular distance, r, from the wire as

$$B = \frac{\mu_o i}{2\pi r}$$

where B is the magnetic field at a distance r from the wire, and μ_o is the permeability of free space ($4\pi \times 10^{-7}$ tesla·meter/ampere $= 1.26 \times 10^{-6}$ T·m/A). The equation demonstrates an inverse relationship between the magnitude of the magnetic field and the distance from the current.

The shape of the magnetic fields surrounding a current is concentric perpendicular circles of magnetic field vectors. To determine the direction of the field vectors, you can use a **right-hand rule.** This right-hand rule is one of three right-hand rules that you will use in the context of magnetism. In this rule, your right thumb points in the direction of the current. Your other right-hand fingers mimic the circular magnetic field lines, curling around your thumb in the same direction that the magnetic field lines curl around the current. Your fingers show you the direction of the magnetic field lines and the direction of B itself at any point. This right-hand rule works for both a straight-line wire and a circular loop of wire. (You must use your right hand for this and all other right-hand rules.)

Key Equation

$$B = \frac{\mu_o i}{2\pi r}$$

$$T = \frac{(T \cdot m/A)(A)}{m}$$

$$T = T$$

Use this equation to determine the magnitude of the magnetic field produced by a straight current-carrying wire at a chosen point in space.

Example: A straight wire carries a current of 5 A toward the top of the page (see Figure 7.3a). What is the magnitude and direction of the magnetic field at point P, which is 10 cm to the left of the wire? What is the magnitude and direction of the magnetic field at point Q, which is 2 cm to the right of the wire?

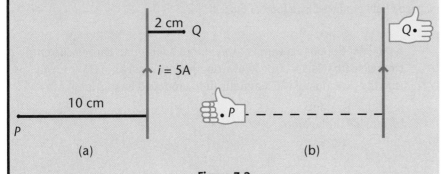

Figure 7.3

Solution: Find the magnitude at point P:

$$B = \frac{\mu_o i}{2\pi r}$$

$$= \frac{(4\pi \times 10^{-7})(5)}{2\pi(0.1)}$$

$$= 10^{-5}\ \text{T} = 0.1\ \text{gauss}$$

Find the magnitude at point Q:

$$B = \frac{(4\pi \times 10^{-7})(5)}{2\pi(0.02)}$$

$$= 5 \times 10^{-5} \text{ T} = 0.5 \text{ gauss}$$

Now to get the direction of the field for each of these points, we use the right-hand rule. Hold your **right thumb** toward the top of the page. Now curl your fingers around the wire. At Q your fingers should point into the page. Keep curling around and you notice that at point P your fingers come out of the page. (See Figure 7.3b). So your answer should be: B (at P) = 0.1 gauss, pointing out of the page, and B (at Q) = 0.5 gauss, pointing into the page. Note that as we move farther from the wire, the magnitude of magnetic field decreases.

Key Equation

$$B = \frac{\mu_o i}{2r}$$

$$\text{T} = \frac{(\text{T·m/A})(\text{A})}{\text{m}}$$

Use this equation to determine the magnitude of the magnetic field produced by a circular loop of current-carrying wire at the center of the loop.

For a **circular loop of current-carrying wire** of radius r, the magnitude of the magnetic field at the center of the circular loop is given as

$$B = \frac{\mu_o i}{2r}$$

You'll notice that the two equations are quite similar, the obvious difference being that the equation for the magnetic field at the center of the circular loop of wire does not include the constant π. The less obvious difference is that the first expression gives the magnitude of the magnetic field at any perpendicular distance, r, from the current-carrying wire, while the second expression gives the magnitude of the magnetic field only at the center of the circular loop of current-carrying wire with radius r. The following example illustrates how to determine the directions of the magnetic field produced by a loop of current.

Example: Suppose a wire is formed into a loop that carries current clockwise (that is, electrons flow counterclockwise) as in Figure 7.4a. Find the direction of the magnetic field produced by this loop

a. within the loop.
b. outside of the loop.

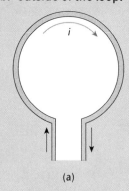 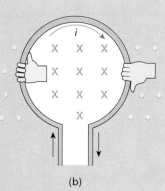

(a)   (b)

Figure 7.4

Solution: Look at Figure 7.4b. By holding your right thumb anywhere around the loop in the direction of current flow (clockwise) and encircling the wire with the remaining fingers of the right hand, your right fingers should point

a. into the page. Thus, the magnetic field within the loop points into the page.
b. out of the page. Thus, the magnetic field outside the loop points out of the page.

MCAT Concept Check 7.1

Before moving on, ensure that you are able to:

✓ Define the magnetic field **B**

✓ Identify the various types of magnetic materials

✓ Calculate the magnetic field produced by a straight or circular loop of current-carrying wire

---

7.2 The Magnetic Field Force   ★★★★☆☆

Now that we've reviewed the ways in which magnetic fields can be created, we need to examine the forces that are exerted by magnetic fields on moving charges. Magnetic fields, as we've seen, are created by magnets or moving charge, and magnetic fields exert forces only on other moving charges. Charges do not "sense" their own fields; they only sense the field established by some other charge or collection of charges. That is to say, charges feel forces only from external electric or magnetic fields. Therefore, in our discussion of the magnetic force on moving charges and on current-carrying wires, we will assume the presence of a fixed and uniform magnetic field B. This field is produced, of course, by some external source, such as a magnet or arrangement of moving charge (such as a configuration of current-carrying wires), but for our purposes, we are only concerned with the strength and direction of this external field.

Bridge

As with electric field lines, magnetic field lines never cross.

FORCE ON A MOVING CHARGE

When a charge moves in a magnetic field, a **magnetic force** may be exerted on it, the magnitude of which can be calculated as follows:

$$F = qvB \sin \theta$$

where q is the charge (including the sign of the charge), v is the velocity of the charge, B is the magnitude of the magnetic field, and θ is the smallest angle between the vector qv and the magnetic field vector B. Notice that the magnetic force is a function of the sine of the angle, which means that the charge must have a perpendicular component of velocity

Key Equation

$F = qvB \sin \theta$
N = (C)(m/s)(T) = (C)(m/s)(N·s/m·C)
N = N
Use this equation to determine the magnetic force on a moving charge in an external magnetic field.

Key Concept

Remember that sin 0° and sin 180° equal zero. This means that any charge moving parallel or antiparallel to the direction of the magnetic field will experience *no force* from the magnetic field.

Key Concept

Another version of the right-hand rule (depicted in Figure 7.5) has your thumb point in the direction of velocity, your index finger in the magnetic field, and then the palm of your hand in the direction of force. As long as your own method works for you, *use it*!

in order to experience a magnetic force. If the charge is moving with a velocity that is parallel or antiparallel to the magnetic field vector, it will experience no magnetic force.

Here we will introduce the second **right-hand rule** that you should practice in anticipation for Test Day. To determine the direction of the magnetic force on a moving charge, you must position your right-hand thumb in the direction of the vector qv. Now, pay close attention because this is very important and the first place where students typically make a mistake: The vector qv takes into account not only the direction of the velocity vector but also the sign on the charge. If the charge is positive, then your thumb will point in the direction of v, but if the charge is negative, your thumb will point in the direction opposite to v. Of course, if either q or v is zero, then you have either no charge or stationary charge, your thumb has nowhere to point, and there is no magnetic force to be calculated.

Once you've figured out what direction your thumb needs to point, extend your fingers in the direction of the magnetic field. Your fingers should point away from you if the magnetic field vector is going "into the page" and represented by Xs; they should point toward you if the magnetic field vector is coming "out of the page" and represented by dots. You may need to rotate your wrist this way or that to get the correct configuration of thumb and fingers. Once your thumb and fingers are in their proper positions, your palm, which has no choice but to face a particular direction, will indicate the direction of the magnetic force vector F on the moving point charge q.

(You may have learned a version of the right-hand rule that is different from what is described here. For example, some students learn to point the right index finger in the direction of qv and the right middle finger in the direction of B, and when you hold the thumb perpendicular to these two fingers, it points in the direction of F. *It makes no difference which version of the right-hand rule you use, as long as you are comfortable with it and are skilled in its proper use.*)

Example: Suppose a proton, whose charge is $+1.6 \times 10^{-19}$ C, is moving with a speed of 15 m/s in a direction parallel to a uniform magnetic field of 3.0 T. What is the magnitude and direction of the magnetic force on the proton?

Solution: Because the proton is positively charged, the vector qv is in the same direction as v, which is the same direction as B, as stated in the problem. Because qv and B are pointing in the same direction, the angle between the vectors is zero. Because sin 0° = 0 and $F = qvB \sin \theta$, the magnetic force on the proton is zero, too. Note that if the charge had been negative (an electron, for example), the angle between qv and B would have been 180°, and because sin 180° = 0, the magnetic force on a negative charge moving parallel to a uniform magnetic field would be zero as well. In general, the magnetic force on a moving charge will be zero if the charge is moving parallel or antiparallel to the magnetic field.

Example: Suppose a proton whose charge equals $+1.6 \times 10^{-19}$ C is moving with a speed of 15 m/s toward the top of the page and through a uniform magnetic field of 3.0 T directed into the page (see Figure 7.5a). What is the magnitude and direction of the magnetic force on the proton?

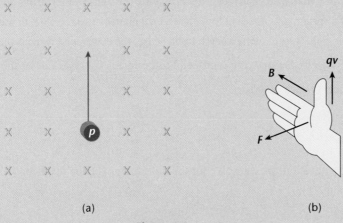

(a)   (b)

Figure 7.5

Solution: Because the proton is positively charged, the vector qv is in the same direction as v, which is perpendicular to B as stated in the problem. (B is perpendicular to the plane of the page.) Because qv and B are perpendicular, the angle between the vectors is $\theta = 90°$, and because $\sin 90° = 1$, the magnetic force on the proton is

$$F = qvB \sin \theta$$
$$= qvB$$
$$= (1.6 \times 10^{-19})(15)(3.0)$$
$$= 7.2 \times 10^{-18} \text{ N}$$

By holding the thumb of the **right hand** so that it is directed toward the top of the page, then holding the remaining fingers of the **right hand** so that they point towards (into) the page, one's **right-hand** palm points to the left (see Figure 7.5b). Hence, the proton is deflected to the left on its upward journey. As the velocity of the proton changes, so does the magnetic force that it experiences. Note that if the charge had been negative (an electron, for example), the angle between qv and B still would have been 90°, but the right-hand rule would have required that qv point toward the bottom of the page, meaning that one's right-hand palm would point to the right. Hence, an electron is deflected to the right on its upward journey. One can readily see that the direction of the magnetic force on a negative charge moving through a magnetic field is opposite to the direction of the magnetic force acting on a positive charge moving in the same direction.

When a charged particle moves perpendicular to a constant, uniform magnetic field, the resulting motion is circular motion with constant speed in the plane perpendicular to the magnetic field. Charged particles assume circular motion with constant speed when they move into a constant, uniform magnetic field perpendicular to the field vector. This is uniform circular motion, a topic of discussion in Chapter 2, Newtonian Mechanics. A centripetal force is always associated with circular motion. In other words, an external force, which we call the centripetal force, must always be applied to an object demonstrating circular motion since that object must constantly change direction. The centripetal force may be the tension in a string, the restoring force of a spring, gravitational force between a planet and a satellite, or the force of a magnetic field (just to name a few). In this case, the centripetal force is the magnetic force ($F = qvB$). Because the centripetal force equals $\dfrac{mv^2}{r}$, we can set the two equations equal to each other:

$$F = qvB = \frac{mv^2}{r}$$

From this equation, we can solve for the orbit radius (r), the magnetic field (B), and the velocity (v):

$$r = \frac{mv}{qB} \qquad B = \frac{mv}{qr} \qquad v = \frac{qrB}{m}$$

If you look closely at these equations, you can see that, assuming constant mass and charge of the charged particle, both the velocity and radius of the uniform circular motion seem to be a function of the magnetic field. This is to say, it seems to be the case that changing the magnitude of the magnetic field will either result in an increase in the velocity or a decrease in the radius (or some combination of both). We can approach this question using the equation for work and the work-energy theorem. Let's apply the work equation first. We know that work is done when a force is applied through some distance and there is a dependency of work on the cosine of the angle between the force vector and the displacement vector. In circular motion, the centripetal force is always perpendicular to the instantaneous velocity vector (angle equals 90°; cos 90° = 0); therefore, no work is done by the centripetal force on the moving charged particle. According to the work-energy theorem, if no (net) work is done on an object, its kinetic energy will not change, and there will be no change in the magnitude of the object's velocity. This is exactly what happens in uniform circular motion: The speed of the object is constant as it travels through its circular pathway. For this charged particle, which demonstrates uniform circular motion, it must be the case that the magnitude of its velocity is constant. Thus, a change in the strength of the magnetic field will result in a change in the radius of the circular pathway of the charged particle but not in the magnitude of the velocity.

Example: Suppose the proton of the previous example is allowed to circle (counterclockwise) in the same perpendicular magnetic field of 3.0 T with the same speed of 15 m/s (as in Figure 7.6a). What is the orbit radius r? (The mass of a proton is 1.67×10^{-27} kg.)

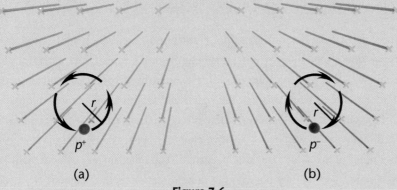

(a)   (b)

Figure 7.6

Solution: Equate the centripetal force to the magnetic force and solve for the orbit radius as shown above:

$$r = \frac{mv}{qB}$$

$$= \frac{(1.67 \times 10^{-27})(15)}{(1.6 \times 10^{-19})(3)}$$

$$= 5.2 \times 10^{-8} \, \text{m}$$

Note that the direction of the magnetic force on a negative charge moving through a uniform magnetic field is opposite to the direction of the magnetic force acting on a positive charge moving in the same direction. Therefore, if the charge had been negative (such as an antiproton, for example, which has the mass of the proton but is negatively charged), it would have circled in the **clockwise** direction with the same orbit radius (see Figure 7.6 b).

FORCE ON CURRENT-CARRYING WIRE

We've just examined the force that can be created by a magnetic field when a point charge moves through the field, so it should not come as a surprise that a current-carrying wire placed in a magnetic field may also experience a magnetic force. For a straight wire of length L carrying a current i in a direction that makes an angle θ with a uniform magnetic field B, the magnitude of the magnetic force on the current-carrying wire can be calculated by

$$F = iLB \sin \theta$$

This equation is not actually any different from the equation you learned to apply to a point charge moving through a magnetic field. What is current? It is a quantity of

Key Equation

$F = iLB \sin\theta$
N = (A)(m)(T) = (C/s)(m)(N·s/m·C)
N = N

Use this equation to determine the magnetic force on a current-carrying wire in a uniform external magnetic field.

charge per unit time. And the length of the wire running through the field is measured in meters, so when we put it all together, we get:

$$F = \left(\frac{\Delta q}{\Delta t}\right)(L)(B)\sin\theta = (\Delta q)\left(\frac{L}{\Delta t}\right)(B)\sin\theta = qvB\sin\theta$$

$F = iLB\sin\theta$ and $F = qvB\sin\theta$ are the same equation!

We need to discuss the third and final **right-hand rule,** which applies to current-carrying wire placed in an external magnetic field. It's actually the same right-hand rule you will use to determine the force exerted by a magnetic field on a point charge; the only difference is that the right-hand thumb always points in the direction of the current, never opposite to that direction. Because current, by convention, is the direction of movement of positive charge, it makes sense that the thumb will always point in the same direction as current. The other fingers of your right hand are positioned so that they point in the same direction as the magnetic field vector *B*. The palm of your right hand will automatically be facing in the direction of the magnetic force vector. The force acting on the current-carrying wire will always be perpendicular to the plane defined by *B* and the direction of the current. Your palm will indicate which of the two perpendicular directions the force is acting.

Example: Suppose a wire of length 2.0 m is conducting a current of 5.0 A toward the top of the page and through a 30 gauss uniform magnetic field directed into the page (see Figure 7.7a). What is the magnitude and direction of the magnetic force on the wire?

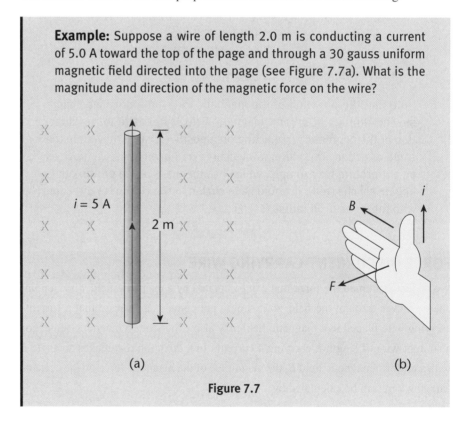

(a)

(b)

Figure 7.7

Solution: Since 1 T = 10^4 gauss, 1 gauss = 10^{-4} T, 30 gauss = 30×10^{-4} T = 3×10^{-3} T. The wire is conducting current toward the top of the page, and the magnetic field points into the page; therefore, the current is perpendicular to B. The angle between them is $\theta = 90°$, and since sin 90° = 1, the magnetic force on the wire is

$$F = iLB \sin \theta = iLB$$
$$= 5.0(2.0)(3.0 \times 10^{-3})$$
$$= 3.0 \times 10^{-2} \text{ N} = 0.03 \text{ N}$$

By holding the thumb of the right hand so that it is directed toward the top of the page, then holding the remaining fingers towards (into) the page, the palm of the right hand points to the left. Hence, the force on the wire is to the left.

MCAT Concept Check 7.2

Before moving on, ensure that you are able to:

✓ Identify the direction of force on a moving charge or current-carrying wire in a magnetic field

✓ Calculate the force on a moving charge or current-carrying wire in a magnetic field

Conclusion

This chapter continued our investigation and review of charge that began in Chapter 6, Electrostatics. Here, we discussed the magnetic field created by moving charge(s) and magnets and the forces that are exerted by magnetic fields when charges move through them. We reviewed the different types of magnet materials: diamagnetic, paramagnetic, and ferromagnetic. We also demonstrated the use of the various equations for calculating the strength of magnetic fields at different distances from a straight, current-carrrying wire and at the center of a circular loop of current-carrying wire, as well as two equations for calculating the magnitude of force acting on either a point charge moving through a magnetic field or a current-carrying wire placed in a magnetic field.

CONCEPT SUMMARY

Sources of Magnetic Field

☐ **Magnetic fields** (p. 198) are created by magnets and moving charges

☐ The SI unit for the magnetic field is the **tesla (T)** (p. 198) (1 T = 1 N·s/m·C)

☐ **Diamagnetic materials** (p. 198) are weakly antimagnetic materials in which all electrons are paired

☐ **Paramagnetic materials** (p. 198) possess some unpaired electrons and become weakly magnetic in an external magnetic field

☐ **Ferromagnetic materials** (p. 198) possess some unpaired electrons with atoms organized in magnetic domains; the materials are strongly magnetic

☐ **Straight current-carrying wires** (p. 201) create magnetic fields that are perpendicular concentric circles surrounding the wire

☐ **Circular loops of current-carrying wire** (p. 202) create magnetic fields that are perpendicular concentric circles surrounding the wire

The Magnetic Field Force (p. 203)

☐ External magnetic fields exert forces on charges only if they are moving with a velocity that has a component that is not parallel or antiparallel to the magnetic field vector

☐ Point charges moving into a magnetic field perpendicular to the magnetic field vector will assume uniform circular motion for which the centripetal force is the magnetic force acting on the point charge

☐ For a charge moving in uniform circular motion due to an external magnetic field, a change in strength of the external magnetic field will result in a change in the radius of the circular pathway of the charged particle but *not* in the magnitude of its velocity

☐ A current-carrying wire placed in an external magnetic field will experience a magnetic force as long as the current has a directional component that is not parallel or antiparallel to the magnetic field vector

☐ The direction of the magnetic force on a moving charge or current-carrying wire is determined using the right-hand rule

EQUATIONS TO REMEMBER

☐ $B = \dfrac{\mu_o i}{2\pi r}$ (for straight current-carrying wire)

☐ $B = \dfrac{\mu_o i}{2r}$ (for circular loop of current-carrying wire)

☐ $F = qvB \sin \theta$ (for point charge moving through magnetic field)

☐ $F = iLB \sin \theta$ (for current-carrying wire in magnetic field)

SHARED CONCEPTS

HIGH-YIELD PRACTICE PROBLEMS

Practice Questions

1. A moving negative charge placed in an external magnetic field circulates counterclockwise in the plane of the paper as shown. In which direction is the magnetic field pointing?

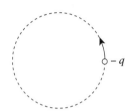

   A. Into the page
   B. Out of the page
   C. Toward the center of the circle
   D. Tangent to the circle

2. If, as in the accompanying figure, an electron is traveling straight out of the page crossing a magnetic field that is directed from left to right, in which direction will the electron be deflected?

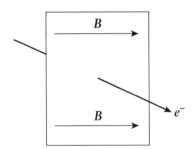

   A. Downward
   B. Upward
   C. To the right
   D. To the left

3. Which of the following is NOT a necessary condition for having a magnetic force on a particle?

   A. The particle must have a charge other than zero.
   B. The particle must move in a direction that is neither parallel nor antiparallel to the direction of the magnetic field.
   C. There must be a current.
   D. The particle must have a certain length.

4. If the magnetic field a distance r away from a current carrying wire is 10 T, what will be the total magnetic field at r if another wire is placed a distance $2r$ from the original wire and has a current twice as strong flowing in the opposite direction? The magnetic field generated by a current carrying wire is $B = \dfrac{\mu_0 i}{2\pi r}$.

   A. 0 T
   B. 15 T
   C. 20 T
   D. 30 T

5. A long, straight wire carries a current of 5×10^{-4} A as shown in the figure. A charged particle moving parallel to the wire experiences a force of 1×10^{-6} N at point P. Assuming the particle maintains the same charge and same velocity, what is the magnetic force on the particle at point R and at point S?

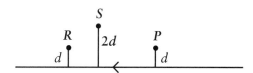

A. $F_R = 1 \times 10^{-6}$ N; $F_S = 5 \times 10^{-7}$ N
B. $F_R = 0.5 \times 10^{-6}$ N; $F_S = 0.5 \times 10^{-6}$ N
C. $F_R = 1 \times 10^{-6}$ N; $F_S = 5 \times 10^{-6}$ N
D. $F_R = 1 \times 10^{-6}$ N; $F_S = 1 \times 10^{-6}$ N

6. A positively charged particle enters a region with a uniform electric field, as shown, and is initially moving perpendicular to the field. In what direction must a uniform magnetic field be oriented so that the net force on the particle is zero (assuming that the strength of the magnetic field can be appropriately adjusted)?

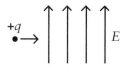

A. Into the page
B. Out of the page
C. Top of the page
D. Bottom of the page

7. A circular loop of wire of radius 20 cm carries a current of 5 A. A positively charged particle with velocity perpendicular to the plane of the loop passes directly through the center of the loop. What is the force on the charged particle the instant it passes through the center? (The magnetic field at the center of a circular loop is $B = \dfrac{\mu_0 I}{2r}$ and $\mu_o = 4\pi \times 10^{-7}$ T·m/A.)

A. 0 N
B. π N
C. $\pi \times 10^{-6}$ N
D. $0.5\pi \times 10^{-5}$ N

8. A certain urban hospital wants to expand its radio-oncology department and will need a source of short-lived radioisotopes. A 6.5 MeV proton cyclotron is to be built, but it must fit into an existing 10 m × 10 m room in the basement of the hospital. Assuming that the maximum magnetic field attainable is 1 T, can the hospital go ahead with its plans? (The mass of a proton is 1.67×10^{-27} kg, and the charge of a proton is $+1.6 \times 10^{-19}$ C.)

A. Yes, because the magnetic field needed is smaller than the maximum magnetic field attainable.
B. No, because the cyclotron would be too big for the room in the basement.
C. It depends on the number of short-lived radioisotopes needed.
D. The answer cannot be determined.

9. Two positive charges are traveling in opposite directions parallel to the uniform magnetic field. It can be inferred that the magnetic force on both charges

A. is equal in magnitude and opposite in direction.
B. has the same direction but different magnitudes.
C. is zero.
D. is different in both magnitude and direction.

10. A negatively charged particle of 2 C and 0.005 g is spinning in a uniform magnetic field along the circle with a radius of 8 cm. Knowing that the strength of the magnetic field is 5 T, calculate the speed of the particle.

A. 1.3×10^{-2} m/s
B. 160 m/s
C. 1.6×10^{5} m/s
D. 1.3×10^{-5} m/s

11. A power cable, stretched 8 m above the ground, is carrying 50 A of current. Determine the magnetic field produced by the current at the ground level under the wire if μ_o, the permeability of free space, is 1.26×10^{-6} T·m/A.

A. 1.26×10^{-6} T
B. 4.5×10^{-6} T
C. 33×10^{-6} T
D. 0.5×10^{-6} T

12. A researcher is interested in creating a particle accelerator that can spin particles in the uniform magnetic field at the highest possible speed. This can be achieved by all of the following EXCEPT

A. increasing magnetic field strength.
B. increasing mass of the particles.
C. increasing orbital radius.
D. increasing charge of the particle.

13. A proton and an electron are traveling in the uniform magnetic field with identical velocities. If the movement of both particles is perpendicular to the magnetic field lines, which of the following is/are NOT true?

I. The acceleration of the proton is greater than that of the electron.

II. The proton will experience a greater kinetic energy change than the electron.

III. The magnetic force on both particles is zero.

A. III only
B. I and III only
C. II and III only
D. I, II, and III

14. A velocity filter detects particles of particular speed at the point when electric force $F = Eq$ and magnetic force $F = qvB$ produced by the filter are equal. It can be reasonably assumed that, in order to select a particle with a higher speed, one should increase

A. the electric field.
B. the charge of the particle.
C. the magnetic field.
D. both electric and magnetic fields.

Small Group Questions

1. Suppose a magnetic field is applied to a moving electron so that the electron travels in a circular path perpendicular to the magnetic field. As the strength of the magnetic field increases, would the radius of the electron's circular path increase, decrease, or stay the same?

2. While the Earth has a magnetic field detectable by a compass, some planets, like Venus, have almost no discernible magnetic field. Use your knowledge of the source of magnetic fields to deduce what factors might explain why Venus does not produce a magnetic field.

Explanations to Practice Questions

1. B

This problem is an application of the right-hand rule. The velocity vector v is always tangent to the circle. Because you are dealing with a negative charge, qv is also tangent to the circle but going clockwise the other way. The magnetic force is the centripetal force and points toward the center of the circle. Knowing the directions of qv and F, use the right-hand rule to find the direction of B. Pick a convenient point along the circular path. Using your right hand, put your thumb in the clockwise direction. Now the direction of B is unknown, but you know that F points toward the center of the circle. With your thumb pointing in the direction of qv and the palm facing the center of the circle, your remaining fingers should be pointing out of the page. Therefore, the direction of the magnetic field is out of the page. Choice (B) is the correct answer.

2. A

The problem asks only for the direction of deflection, so it will only be necessary to apply the right-hand rule to find the direction of the force. An electron travels straight out of the page, so v is out of the page and qv is into the page (the electron is negatively charged). Holding the thumb of the right hand into the page and the remaining fingers pointing toward the right, your palm, and therefore the force, points downward. The electron therefore will be deflected downward, just as (A) states.

3. D

Three main conditions must be satisfied in order for a magnetic force to be exerted on a particle in a magnetic field. The fastest way for determining these conditions is to look at the two formulas for the magnetic force:

$$F = qvB \sin \theta$$
$$F = iLB \sin \theta$$

where q is the charge of the particle, v is the velocity, B is the magnetic field, θ is the angle between v and B, i is the current, and L is the length of the wire through which current runs. The first formula describes the force on a particle, while the second formula describes the magnetic force on a current-carrying wire. Thus, we can infer that for F to exist, the particle must be charged; that is, it cannot be neutral. Cross out (A). Furthermore, the velocity cannot be zero; that is, the particle must be moving. The flow of charge is called electric current. Choice (C) is also out. Finally, for $\sin \theta$ to have a nonzero value, θ must be different from $180°, 360°$, or any multiple of these numbers; in other words, the direction of the velocity vector with respect to the magnetic field vector has to be other than parallel or antiparallel. Because (B) is a true statement, you are left with (D) as the correct answer. Indeed, the length L that we see in the second formula refers to the length of the current-carrying wire, not the length of the particle.

4. D

The safest way to answer this question is to quickly draw a diagram:

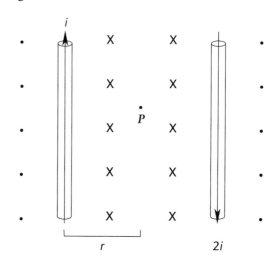

Notice right away that between the two wires, the direction of the magnetic field is the same, into the page. Therefore, since the vector direction is the same, we can just focus on the magnitude of the two magnetic fields. We know that $B_1 = 10$ T at a distance r. B_2 can be calculated using this formula:

$$B = \frac{\mu_o i}{2\pi r}$$

Given that the current in the second wire is twice as strong as the one in the first wire, at a distance r from each wire, B_2 is equal to

$$B_2 = \frac{\mu_o 2i}{2\pi r} = 2 \times B_1 = 20 \text{ T}$$

Thus, overall, the magnitude of the magnetic field at a distance r away from each wire is $10 \text{ T} + 20 \text{ T} = 30 \text{ T}$, making (D) the correct answer.

5. A

The magnetic force on a charge moving in the vicinity of the given wire is $F = qvB \sin \theta$, where B is given by the magnetic field of a long, straight wire and is equal to $B = \frac{\mu_o i}{2\pi r}$. Thus,

$$F = qv\left(\frac{\mu_o i}{2\pi r}\right)\sin \theta$$

In other words, F is inversely proportional to the distance between the charge and the wire. Because point R is the same distance from the wire as point P, the force at R is the same as at P. Point S is twice as far from the wire as point P, so the magnetic force at S will be half the force at P. Plugging in numbers, determine the following values for the force at R and S, respectively:

$$F_R = 1 \times 10^{-6} \text{ N}$$
$$F_S = 0.5 \times 10^{-6} \text{ N} = 5 \times 10^{-7} \text{ N}$$

Choice (A) matches our result and is thus the correct answer.

6. B

The electric field lines always point from positive to negative; in the diagram, the positive end is therefore on the bottom of the page, and the negative end is toward the top of the page, in the direction of the field lines. The positively charged particle will experience a force in the direction of the electric field, pushing it toward the top of the page (i.e., toward the negative end). Using the right-hand rule for magnetic forces on charged particles, you can see that a magnetic field coming out of the page will give a force toward the bottom of the page. Assuming that the strength of the magnetic field is appropriately set (the assumption stated in the question), the net force on the charged particle due to both the electric and magnetic fields will be zero. Thus, (B), out of the page, correctly describes the direction of the magnetic field.

7. A

The magnetic field at the center of the loop is directly perpendicular to the plane of the loop. Therefore, the particle's velocity is parallel to the magnetic field, which means that the field doesn't exert any force on the particle. Remember that $F = iLB \sin \theta$, and if the velocity (or current) is parallel ($\theta = 360°$) or antiparallel ($\theta = 180°$), $\sin \theta = 0$. Choice (A) is the correct answer.

8. A

The problem is asking whether the proposed cyclotron will fit in the room with the given dimensions. You could assume the maximum value of the magnetic field and then calculate the cyclotron orbit radius to see if it will fit in the room. Alternatively, you could assume that the protons in the cyclotron will orbit such that they are just contained by the room, then calculate the necessary field and see if it is feasible. Because the cost of providing a strong magnetic field is high, take the latter approach. For circular motion, the centripetal acceleration $a = \frac{v^2}{r}$. The centripetal force is the magnetic force $F = qvB$. From $F = ma$, we obtain the following:

$$F = ma = \frac{mv^2}{r} = qvB$$

Now solve for B:

$$B = \frac{mv}{qr}$$

Let the energy be denoted by E. $E = 6.5\,\text{MeV} = 6.5 \times 10^6\,\text{eV} = (6.5 \times 10^6)(1.6 \times 10^{-19}) \approx 1 \times 10^{-12}\,\text{J}$. We can find mv by using the definition of kinetic energy:

$$E = \frac{1}{2}mv^2$$

$$v^2 = \frac{2E}{m}$$

$$v = \sqrt{\frac{2E}{m}}$$

The orbit diameter must fit into the 10×10 m room, so the orbit radius must be about 5 m (actually less than this to allow room for the walls of the cyclotron and various wires, etc.). At any rate, combining the above expressions yields an upper limit to the required field:

$$B = \frac{mv}{qr}$$

$$B = \frac{m\sqrt{\frac{2E}{m}}}{qr} = \frac{\sqrt{2mE}}{qr}$$

$$B = \frac{\sqrt{2(1.67 \times 10^{-27})(1 \times 10^{-12})}}{(1.6 \times 10^{-19})(5)}$$

$$B \approx 0.08\,\text{T}$$

So if the maximum field needed is only 0.08 T and the materials are available to make a field up to 1 T, then clearly it will be possible to go ahead with the project. Choice (A) mirrors this decision and is thus the correct answer.

9.   C

The magnetic force experienced by both charges is zero, as one charge is traveling parallel and another charge antiparallel to the direction of magnetic field. That makes the angle between v and $B = 0°$. $\sin 0° = 0$; thus, $F = qvB \sin 0° = 0$.

10.   C

A charged particle moving perpendicular to the direction of a uniform magnetic field is rotating. A centripetal force associated with circular motion is the magnetic force

acting on the particle. Thus, $\frac{mv^2}{r} = qvB$. Eliminating v on both sides yields $\frac{mv}{r} = qB$, and from there, $v = \frac{qBr}{m}$. For the question, convert mass to kg ($0.005\,\text{g} = 5 \times 10^{-6}\,\text{kg}$) and circle radius to meters ($8\,\text{cm} = 8 \times 10^{-2}\,\text{m}$). Plugging the numbers into the equation, we have

$$v = \frac{(2)(5)(8 \times 10^{-2})}{5 \times 10^{-6}} = 1.6 \times 10^5\,\text{m/s·}$$

11.   A

The magnetic field produced by the current at particular distance from the wire can be calculated by applying the formula $B = \frac{\mu_0 i}{2\pi r}$, where μ_0 is the permeability of free space and r is a distance away from the wire, in this case 8 m. Plugging values into the formula, we can estimate our answer:

$$B = \frac{\mu_0 i}{2\pi r} = \frac{(1.26 \times 10^{-6})(50)}{(2\pi)(8)} = \frac{1.26 \times 10^{-6}}{\pi} \times \frac{50}{16}$$

$$\approx \frac{1 \times 10^{-6}}{3}(3) \approx 1 \times 10^{-6}$$

This matches most closely with (A).

12.   B

A charged particle moving perpendicular to the direction of a uniform magnetic field is rotating. A centripetal force associated with circular motion is the magnetic force acting on the particle. Thus, $\frac{mv^2}{r} = qvB$, and eliminating v on both sides, we have $\frac{mv}{r} = qB$. From there, you get $v = \frac{qBr}{m}$. From this formula, to obtain the highest value for v, the charge of the particle (D), the magnetic field strength (A), and orbital radius (C) can be increased, but increasing the mass of the particles (B) would decrease the speed of rotation.

13.   D

All of the statements are false. The magnetic force on both particles is not zero, as the particles move perpendicular to the magnetic field lines and not parallel (III). Acceleration of the proton would be less than that of an electron, as the net force $F = ma$ according to Newton's second law, and F_{net} is the same for both proton and electron. Thus, as the proton's mass is greater, its acceleration would be less (I). The magnetic force does not do work, so it cannot change the kinetic energy of either particle (II).

14. A

According to the question, particle speeds are detected when $F_{electric}$ equals $F_{magnetic}$ or $Eq = qvB$; from here, $v = \dfrac{E}{B}$. To increase the velocity of a charge, you would need to increase the electric field strength, (A), or decrease the magnetic field strength. As the particle charge, (B), is not in the equation, increasing it would not bring the result needed. Increasing both electric and magnetic fields, (D), would cause the effects to oppose each other, resulting in no change in velocity.

Explanations to Small Group Questions

1. The radius of the electron's circular path would decrease with increasing magnetic field strength. In other words, the electron will move in a smaller circle. Since $F = qvB$ (use $\sin 90° = 1$ because the magnetic field is perpendicular to the electron's velocity), the force due to the magnetic field, F, and the magnitude of the magnetic field, B, are directly proportional. Furthermore, the magnetic force is a centripetal force that causes the electron to move in a circular path. Thus F can also be defined using the centripetal force equation, $F = \dfrac{mv^2}{r}$ (see Chapter 2, Newtonian Mechanics), in which the force, F, and radius, r, are inversely proportional. Finally, we can equate the two expressions for F: $qvB = \dfrac{mv^2}{r}$; as B increases, r decreases.

2. A magnetic field is produced by moving charges. Therefore, Venus must lack either sufficient charged particles or sufficient movement to create a magnetic field. The Earth contains molten conducting material (liquid metal) beneath its surface. When the Earth rotates, electrons within the Earth flow around the Earth's core. This movement generates a magnetic field. Some scientists speculate that Venus may not contain conductive liquid, but presently we have only indirect evidence for the interior composition of Venus. Another possible reason is that Venus spins at a rate about 243 times slower than that of the Earth, so its particles may not move fast enough to generate a magnetic field.

8

DC and AC Circuits

In this Chapter:

Introduction

Batteries, electric circuits, and electrical equipment pervade our everyday world. Think of any piece of equipment, tool, or toy that has a battery or a power cord, and you've just identified an object whose very function depends on the movement of electrons and the delivery of electric potential energy. Turn on a light, ring a buzzer, or toast bread, and you are witnessing moving electrons at work (literally).

This chapter reviews the essentials of DC (direct current) circuits and briefly considers AC (alternating current) circuits. Within this broader coverage of circuits, we will review the many topics of circuit theory: emf, resistance, power, Kirchoff's laws, resistors, capacitors, and series and parallel arrangement of circuit components. As you encounter the lessons of this chapter and the equations associated with them, remember this: The MCAT approaches the topic of circuits with a greater emphasis on the concepts than on the math. You will be expected to calculate, say, the resultant resistance for resistors in series and/or parallel, but the circuits you encounter on Test Day will, on the whole, be simpler than what you may have seen in your college physics class.

8.1 Current ★★★★☆☆

Some materials allow free flow of electric charge within them; these materials are called **electrical conductors**. Metal atoms can easily lose one or more of their outer electrons, which are then free to move around in the metal, and this makes most

Bridge

A good thing about the divisions of science is that they are all related. This topic is a perfect bridge to General Chemistry. Remember that the metals on the periodic table are on the left side. These are the atoms that are the least electronegative; thus, it is easiest for these atoms to lose electrons. Due to this weak hold on their electrons, they are free to move around in the metal, conducting electrical charges.

metals good electrical conductors. In fact, in bulk metal, metallic bonding results from an equal division of the charge density of the "free" (conduction) electrons across all of the (neutral) atoms within the metallic mass. This is a correction of the earlier model of the "metallic bond," which posited a "sea of free electrons" flowing over and past a rigid lattice of metal cations.

Other materials hold on to electrons more tightly and severely hinder or retard the flow of electrons. These materials are called insulators. Most nonmetals are good insulators, and you are probably quite familiar with the insulating plastic or rubber tubing that surrounds most electrical wires. Glass, wood, air, and even distilled water are good insulators. (Although water has a reputation as a conductor with the ability to "short-circuit" electrical appliances, it is actually a good insulator as long as the water has no ions in it. Distilled water has a conductivity of almost zero.)

Chapter 7 introduced the concept of electric current: the flow of charge between two points at different electric potentials connected by a conductor (such as a copper wire). The magnitude of the current i is the amount of charge Δq passing through the conductor per unit time Δt, and it can be calculated by

$$i = \frac{\Delta q}{\Delta t}$$

The SI unit of current is the **ampere** (1 A = 1 coulomb/second). Charge is transmitted by a flow of electrons in a conductor, and because electrons are negatively charged, they move from a point of lower electric potential to a point of higher electric potential (and in doing so reduce their electrical potential energy). *By convention, however, the direction of current is the direction in which positive charge would flow from higher potential to lower potential. Thus, the direction of current is opposite to the direction of actual electron flow.* The two patterns of current flow are direct current (DC), in which the charge flows in one direction only, and alternating current (AC), in which the flow changes direction periodically. Direct current is produced by household batteries, while the current supplied over long distances to homes and other buildings is alternating current. Our discussion of circuits will presume direct current, which is tested on the MCAT much more often than alternating current.

A potential difference (voltage) can be produced by an electric generator, a voltaic (galvanic) cell, a group of cells wired into a battery, or even a potato! When no charge is moving between the two terminals of a cell that are at different potential values, the voltage is called the electromotive force (emf or ε). Do not be misled by this term; emf is *not* a force; it is a potential difference (voltage) and as such has units of joules per coulomb (1 V = 1 J/C). You may find it helpful to think of emf as a "pressure to move" that results in current, in much the same way that a pressure difference between two points in a fluid-filled tube causes the fluid to flow.

CIRCUIT LAWS

Circuits and currents are governed by the laws of conservation. Charge and energy must be fully accounted for at all times: They can be neither created nor destroyed. An electric circuit is a conducting path that usually has one or more voltage sources (such as a battery) connected to one or more passive circuit elements (such as resistors). Kirchhoff's laws are two rules that deal with the conservation of charge and energy within a circuit.

Kirchhoff's Junction Rule

At any point or junction in a circuit, the sum of currents directed into that point equals the sum of currents directed away from that point. This is an expression of conservation of electrical charge.

Example: Three wires (a, b, and c) meet at a junction point P, as in Figure 8.1. A current of 5 A flows into P along wire a, and a current of 3 A flows away from P along wire b. What is the magnitude and direction of the current along wire c?

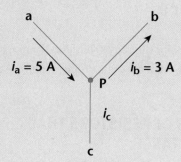

Figure 8.1

Solution: The sum of currents entering P must equal the sum of the currents leaving P. Assume for now that i_c flows out of P. If we find that it is negative, then we know that it flows into P.

$$i_a = i_b + i_c$$
$$i_c = 5 - 3$$
$$i_c = 2 \text{ A}$$

Thus a current of 2 A flows out of P along wire c. Note that the total current into and out of P is then zero.

Kirchhoff's Loop Rule

Around any closed circuit loop, the sum of voltage sources will always be equal to the sum of voltage (potential) drops. This is a consequence of the conservation of energy. All the electrical energy supplied by a source gets fully used up by the other elements of the circuit. No excess energy appears, and no energy

Real World

Once again, think of a river. There are a certain amount of water molecules in a river, and at any junction, that number has to go in one of the diverging directions; nothing magically appears or disappears. The same holds true for the amount of current at any junction.

disappears that can't be accounted for. Of course, energy can be changed from one form to another, so the kinetic energy of the electrons can be converted to heat or light (or sound, etc.) by the particular apparatus that is connected into the circuit. Remember that though Kirchhoff's loop rule is a consequence of the law of conservation of energy, this law is in terms of voltage (joules per coulomb), not just energy (joules).

MCAT Concept Check 8.1

Before moving on, ensure that you are able to:

✓ Summarize the theory behind conductivity

✓ List several common conductors and insulators

✓ Define current, voltage, and electromotive force (emf)

✓ Apply Kirchhoff's laws

8.2 Resistance   ★★★★★☆

Resistance is the opposition within any material to the movement and flow of charge. Electrical resistance can be thought of like friction, air resistance, or fluid resistance: Motion is being opposed.

CHARACTERISTICS OF RESISTORS THAT DETERMINE RESISTANCE

Materials that offer low resistance are called conductors, and those materials that offer very high resistance are called insulators. Conductive materials that offer amounts of resistance between these two extremes are called **resistors**. The resistance of a resistor is dependent upon certain characteristics of the resistor, which we will now examine.

Resistivity of the Conductive Material

Some materials are intrinsically better conductors of electricity than others. For example, copper conducts electricity better than plastic, which is why electrical cords have a copper core surrounded by a layer of plastic rather than the other way around. The number that characterizes the intrinsic resistance to current flow in a material is called the **resistivity** (ρ), for which the SI unit is the ohm-meter ($\Omega \cdot$m). Resistivity is the proportionality constant that relates a conductor's resistance (R) to the ratio of its cross-sectional area (A) to the length of the resistor (L). The equation for resistance is:

$$R = \frac{\rho L}{A}$$

Length

From the previous equation, you can see that the resistance of a conductor is directly proportional to the length of the resistor. A longer resistor means that electrons will have to travel a greater distance through a resistant material. For example, if we were to compare the resistances of two wires, identical in every way except for their length, the longer wire would offer the greater resistance to the current. This factor scales linearly: If the longer wire were twice the length of the shorter wire, it would have twice the resistance of the shorter wire.

Cross-Sectional Area

The equation for resistance also shows you that there is an inversely proportional relationship between resistance and the cross-sectional area of the resistor. The basis for the decrease in resistance as cross-sectional area increases is the increased number of pathways, called conduction paths, that are available to the moving electrons. For example, if we were to compare the resistances of two wires, identical in every way except for their cross-sectional area, the thicker wire would offer the lesser amount of resistance to the current. This is also a linear relationship, albeit an inverse one: If the thicker wire had twice the cross-sectional area of the thinner wire, it would have half the resistance of the thinner wire.

Temperature

Although not evident from the resistance equation, most conductors have greater resistance at higher temperatures. This is due to increased thermal oscillation of the atoms in the conductive material, which produces a greater resistance to electron flow. Because temperature is an intrinsic quality of all matter, you can think of the resistivity as a function of temperature. A few materials do not follow this general rule, including glass, pure silicon, and most semiconductors.

If you're having trouble remembering the major factors that contribute to resistance, it may help to imagine electrons moving through a wire as cars driving down a highway. For cars on a highway, a road made of gravel (representing high ρ) will impede the flow of traffic more than a smooth road (representing low ρ); a multi-lane highway (representing large A) will allow for an easier flow of traffic than a single-lane highway (representing small A); and any impediments to traffic flow will accumulate more on a longer road (one with large L) than on a shorter road (one with small L).

OHM'S LAW

Associated with electrical resistance is an energy loss that results in a drop in electric potential. The voltage drop between any two points in a circuit can be calculated according to **Ohm's law**:

$$V = iR$$

where V is the voltage drop, i is the current, and R is the magnitude of the resistance, measured in the SI unit of resistance, the **ohm** (Ω). Ohm's law is the basic law of

---

MCAT Expertise

It is always good practice to derive the units of a term from the equation for it. If you were to solve for resistivity (ρ) in the above resistance equation, you'd end up with $(AR)/L$. Because A is in meters squared and L is in meters, it simplifies to just meters times ohms, which are the units for resistivity. This is a trick that can often help solve a problem on the MCAT without having to jump into the math.

Real World

Returning to the example of a river, the wider the river, the more current that can flow through. The same holds true for a wire: The bigger the cross-sectional area, the more current that can flow through. Note, however, that electric current does *not* follow the continuity principle that applies to incompressible fluids ($A_1v_1 = A_2v_2$). Smaller cross-sectional area does not increase the velocity of electrons through a wire in this way—higher resistance does speed electrons up, but this relationship is not linear, and its nature is far outside the scope of the MCAT.

Key Equation

$V = iR$
$V = (A)(\Omega)$
$J/C = (C/s)(J \cdot s/C^2) = J/C$
Use this equation to determine the drop in electric potential across a resistor.

electricity. It states that for a given magnitude of resistance, the voltage drop across the resistor will be proportional to the magnitude of the current. Likewise, for a given resistance, the magnitude of the current will be proportional to the magnitude of the emf (voltage) impressed upon the circuit. The equation applies to a single resistor within a circuit, to any part of a circuit, or to an entire circuit (provided you correctly calculate the resultant resistance from resistors connected in series and/or parallel). As current moves through a set of resistors in a circuit, the voltage changes, dropping some amount as the current encounters each resister in succession; the current (or sum of currents for a divided circuit) is constant. No charge is gained or lost through resistors. If resistors are connected single-file (that is, in series), all current must pass through each resistor.

Conductive materials, such as copper wires, act as weak resistors themselves, offering some magnitude of resistance to current and causing a drop in electric potential (voltage). Even the very source(s) of emf, such as batteries, have some measurable but small amount of internal resistance r_{int}. As a result of this small internal resistance, the voltage supplied to a circuit is reduced by an amount equal to ir_{int}. Thus, the actual voltage supplied by a cell to a circuit is calculated as follows:

$$V = \varepsilon_{cell} - ir_{int}$$

Of course, if the cell is not actually driving any current (e.g., when a switch is in the open position), then the internal resistance is zero, and the emf of the cell is the voltage. For cases when the current is not zero and the internal resistance is not negligible, then voltage will be less than emf ($V < \varepsilon$).

When a cell is discharging, it supplies current, and the current flows from the positive, higher voltage end of the cell to the negative, lower voltage end. (Remember that current, by convention, is the movement of positive charge. Negatively-charged electrons are the particles that are actually in motion, so they flow in the direction opposite to current.) Certain types of cells (called secondary batteries) can be recharged. You'll find one in your cell phone. When these batteries are being recharged, an external voltage is applied in such a way to drive current toward the positive end of the secondary battery. Think about your cell phone battery: When it "dies," you don't just toss it out; you plug your phone into the wall outlet to recharge it.

MEASURING POWER OF RESISTORS

In Chapter 3, we briefly mentioned that power is the rate at which energy is transferred or transformed. Power is measured as the ratio of energy to time and can be expressed as follows:

$$P = \frac{E}{\Delta t}$$

In electric circuits, energy is supplied by the cell that houses a spontaneous redox reaction, which when "allowed" to proceed (by the closing of a switch, for example), generates a

---

MCAT Expertise

Most batteries on the MCAT will be considered "perfect batteries," and you will not have to accommodate their internal resistances.

Key Equation

$V = \varepsilon_{cell} - ir_{int}$
$V = V - (A)(\Omega)$
$V = V$
Use this equation to determine the actual voltage supplied by a cell to a circuit.

Real World

Superconductors, a special class of materials, are the one major exception to the rules of internal resistance and resistive conductors. When these elements and compounds are cooled to very low temperatures (usually well below 100 K, but the exact threshold varies by material), the resistivity of the material (ρ) completely dissipates, dropping to zero. Because these materials break a generally applicable law of physics, superconductors have many interesting and spectacular applications.

flow of electrons. These electrons, which have electric potential energy, convert that energy into kinetic energy (the energy of their motion), "motivated" as they are by the emf of the cell. Think of emf as a pressure to move, exerted by the cell on the electrons. Current delivers energy to the various resistors, which convert this energy to heat or some other form, depending on the particular configuration of the resistor. All electric appliances work in this way, but one particularly recognizable example of resistors at work is the coils inside a toaster. The coils turn red-hot when the toaster is powered on, which is a direct consequence of the resistance that the coils pose to the current running through them.

The rate at which energy is dissipated by a resistor is the **power** of the resistor and is calculated as

$$P = iV$$

where i is the current through the resistor and V is the voltage drop across the resistor. Using Ohm's law ($V = iR$), the power expression can also be written as

$$P = i^2R = \frac{V^2}{R}$$

These equations for calculating the power of a resistor or collection of resistors are extremely helpful for the MCAT. Commit them to your memory—and more importantly, to your understanding—and your efforts will be rewarded (in the form of points) on Test Day!

RESISTORS IN SERIES

Resistors can be connected into a circuit in one of two ways: either in series, in which all current must pass sequentially through each resistor connected in a linear arrangement, or in parallel, in which the current will divide to pass through resistors connected in parallel arrangement. For resistors connected in **series**, the current has no "choice" but to travel through each resistor in order to return to the cell. As the electrons flow through each resistor, energy is dissipated, and there is a voltage drop. The voltage drops are additive; that is, for a series of resistors, R_1, R_2, R_3...R_n (see Figure 8.2), the total voltage drop will be

$$V_s = V_1 + V_2 + V_3 + \cdots + V_n$$

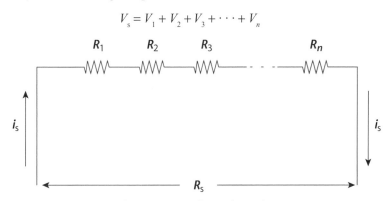

Figure 8.2. Resistors in Series
R_s increases as more resistors are added

Key Concept

A good relationship to distinguish in these equations is that $P = i^2R$ solves for power *lost* during transmission. A good way to understand this relationship is to understand how power companies send electricity down power lines. Because power equals voltage times current, they can manipulate these two values while keeping power constant. One option is to increase current, which results in a decrease in voltage. The other option would be to increase voltage, thus decreasing the current. If you think of actual power lines, remember that they are known as *high-voltage* lines. The reason power companies use high-voltage lines is to keep the current smaller. Because the amount of power *lost* in the line is $P = i^2R$, with current is squared in this relationship, having a large current exponentially increases the amount of power lost.

Key Equation

$P = iV = i^2R = \dfrac{V^2}{R}$

$J/s = (C/s)(J/C) = (C/s)^2(J \cdot s/C^2) = (J/C)^2/(J \cdot s/C^2)$

Use this equation to determine the power dissipated by a given resistor.

Key Concept

When there is only one path for the current to take, the current will be the same at every point in the line, including through every resistor. Once you know the current of the full circuit, you can use $V = iR$ to solve for the voltage drop across each resistor (assuming you know the resistances of the resistors).

Example: A circuit is wired with one cell supplying 5 V (neglect the internal resistance of the cell) in series together with three resistors of 3 Ω, 5 Ω, and 7 Ω, also wired in series as shown in Figure 8.3. What is the resulting voltage across and current through each resistor of this circuit, as well as the entire circuit?

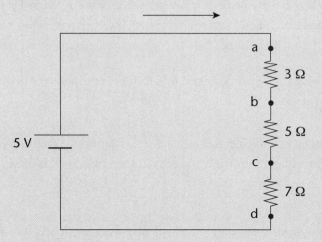

Figure 8.3

Solution: The total resistance of the resistors is

$$R_s = R_1 + R_2 + R_3$$
$$= 3 + 5 + 7$$
$$= 15 \, \Omega$$

Now use Ohm's law to get the current through the entire circuit (because everything is in series, this is also the current through each element):

$$i_s = \frac{V_s}{R_s} = \frac{5}{15} = \frac{1}{3} A$$

Now use Ohm's law for each of the resistors in turn. From a to b, the voltage drop across R_1 is

$$iR_1 = (1/3)(3)$$
$$= 1.0 \, V$$

From b to c, the voltage drop across R_2 is

$$iR_2 = (1/3)(5)$$
$$= 1.67 \, V$$

From c to d, the voltage drop across R_3 is

$$iR_3 = (1/3)(7)$$
$$= 2.33 \, V$$

Because $V = iR$, we can also see that the resistances of resistors in series are additive, such that

$$R_s = R_1 + R_2 + R_3 + \cdots + R_n$$

The set of resistors wired in series can be treated as a single resistor whose resistance is equal to the sum of the individual resistances ($R_1, R_2, \ldots, R_n$). This single, end-result resistor (R_s) is called a resultant resistor.

RESISTORS IN PARALLEL

When resistors are connected in **parallel,** they are wired with a common high-potential terminal and a common low-potential terminal (see Figure 8.4). This configuration allows charge to follow different, parallel paths between the high-potential terminal and the low-potential terminal. In this arrangement, electrons have a "choice" regarding which path they will take: Some will choose one pathway, while others will choose a different pathway. No matter which path is taken, however, the voltage drop experienced by each division of current is the same, because all pathways originate from a common point and end at a common point within the circuit. This is analogous to a river that splits into multiple streams before plunging over different waterfalls. If all the water starts at some common height and ends at a lower common height, then it doesn't matter how many "steps" the water fell over to get to the bottom of the falls: The change in gravitational potential energy for each individual stream will be the same as long as the total height displacement is the same for each individual waterfall. In circuits with parallel arrangements of resistors, this is expressed mathematically as follows:

$$V_p = V_1 = V_2 = V_3 = \cdots = V_n$$

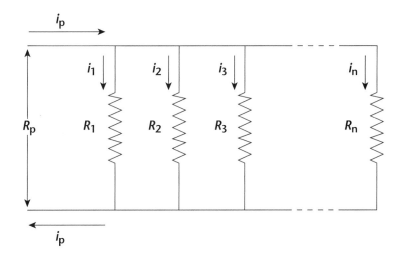

Figure 8.4. Resistors in Parallel
R_p decreases as more resistors are added

Key Equations

$V_s = V_1 + V_2 + V_3 + \cdots + V_n$
$V = V$
Use this equation to determine the total voltage drop across multiple resistors in series.
$R_s = R_1 + R_2 + R_3 + \cdots + R_n$
$\Omega = \Omega$
Use this equation to determine the resultant resistance of multiple resistors in series.

Key Concept

When resistors are in series, the current *must* pass through every resistor; this is why you find the total resistance by adding together every resistor.

Key Concept

Remember Kirchhoff's loop rule: If every resistor is in parallel, then the voltage drop across each pathway must be the voltage of the entire circuit.

Key Equations

$$V_p = V_1 = V_2 = V_3 = \ldots = V_n$$
$$V = V$$

Use this equation to determine the total voltage drop across multiple resistors in parallel.

$$\frac{1}{R_p} = \frac{1}{R_1} + \frac{1}{R_2} + \frac{1}{R_3} + \ldots + \frac{1}{R_n}$$

$$\Omega^{-1} = \Omega^{-1}$$

Use this equation to determine the resultant resistance of multiple resistors in parallel.

MCAT Expertise

These equations regarding current in the various branches of a parallel circuit do not need to be memorized in their own right. They are just algebraic reorganizations of Ohm's Law ($V = iR$), applied to resistors in parallel.

Nevertheless, the parallel pathways may differ in the amount of resistance that each offers to the flow of the electrons if the resistor(s) in each branch of the circuit have different values or add up to different values. In this case, electrons embody an old adage you may know: They prefer the path of least resistance. We will see, from the following equations, that there is an inverse relationship between the magnitude of the divided current that travels through a particular pathway and the resistance offered by that pathway.

The resistance equation previously discussed shows us that there is an inverse relationship between the cross-sectional area of a resistor and the resistance magnitude of that resistor. Like opening up rush-hour lanes on a highway to reduce traffic congestion, the configuration of resistors in parallel allows for a greater total number of conduction paths, and the effect of connecting resistors in parallel is a reduction in the resultant resistance. In effect, we could replace all resistors in parallel with a single resistor whose resistance is less than the resistance of the smallest resistor (in the circuit), and the circuit as a whole would move the same amount of current. The resultant resistance of resistors in parallel is calculated by

$$\frac{1}{R_p} = \frac{1}{R_1} + \frac{1}{R_2} + \frac{1}{R_3} + \ldots + \frac{1}{R_n}$$

Because the voltage drop across any one circuit branch must be same as the voltage drops across each of the other parallel branches, applying Ohm's law to each branch, we can see that the magnitude of the current in each branch will be inversely proportional to the resistance offered by each branch. So if a circuit divides into two branches and one branch has twice the resistance of the other, the one with twice the resistance will have half the magnitude of current in the lower-resistance division. The sum of the currents going into each division, according to Kirchhoff's junction rule, must equal the total current going into the point at which the current divides, such that

$$i_{tot} = i_1 + i_2 + i_3 + \cdots + i_n \quad \text{and} \quad i_1 = \frac{V_p}{R_1}, i_2 = \frac{V_p}{R_2}, i_3 = \frac{V_p}{R_3}, \text{etc.}$$

Example: Consider two equal resistors wired in parallel. What is the equivalent resistance of the two?

Solution: The equation for summing resistors in parallel is

$$\frac{1}{R_p} = \frac{1}{R_1} + \frac{1}{R_2}$$

Find the common denominator of the right side and take the inverse to find

$$R_p = \frac{R_1 R_2}{R_1 + R_2}$$

Since $R_1 = R_2$ in this special case, let $R = R_1 = R_2$:

$$R_p = \frac{R^2}{2R} = \frac{R}{2}$$

In the example above, we can see that the total resistance is halved by wiring two identical resistors in parallel. More generally, when n identical resistors are wired in parallel, the total resistance is given by $\frac{R}{n}$. Note that the voltage across each of the parallel resistors is equal and that, for equal resistances, the current flowing through each of the resistors is also equal (a current of $\frac{i_{tot}}{n}$ runs through each).

MCAT Expertise

Whenever approaching circuit problems, the first things you need to find are the total values: the total voltage (almost always given as the voltage of the battery), the total resistance, and the total current. To find the total current, first find the total resistance of the circuit.

Example: Consider two resistors wired in parallel with $R_1 = 5 \ \Omega$ and $R_2 = 10 \ \Omega$. If the voltage across them is 10 V, what is the current through each of the two resistors?

Solution: First, the current flowing through the whole circuit must be found. To do this, the combined resistance must be determined:

$$\frac{1}{R_p} = \frac{1}{R_1} + \frac{1}{R_2}$$

$$= \frac{1}{10} + \frac{1}{5}$$

$$= \frac{3}{10}$$

$$R_p = \frac{10}{3} \ \Omega$$

Using Ohm's law to calculate the current flowing through the circuit gives

$$i_p = \frac{V_p}{R_p}$$

$$= \frac{10}{(10/3)}$$

$$= 3 \ A$$

Three amps flow through the combination R_1 and R_2. Since the resistors are in parallel, $V_p = V_1 = V_2 = 10$ V. Apply Ohm's law to each resistor individually:

$$i_1 = \frac{V_p}{R_1} = \frac{10}{5} = 2 \ A$$

$$i_2 = \frac{V_p}{R_2} = \frac{10}{10} = 1 \ A$$

As a check, note that $i_p = 3 \ A = i_1 + i_2 = 2 + 1 = 3 \ A$. More current flows through the smaller resistance. In particular, note that R_1, with half the resistance of R_2, has twice the current. Once i_p was found to be 3 A, the problem could have been solved by noting that because R_1 is half of R_2, $i_1 = 2i_2$, and $i_1 + i_2 = 3$ A.

MCAT Concept Check 8.2

Before moving on, ensure that you are able to:

✓ Compare resistors across different resistivities, lengths, and cross-sectional areas

✓ Recall and apply Ohm's law to multiple situations

✓ Explain and apply the concept of a battery's internal resistance

✓ Determine the power dissipated over each resistor in a circuit

✓ Calculate the resultant resistance for circuits with resistors arranged in series or in parallel

---

8.3 Capacitance and Capacitors ★★★★★☆

Aside from resistors and batteries, the last major circuit element tested on the MCAT is the capacitor. Capacitors have a more complicated function than resistors (and formulas that are somewhat less intuitive), but just as the hot coils of a toaster can help illustrate the principles of resistance, so there are excellent real-world examples of capacitance as well. Perhaps the most commonly known capacitor in popular culture is a defibrillator, used on heart attack patients in hospital dramas and real-life emergency rooms alike. While a defibrillator is charging, a high-pitched electronic tone sounds as electrons build up on one plate of the capacitor. When the defibrillator is fully charged, that charge can be released in one surge of power (after the operator yells "Clear!"). The clouds and the ground during a lightning storm also act as a capacitor, with the charge that builds up between them eventually discharging as a bolt of lightning. Even batteries function as a form of capacitor, but with the ability to hold charge for longer periods and release it more slowly. The MCAT focuses on a particular type of capacitor called a parallel plate capacitor, and all of our discussion will be regarding capacitors of this type.

PARALLEL PLATE CAPACITORS

When two electrically neutral metal plates are connected to a voltage source, positive charge builds up on the plate connected to the positive (higher voltage) terminal, and negative charge builds up on the plate connected to the negative (lower voltage) terminal. The two-plate system stores charge at a particular voltage and is called a **capacitor**. Charge will collect on the plates of a capacitor anytime there is a potential difference between the plates. The capacitance C of a capacitor is defined as the ratio of the magnitude of the charge stored on one plate (taking the absolute value of the charge) to the total potential difference, voltage, across the capacitor (that is, between the two plates of a parallel plate capacitor). Therefore, if a voltage difference

V is applied across the plates of a capacitor and a charge Q collects on it (with $+Q$ on the positive plate and $-Q$ on the negative plate), then the **capacitance** is given by

$$C = \frac{Q}{V}$$

The SI unit for capacitance is the farad (1 F = 1 coulomb/volt). Because one coulomb is such a large quantity of charge, one farad is a very large capacitance. Capacitances are usually given in submultiples of the farad, such as microfarads (1 μF = 1×10^{-6} F) or picofarads (1 pF = 1×10^{-12} F). Be careful not to confuse the farad with the Faraday constant, which is the amount of charge equal to the charge on a mole of electrons (96,485 coulombs/mole e^-).

The capacitance of a parallel plate capacitor is dependent upon the geometry of the two conduction surfaces. For the simple case of the parallel plate capacitor, the capacitance is given by

$$C = \varepsilon_{o} \left(\frac{A}{d} \right)$$

where ε_{o} is the permittivity of free space (8.85×10^{-12} F/m), A is the area of overlap of the two plates, and d is the separation of the two plates. The separation of charges sets up an electric field between the plates of a parallel plate capacitor. The electric field between the plates of a parallel plate capacitor is a uniform field (parallel field vectors) whose magnitude at any point can be calculated as

$$E = \frac{V}{d}$$

The direction of the electric field at any point between the plates is away from the positive plate and toward the negative plate. If we imagine placing a positively charged particle between the oppositely charged plates, we would expect the particle to accelerate in the direction from the positively charged plate toward the negatively charged plate. This ought not to surprise us, given our understanding of the nature of interaction between like and unlike charges.

Regardless of the particular geometry of a capacitor (parallel plate or otherwise), the function of a capacitor is to store an amount of energy in the form of charge separation at a particular voltage. This is akin to the function of a dam whose purpose is to store gravitational potential energy by holding back a mass of water at a given height. The potential energy stored in a capacitor is

$$U = \frac{1}{2}CV^2$$

DIELECTRIC MATERIALS

The term **dielectric material** is just another way of saying *insulation*. When an insulating material, such as air, glass, plastic, ceramic, or certain metal oxides, is placed between the

Key Concept

If you look back to the equations discussed at the end of the last chapter, you can see that the equation for E here can be derived from the four fundamental electrostatics equations. The only difference between V and E is that E has radius (or distance) squared in the denominator. You can derive E from V by simply dividing V by distance, making the distance in the denominator squared.

Key Equations

$C = \dfrac{Q}{V}$

$F = C/V = \dfrac{C}{V}$

Use this equation to determine the capacitance of a capacitor.

$C = \varepsilon_{o} \left(\dfrac{A}{d} \right)$

$F = (F/m) \left(\dfrac{m^2}{m} \right)$

$F = F$

Use this equation to determine the capacitance of a parallel plate capacitor.

$E = \dfrac{V}{d}$

$N/C = \dfrac{V}{m} = \dfrac{N \cdot m/C}{m}$

$N/C = N/C$

Use this equation to determine the electric field at a point in space between the plates of a parallel plate capacitor.

$U = \dfrac{1}{2}CV^2$

$J = (F)(V)^2 = \left(\dfrac{C}{V} \right) \left(\dfrac{J}{C} \right)^2 = \left(\dfrac{C}{J/C} \right) \left(\dfrac{J^2}{C^2} \right)$

$J = J$

Use this equation to determine the potential energy stored in a capacitor.

plates of a charged capacitor, the voltage across the capacitor decreases. This is the result of the dielectric material "shielding" the opposite charges from each other. Because they feel each other less, the voltage (energy per coulomb) across the capacitor decreases. By lowering the voltage across a charged capacitor, the dielectric has in effect "made room" for more charge, and the capacitance of the capacitor increases by a factor equal to a dimensionless number called the **dielectric constant K**, which is a measure of the insulating capability of a particular dielectric material. For your reference (but not necessary to memorize for the MCAT), the dielectric constant for air is about 1, for glass is 4.7, and for rubber is 7. The increase in capacitance due to a dielectric material is

$$C' = KC$$

where C' is the new capacitance with the dielectric and C is the original capacitance.

All the stored charge (stored energy) on a capacitor won't do any good unless it is allowed to discharge. The charge will be "released" from its holding plates either by discharging across the plates or through some conductive material with which the plates are in contact. For example, capacitors can discharge into wires, causing a current to pass through the wires in much the same way that batteries cause current to move through a circuit. The paddles of the defibrillator machine, once charged, are placed on either side of a heart that has gone into a life-threatening abnormal rhythm (such as ventricular tachycardia). The reason the doctor yells "Clear!" before discharging the paddles is because the current needs to travel through the patient's heart, not through any other people who might be touching the patient. And on a much larger scale, lightning occurs when a very, very large amount of charge exceeds the capacitance of the Earth's surface and underside of the cloud (the two serving, approximately, as a parallel plate capacitor).

> **Key Concept**
>
> A dielectric material can never decrease the capacitance; thus K can never be less than 1.

> **Key Equation**
>
> $C' = KC$
> F = (dimensionless)(F)
> Use this equation to determine the increase in capacitance due to a dielectric material.

Example: The voltage across the terminals of an isolated 3 μF capacitor is 4 V. If a piece of ceramic having dielectric constant $K = 2$ is placed between the plates, find

    a. the new charge on the capacitor.
    b. the new capacitance of the capacitor.
    c. the new voltage across the capacitor.

Solution:

a. The introduction of a dielectric by itself has no effect on the charge stored on the isolated capacitor. There is no new charge, so the charge is the same as before. The charge stored is therefore given by

$$\begin{aligned} Q' &= Q \\ &= CV \\ &= (3 \times 10^{-6})(4) \\ &= 12 \times 10^{-6} \text{ C} \\ &= 12 \text{ μC} \end{aligned}$$

b. By introducing a dielectric with a value of 2, the capacitance of the capacitor is doubled ($C' = KC$). Hence, the new capacitance is 6 µF.

c. Using the relationship $V' = Q'/C'$, the new voltage across the capacitor may be determined. Putting numbers into the equation gives

$$V' = \frac{12 \times 10^{-6}}{6 \times 10^{-6}}$$

$$= 2\,V$$

Example: The voltage across the terminals of a 3 µF capacitor is 4 V. Now suppose a piece of ceramic having dielectric constant $K = 2$ is placed between the plates **and the voltage is held constant** (e.g., by a battery). What is the new charge on the capacitor?

Solution: With the introduction of the dielectric ceramic, the capacitance of the capacitor has been altered. But because the voltage was held constant, the charge on the capacitor plates must have been altered. From the definition of dielectric constant and the above example, it is clear that the new capacitance is

$$C' = KC$$

$$= 6\,µF$$

But the new voltage is still 4 V, so the new charge must be

$$Q' = C'V'$$

$$= (6 \times 10^{-6})(4)$$

$$= 24 \times 10^{-6}\,C$$

$$= 24\,µC$$

Because the original charge was $Q = CV = (3 \times 10^{-6})(4) = 12$ µC, by keeping the voltage constant, the battery had to supply an additional +12 µC of charge to the positive plate and 12 µC to the negative plate.

CAPACITORS IN SERIES

When capacitors are connected in **series,** the total capacitance decreases in similar fashion to the decrease in resistance for resistors in parallel (see Figure 8.5). This may not be as conceptually clear as in the case of parallel resistors, so rather than memorizing the following equations independently, we recommend that you understand the conceptual basis for the mathematics of resistors (in parallel and in series) and then simply reverse that mathematical approach for capacitors (e.g., treat capacitors in series in the same manner that you approach resistors in parallel). The equation for calculating the resultant capacitance for capacitors in series, such as those in Figure 8.5, is

$$\frac{1}{C_s} = \frac{1}{C_1} + \frac{1}{C_2} + \frac{1}{C_3} + \ldots + \frac{1}{C_n}$$

For capacitors in series, the total voltage is the sum of the individual voltages, such that

$$V_s = V_1 + V_2 + V_3 + \ldots + V_n$$

This rule for voltage is similar to that for resistors in series.

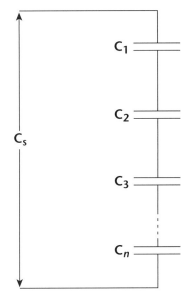

Figure 8.5. Capacitors in Series
C_s decreases as more capacitors are added

CAPACITORS IN PARALLEL

Capacitors wired in parallel produce a resultant capacitance that is equal to the sum of the individual capacitances (see Figure 8.6). It is as if all the capacitors in parallel can be replaced by a single resultant capacitor whose capacitance is equal to the sum of all the capacitances.

$$C_p = C_1 + C_2 + C_3 + \ldots + C_n$$

Because the wire from one capacitor to the next is a conductor and equipotential surface, the potential of all the plates on one side are the same. Just as we saw with resistors in parallel, the voltage across each parallel capacitor is the same and is equal to the voltage across the entire combination.

$$V_p = V_1 = V_2 = V_3 = \ldots = V_n$$

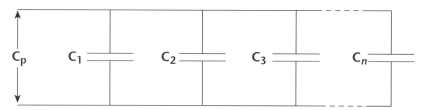

Figure 8.6. Capacitors in Parallel

C_p increases as more capacitors are added

SUMMARY OF CIRCUIT ELEMENT MATHEMATICS

SERIES

$$R_s = R_1 + R_2 + R_3 + \ldots + R_n$$

$$\frac{1}{C_s} = \frac{1}{C_1} + \frac{1}{C_2} + \frac{1}{C_3} + \ldots + \frac{1}{C_n}$$

$$V_s = V_1 + V_2 + V_3 + \ldots + V_n$$

PARALLEL

$$\frac{1}{R_p} = \frac{1}{R_1} + \frac{1}{R_2} + \frac{1}{R_3} + \ldots + \frac{1}{R_n}$$

$$C_p = C_1 + C_2 + C_3 + \ldots + C_n$$

$$V_p = V_1 = V_2 = V_3 = \ldots = V_n$$

> **Key Concept**
>
> The sum of the voltage drops across any combination of resistors or capacitors will always equal the voltage of the entire system (the voltage of the battery).

MCAT Concept Check 8.3

Before moving on, ensure that you are able to:

✓ Visualize the buildup and discharge of energy in a parallel plate capacitor

✓ Compare the capacitance of parallel plate capacitors that have different areas, plate distances, and dielectrics

✓ Apply the equations for electric field and, for fully-charged capacitors, total stored energy

✓ Calculate the resultant capacitance for circuits with capacitors arranged in series or in parallel

---

8.4 Alternating Current

Alternating current is not fundamentally different from direct current. As currents, both are formed by moving electrons from low potential to high potential; therefore, both are motivated by emf. Both conform to Ohm's law and Kirchhoff's laws. The difference is that direct current flows in one direction only, while alternating current, as its name suggests, reverses direction periodically. For the devices that rely on electrical current for energy, the direction of the current makes no difference: Energy will be delivered as long as charge is moving. ($P = i^2R$; by squaring the current, you "remove" direction from consideration. If this doesn't make sense, think of it this way: Power is energy over time, and energy is scalar.) The reason why electricity delivered to buildings is AC is because it is easier to produce than DC and easier to transport over long distances. Because alternating current and voltage can be "stepped down" or "stepped up" by transformers (which is an interesting topic but beyond the scope of the MCAT), it can be transported through wires over long distances at high voltage and low current, which minimizes resistance and energy dissipation, and then delivered into a building at a lower voltage and higher current.

MCAT Expertise

On the MCAT, AC currents are largely tested only *qualitatively*.

The most common form of alternating current oscillates in a sinusoidal way, as shown in Figure 8.7. Notice that for half of the cycle, the current flows in one direction, and for the other half of the cycle, the current flows in the opposite direction. This current can be described by this equation:

$$i = I_{max}\sin(2\pi ft) = I_{max}\sin(\omega t)$$

where i is the instantaneous current at the time t, I_{max} is the maximum current, f is the frequency, and ω is the angular frequency ($\omega = 2\pi f$).

Real World

Ordinary household alternating current oscillates with a frequency f of 60 Hz in North America but with a frequency f of 50 Hz in Europe and other parts of the world.

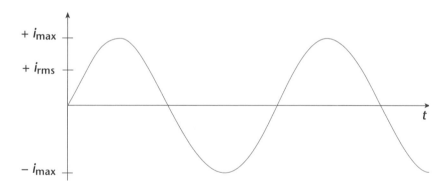

Figure 8.7. Alternating Current
Over time, current fluctuates sinusoidally from $+i_{max}$ to $-i_{max}$

RMS CURRENT

If you were to take the average value for alternating current at any frequency, the result would be zero because the sum of the current flowing in one direction is exactly cancelled by the sum of the current flowing in the opposite direction. This presents a problem, but only a mathematical one, because we've already noted that electrical appliances "don't care" what direction current is flowing. However, an average current of zero makes calculations of Ohm's law rather difficult. This is why rms current and rms voltage are used instead.

Energy is dissipated by a resistor carrying alternating current i according to the equation $P = i^2R$. If we want to find the average power in one cycle of alternating current, we must find the average of i^2 over one period. This is equal to I_{rms}^2, where I_{rms} is the **root-mean-square (rms) current** given by

$$I_{rms} = \frac{I_{max}}{\sqrt{2}}$$

Example: What is the rms current of an AC signal that will produce a maximum current of 1.00 A?

Solution:
$$I_{rms} = \frac{I_{max}}{\sqrt{2}}$$
$$= \frac{1.00}{\sqrt{2}}$$
$$= \frac{1.00}{1.41}$$
$$= 0.71\,A$$

RMS VOLTAGE

Because the direction of current reverses at some frequency in alternating current, this must mean that the voltage is also reversing direction (remember, current always flows from higher potential to lower potential). You're probably not surprised to learn that the graph of AC voltage is sinusoidal and oscillates at the same frequency as the current for a given alternating current. Mathematically, this again presents the problem of taking the average of AC voltage (which would be zero). The solution is to calculate the **root-mean-square voltage (V_{rms})**, using the same form of equation that we used to calculate the root-mean-square current:

$$V_{rms} = \frac{V_{max}}{\sqrt{2}}$$

Example: The AC current used in a home is frequently called "120 V AC." Assuming that this refers to the rms voltage, what is the maximum voltage?

Solution: Using the above equation gives
$$V_{max} = V_{rms}\sqrt{2}$$
$$= \sqrt{2}\,(120)$$
$$= 170\ V$$

Once you have calculated the values for I_{rms} and V_{rms}, you can use these values in applications of Ohm's law to AC circuits just as you would use values of current and voltage in applications of Ohm's law to DC circuits. In other words, there is nothing additional that you need to understand in order to properly and correctly solve any AC circuit problem on Test Day! Just remember how to calculate the rms values for current and voltage, and you will be set.

MCAT Concept Check 8.4

Before moving on, ensure that you are able to:

✓ Explain the process that generates alternating current

✓ Contrast alternating current with direct current

✓ Find the root-mean-squared current and voltage when given maximum current and voltage (and vice versa)

MCAT Expertise

The only AC equations to remember are the equations for I_{rms} and V_{rms}. Just realize that these two equations state the exact same thing for both current and voltage, so in reality, there is only one AC equation we need to know.

Conclusion

This chapter covered a lot of material. We began with a review of current, taking special note of the conventional definition of current as the movement of positive charge (when in fact, negatively-charged electrons are actually moving). We considered the basic laws of electricity and circuits: Kirchhoff's laws, which are expressions of conservation of charge and energy, and Ohm's law, which relates voltage, current, and resistance. We defined resistance and determined the relationship between resistance and length (directly proportional) and resistance and cross-sectional area (inversely proportional). We also defined capacitance as the ability to store charge at some voltage, thereby storing energy. We stressed the importance of the mathematical treatment of resistors and capacitors in series and in parallel as a major testing topic on the MCAT. Finally, we briefly reviewed the key differences between DC and AC circuits and defined the rms values of current and voltage for AC circuits.

Now, take a moment to rest and relax. When you are refreshed, tackle some MCAT practice problems to reinforce these concepts.

CONCEPT SUMMARY

Current (p. 221)

- ☐ Is the movement of charge that occurs between two points that have different electric potentials
- ☐ By convention, current is defined as the movement of positive charge from the high-potential end of a voltage source to the low-potential end
- ☐ In reality, it is negatively-charged particles (electrons) that move in a circuit, from low potential to high potential
- ☐ The SI unit of current is the **ampere** (coulombs per second)

Kirchhoff's Laws

- ☐ Expressions of conservation of charge and energy
- ☐ **Kirchhoff's junction rule** (p. 223) states that the sum of currents directed into a point within a circuit equals the sum of the currents directed away from that point
- ☐ **Kirchhoff's loop rule** (p. 223) states that in a closed circuit loop, the sum of voltage sources is always equal to the sum of voltage drops

Resistance (p. 224)

- ☐ Is opposition to the movement of electrons through a material
- ☐ **Conductors** are materials with low resistance (unless otherwise noted, conductors are assumed to have a resistance of zero on the MCAT)
- ☐ **Insulators** are materials with very high resistance that essentially stop the flow of electrons
- ☐ **Resistors** are conductive materials with a moderate amount of resistance, which slow down electrons without stopping them
  - ○ Resistance is calculated using the resistivity, length, and cross-sectional area of the material in question

Ohm's Law (p. 225)

- ☐ States that for a given resistance, the magnitude of the current through a resistor is proportional to the voltage drop across the resistor

Resistors in Circuits

- ☐ Can be combined to calculate the resultant resistance of a full or partial circuit
- ☐ Across each resistor in a circuit, a certain amount of **power** (p. 226) is dissipated, which is dependent on the current through the resistor and the voltage drop across the resistor
- ☐ **Resistors in series** (p. 227) are additive and sum together to create the total resistance of a circuit
- ☐ **Resistors in parallel** (p. 229) cause a decrease in resultant resistance of a circuit

Capacitors (p. 233)

- ☐ Have the ability to store electric charge and discharge the energy later
- ☐ **Capacitance** (p. 233) is determined (in parallel plate capacitors) by the area of the plates and the distance between the plates
- ☐ **Capacitors in series** (p. 236) cause a decrease in the resultant capacitance of a circuit

☐ **Capacitors in parallel** (p. 237) sum together to create a larger resultant capacitance

☐ **Dielectric materials** (p. 234) are insulators placed between the plates of a capacitor that increase the capacitance of the capacitor by a factor equal to the material's **dielectric constant, K**

Direct and Alternating Current

☐ **Direct current** (DC) occurs in one direction only

☐ **Alternating current** (p. 238) (AC) reverses direction periodically

    ○ For AC circuits, use the **rms values of current** and **voltage** (p. 240) for Ohm's law applications

EQUATIONS TO REMEMBER

☐ $i = \dfrac{\Delta q}{\Delta t}$

☐ $R = \dfrac{\rho L}{A}$

☐ $V = iR$

☐ $P = iV = i^2 R = \dfrac{V^2}{R}$

☐ $R_s = R_1 + R_2 + R_3 + \ldots + R_n$

☐ $\dfrac{1}{R_p} = \dfrac{1}{R_1} + \dfrac{1}{R_2} + \dfrac{1}{R_3} + \ldots + \dfrac{1}{R_n}$

☐ $C = \dfrac{Q}{V}$

☐ $C = \varepsilon_o \left(\dfrac{A}{d} \right)$

☐ $E = \dfrac{V}{d}$

☐ $U = \dfrac{1}{2} CV^2$

☐ $C' = KC$

☐ $\dfrac{1}{C_s} = \dfrac{1}{C_1} + \dfrac{1}{C_2} + \dfrac{1}{C_3} + \ldots + \dfrac{1}{C_n}$

☐ $C_p = C_1 + C_2 + C_3 + \ldots + C_n$

☐ $V_s = V_1 + V_2 + V_3 + \ldots + V_n$

☐ $V_p = V_1 = V_2 = V_3 = \ldots = V_n$

☐ $i = I_{max} \sin(2\pi f t) = I_{max} \sin(\omega t)$

☐ $I_{rms} = \dfrac{I_{max}}{\sqrt{2}}$

☐ $V_{rms} = \dfrac{V_{max}}{\sqrt{2}}$

SHARED CONCEPTS

HIGH-YIELD PRACTICE PROBLEMS

Practice Questions

1. If a defibrillator passes 15 A of current through a patient's body for 0.1 seconds, how much charge goes through the patient's skin?

   A. 0.15 C
   B. 1.5 C
   C. 15 C
   D. 150 C

2. A charge of 2 μC flows from the positive terminal of a 6 V battery, through a 100 Ω resistor, and back through the battery to the positive terminal. What is the total voltage drop experienced by the charge?

   A. 0 V
   B. 0.002 V
   C. 0.2 V
   D. 6 V

3. If the resistance of two conductors of equal cross-sectional area and equal lengths are compared, they are found to be in the ratio 1:2. The resistivities of the materials from which they are constructed must therefore be in what ratio?

   A. 1:1
   B. 1:2
   C. 2:1
   D. 1:3

4. If a voltaic cell provides a current of 0.5 A, the resistor in the circuit has a resistance of 3 Ω, and the internal resistance of the battery is 0.1 Ω, what is the voltage across the terminals of the battery when there is no current flowing?

   A. 0.05 V
   B. 1.5 V
   C. 1.505 V
   D. 1.55 V

5. A transformer is a device that takes an input voltage and produces an output voltage that can be either larger or smaller than the input voltage, depending on the transformer design. Although the voltage is changed by the transformer, energy is not, so the input power equals the output power. A particular transformer produces an output voltage that is 300 percent of the input voltage. What is the ratio of the output current to the input current?

   A. 1:3
   B. 3:1
   C. 1:300
   D. 300:1

6.

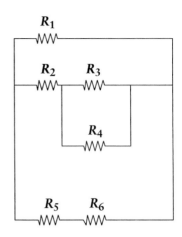

Given that $R_1 = 20\ \Omega$, $R_2 = 4\ \Omega$, $R_3 = R_4 = 32\ \Omega$, $R_5 = 15\ \Omega$, and $R_6 = 5\ \Omega$, what is the total resistance in the circuit shown?

A. $0.15\ \Omega$
B. $6.67\ \Omega$
C. $16.7\ \Omega$
D. $60\ \Omega$

7. How many moles of charge pass over a period of 10 seconds through a circuit with a battery of 100 V and a resistance of 2 Ω? ($F = 9.65 \times 10^4$ C/mol.)

A. 500 moles
B. 5.2×10^6 moles
C. 5.18×10^3 moles
D. 5.18×10^{-3} moles

8.

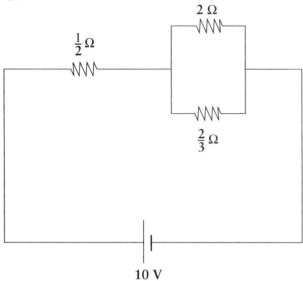

10 V

In the above circuit, what is the voltage drop across the $\frac{2}{3}\ \Omega$ resistor?

A. $\frac{1}{2}$ V
B. $\frac{2}{3}$ V
C. 5 V
D. 10 V

9. If the area of a capacitor's plates is doubled while the distance between them is halved, how will the final capacitance (C_f) compare to the original capacitance (C_i)?

A. $C_f = C_i$
B. $C_f = \frac{1}{2} C_i$
C. $C_f = 2C_i$
D. $C_f = 4C_i$

10. The energy stored in a fully charged capacitor is given by $E = \frac{1}{2}CV^2$. In a typical cardiac defibrillator, a capacitor charged to 7,500 V has a stored energy of 400 W·s. If the charge Q and voltage V on a capacitor are related by $Q = CV$, what is the charge on the capacitor in the cardiac defibrillator?

A. 1.1×10^{-5} C
B. 5×10^{-2} C
C. 1.1×10^{-1} C
D. 3.1×10^{6} C

11. A 10 Ω resistor carries a current that varies as a function of time as shown. What energy has been dissipated by the resistor after 5 s?

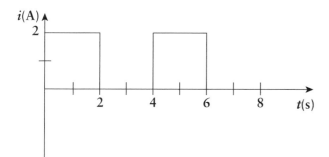

A. 40 J
B. 50 J
C. 80 J
D. 120 J

12. In the figure below, six currents meet at point P. What is the magnitude and direction of the current between points P and x?

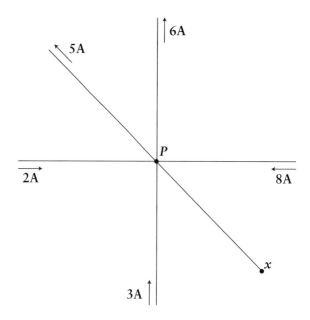

A. 2 A, toward x
B. 2 A, toward P
C. 10 A, toward x
D. 10 A, toward P

13. Which of the following will most likely increase the electric field between the plates of a parallel plate capacitor?

A. Adding a resistor that is connected to the capacitor in series
B. Adding a resistor that is connected to the capacitor in parallel
C. Increasing the distance between the plates
D. Adding an extra battery to the system

14. Each of the resistors shown carries an individual resistance of 4 Ω. Assuming negligible resistance in the wire, what is the overall resistance of the circuit?

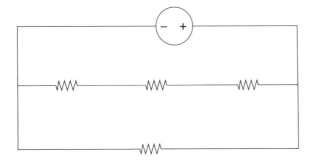

A. 16 Ω

B. 8 Ω

C. 4 Ω

D. 3 Ω

Small Group Questions

1. A 10 V battery is connected to a 3Ω resistor in series with a 7Ω resistor. A 5Ω resistor is also connected in parallel with the two resistors in series. How will the total resistance and current through each circuit element change if the cross-sectional area of each resistor is reduced by one-third?

2. A fully charged capacitor with $C = 60$ μF and two 30 μF capacitors are connected in parallel, and all of them are connected to a 120 V DC power supply. What will be the maximum speed achieved by a 2×10^{-3} C charge weighing 1.5×10^{-12} kg that is placed in the middle of the capacitor?

Explanations to Practice Questions

1. B

This is a straightforward question that tests your knowledge about the current in a circuit. Electric current is defined as charge flow, or in mathematical terms, charge over time:

$$i = \frac{q}{\Delta t}$$

A 15 A current that acts for 0.1 s means that $q = i\Delta t = 15$ A $\times 0.1$ s $= 1.5$ C flowed through the patient's body. Choice (B) matches your answer.

2. A

Kirchhoff's loop rule states that the total voltage drop around a complete circuit loop is zero. Another way of saying this is that the voltage lost through the resistors is gained in going through the battery, so the net change in voltage is zero. Because the voltage is electric potential energy per unit charge, this is also equivalent to saying that the amount of potential energy lost by the charge in going through the resistor is gained back when the charge goes through the battery.

3. B

The resistance of a resistive material is given by this formula:

$$R = \frac{\rho L}{A}$$

For two different materials,

$$R_1 = \frac{\rho_1 L_1}{A_1}$$

$$R_2 = \frac{\rho_2 L_2}{A_2}$$

From the information given in the question stem, $A_1 = A_2$, $L_1 = L_2$ and $R_1 : R_2 = 1:2$. Because the resistance is directly proportional to resistivity, $\rho_1 : \rho_2 = 1:2$, making (B) the correct answer.

4. D

This question tests our understanding of batteries in a circuit. The voltage across the terminals of the battery when there is no current flowing is referred to as the electromotive force (emf or ε of the battery). However, when a current is flowing through the circuit, the voltage across the terminals of the battery is decreased by an amount equal to the current multiplied by the internal resistance of the battery. In other words,

$$V = \varepsilon - ir_{int}$$

To determine the emf of the battery, first calculate the voltage across the battery when the current is flowing. For this, we can use Ohm's law:

$$V = iR$$
$$V = 0.5 \text{ A} \times 3 \text{ } \Omega$$
$$V = 1.5 \text{ V}$$

Because you know the internal resistance of the battery, the current and the voltage, calculate the emf:

$$\varepsilon = V + ir_{int}$$
$$\varepsilon = 1.5 \text{ V} + 0.5 \text{ A} \times 0.1 \text{ } \Omega$$
$$\varepsilon = 1.5 \text{ V} + 0.05$$
$$\varepsilon = 1.55 \text{ V}$$

The answer makes sense in the context of a real battery, because its internal resistance is supposed to be very small so that the voltage provided to the circuit is as close as possible to the emf of the cell when there is no current running. Choice (D) matches the result and is thus the correct answer.

5. A

You are told that transformers conserve energy so that the output power equals the input power. Thus $P_{out} = P_{in}$, where $P_{out} = i_{out}V_{out}$ and $P_{in} = i_{in}V_{in}$. So $i_{out}V_{out} = i_{in}V_{in}$, which means that $\dfrac{i_{out}}{i_{in}} = \dfrac{V_{in}}{V_{out}}$. You are told that the output voltage is 300 percent of the input voltage, which means that $\dfrac{V_{out}}{V_{in}}$

$= 300\% = \dfrac{300}{100} = \dfrac{3}{1}$. This means that $\dfrac{V_{in}}{V_{out}} = \dfrac{1}{3}$ and $\dfrac{i_{out}}{i_{in}} = \dfrac{1}{3}$,

making (A) the correct answer.

6. B

The fastest way to tackle these kinds of questions is to simplify the circuit as much as possible. For example, notice that R_3 and R_4 are in parallel and in series with R_2; similarly, R_5 and R_6 are in series. If you determine the total resistance on each branch, you will be left with three branches in parallel, each with a different resistance. To start, find the total resistance in the middle branch:

$$\frac{1}{R_{3,4}} = \frac{1}{R_3} + \frac{1}{R_4}$$
$$\frac{1}{R_{3,4}} = \frac{1}{32} + \frac{1}{32} = \frac{2}{32} = \frac{1}{16}$$
$$R_{3,4} = 16\ \Omega$$
$$R_{2,3,4} = 4\ \Omega + 16\ \Omega = 20\ \Omega$$

Next, take a look at the total resistance in the bottom branch:

$$R_{5,6} = R_5 + R_6$$
$$R_{5,6} = 15\ \Omega + 5\ \Omega = 20\ \Omega$$

The circuit can now be viewed as three resistors in parallel, each providing a resistance of 20 Ω. The total resistance in the circuit is thus

$$\frac{1}{R_{tot}} = \frac{1}{R_1} + \frac{1}{R_{2,3,4}} + \frac{1}{R_{5,6}} = \frac{1}{20} + \frac{1}{20} + \frac{1}{20} = \frac{3}{20}$$

Therefore, $R_{tot} = \dfrac{20}{3} \approx 7\ \Omega$. Choice (B) most closely matches our result and is thus the correct answer.

7. D

This question is testing your understanding of circuits and charge. To determine the moles of charge that pass through the circuit over a period of 10 s, first calculate the amount of charge using Faraday's constant. Obtain the amount of charge from the current in the circuit, which can be calculated using Ohm's law:

$$i = \frac{V}{R}$$
$$i = \frac{100\ \text{V}}{2\Omega}$$
$$i = 50\text{A}$$

Your result implies that every second, 50 A worth of current pass through the circuit. Determine the amount of charge for 10 seconds by using the following calculation:

$$i = \frac{q}{\Delta t}$$
$$q = i\Delta t$$
$$q = (50\ \text{A})(10\ \text{s})$$
$$q = 500\ \text{C}$$

Lastly, calculate the number of moles of charge that this represents by using the Faraday constant and approximating F as 10^5 C/mol.

$$\text{moles of charge} = \frac{500\ \text{C}}{10^5\text{C/mol}} = 5 \times 10^{-3}\ \text{mol}$$

Choice (D) is closest to our result and is thus the correct answer.

8. C

To determine the voltage drop across the $\dfrac{2}{3}\ \Omega$ resistor, simply calculate the voltage drop across both parallel resistors. Because they are arranged in parallel, the voltage drop will be the same. To begin, calculate the total resistance in the circuit. For the resistors in parallel, the total resistance is $\dfrac{1}{R_{tot}} = \dfrac{1}{2} + \dfrac{3}{2} = \dfrac{4}{2} = 2$, so $R_{tot} = \dfrac{1}{2}\ \Omega$. The total resistance in the circuit is the sum of the two main resistances: R_{tot} $= \dfrac{1}{2}\ \Omega + \dfrac{1}{2}\ \Omega = 1\ \Omega$. The current in the circuit is therefore $i = \dfrac{V}{R_{tot}} = \dfrac{10\text{V}}{1\Omega} = 10$ A. Lastly, determine the voltage drop across the two parallel resistors. Their resistance added together is $\dfrac{1}{2}\ \Omega$. Given that the current that goes through both of them together is 10 A, the voltage drop is $V = iR = 10$

across the $\frac{1}{2}$ Ω resistor must also be 5 V, which adds up to the total voltage of the battery. The voltage drop across the $\frac{2}{3}$ Ω resistor is thus 5 V, making (C) the correct answer.

9. D

To answer this question, you have to make use of our knowledge of capacitance. Because $C = \varepsilon_0 \frac{A}{d}$, where ε_0 is the permittivity of free space, A is the area of the plates, and d is the distance between the plates, you can infer that doubling the area will double the capacitance, while halving the distance will also double the capacitance. Therefore, the new capacitance is four times larger than the initial one, making (D) the correct answer.

10. C

Because the question is asking you to calculate the charge on the capacitor, use the $Q = CV$ formula. You are given $V = 7{,}500$ V and can calculate C from the formula for energy, $E = \frac{1}{2}CV^2$.

$$E = \frac{1}{2}CV^2$$

$$C = \frac{2E}{V^2}$$

Lastly, to calculate the charge, simply plug in the equation for capacitance into the $Q = CV$ formula:

$$Q = \left(\frac{2E}{V^2}\right)V$$

$$Q = \frac{2E}{V}$$

$$Q = \frac{2(400 \text{ W} \cdot \text{s})}{7{,}500 \text{ V}}$$

$$Q \approx \frac{800}{8{,}000} = 0.1\text{C}$$

Our result best matches with (C), the correct answer.

11. D

Power is energy dissipated per unit time; therefore, the energy dissipated is

$$E = Pt$$

The power dissipated in a resistor R carrying a current I is

$$P = i^2R$$

Therefore, the energy dissipated in the first 2 s is

$$E = i^2Rt$$
$$E = 4\text{A}^2 \times 10\text{ }\Omega \times 2\text{ s}$$
$$E = 80\text{ J}$$

The energy dissipated in the next 2 s is zero, because there is no current, and therefore no power is dissipated. The energy dissipated during the one second interval from $t = 4$ s to $t = 5$ s is

$$E = i^2Rt$$
$$E = 4\text{A}^2 \times 10\text{ }\Omega \times 1\text{ s}$$
$$E = 40\text{ J}$$

The total energy dissipated is therefore

$$80\text{ J} + 40\text{ J} = 120\text{ J}$$

Choice (D) is thus the correct answer.

12. A

Kirchhoff's junction rule states that the sum of all currents directed into a point is always equal to the sum of all currents directed out of the point. The currents directed into point P are equal to 8 A, 2 A, and 3 A, so the sum is 13 A. The currents directed out of point P are equal to 5 A and 6 A, so the total is 11 A. Because the two numbers must always be equal, an additional current of 2 A must be directed away from point P, which is (A).

13. D

The electric field between two plates of a parallel plate capacitor is related to the potential difference between the plates of the capacitor and the distance between the plates (according to the formula $E = \frac{V}{d}$). The addition of another battery will increase the total voltage applied to the circuit, which, consequently, is likely to increase the electric field. Choice (D) is correct. The addition of a resistor, whether in series (A) or parallel (B), will increase the resistance and decrease the voltage applied to the capacitor. Increasing the distance between the plates, (C), would not work because electric field is inversely proportional to the distance between the plates.

14. D

The resistance of the three resistors wired in series is equal to the sum of the individual resistances (12 Ω). This means that the circuit essentially contains a 12 Ω resistor and a 4 Ω resistor. To determine the overall resistance of this system, use the formula $\frac{1}{R} = \frac{1}{R_1} + \frac{1}{R_2} + \cdots$ where R is equal to the overall resistance when R_1 and R_2 are wired in parallel. Based on this formula, the resistance is equal to 3 Ω. Choice (D) is therefore the correct answer.

Explanations to Small Group Questions

1. The resultant resistance of the original circuit is 3.33 Ω and the total current traveling through the circuit is 3A, with 2A passing through the 5 Ω resistor and 1 A passing through the other two resistors in series. A resistor's resistance is inversely proportional to the cross sectional area, so as the area decreases, the resistance of the element increases. The new resistance for each resistor is three times the original resistance, with the 3 Ω, 7 Ω, and 5 Ω resistors becoming 9 Ω, 21 Ω, and 15 Ω, respectively. This gives a new resultant resistance of 2.5 Ω and total current of 5A, with 3.33A passing through the 5 Ω resistor and 1.67A passing through the other two resistors in series.

2. Since the capacitors are wired in parallel, the voltage across each capacitor will be the same and equal to the voltage of the power source, 120 V. Thus, the voltage across the 60 μF capacitor in question is 120 V. The electric field generated by the capacitor will perform work on the charge. From the work-energy theorem we know that the work done by a conservative force on an object equals the change in kinetic energy of that object. Therefore, we can use the relationship $qV = \frac{1}{2}mv^2$, where $V = Ed$ in the case of the capacitor. Our charge starts in the middle of the capacitor, so the distance over which the charge is accelerated is $\frac{d}{2}$. Thus, the equation simplifies to:

$$qE\left(\frac{d}{2}\right) = \frac{1}{2}mv^2$$
$$qEd = qV = mv^2$$
$$v^2 = \frac{(2 \times 10^{-3}\,\text{C})(120\,\text{V})}{1.5 \times 10^{-12}\,\text{kg}}$$
$$v = 4.0 \times 10^5\,\text{m/s}$$

9

Periodic Motion, Waves, and Sound

In this chapter:

Introduction

In the ongoing battle between convenience store owners and groups of bored teenagers, there's a new weapon that may finally bring victory to merchants in the quest against loitering. It doesn't involve parents or the police, and it is safe and effective. So, what is it?

It's a noise machine, but not just any noise machine. Anyone over the age of 25 is completely unaffected since it emits a high frequency sound that people lose the ability to detect with age. Thus, the shopkeepers are spared the fingernails across chalkboard sound while at the same time dispersing the marauding youth on their property. While we leave it for the courts to decide whether this is a violation of the civil liberties of the young, we marvel at the unique way this device uses the wave character of sound.

This chapter lays the foundation for understanding wave phenomena by reviewing the subject of simple harmonic motion. Then the general properties of waves will be introduced, including a discussion of wavelength, frequency, wave speed, amplitude, and resonance. We will also review the interaction of waves meeting at a point in space (constructive or destructive interference) and examine the mathematics of standing waves (the means by which musical instruments produce their characteristic sounds). Finally, the subject of sound is reviewed as a specific example of the longitudinal waveform with a focus on wave phenomena, like the Doppler effect, that can be observed through our sense of hearing.

9.1 Simple Harmonic Motion ★★★★★★

We recognize oscillating systems by their repetitive motion about some point or position. There are many naturally occurring and manufactured oscillating systems, such as water waves, the pendulum of a grandfather clock, swing sets, springs, sound, and light (electromagnetic waves). The repetitive motion of an oscillating system is also called periodic motion, and a very important type of periodic motion is **simple harmonic motion (SHM).** In SHM, a particle or mass oscillates about an equilibrium position and is subject to a linear restoring force. The name of this force is perfectly descriptive of its function and character. First, it always acts to restore the particle or object to its equilibrium position any time it is displaced. That is, the direction of the restoring force is always toward the equilibrium position. Second, the magnitude of the force is directly proportional to the magnitude of the displacement of the particle or object from its equilibrium position. From Newton's second law, we can predict that the acceleration of the particle or object is always directed toward the equilibrium position and is also proportional to its displacement from the equilibrium position. Two systems that demonstrate simple harmonic motion are springs and pendulums. The MCAT takes these as paradigms for the testing of SHM.

SPRINGS

When a **spring** with a mass attached to one end is compressed or stretched and then released, it will oscillate in simple harmonic motion about its equilibrium position (the spring's natural length). The material of the spring itself is responsible for generating the restoring force according to the following equation:

$$F = -kx$$

F is the restoring force, k is a constant called the spring constant, and x is the displacement of the spring from its equilibrium (natural) length. The spring constant k is a measure of the spring's stiffness. The higher the k value, the stiffer the spring and the greater the magnitude of the restoring force for any given displacement. The negative sign in front of the right side of the equation tells us that the restoring force is always in the direction opposite to the direction of displacement. That is, if the spring is stretched, the restoring force with be directed "inward" toward the equilibrium position, but if the spring is compressed, the restoring force will be directed "outward" toward the equilibrium position. The equation $F = -kx$ is called **Hooke's law.** Figure 9.1a shows a spring-mass system with the mass at the equilibrium position ($x = 0$). Figure 9.1b shows the same spring-mass system with the spring stretched out and the mass displaced a distance x_1.

Key Equation

Restoring Force
$F = -kx$
$N = (N/m)(m)$
$kg \cdot m/s^2 = (kg/s^2)(m)$

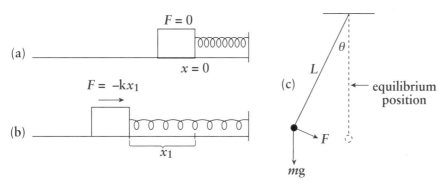

Figure 9.1. Oscillating Systems
(a) Spring-mass system with mass at $x = 0$
(b) Spring-mass system with mass displaced to x_1
(c) Pendulum of length L and maximum displacement of θ

The acceleration of the spring toward its equilibrium position is, as we've stated, proportional to the restoring force according to Newton's second law and, therefore, also proportional to the displacement of the spring from its equilibrium length. A spring with spring constant k and mass m, having been displaced x meters, will have an acceleration a calculated as $a = -\omega^2 x$, where ω is the **angular frequency** and is given by

$$\omega = 2\pi f = \sqrt{\frac{k}{m}}$$

Let's make sure you are clear on what exactly angular frequency is. First, it is a frequency and therefore a rate, but it is not a linear rate, like velocity. Rather, it is a measure of the rate at which cycles of oscillation are being completed. **Frequency** f is measured in **hertz** (Hz), which is cycles per second. Angular frequency ω is measured in **radians per second.** As the term suggests, angular frequency is a measure of the rate at which the oscillating object would move through an arc of a particular size if the object were traveling around a perfect circle (for which one revolution around the circle equals one cycle). The size of a radian is equal to $180/\pi$ degrees, so a circle (360°) is equal to 2π radians (see Figure 9.2). The value of 2π is therefore the conversion between frequency and angular frequency: They measure the same thing (the rate at which an oscillating particle or mass completes a cycle) but in different units.

Another point to pay close attention to (as it is a source of potential error on the MCAT) is the dependency of frequency/angular frequency on the spring constant and mass attached to the spring but not on the displacement x of the spring. Two springs with identical k and m values but stretched to different lengths will have the same frequency of oscillation. Of course, the spring that is stretched out to the greater length (larger displacement x) will generate a larger restoring force F_x, will

Key Equations

Angular Frequency for a Spring
$\omega = 2\pi f$
radians/s = (radians)(1/s)(or Hz)

$$\omega = \sqrt{\frac{k}{m}}$$

radians/s $= \sqrt{\dfrac{kg/s^2}{kg}}$ (where radians
are implied and not officially part of the units of k)

Key Concept

Angular frequency is measured in radians; one full rotation equals 2π radians or 360 degrees.

Key Concept

The angular frequency equation tells us the stiffer the spring (the larger the value of k) or the smaller the mass attached, the faster the spring will oscillate.

experience greater acceleration, and will reach greater linear velocity magnitudes, but all of this only means that it will complete a larger cycle in the same amount of time it takes the spring stretched out to the lesser length to complete its smaller cycle. Frequencies measure the rate at which cycles are completed, irrespective of cycle size.

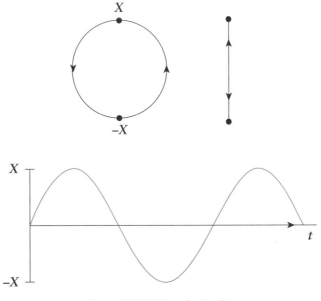

Figure 9.2. Value of a Radian

You can calculate the position of a spring as it moves through its cycle as a function of time according to the following equation:

$$x = X \cos (\omega t)$$

Key Concept

The frequency describes the number of oscillations per second. The period (T) describes how many seconds it takes for one oscillation to occur. These two are inverse to each other.

where X is the amplitude (maximum displacement from equilibrium), ω is the angular frequency ($\omega = 2\pi f = \dfrac{2\pi}{T}$, where T is the period, $\dfrac{1}{f}$, the time to complete one cycle), and t is time. In calculating the displacement as a function of time, we have assumed that the spring has maximum displacement at $t = 0$.

For small oscillations and short periods of time, we can treat springs as conservative systems. Although the energy of the spring will eventually be dissipated in the form of thermal energy as the molecules of the spring bump up against each other, for short periods of time, we can assume that all of the potential energy of the spring will be converted to kinetic energy as it oscillates. When a spring is stretched or compressed from its equilibrium length, the spring has potential energy, which can be determined by

Key Equation

Potential Energy of a Spring

$U = \dfrac{1}{2} kx^2$

$J = kg \cdot m / s^2 = (kg/m \cdot s^2)(m^2)$

$$U = \frac{1}{2}kx^2$$

where x is the displacement from equilibrium. Upon being released, the spring will accelerate in proportion to the restoring force, and the potential energy will be converted to kinetic energy:

$$K = \frac{1}{2}mv^2$$

Because the spring generates a restoring force for all positions of displacement, it will accelerate continuously as it returns to its equilibrium length, at which point all the potential energy of the spring will have been converted into kinetic energy. The spring will reach its maximum velocity upon its return to its equilibrium length. As the spring moves through the equilibrium length to become displaced in the other direction, the restoring force opposes the spring's velocity and slows it down. The spring has a velocity of zero at its maximum displacement (amplitude), and all of the kinetic energy has been converted back into potential energy. Thus, as for all conservative systems,

$$E = K + U = \text{constant}$$

PENDULUMS

Unlike a spring, which is displaced by stretching or compressing, resulting in a change in the spring's length, a **simple pendulum** is displaced by drawing the distal end of the pendulum, where the mass is located, through some angle from the vertical equilibrium position. The displacement of a pendulum is not linear, but angular, and is measured in degrees. When a pendulum, such as that of a grandfather clock or a child on a swing, is swung back from the vertical position by some angle, the restoring force is generated by gravity and is a component of the weight of the mass attached to the pendulum according to the following equation:

$$F = -mg \sin \theta$$

where m is the mass attached to the end of the pendulum, g is the acceleration of gravity (9.8 m/s^2), and θ is the angle between the pendulum arm and the vertical (see Figure 9.1c). You'll notice that, once again, the right side of the force equation has a negative sign, reminding us that this is a restoring force, always directed in the direction opposite to the displacement and in the direction of the equilibrium position.

Key Equation

Angular Frequency for a Pendulum

$$\omega = 2\pi f = \sqrt{\frac{g}{L}}$$

Bridge

Notice how there are only two factors that affect frequency in both situations. In springs, it is mass and the spring constant. In pendulums, it is gravity and the length of the pendulum.

For a pendulum with a length L, the angular frequency can be determined by

$$\omega = 2\pi f = \sqrt{\frac{g}{L}}$$

Please pay close attention to which factors contribute to the angular frequency: only the acceleration of gravity and the length of the pendulum. Neither the mass m attached to the pendulum nor the angular displacement θ determines the angular frequency ω (don't confuse angular frequency and angular displacement!). Therefore, if two pendulums have the same length, they will demonstrate the same angular frequency irrespective of the masses attached to them or their respective initial displacements. As with two identical springs stretched to different lengths with the same angular frequency but different linear velocities, the two pendulums will be traveling at different velocities. This is because the pendulum pulled back at the greater angle will have to travel a longer path to complete its cycle in the same amount of time that the pendulum pulled back at the lesser angle travels its shorter path.

This means every single person on a swing set will swing at exactly the same frequency, as long as the length of the swing is the same, regardless of how large his or her amplitude is. Other than changing the length, the only other way we can change frequency is by changing gravity, something that can be simulated by accelerating either up or down in an elevator. Try this on your own, though remember that if you are going upward but slowing down, it means that you are accelerating in the downward direction.

A pendulum can also be approximated as a conservative system if we discount air resistance and friction between the pendulum and the mechanism supporting the pendulum from above. When a pendulum is pulled back to its maximum displacement, θ, the pendulum has maximum potential energy equal to

$$U = mgh$$

where h is the vertical height difference between the pendulum's mass in the equilibrium position and the mass at the given angular displacement. When the pendulum is released and allowed to swing, it experiences an acceleration that is a function of the restoring force, and the potential energy is converted to kinetic energy. Like the spring, a pendulum has maximum kinetic energy (and minimum potential energy) at the equilibrium position and maximum potential energy (and minimum kinetic energy) at maximum displacement. The kinetic energy of the mass attached to the pendulum is

$$K = \frac{1}{2}mv^2$$

Therefore, the conservation of energy is, once again,

$$E = K + U = \text{constant}$$

Table 9.1 contains important information on both the mass-spring system and the simple pendulum and shows the similarities between them.

Table 9.1. Comparison of Mass-Spring System and Pendulum

	Mass-Spring	Simple Pendulum
force constant k	spring constant k	$\dfrac{mg}{L}$
period T	$2\pi\sqrt{\dfrac{m}{k}}$	$2\pi\sqrt{\dfrac{L}{g}}$
ang. freq. ω	$\sqrt{\dfrac{k}{m}}$	$\sqrt{\dfrac{g}{L}}$
frequency f	$\sqrt{\dfrac{1}{T}}$ or $\sqrt{\dfrac{\omega}{2\pi}}$	$\sqrt{\dfrac{1}{T}}$ or $\sqrt{\dfrac{\omega}{2\pi}}$
kinetic energy K	$\dfrac{1}{2}mv^2$	$\dfrac{1}{2}mv^2$
K_{max} occurs at	$x = 0$	$\theta = 0$ (vertical position)
potential energy U	$\dfrac{1}{2}kx^2$	mgh
U_{max} occurs at	$x = \pm X$	max value of θ
max acceleration at	$x = \pm X$	max value of θ

Example: What is the length of a pendulum that has a period of one second?

Solution: Using our equation for the period of a simple pendulum we can find the length:

$$T = 2\pi\sqrt{\frac{L}{g}}$$

$$L = \frac{T^2 g}{4\pi^2}$$

$$= \frac{g}{4\pi^2}$$

$$= 0.25 \text{ m}$$

MCAT Concept Check 9.1

Before moving on, ensure that you are able to:

✓ Define the terms simple harmonic motion, period, frequency, and angular frequency

✓ Calculate the restoring force using Hooke's Law

✓ Apply the law of conservation of energy to spring displacement

✓ Describe the motion of a pendulum

9.2 General Wave Characteristics

Having considered two cases of simple harmonic motion, we are now ready to examine more closely the characteristics of waves and the particular physical phenomena that demonstrate wave behavior. After we have reviewed the general characteristics of waves, we will turn our attention to sound and, in the next chapter, to light.

TRANSVERSE AND LONGITUDINAL WAVES

The MCAT is primarily concerned with sinusoidal waves. In such waves, the individual particles oscillate back and forth with simple harmonic motion. Transverse and longitudinal waves are sinusoidal waves.

We are all familiar with the way that a beach ball will bob up and down on the surface of a lake or ocean. The reason why beach balls bob is that water waves are transverse, a waveform in which the direction of particle oscillation is perpendicular to the movement (propagation) of the wave. Electromagnetic radiation, such as visible light, microwaves, and x-rays, is a transverse waveform. By holding a piece of string that has been secured at the other end, you can make a transverse wave by moving your hand up and down. This is demonstrated in Figure 9.3a. The string particles oscillate up and down in a manner that is perpendicular to the direction the wave travels through the string from one end (the end you're holding) to the other (the end attached, say, to a doorknob). In any waveform, energy is delivered in the direction of wave travel, so we can say that for a transverse wave, the particles are oscillating perpendicular to the direction of energy transfer. This is why, discounting air currents or undertows, beach balls and swimmers tend to get pushed into shore by waves: Water waves are delivering their energy in the direction of the beach.

The longitudinal wave is a sinusoidal wave in which the particles of the wave oscillate along the direction of travel of the wave motion; that is, the wave particles are oscillating along the direction of energy transfer. Sound waves are the classic example of longitudinal waves, but since we can't "see" sound, this waveform is a little more difficult to picture. Figure 9.3b helps us visualize what a longitudinal waveform traveling through air would "look" like. In this case, the longitudinal wave created by the person moving the piston back and forth consists of oscillating air molecules that go through cycles of compression and rarefaction (decompression) along the direction of motion of the wave. If you are having trouble picturing this, think of the way that the bellows of an accordion are compressed and pulled apart by the accordionist.

Real World

Most waves we see are transverse waves (even "the wave" at sporting events is a transverse wave). The only longitudinal waves we are likely to encounter are sound waves.

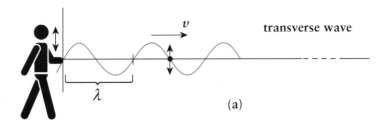

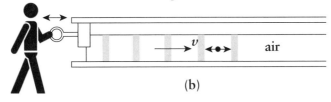

Figure 9.3. Wave Types
(a) Transverse: particles are perpendicular to the direction of motion
(b) Longitudinal: particles are parallel to the direction of motion

DESCRIBING WAVES

The displacement y of a particle in a wave may be plotted at each point x along the direction of the wave's motion. It is given mathematically by

$$y = Y \sin (kx - \omega t)$$

where Y is the amplitude (maximum displacement), k is the wavenumber (don't confuse this k, wavenumber, with the spring constant k in Hooke's law!), ω is the angular frequency, and t is the time. You'll notice how similar this equation is to the equation for calculating the displacement of a spring at time t.

The distance between one maximum (crest) of the wave to the next is the wavelength λ. The frequency f is the number of wavelengths passing a fixed point per second (measured in hertz [Hz] or cycles per second [cps]). On the MCAT, you will be expected to be able to calculate the **speed of the wave v** as it relates to the frequency and wavelength of the wave according to

$$v = f\lambda$$

The following relations define wavenumber k and angular frequency ω:

$$k = \frac{2\pi}{\lambda}$$
$$\omega = 2\pi f = \frac{2\pi}{T}$$

where the period T is the time for the wave to move one wavelength ($f = \frac{1}{T}$). Combining the equations above with the equation for wave speed,

$$v = f\lambda = \frac{\omega}{k} = \frac{\lambda}{T}$$

> ## Key Concept
>
> As long as velocity remains constant, frequency and wavelength are inverse to each other. A large wavelength will have a small frequency, and a small wavelength will have a large frequency.

> ## Key Equation
>
> **Speed of a Wave**
> $v = f\lambda$
> m/s = (1/s)(m)

Example: If a wave on a string is described by the equation $y = (0.01)\sin(2x - 10t)$, find the frequency, wavelength, and speed of the wave. (Assume units of meters and seconds.)

Solution: Everything that is needed to find the frequency, wavelength, and speed is given in the wave's equation, $y = Y\sin(kx - \omega t) = (0.01)\sin(2x - 10t)$. Remembering that frequency is given by $f = \frac{1}{T}$ and that $T = \frac{2\pi}{\omega}$,

$$f = \frac{\omega}{2\pi}$$
$$= \frac{5}{\pi}$$
$$= 1.59 \text{ Hz}$$

The wavelength is given by

$$\lambda = \frac{2\pi}{k}$$
$$= \frac{2\pi}{2}$$
$$= \pi$$
$$= 3.14 \text{ m}$$

And the speed by

$$v = f\lambda$$
$$= \left(\frac{5}{\pi}\right)\pi$$
$$= 5 \text{ m/s}$$

PHASE

> **Key Concept**
>
> If the two waves have different but similar frequencies, they will periodically go in and out of phase, resulting in "beats," which will later be discussed.

When analyzing waves that are passing through the same space, we often speak about a **phase difference,** which describes how "in step" or "out of step" two waves are with each other. If we consider two waves that have the same frequency, wavelength, and amplitude and that pass through the same space at the same time, we can say that they are in phase if their respective maxima (crests) and minima (troughs) coincide (i.e., they occur at the same point in space). When waves are perfectly in phase, we say that the phase difference is zero. However, if the two waves occupy the same space in such a way that the crests of one wave coincide with the troughs of the other, then we would say that they are out of phase, and the phase difference would be one-half of a wave, or 180°. Of course, waves can be out of phase with each other by any definite fraction of a cycle. For example, Figure 9.4a illustrates two waves that are nearly in phase with each other (phase difference is almost zero), and Figure 9.4b illustrates two waves that are out of phase by nearly one-half a wavelength so that the phase difference is almost 180°.

PRINCIPLE OF SUPERPOSITION

The principle of superposition states simply that when waves interact with each other, the result is a sum of the waves. When the waves are in phase, the amplitudes add together (**constructive interference**), and the resultant wave has greater amplitude. When waves are out of phase, the resultant wave's amplitude is the difference between the amplitudes of the interacting waves (**destructive interference**). Figures 9.4a and 9.4b show the constructive interference between waves that are nearly in phase and destructive interference between waves that are nearly out of phase, respectively.

Noise-canceling headphones that construction workers and frequent flyers use to protect their ears from the damaging noises of jackhammers and screaming babies, respectively, operate on the principle of superposition. They do not simply "muffle" sound, as you might do by covering your ears with the palms of your hands. They actually capture the environmental noise and, using computer technology, produce a sound wave that is one-half wavelength out of phase. The combination of the two waves inside the headset results in destructive interference, thereby canceling—or nearly canceling—the ambient noise.

Key Concept

If the two waves were exactly 180 degrees out of phase, then the resultant wave would have zero amplitude; thus, there would be no wave.

Real World

In noise-canceling headphones, pressure waves from noise are canceled by destructive interference; the speaker creates a wave that is 180 degrees out of phase and of similar amplitude. Many frequencies are present in the noise.

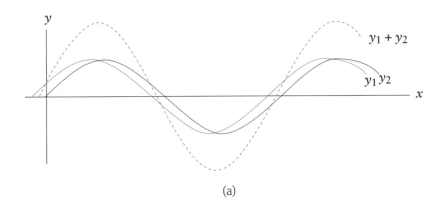

(a)

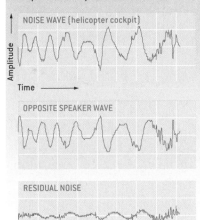

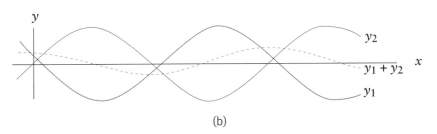

(b)

Figure 9.4. Phase Difference
(a) In phase with a difference of almost zero
(b) Out of phase with a difference of almost 180 degrees

TRAVELING AND STANDING WAVES

If a string fixed at one end is moved up and down, a wave will form and travel, or propagate, toward the fixed end. Because this wave can be seen to be moving, it's called a **traveling wave**. When the wave reaches the fixed boundary, it is reflected and inverted (see Figure 9.5). If the free end of the string is continuously moved up and down, there will then be two waves: the original wave moving down the string toward the fixed end and the reflected wave moving away from the fixed end. These waves will then interfere with each other.

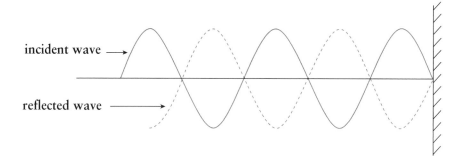

incident wave ⟶

reflected wave ⟶

Figure 9.5. Traveling Wave

Now consider the case when both ends of the string are fixed and traveling waves are excited in the string. Certain wave frequencies can result in a waveform that appears to be stationary, with the only apparent movement of the string being fluctuation of amplitude at fixed points along the length of the string. These waves are known as **standing waves**. Points in the wave that remain at rest (i.e., points where amplitude is constantly zero) are known as **nodes**, and points that are midway between the nodes are known as **antinodes**. Antinodes are points that fluctuate with maximum amplitude. In addition to strings fixed at both ends, pipes that are open at both ends can support standing waves, and the mathematics relating the standing wave wavelength and the length of the string or the open pipe are similar. Pipes that are open at one end and closed at the other can also support standing waves, but because the open end supports an antinode rather than a node, the mathematics are different. Standing waves in strings and pipes are discussed in more detail next, within the context of sound, because standing wave formation is integral to the formation of sound in musical instruments.

RESONANCE

Why are flutes, trumpets, and even water goblets considered musical instruments but not pencils, rulers, or spoons? It has a lot to do with the phenomenon of natural frequency. Almost any object, when hit, struck, rubbed, or disturbed in any way will begin to vibrate. Strike a gong, and it will vibrate. Blow into a flute, and it will vibrate. Throw a spoon against a hard surface, and it will vibrate. The frequency or frequencies at which an object will vibrate when disturbed is the **natural frequency**.

If the frequency is within the frequency detection range of the human ear, the sound will be audible. The quality of the sound, called timbre, is determined by the natural frequency or frequencies of the object. Some objects vibrate at a single frequency, producing a pure tone, while others vibrate at multiple natural frequencies that are related to each other by whole number ratios, producing a rich tone. Flutes, for example, tend to vibrate at a single frequency and thus produce a pure tone, while tubas naturally vibrate at many frequencies that are whole number multiples of the lowest frequency vibration and thus produce a rich tone. However, throw a spoon or pencil against a hard surface and what you hear is *clink, clank, clunk*. Not particularly pleasing to listen to, and that's because the natural frequencies of such objects are multiples but not whole-number multiples. The frequencies (those that are within the human audible range) combine to form a sound that we do not find musical. We call it noise.

The natural frequency of most objects can be changed by changing some aspect of the object itself. For example, a set of eight identical goblets can be filled with different levels of water so that each vibrates at a different natural frequency, producing the eight notes of the musical octave. Strings have an infinite number of natural frequencies that depend on the length, linear density, and tension of the string. A pendulum of length L, however, has a single natural frequency, and there is no way to change that except to change the value of g, since $f = \frac{1}{2\pi}\sqrt{\frac{g}{L}}$.

If a periodically varying force is applied to a system, the system will then be driven at a frequency equal to the frequency of the force. This is known as **forced oscillation**. The amplitude of this motion will generally be small. However, if the frequency of the applied force is close to that of the natural frequency of the system, then the amplitude of oscillation becomes much larger. This can easily be demonstrated by a child on a swing being pushed by a parent. If the parent pushes the child at a frequency nearly equal to the frequency at which the child swings back toward the parent, the arc of the swinging child will become larger and larger: The amplitude is increasing because the force frequency is nearly identical to the swing's natural frequency (which, remember, is a function of only the length of the swing and the acceleration of gravity).

If the frequency of the periodic force is equal to a natural frequency of the system, then the system is said to be resonating, and the amplitude of the oscillation is at a maximum. If the oscillating system were frictionless the periodically varying force would continually add energy to the system, and the amplitude would increase indefinitely. However, because no system is completely frictionless, there is always some dampening, which results in a finite amplitude of oscillation. Furthermore, many objects cannot withstand the large amplitude of oscillation and break or crumble. A dramatic demonstration of resonance is the shattering of a wineglass by

Real World

It may sound strange that a pendulum has a resonant frequency, but if you've ever pushed someone on a swing set, you've experienced it for yourself. When pushing someone on a swing, the best results are obtained when you push at the same tempo that the swing is already moving. By pushing faster or slower, you actually end up slowing the swing down. The natural tempo at which the swing is moving *is* the resonant frequency, and when you push at that frequency, maximum amplitude is obtained.

directing toward the glass a sound whose frequency is equal to the natural frequency of the glass. The glass will resonate (oscillate with maximum amplitude) and eventually shatter. Operatic sopranos have the ability to perform this little feat. Musical instruments rely on resonance to produce their sounds.

> **MCAT Concept Check 9.2**
> Before moving on, ensure that you are able to:
> ✓ Recognize the differences between transverse and longitudinal waves
> ✓ Determine the wave speed using wavelength and frequency
> ✓ Identify phase differences and explain the principle of superposition
> ✓ List the components of standing waves and resonance

9.3 Sound

Sound is transmitted by the oscillation of particles along the direction of motion of the sound wave. Therefore, sound waves are longitudinal. Furthermore, sound waves propagate as mechanical disturbances through a deformable medium and can travel through solids, liquids, and gases, but they cannot travel through a vacuum. (All sci-fi movies that depict loudly booming explosions in the vacuum of space have only got it half right: Explosions are certainly possible, but they would be silent.) The **speed of sound** is inversely proportional to the square root of density but directly proportional to the square root of the bulk modulus. As a result, sound travels fastest through a solid and slowest through a gas. The speed of sound in air at 0°C is 331 m/s.

The behaviors of sound that are tested on the MCAT involve sound waves whose wavelengths and frequencies are within the human range of audible sound. These **audible waves** have frequencies that range from 20 Hz to 20,000 Hz. Sound waves whose frequencies are below 20 Hz are called **infrasonic waves**, and those whose frequencies are above 20,000 Hz are called **ultrasonic waves**. We've already mentioned one instance of sound at the upper limit of human detection—the antiloitering device used by some business owners emits a sound of a frequency that most people lose the ability to hear by their early 20s. Another example is a dog whistle, which emits a sound whose frequency is usually between 20 and 22 kHz.

PRODUCTION OF SOUND

Sound is produced by the mechanical disturbance of the particles of a material, creating oscillations of particle density that are along the direction of movement of the sound wave. Although the particles themselves do not travel along with the wave, they do vibrate or oscillate about an equilibrium position, which causes small regions of compression to alternate with small regions of rarefaction (decompression). These alternating regions of increased and decreased particle density shift linearly through the material, and this is the way that sound waves propagate.

Because sound involves vibration of material particles, the source of any sound is ultimately a mechanical vibration of some frequency. They can be produced by the vibration of solid objects or the vibration of fluids, including gases. Solid objects that can vibrate to produce sound include strings (on a piano, violin, guitar, etc.), metal, wood bars (e.g., on a xylophone), or bells. A guitar, for example, typically has six strings, which are locked down at both ends. When the strings are plucked or strummed, they are set in motion and vibrate at their natural frequencies. Because the strings are very thin, they are very ineffective in transmitting their mechanical vibrations to the particles of the air, which is necessary for us to hear the sounds produced by the vibrating guitar strings. The strings are locked down to a solid object called the bridge, which transfers the vibrations of the strings to the hollow soundboard, which causes a much larger volume of air to vibrate (at the same frequency as the strings) and is more effective in transmitting the sound.

Sound can also be produced by the vibration of fluids, including gases, that are moved through hollow objects or across small openings in objects. Flutes, trumpets, trombones, clarinets, oboes, and pipe organs produce sounds in this manner. Even a soda bottle can become a musical instrument if you blow across the open top. Sounds are produced in these types of instruments by the vibration of air that is set into motion by blowing across a small opening or into a mouthpiece that contains a reed that vibrates. For brass instruments, such as the trumpet, trombone, and tuba, there is no reed. Instead the player vibrates her lips while blowing into the mouthpiece, and this causes the air to vibrate. The pitch, or frequency, at which the air column within the instrument vibrates is determined by the length of the air column, which can be changed either by covering holes in the instrument (as in oboes, flutes, and clarinets), opening and closing valves (as in trumpets, tubas, and french horns), or sliding loops of metal tubes to make the instrument longer or shorter (as in the trombone).

The human voice is no less a musical instrument than any of those listed above. Sound is created by passing air between the vocal cords, which are a pair of thin membranes stretched across the larynx. As the air moves past the cords, they vibrate like the reed of a clarinet or oboe, causing the air to vibrate at the same frequency. The pitch of the sound is controlled by varying the tension of the cords. Adult male vocal cords are larger and thicker than those of the adult female; thus, the male voice is typically lower in pitch.

INTENSITY AND LOUDNESS OF SOUND

The loudness of sounds is the way in which we perceive the intensity of the sound waves. Every one of us will perceive the loudness of sounds differently, depending on our age and prior exposure to loud sounds. Perception of loudness is subjective,

Key Equation

Intensity

$I = \dfrac{P}{A}$

$W/m^2 = (J/s)/m^2$
$\qquad = kg \cdot m^3/s$

but sound intensity is objectively measurable. Intensity is the average rate per unit area at which energy is transferred across a perpendicular surface by the wave. In other words, intensity is the power transported per unit area. The SI units of intensity are watts per square meter, W/m^2. Intensity is calculated as follows:

$$I = \frac{P}{A}$$

Thus, the power delivered across a surface, such as the eardrum, is equal to the product of the intensity I and the surface area A, assuming the intensity is uniformly distributed. This can be expressed as

$$P = IA$$

The amplitude of a sound wave and the intensity of that sound are related to each other: Intensity is proportional to the square of the amplitude. Doubling the amplitude produces a sound wave that has four times the intensity. Intensity is also related to the distance from the source of the sound wave. You can think of sound waves traveling from their source in three-dimensional space as if the waves were pushing up against the interior wall of an ever-expanding spherical balloon. Because the area of a sphere increases as a function of the square of the radius, sound waves transmit their power over larger and larger areas the farther from the source they travel. Intensity, therefore, is inversely proportional to the square of the distance from the source. For example, sound waves that have traveled 2 meters from their source have spread their energy out over a surface area that is four times larger than that for sound waves of the same amplitude and frequency that have traveled 1 meter from their source.

The softest sound that the average human ear can hear has an intensity equal to 1×10^{-12} W/m^2. Remember that sound is produced by mechanical disturbances that result in oscillations of particle density. The mechanical disturbance associated with the threshold of hearing is the displacement of air particles one-billionth of a centimeter! The proverbial pin drop creates a sound whose intensity is about 10 times greater than the threshold. At the other end, the intensity of sound in the front rows of a rock concert is about 1×10^{-1} W/m^2. The number itself may not strike you as particularly large, but realize that the rock concert is 1×10^{11} times more intense than the threshold of hearing and about 100,000 times more intense than normal conversation. Is it any wonder that most people are temporarily deaf for at least a day or two after attending a concert? The intensity of sound at the threshold of pain is 1×10^{1} W/m^2, which is 100 times more intense than the music (noise) of the rock concert. The range of intensity from the threshold of hearing to instant perforation of the eardrum is 1×10^{16}. This is a huge range and would be totally unmanageable to express on a linear scale. To make this range easier to work with, we use a logarithmic scale, called the **sound level (β)**, measured in **decibels (dB)** and defined as follows:

$$\beta = 10 \log \frac{I}{I_0}$$

MCAT Expertise

We use logarithms with scales that have an extremely large range. The MCAT will mostly deal with logs with a base of 10. As an example, the $\log_{10}$ of 1,000 equals 3, because 10 to the power of three equals 1,000. As another example, the $\log_{10}$ of 1 equals 0, because 10 (and every other number) to the power of 0 equals 1.

where I_o is a reference intensity set at the threshold of hearing, 1×10^{-12} W/m². When the intensity of a sound is changed by some factor, you can calculate the new sound level according to the following equation:

$$\beta_f = \beta_i + 10 \log \left(\frac{I_f}{I_i} \right)$$

where $\frac{I_f}{I_i}$ is the ratio of the final intensity to the initial intensity.

Example: A detector with a surface area of 1 square meter is placed 1 meter from an operating jackhammer. It measures the power of the jackhammer's sound as being 10^{-3} W. Find

a.   the intensity and the sound level of the jackhammer.

b.   the ratio of the intensities of the jackhammer and a jet engine (assume $\beta_{jet} = 130$ dB).

Solution:

a.   Intensity is equal to power divided by area.

$$I = \frac{P}{A}$$

$$= \frac{10^{-3}}{1}$$

$$= 10^{-3} \text{ W/m}^2$$

The sound level is given by

$$\beta = 10 \log \frac{I}{I_o}$$

$$= 10 \log \left(\frac{10^{-3}}{10^{-12}} \right)$$

$$= 10 \log 10^9$$

$$= 90 \text{ dB}$$

b.   The ratio of two intensities of sound can be found from the difference of their sound levels:

$$\beta_{jet} - \beta_{jack} = 10 \log \left(\frac{I_{jet}}{I_{jack}} \right)$$

$$130 - 90 = 10 \log \left(\frac{I_{jet}}{I_{jack}} \right)$$

$$4 = \log \left(\frac{I_{jet}}{I_{jack}} \right)$$

$$10,000 = \left(\frac{I_{jet}}{I_{jack}} \right)$$

Thus, the jet engine's sound is 10,000 times more intense than the jackhammer's.

Key Concept

If $\log_{10} x = y$, $10^{\log_{10} x} = 10^y$, which yields $x = 10^y$.

FREQUENCY AND PITCH

We've discussed frequency as the rate at which a particle or wave completes a cycle. Frequency is measured in hertz (Hz) or cycles per second (cps). Angular frequency is related to frequency ($\omega = 2\pi f$) and is measured in radians. Our perception of the frequency of sound is called the **pitch**. Lower-frequency sounds have lower pitch, and higher-frequency sounds have higher pitch. Pitch is a subjective quality and cannot be measured with instruments. People who possess absolute pitch, commonly known as perfect pitch, have the ability to identify any pitch played on an instrument or to sing any pitch without an external reference such as a pitch pipe.

Beats

We ought not to forget that sound waves are just a particular type and example of waveforms. The characteristics and behaviors that describe a waveform can generally be applied to sound waves. In our review of the general characteristics of waves, we discussed the phenomenon of superposition and interference. When two waves pass through a region of space at the same time, the waves will interact with each other in such a way that their amplitudes will add or subtract to produce a resultant wave whose amplitude is the sum or difference of the original waves. When two sound waves pass through a region of space at the same time, they too will interact resulting in constructive and/or destructive interference. If the two sound waves have nearly equal frequencies in the audible range, the resultant wave will have periodically increasing and decreasing amplitude, which we hear as **beats**. Because the amplitude, not the frequency, of the resultant wave varies periodically, we perceive this as periodic variation in the loudness, not the pitch. The beat frequency is

$$f_{\text{beat}} = |f_1 - f_2|$$

Beat frequencies less than 20 Hz are heard as a "wah, wah, wah" fluctuation in sound loudness. Above 20 Hz, the beat frequency is perceived less as a fluctuation in volume and more as a fluttering or roughness in the quality of the sound. Some musical traditions consider beat frequencies undesirable and consider them a source of dissonance (that is, the presence of beat frequencies is evidence of instruments that are playing "out of tune"), while other musical traditions consider them desirable.

> **Example:** Two tuning forks are sounded. One has a frequency of 250 Hz, while the other has a frequency of 245 Hz. What is the frequency of the beats?
>
> **Solution:** The frequency of the beats is the difference of the frequencies of the interacting waves:
>
> $$\begin{aligned} f_{\text{beat}} &= |f_1 - f_2| \\ &= 250 - 245 \\ &= 5 \text{ Hz} \end{aligned}$$

Real World

Beats can be heard as periodic increases in loudness when an orchestra is tuning.

Real World

THE COMBINED SOUND of two tuning forks, one of them slightly out of tune, produces the phenomenon known as beating: The sound's volume oscillates up and down at a rate that is the beat frequency—the difference in frequency of the two forks. Beating of light waves is used in many laser measurements, including those involving optical combs.

Doppler Effect

We've all experienced the Doppler effect: An ambulance or fire truck with its sirens blaring is quickly approaching you from the other lane, and as it passes you, you hear a distinct drop in the pitch of the siren. This phenomenon of frequency is called the **Doppler effect**, which describes the difference between the perceived frequency of a sound and its actual frequency when the source of the sound and the sound's detector are moving relative to each other. If the source and detector are moving toward each other, the perceived frequency f' is greater than the actual frequency f, but if the source and detector are moving away from each other, the perceived frequency f' is less than the actual frequency f. This can be seen from the following equation for calculating the Doppler effect:

$$f' = f\left[\frac{v \pm v_D}{v \mp v_S}\right]$$

where v is the speed of sound in the medium, v_D is the speed of the detector relative to the medium, and v_S is the speed of the source relative to the medium. The upper sign on v_D and v_S is used when the detector and the source are getting closer together. The lower sign is used when the detector and the source are going farther away from each other.

We would urge you to use your common-sense, experiential understanding of the Doppler effect to ensure proper treatment of the mathematics. We all understand, from experience, that when an ambulance, fire truck, or train sounding its siren passes us, the siren pitch seems to drop. This must mean that the apparent frequency is less than the actual frequency. The apparent (perceived) frequency is found by multiplying the actual frequency by a ratio. If the apparent frequency is lower than the actual frequency, then that means that the ratio must be less than 1. If the apparent frequency is greater than the actual frequency, then the ratio must be greater than 1.

Key Equation

Perceived Frequency from the Doppler Effect

$$f' = f\left[\frac{v \pm v_D}{v \mp v_S}\right]$$

Determine the sign conventions that best define the the relationship between the objects in motion.

Key Concept

The easiest way to approach this equation is by approaching the detector and the source separately. Realize that either one moving toward the other will increase the frequency, so you want to see if each object is working toward increasing or decreasing the frequency. Because the detector is in the numerator, if it is working to increase the frequency, then ADD, giving a larger number. Because the source is in the denominator, if it is working to increase the frequency, then SUBTRACT, resulting in a larger number after dividing. Practice using this equation with objects moving in both the same and opposite directions.

Example: The siren of a police car cruising at 144 km/hr is sounding while the car is in pursuit of a speeding motorist. Assume that the speed of sound is 330 m/s. The siren emits sound at a frequency of 1,450 Hz. What is the frequency heard by a stationary observer when

a. the police car is moving towards the observer?
b. the police car has passed the observer?

Solution:

a. To do this problem, the speed of the police car (v_s) must first be converted to m/s.

$$v_s = \frac{144\,\text{km}}{\text{hr}} \cdot \frac{10^3\,\text{m}}{\text{km}} \cdot \frac{\text{hr}}{3,600\,\text{s}} = 40\,\text{m/s}$$

Bridge

The Doppler effect works with all waves, including light. This means that if a source of light is moving toward a detector, the observed frequency will increase (blue shift), and if the source is moving away from a detector, the frequency will decrease (red shift). Observing any distant galaxy, we can see that every one is red shifted, meaning that every galaxy is moving away from our own.

Because the police car is moving toward the stationary observer, the denominator is $v - v_S$, and the numerator is simply v (since $v_D = 0$). This gives

$$f' = f\frac{v}{v - v_S}$$

$$= \frac{1,450\,(330)}{330 - 40}$$

$$= 1,650 \text{ Hz}$$

b. In this part of the question, the police car is now moving away from the observer, so the denominator is $v + v_S$. The numerator remains unchanged because the observer is still stationary.

$$f' = f\frac{v}{v + v_S}$$

$$= \frac{1,450\,(330)}{330 + 40}$$

$$= 1,293 \text{ Hz}$$

This example shows precisely why the pitch of a siren changes when an ambulance or police car passes you on the street. In this case, when the police car is moving toward the observer, the perceived frequency is 1,650 Hz, whereas when the car has passed the observer, the perceived frequency has decreased to 1,293 Hz.

STANDING WAVES

Remember that **standing waves** are produced by the constructive and destructive interference of a traveling wave and its reflected wave. More broadly, we can say that a standing wave will form whenever two waves of the same frequency traveling in opposite directions interfere with one another as they travel through the same medium. The MCAT limits the consideration of standing wave formation, however, to situations involving boundary conditions and wave reflection. Standing waves appear to be "standing still"—that is, not propagating—because the interference of the wave and its reflected wave produce a resultant that fluctuates only in amplitude. As the waves move in opposite directions, they interfere to produce a new wave pattern characterized by alternating points of maximum amplitude displacement (in the positive and negative direction) and points of no displacement. The point(s) in a standing wave with no amplitude fluctuation are called nodes. The points with maximum amplitude fluctuation are called antinodes.

When boundary conditions are present, not every wavelength of traveling wave will result in standing wave formation. The length of the medium dictates the wavelengths of traveling wave that are necessary for establishing the standing wave. Furthermore, the nature of the boundary dictates the appearance of a node or antinode at the boundary itself. Closed boundaries are those that do not allow oscillation and that support nodes. The closed end of a pipe and the secured ends of a string are both closed boundaries. Open boundaries are those that allow oscillation and support antinodes. The open end of a pipe and the free end of a flag are both open boundaries.

Strings

Consider a string, such as a guitar or violin string or a piano wire, fixed rigidly at both ends. Because the string is secured at both ends and therefore immobile, these two points can only support a node of a standing wave. If a standing wave is set up such that there is only one antinode between the two nodes at the end, the length of the string corresponds to one-half the wavelength of this standing wave. (On a sine wave, the distance from one node to the next immediate node is one-half a wavelength.) If a standing wave is set up such that there are two antinodes between the two nodes at the ends and a third node between the antinodes, the length of the string corresponds to the wavelength of this standing wave. (The distance on a sine wave from a node to the second consecutive node is one wavelength.) This pattern suggests that the length L of a string must be equal to some integer multiple of a half-wavelength (e.g., $L = \frac{\lambda}{2}, \frac{2\lambda}{2}, \frac{3\lambda}{2}$, etc.). The equation that relates the wavelength λ of a standing wave and the length L of a string that supports it is

$$\lambda = \frac{2L}{n}$$

where n is a positive nonzero integer ($n = 1, 2, 3,\ldots$). From the relationship that $f = \frac{v}{\lambda}$, where v is the wave speed, the possible frequencies are

$$f = \frac{nv}{2L}$$

where n is a positive nonzero integer ($n = 1, 2, 3,\ldots$). The lowest frequency (longest wavelength) of a standing wave that can be supported in a given length of string is known as the **fundamental frequency (first harmonic)**. The frequency of the standing wave given by $n = 2$ is known as the first **overtone** or second harmonic. This standing wave has one-half the wavelength and twice the frequency of the first harmonic. All the possible frequencies that the string can support form its harmonic series. The waveforms of the first three harmonics for a string of length L are shown in Figure 9.6. (Note: N stands for node and A stands for antinode.)

Key Concept

For strings attached at both ends, the number of antinodes present will tell you which harmonic it is.

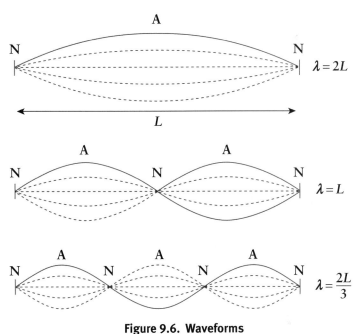

Figure 9.6. Waveforms
The first 3 harmonics for a string of length L

Open Pipes

Pipes can support standing waves and produce sound. Many musical instruments are straight or curved pipes or tubes within which air will oscillate at particular frequencies to set up standing waves. The boundary conditions of pipes are either open or closed. If the end of the pipe is open, it will support an antinode, but if it is closed, it will support a node. One end of the pipe must be open at least a little to allow for the entry of air, but sometimes these openings are small and covered by the musician's mouth and function as a closed end. Pipes that are open at both ends are called open pipes, while those that are closed at one end (and open at the other) are called closed pipes. The flute is an open pipe instrument, and the clarinet is a closed pipe instrument.

An open pipe, being open at both ends, supports antinodes corresponding to the amplitudes of the variation in the movement of the air. At the closed end, there is no variation in the movement of the air (because of the physical boundary), so this is a node. If a standing wave is set up in an open pipe of length L such that there is only one node between the two antinodes at the open ends of the pipe, the length of the pipe corresponds to one-half the wavelength of the standing wave. (The distance from one antinode to the subsequent antinode is one-half the wavelength.) If a standing wave is set up such that there are two nodes between the antinodes at the open ends (with a third antinode between the two nodes), the length of the pipe corresponds to the wavelength of the standing wave. (The distance from one antinode to the second consecutive antinode is one wavelength.) This pattern suggests that the length L of an open pipe must be equal to some integer multiple of a half wavelength (e.g., $L = \frac{\lambda}{2}, \frac{2\lambda}{2}, \frac{3\lambda}{2}$, etc.). The happy news is that this relationship is identical to the one described above for strings and standing waves! The equation that relates the wavelength λ of a standing wave and the length L of an open pipe that supports it is

$$\lambda = \frac{2L}{n}$$

where n is a positive nonzero integer ($n = 1, 2, 3,\ldots$). From the relationship that $f = \frac{v}{\lambda}$, where v is the wave speed, the possible frequencies are

$$f = \frac{nv}{2L}$$

where n is a positive nonzero integer ($n = 1, 2, 3,\ldots$) and v is the speed of sound in air at room temperature, 344 m/s. Figure 9.7 gives a symbolic representation of the first three harmonics in an open pipe. We use the word *symbolic* in recognition that the conventional way of diagrammatically representing sound waves is with transverse, rather than longitudinal, waves (which are much harder to draw).

> ## Key Concept
> For pipes with two open ends, the number of nodes present will tell you which harmonic it is.

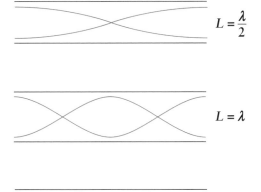

$$L = \frac{\lambda}{2}$$

$$L = \lambda$$

$$L = \frac{3\lambda}{2}$$

Figure 9.7. Harmonics (Open Pipe)
The first three harmonics in an open pipe

Closed Pipes

In the case of a closed pipe, such as a clarinet (or a milk jug), the closed end will support a node, and the open end will support an antinode. The first harmonic in a closed pipe consists of only the node at the closed end and the antinode at the open end. In a sinusoidal wave, the distance from node to antinode is one-quarter of a wavelength. Because the closed end must always have a node and the open end must always have an antinode, there can only be odd harmonics, since an even harmonic is an integer multiple of the half-wavelength and would necessarily have either two nodes or two antinodes at the ends. The first harmonic has a wavelength that is four times the length of the closed pipe, the third harmonic has a wavelength that is four-thirds the length of the closed pipe, the fifth harmonic has a wavelength that is four-fifths the length of the closed pipe, etc. This can be represented as follows:

$$\lambda = \frac{4L}{n}$$

where n is odd integers only ($n = 1, 3, 5,...$). The frequency of the standing wave in a closed pipe is

$$f = \frac{nv}{4L}$$

where n is odd integers only ($n = 1, 3, 5, ...$) and v is the speed of sound at room temperature, 344 m/s. Figure 9.8 symbolically represents the first, third, and fifth harmonics for a closed pipe.

> **Key Concept**
>
> For pipes with one open end, finding the harmonic works the same way as with pipes with two open ends, though there is one important difference. Because the pipe only has one open end, the sound must go through the pipe, bounce off the wall, and go out again. This means that each sound wave will travel double the length of the pipe. This is why the equations for these pipes have four in the fraction instead of two. Once again, counting the number of nodes the sound wave passes through (accounting for both passes) will tell you which harmonic it is.

$$L = \frac{\lambda}{4}$$

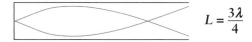
$$L = \frac{3\lambda}{4}$$

$$L = \frac{5\lambda}{4}$$

Figure 9.8. Harmonics (Closed Pipe)
First, third, and fifth harmonics for a closed pipe

MCAT Concept Check 9.3

Before moving on, ensure that you are able to:

✓ Describe the production of sound

✓ Assess the intensity of sound using the decibel scale

✓ Define beat frequencies and pitch

✓ Explain the Doppler effect

✓ Solve standing wave problems (open and closed pipes as well as strings)

Conclusion

Periodic motion is repetitive motion about an equilibrium position. We reviewed simple harmonic motion demonstrated by spring-mass systems and simple pendulums. These conservative systems (ignoring friction) experience restoring forces that are proportional to their displacements. Restoring forces are always directed opposite to displacement in the direction of the equilibrium position. At maximum displacement, the system has maximal potential energy, which is converted to kinetic energy as it accelerates toward its equilibrium position. Maximum kinetic energy is reached as the system reaches its equilibrium position. We then reviewed the general characteristics of waves, including the phenomena of interference and resonance, and analyzed the characteristics and behaviors of sound as an example of a longitudinal waveform. Sound is the mechanical disturbance of particles creating oscillating regions of compression and rarefaction along the direction of wave movement. The intensity of a sound wave is perceived as the loudness of the sound and is measured in decibels, which is a logarithmic scale used to describe the ratio of a sound's intensity to a reference intensity (usually the intensity of the threshold of hearing). The Doppler effect is a phenomenon of a sound's frequency, perceived as pitch, that occurs when the source of a sound and the detector of the sound are moving relative to each other. The perceived frequency is either higher or lower than the actual frequency, depending on whether the source and detector are moving toward each other or away from each other, respectively. Finally, we reviewed the mathematics governing the formation of standing waves, important in the formation of musical sounds in strings, open pipes, and closed pipes.

Continue to review these important topics for the MCAT, taking time to apply what you've learned to MCAT-style passages and questions. Practice is the best way to ensure that you'll be ready to tackle any problem on Test Day!

CONCEPT SUMMARY

Periodic Motion

- ☐ Repetitive motion about an equilibrium position
- ☐ **Simple harmonic motion** (p. 256) is a special type of periodic motion demonstrated by springs and pendulums

Springs

- ☐ **Hooke's law ($F = -kx$)** (p. 256) governs springs by showing that the restoring force is proportional to the displacement and directed toward the equilibrium position
  - ○ **At maximum displacement** springs experience the maximum restoring force, maximum acceleration, maximum potential energy, and minimum kinetic energy
  - ○ **At minimum displacement** springs experience minimum restoring force, minimum acceleration, minimum potential energy, and maximum kinetic energy
- ☐ **Angular Frequency** (p. 257) of a spring is a function of the spring constant (k) and the mass (m) attached to the spring (not its displacement)

Pendulums (p. 259)

- ☐ Governed by a restoring force that is a function of gravity
- ☐ **Equilibrium position** is the alignment with the vertical position (gravitational acceleration vector)
  - ○ **At maximum angular displacement** pendulums experience maximum restoring force, maximum acceleration, maximum potential energy, and minimum kinetic energy
  - ○ **At minimum angular displacement** pendulums experience minimum restoring force, minimum acceleration, minimum potential energy, and maximum kinetic energy
- ☐ **Angular frequency** (p. 260) of a pendulum is a function of the acceleration due to gravity and the length of the pendulum arm

Waves (p. 262)

- ☐ **Transverse** waves have oscillation of wave particles perpendicular to the direction of wave propagation (e.g., water and EM waves)
- ☐ **Longitudinal** waves have oscillation of wave particles along the direction of wave propagation (e.g., sound waves)
- ☐ **Interference** (p. 265) describes waves meeting in space
  - ○ **Constructive interference** describes waves meeting in space in phase
  - ○ **Destructive interference** describes waves meeting in space out of phase

Sound (p. 268)

- ☐ Defined as longitudinal waves of oscillating mechanical disturbances of a material
- ☐ **Loudness** (p. 269) of sound is related to its intensity (which is related to its amplitude)
- ☐ **Pitch** (p. 272) of sound is related to its frequency

- ☐ **The Doppler effect** (p. 273) is a shift in the perceived frequency of a sound compared to the actual frequency of the emitted sound when the source of the sound and its detector are moving relative to each other
    - ○ The apparent frequency will be higher when they are moving toward each other
    - ○ The apparent frequency will be lower when they are moving away from each other

Standing Waves (p. 274)

- ☐ Produced by the constructive and destructive interference of two waves of the same frequency traveling in opposite directions in the same space
    - ○ **Antinodes** are points of maximum oscillation of amplitude
    - ○ **Nodes** are points where there is no oscillation of amplitude
- ☐ **Open pipes** (p. 276) (open at both ends) and strings support standing waves, and the length of the string or pipe is equal to integer multiples of the half wavelength
- ☐ **Closed pipes** (p. 277) (closed at one end) support standing waves, and the length of the pipe is equal to odd integer multiples of the quarter wavelength

EQUATIONS TO REMEMBER

- ☐ $F = -kx$

- ☐ $\omega = 2\pi f = \sqrt{\dfrac{k}{m}}$

- ☐ $U = \dfrac{1}{2}kx^2$

- ☐ $F = -mg \sin\theta$

- ☐ $\omega = 2\pi f = \sqrt{\dfrac{g}{L}}$

- ☐ $v = f\lambda$

- ☐ $\beta = 10 \log \dfrac{I}{I_o}$

- ☐ $\beta_f = \beta_i + 10 \log \left(\dfrac{I_f}{I_i}\right)$

- ☐ $f_{beat} = |f_1 - f_2|$

- ☐ $f' = f\left[\dfrac{v \pm v_D}{v \mp v_S}\right]$

- ☐ $\lambda = \dfrac{2L}{n}$ (for strings and open pipes; where n is a positive non-zero integer)

- ☐ $\lambda = \dfrac{4L}{n}$ (for closed pipes; where n is an odd integer)

SHARED CONCEPTS

HIGH-YIELD PRACTICE PROBLEMS

Practice Questions

1. If the length of a pendulum is increased from 2 m to 8 m, how will the period of oscillation be affected?

   A. It will double.
   B. It will be halved.
   C. It will quadruple.
   D. It will decrease by one-fourth.

2. A child is practicing the second harmonic on his flute. If his brother covers one end of the flute for a brief second, how will the sound change?

   A. The pitch of the sound will be higher.
   B. The pitch of the sound will be lower.
   C. The pitch of the sound will not change.
   D. The pitch of the sound depends on the song the boy is playing.

3. A mass is attached to a horizontal spring and allowed to move horizontally on a frictionless surface. The mass is displaced from equilibrium and released. At what point does the mass experience the minimum force from the spring and its maximum acceleration, respectively?

   A. At the equilibrium point; at the equilibrium point
   B. At maximum compression or expansion; at the equilibrium point
   C. At the equilibrium point; at maximum compression or expansion
   D. At maximum compression or expansion; at maximum compression or expansion

4. How far away from equilibrium will the kinetic energy be equal to the potential energy for a spring that has a spring constant $k = 0.1$ N/m, a speed of 3 m/s, and a 0.4 kg mass attached?

   A. 3 m
   B. 6 m
   C. 12 m
   D. 18 m

5. At what frequency will a spring with an attached mass resonate?

   A. $\dfrac{1}{2\pi}\sqrt{\dfrac{k}{m}}$

   B. $2\pi\sqrt{\dfrac{k}{m}}$

   C. $\dfrac{5}{2\pi\sqrt{\dfrac{m}{k}}}$

   D. $\pi\sqrt{\dfrac{m}{k}}$

6. If the speed of a wave is 3 m/s and its wavelength is 10 cm, what is its period?

   A. 0.01 s
   B. 0.03 s
   C. 0.1 s
   D. 0.3 s

7. What is the angular frequency of a sound in the third harmonic that comes out of a pipe with one end closed? (The length of the pipe $L = 0.6$ m, and the speed of the sound is 340 m/s.)

   A. 200
   B. 400π
   C. 400
   D. 800π

8. A certain sound level is increased by an additional 20 dB. By how much does its intensity increase?

   A. 2
   B. 20
   C. 100
   D. $\log 2$

9. If two waves are 180° out of phase, what is the amplitude of the resultant wave if the amplitudes of the original waves are 5 cm and 3 cm?

   A. 2 cm
   B. 3 cm
   C. 5 cm
   D. 8 cm

10. A student is standing on the side of a road, facing east, and measuring sound frequencies. For which of the following situations would the student determine that the difference between the perceived frequency and the actual emitted frequency is zero?

   A. A plane flying directly above him from east to west
   B. A police car chasing a driver with its siren on
   C. A person playing piano right behind the student
   D. A dog barking in a car that moves from north to south

11. In which of the following media does sound travel the fastest?

   A. Vacuum
   B. Air
   C. Water
   D. Glass

12. A mass on a pendulum oscillates via simple harmonic motion. A student wants to double the period of the system. She can do this by taking which of the following actions?

   I. Increasing the mass
   II. Dropping the mass from a higher height
   III. Increasing the length of the pendulum string

   A. I only
   B. III only
   C. II and III only
   D. I and III only

13. An officer walks at a velocity of 2 m/s directly toward a student who is stationary and holding a radio playing loud music. Which of the following statements is true about this situation?

I. The officer hears the music at a higher frequency than the student does.

II. The officer hears the exact same frequency of sound that he would if he were standing still and the student were walking directly towards him at 2 m/s.

III. The officer observes the sound waves from the radio to be moving at a lower velocity than the student does.

    A. I only
    B. II only
    C. I and II only
    D. I, II, and III

14. If the frequency of a pendulum is four times greater on an unknown planet than it is on earth, then the gravitational constant on that planet is

    A. 16 times greater.
    B. 4 times greater.
    C. 4 times lower.
    D. 16 times lower.

Small Group Questions

1. As an orchestra tunes its instruments together before a concert, the volume of the orchestra is heard to increase. Why?

2. A flag at the top of a flagpole gently waves in the wind. Is the waving end of the flag a node or an antinode?

Explanations to Practice Questions

1. A

To answer this question, first determine the relationship between the length of a pendulum and its period of oscillation. You know that the angular frequency, ω, of a pendulum is given by

$$\omega = 2\pi f$$

$$\omega = \sqrt{\frac{g}{L}}$$

Since $f = \frac{1}{T}$, rewrite the first formula as

$$\omega = \sqrt{\frac{2\pi}{T}}$$

Equating these two equations, you obtain the following equality:

$$2\pi / T = \sqrt{\frac{g}{L}}$$

From here, you see that the period is equal to

$$T = 2\pi\sqrt{\frac{L}{g}}$$

Finally, you can see that quadrupling the length of the pendulum will double the period, making choice (A) the correct answer.

2. B

This question is basically testing your understanding of pipes open at one or both ends. To begin with, establish the relationship between the sound change and the type of pipe. A change in sound can best be characterized by a change in its frequency; low-frequency sounds have a low pitch (e.g., bass), while high-frequency sounds have a high pitch (e.g., soprano). Your task is to determine how the frequency of a second harmonic differs between a pipe that is open at both ends from one that is open at only one end. For a pipe open at both ends and of length L, the wavelength for the second harmonic is equal to L. In contrast, for a pipe open at one end and closed at the other, the wavelength is equal to $\sqrt{\frac{4L}{3}}$. In other words, when the brother covers one end of the flute, the wavelength increases by $\frac{4}{3}$. Given that the wavelength and the frequency of a sound are inversely proportional, an increase of $\frac{4}{3}$ in wavelength corresponds to a decrease of $\frac{3}{4}$ in frequency. In other words, when the brother covers one end of the flute, the sound produced by the instrument will be slightly lower in pitch than the original sound. The explanation matches choice (B), the correct answer.

3. C

Hooke's law gives the force, F, of the spring on the mass: $F = -kx$. The minimum force is actually zero and occurs where $x = 0$. By definition, $x = 0$ is the equilibrium point (i.e., the position of the mass when the spring is neither stretched nor compressed). Based on this, eliminate choices (B) and (D). Newton's second law tells you that $F = ma$ and therefore $a = \frac{F}{m}$, so the point of maximum acceleration is the point at which the mass experiences the greatest force. From Hooke's law, the greatest force occurs at the point of the largest displacement from equilibrium. Because the displacement at maximum expansion equals the displacement at maximum compression, the largest force and therefore largest acceleration occurs at either maximum expansion or maximum compression. Choice (C) matches the explanation and is thus the correct answer.

4. B

This question is testing your understanding of springs and how they conserve energy. The kinetic energy of a spring is given by $KE = \frac{1}{2}mv^2$, while the potential energy is equal to $U = \frac{1}{2}kx^2$. Your task is to determine at what speed and distance from the equilibrium point the two energies will be equal. Equate the two equations:

$$\frac{1}{2}mv^2 = \frac{1}{2}kx^2$$
$$mv^2 = kx^2$$
$$x^2 = \frac{mv^2}{k}$$
$$x = \sqrt{\frac{mv^2}{k}} = v\sqrt{\frac{m}{k}} = 3\sqrt{\frac{0.4}{0.1}} = 3(2) = 6 \text{ m}$$

Choice (B) is therefore the correct answer.

5. A

The resonance frequency of a mass on a spring is just the natural frequency:

$$\omega = 2\pi f = \sqrt{\frac{k}{m}}$$
$$f = \frac{1}{2\pi}\sqrt{\frac{k}{m}}$$

At this frequency and any multiple of it, the spring will be in resonance. Choice (A) is thus the correct answer.

6. B

This question is testing your understanding of traveling waves. To find the period of the wave, manipulate the calculation for frequency. Since one knows the speed and wavelength, the frequency and period can be calculated using the following equation:

$$v = \lambda f$$
$$f = \frac{v}{\lambda} = \frac{1}{T}$$
$$T = \frac{\lambda}{v}$$
$$T = \frac{0.1\text{m}}{3 \text{ m/s}} \approx 0.03 \text{ s}$$

Choice (B) is therefore the correct answer.

7. D

You know that the angular frequency is related to the frequency of a wave through the following formula: $\omega = 2\pi f$.

Thus, your initial task is to calculate the frequency of the wave. Knowing its speed, determine the frequency by first calculating its wavelength. For the third harmonic of a standing wave in a pipe with one end closed, the wavelength is

$$\lambda = \frac{4L}{n}$$

where n is the harmonic. In this case, $n = 3$. The wavelength is

$$\lambda = \frac{4(0.6\text{m/s})}{3}$$
$$\lambda = 0.8 \text{ m}$$

The frequency of the wave is therefore

$$v = \lambda f$$
$$f = \frac{v}{\lambda}$$
$$f = \frac{340\text{m/s}}{0.8\text{m}}$$
$$f \approx 400 \text{ s}^{-1}$$

Finally, obtain the angular frequency simply by multiplying the frequency of the wave by 2π:

$$\omega = 2\pi f$$

$$\omega = 800\pi$$

Choice (D) matches your result and is thus the correct answer.

8. C

Let I_a be the intensity before the increase and I_b the intensity after the increase. Using the equation that relates decibels to intensity, obtain the ratio of I_b to I_a.

$$\Delta\beta = 10 \log\left(\frac{I_a}{I_b}\right)$$
$$\log\left(\frac{I_a}{I_b}\right) = \frac{\Delta\beta}{10}$$
$$\log\left(\frac{I_a}{I_b}\right) = \frac{20}{10}$$
$$\frac{I_b}{I_a} = 10^2$$

$$\frac{I_b}{I_a} = 100$$
$$I_b = 100 I_a$$

The intensity is increased by a factor of 100, making choice (C) the correct answer.

9. A

When two waves are out of phase by 180°, the resultant amplitude is the difference between the two separate amplitudes. Because this is destructive interference, expect that the amplitude of the resulting wave will be less than the amplitude of each individual wave. In this case, the resulting wave will have an amplitude of $5 - 3 = 2$ cm, making choice (A) the correct answer.

10. C

This question is testing us on your understanding of the Doppler effect. A difference of zero between the perceived and the emitted frequencies implies that the source of the sound is not moving. From the given choices, the only source of sound that is not moving is the person playing the piano right behind the student. Choice (C) is therefore the correct answer.

11. D

Sound is a mechanical disturbance propagated through a deformable medium; it is transmitted by the oscillation of particles along the direction of motion of the sound wave. As such, sound needs a medium to travel through, and the more tightly packed the particles are within that medium, the faster the propagation of vibration of the sound waves. Therefore, sound cannot be transmitted in a vacuum, and its speed of propagation increases as it moves from gas to liquid to solid. Sound will thus travel fastest through glass, making choice (D) the correct answer.

12. B

Recall the formula for the period of a pendulum, $T = 2\pi\sqrt{\frac{L}{g}}$. It is a common misconception that mass has an effect on the frequency of a pendulum. Remember that this is a pendulum and not a spring! In a pendulum system, the only factors that affect the motion are the ones in the formula: L, the length of the string, and g, the gravitational acceleration (usually 9.8 m/s², unless the pendulum is on a different planet or under special conditions). Only item III is correct.

13. A

Here, an observer is moving closer to a stationary source. The formula needed is $f' = f\left(\frac{v + v_D}{v}\right)$, where v is the velocity of the sound. Because the numerator is greater than the denominator, f' will be greater than f; therefore, item I is true. Choice (A) is the correct answer. The scenario described in item II will produce a similar, but not identical, frequency for the officer: the frequency formula would be $f' = f\left(\frac{v}{v - v_s}\right)$. The listener's frequency will increase, but the increase will not be exactly the same as if the officer is moving. So item II is false. And item III is false because we already know the frequency increases for the officer, but a decrease in velocity would correspond to a decrease in frequency. Choice (A), I only, is the correct answer.

14. A

The frequency of a pendulum is defined as $f = \frac{1}{2\pi}\sqrt{\frac{g}{L}}$. Because g is under a square root, the gravitational constant has to be f^2 as large, or 16 in this case. Choice (A) is the correct answer. Choices (B) and (C) assume that the relationship between frequency and gravitational acceleration is 1:1. Choices (C) and (D) may be obtained if you mistakenly wrote g in the denominator instead of the numerator when solving the equation.

Explanations to Small Group Questions

1. The volume of the orchestra will increase as the instruments become in tune, even if the musicians are not playing more loudly. This is because in-tune instruments will produce sound waves that are in phase and will constructively interfere. The constructive interference means that the amplitudes of the sound waves will add together, thus increasing the intensity and loudness of the orchestra.

2. The loose end of the flag would have a maximum amplitude because it can move freely. Therefore, it would behave as an antinode. In contrast, the end of the flag that is tied to the flagpole does not move. Because the tied end has no displacement, it is a node. The flag in the wind can be thought of as a standing wave much like the standing wave in a pipe with one closed end.

Light and Optics

In this chapter:

Introduction

The next time you're browsing your local convenience store, look for the security mirrors; they're the ones that bulge out from the wall, usually above eye level. There should be at least a couple within view of the cash register. Looking into one of these mirrors, notice not just that the image you see of the world is distorted but *how* it is distorted: The image is still right-side up, but everything is much smaller than you'd expect, and the curve of the mirror introduces some slopes that aren't there in reality. Additionally (and this is why security mirrors are convenient, low-tech solutions that allow the cashier to survey the entire store), you see a much wider field of vision than you would if the mirror were a simple plane mirror like the one in your bathroom. All these features result from the fact that the security mirror is a convex, diverging optical system. Parallel light rays that hit the mirror are reflected in multiple directions, which allow observers to see more of the mirror's field of vision, even if the image is somewhat distorted and the objects in the image are closer than they appear. And yes, the passenger-side mirror of your car that has that same message is also a convex mirror, allowing you to see a wider view of the cars behind you.

Optical phenomena can be observed in cars, convenience stores, cameras, contact lenses, cosmetic mirrors, magnifying glasses, rainbows, and many other settings, including on your MCAT. This chapter will first complete a topic from the previous chapter (Chapter 9, Periodic Motion, Waves, and Sound) by analyzing the transverse waveform of visible light and other electromagnetic (EM) waves. It will then consider in detail the rules of optics, which describe the behavior of electromagnetic waves as they bounce off and travel through various shapes and compositions of matter. The optical systems covered are those tested on the MCAT: concave and convex mirrors, which produce images by reflection, and concave and convex lenses, which produce images by refraction. To close, we will discuss the high-level implications of thin-slit experiments and light polarization.

10.1 Electromagnetic Spectrum ★★★★★☆

The full electromagnetic spectrum includes radio waves on one end (long wavelength, low frequency, low energy) and gamma rays on the other (short wavelength, high frequency, high energy). Between the two extremes, we find, in order from lower energy to higher energy, microwaves, infrared, visible light, ultraviolet, and x-rays. This chapter will focus primarily on the range of wavelengths corresponding to the visible spectrum of light (380 nm–760 nm).

ELECTROMAGNETIC WAVES

A changing magnetic field can cause a change in the electric field, and a changing electric field can cause a change in the magnetic field. Because changing electric fields affect changing magnetic fields that affect changing electric fields (and so on and so on), we can see how **electromagnetic waves** occur in nature. One field affects the other, totally independent of matter, and electromagnetic waves can even travel through a vacuum.

Electromagnetic waves are transverse waves because the oscillating electric and magnetic field vectors are perpendicular to the direction of propagation. Furthermore, the electric field and the magnetic field are perpendicular to each other. This is illustrated in Figure 10.1.

Bridge

This perpendicular relationship is described by the right-hand rule, discussed in Chapter 7.

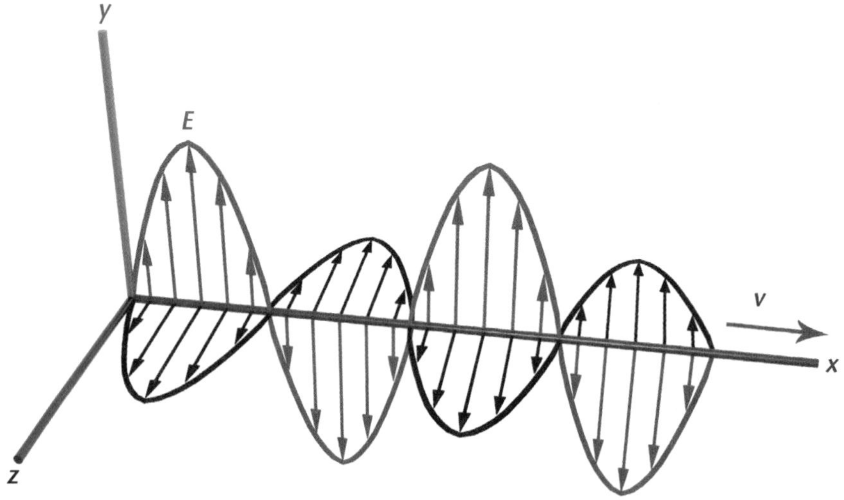

Key Equation

$c = f\lambda$
$m/s = (s^{-1})(m)$

Use this equation to determine the wavelength or frequency of light traveling in air or a vacuum.

Figure 10.1. Electromagnetic Wave
The electric field (E) oscillates up and down the page
The magnetic field (B) oscillates into and out of the page

The **electromagnetic spectrum** is a term used to describe the full range of frequency and wavelength of electromagnetic waves. The following units are often used when quoting wavelengths: 1 mm = 10^{-3} m, 1 μm = 10^{-6} m, 1 nm = 10^{-9} m, and 1 Å (angstrom) = 10^{-10} m. The full spectrum is broken up into many regions, which in descending order of wavelength are radio (10^9 m–1 m), microwave (1 m–1 mm), infrared (1 mm–700 nm), visible light (700 nm–400 nm), ultraviolet (400 nm–50 nm), x-ray (50 nm–10^{-2} nm), and gamma rays (less than 10^{-2} nm). This range of wave types is pictured in Figure 10.2.

Electromagnetic waves vary in frequency and wavelength, but in a vacuum, all electromagnetic waves travel at the same speed, called the **speed of light**. This constant is represented by c and is approximately 3×10^8 m/s. To a first approximation—and for all MCAT-related equations—electromagnetic waves also travel in air with this velocity. In reference to electromagnetic waves, the familiar equation $v = f\lambda$ becomes

$$c = f\lambda$$

where c is the speed of light in a vacuum and, to a first approximation, also in air.

COLOR AND THE VISIBLE SPECTRUM

We just mentioned that the electromagnetic spectrum is divided into many regions. The only part of the spectrum that is perceived as light by the human eye is named, quite appropriately, the visible region. Within this region, different wavelengths induce sensations of different colors, with violet at one end of the visible spectrum (380 nm) and red at the other (760 nm).

Light that contains all the colors in equal intensity is seen as white. The color of an object that does not emit its own light is dependent on the color of light that it reflects. So an object that appears red is one that absorbs all light except red. This implies that a red object receiving green light will appear black, because it absorbs the green light and has no light to reflect. The term *blackbody*, used to describe an ideal radiator (see Chapter 11, Atomic Phenomena), refers to the fact that such an object is also an ideal absorber and would appear totally black if it were at a lower temperature than its surroundings.

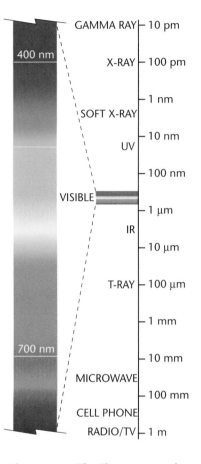

Figure 10.2. The Electromagnetic Spectrum

Mnemonic

To recall the order of the colors in the visible spectrum, remember the grade-school "rainbow" mnemonic of ROY G. BIV (red, orange, yellow, green, blue, indigo, violet).

MCAT Expertise

The wavelengths of the visible spectrum appear on the MCAT often. Remembering its boundaries (about 400 nm–700 nm) will save you time and energy on Test Day.

MCAT Concept Check 10.1

Before moving on, ensure that you are able to:

✓ List the basic properties and describe the structure of electromagnetic waves

✓ Identify the location of various types of light and radiation on the electromagnetic spectrum

✓ Recall the traits of the speed of light and its relation to wavelength and frequency

✓ Describe the different energy levels within the visual spectrum

10.2 Geometrical Optics

When light travels through a single homogeneous medium, it travels in a straight line. This is known as **rectilinear propagation.** The behavior of light at the boundary of a medium or interface between two media is described by the theory of **geometrical optics**. Because the light travels in a straight-line path, we can apply simple geometry to determine its behavior. Geometrical optics pertains to the behavior of reflection and refraction, as well as the study of mirrors and lenses.

REFLECTION

Reflection is the rebounding of incident light waves at the boundary of a medium. Light waves are not absorbed into the second medium; rather, they bounce off of the boundary and travel back through the first medium. Figure 10.3 illustrates reflection.

The **law of reflection** is

$$\theta_1 = \theta_2$$

Figure 10.3. Reflection
According to the law of reflection,
$\theta_1 = \theta_2$

where θ_1 is the **incident angle** and θ_2 is the **reflected angle**, both measured from the normal. We don't anticipate that you will have any difficulty remembering this particular law of optics. Do note that, in optics, angles are always measured from a line drawn perpendicular to the boundary of a medium, usually referred to as the **normal.**

Plane Mirrors

In general, images created by a mirror can be either real or virtual. An image is said to be **real** if the light actually converges at the position of the image. An image is **virtual** if the light only *appears* to be coming from the position of the image but does not actually converge there.

Parallel incident light rays remain parallel after reflection from a plane mirror; that is, plane mirrors—being flat reflective surfaces—cause neither convergence nor divergence of reflected light rays. Because the light does not converge at all, plane mirrors always create virtual images. In a plane mirror, the image appears to be the same distance behind the mirror as the object's distance in front of it (see Figure 10.4). In other words, plane mirrors create the appearance of light rays originating behind the mirrored surface. Of course, this is a physical impossibility; nevertheless, the appearance is there. Because the reflected light remains in front of the mirror but the image is behind the mirror, the image is virtual. We are very familiar with plane mirrors, as they are the common mirrors found in our homes (bathroom mirrors, full-length mirrors, etc.).

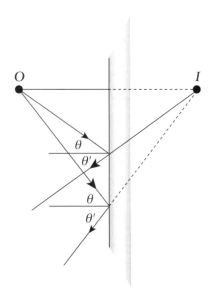

Figure 10.4. Reflection in a Plane Mirror
O is the object and *I* is the (virtual) images incident angles (θ) are equal to their respective reflected angles (θ')

Spherical Mirrors

Spherical mirrors come in two varieties, **concave** and **convex**. The word *spherical* implies that the mirror can be considered a small portion of the surface of the mirrored ball (sphere). In other words, if you had a sphere made out of a mirror-like material, a spherical mirror would be a small portion cut out of that sphere. Spherical mirrors have a **center of curvature** (C) and a **radius of curvature** (r) associated with them. The center of curvature is a point on the optical axis located at a distance equal to the radius of curvature from the vertex of the mirror; in other words, where the center of the mirrored sphere would be, were it a complete sphere.

If you were to look from the inside of a sphere to its surface, you would see a concave surface (con*cave* = looking into a *cave*). However, if you were to look from outside the sphere, you would see a convex surface. For a convex surface (mirror on the outer curvature), the center of curvature and the radius of curvature are located behind the mirror. For a concave surface (mirror is on inner curvature), the center of curvature and the radius of curvature are in front of the mirror. Concave mirrors are called **converging mirrors**, and convex mirrors are called **diverging mirrors**, because they cause parallel incident light rays to reflect convergently and divergently, respectively.

There are several important distances associated with mirrors. The focal length (f) is the distance between the focal point (F) and the mirror (for all spherical mirrors, $f = \dfrac{r}{2}$, where the radius of curvature (r) is the distance between C and the mirror); the distance of the object from the mirror is o; the distance of the image from the mirror is i (see Figure 10.5 for an illustration of these distances).

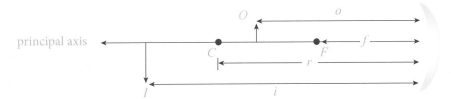

Figure 10.5. Key Variables for Geometrical Optics
The mirror pictured is a concave mirror; light rays are not shown

There is a simple relation satisfied by these distances:

$$\frac{1}{o} + \frac{1}{i} = \frac{1}{f} = \frac{2}{r}$$

While it is not important which units of distance are used in this equation, it is important that all values used have the same units, be they centimeters, meters, and so on.

On the MCAT, you will most often use this equation to calculate the image distance. (This equation applies not only to both types of mirrors but also to both types of

Real World

The passenger-side mirrors in cars are an example of convex mirrors; the small circular mirrors used for applying makeup are an example of concave mirrors.

Key Concept

The focal point of converging mirrors (and converging lenses) will always be positive. The focal point of diverging mirrors (and diverging lenses) will always be negative.

Key Equation

Mirror Equation

$$\frac{1}{o} + \frac{1}{i} = \frac{1}{f} = \frac{2}{r}$$

$m^{-1} + m^{-1} = m^{-1} = m^{-1}$

Use this equation to determine the object or image distance from a mirror, focal length, or radius of curvature.

Key Concept

Any time the object is at the focal point, the reflected rays will be parallel, and thus, the image will be at infinity.

Key Equation

$$m = -\frac{i}{o}$$

Use this equation to find the magnification of an image.

lenses! It is a very high-yield equation, to say the least.) If the image has a positive distance, it is a real image, which implies that the image is in front of the mirror. If the image has a negative distance, it is virtual and thus located behind the mirror. Plane mirrors can be thought of as infinitely large spherical mirrors. As such, for a plane mirror, $r = f = \infty$, and the equation becomes $\frac{1}{o} + \frac{1}{i} = 0$ or $i = -o$ (virtual image at distance behind mirror equal to distance of object in front of mirror).

The **magnification** (m) is a dimensionless value that is the ratio of the image's height to the object's height. Following the sign convention given below, the orientation of the image compared with the object can also be determined. A negative magnification signifies an inverted image, while a positive value means the image is upright.

$$m = -\frac{i}{o}$$

If $|m| < 1$, the image is reduced; if $|m| > 1$, the image is enlarged; and if $|m| = 1$, the image is the same size as the object.

Figure 10.6 shows ray diagrams for a concave spherical mirror with the object at three different points. A ray diagram is useful for getting an approximation of where the image is. On Test Day, ray diagrams will be especially helpful for getting a quick understanding of the type of image (real versus virtual, inverted versus upright, and magnified versus reduced) that will be produced by an object some distance from the mirror (or lens). In general, there are three important rays to draw. For a concave mirror, a ray that strikes the mirror parallel to the horizontal is reflected back through the focal point. A ray that passes through the focal point before reaching the mirror is reflected back parallel to the horizontal. A ray that strikes the mirror right where the normal intersects it gets reflected back with the same angle (measured from the normal). In Figure 10.6a, the object is placed between F and C, and the image produced is real, inverted and magnified. In Figure 10.6b, the object is placed at F, and no image is formed because the reflected light rays are parallel to each other. In terms of the mirror equation, we say that the image distance $i = \infty$ here. For the scenario in Figure 10.6c, the object is placed between F and the mirror, and the image produced is virtual, upright, and magnified.

A single diverging mirror forms only a virtual, upright, and reduced image, regardless of the position of the object, and the further away the object, the smaller the image will be. (To quickly remember these rules, recall the convenience store security mirrors and the side-view mirror on an automobile. If you're wondering what a ray diagram for a diverging mirror would look like, just swap the image and the object in Figure 10.6c.)

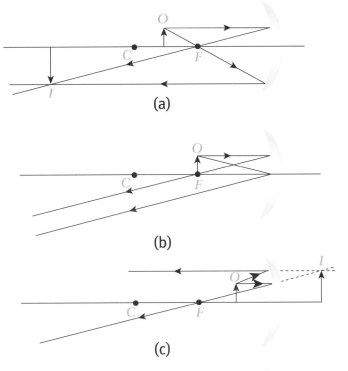

(a)

(b)

(c)

Figure 10.6. Ray Diagrams for Concave Mirrors
(a) Object is placed between *C* and *F*
(b) Object is placed at *F*
(c) Object is placed between *F* and the mirror

Sign Convention for Single Mirrors

Table 10.1 gives the proper signs for various instances when dealing with single mirrors. Note that *R* side is used to denote *R*eal side, which for mirrors is in front of the mirror. Similarly, *V* side stands for *V*irtual side, which is behind the mirror. Note that on the MCAT, for almost all problems involving mirrors, the object will be placed in front of the mirror, and the object distance *o* will thus be positive.

Table 10.1. Sign Chart for Single Mirrors

Symbol	Positive	Negative
o	object is in front of mirror (*R* side)	object is behind mirror (*V* side)
i	image is in front of mirror (*R* side)	image is behind mirror (*V* side)
r	concave mirrors	convex mirrors
f	concave mirrors	convex mirrors
m	image is upright (erect)	image is inverted

Example: An object is placed 7 cm in front of a concave mirror that has a 10 cm radius of curvature. Determine the image distance, the magnification, whether the image is real or virtual, and whether it is inverted or upright.

Solution: Use the mirror equation:

$$\frac{1}{i} + \frac{1}{o} = \frac{2}{r}$$

$$\frac{1}{i} = \frac{2}{r} - \frac{1}{o}$$

$$\frac{1}{i} = \frac{2}{10} - \frac{1}{7}$$

$$i = +17.5 \text{ cm}$$

The magnification m is

$$m = -\frac{i}{o}$$

$$= -\frac{17.5}{7}$$

$$= -2.5$$

The image is in front of the mirror (i is positive) and therefore real. The image is inverted (m is negative) and 2.5 times larger ($|m| = 2.5$).

REFRACTION

Refraction is the bending of light as it passes from one medium to another and changes speed. The speed of light through any medium is always less than its speed through a vacuum. We've already mentioned that the speed of light through air can be approximated as the speed of light through a vacuum (3.00×10^8 m/s).

The Law of Refraction: Snell's Law

When light is not in a vacuum, its speed is less than c. For a given medium,

$$n = \frac{c}{v}$$

where c is the speed of light in a vacuum, v is the speed of light in the medium, and n is a dimensionless quantity called the **index of refraction** of the medium. For air, n is essentially equal to 1 because $v \approx c$. But for all other materials you encounter on the MCAT, $v < c$ and $n > 1$. Refracted rays of light obey **Snell's law** as they pass from one medium to another:

$$n_1 \sin \theta_1 = n_2 \sin \theta_2$$

Real World

When a pencil (or any straight object) is dipped into a glass of water at an angle, it looks impossibly bent where it intersects the surface of the water. This is because of the refraction of light through the water.

Key Equation

Snell's Law (Law of Refraction)
$n_1\sin\theta_1 = n_2\sin\theta_2$
Use this equation to find the degree of refraction of a light ray upon entering a new medium.

where n_1 and θ_1 are for the medium from which the light is coming and n_2 and θ_2 are for the medium into which the light is entering. Note that θ is once again measured with respect to the perpendicular (normal) to the boundary (see Figure 10.7).

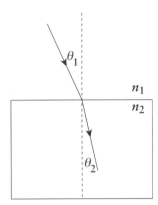

Figure 10.7. Snell's Law
The light is moving from a medium with a lower index of refraction (n_1)
to a medium with a higher index of refraction (n_2)

A helpful generalization to keep in mind for Test Day is that when light enters a medium with a higher index of refraction ($n_2 > n_1$), it bends towards the normal so that $\theta_2 < \theta_1$ (see Figure 10.8). Conversely, if the light travels into a medium where the index of refraction is smaller ($n_2 < n_1$), the light will bend away from the normal so that $\theta_2 > \theta_1$.

> **Key Concept**
>
> The most important thing to remember is that when light enters a medium with a higher index of refraction, it bends *toward* the normal. When light enters a medium with a lower index of refraction, it bends *away* from the normal.

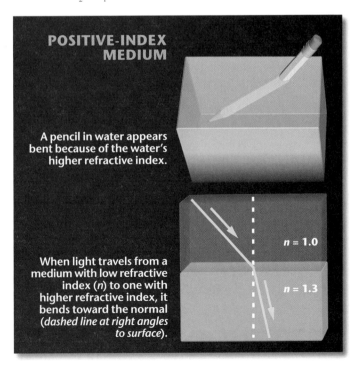

Figure 10.8. Refraction, Air to Water

Example: A penny sits at the bottom of a pool of water ($n = 1.33$) at a depth of 3.0 m. If an observer 1.8 m tall stands 30 cm away from the ledge, how close to the side can the penny be and still be visible?

Solution: First draw a picture of the situation as in Figure 10.9. Note that the light is coming from the water ($n_1 = 1.33$) and going into the air ($n_2 = 1$), so the light is bent away from the normal ($\theta_2 > \theta_1$).

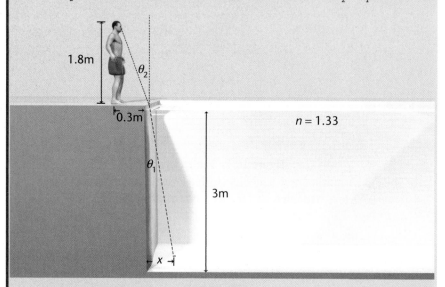

Figure 10.9

We need to find the angles that the light rays make with the normal to the water's surface:

$$\tan \theta_2 = \frac{0.3}{1.8}$$
$$\theta_2 = 9.5°$$

Using Snell's law, we can solve for θ_1:

$$\sin \theta_1 = \frac{n_2}{n_1} \sin \theta_2$$
$$= \frac{0.165}{1.33}$$
$$\theta_1 = 7.1°$$

We can find x using trigonometry:

$$x = 3 \tan \theta_1$$
$$= 0.37 \text{ m}$$
$$= 37 \text{ cm}$$

Real World

It is this property of water that makes spearfishing so difficult. Just remember, the fish is actually *closer* than it looks.

Total Internal Reflection

Have you ever noticed that sometimes objects underwater (like coins in a fountain) will "disappear" from your view only to reappear when you move closer to the edge of the water? If you have, then you've experienced the optical phenomenon called **total internal reflection**. You may not have called it that, but that's what you experienced.

When light travels from a medium with a higher index of refraction (such as water) to a medium with a lower index of refraction (such as air), the refracted angle is larger than the angle of incidence ($\theta_2 > \theta_1$); that is, the refracted light ray bends away from the normal. As the angle of incidence is increased, the refracted angle also increases, and eventually, a special incident angle is reached called the **critical angle** (θ_c), for which the refracted angle θ_2 equals 90 degrees. At the critical angle of incidence, the refracted light ray passes along the interface between the two media. The critical angle can be found from Snell's law:

$$n_1 \sin \theta_1 = n_2 \sin \theta_2$$
$$n_1 \sin \theta_c = n_2 \sin 90° = n_2$$
$$\sin \theta_c = \frac{n_2}{n_1}$$

Total internal reflection, a phenomenon in which all the light incident on a boundary is reflected back into the original material, results for any angle of incidence greater than the critical angle, θ_c (see Figure 10.10).

> **Key Concept**
>
> Remember that the sine of 90 degrees equals 1. This is why the second θ simply cancels out.

> **Key Concept**
>
> When drawing these diagrams, it may seem counterintuitive to make the light come from the water, but you always want to have light traveling toward the observer's eye.

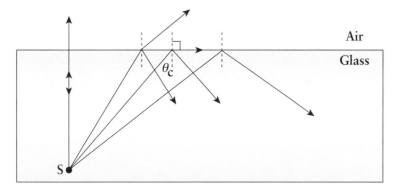

Figure 10.10. Total Internal Reflection
At incident angle θ_c, the refracted angle is equal to 90°; incident angles greater and less than θ_c are also shown

Example: From the previous example, suppose another penny is 10 times farther out than the first one. Will a light ray going from this penny to the top edge of the pool emerge from the water?

Solution: First find the critical angle:

$$\sin \theta_c = \frac{n_2}{n_1}$$
$$= \frac{1}{1.33}$$
$$\theta_c = 48.8°$$

The angle made by the second penny's light ray is

$$\tan \theta_1 = \frac{0.37 \times 10}{3} = 1.23$$

$$\theta_1 = 51°$$

$\theta_1 > \theta_c$; therefore, the light ray will be totally internally reflected and will not emerge.

Bridge

It is important to realize that concave mirrors and convex lenses (we will discuss these soon) are both converging and thus have similar properties. Similarly, convex mirrors and concave lenses have similar properties and are both diverging.

Real World

Converging lenses are needed for people who are "farsighted." These tend to be reading glasses. Diverging lenses are needed for people who are "nearsighted," or those who can't see the board when sitting in the back of the classroom.

Key Concept

If the rays you draw do not intersect, reflect the rays back to the side of the lens the light came from, resulting in a virtual image.

THIN SPHERICAL LENSES

There is an important difference between lenses and mirrors, aside from the fact that lenses refract light while mirrors reflect it. When working with lenses, you are dealing with *two* surfaces that affect the light path. For example, a person wearing glasses sees light that travels from an object through the air into the glass lens (first surface). Then the light travels through the glass until it reaches the other side, where again it travels out of the glass into the air (second surface). The light refracts twice as it passes from air to lens and from lens back to air.

On the MCAT, you'll be working with thin lenses whose thickness can be neglected. Because light can be coming from either side of a lens, a lens has two focal points (one on each side of the lens) and the focal length can be measured in either direction from its center (see Figure 10.11). For thin spherical lenses, the focal lengths are equal, so we speak of the focal length.

Figure 10.11(a) also illustrates that a **converging lens** is always thicker at the center, while Figure 10.11(b) illustrates that a **diverging lens** is always thinner at the center.

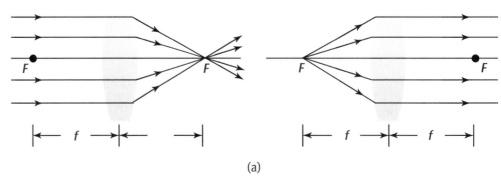

(a)

Figure 10.11. Ray Diagrams for Single Lenses
(a) Convex (converging) lenses

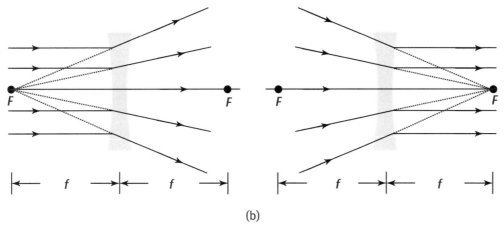

(b)

Figure 10.11. Ray Diagrams for Single Lenses (continued)
(b) Concave (diverging) lenses

The basic formulas for finding image distance and magnification for spherical mirrors (except $r = 2f$) also apply to lenses. The object distance o, image distance i, focal length f, and magnification m, are related by

$$\frac{1}{o} + \frac{1}{i} = \frac{1}{f}$$

$$m = \frac{-i}{o}$$

For lenses where the thickness cannot be neglected, the focal length is related to the curvature of the lens surfaces and the index of refraction of the lens by the **lensmaker's equation:**

$$\frac{1}{f} = (n-1)\left(\frac{1}{r_1} - \frac{1}{r_2}\right)$$

where n is the index of refraction of the lens material, r_1 is the radius of curvature of the first lens surface and r_2 is the radius of curvature of the second lens surface.

Note that the sign conventions change slightly for lenses. (Sign conventions are the trickiest part of optics, so be sure to get plenty of practice using them before Test Day.) For both lenses and mirrors, positive magnification means upright images, and negative magnification means inverted images. Also, for both lenses and mirrors, a positive image distance means that the image is real and is located on the R side, whereas a negative image distance means that the image is virtual and located on the V side. Table 10.2 summarizes the sign conventions for single lenses.

However, the designations of the R side and V side confuse many students because they are different for mirrors and lenses. To identify the R side, remember that the R side is where the light really goes after interacting with the mirror or lens. For

Key Concept

To find where the image is, draw these rays and find a point where any two rays intersect. This point of intersection will show you where the image is.

Bridge

To simplify sign conventions, just think about if the image is on the side it's supposed to be on or not. Mirrors reflect light back; lenses let light pass through. If the image is on the wrong side, then it is a virtual image.

mirrors, light is reflected and, therefore, stays in front of the mirror. The image may either appear in front of or behind the mirror, but the light rays always remain in front of the mirror. Because the R side is in front of the mirror, the V side is behind the mirror. For lenses, it is different: Light travels through the lens and comes out on the other side. The light really travels to the other side of the lens, and therefore, for lenses, the R side is opposite to the side of the lens from which the light originated; in other words, it is the side *to* which the light travels after it passes through the lens. In addition, the V side is the side of the lens from which the light originates; in other words, it is the side *from* which the light passes through the lens. Although the object of a single lens is on the V side, this does not make the object virtual. Objects are real, with a positive object distance, unless they are placed in certain multiple lens systems (a scenario which is rarely encountered on the MCAT).

Focal lengths have a simple sign convention. For both mirrors and lenses, converging lenses and mirrors have positive focal lengths, and diverging mirrors and lenses have negative focal lengths. For radii of curvature, you have to remember that a lens has two surfaces, each with its own radius of curvature (r_1 and r_2, where the surfaces are numbered in the order that they are encountered by the traveling light). For both mirrors and lenses, a radius of curvature is positive if the center of curvature is on the R side and negative if the center of curvature is on the V side.

Table 10.2. Sign Chart for Single Lenses

Symbol	Positive	Negative
o	object on side of lens light is coming from (V side)	object on side of lens light is going to (R side)
i	image on side of lens light is going to (R side)	image on side of lens light is coming from (V side)
f	converging lens	diverging lens
m	image erect	image inverted
r	when on R side (convex surface as seen from side the light is coming from)	when on V side (concave surface as seen from side the light is coming from)

Optometrists often describe a lens in terms of its **power (P)**. This is measured in **diopters**, where f (the focal length) is in meters and is given by this equation:

$$P = \frac{1}{f}$$

P has the same sign as f and is, therefore, positive for a converging lens and negative for a diverging lens. People who are nearsighted (can see near objects clearly) need diverging lenses, while people who are farsighted (can see distant objects clearly) need converging lenses. Bifocal lenses are corrective lenses that have two distinct regions, one that causes convergence of light to correct for farsightedness (hyperopia) and a second that causes divergence of light to correct for nearsightedness (myopia) in the same lens.

Multiple Lens Systems

Lenses in contact are a series of lenses with negligible distances between them. These systems behave as a single lens with equivalent focal length given by

$$\frac{1}{f} = \frac{1}{f_1} + \frac{1}{f_2} + \cdots + \frac{1}{f_n}$$
$$P = P_1 + P_2 + \cdots + P_n$$

A good example of lenses in contact is a corrective contact worn directly on the eye. In this case, the lens of the eye (a converging lens) is in contact with a contact lens (either converging or diverging, depending on the necessary correction), and their focal lengths and powers would be added.

For **lenses not in contact**, the image of one lens is used to make the object of another lens. The image from the last lens is the image of the system. Microscopes and telescopes are good examples of multiple lenses not in contact. The magnification for the system is

$$M = m_1 \times m_2 \times m_3 \times \ldots \times m_n$$

> ### MCAT Expertise
>
> Because the MCAT is a timed test, you will not be given a massive multiple lens system to calculate, though they might test a multiple-lens system conceptually.

Example: An object is 15 cm to the left of a thin diverging lens with a 45 cm focal length as shown in Figure 10.12. Find
a. where the image is formed, if it is upright or inverted, and if it is real or virtual.
b. the radii of curvature, assuming the lens is symmetrical and made of glass ($n = 1.50$).

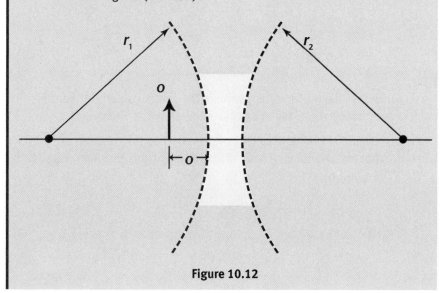

Figure 10.12

Solution:

a. The image distance (i) is found using this equation:

$$\frac{1}{i} + \frac{1}{o} = \frac{1}{f}$$

$$\frac{1}{i} = \frac{1}{f} - \frac{1}{o}$$

Because the lens is diverging, the focal length takes a negative sign, $f = -45$ cm. The object (like any object in a single lens system) has a positive sign, $o = 15$ cm. Solve for i:

$$\frac{1}{i} = \frac{-1}{45} - \frac{1}{15}$$

$$= \frac{-1}{45} - \frac{3}{45}$$

$$= \frac{-4}{45}$$

$$i = -11.25 \text{ cm}$$

The negative sign indicates that the image is on the left side of the lens and, therefore, virtual (the light went through the lens to the right side). To find out whether the image is upright or inverted, we need to calculate the magnification:

$$m = -\frac{i}{o}$$

$$= -\frac{-11.25}{15}$$

$$= \frac{11.25}{15}$$

$$= 0.75$$

Since the magnification is positive, the image is upright. Furthermore, since $|m| < 1$, the image is smaller than the object.

b. Because the lens is symmetrical, the radii are equal but opposite in sign. They can be found from the lensmaker's equation:

$$\frac{1}{f} = (n-1)\left(\frac{1}{r_1} - \frac{1}{r_2}\right)$$

As the light progresses from left to right, the first surface of the lens is concave (r_1 negative), and the second surface of the lens is convex (r_2 positive). Thus,

$$\frac{1}{f} = (n-1)\left(\frac{1}{r_1} - \frac{1}{r_2}\right)$$

$$= (n-1)\left(-\frac{2}{r}\right)$$

We know that $f = -45$ cm (diverging lens). Therefore,

$$-\frac{1}{45} = (1.5-1)\left(-\frac{2}{r}\right)$$

$$-\frac{1}{45} = \frac{-1}{r}$$

$$r = 45 \text{ cm}$$

DISPERSION

As we discussed earlier, the speed of light in a vacuum is the same for all wavelengths. However, when light travels through a medium, different wavelengths travel at different velocities. This fact implies that the index of refraction of a medium is a function of the wavelength, because the index of refraction is related to the velocity of the wave by $n = \frac{c}{v}$. When the speed of the light wave varies with wavelength, a material exhibits **dispersion**. The most common example of dispersion is the splitting of white light into its component colors using a prism.

If a source of white light is incident on one of the faces of a prism, the light emerging from the prism is spread out into a fan-shaped beam, as shown in Figure 10.13. The light has been dispersed into a spectrum. This occurs because violet light experiences a greater index of refraction than red light and so is bent to a greater extent. Because red experiences the least amount of bending, it is always on top of the spectrum; violet, having experienced the greatest amount of bending, is always on the bottom of the spectrum. You can prove this to yourself the next time you see a rainbow (raindrops act as miniature prisms): The outermost band of light will be red, and the innermost band of light will be violet.

Bridge

Remember the relative wavelengths and frequencies of the visible colors and the order of the colors. Violet has the largest frequency and thus the smallest wavelength. Red has the smallest frequency and thus the largest wavelength.

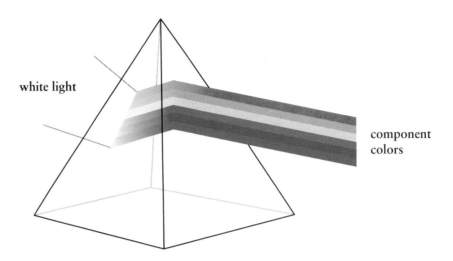

white light

component colors

Figure 10.13. Dispersion in a Prism
Due to their different speeds while inside the prism, the various wavelengths of
light are bent to different degrees

MCAT Concept Check 10.2

Before moving on, ensure that you are able to:

✓ Recall the most important equations regarding mirrors and lenses, including sign conventions

✓ Determine the location and properties of a resulting image, given an object location and an optical setup (reflective or refractive)

✓ Compare and contrast the optical and mathematical properties of mirrors and lenses

✓ Explain the process of refraction and apply Snell's law

✓ Identify the conditions necessary for total internal reflection

✓ Define the causes and process of dispersion

10.3 Diffraction

Although it is usually safe to assume that non-refracted light travels in a straight line, there are situations where light will not actually travel in a straight-line path. For example, when light passes through a narrow opening (an opening whose size is on the order of light wavelengths), the light waves seem to spread out, as is seen in Figure 10.14. As the slit is narrowed, the light spreads out more. This spreading out of light as it passes through a narrow opening is called **diffraction**.

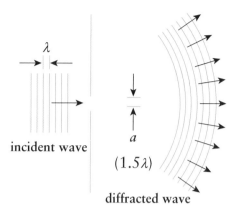

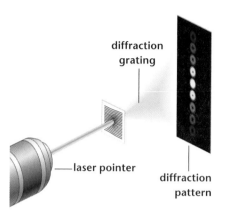

Diffraction Grating and Light Scattering

Figure 10.14. Diffraction
Light emerges from a narrow slit in a wide arc, not a narrow beam

If a lens is placed between a narrow slit and a screen, a pattern is observed consisting of a bright central fringe with alternating dark and bright fringes on each side (see Figure 10.15). The central bright fringe is twice as wide as the bright fringes on the sides, and as the slit becomes narrower, the central maximum becomes wider. The location of the dark fringes is given by the following formula:

$$a \sin \theta = n\lambda \ (n = 1, 2, 3, \dots)$$

where a is the width of the slit, λ is the wavelength of the incident wave, and θ is the angle made by the line drawn from the center of the lens to the dark fringe and the line perpendicular to the screen. Note that bright fringes are halfway between dark fringes.

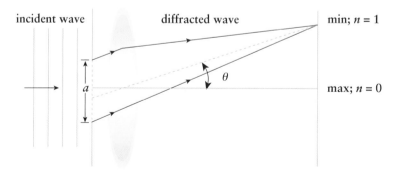

Figure 10.15. Single-Slit Diffraction with Lens

MCAT Concept Check 10.3

Before moving on, ensure that you are able to:

✓ Recognize when diffraction will occur

✓ Describe the changes to a diffraction pattern when a lens is placed near the slit

---

10.4 Interference

By the superposition principle, when waves interact with each other, the amplitudes of the waves add together in a process called interference (see Chapter 9, Periodic Motion, Waves, and Sound). In his famous double-slit experiment, Thomas Young showed that two light waves can interfere with one another, and this finding contributed to the wave theory of light. Figure 10.16a shows the typical setup for Young's double-slit experiment. When coherent monochromatic light illuminates the slits, an interference pattern is observed on a screen placed behind the slits. (Monochromatic light is light that consists of just one wavelength, and coherent light consists of light waves whose phase difference does not change with time.) Regions of constructive interference between the two light waves appear as regions of maximum light intensity on the screen. Conversely, in regions where the light waves interfere destructively, the light is at a minimum intensity, and the screen is dark. An interference pattern produced by a double slit setup is shown in Figure 10.16b.

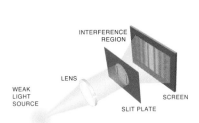

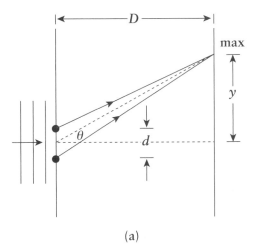

(a)

zeroth fringe

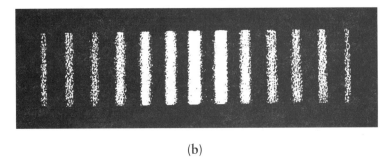

(b)

Figure 10.16. Double-Slit Interference
(a) Setup for Young's double-slit experiment
(b) Interference pattern caused by a double-slit setup

The position of maxima and minima on the screen can be found from the following equations:

(maxima) $d \sin \theta = m\lambda$ $m = 0, 1, 2, \dots$
(minima) $d \sin \theta = (m + \frac{1}{2})\lambda$ $m = 0, 1, 2, \dots$

where d is the distance between the slits, θ is the angle between the dashed lines shown in Figure 10.16a, λ is the wavelength of the light, and m is an integer representing the order.

Example: In a certain double-slit experiment, what is the linear distance y between the sixth and eighth maxima on the screen? The wavelength λ is 550 nm, the slits are separated by 0.14 mm, and the screen is 70 cm from the slits.

Solution: Using the small angle approximation $\sin \theta \approx \tan \theta \approx \theta$, the equation for the distance between maxima is derived as follows:

$$\sin \theta = \frac{m\lambda}{d}$$

$$\tan \theta = \frac{y}{D} \approx \frac{m\lambda}{d}$$

$$\Delta y \approx \frac{\Delta\, m\lambda D}{d}$$

where D is the distance to the screen and Δm is the difference between fringe numbers. Substituting the numbers gives

$$y = \frac{2(550 \times 10^{-9})(0.70)}{0.14 \times 10^{-3}}$$

$$= 5.5 \text{ mm}$$

MCAT Concept Check 10.4

Before moving on, ensure that you are able to:

✓ Explain the important aspects of Young's double-slit experiment
✓ Describe the visual pattern of double-slit interference and its causes
✓ Contrast double-slit interference with single-slit diffraction

10.5 Polarization

Plane-polarized light is light in which the electric fields of all the waves are oriented in the same direction (i.e., their electric field vectors are parallel). It is true that their magnetic fields vectors are also parallel, but convention dictates that the plane of the electric field identifies the plane of polarization. **Unpolarized light** has a random orientation of its electric field vectors; sunlight and light emitted from a light bulb are prime examples. One of the most common applications of plane-polarized light on the MCAT is in the Biological Sciences section, in the context of optically active organic compounds. The optical activity of a compound, due to the presence of chiral centers, causes plane-polarized light to rotate clockwise or counterclockwise by a given number of degrees.

There are filters called polarizers, often used in cameras and sunglasses, that allow only light whose electric field is pointing in a particular direction to pass. If you hold one polarizer in a beam of light, it will let through only that portion of the light that has a given **E** vector orientation. If you then hold up another polarizer directly above or below the first and slowly turn it, you will see the light transmitted through the two polarizers vary from total darkness to the level of the original polarizer alone. When both polarizers are polarizing in the same direction, all the light that passed through the first also passes through the second. When the second polarizer is turned so that it polarizes in a direction perpendicular to the first, no light gets through at all.

MCAT Concept Check 10.5

Before moving on, ensure that you are able to:

✓ Summarize the differences between polarized and unpolarized light
✓ Solve conceptual problems involving polarized light

Conclusion

This chapter illuminated some information about the behaviors and characteristics of light and optical systems. First, we described the nature of the electromagnetic wave, noting the full spectrum of EM waves, of which visible light is the only segment that we can perceive visually. We then focused on geometrical optics to consider the reflective and refractive behaviors of light, noting the ways in which mirrors reflect light to produce images and lenses refract light to produce images. We acknowledged the fact that light doesn't always travel in straight-line pathways but can bend and spread out through diffraction. Finally, we examined the pattern of interference that occurs when light passes through a double slit, as demonstrated in Young's double-slit experiment.

CONCEPT SUMMARY

Electromagnetic Waves (p. 294)

- ☐ **Electromagnetic (EM) waves** are transverse waves
- ☐ They consist of an oscillating electric field and an oscillating magnetic field
  - ○ The two fields are perpendicular to each other and to the direction of propagation of the wave
- ☐ The **electromagnetic spectrum** (p. 295) is the range of frequencies and wavelengths found in EM waves
  - ○ The EM spectrum includes, from lowest to highest energy, radio waves, microwaves, infrared, visible light, ultraviolet, x-rays, and gamma rays

Reflection (p. 296)

- ☐ Is the rebounding of incident light waves at the boundary of a medium
- ☐ The **law of reflection** (p. 296) states that the angle of incidence will equal the angle of reflection, as measured from the normal

Mirrors (p. 296)

- ☐ **Mirrors** reflect light to form images of objects
- ☐ **Spherical mirrors** (p. 297) have centers and radii of curvature as well as focal points
  - ○ **Concave mirrors** (p. 297) are converging systems and can produce real, inverted images or virtual, upright images, depending on the placement of the object relative to the focus
  - ○ **Convex mirrors** (p. 297) are diverging systems and will only produce virtual, upright images
- ☐ **Plane mirrors** (p. 296) also produce virtual, upright images; these images are always the same size as the object
  - ○ Plane mirrors may be thought of as spherical mirrors with infinite radii of curvature

Refraction (p. 300)

- ☐ Is the bending of light as it passes from one medium to another
- ☐ The speed of light changes depending on the density of its medium. This speed change is what causes refraction.
- ☐ The amount of refraction depends on the wavelength of the light involved
  - ○ This behavior causes **dispersion** (p. 309) of light through a prism
- ☐ **Snell's law** (the law of refraction) (p. 300) states that there is an inverse relationship between the index of refraction and the sine of the angle of refraction (measured from the normal)

Total Internal Reflection (p. 303)

- ☐ Occurs when light leaving a medium is instead reflected back inside it
- ☐ This happens when light moves from a medium with a higher index of refraction to a medium with a lower index of refraction with a high angle of incidence
- ☐ The minimum angle of incidence at which total internal reflection occurs is called the **critical angle** (p. 303) for that substance

Lenses (p. 304)

- ☐ Refract light to form images of objects
- ☐ Thin, bilaterally symmetrical lenses have focal points on each side
- ☐ **Convex lenses** are converging systems and can produce real, inverted images or virtual, upright images
- ☐ **Concave lenses** are diverging systems and will only produce virtual, upright images

Diffraction (p. 310)

- ☐ Is the bending and spreading out of light waves as they pass through a narrow slit

Interference (p. 312)

- ☐ Demonstrates the wave/particle duality of light
- ☐ **Young's double-slit experiment** (p. 313) shows the constructive and destructive interference of waves that occur as light passes through a double slit
- ☐ This interference pattern shows **minima and maxima** (p. 312) of intensity

Plane-polarized Light (p. 314)

- ☐ Has all of its electric fields oriented in the same direction (parallel to each other)
- ☐ Plane-polarized light is created by passing unpolarized light through a **polarizer** (p. 314)

EQUATIONS TO REMEMBER

- ☐ $c = f\lambda$

- ☐ $\theta_1 = \theta_2$ (law of reflection)

- ☐ $\dfrac{1}{o} + \dfrac{1}{i} = \dfrac{1}{f} = \dfrac{2}{r}$ (for mirrors)

- ☐ $n = \dfrac{c}{v}$ (index of refraction)

- ☐ $n_1 \sin \theta_1 = n_2 \sin \theta_2$ (law of refraction: Snell's law)

- ☐ $\sin \theta_c = \dfrac{n_2}{n_1}$ (determining critical angle)

- ☐ $\dfrac{1}{o} + \dfrac{1}{i} = \dfrac{1}{f}$ (for lenses)

- ☐ $m = \dfrac{-i}{o}$ (for mirrors and lenses)

- ☐ $\dfrac{1}{f} = (n-1)\left[\left(\dfrac{1}{r_1}\right) - \left(\dfrac{1}{r_2}\right)\right]$ (for lenses of non-negligible thickness)

- ☐ $a \sin \theta = n\lambda$ ($n = 1, 2, 3, \ldots$) (for determining location of dark fringes of diffraction)

- ☐ $d \sin \theta = m\lambda$ (for maxima of interface $m = 0, 1, 2, 3 \ldots$)

- ☐ $d \sin \theta = (m + \frac{1}{2})\lambda$ (for minima of interface $m = 0, 1, 2, 3 \ldots$)

SHARED CONCEPTS

HIGH-YIELD PRACTICE PROBLEMS

Practice Questions

1. If a light ray has a frequency of 5.0×10^{14} Hz, in which region of the electromagnetic spectrum can it be located?

   A. X-ray
   B. UV
   C. Visible
   D. Infrared

2. A standing child has a plane mirror 5 m away from his left arm and another plane mirror 7 m away from his right arm. How far apart are the two images produced by the mirrors if the child has an arm span of 0.5 m?

   A. 2 m
   B. 12 m
   C. 12.5 m
   D. 24.5 m

3. An object is placed at the center of curvature of a concave mirror. Which of the following is true about the image?

   A. It is real and inverted.
   B. It is virtual and inverted.
   C. It is virtual and upright.
   D. It is real and upright.

4. When monochromatic light is refracted as it passes from air to glass, which of the following does not remain the same? (Assume that the wave is fully transmitted.)

   A. Wavelength
   B. Frequency
   C. Amplitude
   D. Period

5. A ray of light ($f = 5 \times 10^{14}$ Hz) travels from air into crystal into chromium. If the indices of refraction of air, crystal, and chromium are 1, 2, and 3, respectively, and the angle of incidence is 30°, which of the following describes the frequency and the angle of refraction in the chromium? (The speed of the light ray is 3×10^8 m/s in air, 2.0×10^4 m/s in crystal, and 1.0×10^3 m/s in chromium.)

   A. 5×10^{14} Hz; 9.6°
   B. 5×10^{14} Hz; 57°
   C. 1.0×10^{10} Hz; 9.6°
   D. 1.0×10^{10} Hz; 57°

6. A source of light ($f = 3.0 \times 10^8$ Hz) passes through three polarizers. The first two polarizers are in the same direction, while the third is rotated 90° with respect to the second polarizer. What is the frequency of the light that comes out of the third polarizer?

   A. Light will not pass through the third polarizer.
   B. 3.0×10^8 Hz
   C. 6.0×10^8 Hz
   D. 9.0×10^8 Hz

7. Which phenomenon would cause monochromatic light entering the prism along path AB to leave along path CD?

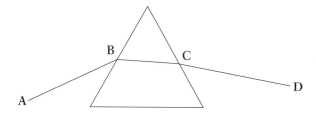

   A. Reflection
   B. Refraction
   C. Diffraction
   D. Polarization

8. Which of the following describes the image formed by an object placed in front of a convex lens at a distance smaller than the focal length?

   A. Virtual and inverted
   B. Virtual and upright
   C. Real and upright
   D. Real and inverted

9. A submarine is inspecting the surface of the water with a laser that points from the submarine to the surface of the water and through the air. At what angle will the laser not penetrate the surface of the water but rather reflect entirely back into the water? (Assume $n_{water} = 2$ and $n_{air} = 1$.)

   A. 15°
   B. 25°
   C. 30°
   D. 35°

10. A student is analyzing the behavior of a light ray that is passed through a small opening and a lens and allowed to project on a screen a distance away. What happens to the central maximum (the brightest spot on the screen) when the slit becomes narrower?

    A. The central maximum remains the same.
    B. The central maximum becomes narrower.
    C. The central maximum becomes wider.
    D. The central maximum divides into smaller light fringes.

11. Which of the following are able to produce a virtual image?

    I. Convex lens

    II. Concave lens

    III. Plane mirror

    A. I only
    B. III only
    C. II and III only
    D. I, II, and III

12. Monochromatic red light is allowed to pass between two different media. If the angle of incidence in medium 1 is 30° and the angle of incidence in medium 2 is 45°, what is the relationship between the speed of the light in medium 2 compared to that in medium 1?

    A. $v_2 = v_1\sqrt{2}$
    B. $v_2\sqrt{2} = v_1$
    C. $v_2 = v_1\sqrt{3}$
    D. $v_2\sqrt{3} = v_1$

13. The near point, or nearest point at which an object can be seen clearly, of one of your eyes is 100 cm. You wish to see your friend's face clearly when she stands 50 cm in front of you. If you use a contact lens to adjust your eyesight, what must be the focal length and power of the contact lens?

   A. $f = 100$ cm; $P = 4$ diopters
   B. $f = -100$ cm; $P = 3$ diopters
   C. $f = -100$ cm; $P = 2$ diopters
   D. $f = 100$ cm; $P = 1$ diopter

14. Imagine that a beam of monochromatic light originates in air and is allowed to shine upon the flat surface of a piece of glass at an angle of 60° with the horizontal. The reflected and refracted beams are perpendicular to each other. What is the index of refraction of the glass?

   A. $\dfrac{1}{\sqrt{3}}$
   B. 1
   C. $\sqrt{3}$
   D. This scenario is not possible.

Small Group Questions

1. Predict the final positions on a screen of the first and second maxima of a beam of light with wavelength 500 nm that is passed through slits separated by 0.75 mm with a 3 cm-thick piece of glass ($n = 1.50$) set 10 cm behind them. The distance from the slits to the screen is 60 cm.

2. The sun falls on a concave mirror and forms an image 3 cm from the mirror. If an object 24 mm high is placed 12 cm from the mirror, where will its image be formed? Construct the ray diagram. How high is the image? Find the magnification of the mirror.

Explanations to Practice Questions

1. C

To determine the region of the spectrum in which this light ray is located, calculate its wavelength:

$$c = \lambda f$$
$$\lambda = \frac{c}{f}$$
$$\lambda = (3 \times 10^8 \text{ m/s})/(5.0 \times 10^{14} \text{ s}^{-1})$$
$$\lambda = 6.0 \times 10^{-7} \text{ m}$$
$$\lambda = 600 \text{ nm}$$

This wavelength falls within the visible spectrum (400–700 nm) and it has an orange-red color. Choice (C) correctly identifies this light ray.

2. D

To answer this question, you must understand that in plane mirrors, the image is as far away from the mirror as the object. In other words, the image produced by the left mirror is 5 m away from the mirror because the child is standing 5 m away from the mirror. Similarly, the right mirror produces an image that is 7 m away from the center of the mirror. To calculate how far away the two images are, you have to take into consideration not only the image distance but also the distance of the object (the child) from the mirrors and the child's arm span of 0.5 m. Therefore, the images are 5 + 5 + 0.5 + 7 + 7 = 24.5 m apart, making (D) the correct answer.

3. A

First draw a diagram:

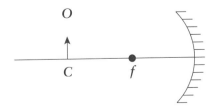

With the mirror equation and what we're given, it should be no problem to find the answer:

$$\frac{1}{i} = \frac{1}{f} - \frac{1}{o}$$

We know $o = r$, and since $\frac{1}{f} = \frac{2}{r}$, we can substitute into the equation:

$$\frac{1}{i} = \frac{2}{r} - \frac{1}{r}$$
$$= \frac{1}{r}$$
$$i = r$$

Because i is positive, the image is real, eliminating choices (B) and (C). The magnification will then tell us the image's orientation:

$$m = -\frac{i}{o}$$
$$= -\frac{r}{r}$$
$$= -1$$

The negative sign tells us the image is inverted, which means the correct choice is (A).

4. A

If you did not know right away that (A) was the correct answer, you could have solved this question by process of elimination. Frequency is related to period ($f = \frac{1}{T}$), so if either of these quantities changes, the other would have to change as well. Because they cannot both be correct, (B) and (D) can both be eliminated. Further, because the wave is fully transmitted, there is no absorption or reflection, and the amplitude should not change. Therefore, (C) is eliminated. Looking at the equation $c = f\lambda$, you might be tempted to eliminate wavelength, too. However, when light is refracted, its speed changes; therefore; although the frequency cannot change, the wavelength will.

5. A

This question contains two parts—you have to determine the frequency *and* the angle of refraction of the light ray. The first part, however, is straightforward because the frequency of a light ray traveling from one medium to another does not change. Because the frequency must be 5×10^{14} Hz, you can cross out (C) and (D). For the angle of refraction, you can either calculate it or determine it using logic. First, the light ray goes from air into crystal; that is, from a low index of refraction to a higher one. According to Snell's law, the angle of refraction will be lower (i.e., closer to the perpendicular). When the light ray moves from crystal to chronium, it again goes from a lower index of refraction into a higher one, thus making the angle of refraction even smaller. Between (A) and (B), the only one that illustrates this situation is (A), the correct answer. This question could also be answered by calculation using Snell's law, but the calculations are time consuming and unnecessary.

6. A

Plane-polarized light is light in which the electric fields of all the waves are oriented in the same direction. Light passing through the first two polarizers will change so that all the electric field vectors point in the same direction. When it reaches the third polarizer, however, the light will not be able to pass through because all the light rays will be oriented in the direction dictated by the first and second polarizer. Because no light will exit the third polarizer, the answer matches (A).

7. B

Even though the light is traveling through a prism, the change in the light's direction is caused by refraction, not dispersion. Dispersion involves the breaking up of polychromatic light into its component wavelengths because of the index of refraction's dependence on wavelength. You are told that the incident light is monochromatic or, in other words, of only one wavelength; therefore, light will not be dispersed.

8. B

The image produced by a convex lens can be either real or virtual: It is real if the object is placed at a distance greater than the focal point, virtual if the object is placed at a distance less than the focal point (between the focal point and the lens). It is also important to keep in mind that an image that is real must be inverted and one that is virtual must be upright. In this question, the object is placed in front of the focal point, so the image must be virtual and, therefore, upright. Choice (B) matches your prediction.

9. D

This question is testing your understanding of total internal reflection. As the laser beam travels from water to air—that is, from a higher to a lower index of refraction—the angle of refraction increases. However, there is a limit to this increase. At a certain angle of incidence (θ_i), the angle of refraction becomes 90°; at this point, the refracted ray is parallel to the surface of the water. When the angle of incidence is greater than the critical angle, all the light is reflected back into the water. The question asks you to determine the angle at which the laser beam will reflect entirely into the water. To find this, first calculate the critical angle of the beam using Snell's law:

$$n_{water} \sin \theta_i = n_{air} \sin \theta_r$$
$$n_{water} \sin \theta_i = n_{air} \sin 90°$$
$$n_{water} \sin \theta_i = n_{air}$$
$$\sin \theta_i = \frac{n_{air}}{n_{water}}$$

This is the sine of the critical angle, and you can memorize this last equation so that you don't have to derive it each time.

$$\sin \theta_c = \frac{n_{air}}{n_{water}} = \frac{1}{2}$$
$$\theta_c = 30°$$

What this tells you is that at exactly 30°, the refracted laser beam will be parallel to the surface of the water. Above 30°, the laser beam will reflect itself entirely back into the water, an event known as total internal reflection. Choice (D) is therefore the correct answer, because it is greater than 30°.

10. C

This question is testing your understanding of diffraction. When light passes through a narrow opening, the light waves spread out; as the slit narrows, the light waves spread out even more. When a lens is placed between the narrow slit and the screen, a pattern consisting of alternating bright and dark fringes can be observed on the screen. As the slit becomes narrower, the central maximum (the brightest and most central fringe) becomes wider. Imagine doing the experiment yourself. If you let the opening be as wide as a door, you wouldn't even notice bright and dark fringes because each fringe is extremely small. As you make the opening smaller and smaller, you are allowing only certain rays to penetrate, and the bright and dark fringes become wider. Choice (C) matches your explanation and is thus the correct answer.

11. D

All images produced by plane mirrors will be virtual (III). The same goes for mirrors that are convex. Lenses are a bit different; all concave lenses (II) will produce virtual images, but this is not necessarily true for convex lenses. Virtual images will not typically be produced unless an object is placed between the center and the focal point of the lens, but it is still possible (I). Since I, II, and III can all produce virtual images, choice (D) is the correct answer.

12. A

First, the color of the light is irrelevant here; the ratio would be the same even if the specific color were not mentioned. Second, recall Snell's Law: $n_1 \sin \theta_1 = n_2 \sin \theta_2$. Although you don't know the value of n for either medium, you do know the simple relationship $n = \dfrac{c}{v}$. Replacing n in the first equation, canceling out c, and rearranging, you can ultimately get $\dfrac{\sin \theta_2}{\sin \theta_1} = \dfrac{v_2}{v_1}$. You're asked for the ratio between 2 and 1, so rearrange accordingly:

$$\frac{c}{v_1} \sin \theta_1 = \frac{c}{v_2} \sin \theta_2$$

$$\frac{1}{v_1} \sin \theta_1 = \frac{1}{v_2} \sin \theta_2$$

$$\frac{v_2}{v_1} = \frac{\sin \theta_2}{\sin \theta_1} = \frac{\sin 45}{\sin 30} = \frac{\sqrt{2}/2}{1/2} = \sqrt{2}$$

Thus, $v_2 = v_1 \sqrt{2}$. This is choice (A).

13. D

A basic optics principle is tested here, but you need to know how to discern between and assign values to variables, as well as choose the correct equation. Here, your choice of equation should not be very difficult. The question points to $\dfrac{1}{o} = \dfrac{1}{i} = \dfrac{1}{f}$. You know that the goal of the lens is to create a virtual image of your friend's face at the near point of your eye. Consider this when assigning amounts to variables: $\dfrac{1}{50\,\text{cm}} = \dfrac{1}{100\,\text{cm}} = \dfrac{1}{f}$; therefore, $f = 100$ cm. Pay attention to signs! Finally, to get power, you know that $P = \dfrac{1}{f}$. This means that $P = 1$ diopter.

14. D

Drawing a diagram is best here. Because the angle given is with respect to the horizontal, you know that the angle in question, θ_1, must equal 30°. You know that the reflected beam will produce a mirror image of the incident beam on the other side of the plane of symmetry. Therefore, the reflected beam will make an angle of 60° with the horizontal. Because you're given that the reflected and refracted beams are perpendicular to each other, the refracted beam will make a 30° angle with the horizontal. θ_2 must be expressed with respect to the plane of symmetry, so it equals 60°. Be careful in this analysis: Confusing 30° and 60° throughout will lead to an incorrect $n_2 = \sqrt{3}$. Using $n_1 \sin \theta_1 = n_2 \sin \theta_2$, you have $1 \sin 30° = n_2 \sin 60°$, and $n_2 = \dfrac{1}{\sqrt{3}}$, which matches (A). However, the index of refraction can never be less than 1 because that would imply that v is larger than c in $n = \dfrac{c}{v}$, which is impossible, so (D) is correct.

Explanations to Small Group Questions

1. To determine the position of the maxima produced by a double-slit setup we can use the equation $d\sin\theta = m\lambda$, where $d = 7.5 \times 10^{-4}$ m and $\lambda = 500 \times 10^{-9}$ m, to determine the angle of the light leaving the double slit for $m = 1$ and $m = 2$ (θ_{1a} and θ_{2a}, respectively). We find that $\theta_{1a} = 0.038°$ and $\theta_{2a} = 0.076°$. To find the lateral position of the maxima from the center of the slits at the point where the light enters the glass, we rearrange $\tan\theta = \dfrac{y}{D}$ to solve for y, with $D = 10$ cm, and find that the first maximum is at $y = 6.67 \times 10^{-5}$ m and the second is at $y = 1.33 \times 10^{-4}$ m. When the rays enter the glass, the angle with the normal decreases according to Snell's law:

$n_1\sin\theta_1 = n_2\sin\theta_2$, with $n_1 = 1.00$ and $n_2 = 1.50$.

The new angles the rays take within the piece of glass are $\theta_{1b} = 0.025°$ for the first maximum ray and $\theta_{2b} = 0.051°$ for the second maximum ray.

We can again use $y = D\tan\theta$ to determine how the lateral positions of the maxima change as the rays pass through the glass, this time with $D = 3$ cm. The new positions are $y = 1.33 \times 10^{-5}$ m and $y = 2.67 \times 10^{-5}$ m for the first and second maxima, respectively. Once the rays pass from the glass back into the air, the angles return to their original values. We can then use $y = D\tan\theta$ one more time, with $D = 60$ cm, to calculate the final positions of the maxima as they reach the screen. The final positions of the first and second maxima are, respectively, $y_1 = 3.98 \times 10^{-4}$ m and $y_2 = 7.87 \times 10^{-4}$ m.

2. The sun, acting as the initial object, forms an image 3 cm from the mirror. In this case, the object distance is much, much greater than the image distance and can be assumed to be infinite. We use the equation $\dfrac{1}{o} + \dfrac{1}{i} = \dfrac{1}{f}$ to determine the focal length of the mirror, which we find is $f = 3$ cm. Now that we know the focal length, we use the same equation to determine where the image of the object will form, and we find $i = 4$ cm. The mirror's magnification is determined using the equation $m = -\dfrac{i}{o}$ and is $m = -0.33$. This indicates the image of the object is reduced to 8 cm, one-third its original height. The ray diagram for the object is shown below.

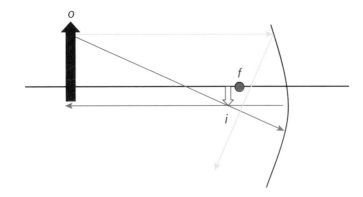

11

Atomic Phenomena

In this chapter:

Introduction

The great 45-carat Hope Diamond is currently housed in the Smithsonian Institute. Mined in the 1600s, the diamond originally had a weight of over 112 carats. Part of the modern allure of the diamond is its behavior under UV light. A small percentage of diamonds fluoresce under UV light and typically emit a bluish glow that ranges from very faint to deep. The Hope Diamond, in keeping with its stature, is extraordinary. Not only does it fluoresce, it fluoresces a faint red, an exceeding rare phenomenon for diamonds, and then glows a brilliant red for a few seconds after the UV light has been removed. This phenomenon of "afterglow" is called phosphorescence. Phosphorescence is similar to fluorescence and is the result of electrons that have been excited by high-frequency radiation returning to their ground state in multiple steps by releasing lower-frequency radiation, typically in the visible range. The difference is that the electrons get "stuck" in unusual energy states and can exit from them only through classically "forbidden" transitions; although possible, these are kinetically unfavorable, so the return of the excited electrons to their ground state is delayed. The slower return to the ground state results in prolonged release of photons whose frequencies correspond to the visible range. The object glows, even after the removal of the UV light, for anywhere from a few seconds to many hours.

Fluorescence and phosphorescence are atomic phenomena that we now understand through the theory of quantum mechanics. From the end of the 19th century through today, research has shown that different sets of physical laws take effect at the atomic scale due to the dual (wave and particle) nature of light. This chapter will discuss a few high-yield applications of quantum mechanical ideas, but the MCAT does not test the theory of quantum mechanics itself, so the details of the modern model will not be covered here. Our first topics will be blackbody radiation and the photoelectric effect, each of which are observable phenomena that reveal mechanisms at the atomic level. We will then cover Bohr's model of the hydrogen atom, which, although not a fully comprehensive quantum mechanical theory, is sufficient to explain many behaviors of one-electron systems, including their emission spectra. Finally, we will briefly review the source and process of fluorescence.

11.1 Thermal Blackbody Radiation

Key Concept

Absolute zero is 0 degrees Kelvin. At this temperature, all random atomic movement stops.

We know from the third law of thermodynamics that it is impossible to achieve absolute zero, the temperature at which the movement of all molecules or particles would stop and entropy would be zero. At any temperature above absolute zero, the particles that make up matter demonstrate some form of movement (vibration, bending, stretching, translation, and rotation) and therefore emit electromagnetic radiation. The amount of radiant energy emitted at a given wavelength depends on the temperature of the emitter. Furthermore, different materials may emit different amounts of radiant energy at a particular wavelength due to the differences in their atomic structure. Because of these complications, physicists at the turn of the 20th century conceptualized an **ideal radiator**, known as a **blackbody**. The term *blackbody* is used, because an ideal radiator is also an ideal absorber and would appear totally black if it were at a temperature lower than that of its surroundings. This is because it would absorb all wavelengths of electromagnetic radiation, including those corresponding to the visible light range. In practice, a blackbody radiator can be approximated rather closely by radiation produced in a cavity within a hot object, such as an oven with a small hole in the door. Hence, blackbody radiation is approximated by what is called **cavity radiation**.

Physicist Max Planck developed the theoretical derivation of the blackbody spectrum. His radiant spectrum for two blackbodies at different temperatures is shown in Figure 11.1. In the derivation, Planck used a number that we now know as Planck's constant (h), whose value is

$$h = 6.63 \times 10^{-34} \text{ J} \cdot \text{s} = 4.14 \times 10^{-15} \text{ eV} \cdot \text{s}$$

There is no need to memorize this value for the MCAT, as all such constants will be provided for you in the passage or question stem as necessary.

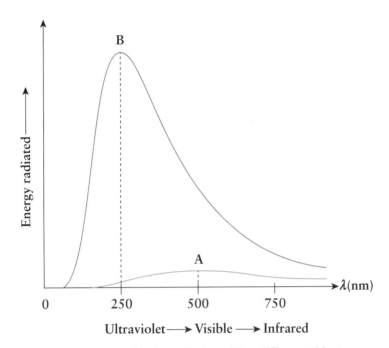

Figure 11.1. Blackbody Radiation of Two Different Objects
λ_{peak} of objects A and B are located at 500 nm and 250 nm, respectively

Real World

If you examine the flame of a candle, you will see that the upper parts of the flame are red (lower temperatures, higher wavelengths), and the lower, hotter parts of the flame shade progressively to orange, yellow, then white as you approach the hottest part of the wick. This color gradient is largely due to the changing blackbody radiation and λ_{peak} of soot burning at different temperatures within the flame. The infrared light given off by human bodies is also a form of blackbody radiation; its wavelength is indicative of the λ_{peak} of the human body temperature of about 300 K.

Because a blackbody is a theoretical "ideal emitter," the graph of blackbody radiation depends only on the temperature of the blackbody and not at all on the body's composition, size, or shape. An analysis of Planck's formula for the blackbody spectrum shows that for a blackbody, there is one wavelength at which the maximum amount of energy is emitted (λ_{peak}). This wavelength depends on the absolute temperature of the blackbody in a relation known as Wien's displacement law, which is expressed mathematically as

$$(\lambda_{peak})(T) = \text{constant}$$

The value of the constant in this law is 2.90×10^{-3} m · K. Please note that λ_{peak} is the wavelength at which more energy is emitted than at any other wavelength. λ_{peak} does not refer to the maximum wavelength emitted. A blackbody will emit wavelengths that are both greater and lesser than λ_{peak}, but the body will emit less energy at those wavelengths than at λ_{peak}. In Figure 11.1, object A is cooler than object B, and object A radiates less energy than object B. Furthermore, object A has a peak wavelength around 500 nm (visible light), while object B has a peak wavelength at 250 nm (UV). Because the peak wavelength for object B is half the peak wavelength of object A, object B's absolute temperature is twice that of object A according to Wien's displacement law.

Key Equation

Wien's Displacement Law
$(\lambda_{peak})(T) = \text{constant} = 2.90 \times 10^{-3}$ m·K
$(m)(K) = m \cdot K$
Use this equation to determine the peak wavelength emitted by an object at a given temperature.

According to the Stefan-Boltzmann law, the total energy a blackbody emits per second per unit area (W/m^2) is proportional to the fourth power of the absolute temperature:

$$E_T = \sigma T^4$$

where σ is the Stefan-Boltzmann constant (5.67×10^{-8} $J/s \cdot m^2 \cdot K^4$).

> **MCAT Concept Check 11.1**
>
> Before moving on, ensure that you are able to:
> ✓ Define the unique properties of a blackbody radiator
> ✓ Explain the relationship of blackbody temperature to both peak wavelength and radiation intensity (as described by Wien's displacement law and the Stefan-Boltzmann law)

11.2 Photoelectric Effect

When light of a sufficiently high frequency (typically, blue or ultraviolet light) is incident on a metal in a vacuum, the metal atoms emit electrons. This phenomenon, discovered by Heinrich Hertz in 1887, is called the **photoelectric effect**. The minimum frequency of light that causes this ejection of electrons is known as the **threshold frequency** f_T. The threshold frequency depends on the type of metal being exposed to the radiation. Einstein's explanation of these results was that the light beam consists of an integral number of light quanta, called photons, with the energy of each photon proportional to the frequency f of the light:

$$E = hf$$

where h is Planck's constant. Once you know the frequency, you can easily find the wavelength λ according to the following equation:

$$\lambda = \frac{c}{f}$$

where c is the speed of light (3.00×10^8 m/s). According to these equations, waves with higher frequency have shorter wavelengths and higher energy (toward the blue and ultraviolet end of the spectrum); waves with lower frequency have longer wavelengths and lower energy (toward the red and infrared end of the spectrum). Common units for wavelengths of light include nanometers (1 nm = 10^{-9} m) and angstroms (1 Å = 10^{-10} m).

If the frequency of a photon incident on a metal is *at* the threshold frequency for the metal, the electron barely escapes from the metal. However, if the frequency of an incident photon is *above* the threshold frequency of the metal, the photon will have more than enough energy to eject a single electron, and the excess energy will be converted to kinetic energy in the ejected electron. We can calculate the maximum kinetic energy of the ejected electron with the formula:

$$K_{max} = hf - W$$

where W is the **work function** of the metal in question. (This formula yields maximum kinetic energy rather than exact kinetic energy because the actual energy of an ejected electron can be anywhere between 0 and K_{max}, depending on the specific subatomic interactions between the photon and the metal atom. K_{max} is only achieved when all possible energy from the photon is transferred to the ejected electron.) The work function is the minimum energy required to eject an electron and is related to the threshold frequency of that metal by

$$W = hf_T$$

The photoelectric effect is (for all intents and purposes) an "all-or-none" response: If the frequency of the incident photon is less than the threshold frequency ($f < f_T$), then no electron will be ejected because the photon doesn't have sufficient energy to dislodge the electron from its atom. But if the frequency of the incident photon is greater than the threshold frequency ($f > f_T$), then an electron will be ejected, and the maximum kinetic energy of the ejected electron will be equal to the difference between hf and hf_T.

Electrons liberated from the metal by the photoelectric effect will produce a net charge flow per unit time, or current. Provided that the light beam's frequency is above the threshold frequency of the metal, light beams of greater intensity produce larger current in this way. The higher the intensity of the light beam, the greater the number of photons per unit time that fall on an electrode, producing a greater number of electrons per unit time liberated from the metal. When the light's frequency is above the threshold frequency, the magnitude of the resulting current is directly proportional to the intensity of the light beam.

> **Example:** If the work function of a metal is 2.00 eV and blue light of frequency 6.00×10^{14} Hz is incident on the metal, will there be photo-ejection of electrons? If so, what is the maximum kinetic energy that an ejected electron will carry away?
>
> **Solution:** If the photons have a frequency of 6.00×10^{14} Hz, each photon has an energy given by
>
> $$\begin{aligned} E &= hf \\ &= (4.14 \times 10^{-15})(6.00 \times 10^{14}) \\ &= 2.48 \text{ eV} \end{aligned}$$

Key Equation

$K_{max} = hf - W$

$J = (J \cdot s)(s^{-1}) - J$

$J = J$

Use this equation to determine the maximum kinetic energy of an electron ejected by an incident photon.

MCAT Expertise

This concept appears often on the MCAT. The energy of the photon is converted into ejecting the electron (the amount required by the work function will be given in the problem), and any excess energy is converted into the kinetic energy of the electron.

Real World

Trying to cause the photoelectric effect with a low-frequency beam of light is like trying to bridge a 6-foot-wide chasm with a single toothpick; just as no single toothpick will ever bridge that gap, no individual photon under the threshold frequency will eject an electron from the metal. In this analogy, incident light at f_T would be like a 6-foot beam: just large enough to bridge the gap with one plank, or to eject an electron with one photon.

Making Waves and Particles

The photoelectric effect, exploited in sensors, solar cells, and other electronic light detectors, refers to the ability of light to dislodge electrons from a metal surface. One aspect of the effect is that the speed of ejected electrons depends on the color of the light, not its intensity. Classical physics, which describes light as a wave, cannot explain this feature. By deducing that light could also act as a discrete bundle of energy—that is, a particle—Einstein accounted for the observation.

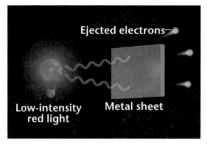

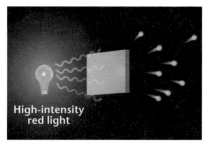

1 Red light sends electrons flying off a piece of metal. In the classical view, light is a continuous wave whose energy is spread out over the wave.

2 Increasing the brightness ejects more electrons. Classical physics also suggests that ejected electrons should move faster with more waves to ride—but they don't.

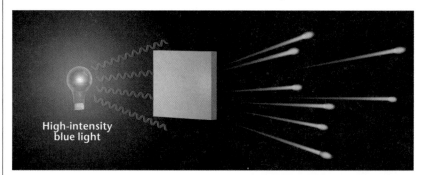

3 Changing the light to blue results in much speedier electrons. The reason is that light can behave not just as continuous waves but also as discrete bundles of energy called photons. A blue photon packs more energy than a red photon and essentially acts as a billiard ball with greater momentum, thereby hitting an electron harder (right). The particle view of light also explains why greater intensity increases the number of ejected electrons—with more photons impinging the metal, more electrons are likely to be struck.

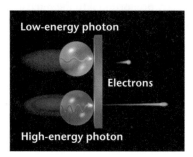

Figure 11.2. The Photoelectric Effect

(*continued from page* 331)

Clearly then, any given photon has more than enough energy to allow an electron in the metal to overcome the 2.00 eV barrier. In fact, the maximum excess kinetic energy carried away by the electron turns out to be

$$K = hf - W$$
$$= 2.48 - 2.00$$
$$= 0.48 \text{ eV}$$

MCAT Concept Check 11.2

Before moving on, ensure that you are able to:

✓ Recognize the conditions that cause incident light to eject electrons from a metal
✓ Describe the role of Planck's constant in the energy of a photon
✓ Recall the characteristics of the electric current propagated by the photoelectric effect
✓ Solve problems involving threshold frequency and work functions

---

11.3 The Bohr Model of the Hydrogen Atom

Danish physicist Niels Bohr, in 1913, used the work of Rutherford and Planck to develop his model of the electronic structure of the hydrogen atom. Starting from Rutherford's findings, Bohr assumed that the hydrogen atom consisted of a central proton around which an electron traveled in a circular orbit and that the centripetal force acting on the electron as it revolved around the nucleus was the electrical force between the positively charged proton and the negatively charged electron.

ENERGY LEVELS

Bohr used Planck's quantum theory to make some corrections to certain assumptions that classical physics made about the pathways of electrons. Classical mechanics postulates that an object, such as an electron, revolving in a circle may assume an infinite number of values for its radius and velocity. The angular momentum ($L = mvr$) and kinetic energy ($K = \frac{1}{2}mv^2$) of the object, therefore, can take any value, but by incorporating Planck's quantum theory into his model, Bohr placed restrictions on the value of the angular momentum of the electron revolving around the hydrogen nucleus.

Analogous to the quantized energy of photons, Bohr predicated that the orbital angular momentum of an electron, is quantized according to the following equation:

$$L = \frac{nh}{2\pi}$$

where *h* is Planck's constant and *n* is the quantum number, which can be any positive integer (the numbers 1, 2, 3, 4,... but none of the decimal values in between). Because the only variable is the quantum number, *n,* the angular momentum of an electron changes only in discrete amounts with respect to the quantum number.

Bohr then related the allowed values of the angular momentum to the energy of the electron to obtain the following equation:

$$E = -\frac{R_H}{n^2}$$

where R_H is an experimentally determined constant known as the Rydberg constant equal to 2.18×10^{-18} J/electron. Therefore, like angular momentum, the energy of the electron changes in discrete amounts with respect to the quantum number. Bohr had to resort to new quantum ideas, since a classical model of hydrogen would require the electron to radiate electromagnetic waves continuously, thereby losing energy and spiraling into the proton. Bohr postulated that there were specific stable, or allowed, orbits of quantized (discrete) energy in which electrons did not radiate energy. This led him to deduce the energy level formula.

The Bohr energy (in electron-volts) corresponding to the closest allowed orbit to the nucleus (ground state; $n = 1$) is −13.6 eV. This number is just the Rydberg constant in more convenient units (eV). The energies corresponding to orbits farther away from the nucleus are less negative and therefore greater, and increase until the electron is given so much energy that it is free of the electrostatic (coulombic) pull of the nucleus and can have any positive energy. The quantum energy levels in the Bohr model of the hydrogen atom can be arranged from lowest to highest, each with an associated principle quantum number (*n*). The energy levels for hydrogen are given in electron-volts by this formula:

$$E_n = -\frac{13.6\ eV}{n^2}$$

The state in which the proton and electron are separated completely, meaning that there is no attractive force between them, has an *n* value of infinity and an E_n value of 0. Positive energy states have no principle quantum number because the electron is not bound to the proton. Therefore, the electron in any of its quantized states in the atom will have a *negative* energy as a result of the attractive forces between the electron and proton; hence the negative sign in the energy equation above. The main conceptual point of the energy equation is that the energy of an electron increases the farther from the nucleus the electron is located. As the denominator (n^2, in this case) increases, the fraction itself gets smaller, but the negative sign in front means that energy increases as n² increases. (The absolute values of negative numbers get smaller as they move to the right on the number line, toward zero, so even though the absolute values of the numbers are decreasing—for example, as you move from –8 to –6—the value of the negative number as a whole is increasing.)

The Bohr model describes the structure of the hydrogen atom as a nucleus with one proton forming a dense core around which a single electron revolves in a defined pathway with a discrete energy value. Transferring an amount of energy exactly equal to the difference in energy between one pathway, or **orbit**, and another results in the electron "jumping" from the one pathway to the higher-energy pathway. These pathways or orbits have increasing radii, and the orbit with the smallest radius in which hydrogen's electron can be found is called the **ground state** and corresponds to $n = 1$. When the electron is promoted to a higher-energy orbit (one with a larger radius and $n = 2, 3, 4,\ldots$), the atom is said to be in the **excited state** (see Table 11.1). Bohr likened his model of the hydrogen atom to the planets orbiting the sun, in which each planet travels along a (roughly) circular pathway at set distances (and energy values) with respect to the sun.

Real World

The concept of quantized energy can be thought of as the change in gravitational potential energy that you experience when you ascend or descend a flight of stairs. Unlike a ramp, on which you could take any infinite number of steps associated with a continuum of potential energy changes, a staircase only allows you certain changes in height, and as a result, only certain, discrete (quantized) changes of potential energy are allowed.

Key Concept

An excited state is any orbit higher than the electron's ground state and, thus, has more energy than the ground state.

Table 11.1. Electron Energy Levels in Hydrogen

Principal quantum number	Energy level
n	E_n
1	$\frac{-13.6}{1}$ eV $= -13.6$ eV
2	$\frac{-13.6}{4}$ eV $= -3.40$ eV
3	$\frac{-13.6}{9}$ eV $= -1.51$ eV
4	$\frac{-13.6}{16}$ eV $= -0.85$ eV
$\cdot$	$\cdot$ $\cdot$
$\cdot$	$\cdot$ $\cdot$
$\cdot$	$\cdot$ $\cdot$
∞	$\frac{-13.6}{\infty}$ eV $= 0$ eV

EMISSION AND ABSORPTION OF LIGHT

Experimental results demonstrated that hydrogen atoms radiate light only at particular frequencies. Bohr proposed a set of four postulates that form the basis of his model:

1. Energy levels of the electron are stable and discrete. They correspond to specific orbits.

2. An electron emits or absorbs radiation only when making a transition from one energy level to another (from one allowed orbit to another).

3. To jump from a lower energy (inner orbit) to a higher energy (outer orbit), an electron must absorb a photon of precisely the right frequency such that the photon's energy (hf) equals the energy difference between the two orbits.

4. When jumping from a higher energy (outer orbit) to a lower energy (inner orbit), an electron emits a photon of a frequency such that the photon's energy (hf) is exactly the energy difference between the two orbits.

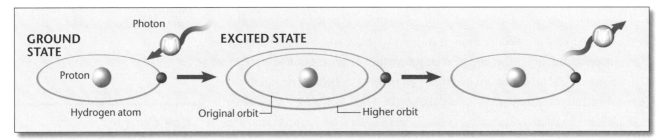

Figure 11.3. Bohr's Postulates

Bohr's initial ideas, illustrated in Figure 11.3, were replaced with the advent of full quantum mechanical theories of atomic structure. In contemporary theories, the electron is not envisioned as following a circular or elliptical path like the planets orbiting the sun. However, the Bohr model is still useful for certain calculations and for this reason it is still an important topic on the MCAT.

An electron in the lowest allowed energy level (the ground state; $n = 1$) cannot emit any more energy (although it could absorb radiation and jump to a higher energy level). An electron occupying an excited state can either emit radiation when it jumps down to a lower energy level or absorb radiation when it jumps to an even higher energy level. We can use Bohr's third and fourth postulates to find the frequency of radiation emitted or absorbed by an electron when it jumps from energy level i to energy level f. The change in the electron's energy is

$$\Delta E = E_f - E_i$$

(The values of E_i and E_f can be determined by finding the electron's energy at energy levels i and f with the Bohr model's energy equation. Remember that these values will be always be negative.) If ΔE is negative, the electron has jumped from a higher, less negative energy state (less tightly bound state) to a lower, more negative energy state (more tightly bound state). There is therefore an *emission* of a photon that has a frequency related to the energy change:

$$hf = -\Delta E$$

Key Equations

$\Delta E = E_f - E_i$

$J = J$

Use this equation to determine the change in energy of an electron due to absorption or emission of a photon.

$hf = |\Delta E|$

$(J\cdot s)(s^{-1}) = J$

$J = J$

Use this equation to determine the change in energy of an electron due to absorption or emission of a photon. The absolute value sign around ΔE represents the fact that negative frequencies do not exist, so the apparent sign of ΔE is irrelevant once you know whether the photon is being emitted or absorbed.

On the other hand, if ΔE is positive, then the electron has *absorbed* a photon and jumped from a lower, more negative energy state to a higher, less negative energy state. The absorbed photon has a frequency that is related to the electron's energy change:

$$hf = \Delta E$$

Example: What wavelength of light is emitted by a hydrogen electron going from the $n = 5$ to the $n = 2$ energy levels?

Solution: For hydrogen, the energy for a given principle quantum number n is given in electron-volts by

$$E = \frac{-13.6}{n^2}$$

Since the electron goes **from** $n = 5$ **to** $n = 2$, the initial energy level is

$$E_i = E_5 = \frac{-13.6}{25} = -0.544 \text{ eV}$$

The final energy level is

$$E_f = E_2 = \frac{-13.6}{4} = -3.40 \text{ eV}$$

Therefore,

$$\begin{aligned} \Delta E &= E_f - E_i \\ &= -3.40 + 0.544 \\ &= -2.856 \text{ eV} \end{aligned}$$

The negative value of ΔE confirms that the light is emitted. The frequency is found by

$$\begin{aligned} f &= \frac{|\Delta E|}{h} \\ &= \frac{2.856}{4.14 \times 10^{-15}} \\ &= 6.90 \times 10^{14} \text{ Hz} \end{aligned}$$

Now we can easily find the wavelength (and convert to different units for comparison):

$$\begin{aligned} \lambda &= \frac{c}{f} \\ &= \frac{3.00 \times 10^8}{6.90 \times 10^{14}} \\ &= 4.35 \times 10^{-7} \text{ m} \\ &= 435 \text{ nm} \\ &= 4{,}350 \text{ Å} \end{aligned}$$

Example: What is the minimum wavelength of light needed to free an electron from the ground state of hydrogen?

Solution: Freeing an electron means that the electron is being completely removed from the hydrogen nucleus, ionizing the atom. This final, free state corresponds to a quantum number of $n = \infty$ and an energy of $E_\infty \geq 0$. As previously mentioned, the electron in the ground state ($n = 1$) of hydrogen has an energy of -13.6 eV. Therefore, according to the equation $\Delta E = E_f - E_i$, it would take a photon of at least $+13.6$ eV to free the electron. Find the frequency:

$$f = \frac{E}{h}$$
$$= \frac{13.6}{4.14 \times 10^{-15}}$$
$$= 3.29 \times 10^{15} \text{ Hz}$$

Now the wavelength is given by

$$\lambda = \frac{c}{f}$$
$$= \frac{3.00 \times 10^8}{3.29 \times 10^{15}}$$
$$= 9.12 \times 10^{-8} \text{ m}$$
$$= 91.2 \text{ nm}$$
$$= 912 \text{ Å}$$

MCAT Concept Check 11.3

Before moving on, ensure that you are able to:

✓ Summarize the physical arrangement of subatomic particles in the Bohr model

✓ Explain the nature and cause of emission spectra

✓ Calculate the energy and frequency of a photon emitted by an electron changing energy levels

---

11.4 Fluorescence

Another phenomenon related to electron energy levels and absorbed and emitted photons is **fluorescence**, which is often seen in its namesake, fluorescent lights. If you excite a fluorescent substance, such as a ruby, an emerald, or the phosphors found in fluorescent lights, with ultraviolet radiation, it will begin to glow with visible light. Photons corresponding to ultraviolet radiation have relatively high frequencies (short wavelengths). After being excited to a higher energy state by the ultraviolet radiation, the electron in the fluorescent substance returns to its original state in two or more steps. By returning in two or more steps, each step involves less energy, so at each step, a photon is emitted with a lower frequency (longer wavelength) than the absorbed ultraviolet photon. If the wavelength of this emitted photon is within the visible range of the electromagnetic spectrum, it will be seen as light of the particular color corresponding to that wavelength. The wide range of colors in fluorescent lights, from the whitish-green of office lighting to the glaring colors of neon signs, is the result of the distinct multi-step emissions spectra of different fluorescent materials.

MCAT Concept Check 11.4

Before moving on, ensure that you are able to:

✓ Explain the concept of fluorescence

Conclusion

Quantum mechanical theory helps us understand phenomena that occur at the molecular level, phenomena that would otherwise seem counter to our understanding based on classical physics. This chapter examined a few behaviors and characteristics of substances that are best understood through quantum mechanical theory. We first discussed blackbody radiation, noting the significance of the relationships of the peak wavelength and the intensity of radiation to absolute temperature for blackbody objects. We then analyzed the photoelectric effect, paying particular attention to the fact that quantum theory explains why ejection is a function of the frequency of the photon, not its intensity. (Also, the magnitude of the current of ejected electrons is a function of the intensity of the incident beam of photons once the threshold frequency of the metal has been exceeded.) We then examined Bohr's model of the hydrogen atom, which he developed by incorporating the work of Rutherford and Planck. Although his model is inadequate for describing more complex atoms, the Bohr model works well to predict the discrete energy levels that the single electron may have in the hydrogen atom. Finally, we concluded our discussion of atomic phenomena with the topic of fluorescence. When a fluorescent substance is excited by high-energy radiation, typically UV radiation, the substance's excited electrons will return to their ground state through multiple steps and, in the process, will emit photons of lower energy whose frequencies correspond to the visible light range.

Only one more chapter to go! You are well on your way to achieving great success on physics portion of your MCAT. Keep up the hard work, the focus, and the energy. We know this is a tough road to Test Day, but you are mere steps away from reaching a major milestone!

CONCEPT SUMMARY

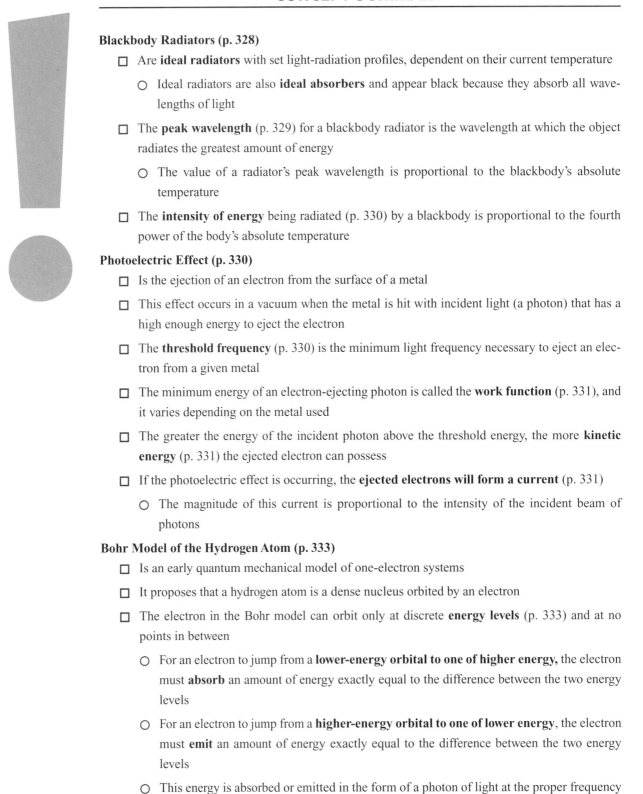

Blackbody Radiators (p. 328)

- [ ] Are **ideal radiators** with set light-radiation profiles, dependent on their current temperature
  - ○ Ideal radiators are also **ideal absorbers** and appear black because they absorb all wavelengths of light
- [ ] The **peak wavelength** (p. 329) for a blackbody radiator is the wavelength at which the object radiates the greatest amount of energy
  - ○ The value of a radiator's peak wavelength is proportional to the blackbody's absolute temperature
- [ ] The **intensity of energy** being radiated (p. 330) by a blackbody is proportional to the fourth power of the body's absolute temperature

Photoelectric Effect (p. 330)

- [ ] Is the ejection of an electron from the surface of a metal
- [ ] This effect occurs in a vacuum when the metal is hit with incident light (a photon) that has a high enough energy to eject the electron
- [ ] The **threshold frequency** (p. 330) is the minimum light frequency necessary to eject an electron from a given metal
- [ ] The minimum energy of an electron-ejecting photon is called the **work function** (p. 331), and it varies depending on the metal used
- [ ] The greater the energy of the incident photon above the threshold energy, the more **kinetic energy** (p. 331) the ejected electron can possess
- [ ] If the photoelectric effect is occurring, the **ejected electrons will form a current** (p. 331)
  - ○ The magnitude of this current is proportional to the intensity of the incident beam of photons

Bohr Model of the Hydrogen Atom (p. 333)

- [ ] Is an early quantum mechanical model of one-electron systems
- [ ] It proposes that a hydrogen atom is a dense nucleus orbited by an electron
- [ ] The electron in the Bohr model can orbit only at discrete **energy levels** (p. 333) and at no points in between
  - ○ For an electron to jump from a **lower-energy orbital to one of higher energy,** the electron must **absorb** an amount of energy exactly equal to the difference between the two energy levels
  - ○ For an electron to jump from a **higher-energy orbital to one of lower energy**, the electron must **emit** an amount of energy exactly equal to the difference between the two energy levels
  - ○ This energy is absorbed or emitted in the form of a photon of light at the proper frequency

Fluorescence (p. 338)

- ☐ Is a method by which absorbed high-frequency light (usually UV light) is emitted by a substance as lower-frequency light (usually visible light)

- ☐ The electrons in a fluorescent substance jump to an excited state by absorbing the high-frequency photons

- ☐ The electrons then return to their ground state in multiple steps, releasing lower-frequency photons with each step.

EQUATIONS TO REMEMBER

- ☐ $(\lambda_{peak})(T) = \text{constant}$

- ☐ $E_T = \sigma T^4$

- ☐ $E = hf$

- ☐ $K = hf - W$

- ☐ $W = hf_T$

- ☐ $E = -\dfrac{R_H}{n^2}$ (energy in joules)

- ☐ $E_n = -\dfrac{13.6\ \text{eV}}{n^2}$ (energy in electron-volts)

SHARED CONCEPTS

HIGH-YIELD PRACTICE PROBLEMS

Practice Questions

1. The Stefan-Boltzmann law says that E is proportional to T^4, where E is the power per unit area radiated by a body of absolute temperature T. A given body is heated to 380 K and then subsequently further heated to 760 K. What is the ratio of the power per unit area radiated at the higher temperature to that at the lower temperature?

   A. 2
   B. 16
   C. 24
   D. 64

2. If the work function of a metal is 2,130 J and a ray of light with a frequency of 1.0×10^{37} Hz is incident on the metal, what will be the speed of the electrons ejected? ($h = 6.63 \times 10^{-34}$ J•s and $m_{electron} = 9.1 \times 10^{-31}$ kg.)

   A. 4,500 m/s
   B. 3×10^{-29} m/s
   C. 10^{17} m/s
   D. 10^{34} m/s

3. If the work function of a certain metal is 4.14 eV and light of frequency 2.42×10^{14} Hz is incident on this metal, will there be an ejection of electrons? What is the threshold frequency of the metal? (Use $h = 4.14 \times 10^{-15}$ eV•s.)

   A. Electrons will not be ejected; $f_T = 1.0 \times 10^{15}$ Hz
   B. Electrons will not be ejected; $f_T = 1.0 \times 10^{-15}$ Hz
   C. Electrons will be ejected; $f_T = 10 \times 10^{15}$ Hz
   D. Electrons will be ejected; $f_T = 10 \times 10^{-15}$ Hz

4. A light of what wavelength must be incident on a metal for the ejected electrons to have a kinetic energy of 50 J? (The work function of the metal is 16 J, and $h = 6.63 \times 10^{-34}$ J•s.)

   A. 3×10^{-27} m
   B. 3×10^{-26} m
   C. 1.0×10^{-34} m
   D. 1.0×10^{35} m

5. In the hydrogen atom, how many electron states fall in the energy range −10.2 eV to −1.4 eV?

   A. 1
   B. 2
   C. 3
   D. 4

6. Which of the following statements is NOT consistent with Bohr's set of postulates regarding the hydrogen atom model with regard to the emission and absorption of light?

   A. Energy levels of the electron are stable and discrete.
   B. An electron emits or absorbs radiation only when making a transition from one energy level to another.
   C. To jump from a lower energy to a higher energy, an electron must absorb a photon of precisely the right frequency such that the photon's energy equals the energy difference between the two orbits.
   D. To jump from a higher energy to a lower energy, an electron absorbs a photon of a frequency such that the photon's energy is exactly the energy difference between the two orbits.

7. What is the difference in ionization energy for a hydrogen atom with its electron in the ground state and a hydrogen atom with its electron in the $n = 4$ state?

   E. 0 eV
   F. 0.85 eV
   G. 12.75 eV
   H. 13.6 eV

8. When a hydrogen atom electron falls to the ground state from the $n = 2$ state, 10.2 eV of energy is emitted. What is the wavelength of this radiation? (Use 1 eV = 1.60×10^{-19} J, $h = 6.63 \times 10^{-34}$ J·s.)

   A. 1.22×10^{-7} m
   B. 3.45×10^{-7} m
   C. 5.76×10^{-9} m
   D. 2.5×10^{15} m

9. Radiation is emitted from a small window in a large furnace. When the temperature of the furnace is doubled, the peak emitted energy

   A. remains constant.
   B. increases by a factor of 2.
   C. increases by a factor of 4.
   D. increases by a factor of 16.

10. The figure shown here illustrates an electron with initial energy of -10 eV moving from point A to point B. What change accompanies the movement of the electron?

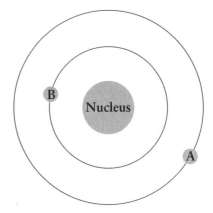

   A. Absorption of a photon
   B. Emission of a photon
   C. Decrease in the atom's work function
   D. Increase in the atom's total energy

11. Ultraviolet light is more likely to cause a photoelectric effect than visible light. This is because photons of ultraviolet light

   A. have a longer wavelength.
   B. have a higher velocity.
   C. are not visible.
   D. have a higher energy.

12. All of the following are characteristics of the photoelectric effect EXCEPT

    A. The intensity of the light beam does not affect the photocurrent.

    B. The kinetic energies of the emitted electrons do not depend on the light intensity.

    C. A weak beam of light of frequency greater than the threshold frequency yields more current than an intense beam of light of frequency lower than the threshold.

    D. For light of a given frequency, the kinetic energy of emitted electrons increases as the value of the work function decreases.

Small Group Questions

1. How do solar panels turn light into electricity?

2. Would light emitted from a hydrogen atom always have the same color? Why or why not?

Explanations to Practice Questions

1. B

Although this question may seem complicated, it is actually rather straightforward. The ratio of the power per unit area radiated at the higher temperature to that at the lower temperature is: $\dfrac{T^4_{higher}}{T^4_{lower}}$. Since $T_{higher} = 760$ K and $T_{lower} = 380$ K, you can obtain the ratio $\dfrac{760}{380} = 2^4 = 16$, making (B) the correct answer.

2. C

To determine the speed of the electrons ejected, you must first calculate their kinetic energy:

$$K = hf - W$$
$$K = (6.63 \times 10^{-34}\ \text{J}\cdot\text{s})(1.0 \times 10^{37}\ \text{Hz}) - 2{,}130\ \text{J}$$
$$K = 6{,}630\ \text{J} - 2{,}130\ \text{J}$$
$$K = 4{,}500\ \text{J}$$

Using the formula for the kinetic energy, we can now calculate the speed of the ejected electrons:

$$K = \frac{1}{2}mv^2$$
$$v = \sqrt{\frac{2K}{m}}$$
$$v = \sqrt{\frac{2(4{,}500\ \text{J})}{9 \times 10^{-31}\ \text{kg}}} = \sqrt{\frac{9 \times 10^3\ \text{J}}{9 \times 10^{-31}\ \text{kg}}}$$
$$v = \sqrt{10^{34}}$$
$$v = 10^{17}\ \text{m/s}$$

Choice (C) matches the result and is thus the correct answer.

3. A

First determine if electrons will be ejected. Each photon has an energy given by

$$E = hf$$

$$E \approx (4 \times 10^{-15}\ \text{eV}\cdot\text{s})(2.5 \times 10^{14}\ \text{s}^{-1})$$
$$E \approx 1\ \text{eV}$$

Therefore, the photons do not have enough energy to allow an electron in the metal to overcome the 4.14 eV barrier, and there will be no ejection of electrons. You can eliminate (C) and (D). Next, from the relation between the work function and the threshold frequency of a metal, $W = hf_T$, we can solve for the threshold frequency:

$$W = hf_T$$
$$f_T = \frac{W}{h}$$
$$f_T = \frac{4.14\,\text{eV}}{4.14\,\text{eV} \times 10^{-15}\ \text{eV}\cdot\text{s}}$$
$$f_T = 1.0 \times 10^{15}\ \text{Hz}$$

Choice (A) matches the result and is thus the correct answer.

4. A

To determine the wavelength of the light ray, first calculate its frequency from the following equation:

$$K = hf - W$$
$$f = \frac{K + W}{h}$$
$$f = \frac{50\,\text{J} + 16\,\text{J}}{6.63 \times 10^{-34}\ \text{J}\cdot\text{s}} = \frac{66\,\text{J}}{6.63 \times 10^{-34}\ \text{J}\cdot\text{s}}$$
$$f = 10^{35}\ \text{Hz}$$

Next, determine the wavelength of the incident ray of light by relating the frequency to the speed of light:

$$c = \lambda f$$
$$\lambda = \frac{c}{f}$$
$$\lambda = \frac{3 \times 10^8 \, \text{m/s}}{10^{35} \, \text{s}^{-1}}$$
$$\lambda = 3 \times 10^{-27} \, \text{m}$$

(A) best matches your result and is thus the correct answer.

5. B

The energy states of an electron in hydrogen are given by this equation:

$$E_n = \frac{-13.6 \, \text{eV}}{n^2}$$

where $n = 1, 2, 3,\ldots$ For $n = 1$, $E_1 = -13.6$ eV. For $n = 2$, $E_2 = -13.6/4 = -3.4$ eV. For $n = 3$, $E_3 = -13.6/9 = -1.5$ eV. For $n = 4$, $E_4 = -13.6/16 = -0.85$ eV. Therefore, there are two energy states in the range -10.2 eV to -1.4 eV, at $n = 2$ and $n = 3$. Choice (B) is therefore the correct answer.

6. D

Bohr put forth a set of postulates that forms the basis of the model of the hydrogen atom with regard to the emission and absorption of light. First, energy levels of the electron are stable and discrete; they correspond to specific orbits. Next, an electron emits or absorbs radiation only when making a transition from one energy level to another. To jump from a lower to a higher energy orbital, an electron must absorb a photon of precisely the right frequency such that the photon's energy equals the energy difference between the two orbitals. To jump from a higher to a lower energy orbital, an electron emits a photon of a frequency such the photon's energy is exactly the energy difference between the two orbitals. From the given answer choices, all of them are consistent with the Bohr theory except for (D), the correct answer.

7. C

The energy required to ionize an atom is the energy needed to bring the electron energy up to 0 eV. Using the equation for the energy states of an electron in a hydrogen atom, $E_n = \frac{-13.6 \, \text{eV}}{n^2}$, calculate the ionization energies for the ground state and the $n = 4$ state. For a hydrogen atom with its electron in the ground state, the ionization energy $E_1 = -13.6$ eV. For a hydrogen atom with its electron in the $n = 4$ state, the ionization energy $E_4 = -0.85$ eV. The difference in ionization energies is $[-0.85 - (-13.6)]$ eV $= 12.75$ eV. Choice (C) is therefore the correct answer.

8. A

To solve this question correctly, you must first make sure to be consistent with the units. As such, we have to convert $\Delta E = 10.2$ eV to joules: $\Delta E = 10.2$ eV $(1.60 \times 10^{-19}$ J/eV$) = 1.6 \times 10^{-18}$ J. Next, to determine the wavelength of the radiation, first find the frequency using the following equation:

$$\Delta E = hf$$
$$f = \frac{\Delta E}{h}$$
$$f \approx \frac{1.5 \times 10^{-18} \, \text{J}}{6.5 \times 10^{-34} \, \text{J} \cdot \text{s}}$$
$$f \approx 2.5 \times 10^{15} \, \text{Hz}$$

Lastly, from the wave equation $c = \lambda f$, you can calculate the wavelength of the radiation:

$$\lambda = \frac{c}{f}$$
$$\lambda = \frac{3 \times 10^8 \, \text{m/s}}{2.5 \times 10^{15} \, \text{s}^{-1}}$$
$$\lambda \approx 1 \times 10^{-7} \, \text{m}$$

Choice (A) most closely matches your result and is thus the correct answer.

9. D

A window in a furnace is an approximate replica of a blackbody system. In such a system, the total emitted energy is proportional to the fourth power of the temperature (according to the equation $E_T = \sigma T^4$). If the temperature is doubled, then the total energy must increase by a factor of 16. Therefore, (D) is the correct answer.

10. B

The electron moves from a higher energy level to a lower energy level; this can only occur if the extra energy is dissipated through the emission of a photon. Choice (A) suggests the opposite. Choice (C) is incorrect because the work function is equal to the amount of energy required to eject the electron, which increases as the electron becomes more difficult to separate from the nucleus. Choice (D) is incorrect because the energy of the atom will decrease after it emits a photon. Therefore, (B) is the correct answer.

11. D

The photoelectric effect occurs when a photon of sufficiently high energy strikes an atom with a sufficiently low work function. This means that a photon with higher energy is more likely to produce the effect. Because ultraviolet light has a higher frequency and lower wavelength than visible light, it also carries more energy according to the formula $E = hf$.

12. A

The greater the intensity, the greater the number of incident photons and, therefore, the greater the number of photoelectrons that will be ejected from the metal surface (provided that the frequency of the light is above the threshold). This means a larger current. Choice (A) is not a characteristic of the photoelectric effect and is therefore the answer to the question. All of the other choices are characteristics of the photoelectric effect.

Explanations to Small Group Questions

1. When photons hit the metal or metalloid (usually silicon) in a solar panel, they can liberate electrons. The emitted electrons are picked up by metal conducting strips to generate a current that can be carried by a wire.

2. Photons emitted by a hydrogen atom can have different energies and therefore different colors. Collectively, the light emitted by hydrogen appears bluish, but the light can be separated by a prism into a characteristic emission spectrum consisting of separate colored bands. Excited electrons are in a variety of higher energy orbits and therefore can release different amounts of energy when they return to the ground state. The difference in energy between the excited electron and its ground state will be the same as the energy of the photon released. A particular photon's energy determines its color. Higher energy photons have higher frequencies and lower wavelengths and will appear more violet (see Chapter 10, Light and Optics).

Nuclear Phenomena

In this chapter:

Introduction

This last chapter reviews the organization of the atomic nucleus and describes nuclear phenomena. We will begin with a review of some of the standard terminology used in nuclear physics, then discuss the concept of binding energy and the related concept of the mass defect. We will investigate what Einstein's famous dictum, $E = mc^2$, really means. The remainder of the chapter focuses on nuclear reactions, fission and fusion, and radioactive decay, which will be presented in two parts. The first part deals with the four types of radioactive decay and a discussion of the reaction equations that describe them. The second part covers the general problem of determining the half-life of a decay process and the associated calculations of the number of nuclei that remain after a period of time.

12.1 Nuclei

At the center of an atom lies its nucleus, consisting of one or more **nucleons** (protons or neutrons) held together with considerably more energy than the energy needed to hold electrons in orbit around the nucleus. The radius of the nucleus is about 100,000 times smaller than the radius of the atom. The nucleus can be described by the number of protons and neutrons that it contains.

ATOMIC NUMBER (Z) AND MASS NUMBER (A)

The atomic number (Z) is always an integer and is equal to the number of protons in the nucleus. Each element has a unique number of protons; therefore, the atomic number Z identifies the element. Z is used as a presubscript to the chemical symbol in **isotopic notation**. The chemical symbols and the atomic numbers of all the elements are given in the periodic table.

> **Key Concept**
>
> Protons and neutrons have the same mass; the only difference is that protons have a positive charge while neutrons are neutral.

The **mass number (A)** is equal to the total number of nucleons (neutrons and protons) in a nucleus is represented by the letter A. If we represent the number of neutrons in a nucleus by the letter N, then the equation relating A, N, and Z is simply

$$A = N + Z$$

In isotopic notation, A appears as a presuperscript to the chemical symbol. In other words, immediately to the left of the elemental symbol, the mass number and the atomic number can be read top to bottom, respectively. Remember it this way: *From top to bottom, the mass number and the atomic number tell you everything about the nucleus from A to Z.* So for an element X, the mass number and atomic number are written in isotopic notation as follows:

$$_{Z}^{A}\text{X}$$

Below are three examples of isotopic notation.

$_{1}^{1}\text{H}$ A single proton; the nucleus of ordinary hydrogen

$_{2}^{4}\text{He}$ The nucleus of ordinary helium, consisting of 2 protons and 2 neutrons; also known as an alpha particle (α-particle)

$_{92}^{235}\text{U}$ A fissionable form of uranium, consisting of 92 protons and 143 neutrons

ISOTOPE

The term *isotope* comes from the Greek, meaning "the same place." **Isotopes** are different atoms of the same element, having the same atomic number (hence, occupying the same *place* on the periodic table of the elements), that have different numbers of neutrons and, therefore, have different mass numbers. Isotopes are referred to by the name of the element followed by the mass number (e.g., carbon-12 has 6 neutrons, carbon-13 has 7 neutrons). Only the three isotopes of hydrogen are given unique names. The three isotopes of hydrogen are these:

$_{1}^{1}\text{H}$ A single proton; the nucleus of ordinary hydrogen

$_{1}^{2}\text{H}$ A proton and a neutron together, often called a **deuteron**; the nucleus of one type of heavy hydrogen called **deuterium**

$_{1}^{3}\text{H}$ A proton and two neutrons together, often called a **triton**; the nucleus of a heavier type of heavy hydrogen called **tritium**

Because isotopes have the same number of protons and electrons, they generally exhibit the same chemical properties. The term **radionuclide** is a generic term used to refer to any radioactive isotope, especially those used in **nuclear medicine**.

> **Key Concept**
>
> Looking at the periodic table, we can see that many elements have a mass number that is a noninteger. This is because the periodic table shows the atomic weight, which is the average mass of all known isotopes. This will be discussed further later in this section.

> **Key Concept**
>
> The only difference between hydrogen, deuterium, and tritium is the number of neutrons. All still have one proton and one electron.

ATOMIC MASS AND ATOMIC WEIGHT

Atomic mass is most commonly measured in **atomic mass units** (abbreviated amu or simply u). The size of the atomic mass unit is defined as exactly $\frac{1}{12}$ the mass of the carbon-12 atom, approximately 1.66×10^{-24} g. Because the carbon-12 nucleus has six protons and six neutrons, an amu is really the average of the mass of a proton and a neutron. Because the difference in mass between the proton and the neutron is so small, the mass of the proton and the neutron are each about equal to 1 amu. We essentially discount the mass of carbon's six electrons because they are so tiny—the mass of an electron is $\frac{1}{1,836}$ the mass of a proton. Thus, the **atomic mass** of any atom is simply equal to the mass number (sum of protons and neutrons) of the atom. In terms of more familiar mass units,

$$1 \text{ amu} = 1.66 \times 10^{-27} \text{ kg} = 1.66 \times 10^{-24} \text{ g}$$

A more common convention used to define the mass of an atom is the **atomic weight**. The atomic weight is the mass in grams of one mole of atoms of a given element and is expressed as a ratio of grams per mole (g/mol). A mole is simply the number of "things" equal to **Avogadro's number**: 6.022×10^{23}. For example, the atomic weight of carbon-12 is 12.0 g/mol, which means that 6.022×10^{23} carbon-12 atoms (1 mole of carbon-12 atoms) have a mass of 12.0 grams. It also follows that one gram is the mass of one mole of amu.

Because isotopes exist, atoms of a given element can have different masses. The atomic weight reported on the periodic table refers to a weighted average of the masses of an element. The average is weighted according to the natural abundances of the various isotopic species of an element. That's why the atomic weight that you read off the periodic table may not be a whole number.

> **Example:** Of hydrogen, 99.985499% occurs in the common ^{1}H isotope with a mass of 1.00782504 u. About 0.0142972% occurs as deuterium with a mass (including the electron) of 2.01410 u, and about 0.0003027% occurs as tritium with a mass of 3.01605 u. Calculate the atomic mass of hydrogen $A_r(\text{H})$.
>
> **Solution:** Find the sum of the mass of each isotope multiplied by its natural abundance (x):
>
> $$\begin{aligned} A_r(\text{H}) &= m_{1\text{H}}x_{1\text{H}} + m_{2\text{H}}x_{2\text{H}} + m_{3\text{H}}x_{3\text{H}} \\ &= (1.00782504)(0.99985499) \\ &\quad + (2.01410)(0.000142972) \\ &\quad + (3.01605)(0.000003027) \\ &= 1.00797 \text{ u} \end{aligned}$$

12.2 Nuclear Binding Energy and Mass Defect

> **Key Equation**
>
> $E = mc^2$
>
> $J = (kg)(m/s)$
>
> Use this equation to determine the mass lost as binding energy in a nucleus.

We have just learned how to estimate an element's atomic mass. However, in reality every nucleus (other than protium) has a smaller mass than the combined mass of its constituent protons and neutrons. The difference is called the **mass defect**. Scientists had difficulty explaining why this mass defect occurred until Einstein discovered the equivalence of matter and energy, embodied by the equation

$$E = mc^2$$

where E is energy, m is mass, and c is the speed of light. The mass defect is a result of matter that has been converted to energy. A very small amount of mass will yield a huge amount of energy. For example, the conversion of one gram of mass will produce 89.9 terajoules (1 terajoule = 10^{12} joules) or 21.5 billion kilocalories!

When protons and neutrons come together to form the nucleus, they are attracted to each other by the **strong nuclear force**, which is strong enough to more than compensate for the repulsive electromagnetic force between the protons. Although the strong nuclear force is the strongest of the four basic forces, it only acts over extremely short distances, less than a few times the diameter of a proton or neutron. The nucleons have to get very close together in order for the strong nuclear force to hold them together. The bound system is at a lower energy level than the unbound constituents, and this difference in energy must be radiated away in the form of heat, light, or other electromagnetic radiation (that is, the system has to cool down) before the mass defect becomes apparent. This energy, called **binding energy**, allows the nucleons to bind together in the nucleus. Given the strength of the strong nuclear force, the amount of mass that is transformed into the dissipated energy will be a measurable fraction of the initial total mass. (Note: The binding energy per nucleon peaks at iron, which implies that iron is the most stable atom. In general, intermediate-sized nuclei are more stable than large and small nuclei.)

The mass defect and binding energy of ^{4}He are calculated in the following example.

Example: Measurements of the atomic mass of a neutron and a proton yield these results:

$$\text{proton} = 1.00728 \text{ amu}$$
$$\text{neutron} = 1.00867 \text{ amu}$$

^{4}He consists of 2 protons and 2 neutrons, which should theoretically give a ^{4}He mass of

$$Z(m_p) + N(m_n) = 2(1.00728) + 2(1.00867) = 4.03190 \text{ amu}$$

A measurement of the atomic mass of a ^{4}He nucleus yields this:

$$^4\text{He} = 4.00260 \text{ amu}$$

What is the mass defect and binding energy of this nucleus? (The rest energy of 1 amu is 932 MeV.)

Solution: The difference $4.03190 - 4.00260 = 0.02930$ amu is the mass defect for ^{4}He. It is interpreted as the conversion of mass into the binding energy of the nucleus. Since the rest energy of 1 amu is 932 MeV, using $E = mc^2$, we find that $c^2 = 932$ MeV/amu. Therefore, the binding energy of ^{4}He is

$$E = \Delta mc^2$$
$$= (0.02930)(932)$$
$$= 27.3 \text{ MeV}$$

MCAT Concept Check 12.2

Before moving on, ensure that you are able to:

✓ Recognize the strong nuclear force as the force that binds nucleons

✓ Recognize binding energy as the energy given off by bound nucleons

✓ Interpret the mass defect as the difference between the theoretical mass and actual mass of a nucleus that is lost to binding energy

---

12.3 Nuclear Reactions and Decay

Nuclear reactions, such as fusion, fission, and radioactive decay, involve either combining or splitting the nuclei of atoms. Because the binding energy per nucleon is greatest for intermediate-sized atoms (that is to intermediate-sized atoms are most stable), when small atoms combine or large atoms split, a great amount of energy is released.

FUSION

Fusion occurs when small nuclei combine into a larger nucleus. As an example, many stars (including the sun) power themselves by fusing four hydrogen nuclei to make one helium nucleus. By this method, the sun produces 4×10^{26} joules every second, which accounts for the mass defect that arises from the formation of helium nuclei from hydrogen nuclei. Here on Earth, researchers are trying to find ways to use fusion as an alternative energy source.

FISSION

Fission is a process in which a large nucleus splits into smaller nuclei. Spontaneous fission rarely occurs. However, by the absorption of a low-energy neutron, fission can be induced in certain nuclei. Of special interest are those fission reactions that release more neutrons, because these other neutrons will cause other atoms to undergo fission. This in turn releases more neutrons, creating a **chain reaction**. Such induced fission reactions power commercial nuclear electric generating plants.

> **Example:** A fission reaction occurs when uranium-235 (U-235) absorbs a low-energy neutron, briefly forming an excited state of U-236, which then splits into xenon-140, strontium-94, and x more neutrons. In isotopic notation form, the reactions are
>
> $$^{235}_{92}U + {}^{1}_{0}n \rightarrow {}^{236}_{92}U \rightarrow {}^{140}_{54}Xe + {}^{94}_{38}Sr + x{}^{1}_{0}n$$
>
> How many neutrons are produced in the last reaction?
>
> **Solution:** The question is asking "What is x?" By treating each arrow as an equals sign, the problem is simply asking to balance the last "equation." The mass numbers (A) on either side of each arrow must be equal. This is an application of **nucleon** or **baryon number conservation**, which says that the total number of neutrons plus protons remains the same, even if neutrons are converted to protons and vice versa, as they are in some decays. Since $235 + 1 = 236$, the first arrow is indeed balanced. To find the number of neutrons, solve for x in the last equation (arrow):
>
> $$236 = 140 + 94 + x$$
> $$x = 236 - 140 - 94$$
> $$= 2$$
>
> So two neutrons are produced in this reaction. These neutrons are free to go on and be absorbed by more ^{235}U and cause more fissioning, and the process continues in a chain reaction. Note that it really was not necessary to know that the intermediate state $^{236}_{92}U$ was formed.

RADIOACTIVE DECAY

Radioactive decay is a naturally occurring spontaneous decay of certain nuclei accompanied by the emission of specific particles. On the MCAT, you should be prepared to answer three general types of radioactive decay problems:

1. The integer arithmetic of particle and isotope species
2. Radioactive half-life problems
3. The use of exponential decay curves and decay constants

1. Isotope Decay Arithmetic and Nucleon Conservation

Let the letters X and Y represent nuclear isotopes, and let us further consider the three types of decay particles and how they affect the mass number and atomic number of the **parent isotope** $^A_Z X$ and the resulting **daughter isotope** $^{A'}_{Z'} Y$ in the decay:

$$^A_Z X \longrightarrow {}^{A'}_{Z'} Y + \text{emitted decay particle}$$

a. Alpha decay is the emission of an α-particle, which is a ^{4}He nucleus that consists of two protons and two neutrons. The alpha particle is very massive (compared to a beta particle) and doubly charged. Alpha particles interact with matter very easily; hence, they do not penetrate shielding (such as lead sheets) very extensively.

The emission of an α-particle means that the daughter's atomic number Z will be 2 less than the parent's atomic number and the daughter's mass number will be 4 less than the parent's mass number. This can be expressed in two simple equations:

$$\alpha \textbf{ decay}$$

$$Z_{\text{daughter}} = Z_{\text{parent}} - 2$$
$$A_{\text{daughter}} = A_{\text{parent}} - 4$$

The generic alpha decay reaction is then:

$$^A_Z X \longrightarrow {}^{A-4}_{Z-2} Y + \alpha$$

MCAT Expertise

Whenever you approach radioactive decay problems on the MCAT, count the number of protons and neutrons. Often wrong answer choices will simply have an error in the number of protons.

Key Concept

Alpha particles do not have any electrons, so they carry a charge of +2.

Example: Suppose a parent *X* alpha decays into a daughter *Y* such that

$$^{238}_{92}X \rightarrow {}^{A'}_{Z'}Y + \alpha$$

What are the mass number (*A'*) and atomic number (*Z'*) of the daughter isotope *Y*?

Solution: Since $\alpha = {}^{4}_{2}He$, balancing the mass numbers and atomic numbers is all that needs to be done:

$$238 = A' + 4$$
$$A' = 234$$
$$92 = Z' + 2$$
$$Z' = 90$$

So *A'* = 234 and *Z'* = 90. Note that it was not necessary to know the chemical species of the isotopes to do this problem. However, it would have been possible to look at the periodic table and see that *Z* = 92 means *X* is uranium-238 ($^{238}_{92}U$) and that *Z* = 90 means *Y* is thorium-234 ($^{234}_{90}Th$).

b. Beta decay is the emission of a β-particle, which is an electron given the symbol e⁻ or β⁻. Electrons do not reside in the nucleus, but they are emitted by the nucleus when a neutron in the nucleus decays into a proton and a β⁻ (and an antineutrino). Because an electron is singly charged and about 1,836 times lighter than a proton, the beta radiation from radioactive decay is more penetrating than alpha radiation. In some cases of induced decay, a positively charged antielectron known as a **positron** is emitted. The positron is given the symbol e⁺ or β⁺.

β⁻ decay means that a neutron disappears and a proton takes its place. Hence, the parent's mass number is unchanged, and the parent's atomic number is increased by 1. In other words, the daughter's *A* is the same as the parent's, and the daughter's *Z* is one more than the parent's.

β⁻ decay

$$Z_{daughter} = Z_{parent} + 1$$

$$A_{daughter} = A_{parent}$$

The generic negative beta decay reaction is

$$^{A}_{Z}X \longrightarrow {}^{A}_{Z+1}Y + \beta^{-}$$

In positron decay, a proton (instead of a neutron as in β⁻ decay) splits into a positron and a neutron. Therefore, a β⁺ decay means that the parent's mass number is unchanged and the parent's atomic number is decreased by 1. In

> **Key Concept**
>
> In both types of beta decay, there needs to be conservation of charges. If a negative charge is created, a positive charge must be created as well (via neutron changed into a proton). Conversely, if a positive charge is created, a negative charge must be created as well (via proton changed into neutron). Remember negative beta decay creates a negative beta particle and positive beta decay creates a positive beta particle.

other words, the daughter's A is the same as the parent's, and the daughter's Z is one less than the parent's. This can be written in equation form:

β^+ decay

$$Z_{daughter} = Z_{parent} - 1$$
$$A_{daughter} = A_{parent}$$

The generic positive beta decay reaction is

$$^A_Z X \longrightarrow ^{\ A}_{Z-1} Y + \beta^+$$

Example: Suppose a cobalt-60 nucleus beta-decays as follows:

$$^{60}Co \rightarrow ^{A'}_{Z'} Y + e^-$$

What is the element Y, and what are A' and Z' ?

Solution: Again, balance mass numbers:

$$60 = A' + 0$$
$$A' = 60$$

Now balance the atomic numbers, taking into account that cobalt has 27 protons (you learn this by consulting the periodic table) and that there is one more proton on the right-hand side:

$$27 = Z' - 1$$
$$Z' = 28$$

Look at the periodic table to find that $Z' = 28$ is nickel:

$$Y = ^{60}_{28}Ni$$

---

c. **Gamma decay** is the emission of γ-particles, which are high-energy photons. They carry no charge and simply lower the energy of the emitting (parent) nucleus without changing the mass number or the atomic number. In other words, the daughter's A is the same as the parent's, and the daughter's Z is the same as the parent's.

γ decay

$$Z_{parent} = Z_{daughter}$$
$$A_{parent} = A_{daughter}$$

The generic gamma decay reaction is thus

$$^A_Z X' \longrightarrow ^A_Z X + \gamma$$

Key Concept

While gamma particles are dangerous, they are the easiest problems on the MCAT. *No* changes happen; the parent and daughter are the same.

MCAT Expertise

When the MCAT gives you problems like this, it is easiest to approach them by working backward.

Example: Suppose a parent isotope $^A_Z X$ emits a β^+ and turns into an excited state of the isotope $^{A'}_{Z'} Y'$, which then γ decays to $^{A''}_{Z''} Y$, which in turn α decays to $^{A'''}_{Z'''} W$. If W is ^{60}Fe, what is $^A_Z X$?

Solution: Since the final daughter in this chain of decay is given, it will be necessary to work backward through the reactions. By looking at the periodic table, one finds that $W = $ Fe means $Z''' = 26$; hence, the last reaction is the following α decay:

$$^{A''}_{Z''} Y \rightarrow ^{60}_{26}\text{Fe} + ^4_2\text{He}$$

By balancing the atomic numbers, you find

$$Z'' = 26 + 2 = 28$$

A balancing of the mass numbers implies

$$A'' = 60 + 4 = 64$$

The second-to-last reaction is a γ decay that simply releases energy from the nucleus but does not alter the atomic number or the mass number of the parent. That is, $Z' = Z'' = 28$ and $A' = A'' = 64$. So the second reaction is

$$^{64}_{28} Y' \rightarrow ^{64}_{28} Y + \gamma$$

The first reaction was a β^+ decay that must have looked like this:

$$^A_Z X \rightarrow ^{64}_{28} Y' + e^+$$

Again, balance the atomic numbers:

$$Z = 28 + 1 = 29$$

You carry out a balancing of mass numbers by taking into account that a proton has disappeared on the left and reappeared as a neutron on the right, leaving mass number unchanged:

$$A = 64 + 0 = 64$$

By looking at the periodic table, you find that $Z = 29$ means that X is Cu. $A = 64$, so that means that the solution is

$$^A_Z X = ^{64}_{29}\text{Cu}$$

Even though the problem did not ask for it, it is possible again to look at the periodic table to find that $Z' = Z'' = 28$ means $Y' = Y = $ Ni. The total chain of decays can be written as follows:

$$^{64}_{29}\text{Cu} \longrightarrow ^{64}_{28}\text{Ni}' + \beta^+$$

$$^{64}_{28}\text{Ni}' \longrightarrow ^{64}_{28}\text{Ni} + \gamma$$

$$^{64}_{28}\text{Ni} \longrightarrow ^{60}_{26}\text{Fe} + \alpha$$

d. Electron capture

Certain unstable radionuclides are capable of capturing an inner (K or L shell) electron that combines with a proton to form a neutron. The atomic number is now one less than the original, but the mass number remains the same. Electron capture is a rare process that is perhaps best thought of as an inverse β^- decay.

2. Radioactive Decay Half-Life ($T_{1/2}$)

In a sample of a great many identical radioactive isotopes, the **half-life** ($T_{1/2}$) of the sample is the time it takes for half of the sample to decay.

> **Example:** If the half-life of a certain isotope is 4 years, what fraction of a sample of that isotope will remain after 12 years?
>
> **Solution:** If 4 years is 1 half-life, then 12 years is 3 half-lives. During the first half-life—the first 4 years—half of the sample will have decayed. During the second half-life (years 4 to 8), half of the remaining half will decay, leaving one-fourth of the original. During the third and final period (years 8 to 12), half of the remaining fourth will decay, leaving one-eighth of the original sample. Thus, the fraction remaining after 3 half-lives is $\left(\dfrac{1}{2}\right)$ or $\dfrac{1}{8}$.

3. Exponential Decay

Let n be the number of radioactive nuclei that have not yet decayed in a sample. It turns out that the **rate** at which the nuclei decay $\dfrac{\Delta n}{\Delta t}$ is proportional to the number that remain (n). This suggests this equation:

$$\frac{\Delta n}{\Delta t} = -\lambda n$$

where λ is known as the **decay constant**. The solution of this equation tells us how the number of radioactive nuclei changes with time. The solution is known as an **exponential decay**:

$$n = n_0 e^{-\lambda t}$$

where n_0 is the number of undecayed nuclei at time $t = 0$. The decay constant is related to the half-life by $\lambda = \dfrac{\ln 2}{T_{1/2}} = \dfrac{0.693}{T_{1/2}}$.

MCAT Expertise

Half-life problems are common on the MCAT. Make sure you draw them out; it's easy to lose your place when doing them in your head.

MCAT Expertise

On the MCAT, it will often be much faster and accurate enough to approach these problems the same way as you approached the previous ones. Remember that the MCAT is a timed test; the quickest way either to get an accurate answer or to get rid of the incorrect answers will always be the best route.

Key Equation

$n = n_0 e^{-\lambda t}$

The units of λ (s^{-1}) and t (s) cancel out, and all other variables are dimensionless.

Use this equation to determine the number of undecayed nuclei remaining (n).

Example: If at time $t = 0$ there is a 2-mole sample of radioactive isotopes of decay constant 2 (hour)$^{-1}$, how many nuclei remain after 45 minutes?

Solution: Since 45 minutes is $\dfrac{3}{4}$ of an hour, the exponent is

$$\lambda t = 2\left(\frac{3}{4}\right) = \frac{6}{4} = \frac{3}{2}$$

The exponential factor will be a number smaller than 1:

$$e^{-\lambda t} = e^{-3/2} = 0.22$$

So only 0.22 or 22 percent of the original 2-mole sample will remain. To find n_0, multiply the number of moles we have by the number of particles per mole (Avogadro's number):

$$n_0 = 2(6.02 \times 10^{23}) = 1.2 \times 10^{24}$$

From the equation that describes exponential decay, you can calculate the number that remains after 45 minutes:

$$
\begin{aligned}
n = n_0 e^{-\lambda t} \\
= (1.2 \times 10^{24})(0.22) \\
= 2.6 \times 10^{23} \text{ nuclei}
\end{aligned}
$$

MCAT Concept Check 12.3

Before moving on, ensure that you are able to:

✓ Compare and contrast fusion and fission reactions

✓ Solve for atomic and mass numbers of nuclei in alpha, beta, and gamma decay equations

✓ Calculate the number of undecayed nuclei remaining using half-life and exponential decay equations

---

Conclusion

Our final chapter examined the characteristics and behavior of the atomic nucleus. We began by defining some of the important terms that are used to describe the nucleus and the atom, including atomic number, which is the number of protons in the nucleus and is a unique identifier for each element; atomic mass, which is the total number of protons and neutrons in the nucleus; isotopes, which are atoms of the same element that differ in the number of neutrons and therefore have the same atomic number but different mass numbers; and finally, atomic mass and atomic weight, which are defined as the mass of a single atom (in amu) and the mass of a mole of atoms (in grams) of a given element, respectively. We reviewed the relation between the binding energy and the mass defect and used Einstein's equation $E = mc^2$ to understand that the energy released when the nucleons are bound together by the strong nuclear force is from the conversion of a small amount of mass of the constituent nucleons. We reviewed the different types of radioactive decay in which the nucleus decays and emits a specific type of particle, such as an alpha particle, electron, positron, or gamma photon. Finally, we concluded our discussion of nuclear decay with a brief consideration of radioactive decay half-life and calculation of the remaining radioactive nuclei as a function of time.

Congratulations! You did it! You have accomplished so much in completing this review of physics for the MCAT. We know that you've worked hard and invested much time, effort, and attention to the concepts reviewed in this book. We know that your hard work will pay off in points on Test Day. You've done much, but there's more to do. Continue to review the concepts discussed in these chapters and practice applying them to MCAT passages and questions. Success on Test Day is based not just on your ability to recall important facts, figures, equations, or laws, but also—and even more importantly—on your ability to think critically, analyze new information, and synthesize your knowledge with the passage and questions.

CONCEPT SUMMARY

Atomic Number (p. 351)

☐ Is the number of protons in the nucleus

☐ All the atoms of a given element have the same number of protons and therefore the same atomic number

☐ No two elements have the same atomic number

Mass Number (p. 352)

☐ Is the number of protons and neutrons in the nucleus

☐ **Isotopes** (p. 352) are atoms of the same element that have different mass numbers

○ Isotopes have the same atomic number, but have different numbers of neutrons and therefore, different mass numbers

Atomic Mass (p. 353)

☐ Is the mass of a single atom of a given element in atomic mass units (amu)

○ The average mass of a single proton or neutron is one amu, so the atomic mass of an atom is equal to the mass number of that atom

Atomic Weight (p. 353)

☐ Is the mass of one mole of atoms of a given element in grams

Nuclear Binding Energy (p. 354)

☐ Is the amount of energy that is released when nucleons (protons and neutrons) bind together through the strong nuclear force

☐ The more binding energy per nucleon released, the more stable the nucleus

☐ The **mass defect** (p. 354) is the difference between the mass of the unbound constituents and the mass of the bound constituents in the nucleus

○ The unbound constituents have more energy and, therefore, more mass than the bound constituents

○ The mass defect is the amount of mass converted to energy through the nuclear reactions of fusion or fission

Nuclear Reactions

☐ **Fusion** (p. 356) occurs when small nuclei combine into larger nuclei

☐ **Fission** (p. 356) occurs when a large nucleus splits into smaller nuclei

☐ Energy is released in both fusion and fission since the nuclei formed in both processes are more stable than the starting nuclei

Radioactive Decay

☐ **Alpha (α) decay** (p. 357) is the emission of an alpha particle, a ^{4}He nucleus

☐ **Beta (β⁻) decay** (p. 358) is the decay of a neutron and emission of an electron

☐ **Positron (β⁺) decay** (p. 359) is the decay of proton and emission of a positron

- ☐ **Gamma (γ) decay** (p. 359) is the emission of a gamma photon
- ☐ **Electron capture** (p. 361) is the capture of an electron that combines with a proton to form a neutron
- ☐ **Half-life** (p. 361) is the amount of time required for half of a sample of radioactive nuclei to decay
  - ○ The rate at which radioactive nuclei decay is proportional to the number of nuclei that remain

EQUATIONS TO REMEMBER

- ☐ $n = n_0 e^{-\lambda t}$ (exponential decay)

SHARED CONCEPTS

HIGH-YIELD PRACTICE PROBLEMS

Practice Questions

1. Which of the following correctly identifies the following process?

$$^{96}_{42}X + 1e^- \rightarrow {}^{96}_{41}X$$

A. β^- decay

B. α decay

C. e^- capture

D. γ decay

2. Consider the following fission reaction.

$$^1_0n \;+\; {}^{10}_{5}B \;\rightarrow\; {}^7_3Li \;+\; {}^4_2He$$
$$1.0087 \quad 10.0129 \quad 7.0160 \quad 4.0026$$

The masses of the species involved are given in atomic mass units below each species, and 1 amu = 932 MeV. What is the energy liberated due to transformation of mass into energy?

A. 0.003 MeV

B. 1.4 MeV

C. 2.8 MeV

D. 5.6 MeV

3. Calculate the binding energy of the argon-40 isotope in MeV using the following information: 1 proton = 1.0073 amu, 1 neutron = 1.0087 amu, ^{40}Ar = 39.9132 amu, $c^2 = 932$ MeV/amu.

A. 381.7 MeV

B. 643.8 MeV

C. 0.4096 MeV

D. 40.3228 MeV

4. An α particle and a β^+ particle (positron) possess the same kinetic energy. What is the ratio of the velocity of the β^+ particle to that of the α particle? (Assume that the neutron mass is equal to the proton mass and neglect binding energy.)

A. $\sqrt{\dfrac{m_{proton}}{m_{electron}}}$

B. $2\sqrt{\dfrac{m_{proton}}{m_{electron}}}$

C. $\sqrt{\dfrac{m_{electron}}{m_{proton}}}$

D. $2\sqrt{\dfrac{m_{electron}}{m_{proton}}}$

5. A student is trying to determine the type of nuclear decay for a reaction. Which of the following would be an indication that the reaction he is observing is a gamma decay?

A. $Z_{daughter} = Z_{parent} + 1; A_{daughter} = A_{parent}$

B. $Z_{daughter} = Z_{parent} - 1; A_{daughter} = A_{parent}$

C. $Z_{daughter} = Z_{parent} - 2; A_{daughter} = A_{parent} - 4$

D. $Z_{daughter} = Z_{parent}; A_{daughter} = A_{parent}$

6. Element X is radioactive and decays via α decay with a half-life of four days. If 12.5 percent of an original sample of element X remains after N days, what is the value of N?

A. 4

B. 8

C. 12

D. 16

7. A patient undergoing treatment for thyroid cancer receives a dose of radioactive iodine (^{131}I), which has a half-life of 8.05 days. If the original dose contained 12 mg of ^{131}I, what mass of ^{131}I remains after 16.1 days?

A. 3 mg
B. 6 mg
C. 9 mg
D. 12 mg

8. In an exponential decay, if the natural logarithm of the ratio of intact nuclei (n) at time t to the intact nuclei at time $t = 0$ (n_0) is plotted against time, what does the slope of the graph correspond to?

A. λ
B. $-\lambda$
C. $e^{-\lambda t}$
D. $\dfrac{n}{n_0}$

9. The mass of a proton is about 1.007 amu, and the mass of a neutron is about 1.009 amu. The mass of a helium nucleus is

A. less than 4.032 amu.
B. exactly 4.032 amu.
C. greater than 4.032 amu.
D. Cannot be determined from the information given

10. A certain carbon nucleus dissociates completely into α particles. How many particles are formed?

A. 1
B. 2
C. 3
D. 4

11. $^{292}_{116}\text{Uuh} \rightarrow \, ^{292}_{115}\text{Uup} + 0.96\,\text{MeV} + \text{other particles}$

The reaction here is an example of

A. α decay.
B. β decay.
C. γ decay.
D. election capture.

12. The half-life of ^{14}C is approximately 5,730 years, while the half-life of ^{12}C is essentially infinite. If the ratio of ^{14}C to ^{12}C in a certain sample is 25% less than the normal ratio in nature, how old is the sample?

A. Less than 5,730 years
B. Approximately 5,730 years
C. Significantly greater than 5,730 years, but less than 11,460 years
D. Approximately 11,460 years

13. A nuclide undergoes 2 alpha decays, 2 positron decays, and 2 gamma decays. What is the difference between the atomic number of the parent nuclide and the atomic number of the daughter nuclide?

A. 0
B. 2
C. 4
D. 6

14. A helium nucleus fuses with a hydrogen nucleus and then captures an electron. What is the identity of the daughter nuclide?

A. ^{5}He
B. ^{5}He$^+$
C. ^{5}Li
D. ^{5}Li$^+$

Small Group Questions

1. How much energy is released by radioactive decay in 2 minutes when 0.5 moles of a compound with a half-life of 10 minutes undergoes exponential decay by emitting a positron from its nucleus at 75% the speed of light? The mass of a positron is 9.11×10^{-31} kg.

2. Provide three different possible radioactive decay pathways (each using more than one type of decay particle) in which the atomic number of the parent isotope decreases by 4. Give the final mass number of the daughter isotope for each pathway.

Explanations to Practice Questions

1. C

This process can be described as electron capture. Certain unstable radionuclides are capable of capturing an inner electron that combines with a proton to form a neutron. The atomic number becomes one less than the original, but the mass number remains the same. Electron capture is a relatively rare process and can be thought of as inverse β^- decay. Notice that the equation is similar to that of β^+ decay but not identical. Choice (C) is therefore the correct answer.

2. C

This problem presents a reaction and asks for the energy liberated due to transformation of mass into energy. To convert mass into energy, we are given the conversion factor 1 amu = 932 MeV. (Note that this is actually the c^2 from Einstein's equation $E = \Delta mc^2$). All we need to do now is calculate how much mass, in amu, is lost in the reaction. Because we are given the atomic mass for each of the elements in the reaction, this is simply a matter of balancing the equation:

$$1.0087 + 10.0129 = 7.0160 + 4.0026 + x$$
$$11.0216 = 11.0186 + x$$
$$x = 11.0216 - 11.0186$$
$$x = 0.0030 \text{ amu}$$

This is the amount of mass that has been converted into kinetic energy. To obtain energy from mass, we have to multiply by the conversion factor (1 amu = 932 MeV):

$$K = 0.003 \times 932 \approx 3 \text{ MeV}$$

Choice (C) best matches our prediction and is thus the correct answer.

3. A

Glancing at the periodic table, you can see that argon has an atomic number of $Z = 18$, so we can determine the number of neutrons: $A - Z = 40 - 18 = 22$. Therefore, the masses of the constituent nucleons of ^{40}Ar add up as follows:

$$Z(m_p) + N(m_n) = 18 \times 1.0073 + 22 \times 1.0087$$
$$Z(m_p) + N(m_n) = 18.1314 + 22.2924$$
$$Z(m_p) + N(m_n) = 40.3228 \text{ amu}$$

Therefore, if the actual mass of ^{40}Ar is 39.9132 amu, then the mass defect is

$$\Delta m = 40.3228 - 39.9132 = 0.4096 \text{ amu}$$

Convert this value into binding energy in MeV:

$$E = \Delta mc^2$$
$$E = (0.4096)(932) = 381.7 \text{ MeV}$$

Choice (A) matches our prediction and is thus the correct answer.

4. B

An α particle is a helium nucleus and therefore contains 2 protons and 2 neutrons. Assuming the neutron mass equals the proton mass, and neglecting binding energy, the mass of an α particle is $4m_{proton}$, where m_{proton} is the mass of a proton. A β^+ particle is a positron. (Recall that a positron has the same mass but opposite charge to that of an electron). Thus, the mass of a β^+ particle is $m_{electron}$, where $m_{electron}$ is the mass of an electron. Given that the particles have equal kinetic energy, you have

$$\frac{1}{2}\left(4m_{proton}\right)v_\alpha^2 = \frac{1}{2}m_{electron}v_\beta^2$$

Solving for $\frac{v_\beta}{v_\alpha}$ gives

$$\frac{v_\beta}{v_\alpha} = 2\sqrt{\frac{m_{proton}}{m_{electron}}}$$

Choice (B) is therefore the correct answer.

5. D

Gamma decay is the emission of a γ particle, which is a high-energy photon. In this process, the mass number and the atomic number remain the same. Therefore, (D) is the correct answer.

6. C

Because the half-life of element X is four days, 50 percent of an original sample remains after four days, 25 percent remains after eight days, and 12.5 percent remains after 12 days. Therefore, $N = 12$ days. Another approach is to set $\left(\frac{1}{2}\right)^n = 0.125$, where n is the number of half-lives that have elapsed. Solving for n gives $n = 3$. Thus, 3 half-lives have elapsed, and because each half-life is four days, we know that $N = 12$ days, making (C) the correct answer.

7. A

Given that the half-life of ^{131}I is 8.05 days, you know that 2 half-lives have elapsed after 16.1 days, which means that 25 percent, or one-fourth, of the original amount of ^{131}I is still present. Therefore, only 25 percent of the original number of ^{131}I nuclei remains, which means that only 25 percent of the original mass of ^{131}I remains. Because the original dose contained 12 mg of ^{131}I, only 3 mg remain after 16.1 days. Choice (A) is therefore the correct answer.

8. B

The expression $n = n_0 e^{-\lambda t}$ is equivalent to $\frac{n}{n_0} = e^{-\lambda t}$. Taking the natural logarithm of both sides of the latter expression, you find

$$\ln\left(\frac{n}{n_0}\right) = -\lambda t$$

From this expression, it is clear that plotting $\ln\frac{n}{n_0}$ versus t will give a straight line with a slope of $-\lambda$. Choice (B) is therefore the correct answer.

9. A

The mass of the protons and neutrons is (1.007 amu/proton)(2 protons) + (1.009 amu/neutron)(2 neutrons) = 4.032 amu. Some of this mass is converted to energy in order to overcome the binding energy of the nucleus, so the overall mass must be less than 4.032 amu. Therefore, (A) is the correct answer.

10. C

A typical carbon nucleus contains 6 protons and 6 neutrons. An α particle contains 2 protons and 2 neutrons. Therefore, one carbon nucleus can dissociate into $\frac{6}{2} = 3$ α particles, making choice (C) the correct answer.

11. B

β decay occurs when an electron or a positron is released by the nucleus. This means that a proton is converted to a neutron or vice versa. Therefore, a β particle is emitted in any reaction in which the atomic number of the parent atom increases or decreases by 1 while the mass number stays the same.

12. A

Because the half-life of ^{12}C is essentially infinite, a 25 percent decrease in the ratio of ^{14}C to ^{12}C means the same as a 25 percent decrease in the amount of ^{14}C. If less than half of the ^{14}C has deteriorated, then less than one half-life has elapsed. Therefore, the sample is less than 5,730 years old, making (A) the correct answer.

13. D

In alpha decay, an element loses two protons. In positron decay, a proton is converted to a neutron. Gamma decay, meanwhile, has no impact on the atomic number of the nuclide. Therefore, two alpha decays and two positron decays will yield a daughter nuclide with six less protons than the parent.

14. A

The fusion of a hydrogen nucleus (one proton) and a helium nucleus (two protons, two neutrons) will produce ^{5}Li. If the ^{5}Li nucleus captures an electron, a proton will be converted to a neutron, producing ^{5}He. Although the atom will initially carry a positive charge in most cases, the positive charge is a property of the atom and not of the nuclide.

Explanations to Small Group Questions

1. To calculate the energy loss, we first must identify the amount of material that is emitted due to radioactive decay by using the exponential decay equation, $n = n_0 e^{-\lambda t}$. Plugging $n_0 = 0.5$ moles, $\lambda = 0.069$ min^{-1}, and $t = 2$ min into the equation, we find that after 2 minutes we are left with 2.62×10^{23} nuclei. Having started with $(0.5 \text{ mol})(6.023 \times 10^{23} \text{ nuclei/mol}) = 3.011 \times 10^{23}$ nuclei, 3.91×10^{22} positrons have been emitted. To determine the total energy emitted, we can calculate the total kinetic energy of the positrons emitted.

$$K = \frac{1}{2}mv^2 \text{ , } m = 9.11 \times 10^{-31}\text{kg, } v = 0.75c$$

$$K = \frac{1}{2}(3.91 \times 10^{22})(9.11 \times 10^{-31}\text{kg})(0.75)(3.0 \times 10^8\text{m/s})$$
$$K = 9.02 \times 10^8\text{J}$$

2. One pathway for decreasing the atomic number of the parent by 4 is via two beta decays, which would decrease the mass number by 8. A second pathway would involve four positron decays, in which the final mass number would be unchanged. A third pathway would involve one beta decay and two positron decays, which would decrease the mass number by 4.

High-Yield Problem Solving Guide for Physics

High-Yield MCAT Review

This is a **High-Yield Questions section**. These questions tackle the most frequently tested topics found on the MCAT. For each type of problem, you will be provided with a stepwise technique for solving the question and key directional points on how to solve for the MCAT specifically.

At the end of each topic you will find a "Takeaways" box, which gives a concise summary of the problem-solving approach, and a "Things to Watch Out For" box, which points out any caveats to the approach discussed that usually lead to wrong answer choices. Finally, there is a "Similar Questions" box at the end so you can test your ability to apply the stepwise technique to analogous questions (answers to these questions follow the High-Yield Section).

We're confident that this guide can help you achieve your goals of MCAT success and admission into medical school!

Good luck!

Key Concepts

Chapter 1

Newton's second law: $F = ma$
(N: $kg \cdot m/s^2$)

Kinematics

$v_f = v_0 + at$ (m/s)

$\Delta x = v_0 t + \left(\frac{1}{2}\right) at^2$ (m)

$\Delta x = \frac{v_f + v_0}{2} t$ (m)

Kinematic Motion

A firecracker with a mass of 100 grams is propelled vertically with a launch force of 1.2 newtons applied over 5 seconds, after which the firecreacker explodes and launches two 50 g fragments. The first fragment goes horizontally to the left with an initial velocity of 15 m/s. The second fragment goes to the right at a 53.1° angle from the horizontal with an initial velocity of 25 m/s. Find the distance between the two fragments once they both hit the ground. Ignore air resistance. ($g = 10$ m/s²)

1) Draw a free-body diagram of the object's trajectory.

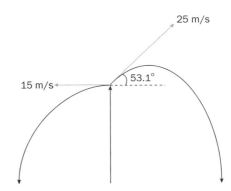

Ignoring air resistance, there are two forces acting on the firecracker initially: gravity and the propulsion provided by the launch. After the explosion, the only force acting is gravity. In our sketch, we must recognize that there are two portions: the linear firing and then the parabolic trajectories of the fragments. The difference between the left and right portions is where the parabola starts.

---

2) Find the acceleration of the object at launch.

$F = ma$

$F_{net} = ma - mg = m(a - g) = ma_{net}$

$1.2\ N = (0.1\ kg)a \rightarrow a = 12$ m/s²

$F_{net} = ma - mg = (0.1)(12) - (0.1)(10) = (0.1)(12 - 10) = 0.2$ N

Because of Newton's second law, we know that force is the product of mass and acceleration. We can determine the net force either by subtracting the weight (mg) from the initial launch force or by finding the acceleration due to the launch force and subtracting out the acceleration due to gravity. Overall, we end up with a 0.2 N force directed upwards and a net acceleration of 2 m/s², which is also directed upwards.

Takeaways

In projectile motion problems, you will need to consider the **X** and **Y** components of motion separately. The equations for kinematics are often tested and should be memorized. Another extremely useful equation that was not used here is $v_f^2 = v_0^2 + 2a\Delta x$.

Things to Watch Out For

Don't forget to add all the different forces acting on the object—in this case, the launch force and the weight. The object's mass will not matter for projectile motion when gravity is the only force acting on the object.

3) Find the velocity and distance of the object after the elapsed period.

With the acceleration, we can find the velocity after five seconds. With that velocity, we can find the distance traveled in the first segment of travel. This is simple "plug-and-chug" mathematics.

$$v_f = v_o + at$$
$$\Delta x = v_o t + \left(\frac{1}{2}\right)at^2$$
$$v_f = 0 + 2(5) = 10 \text{ m/s}$$
$$\Delta x = 0(5) + \left(\frac{1}{2}\right)(2)(5)^2 = 25 \text{ m}$$

OR

$$\Delta x = \bar{v}t = \frac{(v_f + v_i)}{2}t$$
$$\Delta x = \left(\frac{1}{2}\right)(10 + 0)(5) = 25 \text{ m}$$

Remember: *The second equation for distance features $\bar{v}$. This is shorthand for average velocity. It would be incorrect simply to use 10 m/s here because the firecracker did not start out with that speed.*

---

4) Find the time required for the left fragment to hit the ground.

$$\Delta x = v_o t + \left(\frac{1}{2}\right)at^2$$

Y component: $-25 = 0(t) + \left(\frac{1}{2}\right)(-10)t^2 \rightarrow t = \sqrt{5} \approx 2.2 \text{ s}$

The left fragment has a velocity in the left direction. This will determine how far away it lands but has no bearing on how long it will take the fragment to fall to the ground. The fragment moves in a parabolic curve downward starting from a height of 25 m. Because our final height is 0, this means that the distance we travel is negative. In other words, because we defined gravity as negative, when we move with gravity (downward), we are going in a negative direction. Consider only the **Y** component of motion—no initial velocity and acceleration due to gravity.

---

5) Find how far away the left fragment lands.

$$\Delta x = v_o t + \left(\frac{1}{2}\right)at^2$$

X component: $\Delta x = 15(2.2) + \left(\frac{1}{2}\right)(0)(2.2)^2 = 33 \text{ m}$

There is no acceleration due to gravity in the *x*-direction. Because we already found the time that the fragment was falling and we are given its initial velocity, we once again just plug in numbers to the appropriate kinematics formula.

Similar Questions

1) A bottle is thrown with an initial velocity of 4 m/s at 45° from the horizon. Find its final horizontal and vertical velocities before striking the ocean.

2) A pre-1982 penny with a mass of 3.1 grams is dropped from the top of a skyscraper of 1,250 meters. Find the object's acceleration after 5 seconds. If a post-1982 penny with a mass of 2.5 grams is dropped at this point, how far does it travel before the first penny hits the ground?

3) A baseball is thrown vertically with a speed of 3 m/s. Find the total time that the ball has been in flight when it has traveled 50 cm.

Remember: *The horizontal velocity remains constant, so if we instead use* $\Delta x = \bar{v}t = \dfrac{(v_f + v_i)}{2}t$ *, we get the same result.*

---

6) Find the X and Y components of the right trajectory.

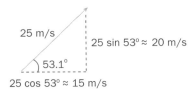

If the right fragment is shot at 25 m/s at a 53.1° angle, we will need to break its movement into **X** (right) and **Y** (up) components. The **X** and **Y** components behave independently. At this point, it is also wise for us to round our numbers. Thus, we consider a 53° angle and find that $v_x \approx 15$ m/s and $v_y \approx 20$ m/s.

Remember: *When working with sine and cosine on the MCAT, be sure to estimate. Knowing that the sine of 30 is 0.5 whereas the sine of 60 is 0.866, you can estimate the sine of 53 to be approximately 0.8, a little less than 0.866.*

---

7) Find the time it takes for the right fragment to hit the ground.

$$\Delta x = v_0 t + \left(\frac{1}{2}\right)at^2$$
Y component: $-25 = 20t + \left(\dfrac{1}{2}\right)(-10)t^2$
$\Rightarrow 5t^2 - 20t - 25 = 0$
$\Rightarrow t^2 - 4t - 5 = 0$
$\Rightarrow (t - 5)(t + 1) = 0$
$\Rightarrow t - 5 = 0$ or $t + 1 = 0$
$\Rightarrow t = 5$ or -1
$\Rightarrow t = 5$ s

If we consider the point of explosion to be at a height of zero, the ground is at −25 m. Though we could find the time it takes for the right fragment to peak and return to "zero" or find the maximum height it reaches in this parabola (using $v_f^2 = v_0^2 + 2a\Delta h$, we find that $\Delta h = 20$ m; that is, maximum height above the ground = 25 + 20 = 45 m), it is faster simply to consider the whole trajectory. If the time of explosion is $t = 0$ s, we see that the fragment won't hit the ground until $t = 5$ s. We disregard the negative solution for t since this would refer to a time *before* rather than after the explosion.

---

8) Find how far away the right fragment lands.

$$\Delta x = v_o t + \left(\frac{1}{2}\right)at^2$$

X component: $\Delta x = 15(5) + \left(\frac{1}{2}\right)(0)(5)^2 = 75$ m

Once again, we're only considering the **X** component. We found the time in flight by working with the **Y** component and now we're simply finding the distance that the object can travel in that time.

---

9) Determine the final distance between the fragments.

$33 + 75 = 108$ m

Add the two segments together. The left fragment lands 33 m away from the launching point, 2.2 s after the explosion. The right fragment lands 2.8 s after that (5 s after the explosion), 75 m from the launching point. The total distance between the two fragments is 108 m.

Key Concepts

Chapter 1

Conservation of energy

Kinetic energy

Potential energy

Nonconservative forces

Kinematics

$E_f = U_f + K_f$ (J)

Projectile Motion and Air Resistance

An arrow with a mass of 80 g is fired at an angle of 30° to the horizontal. It strikes a target located 5 m above the firing point and impacts the target traveling 20 m/s. If 10% of the initial energy of the arrow is lost to air resistance, what was the initial velocity of the arrow?

1) Write an expression for the final energy of the arrow.

$$E_f = U_f + K_f = mgh_f + \left(\frac{1}{2}\right)mv_f^2$$

The total energy of the arrow is its potential energy plus kinetic energy. The potential energy of the arrow is *mgh*. For simplicity, make the height at the firing point equal to zero so that the final height is 5 m.

Remember: Finding a numerical value at this point is not necessary. Writing an expression will save you time because some terms (usually the mass) may cancel out in a later step.

Things to Watch Out For

The mention of lost energy in the question stem should tip you off that you need to use the conservation of energy equation. In general, unless you are asked for an acceleration or time value, the energy approach is easier and faster than the kinematics/Newton's laws approach.

2) Write an expression for the initial energy of the arrow.

$$E_i = U_i + K_i = mgh_i + \left(\frac{1}{2}\right)mv_i^2 = \left(\frac{1}{2}\right)mv_i^2$$

As stated in step 1, the initial height is zero, so the potential energy is zero.

3) Relate the change in energy to the energy lost to air resistance.

$$E_i - E_f = E_{lost}$$

$$\frac{1}{2}mv_i^2 - \left(mgh_f + \left(\frac{1}{2}\right)mv_f^2\right) = E_{lost}$$

The conservation of energy equation tells us that all of the energy of a system must be accounted for. Whatever energy is lost between the beginning and the end must have been due to air resistance.

---

4) Relate the energy lost to the initial energy.

$$E_{lost} = (0.1)E_i = 0.1\left(\frac{1}{2}mv_i^2\right)$$

The question states that 10% of the initial energy is lost. Thus, the energy lost is the initial energy times 0.1.

Remember: In problems with no air resistance (or friction), you can simply set the initial and final energies equal to each other.

---

5) Solve for the initial velocity.

Plug the expression for energy lost from step 4 into the expression in step 3 and solve for velocity.

$$\frac{1}{2}mv_i^2 - \left(mgh_f + \left(\frac{1}{2}\right)mv_f^2\right) = E_{lost}$$

$$\frac{1}{2}mv_i^2 - \left(mgh_f + \left(\frac{1}{2}\right)mv_f^2\right) = 0.1\left(\frac{1}{2}mv_i^2\right)$$

$$\frac{1}{2}v_i^2 - \left(gh_f + \left(\frac{1}{2}\right)v_f^2\right) = 0.1\left(\frac{1}{2}mv_i^2\right)$$

$$\left(gh_f + \left(\frac{1}{2}\right)v_f^2\right) = \frac{1}{2}v_i^2 - 0.1\left(\frac{1}{2}v_i^2\right) = 0.45v_i^2$$

$$v_i^2 = \frac{\left(gh_f + \frac{1}{2}v_f^2\right)}{0.45} = 553.3$$

$$v_i = 23.5 \text{ m/s}$$

Similar Questions

1) A rock is dropped from the top of a 100 m tall building and lands while traveling at a speed of 30 m/s. How much energy was lost due to air resistance?

2) Two different objects are dropped from rest off of a 50 m tall cliff. One lands going 30% faster than the other. The two objects have the same mass. How much more kinetic energy does one object have at the landing than the other?

3) A projectile is fired vertically at a speed of 30.0 m/s. It reaches a maximum height of 44.1 m. What fraction of its initial energy has been lost to air resistance at this point?

Takeaways

Note that the angle and the mass were never used in the calculation. This will often be the case when using the conservation of energy equation to solve problems.

These problems can be worded in many different ways, but the problem-solving process is the same for all of them:

1) Write an expression for the initial energy and an expression for the final energy.

2) If there is friction or air resistance, the difference between final and initial energy is the energy lost to these forces.

3) If there is no friction or air resistance, the energy lost is zero, so set the two expressions equal to each other.

4) Solve for the quantity of interest.

Keep a realistic view of these problems to check your answers for math errors. Note that the initial velocity is faster than the final velocity, which we expect because the target is higher than the firing point and some energy is lost to air resistance.

Universal Law of Gravitation

On a certain planet with radius 7,000 km, the acceleration due to gravity at the surface of the planet is 6 m/s². What is the acceleration due to gravity at an elevation above the surface equal to twice the radius of the planet? By what factor is the acceleration due to gravity changed at this elevation? ($G = 6.6 \times 10^{-11}$ N·m²/kg².)

1) Find the mass of the planet.

Use the Universal Law of Gravitation. In this equation, r is the distance from the center of the mass, so at the surface of the planet it is the radius of the planet. Use Newton's second law, $a = \dfrac{F}{m}$, to get an expression for acceleration. Solve for the mass of the planet.

$$F_{surf} = \frac{Gm_1m_2}{r^2}$$

$$a_{surf} = \frac{F}{m} = \frac{Gm_{planet}}{r_{planet}^2}$$

$$m_{planet} = \frac{(a_{surf})(r_{planet}^2)}{G} = \frac{(6)(7\times10^6)^2}{(6.6\times10^{-11})} = \frac{(6)(49\times10^{12})}{(6.6\times10^{-11})} = 4.5 \times 10^{24} \text{ kg}$$

2) Write an expression for the acceleration at the high elevation.

$$F_{elev} = \frac{Gm_1m_2}{(r+h)^2}$$

This is the same expression as in step 1, except the distance from the center of the planet is now the radius of the planet added to the height above the surface, h. Solve for acceleration.

$$a_{elev} = \frac{F}{m} = \frac{Gm_{planet}}{(r_{planet}+h)^2}$$

$$h = 2(7,000) = 14,000 \text{ km} = 1.4 \times 10^7 \text{ m}$$

$$a_{elev} = \frac{(6.6\times10^{-11})(4.5\times10^{24})}{(7\times10^6 + 1.4\times10^7)^2}$$

$$a_{elev} = \frac{(6.6\times10^{-11})(4.5\times10^{24})}{(2.1+10^7)^2}$$

$$a_{elev} = \frac{(6.6\times10^{-11})(4.5\times10^{24})}{(4.41\times10^{14})}$$

$$a_{elev} = 0.67 \text{ m/s}^2$$

3) Divide the accelerations.

$$\frac{a_{elev}}{a_{surf}} = \frac{(0.67)}{(6)} = 0.11$$

To find the factor by which acceleration has changed, simply divide the elevated acceleration by that at the surface.

---

4) Here is an alternate solution to part 2 of the question.

$$\frac{a_{elev}}{a_{surf}} = \frac{\frac{Gm_{planet}}{(r_{planet}+h)^2}}{\frac{Gm_{planet}}{r_{planet}^2}} = \frac{Gm_{planet}\, r_{planet}^2}{(r_{planet}+h)^2\, Gm_{planet}} = \frac{r_{planet}^2}{(r_{planet}+2r_{planet})^2} = \frac{r_{planet}^2}{9r_{planet}^2} = \frac{1}{9}$$

If we had not solved for the mass of the planet in step 1, we could have solved for the factor of change in acceleration by writing a fraction of the two expressions. It simplifies with algebra to $\frac{1}{9}$. It is three times the distance, and the acceleration is related to the distance squared.

---

5) And here is another solution.

r is getting multiplied by 3. Using the formula $F = \frac{Gm_{planet}m_{object}}{r^2}$, we see that F is inversely proportional to r^2; therefore, F is getting multiplied by $\frac{1}{9}$. Using the formula $a = \frac{F}{m}$, we see that a is directly proportional to F; therefore, a is getting multiplied by $\frac{1}{9}$.

Similar Questions

1) Two masses, $m_1 = 10$ kg and $m_2 = 30$ kg, are 1 m apart. What is the force of gravity acting on m_1 from m_2?

2) At what height above the Earth's surface is the acceleration due to gravity 10% of that at sea level?

3) The moon has $\frac{1}{6}$ the acceleration of gravity of the Earth. What would the mass of the Earth have to be to have this acceleration at its surface (where Earth (radius) = 6378 km and Earth (mass) = 5.97×10^{24} kg)?

Key Concepts

Chapter 2

Newton's laws

Free-body diagram

Drag force

Power

Work-kinetic energy theorem

$F = ma$ (N: kg · m/s²)

$P = \dfrac{\Delta E}{t}$ (W: J/s)

$W = \Delta E$ (J)

Terminal Velocity

> A 5,000 N golf cart experiences a drag force equal to $65v$ kg/s, where v is the speed of the golf cart. If the golf cart has an electric motor that has a maximum power output of 76 kW, what is the golf cart's maximum speed on a level fairway?

1) Draw a free-body diagram.

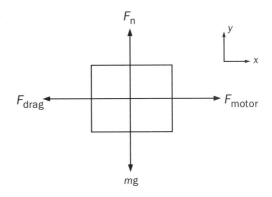

There are two horizontal forces forces acting on the golf cart: the force of the motor (labeled F_{motor}) and the drag force (labeled F_{drag}).

2) Add the forces in the x direction.

$$\Sigma F_x = ma_x = F_{motor} - F_{drag}$$

Add the forces in the x direction. Because there is no friction, it will not be necessary to solve for the normal force, so we can disregard the y direction. Set the sum of the forces equal to ma. This is Newton's second law.

3) Set the acceleration equal to zero.

$$a_x = 0 \rightarrow F_{motor} - F_{drag} = 0$$
$$F_{motor} = F_{drag}$$

The maximum velocity of the cart will occur when the acceleration of the cart is zero—that is, when the cart motor can no longer exert enough force to accelerate the cart. This means that the force of the motor equals the drag force.

Takeaways

This question is solved like all other force/acceleration problems: (1) draw a free-body diagram, (2) add the forces in each direction, and (3) solve. The tricky part of this question is in the units because the power of the motor is given. Use dimensional analysis to guide you.

Things to Watch Out For

Terminal velocity problems will always involve a drag force that depends on velocity.

4) Find the force of the motor from the power.

Power is change in energy per time. Work is equal to the change in energy. Work is also equal to the force times distance. Use these relations and solve for the force of the motor.

$$P = \frac{\Delta E}{t}$$

$$P_{motor} = \frac{\Delta E}{t}$$

$$W = \Delta E \rightarrow P = \frac{w}{t} = \frac{F_{motor}d}{t}$$

$$F_{motor} = \frac{P_{motor}t}{d}$$

Distance divided by time is velocity. Use this to get the force in terms of the power and velocity.

$$\frac{d}{t} = v \rightarrow F_{motor} = \frac{P_{motor}}{v}$$

5) Set the forces equal and solve.

Set the forces equal, as in step 3, and plug in the force expressions from the question and from step 4. Solve for the velocity.

$$F_{motor} = F_{drag}$$

$$\frac{P_{motor}}{v} = 65\,v$$

$$v^2 = \frac{P_{motor}}{65} = 1,169.2$$

$$v = 34.2 \text{ m/s}$$

Key Concepts

Chapter 2

Dimensional analysis

Frequency

Density

Force

Surface tension

Dimensional Analysis

Water is dripping from a leaky faucet. As the drops fall, they oscillate as shown in the diagram above. Given that the frequency depends only on the surface tension T of the water (measured in N/m), the radius of the drops r, and the density of the water, use dimensional analysis to find a proportionality expression for the frequency f of the drops.

Takeaways

It is possible to find the trend for a quantity based solely on units of that quantity. Keep this in mind when facing unfamiliar topics on the MCAT.

1) Identify all of the relevant physical quantities and their units.

T: N/m = kg/s^2
ρ: kg/m^3
r: m
f: Hz = $\dfrac{1}{s}$

As given in the problem, surface tension has units of Newtons per meter. 1 N is 1 kg·m/s^2. Density has units of kg/m^3. Radius is a distance with units of meters. Frequency has units of Hz, or $\dfrac{1}{s}$.

Remember: If you forget what a newton is, remember F = ma, *so newtons =* kg(m/s^2).

Things to Watch Out For

If you are short on time, you can at least determine general trends using a commonsense approach. The larger the radius, the slower the drop will oscillate. The denser the fluid, the slower the drop will oscillate. The surface tension is supplying the force to keep the drop oscillating, so if it is stronger, the drop will oscillate more quickly.

2) Write a hypothetical formula for the frequency.

The frequency is related to the surface tension, T, the radius, r, and the density, ρ. Write an equation for these using variables as exponents.

$f = kT^x r^y \rho^z$, where k is a unitless constant

3) Plug the units into the hypothetical formula.

Plug the units into the hypothetical formula from step 2.

$$f = kT^x r^y \rho^z$$
$$1/s = (kg/s^2)^x (m)^y (kg/m^3)^z$$

---

4) Solve for the variables.

We know that the units on the left must equal the units on the right. Only the first term on the right contains seconds, so we know that the exponent must be $\frac{1}{2}$; thus, we end up with $\frac{1}{s}$ on the right side. After you have this, set up an equation for the other two units, checking the powers of the units on each side of the equation. The power of kg and m on the left side is 0. Solve for y and z. Plug into the hypothetical formula.

$$1/s = (kg/s^2)^x (m)^y (kg/m^3)^z$$
$$x = \frac{1}{2}$$
$$kg: 0 = x + z$$
$$m: 0 = y - 3z$$
$$\Rightarrow z = -\frac{1}{2}, y = -\frac{3}{2}$$
$$\Rightarrow f = k\frac{T^{1/2}}{r^{3/2}\rho^{1/2}} = k\sqrt{\frac{T}{r^3 \rho}}$$

Similar Questions

1) What are the units of G in Newton's law of gravitation?

2) An electric dipole is initially at rest in a uniform electric field. The torque provided by the electric field causes the dipole to oscillate back and forth. For the period of motion, the physicist derives the formula $T = k(E)^{\frac{1}{2}}$. In this equation, T is the period, E is the electric field, and k is a quantity with the appropriate units. Is this equation physically reasonable?

3) What are the units for the permeability of free space, μ_o?

Key Concepts

Chapter 2

Newton's laws

Friction

Pulley

Tension

Two Connected Masses

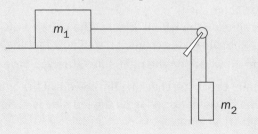

Two masses are connected by a string over a massless pulley as shown below. The coefficient of kinetic friction between mass 1 and the table on which it sits is 0.3. If the system is released from rest, what is the acceleration of mass 1? ($m_1 = 1$ kg; $m_2 = 4$ kg.)

Takeaways

The key here is that if there are two masses involved, you need to draw two free-body diagrams and write two sets of the sum of forces. Any two-mass problem will end in solving a system of two equations.

1) Draw free-body diagrams of both masses.

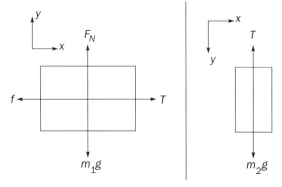

On mass 1, there are four forces acting: the normal force (labeled F_N), the weight (which equals m_1g), the tension in the string (labeled T), and the friction force (labeled f).

On mass 2, there are two forces acting: the weight (labeled m_2g) and the tension in the string (labeled T).

Notice that for mass 2, we have chosen the positive y-direction as down. Because we know that mass 2 will be going downward, this will simplify the calculations in later steps.

Things to Watch Out For

This problem could be made more complex by adding an incline or a third mass. No matter how complex the situation is, you can apply the same problem-solving process.

2) Add the forces in the x- and y-direction for each mass.

Mass 1:
$$\Sigma F_x = m_1 a_{x1} = T - f$$
$$\Sigma F_y = m_1 a_{y1} = F_N - m_1 g$$

Mass 2:
$$\Sigma F_x = m_2 a_{x2} = 0$$
$$\Sigma F_y = m_2 a_{y2} = m_2 g - T$$

According to Newton's second law, the sum of the forces in a given direction is always equal to the mass times the acceleration in that direction. Note that the tension (T in the diagrams) is the same tension in both equations.

---

3) Solve for the normal force of mass 1.

We know the acceleration in the y-direction is zero because mass 1 cannot move in the y-direction. Set $a_{y1} = 0$ and solve.

$a_{y1} = 0$, so $\Sigma F_y = 0$: $F_N - m_1 g = 0$
$F_N = m_1 g$

Remember: *Generally, it is only necessary to solve for the normal force when friction is involved.*

---

4) Write the friction force in terms of the normal force.

$f = \mu_k F_N = \mu_k m_1 g$
$m_1 a_{x1} = T - \mu_k m_1 g$
$m_2 a_{y2} = m_2 g - T$

The force of friction depends on the normal force and the coefficient of friction, μ_k.

---

5) Relate the accelerations of mass 1 and mass 2.

$a_{x1} = a_{y2} = a$

The two masses must accelerate at the same rate because they are tied together. Because we have chosen the positive y-direction to be downward for mass 2, we can say that $a_{x1} = a_{y2}$ and simplify the notation by calling them both a. (If we had chosen the positive y-direction to be upward, we would have to say $a_{x1} = -a_{y2}$).

---

6) Solve the system of equations.

(1) $m_1 a = T - \mu_k m_1 g$
(2) $m_2 a = m_2 g - T$

Solve (1):

$m_1 a = T - \mu_k m_1 g \therefore T = m_1 a + \mu_k m_1 g$

Plug in to (2):

$m_2 a = m_2 g - (m_1 a + \mu_k m_1 g)$
$m_2 a + m_1 a = m_2 g - \mu_k m_1 g$
$(m_1 + m_2)a = m_2 g - \mu_k m_1 g$
$a = \dfrac{m_2 g - \mu_k m_1 g}{m_1 + m_2} = 7.25$ m/s^2

Steps 4 and 5 leave us with two equations (labeled 1 and 2) and two unknowns (a and T). Solve for T in the first equation. Then, plug this expression for T into the second equation. Rearranging, we get an expression for acceleration. Finally, plug in the known values for m_1, m_2, g, and μ_k into the expression for a to get the final answer for the acceleration of m_1.

Similar Questions

1) Two masses are tied together by a string over a massless pulley so that they can both move vertically. Their masses are 1 kg and 3 kg. What is the acceleration of the 1 kg mass?

2) Two masses are connected by a string over a massless pulley. Mass A is on a table, while mass B hangs freely. What is the coefficient of friction necessary between mass A and the table to keep the system at rest?

3) Two masses are tied together by a string over a massless pulley so that they can both move vertically. One mass is 5 kg, and the other is 1 kg. The masses are released from rest. How far does one mass fall to reach a velocity of 10 m/s?

Inclined Plane

A block with a mass of 2 kg is sliding down a plane that is inclined at 30° to the horizontal. The coefficient of kinetic friction between the block and the plane is 0.3. Starting from rest, how far does the block travel in 2 seconds?

1) Draw a free-body diagram of the forces present.

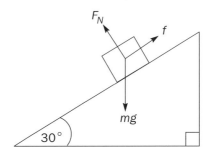

There are three forces acting on the block: the force of gravity (which equals *mg*), which always acts straight down; friction (labeled *f*), which always acts opposite the direction of motion; and the normal force (labeled F_N), which is always perpendicular to the plane.

---

2) Break the weight into X and Y components.

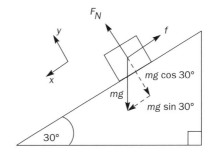

X component of *mg*:	$mg \sin 30°$
generic:	$mg \sin \theta$
Y component of *mg*:	$mg \cos 30°$
generic:	$mg \cos \theta$

Orient the *x–y* axis so that the *x*-axis points down the plane. This will make the calculations much easier because we can solve for the acceleration in the *x*-direction. F_N points in the +*y*-direction, and *f* points in the −*x*-direction. The weight, *mg*, must be broken into components along the axes.

Remember: *When the angle of the plane is given with respect to the horizontal, the component of the weight along the plane will always be* mg sin θ.

3) Write the sum of the forces in each direction.

$$\Sigma F_x = ma_x = mg \sin 30° - f$$
$$\Sigma F_y = ma_y = F_N - mg \cos 30°$$

The sum of the forces in a given direction is always equal to ma. This is Newton's second law.

---

4) Solve for the normal force.

We know that the block is not accelerating in the y-direction because it is not sinking into the plane or coming off of the plane; thus, we can set $a_y = 0$ and solve for F_N.

$$a_y = 0, \text{ so } \Sigma F_y = 0: F_N - mg \cos 30° = 0$$
$$F_N = mg \cos 30°$$

---

5) Solve for the acceleration of the block.

$$f = \mu_k F_N = \mu_k mg \cos 30°$$
$$ma_x = mg \sin 30° - \mu_k mg \cos 30°$$
$$a_x = g \sin 30° - \mu_k g \cos 30° = 9.8 \,(0.5) - 0.3(9.8)(0.866) = 2.35 \text{ m/s}^2$$

The force of friction depends on the normal force, F_N, and the coefficient of kinetic friction, μ_k. Plug in the expression for normal force from step 4 to determine the friction force. Plug this expression for friction force into the forces in the x-direction expression from step 3 to determine the acceleration. Note that the mass cancels out completely.

---

6) Use a kinematics formula to calculate the distance.

$$\Delta x = v_0 t + \frac{1}{2}at^2$$
$$\Delta x = 0 + \frac{1}{2}(2.35)(2)^2 = 4.7 \text{ meters}$$

This is a general kinematics formula that you should have memorized. In this particular problem, the initial velocity of the block, v_0, is zero.

Takeaways

In every force problem, the process is the same: Draw the forces on the object; write the sum of forces in the x- and y-directions; set these equal to ma_x and ma_y, respectively; and then solve. In most single-body problems, the mass will cancel out of the equation. Notice that this problem would be much simpler if the ramp were frictionless.

Things to Watch Out For

The geometry can become confusing on Test Day, so it is helpful to memorize that the component of weight along the plane is $mg \sin \theta$, as long as θ is the angle to the horizontal.

Similar Questions

1) A block of mass 5 kg is placed on an inclined plane at 45° to the horizontal. What is the minimum coefficient of static friction so that the block remains at rest?

2) A block is given an initial velocity of 2 m/s up a frictionless plane inclined at 60° to the horizontal. What is the highest point reached by the block?

3) What is the velocity of a 10 kg block down a frictionless inclined plane at 30° to the horizontal 5 seconds after it is released from rest?

Key Concepts

Chapter 2

Pulley

Inclined plane

Tension

Takeaways

This was a complicated problem solved methodically. On Test Day, be sure to draw the force diagram for each object. Do not be intimidated by multiple objects on a pulley system. It does not matter which way you assume the acceleration of the objects to go. If you chose incorrectly, the acceleration you get will be negative. Just remember to reverse the direction.

Pulley with Multiple Masses

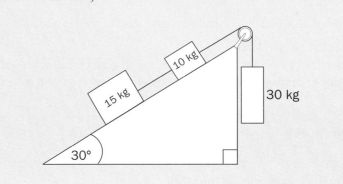

What is the tension on the rope between the 10.0 kg and 15.0 kg masses? (Assume no friction.)

1) Assign tensions of the ropes.

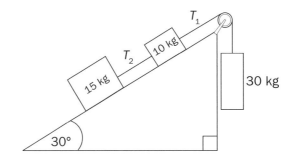

Set down as positive. Tension is a pull.

Let T_1 be the tension in the rope connecting the 10.0 kg and 30.0 kg masses.
Let T_2 be the tension in the rope connecting the 10.0 kg and 15.0 kg masses.

2) Draw force diagrams on each block system.

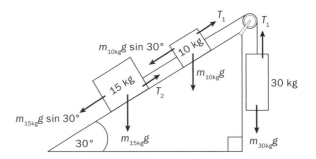

Establish down as positive. Because the right side of the pulley system is heavier than the left side, let us assume that the right object falls down while the other two objects accelerate towards the pulley. Thus, the two objects on the left have negative accelerations, whereas the object on the right has a positive acceleration.

Add the sum of the forces on each object to get a net force equal to mass times acceleration.

Sum of the forces:

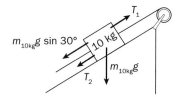

15 kg object: $F_{net} = m_{15kg}g\sin 30° - T_2 = -m_{15kg}a$

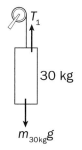

10 kg object: $F_{net} = m_{10kg}g\sin 30° - T_1 + T_2 = -m_{10kg}a$

30 kg

$m_{30kg}g$

30 kg object: $F_{net} = m_{30kg}g - T_1 = m_{30kg}a$

Remember: *It does not matter which way you assign your objects to move, as long as one side is moving up while the other side is moving down. Whatever sign you assign acceleration for one side, the other side needs to be opposite in sign. When you get an answer, compare it to the signs you've assigned.*

3) Solve the equations simultaneously.

(30 kg object solved for T_1)

$$T_1 = m_{30kg}g - m_{30kg}a$$
$$m_{10kg}g\sin 30° + T_2 - m_{30kg}g + m_{30kg}a = -m_{10kg}a$$

(Previous equation solved for T_2)

$$T_2 = m_{30kg}g - m_{10kg}a - m_{30kg}a - m_{10kg}g\sin 30°$$
$$m_{30kg}g\sin 30° - m_{30kg}g + m_{10kg}a + m_{30kg}a + m_{10kg}g\sin 30° = -m_{15kg}a$$

---

4) Get all *a* terms on the left side and all *g* terms on the right side.

Take the last equation from step 3, and get all of the acceleration terms on the left-hand side while leaving the gravity terms on the right-hand side.

$$m_{10kg}a + m_{30kg}a + m_{15kg}a = m_{30kg}g - m_{10kg}g\sin 30° - m_{15kg}g\sin 30°$$

---

5) Solve for the tension of the rope.

$$a(m_{10kg} + m_{30kg} + m_{15kg}) = m_{30kg}g - m_{10kg}g\sin 30° - m_{15kg}g\sin 30°$$

$$a = \frac{(m_{30kg}g - m_{10kg}g\sin30° - m_{15kg}g\sin30°)}{(m_{10kg} + m_{30kg} + m_{15kg})}$$

$$a = \frac{(30.0\,kg \times 9.80\,m/s^2 - 10.0\,kg \times 9.80\,m/s^2 \times \sin 30° - 15.0\,kg \times 9.80\,m/s^2 \times \sin 30°)}{(10.0\,kg + 30.0\,kg + 15.0\,kg)}$$

$$a = 3.12\ m/s^2$$

From step 4, factor out *a*. Then solve for *a* to find the acceleration. Plugging in the numbers gives an acceleration of 3.12 m/s². This confirms our earlier establishment that the object to the right of the pulley is going down. Because we declared that *a* was positive down, the right object will be accelerating down.

Once you have determined *a*, use the 15 kg object equation to solve for T_2.

15 kg object equation:
$$m_{15kg}g\sin 30° - T_2 = -m_{15kg}a$$
$$T_2 = m_{15kg}a + m_{15kg}g\sin 30°$$
$$T_2 = 15.0\ kg \times 3.12\ m/s^2 + 15.0\ kg \times 9.80\ m/s^2 \times \sin 30°$$
$$T_2 = 120\ N$$

High-Yield Problems continue on the next page

Rotational Equilibrium

> Three masses are sitting on a 2 m beam of wood, which rests on a fulcrum. The first mass is 2 kg and rests 30 cm to the left of the fulcrum. The second mass is 5 kg and sits 45 cm from the left side of the beam. The fulcrum is located at the middle of the beam. The third mass is 6 kg. If the system is in rotational equilibrium, where is the third mass located?

1) Draw a diagram of the system.

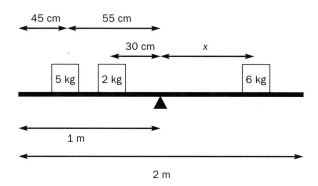

Always draw a sketch of the system in these problems. Because mass 1 and mass 2 are both on the left side of the fulcrum, mass 3 must be on the right side to balance them out. Label the distance from the fulcrum to mass 3 as x.

2) Write an equation for the total torque of the system.
torque = force $\times$ distance
torque = $5g(55) + 2g(30) - 6g(x)$

Write an equation for the torque about the fulcrum. Torque equals force times the distance to the axis of rotation. For each mass, the force is the weight of the mass, mg. Make a torque causing a counterclockwise rotation positive and a clockwise rotation negative.

Remember: You can use cm as units for distance as long as you are consistent throughout the problem.

3) Set the torque equal to zero and solve.
The system is in rotational equilibrium. This means that the net torque on the system is zero. Set the equation for step 2 equal to 0 and solve for x. (Another way to solve this problem would be to say that the magnitude of the torque due to mass 3 must be equal to the sum of the magnitudes of the torques for mass 1 and 2, because these must balance out to stop the beam from rotating.)

torque $= 0 = 5g(55) + 2g(30) - 6g(x)$
$5(55) + 2(30) = 6(x)$
$335 = 6x$
$x = 55.8$ cm

Similar Questions

1) Block A has 2.5 times the mass of block B. They are located 55 cm apart on a beam. Where should the fulcrum be placed relative to block B so that the beam does not rotate?

2) Three equal masses, each of 40 kg, are placed on a 5 m iron beam. They are placed 1.5 meters apart, with one on the far right end of the beam. Where should a fulcrum be placed so that the system is in rotational equilibrium?

3) Mass 1 is located at the far left end of a 90 cm beam. Mass 2 is located at the center of the beam, and mass 3 is located 30 cm from the center on the left side. Mass 3 and mass 1 are the same. If the fulcrum is located 10 cm to the left of the center of the beam, what is the mass of mass 2 if the beam does not rotate?

Key Concepts

Chapter 2

Centripetal acceleration

Friction

Newton's laws

$f \leq \mu_s F_N$

$a_c = \dfrac{v^2}{r} \; (\text{m/s}^2)$

Uniform Circular Motion

A car rounds a curve with a constant velocity of 25 m/s. The curve is a circle of radius 40 m. What must the coefficient of static friction between the road and the wheels be to keep the car from slipping?

1) Draw a free-body diagram of the car.

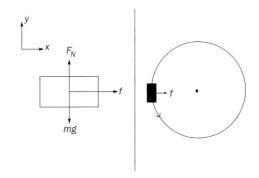

There are three forces acting on the car: the weight of the car, which equals mg (labeled mg); the normal force (labeled F_N); and the force of friction (labeled f). The view shown on the left is a head-on view of the car. The force of friction points toward the center of the circle, as shown in the diagram on the right.

Takeaways

Do not be scared off by the circular motion of this problem. It only adds one step to the solution! The process for solving this problem is the same as for any force problem: Draw the forces on the object; write the sum of forces in the x- and y-directions; set these equal to ma_x and ma_y, respectively; and then solve. The only difference with this problem is that you set the acceleration equal to $\dfrac{v^2}{r}$ at the end.

2) Add up the forces in the x- and y-directions.

$$\Sigma F_x = ma_x = f$$
$$\Sigma F_y = ma_y = F_N - mg$$

The sum of the forces in a given direction is always equal to ma. This is Newton's second law.

Things to Watch Out For

A more complicated version of this problem would have the car traveling around an inclined track. Then we would have to break the weight of the car into its components, much as in an inclined-plane problem.

3) Solve for the normal force.

We know that the car is not accelerating the in y-direction because it is not sinking into the road or coming off of the road; thus, we can set $a_y = 0$ and solve for F_n.

$a_y = 0$, so $\Sigma F_y = 0$: $F_N - mg = 0$

$F_N = mg$

Remember: Solving for the normal force is generally only necessary when the problem involves friction.

4) Write the force of friction in terms of the normal force.

The maximum force of static friction is the coefficient of friction, μ_s, multiplied by the normal force. Plug the expression for normal force from step 3 into the force equation from step 2.

generic: $f \leq \mu_s F_N$
$f = ma_x$
$\mu_s F_N \geq ma_x$
$\mu_s mg \geq ma_x$

---

5) Identify a_x as the centripetal acceleration and solve.

Whenever anything travels in a circle, it has an acceleration directed toward the center of that circle, called the centripetal acceleration. This acceleration has a magnitude given by $a_c = \dfrac{v^2}{r}$.

generic: $a_c = \dfrac{v^2}{r}$

In this problem, the car is going in a circle, and the center of the circle is always pointed in the x-direction. This means that the car is accelerating in the x-direction, and we can set $a_x = \dfrac{v^2}{r}$. Substitute $\dfrac{v^2}{r}$ for a_x into the final equation from step 4, and solve for μ_s.

$$a_x = \frac{v^2}{r}, \text{ so } \mu_s mg \geq \frac{mv^2}{r}$$

$$\mu_s g \geq \frac{v^2}{r}$$

$$\mu_s \geq \frac{v^2}{gr} = \frac{(25)^2}{(9.8 \times 40)} = 1.59$$

Similar Questions

1) What is the minimum radius that a cyclist can ride around at 10 kilometers per hour without slipping if the coefficient of friction between her tires and the road is 0.5?

2) A 1 kg ball is swung around in a 90 cm circle at an angle of 10° below the horizontal. What is the tension in the string?

3) A force how many times greater than that of gravity is felt by a race car driver rounding a turn with a radius of 50 m at a speed of 120 m/s?

Power and Energy

The electricity for a certain industrial-strength space heater costs $1.50 for 40 minutes. The electric company charges 2 cents per kWh. How long would a light with a 100 W lightbulb have to run continuously to use the same amount of energy as the heater uses in 40 minutes?

1) Determine the energy used by the heater.

$$\frac{\$1.50}{(\$0.02/\,kWh)} = 75\,kWh$$

A kWh is a unit of energy, because 1 kW = 1 kJ/s, so 1 kWh = 1 (kJ·h/s).

2) Determine the power of the heater.

$$40\,minutes = \frac{2}{3}\,hour$$

$$75\,kWh = 75\,(kJ\cdot h/s)$$

$$P = \frac{75(kJ\cdot h/s)}{\left(\frac{2}{3}\,h\right)} = 112.5\,kJ/s = 112.5\,kW$$

Power is always energy (or work) divided by time, so divide the energy from step 1 by the time. Pay attention to the units here—the time must be in hours!

3) Determine the time for which the lightbulb could run on the same amount of power.

$$\frac{112.5\,kW}{100\,W} = 1,125$$

$$\left(\frac{2}{3}\,h\right) \times 1,125 = 750\,h$$

Divide the power of the heater by the power of the lightbulb. This tells you that the heater uses 1,125 times as much energy every second as the lightbulb does. Then, multiply the time that the heater operated to use 75 kWh of energy by this factor to determine the time for the lightbulb to use that much energy.

Similar Questions

1) How much heat is given off by a 60 W lightbulb in 1 hour if only 99% of the energy is released thermally?

2) How much heat is dissipated in 10 minutes by a 2 kΩ resistor with a current of 25 mA?

3) A certain laser beam delivers 10,000 J of energy to a sample in 5 minutes, and 10% of the laser energy is lost in transit to the sample. What is the power of this laser?

High-Yield Problems continue on the next page

Key Concepts

Chapter 3

Conservation of energy

Centripetal acceleration

Gravitational potential energy:
$U = mgh$ (J)

Kinetic energy: $K = \left(\dfrac{1}{2}\right)mv^2$ (J)

Circular Loops

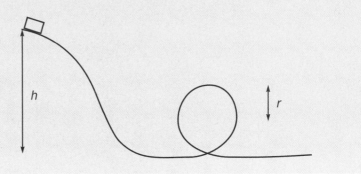

A 1 kg block slides down a ramp and then around a circular loop of radius 10 m, as shown in the diagram below. Assuming that all surfaces are frictionless, what is the minimum height of the ramp required so that the block makes it all the way around the loop without falling?

Takeaways

The key to this problem is knowing that the normal force is zero at the top of the loop in the case where the block is just about to fall.

Notice that the loop problem follows the same process as any other conservation of energy problem but with the added aspect of centripetal acceleration. Draw a free-body diagram and solve for the velocity. After this, your goal is the same as always: (1) write expressions for the energy at two points and (2) set them equal and solve for the unknown quantity.

1) Write an expression for the initial energy of the system.
At the top of the ramp, the block has only potential energy given by the formula $U = mgh$.

$$E_i = mgh$$

Remember: *Leaving the expressions in terms of variables will save time and reduce the chance of calculation error.*

2) Write an expression for the energy of the system at the top of the loop.
At the top of the loop, the block has both potential energy and kinetic energy. The height of the block at the top of the loop is $2r$. Add these to get the total energy.

$$E_{loop} = mg(2r) + \frac{1}{2}mv^2$$

3) Draw a free-body diagram of the block at the top of the loop.

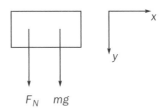

There are two forces acting on the block at the top of the loop: the weight of the block (equal to mg) and the normal force (labeled F_N). Note that the normal force is acting down because the track is above the mass.

High-Yield Problems

Remember: The normal force is always perpendicular to the surface and points from the surface to the object.

4) Add the forces in the *y* direction.
There are no forces acting in the *x*-direction, so add the forces in the *y*-direction only.

$$\Sigma F_y = ma_y = mg + F_N$$

5) Set the normal force equal to zero.
If the block falls off of the ramp at the top of the loop, the normal force will become zero because the ramp is no longer touching the block. By setting the normal force equal to zero, we are solving for the case where the block just starts to fall.

$$F_N = 0 \rightarrow ma_y = mg$$

6) Identify the acceleration as centripetal.
Because the block is traveling in a circle, it has an acceleration directed towards the center of the circle, which is called centripetal acceleration. The magnitude of this acceleration is given by the formula $a_c = \dfrac{v^2}{r}$. Plug this into the equation from step 5 and solve for *v*.

$$a_y = \frac{v^2}{r} \rightarrow \frac{mv^2}{r} = mg$$
$$v = (gr)^{\frac{1}{2}}$$

7) Set the energy expressions equal and solve.
Due to the conservation of energy, we can set the energy at any two points as equal. Do this and set the velocity at the top of the loop equal to the value from step 6. Then solve for *h*. Because we have set the velocity equal to that at which the block starts to fall off the ramp, we have solved for the minimum height of the ramp.

$$E_i = E_{loop}$$
$$mgh = mg(2r) + \frac{1}{2}mv^2$$
$$mgh = mg(2r) + \frac{1}{2}m((gr)^{\frac{1}{2}})^2$$
$$mgh = mg(2r) + \frac{1}{2}m(gr)$$
$$mgh = 2.5mgr$$
$$h = 2.5r = 25 \text{ m}$$

Similar Questions

1) What is the normal force at the bottom of the loop if the height of the ramp is four times that of the radius of the loop?

2) How fast does the block need to be going at the bottom of the ramp so that the acceleration of the block at the top of the loop is 4*g*?

3) What is the speed of the block as it exits the loop if the normal force at the top of the loop was 80 N?

Conservation of Momentum

A rugby player with a mass of 80 kg is running due north with a speed of 4 m/s. He is hit by a 90 kg rival at 5 m/s at an angle of 30° from the south. The two players move together with an unknown velocity before falling to the ground. Find their combined speed and direction.

1) Determine the type of collision.

The question stem states that the two players move together after impact. This indicates an inelastic collision. Energy is lost in an inelastic collision as heat, sound, deformation, and so on, so we cannot use the equation for conservation of kinetic energy. We can, however, use the equation for conservation of momentum.

2) Draw vectors representing the collision.

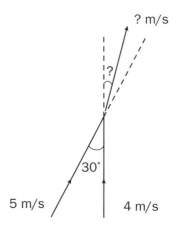

Because we are dealing with angles, we'll need to break the velocity vector down into **X** and **Y** components. First we need to sketch what those components will be.

Remember: Think critically. If the second player hits the first at a 30° angle, the final angle should be between 0 and 30° from the north. Even if the second player had a significantly greater momentum, the final angle could not be greater than the initial one!

3) Break the vectors into X and Y components.

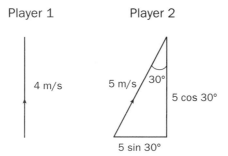

Player 1   Player 2

4 m/s   5 m/s   30°

5 cos 30°

5 sin 30°

Player 1 is moving due north, so all 4 m/s of his speed is oriented upward. Player 2, however, is moving at an angle. We must consider how much of his momentum moves right and how much moves up. Break his velocity into **X** and **Y** components.

Remember: The mnemonic SOH CAH TOA will help you remember which trigonometric function to use for each component.

---

4) Apply the equation for conservation of momentum.

$p_{before} = p_{after}$

$m_1 v_1 + m_2 v_2 = (m_1 + m_2)v_f$ y: $80(4) + 90(5 \cos 30°) = (80 + 90)(v_f \cos \theta) \rightarrow$

$v_f \cos \theta = \dfrac{320 + 389.7}{170} \approx 4.17$

x: $80(0) + 90(5 \sin 30°) = (80 + 90)(v_f \sin \theta) \rightarrow v_f \sin \theta = \dfrac{225}{170} \approx 1.32$

In both elastic and inelastic collisions, momentum is conserved. This means that we can set the momentum of the system before the collision equal to the momentum of the system after the collision. In this case, we are dealing with a totally inelastic collision. This means that the two masses stick together after impact and move off as a unit. Thus, the momentum of the system before the collision is $m_1 v_1 + m_2 v_2$, and afterwards it is $(m_1 + m_2)v_f$. Because this problem deals with two dimensions, we must break the velocity vectors down into **X** and **Y** components and then apply the equation for conservation of momentum to each. We end up having two equations with two variables, v_f and θ, where θ is the angle from north.

---

5) Use the relationship between sinusoidal functions to solve for θ.

$\dfrac{v_f \sin \theta}{v_f \cos \theta} = \dfrac{1.32}{4.17}$

$\dfrac{\sin \theta}{\cos \theta} = \dfrac{1.32}{4.17} = \tan \theta$

$\tan^{-1}(0.316) = 17.6°$

Similar Questions

1) A 1,980 kg car moving at 13 m/s is brought to a stop in 2 seconds when it collides with a wall. If a new model of this car has a longer crumple zone, the passengers experience a 3,217.5 N force upon impact. By what percentage has the period of impact been increased? Has the impulse on the car and its passengers changed?

2) A curler slides a stone across an ice rink with an initial speed of 3 m/s towards the center of a target. It strikes a second stone, which then hits a third stone. All stones have a mass of 44 kg and are hit head on. If the second and third stones move with individual final velocities of 1 m/s, find the velocity of the first stone after it collides with the second.

3) A 4.2 g bullet is fired into a stationary 5 kg block of wood. If the bullet lodges in the block, knocking it back with a speed of 0.81 m/s, find the speed of the bullet prior to impact.

To find θ, we need to get rid of $\mathbf{v}_f$ temporarily. Divide the x-equation by the y-equation. $\mathbf{v}_f$ cancels out, and the components allow us to find θ with the arc tangent.

Remember: Use the mnemonic SOH CAH TOA if you forget how sine and cosine are related to tangent. If you divide sine by cosine, you end up with $(O/H)/(A/H) = O/A$, the definition of tangent.

---

6) Use θ to find the final speed.

y: $80(4) + 90(5 \cos 30°) = (80 + 90)(\mathbf{v}_f \cos 17.6°) \rightarrow$
$\mathbf{v}_f = 4.17 \div (\cos 17.6°) \approx 4.37$ m/s
x: $80(0) + 90(5 \sin 30°) = (80 + 90)(\mathbf{v}_f \sin 17.6°) \rightarrow$
$\mathbf{v}_f = 1.32 \div (\sin 17.6°) \approx 4.37$ m/s

Plug $17.6°$ back into either the x- or y-equation. In both cases, we find $\mathbf{v}_f = 4.37$ m/s. If we find different values with these equations, we should look very carefully for our mistake.

---

7) Here is an alternate solution.

$$\mathbf{p}_x = \mathbf{p}_{1x} + \mathbf{p}_{2x} = m\mathbf{v}_{1x} + m\mathbf{v}_{2x} = 0 + (90)5 \sin 30° = 225$$

$$\mathbf{p}_y = \mathbf{p}_{1y} + \mathbf{p}_{2y} = m\mathbf{v}_{1y} + m\mathbf{v}_{2y} = (80)4 + (90)5 \cos 30° = 709.7$$

$$\mathbf{p} = (\mathbf{p}_x^{\,2} + \mathbf{p}_y^{\,2})^{\frac{1}{2}} = (225^2 + 709.7^2)^{\frac{1}{2}} = 744.5$$

$$\mathbf{p} = (m_1 + m_2)\mathbf{v}_f \rightarrow \mathbf{v}_f = \frac{\mathbf{P}}{m_1 + m_2} = \frac{744.5}{90 + 80} = 4.37 \text{m/s}$$

$$\alpha = \tan^{-1}\left(\frac{\mathbf{p}_y}{\mathbf{p}_x}\right) = \tan^{-1}\left(\frac{709.7}{225}\right) = 72.4° \rightarrow \theta = 90° - 72.4° = 17.6°$$

where α is the angle from east and θ is the angle from north.

An alternate solution is to calculate the **X** and **Y** components of the momentum directly by adding the **X** and **Y** components of the momentum of the system before the collision. Then, use the Pythagorean theorem to calculate the magnitude of the vector. Because momentum is conserved, set this equal to the momentum of the system after the collision and solve for $\mathbf{v}_f$. To find the angle, use trigonometry, and note that to find the angle relative to the horizontal, you must find the complementary angle.

High-Yield Problems continue on the next page

Key Concepts

Chapter 3

Gravitational potential energy:
$U = mgh$ (N·m: kg·m²/s²)

Kinetic energy:
$K = \frac{1}{2}mv^2$ (kg·m²/s²)

Collisions

Conservation of mechanical
energy: $E_i = E_f$

Takeaways

Gravity is a conservative force,
and at any point, the total
energy is found by adding the
gravitational and potential
energies. In an elastic collision,
kinetic energy (as well as
momentum) is conserved.

Elastic Collisions

A circus performer weighing 700 N steps off a platform 9 m high. She
lands on a seesaw to launch her 630 N partner straight into the air.
Compare the landing and launching velocities. Find the height her partner
achieves. Ignore the height of the seesaw and any dissipative forces.

1) Find the potential energy of the first performer.

$U = mgh$

$U = (700 \text{ N})(9 \text{ m}) = 6{,}300 \text{ N·m}$

Gravitational potential energy is given by the equation $U = mgh$. Because
weight is the product of mass and gravitational acceleration, we need only
multiply the performer's weight by her height.

Remember: A joule is defined as a newton-meter.

2) Find the landing velocity of the first performer.

$E = U + K$

$K = \frac{1}{2}mv^2$

$E = 6{,}300 \text{ N·m}$

$6{,}300 \text{ N·m} = \left(\frac{1}{2}\right)(70 \text{ kg})v^2 \rightarrow v \approx 13.4 \text{ m/s}$

Because gravity is a conservative force, the total energy is the sum of the
potential and kinetic energies. When the performer is atop the platform, all
her energy is potential. Thus, $E = 6{,}300$ N·m. Just before the performer hits the
seesaw, all of her energy is kinetic. The equation $K = \frac{1}{2}mv^2$ is used to find her
landing velocity.

*Remember: On the MCAT, you will use 10 m/s² for the acceleration due to
gravity, as in the solution to this question.*

3) Find the launching velocity of the second performer.

$6{,}300 \text{ N·m} = \left(\frac{1}{2}\right)(63 \text{ kg})v^2 \rightarrow v \approx 14.1 \text{ m/s}$

All of the first performer's kinetic energy is transferred to the second performer.
Thus, she also has 6,300 J. She has a smaller mass, so it makes sense that her
velocity is higher.

High-Yield Problems

4) Find the maximal height of the second performer.

After being launched into the air, the second performer's kinetic energy is transferred back to potential energy. Compare the total energy of the system with her weight to find the maximal height she reaches.

$$6{,}300 \text{ N·m} = (630 \text{ N})h \rightarrow h = 10 \text{ m}$$

5) Here is an alternate solution.

$$U_i = U_f$$
$$U = mgh = Wh$$
$$(700 \text{ N})(9 \text{ m}) = (630 \text{ N})h \rightarrow h = 10 \text{ m}$$

At any point, $E = U + K$. When the first performer hits the seesaw, all of her energy is kinetic. It is transferred to her partner, and as the second performer goes higher in the air, her energy increasingly becomes potential. Thus, we can simply equate the potential energy of the first performer with the second.

> **Things to Watch Out For**
>
> Dissipative forces, such as air resistance, heat, and sound, reduce the total mechanical energy of the system such that $E_f < E_i$.

Similar Questions

1) The first step in the fusion reaction that occurs on the sun is $^1\text{H} + {}^1\text{H} \rightarrow {}^2\text{H} +$ antielectron + neutrino. This step is rarely ever successful. If an unsuccessful collision of hydrogen nuclei is considered to be elastic, and they each have a mass of 1.008 amu, how do their kinetic energies compare before and after the collision?

2) A frictionless, vertical wire has two metal beads on it. The beads are held 30 cm apart by horizontal magnets. If the top magnet is removed, the first bead falls under the force of gravity and strikes the second. The first bead bounces back up to a height of 10 cm, and the second is knocked free of the magnet and falls downward. If the two beads each have a mass of 49.7 g, what is the kinetic energy of the second immediately after impact?

3) Two adult bighorn rams butt heads in an elastic collision. The alpha male (136 kg) moves more slowly than his challenger (113 kg). If the challenger collides at 8 m/s and is repelled at 6 m/s, find the kinetic energy of the system and the percent increase in speed that the alpha male experiences.

Key Concepts

Chapter 3

Kinetic energy

Potential energy

Momentum

Collision

$U = mgh$ (N·m: kg·m²/s²)

$K = \frac{1}{2}m\mathbf{v}^2$ (N·m: kg·m²/s²)

$\mathbf{p} = m\mathbf{v}$ (kg·m/s)

Conservation of energy

Conservation of momentum

Takeaways

This problem combines a conservation of energy problem with a conservation of momentum problem. Remember that the conservation of energy is useful for finding velocities or distances, whereas momentum is used exclusively to find the conditions after a collision.

This is an inelastic collision. Momentum is conserved, while energy is not. Therefore, the maximum height reached should be significantly less than the initial height of the block.

Collisions and Energy

> A 10 kg block starts from rest at a height of 20 meters and slides down a frictionless, semicircular track. The block collides with a stationary object of 50 kg at the bottom of the track. If the objects stick together on collision, what is the maximum height that the block-object system could reach?

1) Draw a rough sketch of the collision.

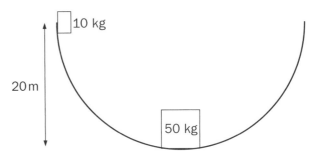

Once you draw the semicircle, draw two objects: one along the top of the semicircle and one at the bottom of the semicircle. Both objects start at rest. The 10 kg block will travel down and reach a velocity **v** before impact with the object. The objects will stick together and travel up the semicircle to a maximum height *h*. The question asks you to find *h*.

---

2) Write an expression for the initial energy of the falling block.

$E_i = U_i + K_i$

$U = mgh$

$K = \frac{1}{2}m\mathbf{v}^2$

$E_i = mgh_i + \frac{1}{2}m\mathbf{v}_i^2$

$E_i = mgh_i$

Write an expression for the energy of the falling block. The total energy of the block is its kinetic energy plus its potential energy. The block is initially at rest, so it has no kinetic energy.

---

3) Write an expression for the final energy of the falling block.

$$E_f = U_f + K_f$$
$$E_f = 0 + \frac{1}{2}mv_f^2$$

Write an expression for the energy of the falling block just before it collides with the other block. At this point it has no potential energy; it has only kinetic energy.

---

4) Set the expressions equal and solve for velocity.

Due to the conservation of energy, we can set the energy at any two points equal and solve. Use the energy found in steps 1 and 2 to solve for the velocity of the block just before impact.

$$E_f = E_i$$
$$mgh_i = \frac{1}{2}mv_f^2$$
$$v_f = (2gh_i)^{\frac{1}{2}} = 19.8 \text{ m/s}$$

---

5) Write an expression for the momentum of the system before the collision.

$$\mathbf{p}_{before} = m_1\mathbf{v}_1$$

Before the collision, only mass 1 is moving. The momentum of the system is entirely due to mass 1.

---

6) Write an expression for the momentum of the system after the collision.

$$\mathbf{p}_{after} = (m_1 + m_2)\mathbf{v}_2$$

After the collision, both masses are stuck together and move with the same velocity.

---

7) Set the expressions equal and solve for velocity.

Due to the conservation of momentum, we can set the momentum of the system before the collision equal to that after the collision. Solve for the velocity.

$$\mathbf{p}_{after} = \mathbf{p}_{before}$$
$$m_1\mathbf{v}_1 = (m_1 + m_2)\mathbf{v}_2$$
$$\mathbf{v}_2 = \frac{m_1\mathbf{v}_1}{(m_1 + m_2)} = \frac{10(19.8)}{(10+50)} = 3.3 \text{ m/s}$$

Remember: Momentum is conserved in all types of collisions: elastic, inelastic, or completely inelastic. Energy is only conserved in elastic collisions (perfect bouncing). Because this is not an elastic collision, you cannot use energy to calculate the velocity after impact.

Things to Watch Out For

Momentum is conserved in all types of collisions in all cases! Energy is conserved only in elastic collisions.

Similar Questions

1) In the above question, determine the height reached by each object if the collision were inelastic and the falling mass rebounded back with a speed of 1 m/s.

2) A man of mass 140 kg standing on a frictionless surface throws a 10 kg rock horizontally away from himself. What is the momentum of the system immediately after the throw?

3) Two baseballs undergo a head-on collision. Ball 1 is twice as heavy as ball 2. Ball 1 was traveling at an initial speed of $\mathbf{v}_1$, while ball 2 had an initial speed of $\mathbf{v}_2$. The type of collision was elastic. If ball 1 travels at a speed of $\frac{7}{5}\mathbf{v}_1$ after impact, what is the speed of ball 2?

8) Write an expression for the energy of the system just after the collision.

$$E_a = U_a + K_a$$
$$E_a = 0 + \frac{1}{2}(m_1 + m_2)\mathbf{v}_2^2$$

The energy of the system after the collision is due to the kinetic energy of the two blocks moving together.

---

9) Write an expression for the energy of the system at the top.

$$E_t = U_t + K_t$$
$$E_t = (m_1 + m_2)gh + 0$$

When the blocks get to the top, they stop moving briefly (before falling back down), so their kinetic energy is zero.

---

10) Set the expressions equal and solve for height.

$$E_a = E_t$$
$$\frac{1}{2}(m_1 + m_2)\mathbf{v}_2^2 = (m_1 + m_2)gh$$
$$\frac{1}{2}\mathbf{v}_2^2 = gh$$
$$h = \frac{\mathbf{v}_2^2}{2g} = \frac{3.3^2}{2(9.8)} = 0.56\,\text{m}$$

High-Yield Problems continue on the next page

Specific Gravity

> A cube, composed of substance X and having a side length of 5 cm, hangs from a string while fully submerged in saltwater ($\rho = 1.1$ g/cm³). The tension in the string is 11 N. What is the specific gravity of substance X?

1) Find the volume of the cube.

The volume of a cube is the side length cubed.

$$V = (\text{side})^3 = (5 \text{ cm})^3 = 125 \text{ cm}^3$$

2) Find the buoyant force on the cube.

generic: $F_B = \rho_{fluid} g V_{submerged}$

The buoyant force depends on the density of the fluid, acceleration due to gravity, and volume of the object submerged. Convert the density of saltwater to kg/cm³ so that the buoyant force will be in newtons.

$$(\rho_{fluid} = \rho_{saltwater} = 1.1 \text{ g/cm}^3 = 1.1 \times 10^{-3} \text{ kg/cm}^3)$$
$$F_B = (1.1 \times 10^{-3} \text{ kg/cm}^3)(9.8 \text{ m/s}^2)(125 \text{ cm}^3) = 1.35 \text{ N}$$

3) Draw a free-body diagram of the cube.

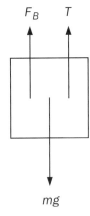

There are three forces acting on the block: the weight of the block (which equals *mg*), the tension in the string (labeled *T*), and the buoyant force (labeled F_B).

Remember: *The buoyant force always acts upward.*

4) Add the forces in the *y*-direction and solve for the mass.

$$\Sigma F_y = ma_y = T + F_B - mg$$

Every time you draw a free-body diagram, the next step is to add the forces in a direction and set them equal to mass times acceleration in that direction. Because the cube is not moving, the acceleration is zero. Solve for mass.

$$a_y = 0 \rightarrow T + F_B - mg = 0$$

$$m = \frac{(T + F_B)}{g} = \frac{(11 + 1.35)}{9.8} = 1.26 \text{ kg}$$

5) Find the density of the cube.

$$1.26 \text{ kg} = 1{,}260 \text{ g}$$

The density of the cube is needed to find the specific gravity. Find the density in g/cm^3 because we know that the density of water is 1 g/cm^3. Density is mass divided by volume.

$$\rho = \frac{m}{V} = \frac{(1{,}260 \text{ g})}{(125 \text{ cm}^3)} = 10.08 \text{ g/cm}^3$$

6) Find the specific gravity of the cube.

$$\text{specific gravity} = \frac{\rho_{material}}{\rho_{water}} = \frac{(10.08 \text{ g/cm}^3)}{(1 \text{ g/cm}^3)} = 10.08$$

The specific gravity of a substance is the density of that substance divided by the density of water. When working in g/cm^3, this is a simple calculation because the density of water is 1.

Similar Questions

1) What is the specific gravity of a substance that weighs 40 N and has a volume of 4 cm^3?

2) Three liters of a certain fluid weigh twice as much as 2 liters of water. What is the specific gravity of the fluid?

3) The specific gravity of a block is 5.6. When fully submerged, what is the buoyant force, in water, on this 2 kg block?

Hydraulic Lift

An automobile hydraulic lift consists of two circular pistons, one with a radius of 25 cm and the other with a radius of 75 cm. They are connected via a tube filled with an incompressible fluid. A constant force is applied to the smaller piston in order to raise a car with a mass of 2,000 kg to a height of 0.5 m. What is the minimum force applied to the smaller piston? How far is the smaller piston compressed?

1) Find the work performed.

The amount of work performed is simply the change in potential energy of the automobile, which equals the potential energy of the automobile at 0.5 meters. It is common to think that there is a more complex relationship because the hydraulic lift is being used, but the idea is that the hydraulic lift has 100 percent efficiency and thus all of the work put into it is used to raise the car.

$$W = mgh = (2,000)(9.8)(0.5) = 9,800 \text{ J}$$

2) Find the force on the larger piston.

The work performed is equal to the force times the distance. You can solve for the force from this formula. However, it is simpler to realize that the minimum force is the weight of the car, which equals mg. Realizing this will save you a step of calculation!

$$W = Fd$$
$$9,800 \text{ J} = F(0.5)$$
$$F = 19,600 \text{ N}$$

3) Find the area of the pistons.

A hydraulic lift is useful because the force is multiplied by the ratio of the areas of the pistons. Any time you see a hydraulic lift problem, count on needing to calculate the areas. You will see in step 4 that explicit calculation of the area is generally not needed, even though it is performed here.

$$A_1 = \pi r_1^2 = \pi(0.25)^2 = 0.196 \text{ m}^2$$
$$A_2 = \pi r_2^2 = \pi(0.75)^2 = 1.77 \text{ m}^2$$

Takeaways

Every time you see hydraulics problems, get ready to set up ratios involving the areas of the cylinders in order to calculate forces, distances, or volumes. All of the same rules of work and energy apply to hydraulics, and 100 percent efficiency is assumed. Remember: The less force used, the greater the distance.

Things to Watch Out For

There are multiple ways to solve hydraulics problems. To avoid confusion, pick a plan at the beginning and stick with it.

4) Set the pressure in the pistons equal to each other and solve.

$$P_1 = \frac{F_1}{A_1} = P_2 = \frac{F_2}{A_2}$$

Pascal's principle states that the pressure on both pistons must be equal. Set them equal and solve, using $P = \dfrac{F}{A}$, the general formula for pressure.

$$F_1 = \left(\frac{A_1}{A_2}\right) F_2 = \frac{\pi(0.25)^2}{\pi(0.75)^2} \times 19{,}600 = \left(\frac{0.25}{0.75}\right)^2 \times 19{,}600$$

$$F_1 = \left(\frac{1}{3}\right)^2 \times 19{,}600 = \frac{1}{9} \times 19{,}600 = 2{,}178 \text{ N}$$

Note that the calculation can be simplified somewhat by leaving the expressions for area in terms of π. This type of thinking will save you time on Test Day.

---

5) Calculate the compression of the small piston.

Fluid is pushed through the tube; none is allowed to escape, nor is it compressed. This means that the volume of fluid moved by each piston must be the same. Set them equal to each other and solve.

$$V_1 = V_2$$
$$d_1 A_1 = d_2 A_2$$
$$d_1 = \left(\frac{A_2}{A_1}\right) d_2 = (9) \times 0.5 = 4.5 \text{ m}$$

This highlights a drawback of hydraulic lifts—even though the force is greatly reduced, the distance is increased. This is because the amount of work performed, given by $W = Fd$, is the same for both pistons:

$$W_1 = F_1 d_1 = (2{,}178)(4.5) = 9{,}800 \text{ J}$$

(Thus, another way to calculate distance is to set the work done by one piston equal to the work by the other piston.)

Similar Questions

1) A hydraulic lift has a cylinder with a radius of 5 cm. What should be the radius of the other cylinder so that the force applied to the first cylinder is multiplied by a factor of 10?

2) The small piston in a hydraulic lift with a piston radius ratio of 10:1 is compressed by 50 cm. How far does the large piston move?

3) What is the volume of fluid moved when the large piston of a hydraulic press is moved 0.2 m (the radii of the pistons are 20 cm and 80 cm)?

Key Concepts

Chapter 5

Gauge pressure

Density

Atmospheric pressure

$P_{total} = P_{atm} + \rho_{fluid}gh$

Takeaways

The gauge pressure of a solution is the pressure due only to the weight of the solution pushing down from above. It does not include the effect of the atmosphere pushing down.

Gauge Pressure

A certain saltwater solution has a density 10% greater than that of water. At what depth in this solution does the gauge pressure equal 2.5 times atmospheric pressure? ($\rho_{water} = 1$ g/cm^3; $P_{atm} = 101$ kPa.)

1) Find the density of the saltwater solution.

$\rho_{saltwater} = \rho_{water} \times 1.1 = 1.1$ g/cm^3

The density of the solution is 10% greater than that of water. This is a factor of 1.1.

Convert this density to kg/m^3 so that it is in SI units.

1.1 g/cm^3 × (1 kg/1,000 g) × (100 cm/m)^3 = 1,100 kg/m^3

2) Write the expression for pressure.

$P_{total} = P_{atm} + \rho_{fluid}gh$

$P_{gauge} = P_{total} - P_{atm} = \rho_{fluid}gh$

The gauge pressure of a solution is the total pressure minus atmospheric pressure. This is simply $\rho_{fluid}gh$, where h is the depth in the solution.

3) Solve for the depth.

Set the gauge pressure equal to 2.5 times atmospheric pressure. Solve for h.

$2.5\,(101,000) = 1,100\,(9.8)(h)$

$z = 2.5\, \dfrac{(101,000)}{[1,100(9.8)]} = 23.4$ meters

Similar Questions

1) The gauge pressure of a solution at a depth of 1 m equals twice the atmospheric pressure. What is the density of this solution?

2) What is the pressure at a depth of 50 m below the surface of a pool of freshwater?

3) By what factor does the gauge pressure increase in going from a depth of 30 m to a depth of 40 m in pure water?

High-Yield Problems continue on the next page

Hydrostatics

> A raft of area 2 m² floats on water with the bottom 2 cm of the raft submerged. Assuming a thick raft, to what depth is the raft submerged when a brick of mass 3 kg is placed on top of the raft?

1) Determine the volume of the submerged part of the raft.

$$V_{\text{submerged}} = \text{area} \times \text{height} = (2 \text{ m}^2) \times (0.02 \text{ m}) = 0.04 \text{ m}^3$$

The part of the raft that is submerged has the shape of a rectangular prism with a height of 2 cm (0.02 m) and a base area of 2 m². In any buoyancy problem, the volume of the portion of the object that is submerged is a useful quantity, so this is a good starting point even if you do not know where to begin.

2) Determine the buoyant force on the raft.

$$F_B = \rho_{\text{fluid}} g V_{\text{submerged}}$$
$$F_B = (1,000 \text{ kg/m}^3)(9.8 \text{ m/s}^2)(0.04 \text{ m}^3) = 392 \text{ N}$$

The buoyant force is given by the formula $F_B = \rho_{\text{fluid}} g V_{\text{submerged}}$. Because the raft is floating (not sinking), the net force on the raft must be zero. This means that the buoyant force equals the weight of the raft. This is the connection that most people will not make on Test Day.

MCAT Pitfall: The buoyant force depends on the density of the fluid, not the density of the object. Also, it depends on the submerged volume of the object, not the total volume (unless the whole object is submerged).

3) Find the new buoyant force with the added mass.

$$F_B = \text{weight}_{\text{raft}} + \text{weight}_{\text{brick}} = 392 + m_{\text{brick}} g = 392 + (3)(9.8) = 421.4 \text{ N}$$

This buoyant force is the force required to support the weight of the raft and the brick.

4) Find the volume of the submerged part of the raft.

$$F_B = \rho_{\text{fluid}} g V_{\text{submerged}}$$
$$V_{\text{submerged}} = \frac{F_B}{(\rho_{\text{fluid}} g)} = \frac{(421.4 \text{ N})}{(1,000 \text{ kg/m}^3 \times 9.8 \text{ m/s}^2)} = 0.043 \text{ m}^3$$

Use the buoyant force found in step 3 in the buoyancy formula. The only unknown is the new submerged volume.

5) Find the submerged depth of the raft.

$$V = Az$$
$$z = \frac{V}{A} = \frac{(0.043 \text{ m}^3)}{(2 \text{ m}^2)} = 2.15 \text{ cm}$$

Once again, we are considering the volume of a rectangular prism with a base area of 2 m².

Things to Watch Out For

A very common pitfall for buoyancy problems is to try to use the density of the object to determine the buoyant force.

Similar Questions

1) A block of mass 5 kg and density 3 g/cm³ is hung from a string while submerged in water. What is the tension in the string?

2) A cube of side length 3 cm floats in water ($\rho = 1$ g/cm³) with 1 cm floating above the water. What is the density of this cube?

3) A piece of cork ($\rho = 0.2$ g/cm³) with mass 5 g is held underwater. When the cork is released, what is its initial acceleration?

Key Concepts

Chapter 5

Pressure

Density

Bernoulli's equation:

$$P + \frac{1}{2}\rho v^2 + \rho g h = \text{constant (N/m}^2)$$

Continuity equation: $Av = $ constant

Takeaways

Bernoulli's equation looks complicated, but it is really just a statement of the conservation of energy. The process is the same for every problem: (1) Write Bernoulli's equation at the two points of interest, (2) eliminate any variables if possible (often via the continuity equation), and (3) solve for the unknown quantity.

Things to Watch Out For

A common use of Bernoulli's equation is with no change in height, so that $P + 1/2\rho v^2 = $ constant. In this situation, a decrease in pressure causes an increase in velocity. This is known as the Bernoulli effect and is responsible for balls curving in flight, windows exploding during hurricanes, and (partially) for airplane wings experiencing lift.

Fluid Dynamics

A water storage tank is located 300 m away from a water outlet, as shown in the diagram below. The empty space in the water tank is held at a pressure of 3 atm. The storage tank has a diameter of 5 m, and the outlet has a diameter of 1 cm. What is the speed of the water exiting the outlet? (1 atm = 101 kPa; $\rho_{\text{water}} = 1{,}000$ kg/m³)

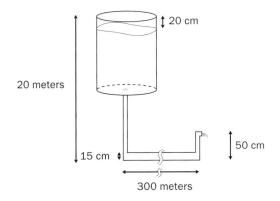

1) Write an expression using Bernoulli's equation.

generic: $P + \frac{1}{2}\rho v^2 + \rho g h = $ constant

Bernoulli's equation is a statement of the conservation of energy for fluids. It has three terms: one analogous to kinetic energy, one analogous to potential energy, and one for pressure (a form of stored energy).

$$P_1 + \frac{1}{2}\rho v_1^2 + \rho g h_1 = P_2 + \frac{1}{2}\rho v_2^2 + \rho g h_2$$

Write the expression for Bernoulli's principle at the two points of interest, just as you would write the total energy of a mechanical system at two points. For this problem, the two points are the top of the water level in the storage tank and the outlet.

---

2) Use the continuity equation.

generic: $Av = $ constant

$A_1 \gg 0$, so $v_1 \approx 0$.

In almost all of Bernoulli's equation applications, you will need to eliminate some of the terms in order to solve the problem. A common one here is velocity. The continuity equation relates fluid-flow velocity to area. It states that the product of the area and velocity is a constant. Because the storage tank has a very large area, we can approximate the velocity as zero. Think about it like this: The level of the water tank is moving down very slowly. This simplifies the equation.

$$P_1 + \rho g h_1 = P_2 + \frac{1}{2}\rho v_2^2 + \rho g h_2$$

3) Plug in the given information and solve.

The pressure inside the tank is 3 atm. Convert this to pascals, the SI unit for pressure.

$P_1 = 3 \text{ (1 atm)} = 3 \text{ (101 kPa)} = 303{,}000 \text{ Pa}$
$P_2 = 1 \text{ atm} = 101{,}000 \text{ Pa}$

The pressure at the outlet is 1 atm because the outlet is exposed to outside air and there is always 1 atm of pressure outside.

$$h_1 = 20 - 0.2 = 19.8 \text{ m}$$
$$h_2 = 50 \text{ cm} = 0.5 \text{ m}$$
$$\rho = 1{,}000 \text{ kg/m}^3$$
$$P_1 + \rho g h_1 = P_2 + \frac{1}{2}\rho v_2^2 + \rho g h_2$$

Plug in the pressures, heights, and density and solve for v_2.

$$v_2^2 = \frac{2(P_1 + \rho g h_1 - P_2 - \rho g h_2)}{\rho}$$

$$v_2^2 = \frac{2 \times [303{,}000 + (1{,}000)(9.8)(19.8) - 101{,}000 - (1{,}000)(9.8)(0.5)]}{1{,}000}$$

$$v_2^2 = 782.3$$
$$v_2 = 28.0 \text{ m/s}$$

Remember: *Any pipe that is exposed to the outside will have a pressure of 1 atm. When using Bernoulli's equation, though, remember to convert this to pascals! Don't get bogged down with arithmetic: Estimate whenever possible.*

Similar Questions

1) The pressure at one point in a horizontal pipe is triple the pressure at another point. How do the fluid velocities compare at these two points?

2) Pipe A has twice the radius of pipe B. Both pipes are placed horizontally and are subjected to a fluid pressure of 1.6 atm. What is the ratio of fluid velocities in these two pipes?

3) A water storage tank is open to air on the top and has a height of 1 meter. If the tank is completely full, and a hole is made at the center of the wall of the tank, how fast will the water exit the tank?

Key Concepts

Chapter 8

Electric field: $E = \dfrac{kq}{r^2}$ (N/C)

Dipoles

$E = \dfrac{V}{d}$ (V/m) (parallel plate

capacitor)

Capacitors

Vector addition

Takeaways

To find the net electric field (or magnetic field), find the effect of each source separately and then add them together. Remember that fields are vectors, so you have to add them like vectors: break the vectors into **X** and **Y** components and add the components separately. Then use trigonometry and the Pythagorean theorem to find the net field.

Things to Watch Out For

Most multiple-charge problems will have a geometry that allows you to cancel out certain components of the fields. Always look for an opportunity to do so, because this will save you time on Test Day.

Net Electric Field with Multiple Sources

The diagram below shows an apparatus assembled using a 120 V battery and a capacitor with 10 cm plate separation. First, switch S was closed for a long time, fully charging the plates of the capacitor. Then, switch S was opened, and a dipole with charges of 1 pC and −1 pC and a separation of 2 mm was placed between the plates of the capacitor, oriented with its positive end on the right-hand side. The dipole is held in a fixed position. What is the magnitude and direction of the electric field at a point 1 mm below the center of the dipole? ($k = 9 \times 10^9$ N·m²/C²)

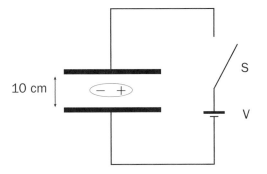

1) Find the electric field due to the plates.

$$E = \frac{V}{d} = \frac{120}{0.1} = 1{,}200 \text{ V/m}$$

The electric field due to a potential difference inside a parallel plate capacitor is given by $E = \dfrac{V}{d}$. The voltage on the plates is the same as the voltage on the battery because the capacitor is fully charged. The top plate of the capacitor is positively charged because it was attached to the positive terminal of the battery (which is always the side with the longer line). Thus, the electric field points vertically from the top plate to the bottom plate.

---

2) Draw the electric field due to the dipole.

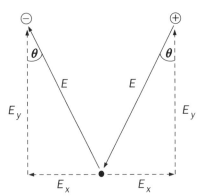

The two charges of the dipole are best treated simultaneously because their effect partially cancels out. The electric field points away from the positive charge and towards the negative charge. Find the **X** and **Y** components of the field for both charges. Note that the **Y** components cancel each other out and that the **X** components are equal and in the same direction. Thus, the electric field due to the dipole is twice the **X** component of the electric field due to either dipole. The **X** component of the electric field is $E \sin \theta$.

3) Calculate the electric field due to the dipole.

$$\theta = \tan^{-1}\frac{1}{1} = 45°$$

$$r = \sqrt{1^2 + 1^2} = 1.41 \text{ mm}$$

$$E_x = E \sin \theta$$

$$E = \frac{kq}{r^2}$$

$$E_x = \left(\frac{kq}{r^2}\right)\sin\theta = \left(\frac{(9\times10^9)(1\times10^{-12})}{(1.41\times10^{-3})^2}\right)\sin45°$$

$$= 3{,}201 \text{ V/m}$$

$$E_{dipole} = 2E_x = 6{,}402 \text{ V/m}$$

Find the angle θ from trigonometry. Find r, the distance from the charges to the point, using the Pythagorean theorem. Then calculate E_x using the formula for electric field due to a point charge. The net electric field is twice E_x and is directed to the left.

4) Find the net electric field.

$$E_{net}^2 = E_x^2 + E_y^2$$

$$E_{net}^2 = (6{,}402)^2 + (1{,}200)^2 = 4.243 \times 10^7$$

$$E_{net} = 6{,}514 \text{ V/m}$$

$$\theta = \tan^{-1}\frac{E_y}{E_x} = 10.6°$$

The net electric field is the vector sum of the electric field due to the plates and the dipole. Because one is in the x-direction and the other is in the y-direction, they form two sides of a right triangle. The length of the hypotenuse of the triangle is the magnitude of the net electric field and is given by the Pythagorean theorem. Find the angle θ from the horizontal using trigonometry.

Key Concepts

Chapter 6

Work: $W = q\Delta V$

Electrostatics

Electric potential energy, U

Charge Distribution and Work

Three charges are lined up along the x-axis. Charge 1 has a charge of $+1$ μC. Charge 2 has a charge of -2 μC. Charge 3 has a charge of $+4$ μC. The charges are all 1 mm away from each other. How much work was required to assemble this distribution of charge, assuming that the charges were initially very far apart? ($k = 9 \times 10^9$ N·m²/C²)

1) Find the work required to place charge 1.

$W = \Delta U = q\Delta V$

$W = 0$

The work done to move a charge equals the charge times the change in electric potential. The work done to place charge 1 is zero because there is no change in electric potential.

Remember: As a matter of convention, the work to place the first charge is always zero.

Takeaways

To find the work required to assemble a distribution of charges, find the work required to place each charge individually and then add. The work to place the first charge is always zero.

Things to Watch Out For

It is common to make sign errors on these types of problems. Keep this in mind when checking your work: Like charges increase in potential energy as they are brought closer; unlike charges decrease in potential energy as they are brought together.

2) Find the work required to place charge 2.

$W = \Delta U = q\Delta V = q_2(V_f - V_i)$

$V_i = 0$

$V_f = \left(\dfrac{kq_1}{r_{12}}\right)$

generic: $V = \dfrac{kq}{r}$

$W = q_2\left[\left(\dfrac{kq_1}{r_{12}}\right) - 0\right]$

$W = (-2 \times 10^{-6})\left[\dfrac{(9 \times 10^9)(1 \times 10^{-6})}{1 \times 10^{-3}}\right] = -18\,\text{J}$

The same formula is used in this step as in step 1. Here, charge 2 has an initial electric potential of zero because it is very far away from charge 1. The final electric potential is given by the formula $V = \dfrac{kq}{r}$, where q is the charge of the stationary charge and r_{12} is the distance between charges 1 and 2.

3) Find the work required to place charge 3.

$$W = \Delta U = q\Delta V = q_3(V_f - V_i)$$

$$V_i = 0$$

$$V_f = \left(\frac{kq_1}{r_{13}}\right) + \left(\frac{kq_2}{r_{23}}\right)$$

$$W = q_3\left[\left(\frac{kq_1}{r_{13}}\right) + \left(\frac{kq_2}{r_{23}}\right) - 0\right]$$

$$W = 4 \; 10^{-6}\left[\frac{(9\times10^9)(1\times10^{-6})}{2\times10^{-3}} + \frac{(9\times10^9)(-2\times10^{-6})}{1\times10^{-3}}\right]$$

$$= 18 - 72 = -54 \; J$$

Much as in step two, the work to place charge 3 equals the magnitude of charge 3 times the change in electric potential. Once again, the initial electric potential is 0. The final potential is the potential due to charge 1 plus the potential due to charge 2. Be careful, because the distances must be from charge 1 to charge 3 (call this r_{13}) and from charge 2 to charge 3 (call this r_{23}), respectively.

---

4) Add the work from steps 1, 2, and 3.

$$W_{net} = 0 - 18 \; J - 54 \; J = -72 \; J$$

Add the work from steps 1, 2, and 3 to find the net work. The net work is negative, meaning that the potential energy of the system has been lowered.

Similar Questions

1) A 1µC charge sits 1 cm from a −2µC charge. How much work is done in tripling the distance between these charges?

2) How much work is done in assembling a square-shaped charge distribution with a side length of 1 µm if all of the charges have a charge of 5 nC?

3) Charges 1, 2, and 3 are lined up, in that order, at 1 mm intervals along the y-axis. Three charges are lined up along the y-axis. Charge 1 has a charge of +4 µC. Charge 2 has a charge of −2 µC. Charge 3 has a charge of −3 µC. What is the change in potential energy of the system if charge 1 is removed?

Key Concepts

Chapter 6

Voltage

Mechanical energy

$U = qV \ (\mathrm{J} = \mathrm{C} \cdot \mathrm{V})$

$E = U + K$

$K = \dfrac{1}{2}mv^2$

Voltage and Energy

A dipole sits at the center of a large wire circle of radius 50 cm that is sitting horizontally in a plane. A small, −2 C charge with a mass of 4 kg is constrained to slide with no friction along the loop. The potential of the dipole is given as $V = V_\mathrm{o} \cos \theta$, where V_o is 5 and θ measures the angle from the vertical. The point charge's initial position on the loop is directly above the dipole ($\theta = 0$) of the loop and is given an initial speed of 3 m/s. How fast is the point charge moving at the point corresponding to $\theta = 90°$?

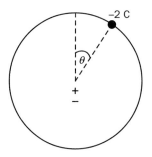

Takeaways

This problem appears complex due to the unusual situation, but it is solved the same way as any other energy problem: (1) Write expressions for the total energy of the system at two points, (2) set the expressions equal, and (3) solve.

1) Write an expression for the initial energy of the system.

$E_\mathrm{i} = U_\mathrm{i} + K_\mathrm{i}$

$U_\mathrm{i} = qV_\mathrm{i} = qV_\mathrm{o} \cos \theta_\mathrm{i}$

$K_\mathrm{i} = \dfrac{1}{2}mv_\mathrm{i}^2$

$E = qV_\mathrm{o} \cos \theta_\mathrm{i} + \dfrac{1}{2}mv_\mathrm{i}^2$

The energy of the system is the sum of the potential energy and the kinetic energy. The potential energy is given by $U = qV$, where the formula for V is given in the question.

Things to Watch Out For

Many students do not realize that problems involving charged particles and voltages can be solved most easily using the conservation of energy equation.

2) Write an expression for the final energy of the system.

$E_\mathrm{f} = U_\mathrm{f} + K_\mathrm{f}$

$U_\mathrm{f} = qV_\mathrm{f} = qV_\mathrm{o} \cos \theta_\mathrm{f}$

$E = qV_\mathrm{o} \cos \theta_\mathrm{f} + \dfrac{1}{2}mv_\mathrm{f}^2$

Much as in step 1, the energy of the system is the sum of the potential energy and the kinetic energy.

3) Set the energy expressions equal to each other and solve.

Due to the conservation of energy, we can set the initial and final energies as equal. This allows us to solve for v_f. Plug in the angles, mass, charge, and initial velocity to find v_f.

$$E_i = E_f$$

$$qV_0 \cos \theta_i + \frac{1}{2}mv_i^2 = qV_0 \cos \theta_f + \frac{1}{2}mv_f^2$$

$$\theta_i = 0 \rightarrow \cos \theta_i = 1$$

$$\theta_f = 90° \rightarrow \cos \theta_f = 0$$

$$qV_0 + \frac{1}{2}mv_i^2 = \frac{1}{2}mv_f^2$$

$$(-2)(5) + \frac{1}{2}(4)(3)^2 = \frac{1}{2}(4)v_f^2$$

$$8 = 2v_f^2$$

$$v_f = 2 \text{ m/s}$$

Similar Questions

1) How fast does a 1 kg ball move after falling from a height of 10 meters if the ball is thrown down with a speed 2 m/sec?

2) An alpha particle, starting from rest, travels through a potential difference of 200 V. What is the final speed of the particle? ($e = 1.6 \times 10^{-19}$ C)

3) Two protons (mass = 1.66×10^{-27} kg) initially are at rest at a distance of 10 nm from each other. They are released and accelerate away from each other. How fast are they both going after they are very far apart? ($k = 9 \times 10^9$ Nm²/C²)

Key Concepts

Chapter 6

Voltage

Electrical potential energy

Conservation of energy

Electrostatics and Velocity

A particle with a mass of 1 g and a charge of $+1\ \mu C$ is released from rest at a distance of 20 cm from another particle with a charge of $+20\ \mu C$, which is held fixed. How fast is the moving particle traveling when it is 150 cm away from the fixed particle? ($k = 9 \times 10^9\ \mathrm{N \cdot m^2/C^2}$)

1) Determine the electrical potential energy at the points of interest.

point 1: $U_1 = \dfrac{kq_1q_2}{r_1} = \dfrac{(9\times10^9)(20\times10^{-6})(1\times10^{-6})}{(0.2)} = 0.9\ \mathrm{J}$

point 2: $U_2 = \dfrac{kq_1q_2}{r_2} = \dfrac{(9\times10^9)(20\times10^{-6})(1\times10^{-6})}{(1.5)} = 0.12\ \mathrm{J}$

Generic: $U = \dfrac{kq_1q_2}{r}$

Potential energy can only be defined as a relative value, but in these types of problems, it is easiest to use the definition that the potential energy is zero at infinite distance. This way, you can use the formula $U = \dfrac{kq_1q_2}{r}$, which saves time compared to using $\Delta U = q\Delta V$ by bypassing the step of first calculating V.

Takeaways

Problems involving charged particles that move around near other charged particles (or in electric fields) are solved most easily using the conservation of energy equation. Do these problems just as you would for gravity. Find the change in potential energy, set that equal to the negative of the change in kinetic energy, and solve for the quantity of interest.

2) Determine the change in potential energy and kinetic energy.

$\Delta U = U_2 - U_1 = -0.78\ \mathrm{J} = -\Delta K$

$\Delta K = 0.78\ \mathrm{J}$

There is a negative change in potential energy. From the conservation of energy equation, this means that there must be a positive change in kinetic energy because the total energy must remain constant. In these types of problems, $\Delta U = -\Delta K$.

3) Determine the velocity of the particle from the kinetic energy.

$\Delta K = \dfrac{1}{2}mv_2{}^2 - \dfrac{1}{2}mv_1{}^2$; ($v_1 = 0$, so $\Delta K = \dfrac{1}{2}mv_2{}^2$)

$0.78\ \mathrm{J} = \dfrac{1}{2}(1 \times 10^{-3})v^2$

$v^2 = \dfrac{0.78(2)}{(1\times10^{-3})} = 1{,}560$

$v = 39.50\ \mathrm{m/s}$

Because the initial velocity is 0, the change in kinetic energy equals the kinetic energy that the particle has at point 2. Set them equal and solve.

Things to Watch Out For

These problems can be presented in several different ways. If you are given the potential at two points, simply multiply by the magnitude of the charge in motion to determine the electrical potential energy at those points. A common mistake is to multiply by the source charge. Remember, the q in the equation $U = qV$ refers to the charge that is moving. Work is often tested with these problems, so remember that work is equal to the change in kinetic energy. For problems involving point charges and speed, you will always use the work energy theorem.

Similar Questions

1) A proton initially at rest is accelerated through a potential difference of 100 V. What is the proton's final speed? ($e = 1.6 \times 10^{-19}$ C; $m_p = 1.67 \times 10^{-27}$)

2) How much work is done in moving an electron from a distance of 1 nm to a distance of 10 nm away from a hydrogen nucleus?

3) What voltage is required to accelerate protons to a speed of 10^4 m/s?

Key Concepts

Chapter 6

Coulomb's law

Vector addition

$$F = \frac{kq_1q_2}{r^2}$$

Electric Force

Find the net force exerted on point charge a by the other two point charges depicted in the diagram below. ($k = 8.99 \times 10^9$ N·m^2/C^2)

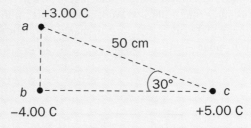

Takeaways

To find the net force on an object:

(1) Choose positive directions for your x- and y-axes.

(2) Break each of the individual forces on the object into **X** and **Y** components.

(3) Add the **X** components of the individual forces to obtain the **X** component of the net force on the object; add the **Y** components of the individual forces to obtain the **Y** component of the net force.

(4) To find the magnitude of the net force, apply the Pythagorean theorem to the **X** and **Y** components of the net force.

(5) To find the direction of the net force (measured as an angle from the x-axis), take the inverse tangent of the **Y** component of the net force divided by the **X** component of the net force.

1) Find the distance from charge a to charge b.

$$\sin 30° = \frac{r_{ab}}{50\,\text{cm}}$$

$$r_{ab} = 50\text{ cm} \times \sin 30°$$

$$r_{ab} = 25\text{ cm}$$

To find the distance between points a and b, use sine. Sine of angle 30 is the hypotenuse over opposite.

___

2) Find the force exerted by charge b on charge a.

Start with Coulomb's law. Plug in the charges located at points a and b. r_{ab} is the distance between points a and b.

$$F = \frac{kq_1q_2}{r^2}$$

$$F_{ab} = \frac{kq_aq_b}{r_{ab}^2}$$

$$F_{ab} = \frac{(8.99\times10^9\text{ N·m}^2/\text{C}^2)(3.00\text{ C})(-4.00\text{ C})}{(0.250\text{ m})^2}$$

$$F_{ab} = -1.73 \times 10^{12}\text{ N}$$

Remember: *The negative sign for the force means that there is an attraction (unlike charges). Because point charge* a *is positive whereas* b *is negative, the direction is straight down toward charge* b.

3) Find the force exerted by charge c on charge a.

Start with Coulomb's law. Plug in the charges located at points a and c. r_{ac} is the distance between points a and c.

$$F = \frac{kq_1q_2}{r^2}$$

$$F_{ac} = \frac{kq_aq_b}{r_{ac}^2}$$

$$F_{ac} = \frac{(8.99\times10^9 \text{ N·m}^2/\text{ C}^2)(3.00 \text{ C})(5.00 \text{ C})}{(0.500 \text{ m})^2}$$

$$F_{ac} = 5.39 \times 10^{11} \text{ N}$$

Remember: *The positive sign for the force means that there is repulsion (like charges). This means that the direction of the force is away from point charge c.*

Things to Watch Out For

This problem shows the nature of the coulomb. One coulomb is a huge charge. Usually you will deal with microcoulombs. Even when you solve for inverse tangent, be sure the angle measurement is pointing in the right direction. Draw force diagrams to confirm.

4) Draw the force diagram and separate into vectors.

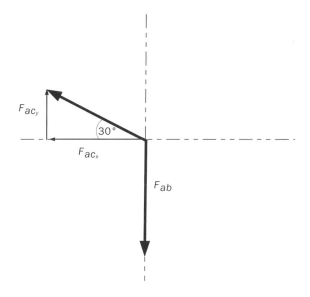

$$F_{ab, x} = 0 \text{ N}$$

$$F_{ab, y} = -1.73 \times 10^{12} \text{ N}$$

$$F_{ac, x} = F_{ac} \times (-1) \cos 30°$$

$$= (5.39 \times 10^{11} \text{ N}) \times (-0.866) = -4.67 \times 10^{11} \text{ N}$$

$$F_{ac, y} = F_{ac} \times \sin 30° = (5.39 \times 10^{11} \text{ N}) \times (0.5)$$

$$= 2.70 \times 10^{11} \text{ N}$$

F_{ab} points toward point b, which is straight down. Thus, F_{ab} has no **X** component—only a **Y** component.

Similar Questions

1) Two point charges, the first with a charge of $+1.97 \times 10^{-6}$ C and the second with a charge of -5.01×10^{-6} C, are separated by 25.5 cm. Find the magnitude of the electrostatic force experienced by the positive charge.

2) Point charge a has a charge of 3.693×10^{-7} C, whereas point charge b has a charge of 1.75×10^{-6} C. They exert an electrostatic force of magnitude 36.1×10^{-3} N on each other. Find the separation between the point charge a and point charge b.

3) Point charge a has a charge of 3.693×10^{-7} C and exerts a force of 36.1×10^{-3} N on point charge b. If the two charges are separated by a distance of 0.025 m, find the charge of point charge b.

F_{ac} points away from point c, which is 30° above the horizontal to the left. F_{ac} has both a horizontal and vertical component. Find the **X** and **Y** components by using the cosine and sine of 30°, respectively.

Remember: F_{ab} *is pointing down, so the x-vector component should be 0 while the y-vector component should be negative.* F_{ac} *is pointing up and to the left, so the x-vector component should be negative while the y-vector component should be positive.*

---

5) Add the vector components.

X components:
$$F_x = F_{ab, x} + F_{ac, x} = 0 + -4.67 \times 10^{11} \text{ N}$$
$$= -4.67 \times 10^{11} \text{ N}$$

Y components:
$$F_y = F_{ab, y} + F_{ac, y} = -1.73 \times 10^{12} \text{ N} + 2.70 \times 10^{11} \text{ N}$$
$$= -1.46 \times 10^{12} \text{ N}$$

$$F_a^2 = F_x^2 + F_y^2$$
$$F_a^2 = (-4.67 \times 10^{11} \text{ N})^2 + (-1.46 \times 10^{12} \text{ N})^2$$
$$F_a = 1.53 \times 10^{12} \text{ N}$$

Add the **X** and **Y** components separately. To find the magnitude, take the square root of the sum of the squares of each component (the Pythagorean theorem).

---

6) Solve for the magnitude and direction.

$$\text{Magnitude} = F_a = 1.53 \times 10^{12} \text{ N}$$
$$\text{Direction} = \tan^{-1}\left(\frac{F_y}{F_x}\right)$$

$$= \tan^{-1}\left(\frac{-1.46 \times 10^{12} \text{ N}}{-4.67 \times 10^{11} \text{ N}}\right)$$

$$= 72.3°$$

The magnitude of F_a was determined in step 5. To solve for direction, take the inverse tangent of the **Y** component over the **X** component. The net force exerted on point charge a is 1.53×10^{12} N exerted at 72.3° south of west.

High-Yield Problems continue on the next page

Key Concepts

Chapter 8

$C = \dfrac{Q}{V}$ (C/V)

$F = ma$ (N: kg·m/s²)

$F = qE$ (N)

$\Delta y = v_{oy}t + \dfrac{1}{2}a_y t^2$

Capacitance

Kinematics

Electrostatics

Voltage

Electric field

Electric force

$E = \dfrac{V}{d}$ (V/m) (parallel plate capacitor)

Takeaways

This is a combination between a capacitor problem, an electrostatics problem, and a kinematics problem. Use the properties of capacitors to find the voltage, which leads you to the force and acceleration of the particle. After you have the acceleration, this problem is no different from a standard free-fall or projectile problem.

Things to Watch Out For

There are several equations you must memorize to solve this problem.

Electron Between Charged Plates

A charged particle of mass 1 µg and charge 10 nC with velocity 2,000 m/s enters the center of the gap in a parallel plate capacitor as shown below. The capacitor holds a charge of 2 C and has a capacitance of 5 mF. The plates of the capacitor are 2.0 mm apart and 10 cm long. Will the particle strike one of the plates of the capacitor before it exits the gap?

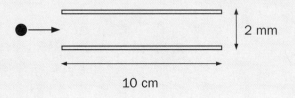

1) Find the voltage across the capacitor.

The capacitance of a capacitor is related to the charge and voltage across the capacitor by $C = \dfrac{Q}{V}$. Solve for V.

$$C = \frac{Q}{V} \rightarrow V = \frac{Q}{C} = \frac{2}{5 \times 10^{-3}} = 400 \text{ volts}$$

2) Find the electric field in between the plates.

$$V = Ed \rightarrow E = \frac{V}{d} = \frac{400}{2 \times 10^{-3}} = 200{,}000 \text{ V/m}$$

The magnitude of the electric field inside a parallel plate capacitor is given by the formula $E = \dfrac{V}{d}$.

3) Find the acceleration of the particle.

$$a = \frac{F}{m}$$

$$F = qE \rightarrow a = \frac{qE}{m} = \frac{(10 \times 10^{-9})(200{,}000)}{1 \times 10^{-9}} = 2{,}000{,}000 \text{ m/s}^2$$

Remember to convert the mass to SI units (kg).

4) Find the time that the particle is between the plates.

Use the standard kinematics formula to find the amount of time it takes the particle to travel the distance across the capacitor. Note that there is no force in the x-direction, so there is no acceleration in the x-direction. Solve for time.

$$\Delta x = v_{ox}t + \frac{1}{2}a_x t^2$$

$$a_x = 0 \rightarrow \Delta x = v_{ox}t$$

$$t = \frac{\Delta x}{v_{ox}} = \frac{0.1}{2,000} = 5 \times 10^{-5}\ s$$

5) Find the deflection of the particle.
Use the standard kinematics formula to find the movement in the *y*-direction based on the acceleration, time, and initial velocity. Note that initially there is no velocity in the *y*-direction.

$$\Delta y = v_{oy}t + \frac{1}{2}a_y t^2$$

$$v_{oy} = 0 \rightarrow \Delta y = \frac{1}{2}a_y t^2 = \frac{1}{2}(2,000,000)(5 \times 10^{-5})^2$$

$$= 2.5 \times 10^{-6}\ m = 2.5\ mm$$

Since the deflection of the particle (2.5 mm) is greater than the distance between the plates (2.0 mm), the particle will strike one of the plates of the capacitor before it exits the gap.

Similar Questions

1) An electron starts from rest at one plate of a parallel plate capacitor and accelerates to the other plate. The plate separation is 2 mm, and it takes 1 ms for the electron to travel from one side to the other. What is the capacitance of this capacitor if there are 2 C of charge stored on the plates? ($m_e = 9.11 \times 10^{-31}$ kg; $e = 1.6 \times 10^{-19}$ C)

2) An electron is brought to rest by a potential difference of 1 kV. What was the initial velocity of the electron?

3) A proton experiences a force of 10 mN as it travels between the plates of a parallel plate capacitor, parallel to the plates. If the capacitor holds 1 mC of charge and has a potential of 10 V, what is the separation between the plates?

Electrostatic Impulse

A +2e charge is sitting on the negative plate of a parallel-plate capacitor. A mechanical error accidentally reverses the charge on the plates such that the test charge is accelerated towards the other plate. In the 7 s that it takes for the technician to correct this mistake, the test charge traverses the entire 20 mm distance between the plates. If the test charge loses 3.2×10^{-16} J of potential energy, what was the impulse created by the electric force? (1 $e = 1.6 \times 10^{-19}$ C)

1) Find the potential difference for the drop in electric potential.

$$\Delta V = \frac{\Delta U}{q_0}$$

$$\Delta V = \frac{3.2 \times 10^{-16} \text{ J}}{(2)(1.6 \times 10^{-19} \text{ C})} = 1,000 \text{ volts}$$

The +2e charge is equal to two fundamental units of charge. Thus, the test charge q_0 is 3.2×10^{-19} coulombs.

2) Find the electric field between the plates.

$\Delta V = Ed$
1,000 V = E(0.02 m) → $E = 5 \times 10^4$ V/m

Once again, we only need to plug in the data appropriate to the equation.

3) Find the electric force.

$F = Eq_0$
$F = (5 \times 10^4$ V/m$)(3.2 \times 10^{-19}$ C$) = 1.6 \times 10^{-14}$ N

Substitute for the relevant quantities and constants.

Remember: Use dimensional analysis to check your work. In this case, we see that $\frac{F}{q_0}$ = E. From the previous step, we found the electric field to have the unit V/m. However, looking at the equation here, we see that the electric field will also have the unit N/C. This means that V/m = N/C. Recognizing this allows us to find alternative ways of defining the units V and C, for instance.

4) Find the impulse.

$$J = F_{av}\Delta t$$
$$J = (1.6 \times 10^{-14} \text{ N})(7 \text{ s}) = 1.12 \times 10^{-13} \text{ N·s}$$

Plug and chug.

Remember: *The impulse on an object is equal to the change in the object's momentum. It is similar to work, as in the equation* W = PΔt.

Similar Questions

1) Three positive charges, +1e, +2e, and +3e, are sitting in a row with 5 mm between them. What is the potential energy of the system? ($k = 9 \times 10^9$ Nm^2/C^2)

2) A −6e charge experiences an electric force upwards when it is fired through a parallel plate capacitor. If the potential difference experienced by the test charge is 1,000 V and the plates are 2 cm apart, what is the force?

3) If a +1e test charge loses 1 J of electric potential energy in moving from equipotential line a to b, which is closer to the positive point charge that creates the field, V_a or V_b?

Key Concepts

Chapter 10

Photoelectric effect

Efficiency

Properties of light

$P = \dfrac{E}{t}$ (W: J/s)

Takeaways

If the work function were greater than the energy of the photons, there would be no current produced, regardless of the power of the light source. This is a major source of confusion for most test takers.

The energy (and thus frequency or wavelength) determines whether the photoelectric effect will occur.

The power (or intensity) is related to the number of photons arriving per second and thus determines how many electrons will be generated.

Problems involving the photoelectric effect often involve tricky, unfamiliar units. Use dimensional analysis to your advantage.

Photoelectric Effect

A beam of monochromatic light of wavelength 550 nm and power of 5 W is incident on a metal wire with work function 1.1 eV. Assuming 60 percent efficiency, what is the maximum possible current produced in the wire? ($1 \text{ eV} = 1.6 \times 10^{-19}$ J; $e = 1.6 \times 10^{-19}$ C; $h = 6.6 \times 10^{-34}$ J·s.)

1) Find the energy of the incident photons.

$550 \text{ nm} = 5.5 \times 10^{-7} \text{ m}$

$$E = hf = \frac{hc}{\lambda} = \frac{(6.6 \times 10^{-34})(3 \times 10^{8})}{(5.5 \times 10^{-7})}$$

$$E = \left[\frac{(6.6)(3)}{(5.5)} \right] \times \left[\frac{(10^{-34})(10^{8})}{(10^{-7})} \right] = 3.6 \times 10^{-19} \text{ J}$$

The energy of a photon depends only on the frequency of that photon and Planck's constant, h. They are related by the formula $E = hf$. The speed, c, wavelength, λ, and frequency, f, of light are related by the formula $c = f\lambda$. Substitute to find the energy in terms of wavelength.

2) Convert units.

$$1 \text{ eV} = 1.6 \times 10^{-19} \text{ J} \rightarrow 1.1 \text{ eV} \times \left(\frac{1.6 \times 10^{-19} \text{ J}}{1 \text{ eV}} \right) = 1.76 \times 10^{-19} \text{ J}$$

Convert the work function of the metal to joules using the conversion factor given in the question. If it is more comfortable, you could work this problem in terms of eV as well.

3) Compare photon energy to work function.

$$3.6 \times 10^{-19} \text{ J} > 1.76 \times 10^{-19} \text{ J}$$

The work function is the amount of energy required to free one electron completely from an atom. The energy of the photons is greater than the work function. This means that each photon has enough energy to liberate an electron from an atom. Any energy above the level of the work function is given to the electron in the form of kinetic energy.

4) Calculate the number of photons arriving per second.

$$P = \frac{E}{t} = 5 \text{ W} = 5 \text{ J/s}$$

$$5 \text{ J/s} \times \left(\frac{1 \text{ photon}}{3.6 \times 10^{-19} \text{ J}} \right) = 1.39 \times 10^{19} \text{ photons/s}$$

The power given in the question tells us that 5 J/s arrive at the wire. Calculate the number of photons in 5 J using dimensional analysis. There are 1.39×10^{19} photons hitting the wire each second. Because each photon produces a free electron, there are 1.39×10^{19} free electrons produced each second.

5) Calculate the charge produced each second (the maximum current).

$$I = \frac{\Delta q}{\Delta t}$$

1.39×10^{19} electrons/s $\times$ $(1.6 \times 10^{-19}$ C/electron$) = 2.22$ C/s $= 2.22$ A

Current equals charge per time, not electrons per time. Use dimensional analysis to find the amount of charge contained in 1.39×10^{19} electrons. This amount of charge per second is the current.

6) Calculate the real current.

$I = 2.22$ A $\times (0.6) = 1.33$ A

The efficiency is only 60 percent, so multiply the current from step 5 by 0.6 to find the real current.

> ## Things to Watch Out For
>
> Light energy can be converted into electrical energy, which can then also be converted to mechanical energy via a generator with a certain efficiency. In that case, you would multiply the electrical energy by the efficiency of the generator to find the useful mechanical work output of the entire system.

> ## Similar Questions
>
> 1) What is the minimum frequency that a photon can have to induce a current in a metal with work function 2 eV?
>
> 2) What is the kinetic energy of an electron ejected from an atom of work function 0.5 eV when it is struck by a photon of wavelength 100 nm?
>
> 3) What power and frequency of incident radiation must be used to strike a metal of work function 1×10^{-18} J to produce 10,000 electrons per second?

Key Concepts

Chapter 7

Magnetic field

Right-hand rule

Vector addition

$B = \dfrac{\mu_0 I}{2\pi r}$ (T) (long straight wire)

$B = \dfrac{\mu_0 I}{2r}$ (T) (center of wire loop)

Magnetic Field

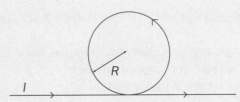

A current of 2 A flows down a long wire with a loop of radius 50 cm in it. The current flows around the loop counterclockwise, as shown in the diagram below. What is the magnitude and direction of the of the magnetic field at the center of the loop?
($\mu_0 = 4\pi \times 10^{-7}$ T·m/A.)

1) Find the magnetic field due to the straight section.

$$B_{\text{straight}} = \frac{\mu_0 I}{2\pi r} = \frac{(4\pi \times 10^{-7})(2)}{2(0.5)} = 8 \times 10^{-7} \text{ T}$$

The magnetic field due to the straight section is given by the formula $B = \dfrac{\mu_0 I}{2\pi r}$.

Takeaways

This problem is another example of considering the sources of a field separately and then adding their effects. This is the same process you use to find the net electric field due to multiple charges.

2) Find the magnetic field due to the circular section.

$$B_{\text{circular}} = \frac{\mu_0 I}{2r} = \frac{(4\pi \times 10^{-7})(2)}{2(0.5)} = 2.5 \times 10^{-6} \text{ T}$$

The magnetic field due to the circular section is given by the formula $B = \dfrac{\mu_0 I}{2r}$.

3) Determine the direction of each of the magnetic fields.

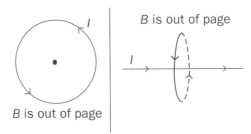

Things to Watch Out For

Many students confuse the right-hand rule, but the rule is essential to getting the correct answer on any magnetic field problem.

Determine the direction of the magnetic field produced by each source separately. To determine the direction of a magnetic field, we use a right-hand rule—essentially the same right-hand rule for a long straight wire as for a circular loop: (i) Grasp a section of the wire, with your thumb pointing in the direction of the current through that section. (ii) Your fingers will now curl in the direction of the magnetic field. To find the direction of the magnetic field at a particular location, position your fingertips at that location (while still gripping the wire with your thumb pointing in the direction from step (i)); your fingertips will now point in the direction of the magnetic field at that location.

MCAT Pitfall: There are two different right-hand rules, one for finding the direction of a magnetic field and one for finding the direction of a magnetic force. Don't confuse them!

To determine the direction of the field generated by the loop: (i) Let's say you grasp the bottom of the loop. Then you should point your thumb to the right. (ii) Your fingers will now curl in the direction of the magnetic field around the bottom of the loop. We want to know the direction of the field inside the loop; therefore, position your fingertips inside the loop. Your fingertips will now be pointing out of the page; therefore, the direction of the magnetic field inside the loop is out of the page.

To determine the direction of the field generated by the straight wire: (i) Grasp the wire, pointing your thumb to the right. (ii) Your fingers will now curl in the direction of the magnetic field. We want to know the direction of the field above the wire; therefore, position your fingertips above the loop. Your fingertips will now be pointing out of the page; therefore, the direction of the magnetic field above the wire is out of the page.

---

4) Find the net magnetic field.

$$B_{net} = B_{straight} + B_{circular} = 8 \times 10^{-7} + 2.5 \times 10^{-6}$$
$$= 3.3 \times 10^{-6} \text{ T}$$

Because the magnetic fields are pointed in the same direction, simply add their magnitudes to find the net field. If they were pointed in opposite directions, you would need to subtract one from the other.

Similar Questions

1) For a long wire with a loop in it as in the previous problem, at what point(s) is there no net magnetic field?

2) Two parallel, straight wires, each carrying a current of 10 mA in the same direction, are located 10 cm apart. What is the net magnetic field halfway between the two wires?

3) Two circular loops of wire are concentric. They both carry a current of 50 mA but in opposite directions. If the radii of the loops are 10 cm and 30 cm, and the inner loop carries a clockwise current, what is the magnitude and direction of the magnetic field at the center of the loops?

Takeaways

From the force relationship above, it can be deduced that the units of magnetic field are $\frac{N \cdot s}{C \cdot m}$ or $\frac{N}{A \cdot m}$. This unit is named the tesla. It is a large unit, and the smaller unit, gauss, is used for small fields like the earth's magnetic field. A tesla is 10,000 gauss.

Things to Watch Out For

The force is perpendicular to both the velocity **(v)** of the charge (*q*) and the magnetic field **(B)**. The magnetic force on a stationary charge or a charge moving parallel to the magnetic field is zero. The direction of the force is given by the right-hand rule.

Magnetic Force

The speed of an alpha particle is 4.5×10^4 m/s, and the magnitude of the magnetic force is 7.5×10^{-15} N. What is the magnitude of the magnetic field if the particle is traveling perpendicular to the field? ($e = 1.6 \times 10^{-19}$ C)

1) Determine the charge of the object that the force is acting on.

$2 \times 1.6 \times 10^{-19}$ C $= 3.2 \times 10^{-19}$ C

The magnetic field is acting on an alpha particle. An alpha particle has two protons and two neutrons. Because the charge of one proton is 1.6×10^{-19} C, multiply that by 2.

Remember: The sign of the charge will depend on the particle. If you have an electron, the charge is negative. If you are dealing with a proton, the charge is positive.

---

2) Set up the force equation.

$F = qvB \sin \theta$

In this formula, *F* is the magnitude of the magnetic force on the moving charge, *q* is the magnitude of the charge, *v* is the magnitude of the velocity of the moving charge, *B* is the magnitude of the magnetic field, and θ is the angle between the magnetic field and the velocity of the charge. The question states that the particle is moving perpendicular to the field, so θ is 90°.

---

3) Solve for the magnitude of the magnetic field.

Solve for B in the equation from step 2 and plug in values.

$$B = \frac{F}{qV}$$

$$= \frac{7.5 \times 10^{-15}\ \text{N}}{(3.2 \times 10^{-19}\ \text{C})(4.5 \times 10^4\ \text{m/s})}$$

$$= 0.521\ \text{T}$$

Similar Questions

1) A beam of electrons moves at right angles to a 0.60 T field. The electrons have a velocity of 2.5×10^7 m/s. What force acts on the electrons? What force acts if the beam of electrons moves at an angle of 45° to the field?

2) What is the force felt from a magnetic field on an electron where the speed of an electron is 5×10^3 m/s, the magnitude of the magnetic field is 1.5 T, and the particle travels at a 30° angle to the field?

3) A proton moves at right angles to a 0.003 T field directed out of the page. The proton moves from right to left with a speed of 5×10^6 m/s. What is the magnitude and direction of the force that the proton experiences?

Key Concepts

Chapter 8

Capacitance

$$C = \frac{\varepsilon_0 A}{d}$$

$$Q = VC$$

Takeaways

When solving electrostatics questions, stop to ask yourself what quantities you have and what quantities you need. In this case, we were presented with a capacitor but asked for voltage. At that point, ask yourself how you can get voltage from capacitance and capacitance from the given information. This is a common strategy that can be applied to many physics-related questions on the MCAT.

Things to Watch Out For

This type of question can be asked in several different ways, but the biggest mistake that most people will make on Test Day is whether the voltage, charge, or capacitance should be held constant. Many students make the mistake of keeping voltage constant in this problem.

Use these facts to guide you: (1) Charge must be supplied by something (generally a battery), (2) a battery will hold a capacitor at a set voltage, and (3) capacitance is determined by the structure of the capacitor.

Parallel Plate Capacitor

A parallel plate air-gap capacitor is constructed from two square plates of side length 100 cm. The separation between the plates is 20 cm. The capacitor is attached to a battery of voltage 10 V. After the capacitor is fully charged, the battery is disconnected, and the separation of the plates is doubled. Afterwards, what is the voltage across the capacitor? ($\varepsilon_0 = 8.85 \times 10^{-12}$ $C^2/N \cdot m^2$)

1) Find the capacitance of the capacitor.

$$C = \frac{\varepsilon_0 A}{d} = \frac{(8.85 \times 10^{-12})(1)^2}{0.2} = 4.4 \times 10^{-11} \text{ F} = 44 \text{ pF}$$

The capacitance is calculated using the physical dimensions of the capacitor. Keep everything in meters because ε_0 is given in terms of meters.

2) Find the initial charge on the capacitor.

$$Q = VC = (10 \text{ V})(44 \text{ pF}) = 440 \text{ pC}$$

This is the general formula relating capacitance, charge, and voltage.

3) Find the new capacitance of the capacitor.

$$C = \frac{\varepsilon_0 A}{d} = \frac{(8.85 \times 10^{-12})(1)^2}{0.4} = 2.2 \times 10^{-11} \text{ F} = 22 \text{ pF}$$

The separation is doubled, so the capacitance is cut in half.

Remember: *The capacitance of a capacitor can only be altered by changes in the physical structure of the capacitor itself: plate size, separation, or gap material.*

4) Find the new voltage across the capacitor.

$$V = \frac{Q}{C} = \frac{440 \text{ pC}}{22 \text{ pF}} = 20 \text{ V}$$

It is very important to understand that because the battery is no longer connected to the capacitor, the charge stored on the capacitor must remain the same—there is nowhere for new charges to come from, nor is there anywhere for excess charge to go! Likewise, the voltage is allowed to change because the battery is no longer holding the capacitor at a set voltage.

Similar Questions

1) A fully charged capacitor is connected to a 120 V power source and holds a charge of 1 μC. What is the charge stored on the capacitor if the voltage is doubled?

2) A 1 μF capacitor holds a charge of 2 μC and is not connected to a battery. Another initially uncharged, 1 μF capacitor is connected in parallel to this capacitor. What is the total charge stored by the second capacitor?

3) A 25 nC parallel plate capacitor is connected to a 12 V battery. By what factor should the separation between the plates be changed so that the charge stored by the capacitor is 30 nC?

Key Concepts

Chapter 8

Capacitors in series:
$$\frac{1}{C_{eq}} = \frac{1}{C_1} + \frac{1}{C_2} + \frac{1}{C_3} + \dots$$

Capacitors in parallel:
$$C_{eq} = C_1 + C_2 + C_3 + \dots$$

$$Q = CV$$

Takeaways

There is a standard process for solving capacitor network problems:

1) Find the equivalent capacitance of the circuit through a number of equivalent capacitance steps.

2) Find the total charge in the circuit.

3) Expand the circuit back out until you have reached the desired capacitor.

Remember that capacitors in series must have the same charge—just like resistors in series must have the same current. If there are branches in the circuit, the charge splits between the branches.

Things to Watch Out For

Many test takers confuse the rules for adding capacitors with those for adding resistors.

Capacitor Networks

In the capacitor network shown below, $C_1 = 30$ μF, $C_2 = 20$ μF, $C_3 = 5$ μF, $C_4 = 6$ μF, and $V = 4$ volts. What is the charge stored in C_2?

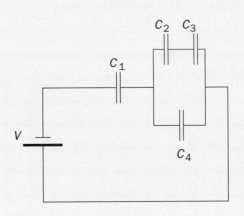

1) Find the equivalent capacitance of the network.

The first step is to combine capacitors 2 and 3. These capacitors are in series. The equivalent capacitance of two capacitors in series is given by

$$\frac{1}{C_{eq}} = \frac{1}{C_A} + \frac{1}{C_B}$$

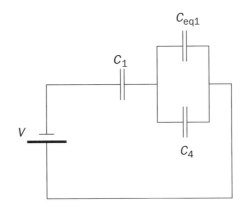

$$\frac{1}{C_{eq1}} = \frac{1}{C_2} + \frac{1}{C_3} = \frac{1}{20} + \frac{1}{5} = \frac{1}{20} + \frac{4}{20} = \frac{5}{20} = \frac{1}{4}$$

$$C_{eq1} = 4 \text{ μF}$$

Remember: *Capacitors add simply in parallel but in a complicated way in series. This is the opposite of resistors.*

2) Find the equivalent capacitance of the network.

Next, find the equivalent of capacitors C_{eq1} and C_4. These capacitors are in parallel, so they add simply.

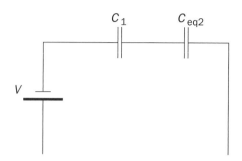

$$C_{eq2} = C_{eq1} + C_4 = 4\ \mu F + 6\ \mu F = 10\ \mu F$$

3) Find the equivalent capacitance of the network.

Finally, find the equivalent of capacitors C_1 and C_{eq2}. Similar to step 1, these capacitors are in series.

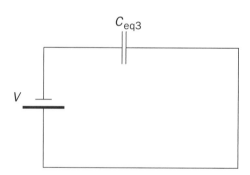

$$\frac{1}{C_{eq3}} = \frac{1}{C_1} + \frac{1}{C_{eq2}} = \frac{1}{30} + \frac{1}{10} = \frac{1}{30} + \frac{3}{30} = \frac{4}{30}$$

$$C_{eq3} = \frac{30}{4} = 7.5\ \mu F$$

4) Find the total charge in the circuit.

The reason to find the equivalent capacitance is so that we can determine the total charge in the circuit. Use the relation $Q = VC$ to find the charge stored in the equivalent capacitor C_{eq3}.

$$Q_{eq3} = VC_{eq3} = (4\ V)(7.5\ \mu F) = 30\ \mu C$$

Similar Questions

1) Four 1 µF capacitors are attached in parallel across a 9 V battery. What is the total charge stored in the circuit?

2) Each capacitor in the diagram below has a capacitance of 10 µF. What is the voltage across C_5?

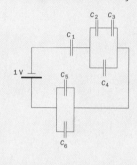

3) In the circuit shown below, $C_1 = C_2 = C_3 = 5\ \mu F$ and $C_4 = C_5 = C_6 = 15\ \mu F$. If the total charge stored in the circuit is 30 µC, what is the voltage of the battery?

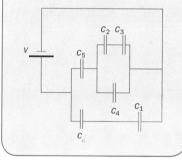

5) Expand the circuit.

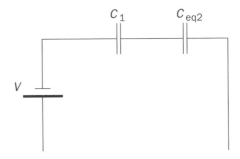

The key to solving capacitor networks is knowing that any capacitors in series must hold the same charge. Solve for the voltage across C_{eq2} so that we can expand the circuit again and determine the charge in each branch.

$$Q_{eq3} = Q_1 = Q_{eq2} = 30 \ \mu C$$

$$V_{eq2} = \frac{Q_{eq2}}{C_{eq2}} = \frac{30 \mu C}{10 \mu F} = 3 \ V$$

Remember: *Think of charge in capacitor problems as being similar to current in resistor problems.*

---

6) Expand the circuit again.

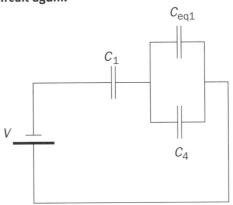

The voltage across any capacitors in parallel must be the same. This is also true for resistors. Once you know the voltage across C_{eq1}, solve for the charge stored on C_{eq1}.

$$V_{eq2} = V_{eq1} = V_4 = 3 \ V$$

$$Q_{eq1} = V_{eq1} C_{eq1} = (3 \ V)(4 \ \mu F) = 12 \ \mu C$$

7) Expand the circuit again.

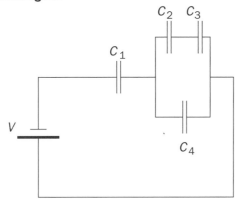

Just like in step 5, the charge on C_{eq1} must equal the charge on C_2 and C_3. Q_{eq1}

$= Q_2 = Q_3 = 12 \ \mu C.$

Key Concepts

Chapter 8

Ohm's law: $V = IR$

Resistors in series: $R_{series} = R_1 + R_2$

Resistors in parallel:

$$\frac{1}{R_{parallel}} = \frac{1}{R_1} + \frac{1}{R_2}$$

Takeaways

There is a standard process for solving these types of resistor problems:

1) Find the equivalent resistance by combining series and parallel resistors.

2) Find the current through the circuit.

3) Expand the circuit back out, step-by-step.

4) Apply knowledge of series and parallel resistors to find the quantity of interest.

Things to Watch Out For

The arithmetic for calculating the equivalent resistance in parallel can be confusing. Another version of the formula is $R_{parallel} = \dfrac{R_1 R_2}{R_1 + R_2}$. Note, however, that this only works for two resistors and cannot be expanded simply to account for three resistors.

Resistor Circuits

What is the current through R_1 in the circuit shown below?
$(R_1 = 30\ \Omega;\ R_2 = 6\ \Omega;\ R_3 = 20\ \Omega;\ R_4 = 10\ \Omega;\ R_5 = 30\ \Omega;\ V = 30\ \text{V})$

1) Find the equivalent resistance of the network.
The first part of this problem is to find the equivalent resistance of the entire circuit. This will take several steps. Begin by combining R_1 and R_2 using the equation for the equivalent of two parallel resistors.

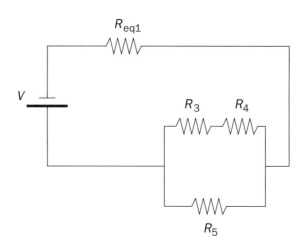

$$\frac{1}{R_{parallel}} = \frac{1}{R_1} + \frac{1}{R_2}$$

$$\frac{1}{R_{eq1}} = \frac{1}{R_1} + \frac{1}{R_2} = \frac{1}{30} + \frac{1}{6} = \frac{1}{30} + \frac{5}{30} = \frac{6}{30}$$

$$R_{eq1} = \frac{30}{6} = 5\ \Omega$$

2) Find the equivalent resistance of the network.

Combine R_3 and R_4, which are in series. Resistors in series add simply.

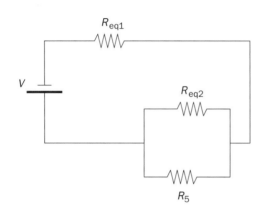

generic: $R_{series} = R_1 + R_2$
$R_{eq2} = R_3 + R_4 = 20 + 10 = 30\ \Omega$

3) Find the equivalent resistance of the network.

Combine the equivalent resistance from step 2, R_{eq2}, with R_5. These resistors are in parallel.

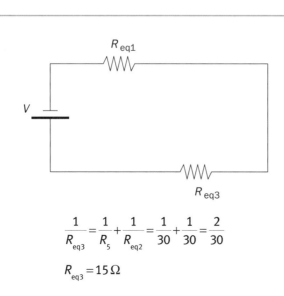

$$\frac{1}{R_{eq3}} = \frac{1}{R_5} + \frac{1}{R_{eq2}} = \frac{1}{30} + \frac{1}{30} = \frac{2}{30}$$

$$R_{eq3} = 15\ \Omega$$

Similar Questions

1) In the circuit shown in the original question, what is the voltage across R_4?

2) Four resistors are attached in parallel to a power supply of 9 V. If the resistances of the resistors are 10 Ω, 20 Ω, 30 Ω, and 40 Ω, what is the current through the battery?

3) There are six resistors in a circuit. R_1, R_2, R_3, R_4, and R_5 are all in parallel with each other, and they are all in series with R_6. If the current leaving the battery is 10 A and all of the resistors have a resistance of 1 Ω except for R_6, which is unknown, what is the resistance of R_6 if $V = 20$ V?

4) Find the equivalent resistance of the network.

Combine the equivalent resistance from step 3, R_{eq3}, with that from step 1, R_{eq1}. These resistors are in series.

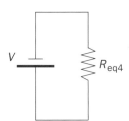

$$R_{eq4} = R_{eq1} + R_{eq3} = 5 + 15 = 20 \ \Omega$$

5) Find the current through the circuit.

$$V = IR \rightarrow I = \frac{V}{R} = \frac{30}{20} = 1.5 \ A$$

The point of finding the equivalent resistance is so that we can find the current through the circuit. This is also often referred to as the current through or leaving the battery. Use Ohm's law to find the current from the voltage and resistance.

6) Expand the circuit.

Now expand the circuit back out and apply what we know about resistors in series and parallel to find the current and voltage through individual resistors. All resistors in series must have the same current, so we know that the current from step 5 must equal the current through R_{eq1} and R_{eq3}. Use Ohm's law to find the voltage across R_{eq1}.

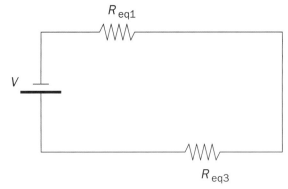

$$I_{eq1} = I_{eq3} = I = 1.5 \ A$$
$$V_{eq1} = I_{eq1} R_{eq1} = (1.5)(5) = 7.5 \ V$$

Remember: *Any number of resistors in series have the same current as one another.*

7) Expand the circuit again.

Because R_{eq1} is a parallel combination of R_1 and R_2, we know that R_1 and R_2 must have the same voltage as R_{eq1}. Any two (or more) circuit components in parallel must have the same voltage as the others. Use the voltage and resistance of R_1 to find the current through R_1.

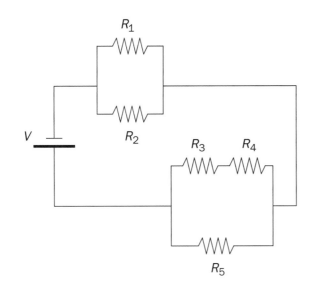

$$V_{R1} = V_{eq1} = 7.5 \text{ V}$$

$$I_1 \; \frac{V_1}{R_1} = \frac{7.5}{30} = 0.25 \text{ A}$$

Remember: *All components attached in parallel have the same voltage as one another.*

Key Concepts

Chapter 9

Conservation of energy

Springs

Gravitational potential energy:
$U = mgh$ (J)

Spring potential energy:
$U = \frac{1}{2}kx^2$ (J)

Kinetic energy: $K = \frac{1}{2}mv^2$ (J)

Takeaways

This problem is solved in the same way as every conservation of energy problem: Write expressions for the total energy of the system at two points, set them equal, and solve for the unknown quantity.

Things to Watch Out For

Variations on this problem could include questions about work required to compress a spring, compression along an incline, or the introduction of nonconservative forces. Apply the process for solving conservation of energy problems, and you will succeed!

Energy and Springs

A block of mass 2 kg falls from a height of 3 meters onto a spring, and the spring reaches a maximum compression of 20 cm. What is the spring constant for this spring? When the block bounces off of the spring, how fast is it going?

1) Write an expression for the initial energy of the system.

$E_i = mg(h + x)$

The initial energy of the system is the gravitational potential energy of the block at a height of 3 meters. However, recognize that the block will fall 3 meters plus an additional distance from the spring compressing. Let $h = 3$ meters and $x =$ the compression of the spring. By doing so, we are saying that the gravitational potential energy of the system is 0 when the spring is fully compressed.

Remember: You can set the potential energy to be zero at whatever point is most convenient, but you must be consistent through the entire problem.

---

2) Write an expression for the final energy of the system.

spring $U = \frac{1}{2}kx^2 \rightarrow E_f = \frac{1}{2}kx^2$

When a spring is stretched or compressed, potential energy is stored in the spring. This energy is given by the formula $U = \frac{1}{2}kx^2$. As we saw in step 1, there is no gravitational potential energy at this point.

---

3) Set the final energy equal to the initial energy and solve for k.

$mg(h + x) = \frac{1}{2}kx^2$

Because of the conservation of energy, we can set the total energy of the system at any two points equal to each other. Set the initial energy equal to the final energy and solve for k.

$mgh + mgx = \frac{1}{2}kx^2$

$(2)(9.8)(3) + 2(9.8)(0.2) = \frac{1}{2}(k)(0.2)^2$

$58.8 + 3.92 = 0.02k$

$k = 3{,}136$ N/m

---

4) Write an expression for energy of the system at the point that the block bounces off of the spring.

$$E_3 = \frac{1}{2}mv^2 + mgx$$

As the block bounces off of the spring, it has kinetic energy equal to $\frac{1}{2}mv^2$. It also has potential energy equal to mgx, because it is now at a height of x. The total energy is the sum of these two amounts.

---

5) Set two energies equal and solve for v.

$$mg(h + x) = \frac{1}{2}mv^2 + mgx$$
$$mgh + mgx = \frac{1}{2}mv^2 + mgx$$
$$gh + gx = \frac{1}{2}v^2 + gx$$
$$gh = \frac{1}{2}v^2$$
$$v = (2gh)^{\frac{1}{2}} = 7.7 \text{ m/s}$$

Much as in step 3, we can set the total energy of the system at any two points equal to each other. The numbers look easier to deal with for the energy expression from step 1, so choosing this one will save some time. (Note that the velocity is the same when it first hits the spring as when it rebounds off of the spring. There is no difference in the energy expression for these two points.)

Similar Questions

1) A spring is compressed vertically 10 cm, and a 5 kg block is placed on top of it. The spring has a spring constant of 50 N/m. If the system is released from rest, what is the maximum height achieved by the block?

2) A spring has a spring constant of 100 N/cm. How much work is required to alter the spring from a compression of 10 cm to a compression of 50 cm?

3) A 5 kg mass and a 2 kg mass are placed on two identical springs ($k = 1.3$ kN/m). What is the ratio of the maximum compressions of these two springs?

Acceleration of a Pendulum

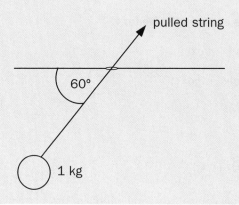

A small ball of mass 1 kg is tied to a string. The string is fed through a small hole as shown in the diagram below. If the ball is held at a 60-degree angle, as shown, and is then released from rest as the string is pulled with a constant force of 10 N at the same angle, what is the initial acceleration (magnitude and direction) of the ball?

1) Draw a free-body diagram.

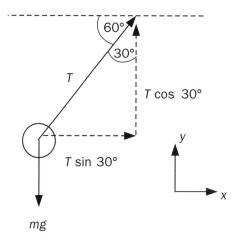

There are two forces acting on the ball: the tension in the string (labeled T) and the weight of the ball (which equals mg). If we use a standard x-y coordinate plane, the tension in the string must be broken into its **X** and **Y** components using trigonometry.

2) Add the forces in the x- and y-directions.

$$\Sigma F_x = ma_x = T \sin 30° = (10)(0.5) = 5 \text{ N}$$
$$\Sigma F_y = ma_y = T \cos 30° - mg = (10)(0.866) - (1)(9.8)$$
$$= -1.14 \text{ N}$$

Add the forces in the *x*- and *y*-directions separately. The net force in a direction always equals the mass times the acceleration in that direction. This is Newton's second law.

---

3) Find the magnitude and direction of the net force.

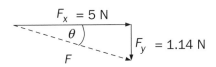

$$F^2 = F_x^2 + F_y^2$$

$$F = (F_x^2 + F_y^2)^{\frac{1}{2}} = [5^2 + (-1.14)^2]^{\frac{1}{2}} = 5.13\,N$$

$$\theta = \tan^{-1}\left(\frac{F_y}{F_x}\right) = \tan^{-1}\left(\frac{-1.14}{5}\right) = -12.8°$$

In step 2, we found the **X** and **Y** components of the net force. These two vectors form the sides of a right triangle. To find the magnitude of the net force, use the Pythagorean theorem. To find the angle of the net force, use trigonometry.

---

4) Find the acceleration.

$$F_{net} = ma \rightarrow a = \frac{F_{net}}{m} = \frac{5.13}{1} = 5.13\ m/s^2$$

$$\theta = -12.8°$$

Use Newton's second law to determine the acceleration from the net force. The direction of the acceleration is the same as the direction of the net force. This is always true.

Similar Questions

1) A car drives around a circular track of radius 100 m at a speed of 120 m/s. What is the magnitude and direction of the acceleration of the car?

2) A 20 kg block is pushed from the east with a force of 100 N, from the west with a force of 20 N, and from the south with a force of 150 N. In what direction does the block travel?

3) A 10 kg sled is pulled at an angle of 35° east of north by a force of 100 N and with a force of 150 N directed due east. A friction force of 50 N acts as well. What is the acceleration (both magnitude and direction) of the sled?

Key Concepts

Chapter 9

Dimensional analysis

Harmonic motion

Friction

Angular frequency $\omega = 2\pi f$ (s^{-1})

Springs

Takeaways

Use dimensional analysis to check your work. Get comfortable with algebraic manipulations.

Things to Watch Out For

Don't be thrown by situations that seem novel or overly complex. Nearly all of the information you need to solve this problem is given explicitly. Keep your units straight! In this example, both the spring constant and the damping constant have the same scalar value, but their units are different.

Dampened Harmonic Motion

A vertical spring-mass system is submerged in oil. The spring has a stiffness coefficient of 3 N/m, and the mass is 1 kg. If the dampened angular frequency ω_d of oscillation is 0.866 Hz, find the damping coefficient b for the oil and how long it takes the spring to reach 50 percent of its original amplitude. The equations for dampened angular frequency and amplitude are provided below.

$$\omega_d = \sqrt{\omega^2 - \left(\frac{b}{2m}\right)^2}$$

$$A = A_0 e^{-\left(\frac{b}{2m}\right)t}$$

1) Find the angular frequency of the spring.

$$\omega = 2\pi f = \sqrt{\frac{k}{m}}$$

$$\omega = \sqrt{\frac{3}{1}} \approx 1.73 \text{ Hz}$$

If the spring-mass system were free of nonconservative forces, it would oscillate indefinitely with an angular frequency of ω. Looking at the equation for dampened frequency ω_d, we see that we're basically adjusting ω for friction by subtracting a quantity specific to the damping coefficient and mass.

Remember: *Use dimensional analysis whenever possible to check your work. In this case, we know that the frequency of oscillation needs to be in Hz or s^{-1}. The spring constant k is in N/m and the mass m is in kg. Even if we forget whether k goes on top or on the bottom in this equation, thinking critically and using dimensional analysis allows us to find the right equation. If you are uncomfortable using the unit of newton, think back to Newton's second law: F = ma. A newton is simply kg(m/s^2).*

2) Use the first equation to find the damping coefficient.

$$\omega_d = \sqrt{\omega^2 - \left(\frac{b}{2m}\right)^2}$$

Here we are being tested on algebra. Square both sides of the equation to get rid of the square root on the right side. Solve for b. Dimensional analysis in the penultimate step shows us that we are multiplying angular frequency with mass. The individual units, respectively, are s^{-1} and kg, so our product, the damping coefficient, must have that unit. (Try using dimensional analysis to prove to yourself that b can also be recorded in $N \cdot s/m$.)

$$\omega_d = \sqrt{\omega^2 - \left(\frac{b}{2m}\right)^2}$$

$$0.866 = \sqrt{(1.73)^2 - \left[\frac{b}{2(1)}\right]^2} \rightarrow 0.75 \approx 3 - \left(\frac{b^2}{4}\right)$$

$$(0.75 - 3)4 = -b^2$$

$$b = 3 \text{ kg/s}$$

---

3) Use the second equation to see how the amplitude of oscillation diminishes with time.

$$A = A_0 e^{-\left(\frac{b}{2m}\right)t}$$

This, too, is a test of our algebraic skills. We are asked to find the time needed to reach 50 percent of the original amplitude of oscillation. Thus, $A = 0.5A_0$. Plug into the equation and cancel the A_0 term.

$$0.5A_0 = A_0 e^{-\left(\frac{3}{2(1)}\right)t}$$

$$0.5 = e^{-\left(\frac{3}{2(1)}\right)t}$$

To find t, we need to get rid of the number e. Take the natural log of both sides (because $\ln(e^x) = x$) to drop t into a workable domain. Then solve for t.

$$\ln 0.5 = -\left(\frac{3}{2(1)}\right)t$$

$$-2(-0.69) \div 3 = t$$

$$0.46 \text{ s} = t$$

Dimensional analysis of the exponent on e reinforces our units are correct. The exponent overall should have no units, so to cancel out s/kg, we need b to have the unit kg/s.

Remember: *On the MCAT, you will not be expected to take natural logs. You should, however, be able to estimate logarithms with the base 10. Occasionally, you will be given the conversion factor between ln and log.*

Similar Questions

1) By what percentage does the frequency diminish in a horizontal spring-mass system where $k = 1 \times 10^3$ N/m and $m = 4$ kg if the motion is dampened by a frictional force that has a damping coefficient of 2 kg/s?

2) What is the period of oscillation of a curled filament with a mass of 100 g and a spring constant of 15 N/m? When heated to 113°C, the filament undergoes a spontaneous exothermic reaction to dissipate the heat. If the new dampening coefficient is 5×10^{-3} kg/s, how much energy is lost in 1.5 minutes? Use the equation $E = E_0 e^{-\left(\frac{b}{m}\right)t}$.

Key Concepts

Chapter 9

Standing waves

Frequency

Wavelength

Standing Waves

When the harmonics of a certain pipe are listed in order of increasing frequency, the second harmonic and third harmonics in the list are at 420 Hz and 700 Hz respectively. Is this pipe open at both ends, or is it closed at one end and open at the other? What is the length of the pipe? (The speed of sound in air at 0°C is 331 m/s.)

1) Identify the pattern in resonant wavelengths in each of the pipe types.

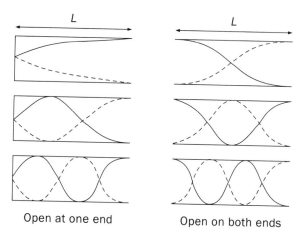

Open at one end   Open on both ends

Takeaways

It is important to understand fully the meanings of the formulas describing standing waves. Make sure that you know how to derive them on a blank piece of paper. This will solidify your understanding. Moreover, it is possible to ask questions about standing waves that test your understanding of what the different harmonics look like, such as in the diagram in step 1. Be sure to understand the visual pattern.

One end open: $\lambda_5 = \dfrac{3}{5}\lambda_3$

Both ends open: $\lambda_3 = \dfrac{2}{3}\lambda_2$

To tell which type of pipe this is, you need to know or be able to derive the formula for the frequency of each type of pipe. The closed end of the pipe must have a node, whereas the open ends must have antinodes. This means that only certain wavelengths are allowed to resonate.

The pipe that is open on one end is shown on the left. For the three harmonics, or modes, shown, the length of the pipe is $\dfrac{1}{4}\lambda$, $\dfrac{3}{4}\lambda$, and $\dfrac{5}{4}\lambda$. This means that the wavelengths for these modes equal $4L$, $\dfrac{4}{3}L$, and $\dfrac{4}{5}L$. The general formula is $\lambda_n = \dfrac{4L}{n}$, where n = 1, 3, 5, and so on. Thus, $\lambda_5 = \dfrac{3}{5}\lambda_3$.

The pipe that is open on both ends is shown on the right. For the three modes shown, the length of the pipe is $\dfrac{1}{2}\lambda$, λ, and $\dfrac{3}{2}\lambda$. This means that the wavelengths for these modes equal $2L$, L, and $\dfrac{2}{3}L$. The general formula is $\lambda_n = \dfrac{2L}{n}$, where n = 1, 2, 3, etc. Thus $\lambda_3 = \dfrac{2}{3}\lambda_2$.

Remember: *If we list the harmonics of a pipe in order of increasing frequency, then in the formula for a pipe open at one end, n = 1 corresponds to the first harmonic in the list, n = 3 corresponds to the second harmonic in the list, n = 5 corresponds to the third harmonic in the list, and so on.*

---

2) Find the resonant frequencies in each of the pipe types.

$$v = f\lambda \rightarrow \lambda = \frac{v}{f}$$

One end open:

$$\frac{v}{f_5} = \left(\frac{3}{5}\right)\left(\frac{v}{f_3}\right)$$

$$f_5 = \frac{5}{3}f_3$$

Both ends open:

$$\frac{v}{f_3} = \left(\frac{2}{3}\right)\left(\frac{v}{f_2}\right)$$

$$f_3 = \frac{3}{2}f_2$$

Use the relationship between velocity, frequency, and wavelength, $v = f\lambda$, to solve the expressions from step 1 for frequency.

---

3) Find the ratio of the harmonic frequencies and determine the type of pipe.

$$\frac{f_{\text{3rd in list}}}{f_{\text{2nd in list}}} = \frac{700}{420} = \frac{5}{3} \rightarrow \text{pipe is open at one end.}$$

The ratio between the harmonics given in the question is $\frac{5}{3}$. From the result in step 2, this means that the pipe is open at one end.

---

4) Find the length of the pipe from the wavelength expression.

$$\lambda_3 = \frac{v}{f_3} = \frac{321}{420} = 0.79\,\text{m}$$

$$\lambda_3 = \frac{4L}{3} \rightarrow L = \frac{3}{4}\lambda_3 = \left(\frac{3}{4}\right)(0.79) = 0.59\,\text{m}$$

Use the formula $v = f\lambda$ once again to solve for the wavelength of the second harmonic in the list. Then use the expression for wavelength from part 1 to solve for the length of the pipe. Remember that for a pipe open at one end, when we list the harmonics in order of increasing frequency, $n = 3$ for the second harmonic in the list.

Similar Questions

1) Where are the nodes located along a pipe, open at both ends, that is resonating at its third harmonic?

2) What is the wavelength of the fourth harmonic of a vibrating string with a length of 30 cm?

3) If we list the harmonics of a certain pipe in order of increasing frequency, the nodes of the third harmonic in the list are located at 40 cm intervals. What is the length of this pipe if one end of the pipe is closed?

Key Concepts

Chapter 9

Doppler effect

Wavelength

Frequency

Takeaways

As the detector approaches the source, the observed frequency will be higher than the emitted frequency, and when the detector moves away from the source, the observed frequency will be smaller than the emitted frequency. The same rule applies to the motion of the source. Therefore, when determining the right form of the Doppler equation, use the sign in the equation that will yield the appropriate observed frequency.

Doppler Effect

Two cars, car A and car B, are moving towards each other at 50 m/s when car B starts to beep its 475 Hz horn. Assuming that the speed of sound is 343 m/s, what is the wavelength of the horn as perceived by the driver of car A?

1) Identify this as a Doppler effect problem and determine the source and detector of the wave.

The source is the object that emits the wave: car B.

The detector or observer is the object that detects the wave: the person in car A.

Whenever you are given two objects with one emitting a wave and are asked to determine a perceived frequency or wavelength, the Doppler effect is involved.

2) Determine the effect of the velocity of the observer on the perceived frequency.

Every Doppler effect problem can be solved using the Doppler effect equation, which states that

$$f_o = f_s \left(\frac{v \pm v_o}{v \mp v_s} \right)$$

where f_o is the frequency observed, f_s is the frequency emitted by the source, v is the speed of the wave, v_o is the speed of the observer, and v_s is the speed of the source.

Remember: Isolate the Doppler effect into two parts: effect of velocity of source and effect of velocity of detector. When solving for what's asked, disregard the other variable.

In this problem, the observer is moving toward the source (car A is moving toward car B), and we are not concerned with the motion of the source, car B. Therefore, the observed frequency (f_o) must be greater than the emitted frequency (f_s), and the numerator must be greater than 1, so we must use the positive sign in the numerator of the problem.

$$f_o = f_s \left(\frac{v + v_o}{v \mp v_s} \right)$$

3) Determine the effect of the velocity of the source on the perceived frequency.

The source is also moving toward the detector (car B is moving toward car A). This should also make the perceived frequency greater than the emitted frequency. Thus, for f_o to be greater than f_s, the denominator must be smaller than 1. Hence, we must use the negative sign in the denominator.

$$f_o = f_s \left(\frac{v + v_o}{v - v_s} \right)$$

Alternate Method: If you look at the first equation in step 2, you will notice that in the denominator, the order of plus and minus signs is switched from the order in the numerator. This is written this way for a specific reason. When an object moves toward another object, the top sign is used. When an object moves away from an object, the bottom sign is used. In our case, because both the observer and source are moving toward each other, we used the top sign in both the numerator and the denominator.

4) Plug the values for the emitted frequency and the different velocities into the Doppler effect equation.

$$f_o = 475 \left(\frac{50 + 343}{50 - 343} \right) = 637 \, s^{-1}$$

5) Convert frequency to wavelength.

$$v = f\lambda$$
$$\lambda = \frac{v}{f}$$
$$\lambda = \frac{343 \, m/s}{637 \, s^{-1}}$$
$$\lambda = 0.54 \, m$$

Things to Watch Out For

Always separate Doppler questions into two parts, the effect of the source and the effect of the observer. Be careful in problems where the object and the source are moving in the same direction. If the source is ahead of the detector, the source will be moving away from the detector while the detector is moving toward the source, regardless of their speed. If the detector is ahead of the source, the detector will be moving away from the source while the source is moving toward the detector.

Similar Questions

1) Suppose a policeman traveling at 5 m/s is firing his gun at a rate of 20 bullets per minute while chasing a bank robber who is peddling his bicycle at 50 m/s. At what rate do the bullets reach the bank robber (use 500 m/s for the speed of a bullet)?

2) A bungee jumper yells in triumph at 350 Hz as he falls off a bridge toward a river at a rate of 20 m/s. What are the frequencies heard by the observers on the bridge and a boat on the river (the speed of sound is 343 m/s)?

Snell's Law

> A gold doubloon rests on a rock 1 m below the surface of the ocean. A glass-bottom boat passes over the area, and a passenger spots the coin at a 60° angle from the normal. If the glass layer is 3 cm thick, find the apparent depth of the coin. The indices of refraction are as follows: air, $n = 1$; glass, $n = 1.5$; salt water, $n = 1.34$.

1) Sketch the situation.

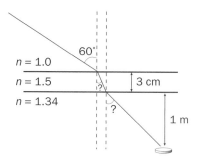

Light bends toward the normal when going from a medium with a lower refractive index to one with a higher refractive index.

Remember: *Our sketch need not be to scale; we use it to approximate what is going on and to keep track of the important data.*

2) Apply Snell's law.

Snell's law shows that light bends towards the normal (decreasing the angle) when it enters a medium with a higher refractive index. Here, we "plug-and-chug" through the formula to find the angles of light entry and exit for the two other substances.

$$n_1 \sin \theta_1 = n_2 \sin \theta_2$$
$$n_{air} \sin (\theta_a) = n_{glass} \sin (\theta_g)$$
$$(1) \sin 60° = (1.5) \sin (\theta_g)$$
$$\frac{(1) \sin 60°}{1.5} = \sin \theta_g \rightarrow \sin^{-1} 0.577 = \theta_g \approx 35°$$

$$n_{glass} \sin(\theta_g) = n_{water} \sin(\theta_w)$$

$$\frac{(1.5) \sin 35°}{1.34} = \sin \theta_w \rightarrow \sin^{-1} 0.642 = \theta_w \approx 40°$$

OR

To do this more quickly, realize that when light passes through multiple layers, the final angle can be determined merely by comparing the first and final media. The glass in this example alters the distance that the light travels in the *x*-direction but has no bearing on the final angle, because the light enters and exits the glass at the same angle.

$$n_{air} \sin(\theta_a) = n_{water} \sin(\theta_w)$$
$$(1) \sin 60° = (1.34) \sin(\theta_w)$$
$$\frac{[(1) \sin 60°]}{1.34} = \sin \theta_w \rightarrow \sin^{-1} 0.646 = \theta_w \approx 40°$$

3) Use trigonometry to determine how far the light goes.

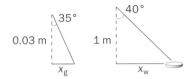

We know the thickness and depth of the glass and water, respectively, so we can use that information to determine how far the coin is from the ray of light the passenger sees. Light travels through a total of three media, but the distance of the observer from the glass doesn't actually matter. As long as he is looking 60° from the normal, he will see the coin. The trigonometry here is direct, using the relationship $\tan \theta = $ opposite/adjacent or, in this case, $\frac{x}{y}$. The triangle in the glass, then, is $\tan 35° = \frac{x_g}{0.03}$, and $x_g \approx 0.02$ m. The triangle in the water is solved the same way, and $x_w = 0.85$ m. The ray of light escapes the water and glass 0.87 meters from the coin.

4) Find the object's image.

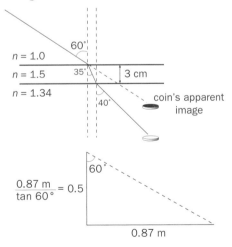

When the passenger sees the coin, his brain interprets light as a straight line. In other words, his brain doesn't consider the bending of light due to the refractive indices, and he perceives the coin to be closer than it actually is. We previously determined the **X** component of the light ray to be 0.87 m. The observer sees the coin at a 60° angle from the normal, so set up a new triangle with this angle. We are trying to find the apparent depth of the coin—the **Y** component of this triangle. Solving $\tan 60° = \frac{0.87}{y}$ gives us $y = 0.50$ m.

Similar Questions

1) A firefighter shines her flashlight through a smoky room at a 45° angle to a window. What angle does the beam of light make with the pane of glass on the outside? The indices of refraction are as follows: air, $n = 1$; glass, $n = 1.5$; smoke, $n = 1.1$.

2) A piece of gallium phosphide is frozen in ice. A beam of light is directed downward through the ice-gallium phosphide boundary at a 25° angle from the normal. The light emerges from the gallium phosphide 12.25 mm away from where it would have, had the solid been pure ice. Find the thickness of the gallium phosphide layer. Gallium phosphide has the highest known optical density (3.5), and ice has the third lowest (1.31).

3) A jeweler is appraising the stone on a ring. He aims a beam of light 35° from the normal at a flat edge of the gem. What angle would he observe in the gem if the stone were diamond ($n = 2.4$)? What angle would he observe if the stone were zircon ($n = 1.9$)?

Key Concepts

Chapter 10

Snell's law

Index of refraction

$n_1 \sin \theta_1 = n_2 \sin \theta_2$

Takeaways

Snell's law gives the relationship between angles of incidence and refraction for a wave striking an interface between two media with different indices of refraction.

Observe that total internal reflection only occurs when the wave is passing from a medium with a higher index of refraction (lower speed) to a medium with a lower index of refraction (higher speed). This is true because the sine cannot be greater than 1.

Things to Watch Out For

The angles in Snell's law are always measured relative to the surface normal.

Refraction

Light is refracted as it travels from a liquid into air unless the angle of incidence is greater than or equal to 51°; otherwise, no light is refracted. What is the index of refraction of the liquid?

1) Write Snell's law.
Use Snell's law to write an equation relating the indices of refraction in the two media to the angles in those media. The angles, θ_1 and θ_2, are measured relative to the surface normals.

$$n_1 \sin \theta_1 = n_2 \sin \theta_2$$
$$n_{liquid} \sin \theta_1 = n_{air} \sin \theta_2$$

2) Set $\theta_2 = 90°$.
When no light is refracted, total internal reflection is occurring. The critical angle is the angle at which light experiences total internal reflection. That is when θ_2 (the exit angle) is 90°. In this case, $\theta_1 = \theta_{critical}$. Solve for n_{liquid}.

$$n_{liquid} \sin \theta_1 = n_{air} \sin \theta_2$$
$$n_{liquid} \sin \theta_{critical} = n_{air}$$
$$n_{liquid} = \frac{n_{air}}{\sin \theta_{critical}}$$

3) Plug in values.
The index of refraction of air is almost 1. Because the critical angle is less than 90°, the sine of the critical angle will be less than 1. Any number divided by a number less than 1 will lead to a larger result.

$$n_{liquid} = \frac{n_{air}}{\sin \theta_{critical}}$$
$$n_{liquid} = \frac{1}{\sin 51°}$$
$$n_{liquid} = 1.29$$

Similar Questions

1) A light ray is incident on crown glass ($n = 1.52$) at an angle of 30° to the normal. It is incident from air. What is the angle of refraction?

2) What is the critical angle for a diamond ($n = 2.42$) to air boundary?

3) A light ray passes from air into an unknown substance. The incident angle is 23°, and the refracted angle is 14°. What is the index of refraction of the unknown substance?

Total Internal Reflection

Light is directed from air ($n = 1$) into a glass tube ($n = 1.3$). A section is shown below. What is the maximum angle x that ensures that no light escapes the horizontal sides of the tube?

$n = 1.0$

$n = 1.3$

Takeaways

Drawing a diagram is key to solving this problem. The angles must be measured relative to the normal.

Note that the formula for a critical angle can be derived from Snell's law by setting $\theta_2 = 90°$.

1) Draw a diagram of the ray traveling through the tube.

Draw a diagram of the ray entering the tube and reflecting off of the horizontal side. Draw the normal to each surface where the ray strikes, because the formulas for refraction are always in terms of the angles measured from the normal. Label the angles θ and y.

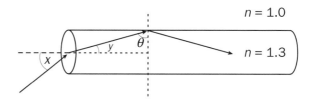

Remember: Light bends in toward the normal when entering a region of higher index of refraction.

2) Set θ equal to the critical angle.

If no light escapes from the horizontal side of the tube, then θ must be greater than or equal to the critical angle for the tube. This is referred to as total internal reflection. The critical angle is given by $\theta_c = \sin^{-1}\left(\dfrac{n_2}{n_1}\right)$, where n_2 is the index of refraction outside of the tube and n_1 is the index of refraction inside the tube.

$$\theta = \theta_c = \sin^{-1}\left(\frac{n_2}{n_1}\right) = \sin^{-1}\left(\frac{1}{1.3}\right) = 50.3°$$

Remember: Total internal reflection can only occur when going from a higher index to a lower index of refraction.

3) Find y from θ.

θ and y are two angles of a right triangle. The sum of the angles of a triangle is $180°$. Solve for angle y.

$$\theta + y + 90 = 180$$
$$y = 90 - \theta = 39.7°$$

4) Use Snell's law to find x.

Snell's law relates the indices of refraction for the two materials to the angles (measured relative to the normal) on both sides of the interface. This law is used to determine what happens when a light ray refracts. Plug in the value for y from step 3 and solve for x.

generic: $n_1 \sin \theta_1 = n_2 \sin \theta_2$
$(1) \sin x = (1.3) \sin 39.7°$
$x = \sin^{-1} [(1.3) \sin 39.7°] = 56.1°$

Similar Questions

1) The critical angle for a certain interface is $35°$. If the index of refraction of one material is 1.6, what is the index of refraction of the other material?

2) Light from air strikes a translucent plastic material. If the light strikes at an angle of $30°$ to the material and bends $15°$, what is the index of refraction of the plastic?

3) Light enters a glass slab ($n = 1.33$) from a vacuum. After traveling through the glass, it travels through a fluid ($n = 1.6$), through another section of glass, and then back into a vacuum. The two glass and fluid sections are parallel to each other. If the light enters the first glass slab at an angle of $35°$ to the normal, at what angle does it leave the final glass slab?

Key Concepts

Chapter 10

Power

Wavelength

Frequency

Planck's constant

Diffraction

Interference

Photon energy

Diffraction and Interference Patterns

A laser beam emits 10^{17} photons per second and has a power of 100 mW. The beam is incident on a single slit of width 0.2 mm. A screen is positioned 1 meter beyond the slit. What is the distance between the first minimum on the left and the first minimum on the right of the central maximum? ($h = 6.6 \times 10^{-34}$ J·s.)

1) Find the amount of energy in 1 photon.

   100 mW = 0.1 W = 0.1 J/s

   $$\frac{0.1 \text{ J/s}}{10^{17} \text{ photons/s}} = 1 \times 10^{-18} \text{ J/photon}$$

Use dimensional analysis to find the amount of energy in one photon. Watts can be written as joules/second. Divide this by the number of photons emitted per second to find the number of joules per photon.

Takeaways

Any problem involving light can feature questions about power, wavelength, frequency, and energy. Solving this problem requires an understanding of all of these topics before you can get to the diffraction step.

In most diffraction problems, you will use the small-angle approximation for sin (θ) and tan (θ).

2) Find the wavelength of the laser beam.

Use the energy of the photon to determine the wavelength from the formula $E = hf$. Use the relation $c = f\lambda$ to get the equation in terms of wavelength, λ.

$$E = hf = \frac{hc}{\lambda}$$

$$\lambda = \frac{hc}{E} = \frac{(6.6 \times 10^{-34})(3 \times 10^{8})}{(10^{-18})} = 1.98 \times 10^{-7} \text{ m}$$

3) Find the angle to the first diffraction minima.

Use the general formula relating the angle of the diffraction minima, θ, to the slit width, a, and wavelength, λ. For the first minima, $m = 1$.

   generic: $a \sin \theta = m\lambda$, $m = 1, 2, 3, \ldots$
   $a = 0.2 \times 10^{-3}$ m
   $m = 1$
   $(0.2 \times 10^{-3}) \sin \theta_1 = (1)(1.98 \times 10^{-7})$
   $\sin \theta_1 = 9.9 \times 10^{-4}$

When angles are extremely small, $\sin \theta \approx \tan \theta \approx \theta$, in radians.

   $\theta_1 \approx 9.9 \times 10^{-4}$

4) Find the distance between the minima.

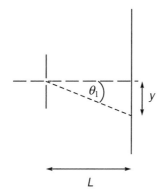

From the diagram, we can see that the angle θ_1 to the first minimum is related by trigonometry to the distance to the minimum along the screen, y, and the distance from the screen to the slit, L. Once again, $\tan \theta \approx \theta$ because the angle is very small. The distance between the two minima equals $2y$. Solve for $2y$.

$$\tan \theta_1 = \frac{y}{L}$$
$$\theta_1 \approx \frac{y}{L}$$
$$y = L\theta_1$$
$$d = 2y = 2L\theta_1 = 2(1)(9.9 \times 10^{-4}) = 1.98 \times 10^{-3}$$
$$d = 1.98 \text{ mm}$$

Similar Questions

1) At what angle is the third diffraction minimum for a beam of 632.8 nm wavelength light incident on a single slit of width 10 μm?

2) What is the angular separation between the first two minima for a double-slit interference pattern when the slit separation is 0.1 mm and the wavelength of the light is 550.1 nm?

3) A single-slit interference pattern has an angle of 1×10^{-5} radians to the first interference minimum. If the wavelength of the light is known to be 714.5 nm, what is the width of the slit?

Chapter 10

Lenses

$$\frac{1}{f} = \frac{1}{o} + \frac{1}{i}$$

$$m = -\frac{i}{o}$$

Takeaways

This question is posed in an unusual way—it does not ask for the object or image distance specifically. However, you should realize that on almost all quantitative lens (or mirror) problems, you will need to solve for the object or image distance or both. When in doubt, write the magnification formula and lens formula and try to combine them.

Ray diagrams, although helpful conceptually, cannot be used to find exact values. A thorough understanding of the mathematical basis for these problems is essential.

Converging Lens

A converging lens with a focal length of 30 cm is used to project an image that is 5 times as large as the object onto a screen. To produce this image, how far from the screen is the object?

1) Write the formula for magnification.

$$m = -\frac{i}{o} = -5$$

For a single-lens system, the magnification is always the negative of the image distance over the object distance. The image is cast onto a screen, meaning that it cannot be a virtual image; it must be a real image. Virtual images cannot be projected, which is why they are called virtual. Because a single lens can either create a virtual, erect image or a real, inverted image, the image must be real and inverted. This means that $m = -5$.

Remember: A negative magnification indicates an inverted image.

2) Write the lens formula.

$$\frac{1}{f} = \frac{1}{o} + \frac{1}{i}$$

$$\frac{1}{30} = \frac{1}{o} + \frac{1}{i}$$

Understanding the sign conventions of this formula is the most important thing in this problem. Always make o, the distance from the object to the lens, a positive number; f is positive for converging lenses, negative for diverging lenses.

For a real (and thus inverted) image, i is always positive, and thus m is always negative (as long as you have taken o to be positive). For a virtual (and thus erect) image, i is always negative, and thus m is always positive.

If i is positive, the image is on the other side of the lens from the object. If i is negative, the image is on the same side as the object.

3) Solve the magnification formula and substitute it into the lens formula.

$$-\frac{i}{o} = -5$$

$$i = 5o$$

$$\frac{1}{30} = \frac{1}{o} + \frac{1}{5o}$$

$$\frac{1}{30} = \frac{6}{5o}$$

$$\frac{5o}{6} = 30$$

$$o = \frac{180}{5} = 36 \text{ cm}$$

Remember: *We know that we are looking for a positive object distance. If you get a negative number here, you have made an error somewhere along the line.*

MCAT Pitfall: *We are not done. The question asks for the distance between the object and the screen, not the object and the lens. We need to do more calculations to get the answer.*

4) Solve for the image distance.

Use the expression for magnification from step 1 with the object distance we solved for in step 3.

$$m = -\frac{i}{o}$$

$$-5 = -\frac{i}{36}$$

$$i = 180 \text{ cm}$$

Remember: *We know that we have to get a positive image distance. If you get a negative number here, you have made an error somewhere along the line.*

5) Add the image and object distance.

The question asks for the distance between the object and the screen or, in other words, the distance between the object and image location. This is simply $o + i$.

$$o + i = 36 + 180 = 216 \text{ cm}$$

Remember: *A real image always appears on the other side of the lens from the object. A virtual image appears on the same side as the object.*

> ## Things to Watch Out For
>
> The biggest mistake on this problem is sign errors caused by a misunderstanding of the sign convention for these formulas. Know it well. Practice!
>
> Many test takers do not understand the physical difference between a real and virtual image: A virtual image cannot be projected. To project an image, we would have to place a screen where the outgoing light rays converge. For a virtual image, though, the outgoing light rays never converge—they only *appear* to converge at the image location.
>
> Also, many test takers do not realize that a single lens cannot produce a virtual, inverted image, nor can it produce a real, erect image. Use these facts to your advantage.

Similar Questions

1) What is the focal length of a lens that produces a real, inverted image 45 cm away from the lens for an object placed 20 cm from the lens?

2) A 2 cm-tall slide is placed 10 cm in front of a diverging lens with a focal length of 20 cm. What are the location and size of the resulting image?

3) A lens produces an inverted image that is the same size as the object when the object is placed 20 cm away from the lens. What is the type and focal length of the lens?

Key Concepts

Chapter 11

Energy levels in hydrogen atoms

Wavelength/frequency

Energy units

Energy Emission from Electrons

An electron in a hydrogen atom moves from the third energy level to the ground state. What is the wavelength of the emitted photon?
$(1 \text{ eV} = 1.6 \times 10^{-19} \text{ J}; h = 6.63 \times 10^{-34} \text{ J} \cdot \text{s}.)$

1) Determine the difference in energy between the energy levels.

For hydrogen, $E = \dfrac{-13.6 \text{ eV}}{n^2}$

$E_1 = \dfrac{-13.6}{(1)^2} = -13.6 \text{ eV}$

$E_3 = \dfrac{-13.6}{(3)^2} = -1.51 \text{ eV}$

$\Delta E = E_3 - E_1 = 12.09 \text{ eV}$

Takeaways

Remember that the energy of the photon must be equal to the energy lost by the electron. This is due to the conservation of energy. Alternately, when a photon is absorbed by an atom, the gain in energy of the electron is the energy of the photon.

The energy values for hydrogen energy levels are given by $E = \dfrac{-13.6 \text{ eV}}{n^2}$, where E will be in electron-volts (eV). The ground state of the atom corresponds to $n = 1$. As the principle quantum number n increases, so does the energy of the electron. As the limit n goes to infinity, note that $E = 0$. Physically, this represents an atom that is completely ionized.

Remember: One eV is the amount of energy required to move an electron through a potential difference of 1 volt. Remember that it is related to joules by the charge of an electron, 1.6×10^{-19}.

2) Find the wavelength of the photon from the energy lost by the electron.

$E = hf = \dfrac{hc}{\lambda}.$

This is a combination of the equations $E = hf$ and $\lambda f = c$: $hc = 1{,}240 \text{ eV} \cdot \text{nm}.$
Therefore,

$\lambda = \dfrac{1{,}240 \text{ eV} \cdot \text{nm}}{12.09 \text{ eV}}$

$\lambda = 103 \text{ nm}$

On Test Day, you can quickly relate photon energy and wavelength by remembering that harmless radio waves with low energy have very large wavelengths; thus the inverse relationship.

Things to Watch Out For

Remember that "completely ionized" means that an electron has an energy equal to zero (this corresponds to an infinite quantum number n).

For any photon, the energy is related to the frequency by $E = hf$. The energy of the photon must be equal to the energy lost by the electron in the transition. Use $c = f\lambda$ to convert to wavelength. Remember that for any photon, $E = \dfrac{1{,}240}{\lambda}$, when E is in eV and λ is in nm. Knowing this will drastically reduce your time spent on these problems.

Similar Questions

1) What energy level is occupied by an electron of a hydrogen atom, which was initially in the ground state, when a photon of wavelength 55 nm is absorbed by the atom?

2) A photon of frequency 6×10^{14} Hz is ejected from an atom when an electron changes energy states. What was the change in energy of the electron, in joules?

3) What is the maximum wavelength that a photon must have to cause a ground-state electron in a hydrogen atom to be completely ejected from the atom?

Nuclear Reactions

A neutral U-238 atom absorbs a neutron and then immediately undergoes two alpha decays, three beta decays, one positron decay, and two gamma decays. Describe the resulting nucleus using isotopic notation. The resulting atom is an isotope of what element?

1) Find the mass number and atomic number of the parent nucleus.

Z = atomic number, A = mass number $\rightarrow {}_Z^A X$

$Z = 92, A = 238 \rightarrow {}_{92}^{238}U$

The notation U-238 indicates a uranium atom with a mass of 238. The letter is always the element symbol, as listed on the periodic table. From the periodic table, the atomic number of uranium is 92. All uranium atoms, by definition, have 92 protons. We call this the Z-number.

The mass number, A, is the sum of the number of protons and neutrons. The mass number is given in the question because a given element may have many different isotopes, which all have the same number of protons but vary in the number of neutrons they contain.

The shorthand notion, called isotopic notation, is ${}_Z^A X$, where X is the element name, A is the mass number, and Z is the atomic number.

MCAT Pitfall: A *is the mass number, not the atomic number. This is counterintuitive.*

---

2) Find the result of the neutron absorption.

${}_Z^A X + {}_0^1 n \rightarrow {}_{Z}^{A+1} X'$

${}_{92}^{238}U + {}_0^1 n \rightarrow {}_{92}^{239}U$

A neutron has a mass number of 1 and an atomic number of 0 because it has no protons. In these problems, write the isotopic notations as a mathematical formula. The rule is that the Z numbers must add up to be the same on each side, as well as the A numbers.

The result of the absorption is the formation of a different isotope of uranium.

---

3) Find the result of the alpha decays.

${}_Z^A X \rightarrow {}_{Z-2}^{A-4} X + {}_2^4 He$

$$A' = A - 2(4) = 239 - 8 = 231$$
$$Z' = Z - 2(2) = 92 - 4 = 88$$

An alpha particle is a helium nucleus: two protons and two neutrons. Thus, for a single alpha decay, **A** decreases by 4 and **Z** decreases by 2. Because there are two alpha decays, multiply these numbers by 2 to find the change in the **Z** and **A** numbers.

Remember: *An alpha particle can be written as $^4_2\alpha$ or ^4_2He.*

4) Find the result of the beta decays.

$$^A_Z X \rightarrow ^A_{Z+1} X' + ^0_{-1}\beta$$
$$A' = A = 231$$
$$Z' = Z + 3(1) = 91$$

A β^--particle is also called a β-particle and is just an electron. In a beta decay, a β-particle is ejected from the nucleus, whereas a neutron is transformed into a proton. Thus, the mass number A stays the same, while the Z number of the daughter nucleus increases by 1. Because there are three beta decays, multiply by 3 to find the result.

Remember: *A β-particle actually increases the atomic number of the daughter nucleus. You can remember this by noting that it is really an electron and is the only type of decay to feature a negative number on the particle.*

5) Find the result of the positron decay.

$$^A_Z X \rightarrow ^A_{Z-1} X' + ^0_{+1}\beta$$
$$A' = A = 231$$
$$Z' = Z - 1 = 90$$

A positron decay is the exact opposite of a beta decay and is often called β^+ decay. A positron (an anti-electron) is ejected from the nucleus, and a proton turns into a neutron. Thus, the mass number stays the same, and the Z number decreases by 1.

6) Find the result of the gamma decays.

$$^A_Z X \rightarrow ^A_Z X' + \gamma$$
$$A' = A = 231$$
$$Z' = Z = 90$$

In gamma decay, a gamma ray (an electromagnetic wave) is ejected from the nucleus. There is no change in atomic number or mass number.

Takeaways

It is important to know the decay types and the decay particles themselves. Once you have these down, the problems are relatively simple.

Things to Watch Out For

Fission occurs when a nucleus splits into smaller nuclei. Fusion is the combination of smaller nuclei to form a larger particle. Transmutation, or radioactive decay resulting in a change of atomic number, is a specific type of fission reaction. Beta particles (electrons) and positrons are very easy to confuse; make sure that you understand the difference.

Similar Questions:

1. Is it possible for neptunium to transmute to an isotope of lead through a series of alpha decays?

2. How many beta particles are ejected when polonium-214 decays to radon-214?

3. Uranium-226 decays radioactively into radon-218 through two positron decays and an unknown number of alpha decays. How many alpha particles must be emitted in this reaction?

7) Write in isotopic notation.

$$^{231}_{90}\text{Th}$$

The resulting nucleus has an atomic number of 90 and a mass number of 231. Thus, it is an isotope of thorium with $231 - 90 = 141$ neutrons.

---

8) Here is an alternate (faster) solution.

$$A' = 238 + 1 - 2(4) = 231$$
$$Z' = 92 - 2(2) + 3(1) - 1 = 90$$

If you are comfortable with the decay types, write one equation for A and one for Z and solve directly, based on the changes to A and Z for each event. Solving the problem this way is your goal for Test Day.

High-Yield Problems continue on the next page

Key Concepts

Chapter 12

Mass defect

Mass Defect

Calculate the nuclear mass defect of cesium-137 if it has a mass of 136.87522 amu. ($m_e = 5.5 \times 10^{-4}$ amu, $m_p = 1.00728$ amu, $m_n = 1.00867$ amu)

1) Tally the number of protons, electrons, and neutrons for cesium.
55 protons + 55 electrons
# of neutrons = 137 − 55 = 82

To find the number of protons, look up cesium on the periodic table. It is element number 55. This means that it has 55 protons. We assume that it is a neutral atom, which means there are also 55 electrons. The 137 indicates that the number of protons plus neutrons is 137. Subtract 55 from 137 to find the number of neutrons.

Takeaways

The mass defect is the mass converted into energy when the atom is made from its components. A larger mass defect creates a larger binding energy. The greater the binding energy per nucleon, the more stable the nucleus.

2) Add up the components.

$$55 \times 1.00728 \text{ amu}$$
$$55 \times 0.00055 \text{ amu}$$
$$+ \ 82 \times 1.00867 \text{ amu}$$
$$138.14159 \text{ amu}$$

Find the total mass of the components of the atom using the masses for each particle given in the question.

Things to Watch Out For

Make sure that your mass defect is a positive number.

3) Calculate mass defect.
mass defect = sum of components − mass of atom
$$= 138.14159 \text{ amu} − 136.87522 \text{ amu}$$
$$= 1.26637 \text{ amu}$$

The mass defect is the difference between the mass of the components and the actual mass of the atom.

Remember: The mass defect will always be a positive value because the sum of the components is greater than the mass of the isotope.

Similar Questions

1) Calculate the mass defect of strontium-84 at 83.9134 amu.

2) Calculate the mass defect of mercury-204 at 203.9735 amu.

3) Calculate the mass defect of tin-122 at 121.9034 amu.

Solutions to Similar Questions

Kinematic Motion

1. The final velocity of the bottle is 2.8 m/s in both the *x*- and *y*-directions.
2. The pre-1982 penny's acceleration after 5 seconds is 9.8 m/s². The post-1982 penny will travel 593 m before the first penny hits the ground.
3. The baseball has been in flight for 0.398 s when it has traveled 50 cm.

Projectile Motion and Air Resistance

1. The rock loses $530m$ J of energy (where *m* is the mass of the rock), or 54.1% of its initial potential energy, due to air resistance.
2. The object with the higher final velocity has 69% more kinetic energy than the other object at landing.
3. The projectile has lost 2% of its initial energy when it reaches its maximum height.

Universal Law of Gravitation

1. The force of gravity acting on m_1 from m_2 is 2×10^{-8} N.
2. At 1.36×10^7 m above Earth's surface, the acceleration due to gravity is 10% of that at sea level.
3. To have the same acceleration due to gravity as the moon, Earth would have to have a mass of 1.03×10^{24} kg.

Terminal Velocity

1. For the ball, $b = 3.3 \times 10^{-2} \dfrac{\text{N} \cdot s^2}{\text{m}^2}$.
2. The terminal velocity of the block is 0.82 m/s.
3. The ratio of the terminal velocities for ball 1 and ball 2 is $\dfrac{v_1}{v_2} = 1.3$.

Dimensional Analysis

1. The units of *G* in Newton's law of gravitation are $\dfrac{\text{N} \cdot \text{m}^2}{\text{kg}^2} = \dfrac{\text{m}^3}{s^2 \cdot \text{kg}}$.
2. The stronger the electric field, the stronger the force, and the faster the dipole oscillates. Hence, the period is a *decreasing* function of the electric field, so the given expression is *unreasonable*.
3. The units of the permeability of free space, μ_0, are $\dfrac{\text{T} \cdot \text{m}}{\text{A}} = \dfrac{\text{kg} \cdot \text{m}^3}{\text{C}^2}$.

Two Connected Masses

1. The acceleration of the 1 kg mass is 4.9 m/s².
2. The coefficient of friction necessary to keep the system at rest is $\mu_s = \dfrac{m_B}{m_A}$.
3. The 5 kg mass needs to fall 7.65 m to reach a velocity of 10 m/s.

Inclined Plane

1. The minimum coefficient of static friction necessary to keep the block at rest is $\mu_s = 1$.
2. The highest point reached by the block is 0.24 m.
3. The velocity of the block after 5 seconds is 24.5 m/s down the plane.

Pulley With Multiple Masses

1. The tension between the 10 kg and 15 kg masses is 127.2 N.
2. The tension on the rope between the 10 kg and 30 kg masses is 200.5 N.
3. The magnitude and direction of acceleration of the 30 kg object is 0.89 m/s^2 straight down.

Rotational Equilibrium

1. Assuming the beam is massless, the fulcrum should be placed between block A and block B at a distance of 39.3 cm from block B.
2. Assuming the beam is massless, the fulcrum should be placed 1.5 m from the right end of the bar (directly under the middle mass).
3. In this configuration, the beam *must* rotate, regardless of the mass of mass 2. In other words, there is no mass of mass 2 that will prevent the beam from rotating.

Uniform Circular Motion

1. The minimum radius that the cyclist can ride without slipping is 4.1 m.
2. The tension in the string is 56.4 N.
3. The race car driver feels a force that is 29 times the force of gravity.

Power and Energy

1. The amount of heat given off by the light bulb in 1 hour is 213,840 J.
2. The amount of heat dissipated in 10 minutes by the resistor is 750 J.
3. The power of the laser is 37 W.

Circular Loops

1. The normal force at the bottom of the loop is 88.2 N.
2. To have an acceleration of $4g$ at the top of the loop, the block needs to travel at 28 m/s at the bottom of the ramp.
3. The speed of the block as it exits the loop is 35.9 m/s.

Conservation of Momentum

1. The new model of the car with a longer crumple zone has a period of impact that has been increased by 300%. The impulse on the car and its passengers has not changed.

2. The velocity of the first stone after it collides with the second is 1 m/s.

3. The speed of the bullet prior to impact is 965 m/s.

Elastic Collisions

1. Kinetic energy is conserved in an elastic collision. If one nucleus is moving faster than the other, it loses some kinetic energy (as velocity) and the other gains some when they collide. If the nuclei are moving at the same speed, there should be no transfer of energy during the collision.

2. The kinetic energy of the second bead immediately after impact is 97.4 kJ.

3. The kinetic energy of the system is 5.2 kJ. The alpha male experiences a 41.5% increase in speed after the collision.

Collisions and Energy

1. The 10 kg block reaches a height of 0.051 m. The 50 kg block reaches a height of 0.883 m.

2. The momentum of the system immediately after the throw is zero.

3. The speed of ball 2 after impact $= 1.6v_1 = 2v_2$.

Specific Gravity

1. The specific gravity of the substance is 1,020.

2. The specific gravity of the fluid is $\frac{4}{3}$.

3. The buoyant force in water of the block is 3.5 N.

Hydraulic Lift

1. The radius of the other cylinder should be 15.8 cm.

2. The large piston moves 0.5 cm.

3. The volume of fluid moved is 0.4 m³.

Gauge Pressure

1. The density of the solution is 20,612 kg/m³.

2. The pressure at a depth of 50 m below the surface of a freshwater pool is 591 kPa.

3. Gauge pressure increases by a factor of $\frac{4}{3}$ when going from a depth of 30 m to 40 m.

Hydrostatics

1. The tension in the string is $32\frac{4}{3}$ N.

2. The density of the cube is $\frac{2}{3}$ g/cm³.

3. The initial acceleration of the cork is 49 m/s².

Hydrodynamics

1. $v_1 = \sqrt{\dfrac{\rho v_0^2 - 4P_0}{\rho}}$, where ρ is the density of the fluid, v_0 is the fluid speed at a point in the pipe where pressure $= P_0$, and v_1 is the fluid speed at the point in the pipe where pressure $= 3P_0$.
2. The ratio of fluid velocities in the two pipes is $v_B : v_A = 4:1$.
3. The water will exit the tank at a velocity of 3.13 m/s.

Net Electric Field with Multiple Sources

1. By symmetry, the electric field halfway between the two protons is zero.
2. There is no point between the proton and electron at which the electric field is zero.
3. The electric field at the center of one of the edges of the triangle is +126 J.

Charge Distribution and Work

1. The amount of work done by tripling the distance between the charges is 1.2 J.
2. The amount of work done by assembling a square-shaped charge distribution is 1.22 J.
3. The change in potential energy of the system if charge 1 is removed is +126 J.

Voltage and Energy

1. The velocity of the ball after falling from a height of 10 m is 14.1 m/s.
2. The final speed of the alpha particle is 1.4×10^5 m/s.
3. The velocity of each proton when they are very far apart is 3.8×10^3 m/s.

Electrostatics and Velocity

1. The proton's final speed is 1.38×10^5 m/s.
2. The amount of work done by moving an electron 10 nm away from a hydrogen nucleus is 2.07×10^{-19} J.
3. The voltage required to accelerate protons to a speed of 10^4 m/s is 0.52 V.

Electric Force

1. The magnitude of the electrostatic force experienced by the positive charge is 1.36 N.
2. The separation between the two point charges is 0.4012 m.
3. The charge of point charge b is 6.796×10^{-9} C.

Electron between Charged Plates

1. The capacitance of the capacitor is 4.4×10^{10} F, which is a huge capacitance!
2. The initial velocity of the electron was 1.9×10^7 m/s.
3. The separation between the plates of the capacitor is 1.6×10^{-16} m.

Electrostatic Impulse

1. The potential energy of the system is 4.38×10^{-25} J.
2. The force on the test charge is 4.8×10^{-14} N.
3. V_a is closer to the positive point charge that creates the field.

Photoelectric Effect

1. For a photon to induce a current in a metal with a work function of 2 eV, the minimum frequency it needs to have is 4.8×10^{14} Hz.
2. The kinetic energy of the ejected electron is 1.9×10^{-18} J.
3. The frequency of incident radiation required is 1.5×10^{15} Hz, and the power required is 10^{-14} W.

Magnetic Field

1. For a set of points outside the loop, the magnetic field is zero.
2. The net magnetic field halfway between the two wires is $B = 0$.
3. The magnitude and direction of the magnetic field at the center of the loops is 2.1×10^{-7} into the page.

Magnetic Force

1. When the electrons move at an angle of 90° to the magnetic field, a force of 2.4×10^{-12} N acts on the elctrons; when they move at an angle of 45°, the force is 1.7×10^{-12} N.
2. The force felt on the electron is 6×10^{-16} N.
3. The magnitude and direction of the force experienced by the proton is 2.4×10^{-15} N up the page.

Parallel Plate Capacitor

1. If the voltage is doubled, the charge stored on the capacitor is 2 μC.
2. The total charge stored by the second capacitor is 1 μC.
3. The separation between the plates should be decreased by a factor of $\frac{5}{6}$.

Capacitor Networks

1. The total charge stored in the circuit is 3.6×10^{-5} C.
2. The voltage across C_5 is 0.23 V.
3. The voltage of the battery is 2.5 V.

Resistor Circuits

1. The voltage across R_4 is 7.5 V.
2. The current through the battery is 1.875 A.
3. The resistance of R_6 is 1.8 Ω.

Energy and Springs

1. The maximum height achieved by the block is 0.0051 m.
2. The amount of work required to alter the compression of the spring is 1,200 J.
3. The ratio of the maximum compression of the spring with the 5 kg mass to that of the spring with the 2 kg mass is 5:2.

Acceleration of a Pendulum

1. The magnitude and direction of the acceleration of the car is 144 m/s^2 toward the center of the circle.
2. The block travels at an angle of 151.9° from the horizontal.
3. The acceleration of the sled is 17.3 m/s^2 at 68.5° east of North.

Dampened Harmonic Motion

1. The frequency of the spring-mass system diminishes by 0.0125%.
2. The period of oscillation of the curled filament is 0.51 s. When heated, 98.9% of the original energy of the filament is lost in 1.5 minutes.

Standing Waves

1. For a pipe open at both ends that is resonating at its third harmonic, the nodes are located at points $\frac{1}{6}$, $\frac{1}{2}$, and $\frac{5}{6}$ of the way along the length of the pipe.
2. The wavelength of the fourth harmonic of the string is 0.15 m.
3. The length of the pipe is 1 m if the end of the pipe is closed.

Doppler Effect

1. The bullets reach the bank robber at a rate of 18 bullets/minute.
2. The perceived frequency by the observers on the bridge is 330.7 Hz. The perceived frequency by the observers on the boat is 371.7 Hz.

Snell's Law

1. The angle that the beam of light makes with the pane of glass on the outside is 51.1°.
2. The thickness of the gallium phosphide layer is 42.2 mm.
3. The jeweler observes an angle of 13.8° if the stone is diamond and an angle of 17.6° if the stone is zircon.

Refraction

1. The angle of refraction in the crown glass is 19.2°.
2. The critical angle for the diamond-air boundary is 24.4°.
3. The index of refraction of the unknown substance is 1.62.

Total Internal Reflection

1. The index of refraction of the other material is 2.79.
2. The index of refraction of the plastic is 1.22.
3. Light leaves the final glass slab at an angle of 35°.

Diffraction and Interference Patterns

1. The third diffraction minimum is at an angle of 0.19 rad.
2. The angular separation between the first two minima is 0.0055 rad.
3. The width of the slit is 0.07145 m.

Converging Lens

1. The focal length of the lens is 14 cm.
2. The image is located $6\frac{2}{3}$ cm in front of the lens. It is $1\frac{1}{3}$ cm tall.
3. The inverted image the same size as the object is produced by a converging lens with $f = 10$ cm.

Energy Emission from Electrons

1. When a photon of 55 nm is absorbed by the atom, the electron is completely ejected from the hydrogen atom, so it does not occupy any of the atom's energy levels.
2. The change in energy of the electron is -4×10^{-19} J.
3. The maximum wavelength that a photon must have to completely eject a ground state electron from a hydrogen atom is 91 nm.

Nuclear Reactions

1. It is not possible for neptunium to transmute to lead through a series of alpha decays. Each alpha decay reduces the atom's atomic number by 2, but the difference in neptunium and lead's atomic numbers (11) is not divisible by 2.
2. When polonium-214 decays to radon-214, 2 beta particles are ejected.
3. Two alpha particles must be emitted when uranium-226 decays to radon-218.

Mass Defect

1. The mass defect of strontium-84 is 0.76206 amu.
2. The mass defect of mercury-204 is 1.68398 amu.
3. The mass defect of tin-122 is 1.08484 amu.

Art Credits for Physics

Figure 1.1—Image credited to Melissa Thomas. From The Great Cosmic Roller-Coaster Ride by Cliff Burgess and Fernando Quevedo. Copyright © 2007 by Scientific American, Inc. All rights reserved.

Page 46—Sidebar. Image credited to Jared Schneidman Designs. From Friction at the Atomic Scale by Jacqueline Krim. Copyright © 1996 by Scientific American, Inc. All rights reserved.

Page 148 Sidebar—Image credited to George Retseck. From Working Knowledge: The Flight of the Frisbee by Louis A. Bloomfield. Copyright © 1999 by Scientific American, Inc. All rights reserved.

Figure 5.3—Image credited to Kent Snodgrass/Precision Graphics. From Working Knowledge: Jet Engines by Mark Fischetti. Copyright © 2006 by Scientific American, Inc. All rights reserved.

Figure 7.1—Image credited to Slim Films. From Spintronics by David D. Awschalom, Michael E. Flatté and Nitin Sarnarth. Copyright © 2002 by Scientific American, Inc. All rights reserved.

Page 261 Sidebar—Image credited to Samuel Velasco; Source: Bose Corporation. From Working Knowledge: Noise-Canceling Headphones by Mark Fischetti. Copyright © 2005 by Scientific American, Inc. All rights reserved.

Page 268 Sidebar—Image credited to David Emmite. From Rulers of Light by Steven Cundiff, Jun Ye and John Hall. Copyright © 2008 by Scientific American, Inc. All rights reserved.

Figure 10.2—Image credited to Laurie Grace. From Ultrashort-Pulse Lasers: Big Payoffs in a Flash by John-Mark Hopkins and Wilson Sibbett. Copyright © 2000 by Scientific American, Inc. All rights reserved.

Figure 10.8—Image credited to Melissa Thomas. From The Quest for the Superlens by John B. Pendry and David R. Smith. Copyright © 2006 by Scientific American, Inc. All rights reserved.

Page 305 Sidebar—Image credited to Samuel Velasco. From News Scan: All Screwed Up by George Musser. Copyright © 2003 by Scientific American, Inc. All rights reserved.

Page 307 Sidebar—Image credited to Michael Goodman. From The Duality of Matter and Light by Berthold-Georg Englert, Marlan O. Scully and Herbert Walther. Copyright © 1994 by Scientific American, Inc. All rights reserved.

Figure 11.2—Image credited to Alfred T. Kamajian. From Everyday Einstein by Philip Yam. Copyright © 2004 by Scientific American, Inc. All rights reserved.

Figure 11.3—Image credited to George Retseck. From The Dark Ages of the Universe by Abraham Loeb. Copyright © 2006 by Scientific American. All rights reserved.

Part II
Practice Sections

INSTRUCTIONS FOR TAKING THE PRACTICE SECTIONS

Before taking each Practice Section, find a quiet place where you can work uninterrupted. Take a maximum of 70 minutes per section (52 questions) to get accustomed to the length and scope.

Keep in mind that the actual MCAT will not feature a section made up of Physics questions alone, but rather a Physical Sciences section made up of both Physics and General Chemistry questions. Use the following three sections to hone your Physics skills.

Good luck!

Practice Section 1

Time—70 minutes

QUESTIONS 1–52

Directions: Most of the questions in the following Physics Practice Section are organized into groups, with a descriptive passage preceding each group of questions. Study the passage, then select the single best answer to the question in each group. Some of the questions are not based on a descriptive passage; you must also select the best answer to these questions. If you are unsure of the best answer, eliminate the choices that you know are incorrect, then select an answer from the choices that remain.

PASSAGE I (QUESTIONS 1–9)

Valence electrons are much more likely to be ejected from an atom than are inner electrons. In the rare cases where an inner electron is ejected, it leaves a hole in the energy level where it originally resided. This hole is quickly filled by an electron from one of the outer energy levels, which drops to a lower energy level and releases the excess energy in the form of an x-ray photon. Occasionally this photon strikes another electron and causes it to be ejected; this second electron is known as an *Auger electron* (Figure 1).

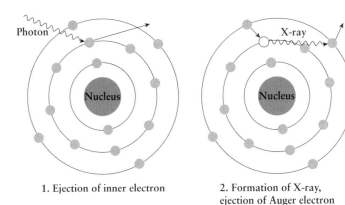

1. Ejection of inner electron

2. Formation of X-ray, ejection of Auger electron

Figure 1

Until the 1950s, Auger electrons were considered to be little more than a source of noise in x-ray measurements. In recent years, however, scientists have used Auger electron spectroscopy (AES) to identify an element by measuring the energy of its Auger electrons. AES is effective for this purpose because each element features a unique spectrum of Auger emissions.

1. Inner electrons are more difficult to eject than outer electrons are because the Bohr energy of outer electrons is
   A. closer to the energy of the photon.
   B. closer to zero.
   C. a more positive value.
   D. a more negative value.

2. Whenever a hole is created by ejected lower-energy electrons, higher-energy electrons drop down to fill this hole because the
   A. emission of an x-ray causes a decrease in the electron's energy.
   B. atom must retain a net neutral charge.
   C. electron is naturally attracted by the gravitational force of the nucleus.
   D. electron is more stable at lower energy.

3. Which of the following transitions is most likely to
produce an Auger electron?

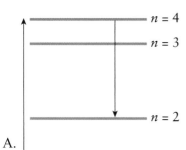

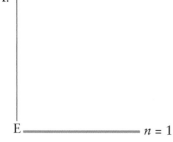

A.

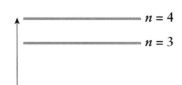

B.

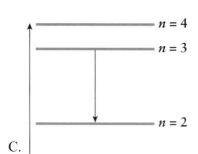

C.

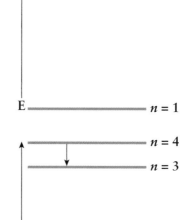

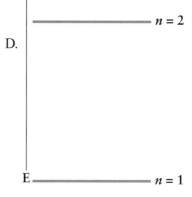

D.

4. An electron carrying 10 eV of energy moves from point A to point B. What is the energy of the accompanying x-ray photon?

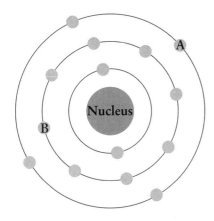

A. 15 eV
B. 10 eV
C. 7.5 eV
D. 5 eV

5. If scientists discovered a new technique to eliminate Auger electrons, how would this most likely impact the measurement of the energy of x-rays?

A. Decreased error in measurements
B. Decreased variability in measurements
C. Improved sensitivity of equipment
D. Improved resolution in readings

6. Samples A and B both contain the same number of energy levels. On average, the Auger electrons produced by sample A carry more energy than those produced by sample B. Which of the following is most likely true about sample A?

A. It contains more electrons per atom.
B. It contains fewer electrons per atom.
C. It carries a positive charge.
D. It carries a negative charge.

7. Which of the following elements cannot be detected accurately by AES?

A. Helium
B. Lithium
C. Beryllium
D. Sodium

8. Which of the following graphs (not to scale) most accurately describes the number of x-rays and Auger electrons produced when an inner electron is struck by photons of various energies?

A.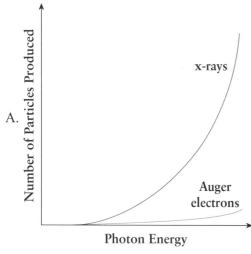

B.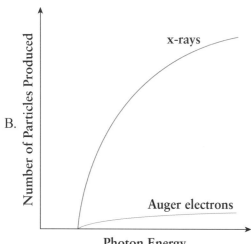

C.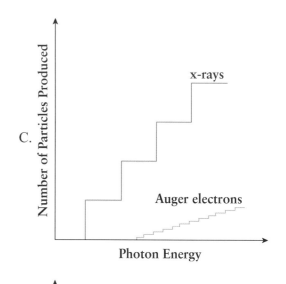

D.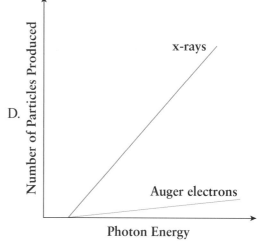

9. When a certain γ-ray causes an electron to drop from energy level a to energy level b, the resultant x-ray produces an Auger electron in energy level c if

A. $E_a + E_b - E_c \geq 0$.
B. $E_a - E_b + E_c \geq 0$.
C. $E\gamma + E_b - E_a + E_c \geq 0$.
D. $E\gamma + E_b + E_a + E_c \geq 0$.

PASSAGE II (QUESTIONS 10–17)

Many automatic temperature-monitoring systems take advantage of a device known as a thermocouple. Thermocouples measure change in temperature by taking advantage of the thermoelectric effect, a reversible phenomenon in which electric voltage is produced as a result of differences in temperature across a circuit. When the temperature changes, a certain voltage is applied to the thermocouple;

this voltage can be measured and converted into a precise temperature reading.

Instead of a thermocouple, some monitoring systems use a resistance temperature detector (RTD), which calculates the temperature by comparing the resistance across a circuit to the expected resistance at any given temperature. The temperature and resistance exhibit a linear relationship. The RTD is based on observations that electrical conductors increase their resistance with increasing temperatures.

10. An increased voltage across a thermocouple indicates a(n)

A. increase in temperature.

B. decrease in temperature.

C. increased temperature difference across the circuit.

D. decreased temperature difference across the circuit.

11. If the voltage applied to an RTD is increased, its resistance will

A. decrease.

B. increase.

C. remain constant.

D. depend on the current.

12. What type of energy imbalance is responsible for the signal produced within a thermocouple?

A. Potential energy imbalance

B. Kinetic energy imbalance

C. Heat imbalance

D. Electric energy imbalance

13. Which type of temperature sensor is likely to require an external power source?

A. A thermocouple, because the voltage can only be measured if external power is available

B. A thermocouple, because the voltage will only be produced if external power is available

C. An RTD, because the resistance can only be measured if external power is available

D. An RTD, because the resistance will only be produced if external power is available

14. A student attempts to use four identical resistors to produce an RTD. Which of the following configurations is likely to detect temperature changes most accurately?

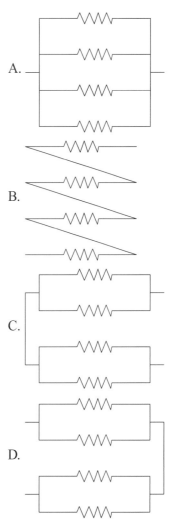

15. Which of the following diagrams best represents the optimal location within a circuit to measure voltage in a thermocouple? "V" is the device used to measure voltage, while T_1 and T_2 are the two individual temperatures.

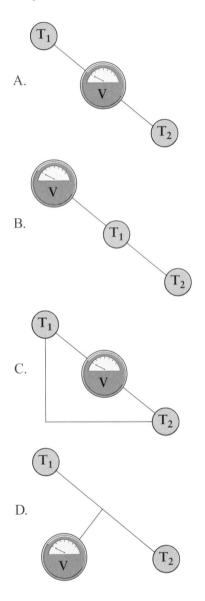

A.

B.

C.

D.

16. The thermoelectric effect CANNOT be used to

A. store electricity.

B. generate electricity.

C. heat an object by applying a voltage.

D. cool an object by applying a voltage.

17. The resistivity of a good RTD will most likely be

A. highly stable with respect to temperature.

B. highly variable with respect to temperature.

C. greater than 1.

D. less than 1.

QUESTIONS 18–21 ARE NOT BASED ON A DESCRIPTIVE PASSAGE.

18. What phenomenon can occur with light but not with sound?

A. Polarization

B. Refraction

C. Doppler effect

D. Interference

19. What is the critical angle for a light wave traveling from a substance with an index of refraction of 2 into a vacuum?

A. 30°

B. 60°

C. 45°

D. 90°

20. Completely destructive interference has been used by the military in the construction of stealth planes. Suppose a new military project was launched to coat all stealth planes with a material that would function as a cloaking device and render them invisible to people. Assuming that white light has an average wavelength of 600 nm, what should the thickness of the cloaking coat be?

A. 300 nm

B. 600 nm

C. 1,200 nm

D. 1,800 nm

21. When an 8 eV photon strikes a photoemissive surface, the surface can eject electrons that have at most a maximum kinetic energy of 6 eV. What is the maximum frequency of the photons being emitted? ($h = 4 \times 10^{-15}$ eV·s)

   A. 5×10^{-14} Hz
   B. 1.5×10^{-15} Hz
   C. 5×10^{-15} Hz
   D. 2×10^{-14} Hz

PASSAGE III (QUESTIONS 22–30)

In the figure below, a plate sits on the edge of a table. As it sits motionless, the plate possesses gravitational potential energy due to its position above the ground. This energy is given by $U = mgh$. Suddenly the plate falls from the table, traveling down to the ground. When it hits the ground, it breaks into three pieces of masses $1M$, $2M$, and $3M$. Assume that gravitational acceleration is 10 m/s².

2 m

22. The plate was initially placed on the ground. If the plate has a mass of 2 kg and force is applied directly upward, how much work is done to move the plate to the table?

   A. 4 J
   B. 10 J
   C. 40 J
   D. 0.1 J

23. How much potential energy does the plate possess as it sits on the table's edge if it has a mass of 40 g and the table's height is changed to 150 cm?

   A. 60 J
   B. 0.06 J
   C. 60,000 J
   D. 0.6 J

24. At the point when the plate has traveled $\frac{1}{3}$ of the distance between the table and the ground

   A. its total energy is $\frac{2}{3}$ of its original energy.
   B. its total energy is equal to its original energy.
   C. its total energy is $\frac{4}{3}$ of its original energy.
   D. it has more potential energy, but less kinetic energy.

25. At what point in its path from the table to the ground does the plate have the greatest kinetic energy?

   A. At the instant after it leaves the table
   B. Halfway to the ground
   C. At the instant before it hits the ground
   D. The kinetic energy is the same throughout the path

26. After the plate breaks, what is the total momentum of all the pieces?

   A. 720M m/s
   B. 240M kg·m/s
   C. 120M m/s
   D. 120M^2 kg·m/s

27. The piece with a mass of $3M$ is traveling at a speed of 5 m/s when it hits a stationary block of mass M. The piece comes to a complete stop and sends the block flying. Assuming that friction is negligible, what is the velocity of the block?

    A. 15 m/s

    B. $15M$ m/s

    C. $75M$ m/s

    D. 75 m/s

28. Assume that the piece with a mass of $1M$ kg is moving at 4 m/s. How much force is required to bring the piece to a complete stop in 3 seconds?

    A. $\dfrac{4}{3}MN$

    B. $\dfrac{3}{4}MN$

    C. $-\dfrac{4}{3}MN$

    D. $-\dfrac{3}{4}MN$

29. If the plate was thrown into the air and then allowed to fall back down to its original position, at what point is its energy the greatest?

    A. At the highest point, because the potential energy is greatest

    B. At the lowest point, because kinetic energy is the greatest

    C. It is the same at all points because energy is conserved

    D. At the halfway point between the highest and lowest points of its path

30. If the plate moves one meter to the left while experiencing a downward force of 2 N that makes an angle of 90 degrees with the horizontal, how much work is done on the plate by the force?

    A. 180 J

    B. 4 J

    C. 0 J

    D. 1 J

PASSAGE IV (QUESTIONS 31–37)

A guitar produces its sound through the vibrations of a string that is fixed at both ends. When a force is applied to this string, it oscillates at its fundamental frequency, which determines the pitch observed by a listener. To adjust the pitch of the sound emitted by the guitar, a guitarist will usually change the effective length of a string by applying his finger to the point where he wants the new "fixed end" of the string to be:

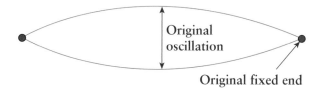

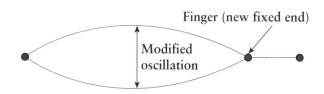

There are two common types of guitars: acoustic guitars and electric guitars. In an acoustic guitar, the waves created on the string move into an empty wooden compartment, where they build up and cause vibrations in the wood. The oscillations in the wood create sound waves in the surrounding air. These sound waves maintain the same frequency as the waves produced by the string, but they have significantly greater amplitude.

An electric guitar uses the same types of strings, but the sound waves are absorbed by a special type of magnetic microphone known as a "pickup." The waves are transmitted through a wire to an amplifier, where electrical energy is used to increase their amplitude. The amplified waves are then converted back into a sound wave by a speaker. The best amplifiers are usually capable of applying more power to the wave, thereby further increasing its amplitude.

31. A beat is produced as a result of the vibrations of two specific guitar strings. If one string is vibrating at 430 Hz and the other is vibrating at 440 Hz, how many beats will an observer hear every minute?

A. 6
B. 10
C. 600
D. 870

32. In order to increase the pitch of a sound emitted by a certain string, a guitarist must

A. move his finger down the string to decrease its effective length.
B. move his finger up the string to increase its effective length.
C. wiggle his finger on the string to increase the number of vibrations.
D. hold his finger steady in order to decrease the number of vibrations.

33. The wooden compartment in the acoustic guitar serves to

A. increase the frequency of the individual sound waves.
B. increase the intensity of the emitted sound.
C. reduce the variation between the frequencies of different sound waves.
D. reduce the background noise in the emitted sound.

34. A certain electric guitar amplifier contains a speaker that is constantly rotating, thereby emitting sounds in different directions at different times. What will happen to the pitch of the sound as the speaker rotates towards a listener?

A. It will increase because of the increased intensity.
B. It will increase because of the Doppler effect.
C. It will decrease because of the increased intensity.
D. It will decrease because of the Doppler effect.

35. Which of the following graphs best describes the relationship between the effective length of a string and the pitch of the tone that it produces?

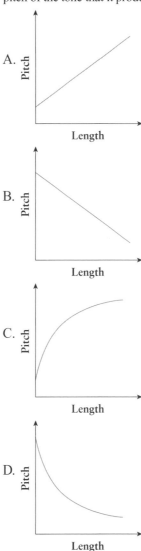

36. One of the two sound waves below represents the sound waves going from an acoustic guitar string to the environment, while the other represents the sound waves going from an electric guitar string to its pickup. The electric guitar is represented by which of the following? (Note: assume each string was played with the same initial displacement.)

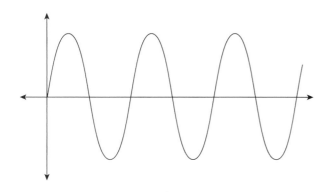

A

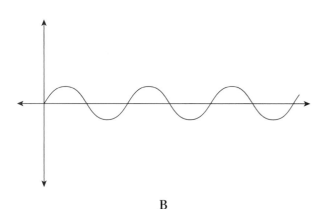

B

A. Graph A, because the sound wave from an electric guitar can be amplified.
B. Graph A, because the pickup is in close proximity to the string.
C. Graph B, because the acoustic guitar emits a sound wave with greater amplitude than the electric guitar string.
D. Graph B, because the acoustic guitar emits a sound wave over a larger area.

37. An acoustic guitarist strikes a note with a frequency of 1,000 Hz. If she applies enough force to displace the wood by 1 cm, what is the intensity of the sound observed at a distance of 1 meter from the string? Assume that the spring constant of the wood is 500 N/m and there is no loss due to friction.

A. 200 W/m²
B. 100 W/m²
C. 50 W/m²
D. 25 W/m²

QUESTIONS 38–45 ARE NOT BASED ON A DESCRIPTIVE PASSAGE.

38. For a projectile thrown with an initial speed of 40 m/s at an angle of 30°, the horizontal component of velocity is closest to

A. 50 m/s.
B. 40 m/s.
C. 35 m/s.
D. 20 m/s.

39. If two different pure substances are placed in an isolated system and a net flow of heat occurs between them, which of the following thermodynamic quantities must be different between the two objects?

A. Initial temperatures
B. Specific heats
C. Masses
D. Heat capacities

40. Which of the following statements is part of the kinetic theory of ideal gases?

A. Molecules transfer energy via collisions.
B. Molecules are always stationary.
C. Intermolecular forces of attraction are significant in guiding a molecule's path.
D. The size of the molecules is large compared to the distance that separates them.

41. A strong resistor in parallel with a voltage source is the essential component of which of the following?

    A. Ammeter
    B. Dynamo
    C. Generator
    D. Voltmeter

42. A perfectly spherical mirror that forms only virtual images has a radius of curvature of 1 meter. What is the focal length of this mirror?

    A. 2 m
    B. 1 m
    C. 0.5 m
    D. Infinity

43. A student is supplied with four 1-ohm resistors. How many functionally different resistors can be made if all resistors must be used in each configuration?

    A. 2
    B. 3
    C. 4
    D. 5

44. If a dielectric is inserted into a parallel plate capacitor that is connected to a constant voltage source, which of the following must happen to the potential difference and charge on each plate, respectively?

    A. Nothing, increase
    B. Nothing, decrease
    C. Nothing, nothing
    D. Increase, increase

45. If the mass of a pendulum is doubled, the frequency of its oscillations

    A. doubles.
    B. quadruples.
    C. halves.
    D. stays the same.

PASSAGE V (QUESTIONS 46–52)

A 100 kg man is conducting research on motorcycle safety. In his first trial, he rides a 400 kg motorcycle around a circular track of radius $R = 100$ m. As his speed increases, his motorcycle tilts toward the center of the circle, making an angle alpha with the ground. When he reaches a speed of 50 m/s, he feels that his body is too close to the ground and decides to stop accelerating. Figure 1 shows some of the forces acting on the motorcycle. It does not show the force of the motor, which accelerates the motorcycle out of the page, or the force of friction that resists that motion. Note that F2 is the centripetal force. The centrifugal force opposing the centripetal force is not shown.

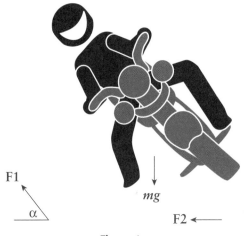

Figure 1

He then conducts another trial during which he accelerates to 50 m/s on a flat surface and then rides inside a cylindrical track of radius R in which he seems to defy gravity. The schematic diagram in Figure 2 shows the motorcyclist in a counterclockwise movement, during which he is upside down at point A:

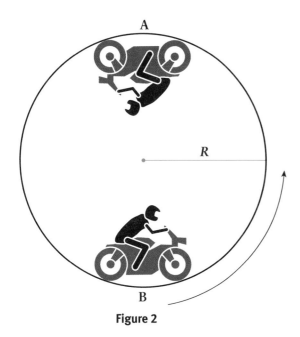

A

R

B

Figure 2

At the end of the second experiment, he observes that his tires are burnt. These observations lead him to make conclusions about motorcycle safety.

46. The man believes that when riding around a circular track, the tires can withstand speeds in excess of 100 m/s because the force of friction would still be smaller than in trial 2. Is he correct?

A. No, although the forces of friction increase as the speed increases, the centrifugal forces on the rotating tires might offset this effect and keep the tires from burning.
B. No, although the force of friction would still be smaller than in trial 2, increasing centripetal forces on the rotating tires might cause the tires to burst.
C. Yes, the force of friction would be smaller than in trial 2 and his prediction is absolutely correct.
D. Yes, the force of friction would be smaller than in trial 2 but this would cause him to lose control at higher speeds.

47. What is the net force acting on the motorcycle in trial 1 at any given moment during the period when he maintains a constant speed of 50 m/s?

A. 0 N
B. 1,000 N
C. 10,000 N
D. 100,000 N

48. What are the directions of forces F1 and F2 from trial 1, if they are measured at point B during trial 2?

A. F1 points into the ground and F2 points toward the center.
B. F1 points toward the center and F2 points in the direction behind the motorcycle.
C. Both F1 and F2 point into the ground.
D. Both F1 and F2 point toward the center.

49. What is the maximum height (diameter) of track 2 that would allow a motorcyclist to execute the gravity-defying stunt while maintaining a minimum speed of 50 m/s?

A. 10 m
B. 50 m
C. 250 m
D. 500 m

50. During trial 2, the engine must supply increasing amounts of power between points B and A in order to maintain constant speed. As the motorcyclist goes up from point B to point A, the

A. force of friction on the tires increases.
B. force of friction on the tires decreases.
C. net force on the motorcycle decreases.
D. net force on the motorcycle increases.

51. If the motorcyclist wishes to increase the safety of trial 1, which of the following are effective strategies for that goal?

   I. Increase the coefficient of friction of the track surface

  II. Increase the radius of the track

 III. Increase the mass of the motorcycle

A. I only

B. II only

C. I and II only

D. II and III only

52. What are the average net forces acting on the motorcyclist during an entire round trip around tracks 1 and 2, respectively?

A. 0 N in both cases

B. 0 N and 10,000 N, respectively

C. 10,000 N in both cases

D. More information is needed

Practice Section 2

Time—70 minutes

QUESTIONS 1–52

Directions: Most of the questions in the following Physics Practice Section are organized into groups, with a descriptive passage preceding each group of questions. Study the passage, then select the single best answer to the question in each group. Some of the questions are not based on a descriptive passage; you must also select the best answer to these questions. If you are unsure of the best answer, eliminate the choices that you know are incorrect, then select an answer from the choices that remain.

PASSAGE I (QUESTIONS 1–9)

An experiment is conducted to test the quality of newly manufactured springs. One spring is attached to the back of a car and another one is attached to the front. The car is driven inside a specialized track (shown below):

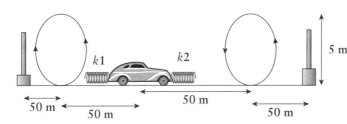

Initially, the car accelerates to the right, travels through a circular loop (with diameter of 5 m), and hits a rectangular brick wall. If the spring causes it to rebound, it goes backward, passes through the two identical circles, and hits the other wall. A device on each wall records the maximum force of impact. This cycle may continue indefinitely.

Each wall is equipped with a transformer that converts mechanical energy into heat. This transformer is a cylinder with an outer part composed of metal and an inner part composed of a liquid. Heat energy is transferred from each wall

to its cylinder according to the formula $\frac{Q}{t} = \frac{kA\Delta T}{L}$ where Q is heat, t is time, A is the cross-sectional area of the cylinder, k is the coefficient of conductivity for the cylinder, L is the length of the boundary between the wall and the inner part of the cylinder, and ΔT is the nonzero temperature difference between the surfaces.

The liquid inside the cylinder will accept heat according to the formula $Q = mc\Delta T$, where c is specific heat capacity ($c = 4.184$ J g^{-1} K^{-1} for water) and m is the liquid's mass in grams.

The car weighs 100 kg. Some of the results of the experiment are shown in the following table:

Trial	k_1	k_2	Speed	Force R	Force L
1	2,000	3,000	50	25×10^6	23×10^6
2	3,000	3,000	20	11×10^6	11×10^6
3	4,000	3,000	7	n/a	n/a
4	10,000	2,000	12	5×10^6	n/a

During each trial the car accelerates to a certain speed in the first 50 m and then the engine is turned off for the duration. Force *R* and Force *L* represent the maximal recorded forces upon the impact with the right or left wall, respectively. k_1 and k_2 are the spring constants of the two springs. All measurements are in standard metric units. (Note: assume that friction is NOT negligible unless otherwise stated.)

1. What was the change in momentum of the car in trial 1 after it hit the right wall? (Note: assume that friction is negligible and that no energy is lost in the collision.)

  A. 0 kg·m/s
  B. 500 kg·m/s
  C. 5,000 kg·m/s
  D. 10,000 kg·m/s

2. Which of the following may explain the results of trial 4?

  A. The car broke after hitting the first brick wall.
  B. The spring constant k_1 was so high that the measuring device on the left wall malfunctioned.
  C. The car lost some kinetic energy due to friction, thereby preventing it from reaching the top of a circle on the way back.
  D. All of the above

3. In trial 1, what is the difference between the time when the car passes the first circle and the time when it comes to a stop at the right wall? (Note: assume that friction is negligible.)

  A. 1 s
  B. 2.3 s
  C. 3.6 s
  D. 4 s

4. What graph best describes the magnitude of the car's acceleration with respect to time as it hits the wall and rebounds?

A.
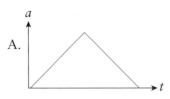

B.

C.

D.
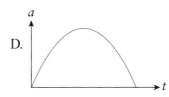

5. If 50 percent of the energy from the spring is converted into heat, how much power is delivered to each liquid cylinder in trial 2?

  A. 90 W
  B. 116 W
  C. 180 W
  D. 232 W

6. If the cylinder contains 1 kg of water and has a cross-sectional area of 1 m², a length of 1 cm, a coefficient of conductivity of 400 W/m·K, how much heat will be added to the water after 5 cycles of trial 2? Assume that 50 percent of energy from the spring is converted into heat.

  A. 100 J
  B. 1,000 J
  C. 12 kJ
  D. 25 kJ

7. Which of the following would NOT affect the temperature change of a liquid inside the cylinder?

   A. The number of times that the cycle is conducted
   B. The magnitude of the spring constant
   C. The speed of the car
   D. The type of liquid inside the cylinder

8. If 50 percent of spring energy is converted into heat, then how many cycles will trial 1 last?

   A. 1
   B. 2
   C. 4
   D. Indefinitely

9. Which of the following graphs best represents the increase in temperature of a cylinder of water with respect to time (*t*) if trial 1 is conducted indefinitely?

A.
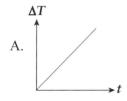

B.
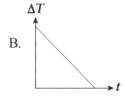

C.
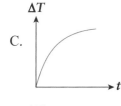

D.
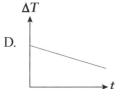

PASSAGE II (QUESTIONS 10–17)

A material's ability to conduct heat is measured by its *thermal conductivity*, *k*. Based on the thermal conductivity of an object, we can determine the rate of heat conduction by using the following formula:

$$\frac{\Delta Q}{\Delta t} = \frac{kA\Delta T}{x}$$

Where $\frac{\Delta Q}{\Delta t}$ is the change in heat per unit time, *A* is the cross-sectional area of the conductor, *x* is the width of the conductor, and ΔT is the difference in temperature between the warmer side of the conductor and the colder side.

To learn more about thermal conductivity, a student divides two compartments containing 100 mL of water total (specific heat = 1 cal/g·K) with a plate made of copper (see figure), whose thermal conductivity is about 400 J/m·s·K. The container is made of glass, which has a thermal conductivity of about 1 J/m·s·K. The student uses a thermometer to measure the change in temperature of the water with respect to time. In order to compare different situations, he uses various thicknesses of copper and various temperatures of water. The total area of contact between the water and the container is 100 cm², while the area of contact between the water and the copper is 50 cm².

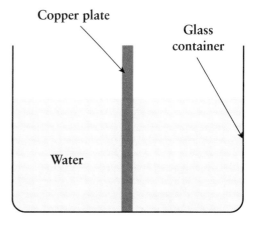

After recording the results of the experiment, the student compares them with the results that would be expected for each setup based on the thermal conductivity formula. In each calculation, the actual value of ΔQ is somewhat lower than the expected value. He notices that increases in this experimental error are almost directly proportional to the thickness of the copper plate. There is also some error present in the rest of the system.

10. The experimental error is proportional to the thickness of the plate because the student did not subtract the

A. specific heat capacity of the plate, which is directly proportional to its mass.

B. specific heat capacity of the plate, which is directly proportional to its thickness.

C. amount of heat stored by the plate, which is directly proportional to its mass.

D. amount of heat stored by the plate, which is directly proportional to its thickness.

11. None of the errors in the calculation come from the fact that the student failed to account for

A. heat transferred by radiation from the warm water to the cold water.

B. heat transferred by conduction from the warm water to the copper plate.

C. heat transferred by conduction from the water to the environment.

D. heat transferred by conduction from the water to the glass.

12. If the environmental temperature is equal to the temperature of the cold water compartment, how much heat is conducted through the copper plate for every 1 J that is conducted through the glass container?

A. 0.5 J

B. 2 J

C. 0.2 kJ

D. 0.5 kJ

13. If one water compartment is at a temperature of 350 K and the other compartment is at 300 K, how much heat is transferred between the two compartments when the copper divider is removed? (Note: assume that no heat is lost to the external environment.)

A. 5 kJ

B. 2.5 kJ

C. 5 Cal

D. 2.5 Cal

14. What would be the primary mode of heat transfer if the copper divider were removed?

A. Convection

B. Conduction

C. Radiation

D. Dissolution

15. The entropy change is

A. positive for the warmer compartment and zero for the cooler compartment.

B. positive for the cooler compartment and zero for the warmer compartment.

C. positive for both compartments.

D. negative for both compartments.

16. Which of the following graphs best represents the rate of heat transfer with respect to time?

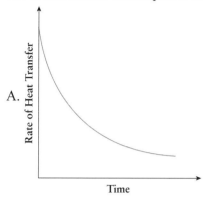

A.

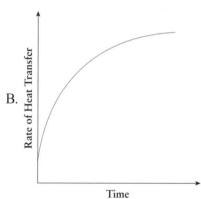

B.

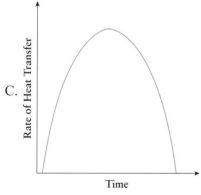

C.

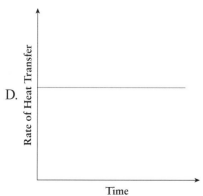

D.

17. The kinetic energy of the molecules most likely decreases in

A. the copper plate.
B. the glass of the container.
C. the warm water compartment.
D. the cold water compartment.

QUESTIONS 18–21 ARE NOT BASED ON A DESCRIPTIVE PASSAGE.

18. A police car speeds toward you at 50 m/s. Its siren wails at 400 Hz. You are driving toward the police car at 20 m/s. What is the frequency of the sound you hear? (velocity of sound in air = 330 m/s)

A. 350 Hz
B. 370 Hz
C. 490 Hz
D. 500 Hz

19. A car moving 10 km/hr skids 15 m while stopping. How far would the car skid if it were originally moving at 100 km/hr?

A. 150 m
B. 300 m
C. 1,500 m
D. 3,000 m

20. Two identical speakers driven by an identical signal each produce 680 Hz waves. If the speakers are facing each other, how far apart must they be placed to completely destructively interfere? Assume that the speed of sound in air is 340 m/s.

A. 0.25 m
B. 0.5 m
C. 0.68 m
D. 1 m

21. A hydraulic lift has a small platform with a surface area of 1 m² and a large platform with a surface area of 100 m², both of which are connected by an enclosed fluid. Approximately how much force must be applied to the small platform in order to lift a 1,000 kg car that sits on the large platform?

    A. 1 N
    B. 5 N
    C. 10 N
    D. 100 N

PASSAGE III (QUESTIONS 22–30)

When operating a flight, pilots need to take into account *tailwinds* and *headwinds*. These components will affect their path and speed of flight. Headwinds will decrease the amount of time required for takeoff and landing, while tailwinds will affect the ground speed of the plane, which must be taken into account during takeoff and landing.

Headwind refers to wind at 180° to the direction of travel that opposes the forward motion of the plane. For example, if a plane is headed west at 850 m/s and the headwind is 150 m/s, then the net speed is calculated by subtracting vectors. The net resultant speed of the plane will be 700 m/s. Conversely, tailwind refers to wind in line with the direction of travel that adds to the forward motion of the plane. Tailwind will, hence, increase the plane's ground speed. In the above example, the net speed of the plane would be 900 m/s. Both headwinds and tailwinds occur at all altitudes. When the incident angle of the headwind or tailwind varies from 180°, vector analysis is required to isolate the component in the direction of travel.

A plane takes off from an airport at 8:00 A.M. and makes a flight path that is 30° north of east. It travels 1,500 meters in 2 seconds before it is met by a tailwind blowing at 400 m/s at an angle of 45° south of east. (cos 30° = $\frac{\sqrt{3}}{2}$; sin 30° = 0.5; sin 45° = cos 45° = $\frac{\sqrt{2}}{2}$)

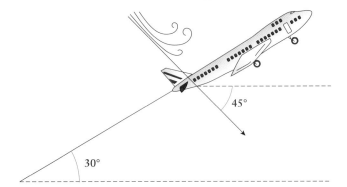

22. Which of the following is an example of a vector?

    A. The speed at which the airplane is flying
    B. The distance that the airplane travels
    C. The velocity at which the airplane is traveling
    D. The angle that the airplane makes with respect to the horizon

23. What is the average velocity of the airplane before it meets the tailwind?

    A. 750 m/s
    B. 750 m/s at 30° north of east
    C. 3,000 m/s
    D. 3,000 m/s at 30° north of east

24. What is the horizontal component of the airplane's velocity vector before it meets the tailwind?

    A. 650 m/s east
    B. 375 m/s east
    C. 650 m/s west
    D. 750 m/s east

25. What is the vertical component of the velocity after the plane meets the tailwind?

A. 92 m/s south
B. 92 m/s north
C. 658 m/s north
D. 658 m/s south

26. What is the resultant velocity of the airplane after it is met by the tailwind?

A. 938 m/s at 84° north of east
B. 1,142 m/s at 35° north of east
C. 1,142 m/s at 55° north of east
D. 938 m/s at 6° north of east

27. If there were no tailwind, how long would it take the plane to travel another 1,000 meters?

A. 1.33 minutes
B. 1.33 seconds
C. 0.75 seconds
D. 0.75 minutes

28. If another plane traveled at 500 m/s east for 3 seconds and then 175 m/s west for 0.5 seconds, what would be its total displacement?

A. 1,325 meters east
B. 675 meters east
C. 1,413 meters east
D. 1,675 meters east

29. If the tailwind were 300 m/s east instead, what would be the plane's total displacement at 3.5 seconds into its journey?

A. 1,500 meters
B. 3,032 meters
C. 1,532 meters
D. 2,625 meters

30. What wind velocity would be required to change the plane's velocity to 500 m/s east?

A. 404 m/s west
B. 250 m/s at 22° south of west
C. 250 m/s west
D. 404 m/s at 68° south of west

PASSAGE IV (QUESTIONS 31–38)

The gas-filled radiation detector was one of the first instruments used to measure radiation. Particles of sufficient energy will ionize the gas molecules, causing a polarization of the gas as the positive ions migrate toward the anode and the negative ions migrate toward the anode. The cathode and anode are connected to a device that measures current and the readings are interpreted in order to determine the activity of the radioactive sample.

More recently, semiconductor detectors have become widespread. The basic principle of these detectors is similar to that of the gas-filled detectors, but the gas is replaced by a sample of solid silicon or germanium, both of which allow the creation of a hole in the valence shell upon contact with radiation of sufficient energy. Instead of measuring the number of gas ions produced (like the gas-filled detector), the semiconductor measures the number of holes.

The readings from most radiation detectors are given in terms of the number of *counts*. Each individual detector must be calibrated in order to relate the number of counts with the exact activity of the radioactive sample. In a certain experiment, a student tests different radionuclides with both types of radiation detectors. Each sample is counted several times in order to account for the error in the detection system; the average readings are reported here.

Sample ID	Activity	Decay Mode	Reading from Detector 1	Reading from Detector 2
None	0	?	12 counts	18 counts
A	1 mCi	α	53 counts	138 counts
B	2 mCi	α	95 counts	257 counts
C	4 mCi	α	?	?
D	0.5 mCi	?	12 counts	26 counts

31. Which of the following types of radiation is LEAST likely to be detected by a gas-filled detector?

  A. α

  B. β

  C. γ

  D. X-rays

32. Which of the following is true regarding the capabilities of both types of detectors?

  A. Gas-filled detectors can measure the activity of a sample, while semiconductor detectors can measure the activity and identify the mode of decay.

  B. Gas-filled detectors can identify the mode of a sample's decay, while semiconductor detectors can measure the activity and identify the mode of decay.

  C. Both detectors can measure the activity of a sample and identify the mode of decay.

  D. Both detectors can measure the activity of a sample, but neither can accurately identify the mode of decay.

33. Why is the semiconductor detector more sensitive than the gas-filled detector?

  A. Semiconductors have a higher atomic mass than gases, making it more likely for any individual atom to interact with radiation.

  B. Semiconductors are denser than gases, making it more likely for any individual atom to interact with radiation.

  C. Semiconductors are less likely than gases to lose an electron.

  D. Semiconductors are more likely than gases to undergo radioactive decay.

34. Why does the student notice a nonzero reading from the detectors when no sample is present?

  A. Erroneous readings are caused by the inherent error in the detection system.

  B. Even identical amounts of radiation may or may not interact with the particles in the detector.

  C. A small amount of ionization occurs even when no radiation source is present.

  D. Small amounts of radiation remain in the detector from the last time that it was used.

35. Which of the following curves is most likely to be produced during the calibration of a radiation detector?

A.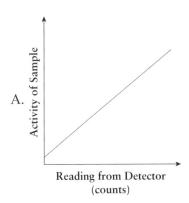

B.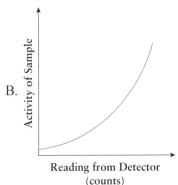

C.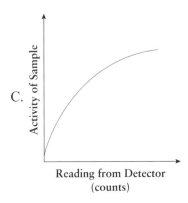

D.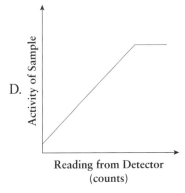

36. If sample C is tested with detector 1, the reading will probably be approximately

    A. 135 counts.

    B. 160 counts.

    C. 175 counts.

    D. 190 counts.

37. When sample A is measured again after 3 days, detector 1 reads 16 counts and detector 2 reads 32 counts. Which of the following is closest to the half-life of sample A?

    A. 1 day

    B. 2 days

    C. 3 days

    D. 4 days

38. If the activity of sample D is doubled, then

    A. the readings from both detectors will definitely increase.

    B. the reading from detector 2 will definitely increase, but the reading from detector 1 might not change.

    C. the reading from detector 1 will definitely increase, but the reading from detector 2 might not change.

    D. neither reading will definitely increase.

PASSAGE V (QUESTIONS 39–46)

Whether objects are in motion or stationary, there are always forces acting upon them. Newton's second law states that a force exerted on an object of mass m will cause it to accelerate in the direction of the force with a magnitude that is proportional to that of the force: $F = ma$. The concept of force is most commonly thought of as an interaction between two objects in direct contact with each other, resulting in some motion. However, one object can exert a force upon another, even across large distances and forces can be acting upon an object even if it is perfectly still. What follows are two examples of such situations.

In the diagram below, a clock of mass $2M$ is placed on a 45° incline. The coefficient of static friction between the two surfaces is 1.2 and the coefficient of kinetic friction is 0.50.

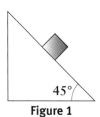

Figure 1

The diagram below shows two spheres. Sphere 1 has a mass of $4M$ and sphere 2 has a mass of M. The spheres are separated by a distance of D.

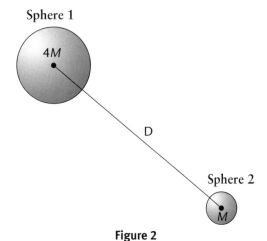

Figure 2

39. Which of the following correctly depicts the direction of the normal force acting upon the block in Figure 1?

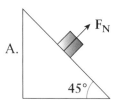

A.

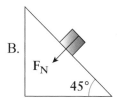

B.

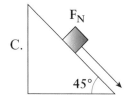

C.

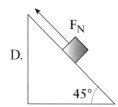

D.

40. What is the magnitude of the normal force acting on the block?

A. $\sin 45° \times 2M$

B. $\cos 45° \times 2M$

C. $\sin 45° \times 2M \times g$

D. $\cos 45° \times 2M \times g$

41. If the block had a mass of 2 kg and was sitting on a flat surface, what would be the minimum force required to move it from its resting position?

A. 2.4 N

B. 1.2 N

C. 24 N

D. 20 N

42. What is the gravitational force between the two spheres in figure 2?

A. $\dfrac{4GM^2}{D^2}$

B. $\dfrac{GM^2}{D^2}$

C. $\dfrac{4GM}{D^2}$

D. $\dfrac{4GM^2}{D}$

43. If the distance D in Figure 2 is increased by a factor of 4, the gravitational force between the spheres will

A. increase by a factor of 4.

B. decrease by a factor of 4.

C. increase by a factor of 8.

D. decrease by a factor of 16.

44. After a certain process, the density of sphere 1 increased while its diameter decreased. The final mass of the sphere is $4M$ and the position of the sphere's center is unchanged. What has happened to the gravitational force between the two spheres?

A. The force increased because the density of sphere 1 has increased.

B. The force decreased because the diameter of sphere 1 has decreased.

C. The force would be multiplied by a factor of 4.

D. The force remained the same because neither mass nor distance was altered.

45. If the block from Figure 1 was placed between the two spheres such that an upward force of 75 N was applied to the block while a downward force of 33 N was also applied, what would be the net force on the block?

A. 42 N upward

B. 108 N upward

C. 42 N downward

D. 108 N downward

46. If an object of mass 1 kg is sitting on the surface of a planet of mass $8M$ and diameter $4D$, what is the force of gravity on the object?

A. $\dfrac{8GM}{16D^2}$

B. $\dfrac{8GM}{4D^2}$

C. $\dfrac{GMm}{D^2}$

D. $\dfrac{GM^2}{D^2}$

PASSAGE VI (QUESTIONS 47–52)

It is often invaluable to determine the blood flow rate in different vessels of the circulatory system so that information about tissue oxygen supply and possible vessel blockage can be obtained. One device commonly used for this purpose is an electromagnetic blood flow meter, which utilizes the movement of charged particles (ions) in the magnetic field. Blood plasma concentrations of different ions are presented in the following table, even though generally only two ions of the highest concentrations are considered when measuring the flow.

Plasma Electrolytes	Concentration
Na^+	140 mmol/L
Cl^-	100 mmol/L
K^+	4.5 mmol/L
Carbonate ion	25 mmol/L
Ca^{++}	2.5 mmol/L

During the measurement, as ions move within the artery with velocity $v = 25$ cm/s, magnetic poles are placed on both sides of the artery creating the magnetic field. Under the influence of these magnetic forces, ions gather at opposite sides of the artery. Polarized plasma electrolytes produce electric fields across the artery, which is considered uniform for the calculations. The voltage across the artery is measured with a voltmeter and calcutaled using $V = Ed$ ($d = 2$ cm is the diameter of the artery). The electric forces $F = qE$ produced by the electric field acting on the ions are in opposite direction to the magnetic forces $F = qvB$. The ions will continue to separate, accumulating on different sides of the artery until the equilibrium is reached and magnetic force equals the electric force.

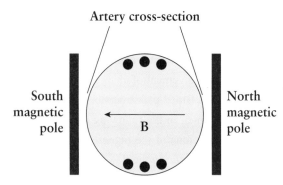

Artery cross-section

South magnetic pole

B

North magnetic pole

Direction of blood flow is into the page

47. What is the direction of the magnetic force on negatively charged ions in the artery?

A. Left
B. Right
C. Up
D. Down

48. Upon the application of a vasoconstricting agent, the radius of the artery decreases by $\frac{1}{2}$. What will happen to the velocity of blood and voltage, respectively?

A. Increase times 4 and decrease by $\frac{1}{2}$
B. Decrease by $\frac{1}{2}$ and increase times 2
C. Both decrease by $\frac{1}{2}$
D. Decrease by $\frac{1}{2}$ and decrease by $\frac{1}{8}$

49. Assume that calcium ion movement is monitored by the flow meter. If a researcher is interested in keeping magnetic force constant for all positive ions, which of the following would need to be performed when monitoring calcium?

A. Increasing particle velocity
B. Decreasing the diameter of the artery
C. Decreasing magnetic field
D. Increasing voltage

50. As sodium and chloride are moving through the artery, what can be concluded about the magnetic force acting on the ions?

A. It is perpendicular to the ions' velocity and parallel to the magnetic field.
B. It is parallel to both the ions' velocity and the magnetic field.
C. It is perpendicular to the magnetic field and parallel to the ions' velocity.
D. It is perpendicular to both the ions' velocity and the magnetic field.

51. If plasma electrolytes were to move from left to right in the cross-section of the artery, which of the following could be inferred?

   A. There is no net magnetic force or torque on the particles.
   B. There is no net magnetic force on the particles.
   C. There is no torque on the particles.
   D. Torque and net magnetic force are acting on the particles.

52. Calculate the current passing through the artery due to the anions' movement if the arterial resistance is $3\ \Omega$ and a magnetic field of 1T is applied across the walls of the artery

   A. $17 \times 10^{-2}\,A$
   B. $1.7 \times 10^{-5}\,A$
   C. $3.4 \times 10^{-5}\,A$
   D. $34 \times 10^{-2}\,A$

Practice Section 3

Time—70 minutes

QUESTIONS 1–52

Directions: Most of the questions in the following Physics Practice Section are organized into groups, with a descriptive passage preceding each group of questions. Study the passage, then select the single best answer to the question in each group. Some of the questions are not based on a descriptive passage; you must also select the best answer to these questions. If you are unsure of the best answer, eliminate the choices that you know are incorrect, then select an answer from the choices that remain.

PASSAGE I (QUESTIONS 1–9)

Automotive audio systems often contain a complex wiring network, which must be optimized in order to maximize their cost-effectiveness. Typically, these systems are based around a 12 V battery, several speakers, and an amplifier, which increases the power delivered to the speakers. More elaborate customized systems often include large capacitors, multiple amplifiers, more speakers, and occasionally extra batteries. The best designs also consider the nature of the wire and the connectors that carry the signal between the various circuit components.

The wiring in a home audio system can be equally elaborate, but there are some clear differences. These systems extract their power from normal electrical outlets, which supply an alternating current with a root-mean-square (RMS) voltage of 110V in most American homes. This eliminates the need for a battery and reduces the need for a capacitor while still permitting the amplifier to produce adequate amounts of power. The remaining circuit components are similar in home systems and automotive systems.

1. Which of the following is increased by the amplifier in order to increase the power delivered to the speakers?

   I. Current
   II. Emf
   III. Resistance

   A. I only
   B. I and II only
   C. I and III only
   D. II and III only

2. A capacitor is added to an automotive system in order to provide an extra 2 A of current for up to 12 seconds at a time. What is the capacitance? (Note: assume a constant current during this interval.)

   A. 2 F
   B. 6 F
   C. 12 F
   D. 24 F

3. Assuming identical lengths, what type of wire should be used in order to optimize power delivery at a temperature of 298 K?

    A. Silver wire (resistivity of 16 nΩ·m) with radius of 1 cm

    B. Aluminum wire (resistivity of 28 nΩ·m) with radius of 2 cm

    C. Copper wire (resistivity of 17 nΩ·m) with radius of 1.5 cm

    D. Gold wire (resistivity of 24 nΩ·m) with radius of 1 cm

4. A system includes six speakers, each of which carries a resistance of 4 Ω. Assuming the speakers are the only source of resistance, what is the resistance of the circuit that would minimize overall power dissipation?

    A. $\frac{2}{3}\,\Omega$

    B. $\frac{3}{2}\,\Omega$

    C. 4 Ω

    D. 24 Ω

5. In a circuit containing a battery, an amplifier, a group of speakers, and a capacitor, the best place to put the capacitor is

    A. between the amplifier and the speakers.

    B. between the battery and the amplifier.

    C. wired in parallel along with the speakers.

    D. wired in series along with the speakers.

6. A car amplifier and a home amplifier are found to produce exactly the same amount of power. Which of the following statements is true?

    A. Both amplifiers draw the same amount of current.

    B. Both amplifiers produce the same amount of resistance.

    C. The home amplifier draws more current.

    D. The car amplifier draws more current.

7. Capacitors are less useful for home systems than for automotive systems because

    A. the components of a home system are more likely to act as natural capacitors than the components of an automotive system.

    B. the electrical outlet stores charge and, therefore, acts as a capacitor.

    C. home amplifiers can extract the necessary current without the help of a capacitor.

    D. car amplifiers cannot extract the necessary current without the help of a capacitor.

8. Although the published potential of most car batteries is 12 V, a typical battery will produce approximately 14 V under normal conditions. Which of the following best explains this phenomenon?

    A. Fluctuations in the DC current can lead to a higher potential.

    B. Fluctuations in the AC current occasionally lead to a higher potential.

    C. The RMS potential is 12 V, while the peak potential is higher.

    D. The RMS potential is 14 V, while the average potential is 12 V.

9. A home amplifier and a car amplifier both have identical resistances. Which amplifier will consume more electrical energy?

    A. A home amplifier, because a higher potential will draw more current

    B. A car amplifier, because more energy is needed to compensate for the decreased potential

    C. Both consume the same energy, because power is directly proportional to resistance

    D. Neither can be determined unless the current is known

PASSAGE II (QUESTIONS 10–17)

Early scientists measured electric charge by using an electroscope, which provides approximate measurements based on the movement of a standard charge with respect to the test object. The two most common types of such devices were the pith-ball electroscope and the gold-leaf electroscope, both of which function through electrostatic induction.

Pith-ball electroscope
The pith-ball electroscope is based on a ball suspended from a hook via a silk thread.

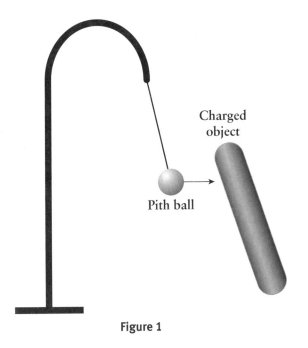

Charged object

Pith ball

Figure 1

The ball is typically made of pith, which is a lightweight electrical insulator. When the electroscope is placed in the vicinity of a positively charged object, the electrons in the ball move slightly toward the object. This motion of the electrons causes the pith ball to have an induced positive side and an induced negative side. Because the electrons are slightly closer to the charged object via their attraction, the ball moves towards the test object (Figure 1).

If the test object touches the pith ball, the ball will become charged. Bringing the now-charged pith ball in the vicinity of objects with a known charge gives the electroscope the ability to distinguish between a positive and a negative charge.

Gold-leaf electroscope

The gold-leaf electroscope consists of a metal ball (or plate) that is attached to two ultra-thin pieces of gold (also known as gold "leaves") via a brass rod.

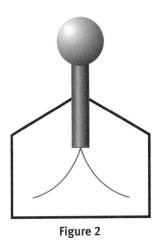

Figure 2

If a charged object is brought near the electroscope, the two gold leaves repel one another through a mechanism similar to the one in the pith-ball electroscope. When the object touches the ball, charge is conducted through the rod, also causing the gold leaves to repel one another.

The instrument was invented a few years after the pith-ball electroscope; it maintains several advantages because the gold leaf is much lighter than the pith ball, but still exerts a similar amount of force.

10. According to the passage, what is the definition of *electrostatic induction*?

A. The transfer of electric charge through an electrical insulator

B. The transfer of electric charge through an electrical conductor

C. A change in the distribution of electric charge in a certain object due to the influence of an outside object

D. A change in the net electric charge in a certain object due to the influence of an outside object

11. How would the pith ball interact with a negatively charged test object?

A. It would repel the test object because the effect should be opposite that of a positively charged object.

B. It would repel the test object because the electrons move slightly toward the object and the protons move slightly away from it.

C. It would attract the test object because metals form positively charged ions.

D. It would attract the test object because the electrons would move slightly away from the object while the protons would stay in place.

12. Some electroscopes contain two suspended pith balls that touch each other when they are uncharged. What would be the final effect of touching one of these pith balls with a negatively charged object?

A. The balls would repel each other and repel the test object.

B. The balls would repel each other and attract the test object.

C. The balls would attract each other and repel the test object.

D. The balls would attract each other and attract the test object.

13. Which of the following can be partially responsible for the movement of the pith ball or the gold leaf?

   I. Electrostatic force

  II. Electric conduction of charges into the pith ball or leaf

 III. Electric field

A. I only

B. I and II only

C. II and III only

D. I, II, and III

14. Why is it important for the pith ball to be light-weight?

A. Heavier objects will contain more atoms, which will make it more difficult for electrons to migrate.

B. Heavier objects will require more force to move, which will reduce the sensitivity of the instrument.

C. Lighter objects are more likely to conduct a charge than heavier objects.

D. Lighter objects are less likely to conduct a charge than heavier objects.

15. Which of the following would be the LEAST effective replacement for gold leaf in a gold-leaf electroscope?

A. Silver leaf

B. Copper wire

C. Gold foil

D. Pith

16. A positively charged object is placed to the right of a pith ball and the pith ball is seen to move toward the object. What is the direction of the electric field?

A. Left

B. Right

C. Up

D. Down

17. Which of the following does NOT describe the interaction between the two gold leaves?

A. Electrostatic repulsion
B. Charge redistribution
C. Production of an electric dipole
D. Production of an electric field

QUESTIONS 18–22 ARE NOT BASED ON A DESCRIPTIVE PASSAGE.

18. The total energy (kinetic plus potential) of a falling object is conserved. If a 5 kg object is dropped from a height of 5 m, approximately how fast is it traveling just before it touches the ground?

A. 1 m/s
B. 10 m/s
C. 25 m/s
D. 100 m/s

19. The distance a car travels relates to its initial velocity and acceleration. Suppose a car traveling at 10 m/s notices a road block the driver of that is 30 m away. The driver instantly presses the brakes, and the car decelerates uniformly at 2 m/s². The car will

A. crash into the roadblock.
B. just barely touch the roadblock.
C. safely miss the roadblock by 5 m.
D. safely miss the roadblock by 10 m.

20. The total resistance of a circuit is related to both the resistances of individual resistors and the orientation of those resistors. If a circuit consists of two 6 ohm resistors in parallel and those resistors are placed in series instead, the total resistance of the circuit will do which of the following?

A. Increase four-fold
B. Increase two-fold
C. Decrease four-fold
D. Decrease two-fold

21. In a perfectly inelastic collision, two objects can be considered one larger object after the collision. If a 150 kg football player traveling south at 3 m/s has a perfectly inelastic collision with a 100 kg player traveling north at 5 m/s, what is the velocity of the two players after the collision?

A. 2 m/s north
B. 0.2 m/s north
C. 0.2 m/s south
D. 2 m/s south

22. The result of two waves interfering with each other can be determined using the principal of linear superposition. If two waves of equal amplitude A_1 interfere in phase, what will be the amplitude of the resultant wave?

A. $2A_1$
B. 0
C. A_1
D. $\frac{1}{2}A_1$

PASSAGE III (QUESTIONS 23–30)

The pentathlon has changed much during the years of its existence. One of the original Olympic games, it comes from the Greek for *five competitions*. Among these were wrestling, long jump, javelin throw, discus throw, and a short foot race. The foot race, or *stadion*, was 180 m long. Though wrestling and the discus throw were similar to their modern forms, the javelin throw was quite different, with the athlete using a leather strap rather than gripping the javelin itself. One of the most remarkable Olympic records in this sport is held by Osleidys Menendez of Cuba, with a throw of 71.53 m obtained in Athens at the start of this century.

The modern Olympics has changed these sports. Starting in 1912 for men, they included 110/100 m hurdles, shot put, high jump, long jump, and 1,500/800 meter run. Today, in addition to this athletic pentathlon, there is a modern pentathlon, which features five completely different sports.

In the shooting competition, participants must use an air pistol to shoot 20 50 g bullets at a 17 cm square target from 10 m away, all in 40 seconds. These bullets typically travel at 500 m/s! Fencing is next and is in the form of a round-robin tournament. Following that is swimming, a freestyle race spanning 200 m. Next is probably one of the most unusual parts, a horse riding competition featuring an obstacle course about 400 m long, with 12 obstacles and 15 jumps. Finally comes the 3 km run. Athletes are assigned handicaps based on their points total from the last four events. This allows the athlete who crosses the finish line first to be given the gold medal.

23. Consider the discus throw from the original Olympics. Which of the following describes the inward pull of the athlete's arm on the discus?

A. It is known as centrifugal force.
B. It is inversely proportional to the speed of the object.
C. It is inversely proportional to the square of the speed.
D. It is proportional to the square of the speed.

24. Imagine that a representative from Chile practices his shot put. As a conditioning exercise, he throws from the top of a peak in the Andes and launches the ball horizontally from 1,000 m above sea level. A microchip in the ball records that it has an initial speed of 30 m/s and hits something (not necessarily at sea level) within 7 seconds of its release. What is its acceleration during the sixth second?

A. 4.2 m/s^2
B. 5.0 m/s^2
C. 10.0 m/s^2
D. 32.2 m/s^2

25. If the record-breaking javelin throw was made at an angle of 45° with the horizon and at an initial speed of 45 m/s, how far had it traveled horizontally in its first 2 seconds in flight?

A. 2.25 m
B. 45.0 m
C. 63.6 m
D. 78.0 m

26. Imagine that the air pistol used in the Olympics operates by spring motion. If the spring is compressed 1 cm while cocked, what is the theoretical spring constant?

A. 1.25 N/m
B. 1.25×10^7 N/m
C. 1.25×10^8 N/m
D. More information is required

27. Two fencers training on ice stand face-to-face, with their sabers crossed and pressed on each other at a single point. If fencers 1 and 2 have a mass of 67 kg and 45 kg, respectively, what is the ratio of fencer 1's speed to fencer 2's speed as they push off in opposite directions?

A. 1:1
B. 1:2
C. 45:67
D. 67:45

28. A rider pushes his horse to the break point, traveling an average of 10 m/s through the first 40 percent of the riding portion of the pentathlon. The horse becomes exhausted and finishes the next 60 percent of the race at half the original rate. What is its average speed for the race?

A. 7.50 m/s
B. 6.25 m/s
C. 7.00 m/s
D. 7.14 m/s

29. A high jump record-holder from Cuba jumped about 2.5 m in 1989. Assuming he fell straight to the ground on his way back down, what was his speed just before he hit the ground?

A. 0.7 m/s

B. 7 m/s

C. 50 m/s

D. 20 m/s

30. An athlete training for the swimming portion of the modern pentathlon spends 30 minutes swimming at a constant rate of 2 m/s. After pushing herself to the limit and surpassing her personal record for round-trip laps swum, she determines that her displacement during this period has been

A. 0 m.

B. 1,800 m.

C. 3,600 m.

D. dependant on her acceleration.

PASSAGE IV (QUESTIONS 31–37)

A student conducts an experiment to study the rules of simple harmonic motion. To do this, he attaches a block to a spring ($k = 100$ N/m) on a horizontal table as shown in the figure below.

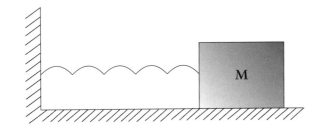

He stretches the block to the right, releases it, and watches it oscillate. After the block comes to rest, he attaches another block of a different mass and records the new findings. He repeats this experiment with varying forces and block masses. He uses formulas from his physics book to compute the measurements. Some of his measurements are shown here.

$E = \frac{1}{2}mv^2 + \frac{1}{2}kx^2 = \frac{1}{2}kA^2$, where A is the maximum amplitude of the system

$\omega = 2\pi f$ (Note: assume that friction is negligible in this system and that no energy is lost to heat.)

Block	Force Applied (F)	Amplitude (A)	Period (T)	Mass (m)
A	50 N	0.5 m		1 kg
B	150 N		7 s	2 kg
C	200 N		1 s	5 kg

31. How many cycles does block A complete in a quarter of a second?

A. $\frac{1}{2\pi}\sqrt{100}$

B. $\pi\sqrt{\frac{1}{100}}$

C. $\frac{\pi}{8}\sqrt{\frac{1}{100}}$

D. $\frac{1}{8\pi}\sqrt{100}$

32. What is the maximum velocity of block C?

A. $2A\sqrt{\frac{k}{m}}$

B. $A\sqrt{\frac{m}{k}}$

C. $A\sqrt{\frac{k}{m}}$

D. $2A\sqrt{\frac{m}{k}}$

33. Which of the following would increase the maximum amplitude of block B?

   I. Increasing the mass of block B

   II. Increasing the spring constant, k

   III. Performing the experiment where the gravity constant is 19.6 m/s^2

A. I only

B. II only

C. I and II only

D. I, II, and III

34. Which of the following could increase the amplitude of the system?

   I. Introducing a coefficient of friction between the table and the block

   II. Introducing an external force (i.e., hitting the block) at the right moment during its motion

   III. Increasing the length of the spring without changing the spring constant

   A. II only

   B. I and III only

   C. II and III only

   D. I, II, and III

35. What is the relationship between the maximum acceleration and amplitude of blocks B and C?

   A. Block B's maximum acceleration and amplitude are both greater than C's.

   B. Block B's maximum acceleration is greater, but its amplitude is less than C's.

   C. Block B's maximum acceleration is less, but its amplitude is greater than C's.

   D. Block B's maximum acceleration and amplitude are both less than C's.

36. The figure below is a graph of velocity versus time for another block. Which of the following statements best describes this block?

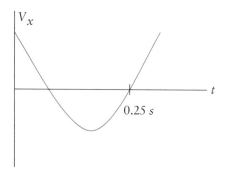

   A. The spring is initially compressed and passes the equilibrium point at 0.25 seconds.

   B. The block is passing the equilibrium position at $t = 0$ and changing direction at 0.25 seconds.

   C. The block is passing the equilibrium position at $t = 0$ and at 0.25 seconds.

   D. The spring is initially extended and is going through the equilibrium position at 0.25 seconds.

37. When the velocity of a block A is zero and the spring is extended, which of the following is true?

   A. The acceleration is at its maximum and points to the left.

   B. The acceleration is at its maximum and points to the right.

   C. The acceleration is zero and points to the left.

   D. The acceleration is zero and points to the right.

PASSAGE V (QUESTIONS 38–44)

Nuclear energy is having a resurgence in popularity as a potential cost-effective way to meet the enormous energy demands in the United States. Together with knowing how radiation and particles affect living organisms, an understanding of basic nuclear processes such as radioactive decay and nuclear fission will influence future energy policy and medical technology. In general, nuclear phenomena involve relatively large quantities of energy for a given amount of material; they also lead to relatively large biological effects.

Equation 1a shows a nuclear fission reaction in which weapons-grade uranium breaks up to form two fission fragments plus some neutrons. Along with protons, these two subatomic particles are collectively known as nucleons. The fission reaction shown in equation 1a involves neutron-induced fission of $^{235}_{92}U$, which temporarily produces a compound nucleus ($^{236}_{92}U$) and then breaks up to form many combinations of nuclei. A typical fission reaction with one possible combination of fission fragments is given in equation 1b. $^{235}_{92}U$ has a half-life of 7.1×10^8 years.

$$^{1}_{0}n + {}^{235}_{92}U \rightarrow {}^{236}_{92}U \rightarrow N_1 + N_2 + \text{neutrons} \qquad (1a)$$

$$^{1}_{0}n + {}^{235}_{92}U \rightarrow {}^{236}_{92}U \rightarrow {}^{92}_{36}Kr + {}^{141}_{56}Ba + 3\,{}^{1}_{0}n \qquad (1b)$$

Radioactive carbon dating is extremely useful for dating events because humans and other living organisms ingest radioactive carbon produced by cosmic rays in our atmosphere. The radioactive carbon mixes with the normal carbon in the environment and is ingested by all living organisms. Once an organism dies, the radioactive carbon in the organism begins to decay, and the ratio of radioactive carbon to ordinary carbon decreases with time. The amount of radioactive carbon can be used to determine approximately when death occurred.

Three naturally occurring isotopes of carbon are currently known to exist on Earth. The most common, making up about 99 percent of the Earth's carbon, is carbon-12.

Carbon-13, a stable isotope, makes up about 1 percent. Finally, carbon-14, a radioactive isotope, makes up trace amounts, but it is this form that is of most interest in radiocarbon dating. This form has a half-life of 5,630 years and a decay rate of 2,000 counts/second. Equation 2 describes this decay.

$$^{6}_{14}C \rightarrow {}^{7}_{14}N + {}^{0}_{-1}e + \text{antineutrino} \quad (2)$$

38. How many neutrons exist in an atom of the uranium intermediary produced during nuclear fission?

A. 92

B. 143

C. 144

D. 236

39. Considering the half-life of $^{235}_{92}U$, the amount of untouched, naturally occurring weapons-grade uranium embedded in the Earth has

A. increased since Earth's formation 4.6×10^9 years ago.

B. remained constant since Earth's formation 4.6×10^9 years ago.

C. decreased by more than a factor of 2 since Earth's formation 4.6×10^9 years ago.

D. decreased by less than a factor of 2 since Earth's formation 4.6×10^9 years ago.

40. Approximately how much of a 200 g sample of $^{14}_{6}C$ remains after 11,260 years?

A. 200 g

B. 100 g

C. 50 g

D. 25 g

41. What will be the decay rate of $^{14}_{6}C$ in 5,630 years?

    A. 2,000 count/s

    B. 1,000 count/s

    C. 500 count/s

    D. 250 count/s

42. $^{14}_{6}C$ decay is best described as

    A. α decay.

    B. β decay.

    C. γ decay.

    D. All of the above

43. Which of the following is true concerning $^{14}_{6}C$ decay?

    A. A proton and an electron are destroyed, while a neutron is created.

    B. A proton and a neutron are destroyed, while an electron is created.

    C. A proton and a neutron are created, while an electron is destroyed.

    D. A proton and an electron are created, while a neutron is destroyed.

44. Assuming 15 decays per minute per gram of carbon in a living organism, how old is a bone containing 100 gram of carbon having a decay rate of 187.5 decays per minute?

    A. 5,630 years

    B. 11,260 years

    C. 16,890 years

    D. 22,520 years

PASSAGE VI (QUESTIONS 45–52)

The Hubble space telescope first went up into orbit in April 1990 and is scheduled to be retrieved around 2013. Remarkable for the quality of its images, Hubble is also known as one of the largest telescopes in the world. Weighing in at 11,110 kg, it orbits quite close to the Earth, about 600 km away from the surface. It orbits the Earth about every 1.5 hours, traveling at a speed of 7,500 m/s.

Many observatories exist around the world with lenses even larger than that of Hubble. However, one of the things that sets it apart from earthbound telescopes is its position relative to the Earth. The near absence of background light allows it to produce exceptionally clear and distinct images. Another unique feature is its ultra deep field abilities, which allows the scope to take images of especially far away objects using only visible light.

The inner-workings of the scope itself are remarkable. Hubble is capable of observing visible, ultraviolet, and near-infrared wavelengths and has a focal length of 57.6 m. The most important aspect of the telescope system is its concave mirror.

There have been several servicing missions since the telescope was launched. The first was scheduled to repair a flawed mirror. Though the mirror had been ground very precisely, it had been produced with an incorrect shape. Because it was too flat at the edges, the mirror caused light reflecting off the edge and light reflecting off the center to focus on different points. This is especially interesting since the length of the imperfection was only a few micrometers! Although this flaw did not disrupt all types of observations, it was catastrophic for some of them.

45. At one point in the construction of Hubble, a company built a blank copy mirror from ultra-low expansion glass, with an index of refraction of 2. Imagine that a thick block of this material had been brought up in space while astronauts were on a service mission. If a laser beam in space had been pointed toward the block, what would the astronaut determine its critical angle to be?

A. 30°

B. 45°

C. 60°

D. None of the above

46. A student builds a scale model of the telescope for a class project. However, his teacher notices that there are several inconsistencies with the actual telescope. In terms of size, everything is accurately 10 percent the size of the original. However, the optical portion consists of converging lenses rather than a single convex mirror. The lenses touch and there are two of them. If the student were to use the model for optical experiments, what would be its total focal length?

A. −2.9 m

B. 0.3 m

C. 2.9 m

D. 5.8 m

47. Rank the following by their wavelength, from highest frequency to lowest frequency.

I. Visible light

II. Ultraviolet

III. Infrared

IV. X-rays

A. III, I, IV, II

B. IV, II, I, III

C. I, II, IV, III

D. II, IV, III, I

48. Imagine that Hubble somehow hits a momentarily stationary spacecraft in the plane of its orbit. Hubble falls to Earth, starting from rest and moving with constant acceleration along a straight line as it falls. You are asked to sketch two graphs of Hubble's fall. Graph A represents speed, while graph B represents distance from the surface of the Earth. Which of the following would describe these graphs?

I. A is a flat line with zero slope.

II. A is a straight line with a nonzero slope.

III. B is parabolic, sloping away from the *x*-axis.

IV. B is parabolic, sloping toward the *x*-axis.

A. I only

B. IV only

C. II and III only

D. II and IV only

49. Suppose that during a maintenance mission, an astronaut drops a hammer (F_g = 10 N) and washer (F_g = 0.01 N) from his hands. Instead of remaining in orbit with the satellite, space station, and astronaut, the objects drop straight down, falling freely. Neglecting air resistance, which of the following statements would be true about the subsequent motion of the two objects?

I. The two fall with the same acceleration.

II. The two have the same speed before hitting the Earth.

III. The hammer has more potential energy before falling.

IV. The two have the same potential energy before falling.

A. III only

B. I and IV only

C. I, II, and III

D. I, II, and IV

50. A scientist monitoring Hubble's speed as it rounds the Earth in orbit notices that the speed has become quite erratic. She looks at a chart of the motion and realizes that over the course of five seconds, Hubble's speed has decreased by 10 percent. As this speed reduction is detrimental to the maintenance of orbit, the scientist needs to get the telescope on track. Among the values she needs is the distance that Hubble has traveled since its speed began to decline. Assuming smooth, constant deceleration, what is this distance?

A. 1,425 m
B. 7,125 m
C. 33,750 m
D. 35,625 m

51. A foil-covered instrument attached to the side of the telescope falls off while Hubble is in a steady orbit. How much time is required for this instrument to reach the Earth's surface? Assume that the acceleration due to gravity is approximately 10 m/s^2.

A. 11 s
B. 1 min
C. 1 min, 16 s
D. 5 min, 46 s

52. Imagine that a ray of light travels parallel to the principal axis of the most important aspect of the telescope, its concave mirror. After reflecting off the mirror, the light ray will travel

A. normal to the mirror's principal axis.
B. parallel to the mirror's principal axis.
C. to a point 57.6 m in front of its initial position.
D. to a point 115.2 m in front of its initial position.

Answers and Explanations

PRACTICE SECTION 1

ANSWER KEY

1.	B	19.	A	37.	B
2.	D	20.	A	38.	C
3.	B	21.	B	39.	A
4.	C	22.	C	40.	A
5.	A	23.	D	41.	D
6.	D	24.	B	42.	C
7.	A	25.	C	43.	D
8.	C	26.	B	44.	A
9.	B	27.	A	45.	D
10.	C	28.	A	46.	B
11.	C	29.	C	47.	C
12.	A	30.	C	48.	D
13.	C	31.	C	49.	D
14.	B	32.	A	50.	B
15.	C	33.	B	51.	C
16.	A	34.	B	52.	A
17.	B	35.	D		
18.	A	36.	C		

PASSAGE I

1. B

The Bohr energy is negative for an atomic electron and zero for a free electron. The largest negative energy values are found in the first energy level; the energy increases for electrons closer to the outer energy levels, but never reaches zero. The electron is only ejected when it is struck by a photon carrying enough energy to bring the electron's energy above zero, and thus permitting it to leave the attractive pull of the nucleus. For this reason, it is easier for a photon to eject a high-energy outer electron than a lower-energy inner electron.

2. D

Electrons always occupy the lowest possible energy level. If one of the inner shells has a vacancy, an electron from an outer shell will immediately occupy it in order to minimize its own energy. Minimizing energy means the same thing as maximizing stability. The energy level drop causes the emission of the x-ray, not vice versa as in (A). The charge on the atom doesn't change when an electron moves from one energy level to another, so (B) is incorrect. The gravitational force between the nucleus and the electron (C) is insignificant compared to the electrostatic force; also, the gravitational force does not change when an empty shell is created.

3. B

Because the x-ray moves in a random direction, only the energy of the photon will impact the likelihood of the production of an Auger electron. A photon carrying more energy, meanwhile, is more likely to carry enough energy to eject a second electron. We can tell by looking at the figures that (A) and (B) involve the largest energy change. A more precise value can be determined by considering the fact that the total energy is inversely proportional to the square of the principal quantum number. If we set the energy of the first level as x, the energy of the drop from level 2 to level 1 (B) is equal to $\frac{x}{(1)^2} - \frac{x}{(2)^2} = \frac{x}{1} - \frac{x}{4} = \frac{3x}{4}$. The energy of the trop from level 4 to level 2 (A), meanwhile, is $\frac{x}{(2)^2} - \frac{x}{(4)^2} = \frac{x}{4} - \frac{x}{16} = \frac{3x}{16}$. Therefore, (B) carries far more energy than (A).

4. C

The passage states that the emission of the x-ray photon is caused by the decrease in energy of the electron, so the photon will carry all of the energy lost by the electron. Because energy is inversely proportional to the square of the principal quantum number, we can say that the energy of an electron in level 3 is equal to $\frac{x}{9}$ and the energy of an electron in level 2 is equal to $\frac{x}{4}$, where x is the energy of an electron in level 1. Since $\frac{x}{9}$ is equal to 10 eV, x must be equal to 90 eV; this means that $\frac{x}{4}$, the energy of level 2, is equal to 2.5 eV. Therefore, the change in energy from level 3 to level 2 is 7.5 eV.

5. A

As the passage suggests, the energy from Auger electrons will slightly distort the measurements of an x-ray's energy. If the Auger electrons are eliminated, this error in the measurements will be decreased. A fairly constant number of Auger electrons is produced (on average) along with an x-ray, so this is not a significant source of variability (B). Auger electrons are unrelated to the sensitivity (C) and resolution (D) of the equipment. Also, no details are provided about the equipment used to measure the energy of x-rays. Even so, noise in a measurement will decrease the precision of the measurement but will have no effect on the resolution of the measurement.

6. D

The number of electrons will change the likelihood of the production of an Auger electron but will not affect the energy of the electron. If a negatively-charged ion is produced through the addition of an extra electron, each of the electrons in orbit will feel a decreased net electrostatic force

with the nucleus; this means that it will take less energy to remove the electron from orbit. Therefore, an Auger electron released from substance A will have a higher kinetic energy because it used up less of its energy when being ejected from orbit.

7. A

Hydrogen and helium have only one energy level, so they do not produce Auger electrons. All the other elements have the potential to produce Auger electrons because they all have multiple energy levels from which an outer electron can drop to fill a hole.

8. C

An increase in photon energy will not directly cause an increase in the number of x-rays unless the increase is significant enough to eject an electron in a lower energy level. Once the energy of the photon reaches this point, the number of x-rays will suddenly increase. The energy of these x-rays, however, will increase continuously. When this energy becomes adequate to start ejecting Auger electrons, it will begin to do so. The number of steps in the Auger electron curve is greater than the number of steps in the x-ray curve because every x-ray has the potential to produce several different Auger electrons.

9. B

When an electron drops from level a to level b, the excess energy will, according to the passage, take the form of an x-ray. This x-ray, whose energy is now equal to $E_a - E_b$, sometimes collides with the potential Auger electron. This electron will be ejected if its new energy (the sum of its energy, E_c, and the x-ray's energy, $E_a - E_b$) is greater than zero. This sum will be equal to the kinetic energy of the electron after it is ejected. Notice that even though the gamma ray caused the electron to drop its energy level, the energy released as an x-ray depends only on the difference between the initial and final energy states of the electron.

PASSAGE II

10. C

According to the passage, the thermocouple measures voltage changes that occur as a result of the temperature difference across the circuit. As this temperature difference increases, the energy difference between the two sides will also increase; this will lead to the production of a larger voltage.

11. C

The resistance does not change when more voltage is applied. According to Ohm's law ($V = IR$), an increase in electric potential (V) will cause an increase in current (I). The amount of current depends on the total resistance in a circuit, but the amount of resistance does not depend on the current (D). The resistance of a material is an innate property of that material and based on $R = \dfrac{\rho L}{A}$, where ρ is the resistivity of the material, L is the length of the resistor, and A is the cross-sectional area of the resistor.

12. A

According to the passage, a thermocouple determines temperature differences based on differences in voltage; you should know that voltage is produced as a result of differences in potential energy. While temperature is a measure of the average kinetic energy of particles in a substance (B), it is not the temperature difference that creates the signal produced. The temperature difference creates the potential energy imbalance, and *that* is what creates the signal within the thermocouple.

13. C

The voltage in a thermocouple is produced as a result of the temperature difference across the circuit; therefore, it can function without an external source of electric current. That means (A) and (B) are incorrect. Resistance, however, cannot be easily measured without applying a current across the circuit. Choice (D) is incorrect because resistance always exists, whether or not external power is present. Because an RTD functions by measuring changes in resistance, a small amount of external power is always necessary in order to accurately determine these changes.

14. B

According to the passage, the RTD measures temperature by measuring changes in resistance. These changes in resistance will be easiest to see if we maximize the resistance of the RTD. That is, a 10% increase in resistance will be much easier to observe and measure if the RTD starts with a large resistance than with a very small resistance. The resistance in a circuit is maximized when the resistors are wired in series, as in (B); in this case, the total resistance is equal to the sum of the individual resistances. In (A), the resistors are wired in parallel, so the total resistance is equal to one-fourth of each individual resistance. Choices (C) and (D) represent a circuit that contains both a series and a parallel connection; no matter how this is organized, the total resistance will be lower than the resistance in a series wiring scheme.

15. C

A complete circuit is always organized in a loop; (C) is the only one that includes such a loop. Choices (B) and (D) disregard the fact that a voltage is always created between two points, so a voltmeter must measure voltage through two different wires. Choice (A) does not feature a loop.

16. A

The thermoelectric effect is used in a thermocouple to generate electricity (B). In general, a circuit can generate and carry electricity, but a circuit cannot store electrical energy unless a capacitor is added. The passage mentions that the thermoelectric effect is reversible, meaning that it can also produce heat from voltage (instead of just producing voltage from heat). Because voltage can be either positive or negative, it can be used for either heating or cooling.

17. B

If the resistivity changes easily with respect to temperature, changes in temperature will lead to significant changes in the readings from the RTD. This will make it more likely for the RTD to detect relatively small changes in temperature.

QUESTIONS 18–21

18. A

How do light and sound waves differ? Polarization requires that the direction of propagation of the wave be perpendicular to the direction of propagation of energy. Electromagnetic waves like light can accomplish this because they are transverse waves. Sound cannot produce this phenomenon because it is a longitudinal wave and so the direction of its propagation is parallel to the direction in which it carries energy. Remember that polarization of light is the alignment of its electric field waves in the same plane.

19. A

The question assumes you know that the index of refraction of a vacuum is, by definition, 1. This assumption is also made on the actual MCAT. The critical angle is the smallest incident angle at which one sees total internal reflection of the light wave; in other words, the refracted angle is 90°. According to Snell's Law, this means $n_i \sin\theta_i = n_r \sin 90°$. For any material with an index of refraction n, the critical angle is $\arcsin\left(\dfrac{1}{n}\right)$. The angle whose sine is $\dfrac{1}{2}$ is 30°. For Test Day, be familiar with the sines and cosines of 0°, 30°, 45°, 60°, and 90° because they occur so commonly in calculations.

20. A

When light reflects off any object, its phase is shifted by pi radians, causing constructive interference. If a material is made that is half the thickness of the wavelength, then as the light passes through the film (once incoming and once outgoing), it will be shifted by another wavelength, causing completely destructive interference.

21. B

This question asks us for the maximum frequency of the emitted photons. Since it tells us the maximum energy is 6 eV, we can use $E = hf$ to find the maximum frequency, where h is Planck's constant. Dividing E by h, we get a maximum value of f of 1.5×10^{-15} Hz.

PASSAGE III

22. C

This problem asks that you calculate work: $W = Fd\cos\theta$, where F is the force, d is the displacement, and θ is the angle between the work and the displacement. Because the force being applied is in the exact same direction as the displacement, θ is equal to 0. $\cos(0) = 1$, so we have $W = Fd$. The force required to lift the plate is equal to the weight of the plate. Weight $= mg = 2$ kg $\times$ 10 m/s^2 $= 20$ N and the displacement is 2 m, so the work is equal to 20 N $\times$ 2 m $=$ 40 J. Choice (C) is Correct. (A) confuses the mass of the plate with its weight. Choice (B) uses the incorrect formula $W = \dfrac{F}{d}$, and (D) uses $W = \dfrac{d}{F}$.

23. D

The formula for potential energy is $U = mgh$, where m is the mass of the object, g is the acceleration due to gravity, and h is the height of the object off the ground. First, make sure that all of the variables are converted into standard units: 40 g $= 0.04$ kg and 150 cm $= 1.5$ m. Then plug in the variables to find the answer. U $= (0.04$ kg$)(1.5$ m$)(10$ m/s$^2)$ $= 0.6$ J. Choices (A) and (C) omit one or more conversions.

24. B

It is important to remember the concept of conservation of energy. Although the energy of the plate may change forms throughout its path, its total energy will remain constant. The plate does not simply lose (A) or gain (C) energy by simply falling. The potential energy of the plate will decrease as its height decreases, while its kinetic energy will increase as its velocity increases (D).

25. C

When the plate sits on the table, all of its energy is potential energy. As it falls, the potential energy is converted to kinetic energy. The farther it falls to the ground, the more the potential energy is converted to kinetic. Thus, although the total energy stays the same, the kinetic energy is greatest right before the plate hits the ground (C).

26. B

Utilizing the concept of conservation of momentum, we know that the individual pieces will have a total momentum equal to the momentum of the plate right before it breaks. Momentum is given by $p = mv$. The mass, as given by the three pieces that form when the plate breaks, must have started as $6M$. The velocity can be determined using kinematics. If the plate started at zero velocity and accelerated at 10 m/s² for 2 seconds, the final velocity is 0 + (2 s)(20 m/s²) = 40 m/s. Since M refers to a particular mass, its units must be kg. The momentum is therefore $(6M$ kg$)(40$ m/s$) = 240M$ kg·m/s.

27. A

Because friction is negligible, momentum will be conserved in this interaction. The piece of the plate has a momentum of $p = (3M)(5$ m/s$) = 15M$ kg·m/s. Because it comes to a complete stop, all of its momentum is transferred to the block. Thus, $15M$ kg·m/s $= (M$kg$)(v)$; $v = 15$ m/s. Choice (A) is correct. Choice (B) is the total momentum, not velocity. Choices (C) and (D) are derived incorrectly using the kinetic energy formula, not the momentum formula.

28. A

Here you must apply the concept of impulse. Impulse is given by $I = Ft = mv_f - mv_o$. If we want to find how much for is required to stop the $1M$ kg piece in 3 seconds, we must plug in our variables ($m = 1M$ kg, $v_o = 4$ m/s, $v_f = 0$ m/s, $t = 3$ s, $F = ?$). Thus, $(F)(3$ s$) = (M)(4$ m/s$) - (M)(0$ m/s$) = \frac{4}{3}M$N. Choice (A) is correct. Choices (C) and (D) confuse the initial velocity with the final velocity.

29. C

Due to conservation of energy, the position of the plate does not matter. As it reaches its highest point, its kinetic energy is decreasing because its velocity is decreasing. However, its potential energy is increasing due to an increase in height from the original position. As it falls, the opposite happens. Overall, the total energy stays constant even if the potential and kinetic energies change. Choice (C) is correct.

30. C

Work is done only by the force that is responsible for an object's movement. Because the force points downward and the plate moves to the left, this particular force does no work on the plate. Choice (C) is correct. Choice (A) multiplies the force by the value of the angle. Choice (B) correctly multiplies force by distance but doesn't consider the fact that the force is not in the same direction as the displacement. Choice (D) also ignores the angle of the force and uses the incorrect formula by dividing the force by the distance.

PASSAGE IV

31. C

Two nearby sound waves will typically emit a beat whose frequency is equal to the difference between the frequencies of the individual waves. In this case, the frequency of the beat is equal to 440 Hz – 430 Hz = 10 Hz, or 10 beats per second. There will be a total of (10 Hz)(60 seconds/minute) = 600 beats per minute.

32. A

The pitch of a sound is determined by its frequency, which is inversely proportional to the length of the string. Therefore, if the length of the string is decreased, the frequency will increase.

33. B

The passage mentions that the sound waves emerging from the compartment have a greater amplitude than those entering the compartment. This means that the waves carry more energy and that the individual sounds are louder. Either of these two observations should lead you to the conclusion that the sound has a greater intensity because the intensity of the wave increases with increasing energy and determines how loud the sound is. Note that increasing the frequency of the wave (A) would increase the pitch of the sound wave.

34. B

As the sound wave approaches the listener, its relative velocity is greater than the typical velocity of sound in air. According to the Doppler effect, this increased velocity will cause the apparent frequency of the sound to increase, since frequency is directly proportional to velocity.

35. D

The length of a fixed string is inversely proportional to its frequency. This means that the pitch of the string will decrease as the length increases. The curve will demonstrate a $y = \dfrac{1}{x}$ curve, which is represented approximately by the graph in (D). Choice (A) represents a curve with the formula $y = x$, Choice (B) represents a curve with the formula $y = -x$, and Choice (C) represents a curve with the formula $y = \sqrt{x}$.

36. C

The passage states that a pickup absorbs a sound wave directly from the electric guitar strings. The acoustic guitar strings, on the other hand, are amplified in the wooden compartment. Therefore, the acoustic guitar produces a louder sound wave than the electric guitar strings; this means that the sine curve will have a larger amplitude.

37. B

Assuming no loss due to friction, the energy transmitted by the string is equal to $\dfrac{1}{2}kx^2$, where k is the spring constant (500 N/m) and x is the total displacement (0.02 m). So $\dfrac{1}{2}kx^2$ is equal to 0.1 J. Power is equal to energy per unit time, which can be determined by multiplying the energy by the frequency (1,000 s^{-1}), so the total power equals 100 W. The intensity of a sound is equal to the power divided by the square of the distance (1 m), so the total intensity is 100 W/m^2.

QUESTIONS 38–45

38. C

A combined approach of test-taking skills and physical reasoning makes this question easier than it seems. First, the horizontal component is always less than the total velocity vector unless the object is moving only in the horizontal

direction. This eliminates (A) and (B). Choice (D) represents the initial velocity in the y-direction. This leaves (C). Since $\cos 30° = \sqrt{\dfrac{3}{2}}$, then (40) $\cos 30° = 20\sqrt{3}$. $\sqrt{3}$ is approximately 1.7, so $20\sqrt{3}$ is about 34. This matches most closely with (C).

39. A

Heat flow is directly proportional to temperature change according to the laws of thermodynamics. For heat exchange to have occurred, there must have been an initial difference in temperature. To eliminate the other answer choices, reason by counterexample: heat can flow from one object to an object of identical composition at a lower temperature, so (B) and (D) are incorrect. The mass (C) will influence the amount of heat transferred but not the fact that heat is transferred.

40. A

Choice (B) is too extreme. Choices (C) and (D) directly contradict the postulates of the kinetic theory of gases.

41. D

Whereas high resistance would increase the error associated with measuring a current because of the creation of a non-negligible current drop across any resistor, it would decrease the error associated with measuring any voltage in parallel because of the very same effect. Both dynamos and generators rely on electromagnetic induction, as can some ammeters.

42. C

How is the focal length related to the radius of curvature? It is one-half the radius of curvature. This is a straightforward application of the formula stating that the focal length of a perfectly spherical mirror is equal to one-half the length of the radius of curvature.

43. D

While this question may seem daunting because these are 1-ohm resistors, the key lies in discovering the symmetry.

They can be arranged as follows: all in series; all in parallel; in a train of two groups of resistors (three then one or two then two); or in a train of three groups of resistors. That makes a total of five combinations.

44. A

A dieletric allows more charge to be stored on each plate in a parallel plate capacitor because it decreases the effective electric field between the plates. Because $F = qE$, at a constant force, the charge stored must go up. The potential difference is unchanged because the addition of additional charge is proportional on both plates.

45. D

The angular frequency (which is directly proportional to the frequency of oscillation) of a pendulum is directly proportional to the square root of acceleration due to gravity, and inversely proportional to the square root of the length of the pendulum's string. The mass has no effect, eliminating all answer choices but (D).

PASSAGE V

46. B

Centripetal forces on the tires are proportional to the speed of the vehicle. This may lead them to expand and burst, even if the force of friction is smaller than in trial 2.

47. C

The net force is not $0\,\text{N}$; it is the centripetal force that causes the constant change in direction, measured by $\frac{mv^2}{R}$. The mass of the motorcycle is 400 kg, so the centripetal force is $\frac{(400\,\text{kg})(50\,\text{m/s})^2}{(100\,\text{m})} = 10,000\,\text{N}$. Choice (C) is the answer.

48. D

F1 and F2 are normal and centripetal forces, respectively. At point B in figure 2, they point toward the center. At point A, they also point toward the center.

49. D

It's important to set the equation up correctly. F_N at point A must be greater than $0\,\text{N}$. $\frac{mv^2}{R} = F_N + mg$. So $\frac{mv^2}{R} = mg \geq 0$, which means $\frac{v^2}{R} \geq g$ and $R \leq \frac{v^2}{g}$. Substituting for v and g, we get $\frac{v^2}{g} = \frac{(50\text{m/s})^2}{10\text{m/s}} = 250\,\text{m}$. This represents the radius of the loop, so the total height is actually 500 m. Of course, the motorcyclist is burning up his engine by going against gravity, but that is not of concern here.

50. B

As the motorcycle moves away from the lowest point (point B), the normal force decreases. The force of friction is proportional to the normal force. To keep constant speed, the net force is always of the same magnitude and points toward the center of the circle.

51. C

Item I is correct: The radial force of friction is responsible for keeping the motorcycle from sliding out of control. (This is what may happen if the road is slick.) This force is equal in magnitude and direction to the horizontal component of the normal force. If it didn't exist, the wheels would slip radially outward. Item II is correct: A greater radius means that a smaller radial force of friction is required to sustain the smaller centripetal force $\frac{mv^2}{R}$. Item III is incorrect; the mass of the motorcycle is proportional to both the centripetal and the frictional forces, creating no net effect. Items I and II are correct, so (C) is the answer.

52. A

In both scenarios the forces are nonzero in magnitude at any given moment, but the summation of force vectors for a circle happens to be $0\,\text{N}$. This indicates that centripetal forces do not do any work over a circular trip.

PRACTICE SECTION 2

ANSWER KEY

1.	D	19.	C	37.	A
2.	C	20.	A	38.	B
3.	B	21.	D	39.	A
4.	A	22.	C	40.	D
5.	B	23.	B	41.	C
6.	D	24.	A	42.	A
7.	B	25.	B	43.	D
8.	C	26.	D	44.	D
9.	C	27.	B	45.	A
10.	C	28.	C	46.	B
11.	B	29.	B	47.	D
12.	C	30.	D	48.	A
13.	D	31.	D	49.	C
14.	A	32.	D	50.	D
15.	C	33.	B	51.	B
16.	A	34.	C	52.	B
17.	C	35.	A		
18.	D	36.	C		

PASSAGE I

1. D

The car maintains its speed when it goes through the circle (change of kinetic energy to potential and back to kinetic) and it also maintains its speed when it hits the wall and rebounds, assuming there is no energy loss to heat. The change in momentum is $m \times (v_i - (-v_i)) = 100$ kg $\times$ 100 m/s = 10,000 kg·m/s.

2. C

Choices (A) and (B) are unlikely to happen because trial 1 used more kinetic energy and, therefore, subjected the car and the wall to greater stress. Choice (C) is reasonable because most collisions are not perfectly elastic.

3. B

If friction is negligible, then the speed of the car after coming out of the circle is the same as the speed when it went in, because no work was done on it. The distance to the wall is 50 m, which can be traversed in 1 second. But the car will have to convert all of its kinetic energy into elastic potential energy before it stops. $\frac{1}{4}\sqrt{\frac{k}{m}} = 1.3$ s. Therefore, the total time is 2.3 s.

4. A

At first, the spring on the car is relaxed ($x = 0$), but as it hits the wall, a force proportional to the length of compression is applied to it: $F = -kx = ma$. Therefore, deceleration grows in magnitude as the spring compresses, until it comes to a stop. After that, the reverse happens as the car rebounds.

5. B

With 50 percent efficiency, half of the kinetic energy will be delivered to the cylinders. The rest will cause the car to rebound with half of its original kinetic energy. So the heat delivered is $50\% \times \frac{1}{2} \times mv^2 = \frac{1}{4} \times 100 \times 20^2 = 10,000$ J. To find power, one must find the time it takes the car to complete one cycle—to go from one wall to another and back. The length of the track is 200 m and the circumference of the circle is 5π, so the time can be found by computing the distance: $x = 2 \times (200 + 5\pi)$ and $t = \frac{x}{v} = \frac{400 + 10\pi}{20} = 21$ s. Power is energy divided by time, which is equal to $\frac{10,000\text{J}}{21\text{ s}}$ = 116 W.

6. D

The heat delivered to the cylinder is equal to the product of power and time. We just calculated how much heat will be delivered in question 5. With 10,000 J per cycle, that means 10,000 J $\times$ 5 = 25 kJ. If you used the heat transfer formula $\frac{Q}{t} = \frac{kA\Delta T}{L}$ to calculate ΔT, you would end up with a small value, which tells you only that the wall of the cylinder quickly transfers heat from the outside to the inside of the cylinder. It does not tell you how much heat will be added to the water inside the cylinder system, only how quickly the temperature is equilibrated. The question asked how much heat was added, and the best way to answer it is to compute how much kinetic energy is delivered to the system.

7. B

The more the car hits the spring, the more energy (and, therefore, more heat) will be delivered to the water cylinder. Unless the water cylinder quickly loses this heat to the environment (which is not mentioned in the passage), its temperature will increase. The speed of the car determines how much energy is delivered. According to the formula $Q = mc\Delta T$ and as explained in the passage, specific heat is different for every liquid and affects the propensity of the liquid to change temperature. The magnitude of the spring constant does not affect the amount of energy generated in the collision. There is no indication in the passage that greater or smaller spring constants increase the efficiency of transfer from elastic to heat energy.

8. C

In order for the car to continue moving from wall to wall, it must overcome the centripetal forces in each of the circular loops (diameter 5 m). If the car does not overcome the centripetal forces in the circular portions of the track, it will not continue moving through the loops. According to the equation $\frac{mv^2}{r} = mg + F_N$, the car always needs a velocity which would provide a normal force greater than 0. This means that $\frac{mv^2}{r} > mg$, so $v^2 > gr$, which means that $v^2 > 25 \text{ m}^2/\text{s}^2$ at the top of the track. The car also needs to overcome the gravitational potential energy while maintaining a speed of at least 5 m/s. The law of conservation of energy is $U_{final} + K_{final} = K_{initial}$, which translates into $gh + \frac{1}{2}v_{final}^2 = \frac{1}{2}v_{initial}^2$. Solving this equation yields $v^2 = 2 \times 10 \times 5 + 25 \text{ m}^2/\text{s}^2 = 125 \text{ m}^2/\text{s}^2$ at the bottom of the track, so v must be > 11 m/s. If the car loses energy and slows down with each collision, eventually it will get stuck between the circles (or fall off the track) if it cannot generate a speed of greater than 11 m/s. If half of its kinetic energy is lost, then its speed declines by a factor of $\sqrt{2}$ with each cycle. After

4 cycles, its speed will be $\frac{50}{\sqrt{2^4}} = \frac{50}{4} = 12.5$ m/s . However, the speed will drop to under 11 m/s right after the next collision, and the car will not be able to continue through the whole track.

9. C

According to the equation $\frac{Q}{t} = \frac{kA\Delta T}{L}$ the rate of heat transfer is proportional to the temperature difference between the hot and cold surfaces. If the cylinder becomes almost as hot as the heated engine, the rate of heat transfer decreases. This means that while water still keeps accepting heat, it will eventually reach a plateau and its rate of cooling will approach its rate of heating.

PASSAGE II

10. C

The amount of heat stored by the copper plate can be calculated by the equation $Q = mc\Delta T$, where m is the mass of the plate, c is its specific heat capacity, and ΔT is the change in its temperature. According to this equation, the plate will absorb some of the heat emitted by the warm water, and this absorption will be directly proportional to the heat capacity. In his calculations, the student did not subtract this heat from the total amount of heat that is transferred from the warm water to the cold water.

11. B

The main purpose of the student's calculation is to determine the amount of heat transferred by conduction from the warm water to the copper plate and from the copper plate to the cold water. Although this is not specifically mentioned in the passage, it is something you should be able to infer. Choices (A), (C), and (D) all mention potential types of heat transfer that the student did not consider in his calculations.

12. C

The passage states that the thermal conductivity of copper is about 400 times the thermal conductivity of glass. Therefore, according to the equation in the passage, the copper plate will conduct 400 times as much heat per unit area. Because the area of the copper is half the area of the glass, then it will conduct 400/2 = 200 times as much heat as the glass. The total amount of heat conducted by the copper is equal to 200 J, or 0.2 kJ.

13. D

The amount of heat transferred can be determined by the formula $Q = mc\Delta T$. In this case, the system reaches equilibrium when the temperature of the warm tank decreases by 25 K and the temperature of the cold tank increases by 25 K, so ΔT is equal to 25 K. Because the mass of 100 mL of water is 100 g and the heat capacity is given as 1 cal/g·K, the total heat transfer equals (100 g)(1 cal/g·K)(25 K) = 2,500 cal. One Cal (with a capital "C") is equal to 1,000 cal (with a lowercase "c"), so the correct answer is 2.5 Cal.

14. A

When the divider is removed, the water will mix together. In cases where heat is transferred as a result of the physical motion of a fluid, the process is known as convection.

15. C

The entropy change is always positive for an irreversible process. When heat is transferred from one side of the system to the other, the process cannot be reversed without artificially heating or cooling either side; therefore, the entropy change is positive.

16. A

The heat transfer, $\frac{\Delta Q}{\Delta t}$, is directly proportional to the difference in temperature between the two sides of the copper plate (ΔT). As heat is transferred from one side of the plate to the other, the temperature of the warm water decreases and the temperature of the cold water increases. This means that ΔT is constantly decreasing, which also causes a decrease in $\frac{\Delta Q}{\Delta t}$. Choice (A) is the only answer choice in which $\frac{\Delta Q}{\Delta t}$ continuously decreases. Think about this question logically: as the two sides get closer in temperature, less heat will be transferred per unit time—only (A) shows this.

17. C

The kinetic energy of the molecules in an object is measured by its temperature; if the kinetic energy is decreasing, then the temperature must also be decreasing. The temperature of the warm water tank will always decrease in the system, because this is the entire purpose of the experimental setup. Conversely, the temperature of the cold water tank will always increase (D). The passage suggests that the copper (A) and the glass (B) are conducting heat, so their temperatures are likely to increase.

QUESTIONS 18–21

18. D

Because both the source and the receiver are heading toward one another, the frequency will be increased, removing (A) and (B). Because (C) and (D) are so close together, one should be careful with this calculation; the change in apparent frequency will be determined by the Doppler equation. Use logic to figure out what signs should be used in the numerator and denominator. Since both you and the police car are driving towards each other, the numerator will have a "plus" in it and the denominator will have a "minus" in it. Both of these signs will cause an increase in the perceived frequency.

$$f' = f\frac{v + v_D}{v + v_S} = 400\,\text{Hz}\left(\frac{330\text{m/s} + 20\text{m/s}}{330\text{m/s} - 50\text{m/s}}\right)$$
$$= 400\,\text{Hz}\left(\frac{380}{310}\right) = 400\,\text{Hz}\left(\frac{5}{4}\right) = 500\,\text{Hz}.$$

19. C

Because the change in velocity in the second case is 10 times that in the first case, the distance skidded is multiplied by a factor of 10 squared since the square difference in velocities is directly proportional to the distance skidded. We can see this through our kinematics equations. If $v_f^2 = v_i^2 + 2ax$, and $v_f = 0$, then $2ax = -v_i^2$. Since acceleration will have a negative sign as the car slows down, we can set up this proportionality, in which x is proportional to v_i^2. Thus, a 10 times increase in velocity corresponds to a 100 times increase in distance. If you just multiplied by 10 and forgot to square, you would get (A).

20. A

Completely destructive interference occurs when two waves are one-half wavelength or 180° out of phase. According to the wave equation $v = f\lambda$, the wavelength is 0.5 m. Half of this wavelength, 0.25 m, would correspond to the two waves being perfectly out of sync. One can eliminate (B) and (D) because they are both even integer multiples of the wavelength and thus cannot both be correct.

21. D

According to Pascal's principle, $\frac{F_1}{A_1} = \frac{F_2}{A_2}$. The force due to the car, F_2, is $mg = 10{,}000\,\text{N}$. The surface area of the larger platform is 100 m², and so $\frac{F_2}{A_2} = 100\,\text{N/m}^2$. Because $A_1 = 1\,\text{m}^2$, then the force which must be applied to the small platform, F_1, is 100 N.

PASSAGE III

22. C

The velocity gives both the speed of the plane and the direction in which the plane is traveling, so (C) is correct. A vector is a quantity that has both a magnitude and a direction. The speed of the plane (A) tells us how fast it is going but nothing about its direction. The distance the plane travels (B) also tells us nothing about its direction. The angle that the airplane makes with the horizon (D) tells us the direction of the plane's velocity, but not the magnitude.

23. B

Average velocity is given by the formula $v = \frac{d}{t}$. We know that the plane traveled 1,500 meters in 2 seconds. Thus, 1,500/2 = 750 m/s. The question asks for velocity and not speed; velocity comprises the direction in addition to the magnitude. To have a complete answer, you must write 750 m/s at 30° north of east (the angle is given in the passage), so (B) is correct. Choice (A) correctly specifies the magnitude of the velocity but fails to give a direction. Choices (C) and (D) miscalculate the magnitude by multiplying distance by time.

24. A

First set up a right triangle with the velocity of the airplane as the hypotenuse.

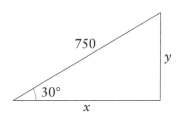

Here you can see that the x- and y-components are the legs of the right triangle. To solve for the x-component, you will utilize the trigonometric formulas: SOH CAH TOA.

$$\sin\theta = \frac{\text{opposite}}{\text{hypotenuse}}$$

$$\cos\theta = \frac{\text{adjacent}}{\text{hypotenuse}}$$

$$\tan\theta = \frac{\text{opposite}}{\text{adjacent}}$$

Here we're looking for the x-component, which is the side adjacent to the 30° angle, so we use the equation $\cos 30° = \frac{x}{750\,\text{m/s}}$. Thus, $x = (750)(\cos 30°)$, which gives us 650 m/s. Because the airplane is traveling in the northeast direction, the x-component is directed east, and (A) is correct. If you had mistakenly used $\sin 30° = \frac{x}{750}$, you would have gotten 375 m/s (B), which is the y-component. Choice (D) pairs the magnitude of the resultant velocity vector with the direction of the x-component.

25. B

To find the sum of the two y-components, you must first break down each velocity vector. Draw a right triangle to represent each vector and its x- and y-components. Then use the trigonometric identities to determine the components that you need.

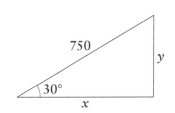

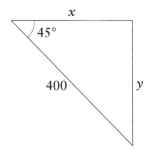

Now you can easily see that the y-component of the plane's velocity will be $y_1 = \sin 30° \times 750 = 375$ m/s heading north. The y-component for the tailwind's velocity is given by $y_2 = \sin 45° \times 400 = 283$ m/s heading south. It is important to note the direction of each vector before you take their sum. To prevent adding together velocities that actually oppose one another, first designate one direction as "positive" and let the opposite direction be "negative." It is most common to indicate north as the positive direction. Thus, we have 375 m/s − 283 m/s = 92 m/s heading north. Choice (B) is correct.

26. D

You can figure out this question by setting up a vector addition problem and solving for each of the components. But that's difficult! Let's use some logic instead to get us to the right answer. The plane is originally flying 30 degrees north of east. We're adding another vector to this that is pointing south of east. What's the overall effect going to be? Well, it should redirect the plane more towards the south—thus, decreasing the angle with the eastern direction. The only answer that shows this is (D). The vector addition shows the same thing: To find the resultant velocity of two separate vectors, you must add the vectors together. Draw the two vectors in a tip-to-tail manner, then draw a final line that connects the two to form a triangle.

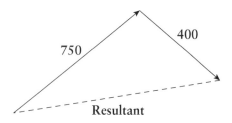

To find the magnitude of this resultant vector you'll need to break down the velocities into their x- and y-components. The x- and y-components are given by:

$$x_1 = \cos 30° \times 750 = 650 \text{ m/s east}$$
$$y_1 = \sin 30° \times 750 = 375 \text{ m/s north}$$

$$x_2 = \cos 45° \times 400 = 283 \text{ m/s east}$$
$$y_2 = \sin 45° \times 400 = 283 \text{ m/s south}$$

Now add up the x- and y-components to get a total for each.

$$x_{total} = 933 \text{ m/s east}$$
$$y_{total} = 92 \text{ m/s north}$$

These sums will be the vectors used to find the resultant velocity of the airplane after it meets the wind.

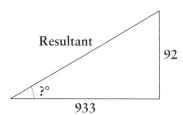

To obtain the magnitude of the velocity, use the Pythagorean theorem ($a^2 + b^2 = c^2$) to determine the hypotenuse of this right triangle. We get a result of 938 m/s. To obtain the direction of the velocity, you will use $\theta = \tan^{-1}\left(\dfrac{\text{opposite}}{\text{adjacent}}\right)$.

$$\theta = \tan^{-1}\left(\frac{92}{933}\right)$$
$$\theta = 6° \text{ north of east}$$

Our full answer will be 938 m/s at 6° north of east, choice (D). You might have gotten (A) if you had used the formula $\tan\theta = \dfrac{\text{opposite}}{\text{adjacent}}$. Notice, though, that solving for the angle here would require calculating an inverse tangent, and you don't get to use a calculator on the MCAT!

27. B

Because the plane traveled 1,500 meters in the 2 seconds before it met the tailwind, we know that its average speed was 1,500/2 = 750 m/s. The question asks how long it takes the plane to travel another 1,000 meters at this speed. Because speed $= \dfrac{d}{t}$, we can solve for time as $t = \dfrac{d}{v}$. Thus, $\dfrac{1,000 \text{ m}}{750 \text{ m/s}} = 1.33$ seconds. Choice (B) is correct.

28. C

You're asked for displacement, not distance. That means it doesn't matter how far the plane travels, but rather how far it is from its original position. The plane traveled at 500 m/s for 3 hours, yielding a total of 1,500 meters east. Then it travels 87.5 meters west, so we can subtract the 87.5 from the 1,500 meters and end up with a total displacement of 1,412.5 meters.

29. B

This question asks for total displacement. When the tailwind meets the plane, the plane has already traveled 1,500 meters. Once the wind and plane meet, a new velocity must be calculated for the next 1.5 seconds. Break the velocities down into their components and add them up to get the totals. The x-component of the plane's velocity is cos 30° × 750 = 650 m/s east. Add the x-component of the wind, 300 m/s east, and the total x-velocity is 950 m/s east. Because there is no y-component for the wind, we just have sin 30° × 750 = 375 m/s north for the plane's velocity. Using these two vectors, 950 m/s E and 375 m/s N, we get a resultant vector of 1,021 m/s. If the plane travels at this speed for another 1.5 seconds, we get a displacement of 1,021 × 1.5 = 1,532 meters. Add this to the original 1,500 meters traveled and we have a total of 3,032 meters, choice (B). Choice (D) assumes that the plane is traveling at 750 m/s for the entire 3.5 seconds. You can also figure this question out using logic. If the plane was traveling at 750 m/s and was NOT affected by the tailwind, the overall displacement would be 750 m/s × 3.5 s = 2,625 m. Tailwinds, according to the passage, will "increase the plane's ground speed." Thus, the total displacement must be more than 2,625 m. The only answer that reflects this is (B).

30. D

Here you need to break up the velocity into its components and then cancel out the parts until you're left with only 500 m/s east. Once you find the x- and y-components that will do this, you can add them to find the resultant vector, which is equal to the velocity of the wind. The x-component of the plane's velocity is 650 m/s east and the y-component is 375 m/s north. Because we want the resultant velocity to be in the east direction, we need to completely cancel out the y-component. This means the wind should have a y-component of 375 m/s south. To reduce the x-component to 500 m/s, we must subtract 150 m/s from the plane's x-component. Therefore, we have the following components for the wind vector:

x-component = 150 m/s west

y-component = 375 m/s south

Using the Pythagorean theorem, we can find a resultant with magnitude 404 m/s and a direction of 68° south of west. Choice (D) is correct. Choices (A) and (C) assume that a wind directed west will cancel out the velocity of the plane and do not give the proper angle. Even if we can't calculate the angle precisely on the MCAT, we know that the wind direction must be more "south" than "west" because the y-component is larger than the x-component.

PASSAGE IV

31. D

According to the passage, a gas-filled detector functions by allowing its particles to be ionized by radiation. You should know that radiation is more likely to ionize a particle if it carries more energy. Also, photons are less likely to interact with atoms because they are infinitely small and they carry no charge. X-rays and γ-rays are the only options that are photons. Because X-rays typically carry much less energy than γ-rays, they are also the least likely to induce ionization.

32. D

Both types of detectors function by ionizing a particle and measuring the extent of the ionization. Radiation with higher energy will produce more ions; however, different modes of decay are capable of carrying the same amount of energy and, consequently, producing the same number of ions. This makes the mode of decay indistinguishable by either of the means mentioned in the passage.

33. B

Because semiconductors are solid, they contain more molecules in the same volume. Therefore, radiation is more likely to interact with an atom in a semiconductor detector. Choice (A) is incorrect because there are several gases that are heavier than silicon and germanium; also, the mass has very little effect on the likelihood of an interaction. Choice (C) is not a true statement. Choice (D) is irrelevant.

34. C

The passage states that ionization occurs as a result of the energy of the radiation; any other form of energy, including the ultraviolet light in the room, can also cause an ionization. For this reason, radiation detectors typically report a small amount of background noise; this noise must be subtracted from any counts in order to get an accurate reading.

35. A

A sample with higher activity simply produces more radiation particles than a sample with lower activity. Every additional radiation particle will produce a constant number of additional ions, so the readings from the detector should be directly proportional to the activity. This is clear based on the data in the table, which suggests a linear trend.

36. C

After the impact of the background radiation is subtracted (12 counts), the ratio of counts to activity for detector 1 is approximately 41 counts/curie. Because the sample in question has a known activity of 4 Ci, it will directly produce $41 \times 4 = 164$ counts. After the background radiation (12 counts) is added, the reading should be close to 175 counts.

37. A

After the background is subtracted, the reading from detector 1 is 4 counts $(16 - 12 = 4)$ and the reading from detector 2 is

14 counts $(32 - 18 = 14)$. On the first day, the reading from detector 1 was 41 counts $(53 - 12 = 41)$ and the reading from detector 2 was 120 counts $(138 - 18 = 120)$. Both of the values recorded after 3 days are slightly less than $\frac{1}{8}$ of the value from the first day. The number of half-lives elapsed can be determined by finding n in the equation $\frac{1}{8} = \left(\frac{1}{2}\right)^{n}$; because n is 3, we know that approximately three half-lives have passed over the course of the 3 days. Therefore, one half-life is equal to approximately one day.

38. B

Detector 1 is unable to detect sample D at its current activity (the measured reading is equal to the background noise from the first trial), so there is no indication that the radiation from the sample will be adequate to ionize the particles in detector 1 if the activity is increased. Detector 2, however, can effectively detect sample D at its current activity; therefore, an increase in activity will clearly lead to an increase in the reading.

PASSAGE V

39. A

The normal force opposes the force of the object on the surface. Thus, the normal force should be drawn perpendicular to the surface of the incline and directed outward. Choice (B) indicates a force perpendicular to the surface, but it is facing into the incline, suggesting that this is the force exerted on the incline by the block. Choices (C) and (D) indicate a component of the force of gravity acting on the block and force of friction, respectively.

40. D

Because of the orientation of the force vectors for an object on an incline, the cosine function should be used to determine this force. We want to use $\cos 45° \times 2M \times g$ to obtain the normal force, and (D) is correct. (C) assumes that a sine function is used to determine the force.

41. C

The force due to friction is equal to the normal force multiplied by the coefficient of friction (static in this case). Thus, to obtain the force of friction we must first calculate the normal force. Because the surface is flat, $F_N = mg = 2$ kg $\times$ 10 m/s^2 = 20 N. This normal force is then multiplied by the coefficient of static friction: 20 N $\times$ 1.2 = 24 N. This is the force of friction that must be overcome in order to move the object. Choice (A) ignores gravity and units by using the mass of the block instead of its weight. Choice (B) is simply the coefficient of static friction.

42. A

For this question you simply need to remember the formula for gravitational force: $F_g = G(m_1 m_2)/D^2$. Now just plug in the variables you are given to derive the formula $(4GM^2)/D^2$. Choice (C) neglects the mass of the second sphere, and Choice (D) does not square the distance between the two spheres.

43. D

Looking at the formula again, $F_g = G(m_1 m_2)/D^2$, we see that the force is inversely proportional to the square of the distance. Therefore, if we alter the distance from D to $4D$, we will change the value of the denominator from D^2 to $16D^2$. That means the force will be decreased by a factor of 16.

44. D

The equation for gravitational force does not include diameter or density $F_g = G(m_1 m_2)/D^2$. If the changes made do not affect the mass of the sphere or the position of its center, then the gravitational force will remain the same between the two spheres.

45. A

Here you simply need to add the two force vectors to get a net result. Because the forces are acting in opposite directions, you must subtract the smaller quantity from the larger one to obtain 42 N. Since the force in the upward direction is greater than that in the downward direction, the overall direction of the force is up and (A) is correct. Choices (B) and (D) both feature the sum of the two vectors without accounting for the direction. Choice (C) correctly states the magnitude but gives the opposite direction.

46. B

To find the gravitational acceleration of a planet on an object that is on its surface, you can use $g = \dfrac{Gm}{r^2}$, where m is the mass of the planet and r is the radius of the planet. If we plug in $8M$ for mass and $2D$ for radius, we get $(8GM)/4D^2$. Choice (A) uses the diameter instead of the radius.

PASSAGE VI

47. D

From the diagram of the flow meter, the direction of the magnetic field is determined to be from right to left (leaving north pole, entering south). Knowing the direction of blood/electrolyte flow and applying the right-hand rule for the negative charge, we determine the direction of magnetic force to be down, perpendicular to both the magnetic field and electrolytes' velocity.

48. A

If the radius is cut in half, the cross-sectional area will be cut in four. According to the continuity formula, $A_1 v_1 = A_2 v_2$, if the area is cut in four, the velocity must quadruple. As for voltage, $V = Ed$, so decreasing the radius by half will decrease both diameter and voltage by half.

49. C

Remember that $F = qvB$. The ions in the passage that are being measured are univalent. However, calcium is bivalent with a 2+ positive charge. Thus, when the charge goes up, the magnetic field must decrease to maintain a constant magnetic force. In other words, the charge and magnetic field are inversely related. The correct answer is (C).

50. D

Applying the right-hand rule for both ions, we can determine that for both positive and negative electrolytes, magnetic force is perpendicular to both the magnetic field and velocity. The most important thing to remember when assessing the direction of current is that it is opposite the direction of electron flow. Using this, and knowing the direction of the magnetic field, you can determine the direction of force. It will always be perpendicular to both magnetic field and current.

51. B

There is no net magnetic force on the particles moving from left to right as they move parallel/antiparallel to magnetic field lines. The torque is indeed present, unlike what is stated in (A) and (C), as the particles would be rotating in the uniform magnetic field at the given direction of magnetic field and particle movement.

52. B

According to Ohm's law $I = \dfrac{V}{R}$. We know from the passage that, at equilibrium, $E = vB$ and $V = Ed = vBd$. Thus, $I = \dfrac{vBd}{R} = \dfrac{(25 \times 10^{-2})(1)(2 \times 10^{-2})}{3} = 17 \times 10^{-4} = 1.7 \times 10^{-5}$A.

PRACTICE SECTION 3

ANSWER KEY

1.	A	19.	C	37.	A
2.	A	20.	A	38.	C
3.	B	21.	B	39.	C
4.	A	22.	A	40.	C
5.	B	23.	D	41.	B
6.	D	24.	C	42.	B
7.	C	25.	C	43.	D
8.	A	26.	C	44.	C
9.	A	27.	C	45.	D
10.	C	28.	B	46.	C
11.	D	29.	B	47.	B
12.	A	30.	A	48.	D
13.	D	31.	D	49.	C
14.	B	32.	C	50.	D
15.	D	33.	A	51.	D
16.	A	34.	A	52.	C
17.	C	35.	B		
18.	B	36.	C		

PASSAGE I

1. A

Based on the equations $P = IV$ and $P = I^2R$, we can tell that power is related to current, voltage, and resistance. The passage states that the battery supplies a constant 12 V of potential, which cannot be increased without the addition of another battery, so item II is incorrect. Item III is incorrect because, although increased resistance would cause the amplifier to *dissipate* more power, the question asks how the amplifier *produces* more power. Therefore, only the current (item I) can be increased by the amplifier.

2. A

The capacitance can be determined by using the formula $C = \dfrac{Q}{V}$, where Q is charge and V is voltage. We also know that $Q = It$, where I is current and t is time, so we can conclude that $C = \dfrac{It}{V}$. The question states that I equals 2 A and t equals 12 seconds, while the passage states that V equals 12 V; therefore, $C = \dfrac{(2\text{A})(12\text{ s})}{12\text{V}} = 2\text{F}$.

3. B

A wire will be more effective if it minimizes resistance, which is directly proportional to resistivity and inversely proportional to the square of the radius. Remember that resistance can be calculated as $R = \dfrac{\rho L}{A}$. Since length is constant in the question, we're asked to minimize the ratio $\dfrac{\rho}{A}$. Cross-sectional area is just πr^2, so we want to minimize $\dfrac{\rho}{r^2}$ (we can ignore π in this case because it is a constant). Plugging in, we get a resistance proportional to 16 for silver, 7 for aluminum, 7.5 for copper, and 24 for gold. Of the four options, the aluminum wire has the smallest ratio of resistivity to the square of the radius.

4. A

Power dissipation can be determined by the formula $P = I^2R$, so it will be decreased if resistance is decreased. This can be accomplished if the speakers are wired in parallel, in which case the reciprocal of the circuit's resistance $\left(\dfrac{1}{R}\right)$ is equal to the sum of the reciprocals of the individual resistances. In this case, this means that $\dfrac{1}{R} = \dfrac{1}{4} + \dfrac{1}{4} + \dfrac{1}{4} + \dfrac{1}{4} + \dfrac{1}{4} + \dfrac{1}{4} = \dfrac{3}{2}\Omega$, so $R = \dfrac{2}{3}\Omega$.

5. B

The purpose of a capacitor is to store charge. It is placed after the battery so that it can provide an extra burst of current whenever the amplifier needs it. If it was placed after the amplifier, the current from the capacitor would not take advantage of the amplifier's ability to increase the power delivered.

6. D

According to the passage, the voltage source is much higher in magnitude for home systems than for automotive systems. This means that to produce the same amount of power, the automotive system would need to draw more current in order to make up for its lack of potential.

7. C

Home amplifiers extract their power from a 110 V emf, while automotive amplifiers can use only a 12 V emf. Because current is directly proportional to electric potential (voltage), the home amplifier can easily acquire all of the necessary current. Capacitance is inversely proportional to electric potential, so the components in a home system (which has more electric potential) are actually less likely to function as a capacitor (A). There is no indication that the power outlet stores charge (B); in fact, it acquires its charge from the power lines outside. Not all car systems include capacitors as per the passage (D), so it is clear that an amplifier can function without a capacitor. Also, be careful of answer (D). Even if it were true, it doesn't quite answer the question. Telling us that automotive systems require a capacitor doesn't *really* tell us *why* capacitors are less useful in home systems. This kind of logical flaw shows up frequently on the MCAT—especially in Verbal Reasoning!

8. A

The easiest way to answer this question is by eliminating the incorrect options. Choices (C) and (D) are incorrect because the ratio of the peak current to the RMS current in an AC circuit is equal to approximately 1.41, which is far from the ratio of 14 V to 12 V. Choice (B) is incorrect because an RMS current only applies to AC circuits, whose average potential

is always equal to zero. DC circuits can, however, experience fluctuations that will affect the exact value of the voltage.

9. A

The current of a circuit can be determined by the formula $V = IR$. Because the resistances are identical, the current must be higher for the system with a higher voltage (the home system). Power is directly proportional to current and voltage, so the home amplifier will consume much more power and, consequently, much more energy.

PASSAGE II

10. C

The passage states that both types of electroscopes function primarily through electrostatic induction. It also mentions that the mechanism of action of the instruments involves the movement of electrons to different locations within any given atom. This is an example of a redistribution of charge.

11. D

According to the passage, a positively charged object pushes protons toward the opposite side of the pith ball, causing the electrons to propel the ball toward the object. A negatively charged object, therefore, will push electrons to the opposite side of the ball. This would mean that the protons are near the test object, which would cause an attractive force.

12. A

A pith ball becomes charged when it is touched by a charged object. When this object is negatively charged, the ball will also gain a negative charge and will be repelled from the object. The second ball will then receive some of the charge from the first ball, causing a repulsive force between the two balls.

13. D

All three items are correct. An object will always move at a constant velocity unless it is acted upon by an external force. In this case, the attraction of the pith ball and the repulsion of the gold leaves are caused by an electrostatic force. In addition, the gold-leaf electroscope requires electric conduction from the ball to the leaves. Finally, electrostatic force is produced by an electric field.

14. B

The pith ball moves as a result of an electrostatic force. Because force is directly proportional to mass and acceleration, a decrease in mass will lead to an increase in acceleration. A heavier pith ball may be too heavy to move as a result of the electrostatic force. The electrons move within an atom, so the number of atoms (A) is irrelevant. Choices (C) and (D) are simply false; there is no trend relating conductivity to weight.

15. D

Pith is an electrical insulator. Gold, silver, and copper are all electrical conductors. An insulator would be unable to absorb the charge conducted through the brass rod.

16. A

For a negatively charged object, the electric field points in the direction opposite that of the electrostatic force. Because the charged object will attract the pith ball, the electrostatic force must be pointing to the right; that means the electric field points to the left.

17. C

Choice (C) is the only item that does not accurately describe the gold leaf interaction. A dipole moment is defined as a pair of charges with opposite sign and equal magnitude. The two gold leaves in the electroscope have charges with the same sign, so they do not form a dipole moment. Electrostatic repulsion (A) is the reason why the leaves spread apart. The charge is conducted from the metal ball through the brass rod and distributed around the gold leaf; this redistribution (B) is the reason for the electrostatic force. An electrostatic force is produced by an electric field (D).

QUESTIONS 18–22

18. B

The total energy of the object is conserved. When the object is dropped, it only has potential energy, which is mgh. Right before the object hits the ground, it has only kinetic energy, which is $\frac{1}{2}mv^2$. Thus, $mgh = \frac{1}{2}mv^2$, and so $v^2 = 2gh = 100 \text{ m}^2/\text{s}^2$, and $v = 10$ m/s.

19. C

In this question, we are given the initial velocity and acceleration. The final velocity, logically, is zero. What kinematics equation relates the initial and final velocity, and the acceleration to displacement? $v_f^2 = v_i^2 + 2ax$. Plugging in our values, we find that $0 = 100 \text{ m}^2/\text{s}^2 - (4 \text{ m/s}^2)(x)$. Remember that a deceleration corresponds to a negative acceleration. Solving, we get $x = 25$ m. The road block is 30 m away when the car starts braking, and so the car misses the road block by 5 m.

20. A

For circuits in parallel, the equation is $\frac{1}{R_P} = \frac{1}{R_1} + \frac{1}{R_2}$, so for two 6 ohm circuits, the total resistance is 3 ohms. For circuits in series, the equation is $R_S = R_1 + R_2$, so the total resistance is 12 ohms. Overall then, the total resistance increases by a factor of 4.

21. B

The linear momentum is conserved. Before the collision, assuming north is positive, total momentum is $m_1v_1 + m_2v_2 = (100 \text{ kg}) \text{ 5 m/s} (-) 150 \text{ kg (3 m/s)} = 50$ kg·m/s north. Because this is a perfectly inelastic collision, the total momentum after the collision is $(m_1 + m_2)v$, and this equals 50 kg·m/s north. Thus, $(100 \text{ kg} + 150 \text{ kg})v = 50$ kg·m/s, and so $v = 0.2$ m/s north.

22. A

If two waves are in phase, constructive interference takes place, and the amplitude of the resultant wave is the sum of the amplitudes of the interfering waves. In this case, the resultant amplitude is $A_1 + A_1 = 2 A_1$.

PASSAGE III

23. D

First, we must know that (A) can't be correct: the pull of the string on the stone is centripetal, not centrifugal force. The expression for centripetal force is $F_c = \dfrac{mv^2}{R}$, leading us to (D) as the correct answer.

24. C

There is a lot of unnecessary information here, included just to annoy and confuse you. If you stick to basics though, you'll realize that horizontal motion has nothing to do with vertical motion. This is basically a projectile motion question. (Though it mentions the shot put, which would be projectile motion with an angle for the initial velocity, in this case the ball is projected horizontally and no arclike motion is observed.) Remembering our basic principles of projectile motion, acceleration is 0 m/s² in the horizontal direction and constant in the vertical direction. Acceleration will always be g, which for our purposes equals 10 m/s². Choice (A) might be your selection had you used $a = \dfrac{v}{t}$, where $v_i = 30$ m/s, $v_f = 0$ m/s, and $t = 7$ s. Choice (B) is half of g and included to make the question more challenging. Choice (D) might be your selection if you had used a one-dimensional motion equation, $x - x_0 = v_0 t + \dfrac{at^2}{2}$. Here, $x - x_0$ is 1,000, v_0 is 30 m/s, and $t = 7$.

25. C

Gathering our facts for this situation, we see that all the required information is provided from the question stem and from the passage. However, the information in the passage might not be necessary. The question only has to do with horizontal motion, as it asks for a distance. We know, then, that we need to find the horizontal component of the given speed. Using the cosine function, we find the following:

$$v_x = v_i \cos \theta$$
$$= (45 \text{ m/s})(\cos 45°)$$
$$= 31.82 \text{ m/s (approx.)}$$

The more complicated kinematics equations aren't necessary here; we can simply work with $v = \dfrac{x}{t}$. Substituting our values, we get the distance traveled to be 63.6, choice (C).

26. C

More firearms work by way of creating explosions, not by using springs. However, this question is theoretical. You might first think you haven't been given enough information, but the passage provided a great deal. You're being asked about spring constants, and there are only a few things required to figure that out. We know here that the loss of potential energy of the spring is equal to the gain in kinetic energy of the bullet. The bullet itself is released from the spring when it is at its equilibrium point. So we have the following:

$$U = K$$
$$\frac{1}{2}kx^2 = \frac{1}{2}mv^2$$
$$k(0.01 \text{ m})^2 = (0.050 \text{ kg})(500 \text{ m/s})^2$$
$$k = 1.25 \times 10^8 \text{ N/m}$$

Notice that we use only variables x, m, and v, and we need to convert m and x to the necessary units.

27. C

In this situation, momentum must be conserved. We know that $p = mv$ and that initially, total momentum is 0. For this reason, we know that the final momenta of each skater must be equal in magnitude and opposite in direction. In other words, they must add up to zero. Using variables, we have $m_1 v_1 = m_2 v_2$. Rearranging, we have $\dfrac{v_1}{v_2} = \dfrac{m_2}{m_1} = \dfrac{45}{67}$.

28. B

To get average speed, we use v = total distance/total time. We know from the passage that the length of the race is 400 m. To get the total time, calculate the time for each part of the race using $t = \dfrac{x}{v}$. For the first 40% = (0.40)(400 m) = 160 m of the race, we have $t = \dfrac{160 \text{ m}}{10 \text{ m/s}} = 16$ s. For the remaining 240 m of the race, we have $t = \dfrac{240 \text{ m}}{5 \text{ m/s}} = 48$ s. So our original equation becomes $v = \dfrac{400 \text{ m}}{16 \text{ s} + 48 \text{ s}} = 6.25$ m/s. Had you averaged 10 m/s and 5 m/s, you would have gotten (A). Had you switched around the percentages, you would have gotten (D).

29. B

We are not provided with much information here, but we can still determine our answer. All we need is the following equation: $v_f^2 = v_i^2 + 2ax$. So $(0) + (2) (-10 \text{ m/s}^2)(-2.5 \text{ m})$ $= 50$. You'll need to know the square root of 50. Thus, v_f is approximately 7 m/s. Another strategy would be to consider the conservation of energy. All of the potential energy from the jumper's height off the ground would be converted to kinetic energy as he nears the ground. Thus, $mgh = \frac{1}{2}mv^2$, or $2gh = v^2$. Plugging in, we again get that the final velocity should be close to 7 m/s.

30. A

This is a trick question that can yield easy points. You're given a lot of information and might be tempted to look back at the passage for details, but all you need to consider is the word *displacement*, a net change in position for the object in question. The athlete has completed round-trips, so you can assume she ends her exercise where she began it. This would mean that she hasn't changed her position at all, and the answer is (A). Choice (D) is definitely incorrect because she is swimming at constant speed. Acceleration in that case would be 0 m/s².

PASSAGE IV

31. D

Know the formula for frequency in simple harmonic motion. Frequency is the number of cycles per second, whereas the period is the number of seconds needed to complete one cycle. This question asks for the frequency, so we need to use $f = \frac{1}{2\pi}\sqrt{\frac{k}{m}}$. Because we're asked about one-quarter of the cycle, we have to divide our answer by 4, which is (D). Choice (A) is the number of cycles for one full second. Choices (B) and (C) are incorrect because initial inspection shows that the locations of k and m are inverted.

32. C

Maximum velocity will be achieved when the kinetic energy of the system is greatest. Because the sum of kinetic and potential energy is always constant, the potential energy is zero when the kinetic energy is maximized. Looking at the

given formula, this reduces to $\frac{1}{2}kA^2 = \frac{1}{2}mv^2_{max}$. If you rearrange the terms to isolate v, you end up with the expression in (C). Choices (A) and (D) are incorrect because there is no "2" term in the equation.

33. A

Only item I is correct. The question asks you to clarify the relationship of amplitude, mass, spring constant, and gravity. $v_{max} = A\sqrt{\frac{k}{m}}$, so if we rearrange, we get $A = v_{max}\sqrt{\frac{m}{k}}$. Now we have an equation that shows the relationship between amplitude, mass, and spring constant. Notice that gravity has no effect because we are conducting this experiment on a horizontal table. Because m is in the numerator, amplitude and mass are directly related. Because k is in the denominator, amplitude and the spring constant are inversely related, and increasing k would decrease amplitude.

34. A

Only item II is correct. Amplitude is just the maximum displacement of a system. If you stretched a block to 2 meters and let it oscillate, the block's amplitude would be 2 meters. If the friction is introduced, this may dampen the oscillation by releasing energy in the form of heat and thus decrease the amplitude. (Item I is incorrect.) If the spring is oscillating and you push it as it is compressing, you can see that the energy introduced will be incorporated by the spring, and it will oscillate with a greater amplitude. (Item II is correct.) The length of the spring has no impact on amplitude, somewhat counter intuitively; all measurements are taken from the equilibrium position of the block and the displacement of the block from that position. (Item III is incorrect.) Consider the fact that amplitude depends only on how far the block is displaced from equilibrium. Even if the spring itself is longer, as long as we displace it the same amount as before, it will oscillate with the same amplitude.

35. B

This is the perfect occasion for using Hooke's law because it incorporates all of the variables into one simple equation, $F = kx$, where x is the maximum displacement. In this case, the maximum displacement is equal to the amplitude because the block cannot oscillate at a greater displacement than the initial displacement unless an external force is applied. So we get $x_B = \dfrac{F_B}{k}$, which is equal to 1.5 m. Repeating the calculation for block C, we get $x_C = 2$ m. This leaves only (B) and (D). Any time you see "acceleration" on the MCAT, think "force" (and vice-versa)! The maximum acceleration can be calculated through Newton's second law: $F = ma$. The maximum acceleration will occur at the point with maximum force, and the maximum force must be equal to the applied force in these trials. Thus, $a_{max} = \dfrac{F_{applied}}{m}$. Plugging in for each block, we get $a_B = 75$ m/s² and $a_C = 40$ m/s². Thus, (B) is correct.

36. C

The graph shows that block has its greatest velocity at the beginning. This occurs when it is at the equilibrium position, so we can eliminate (A) and (D). At the ends, the block comes to a rest and the restoring force pulls/pushes it back. Notice that the velocity changes from negative to positive across 0.25 seconds. This means that the direction is changing, so the block must be reversing. This leaves (C).

37. A

The block has a velocity of zero only when the spring is fully compressed or extended, that is, at the ends of its range of displacement. You can visualize that at these points, the spring wants to jerk the block back toward the equilibrium position, so it is at its maximum acceleration. Mathematically, this can be modeled through Hooke's law and Newton's second law. Hooke's Law says that $F = kx$, and Newton's second law says that $F = ma$. Thus, $kx = ma$. Since both the spring constant (k) and mass (m) are constant, x and a are directly proportional. Thus, at the maximum displacement (at the amplitude), the acceleration is maximized. If the spring is extended, the acceleration will point to the left (see Figure 1), leaving choice (A).

PASSAGE V

38. C

The number of neutrons in a given isotope is determined by subtracting the number of protons in the nucleus from the number of nucleons: $N = A - Z = 236 - 92 = 144$ neutrons for $^{236}_{92}U$. Not realizing that the question refers to the intermediate product would lead us to the other answer choices.

39. C

The amount of untouched naturally occurring weapons-grade uranium, $^{235}_{92}U$, has decreased due to radioactivity by more than a factor of two because the age of the Earth is more than the half-life of this isotope. Half-life is defined as the time it takes for half of the original amount a given radioactive isotope to decay.

40. C

The amount of a radioactive sample decreases exponentially. Here, 11,260 years is equal to two times 5,630 years, which is the half-life for $^{14}_{6}C$. This means that one quarter of the original sample [(0.25)(200 g) = 50 g] will remain after two half-lives.

41. B

The radioactive decay rate, also called the activity, decreases exponentially, just like the amount of a radioactive sample. After one half-life, 5,630 years, the decay rate will be half of the initial value, or 2,000/2 = 1,000 counts/s.

42. B

β decay is defined as the emission of an electron by a nucleus. Equation 2 shows this sort of emission, so it clearly represents a β decay. An anti-neutrino is also emitted in the decay, and has no mass or charge.

43. D

A neutron is converted into a proton, an electron, and an anti-neutrino during the β decay of $^{14}_{6}C$.

44. C

Assuming 15 decays per minute per gram of carbon, a 100-gram sample would initially have a decay rate of 1,500 decays per minute when the organism dies. If the decay rate is currently 187.5 decays per minute, that means that the organism died three half-lives ago, or 3(5,630 years) = 16,890 years ago.

PASSAGE VI

45. D

Critical angles are only a consideration when light moves from a medium of higher index of refraction into a medium of a lower index. In outer space, the originating medium is a vacuum for which the index of refraction is infinity. Had we used the equation for critical angles, $\sin\theta_c = \dfrac{n_2}{n_1} = \dfrac{n_{glass}}{n_{vacuum}}$, we would have gotten a number greater than 1 (and the sine of an angle can never be greater than 1). This might have tempted us to choose (A) over (D). Had we flipped this, however, we would have seen that $\sin\theta_c$ was 0.5 and that θ_c was 30°. Remember, though, that since the question tells us that a laser beam in space was pointed toward the glass block, this critical angle would refer to light *inside* the block, crossing the boundary into the vacuum of space. Choice (D) is indeed the answer, as no critical angle would exist. Total internal reflection cannot occur.

46. C

Although the lenses touch, this should be considered a multiple-lens system. For such a system, there is one very helpful equation from our arsenal of optics equations: $\dfrac{1}{f} = \dfrac{1}{f_1} + \dfrac{1}{f_2}\ldots$ The question is mathematically quite simple after we realize these few points. Our objective is f, because we have f_1 and f_2. We have the focal length of the original, 57.5 m. Ten percent of this is 5.75, or $\dfrac{23}{4}$. The inverse of that is $\dfrac{4}{23}$ and we double this to get $\dfrac{8}{23}$. Setting this equal to $\dfrac{1}{f}$, we find that f is about 2.9 m. Mathematical errors along the way or assuming the focal length of one lens to be sufficient would produce (D). Forgetting to set $\dfrac{8}{23} = \dfrac{1}{f}$ and instead setting it equal to f would produce 0.3 m (B). Using negative focal lengths (A) would give us the negative of our correct answer, and this is incorrect when using converging lenses.

47. B

The relationship between wavelength and frequency is inverse; a wave with a high frequency must have a small wavelength and vice versa. Though we might not know the entire order

of the visible spectrum, we can still make some headway with these options. If we know that wavelength decreases in the order of ROYGBIV, we know that red has the longest wavelength of the visible spectrum. Also recall that infrared light falls right next to red visible light and that it has a higher wavelength. On the other side, ultraviolet light lays next to violet light, which has a smaller wavelength. You should be familiar with the general fact that x-rays are very high-energy waves. The relationship between energy and frequency is direct ($E = hf$) and thus it is inverse between energy and wavelength. We can then say that the order of these waves, from the smallest wavelength, is x-rays, UV, visible, then infrared light.

48. D

This question is a bit time consuming because it requires you to sketch some graphs. Items II and IV are correct. We know that for an object starting from rest and moving with constant acceleration, $a = \dfrac{v}{t}$. Because Graph A reflects speed versus time, we know that the slope of the line is acceleration. We're told that acceleration is constant, so the line representing speed versus time will be straight. However, we know that acceleration is not zero and so item I is incorrect. Next, for distance, we can look to one of our one-dimensional motion equations: $x - x_0 = v_0 t + \dfrac{1}{2}at^2$. The equation shows us that the relationship between distance and time is parabolic and symmetrical about the x-axis. Distance is constantly decreasing. We know, then, that item IV is correct.

49. C

Only item IV is incorrect. Acceleration is the same for all falling objects. Even though acceleration may be different at this height above the Earth's surface, it will affect the two objects identically (as long as we can neglect air resistance). Item I is correct. Next, $v = at$ tells us that the speed of a falling object starting from rest is proportional to the acceleration and the time of fall. These values have nothing to do with the mass of the object. Therefore, item II is correct. Items III and IV differentiate potential energy. Recalling the formula $U = mgh$, in this case g and h are identical for the two objects, though mass is of some consequence. Because potential energy and mass are proportional, the hammer—with greater mass—will have greater potential energy.

50. D

There are several ways to go about this problem. One is to make a graph of the known values. With a graph indicating velocity versus time, we could find the area under the graph. Another way is to use the average speed (we can only do this because acceleration is constant). We simply multiply the average speed by the time traveled. To get the average speed, we add the initial speed to the final speed and divide by 2. We're told the speed has decreased by 10 percent, but what was the speed to begin with? This speed was provided in the passage and we can quickly refer back for this number: 7,500 m/s. When this decreases by 10 percent, we have a new speed of 6,750 m/s. This would give us an average speed of 7,125 m/s, or simply a reduction of 5 percent overall. Stopping here would produce (B), which is an incorrect answer. Multiplying this by 5 seconds, we get that the distance covered is 35,625 m. Dividing would produce (A). Using 6,750 m/s here instead would produce (C).

51. D

While we might be relieved that the passage provides the speed of the telescope, this is not the speed with which we're concerned. In fact, this is only the initial horizontal velocity. Rather, an object falls under the influence of gravity and its descent is not affected by this value. We use the equation $x - x_0 = v_0 t + \frac{1}{2}at^2$. We do not completely dismiss the passage, because we need Hubble's height, 600 km. Plugging this in, we get $600,000 \text{ m} = (0 \text{ m/s})(t) + \frac{1}{2}(10 \text{ m/s}^2)(t^2)$, and $t^2 = 120,000 \text{ s}^2$. Though it would be difficult to know the value of t right off the bat, it is safe at this point to choose from the given answer choices. The only value that comes close is 346 s, or 5 minutes and 46 seconds. Failing to convert km to m would have given you (A), about 11 seconds. Of course, carrying units would prevent that mistake. Using $a = \frac{v}{t}$ would have given you 60 s (1 min), choice (B).

52. C

The concave spherical mirror identified in the passage will be of most help here. Though the equation $1/o + 1/i = 1/f$ might guide you here, you should also be able to visualize the actual rays that produce the images whose distances and heights we calculate. This question tests that ability. First, we must realize that incident rays parallel to the axis of a concave mirror will converge on the focal point. This will be the case for all parallel rays. If we imagine that a certain source of light is producing these rays, a ray that goes through the focal point would reflect back through the focal point. A ray that travels straight to the center of curvature will return back at the same angle as the original ray, with the incident ray *above* the horizontal and refracted ray *below* the horizontal. A reflected ray would not travel normal, or perpendicular, to the axis, so (A) is out. Due to the curvature of the mirror, it would not travel parallel either. This would happen with a plane mirror. Choice (B) is out as well. Choice (C) is the focal length of 57.6 m given in the passage, and (D) uses $2f$ as a value. Knowing that all parallel rays will converge at the focus, we choose (C) over (D).

Glossary

Absolute pressure The actual pressure.

Acceleration A vector quantity; the time-rate of change in velocity.

Adiabatic A process in which heat flows neither into nor out of a system.

Alternating current A current that changes directions periodically, often in a sinusoidal fashion.

Alpha (α) particle A helium ($_2^4$He) nucleus.

Amplitude The maximum displacement from an equilibrium position; the magnitude of the maximum disturbance in a wave.

Antinode Points of maximum amplitude in a standing wave.

Archimedes' principle A body immersed in fluid experiences an upward buoyant force equal to the weight of the displaced fluid.

Atomic mass The mass of an atom of an element in amu (atomic mass units).

Atomic mass unit (amu) One-twelfth $\left(\frac{1}{12}\right)$ of the mass of the carbon-12 ($_6^{12}$C) atom.

Atomic number The number of protons in a nucleus; this number characterizes each element.

Atomic weight The average mass of an element's atoms—a weighted average of the different isotopes, weighted according to each isotope's naturally occurring abundance.

Beats The sound produced by the alternating constructive and destructive interference between sound waves of slightly different frequencies.

Beta (β) particle An electron; usually refers to one emitted in radioactive beta decay.

Binding energy The energy required to separate an electron from an atom or to completely separate the protons and neutrons in a nucleus.

Buoyant force The upward force felt by a body partially or wholly submerged in a fluid that is equal to the weight of the fluid that the submerged body has displaced (see also *Archimedes' principle*).

Capacitance A measure of the ability of a capacitor to store charge; the absolute value of the magnitude of the charge on one plate divided by the potential difference between the plates.

Capacitor Two conducting surfaces that store equal and opposite charges when connected to a voltage source.

Center of gravity A point such that the entire force of gravity can be thought of as acting at that point. If the acceleration of gravity is constant, then the center of gravity and the center of mass are at the same point.

Center of mass The point that acts as if the entire mass was concentrated at that point.

Centripetal acceleration The acceleration of an object that travels in a circle at a constant speed. The magnitude of the acceleration is equal to the velocity squared divided by the radius of the circle. It is always directed towards the center of the circle. (If the velocity is not constant, there is a second component of acceleration tangent to the circle.)

Centripetal force The force responsible for the centripetal acceleration. Its magnitude is equal to the product of the mass and square of the velocity divided by the radius of the circle. Like centripetal acceleration, it is always directed towards the center of the circle, provided that the velocity of the object is constant.

Conductor A material, such as metal, in which electrons can move relatively freely.

Conservative force A force is conservative if the work done on a particle in any round trip is zero, or if the amount of work done by moving a particle from one position to another is independent of the path taken.

Convection The transfer of heat through the bulk motion of the heated material.

Critical angle The critical angle is the angle of incidence such that the refracted angle is 90° when light goes from a medium with a higher index of refraction into a medium with a lower index of refraction.

Decay constant The proportionality constant between the rate at which radioactive nuclei decay and the number of radioactive nuclei remaining.

Decibel A unit of sound level.

Density Mass per unit volume.

Dielectric A nonconducting material often placed between plates of a capacitor to increase the capacitance.

Diffraction The bending of waves as a result of passing through a slit; the bending of waves around an obstacle.

Diopter A measure of a lens's power, defined as the inverse of the focal length in meters.

Dipole moment A vector whose magnitude is the product of the charge of the dipole and the distance separating the two charges. For physicists, the vector points from the negative charge towards the positive charge (chemists sometimes use the reverse direction).

Dispersion The variation of wave-speed with frequency in a medium; the separation of visible light into its constituent colors (for example, by a prism) as a result of this variation.

Displacement A vector quantity; the straight-line distance and direction going from some initial position to some final position.

Doppler effect The change in frequency of a wave as a result of the motion of the source and/or observer along the line joining them.

Electric current The net charge per unit time passing through a given cross section; by convention, the direction is that in which positive charge would flow.

Electric dipole Two equal and opposite electric charges separated by a small distance.

Electric field The electrical force on a stationary positive test charge divided by the charge.

Electric potential The work needed to move a positive test charge from infinity to a given point in an electric field divided by the charge. The electric potential can also be considered the electric potential energy per unit charge.

Electromagnetic wave A transverse wave of changing electric and magnetic fields.

Electromagnetic spectrum The full range in frequency and wavelength of all electromagnetic waves.

Electromotive force The voltage across the terminals of a cell or battery when no current is flowing.

Energy The ability to do work.

Entropy The measure of a system's disorder.

Equilibrium See *Rotational equilibrium, Translational equilibrium.*

Excited state An atom in which an electron occupies an energy state above the minimum energy state or ground state; a nucleus that is in an energy level above its ground state energy level.

Field line A technique used to better visualize electric or magnetic field patterns. The tangent to a field line at any point is the direction of the field itself at that point. The more field lines per unit area, the greater the magnitude of the field.

Fission The splitting of a heavy nucleus into two or more lighter nuclei accompanied by the release of energy.

Fluorescence A process in which certain substances emit visible light when excited by other radiation, usually ultraviolet radiation.

Focal length The distance from a mirror or lens to the focal point.

Focal point The point at which rays of light parallel to the optic axis converge or appear to diverge from when reflected from a mirror or refracted by a lens.

Frequency The number of cycles per second; the number of wavelengths of a traveling sinusoidal wave passing a fixed point per second.

Friction The force that two surfaces in contact exert on each other in a direction parallel to their surfaces and opposite to their motion.

Fundamental frequency The lowest frequency at which a standing wave can be produced on or in a body.

Fusion The combining of lighter nuclei into a heavier nucleus accompanied by the release of energy.

Gamma (γ) radiation High-energy photons, often emitted in radioactive decay.

Gauge pressure The difference between the absolute pressure and atmospheric pressure.

Gravity A fundamental force of attraction between all matter. Its magnitude is directly proportional to the product of the masses and inversely proportional to the square of the distance between their centers.

Ground state The lowest energy state of an atom or nucleus.

Half-life The time in which one-half of the radioactive nuclei that were originally present decay.

Heat The energy that is transferred between two objects as a result of a difference in temperature.

Heat conduction The transfer of heat energy through a body without bulk motion of the material within the body.

Impulse A vector quantity; the force acting on an object multiplied by the time the force acts; also the change of momentum of an object.

Index of refraction The ratio of the speed of light in a vacuum to the speed of light in a medium.

Inertia An object's resistance to a change in its motion when a force is applied.

Insulator A material in which electrons do not move freely.

Intensity The average rate per unit area of energy transported by a wave across a perpendicular surface.

Interference The combined effects of two waves—*constructive* when the waves are in phase, *destructive* when they are out of phase.

Isobaric A process in which the pressure of a system remains constant.

Isothermal A process in which the temperature of a system remains constant.

Isotopes Atoms of a given element whose nuclei have the same number of protons but a different number of neutrons and, therefore, have the same atomic number but different mass numbers.

Kinetic energy The energy a body has as a result of its motion.

Line of force See *Field line*.

Longitudinal wave A wave in which the oscillation is parallel to the direction of propagation.

Magnetic field A magnetic property associated with a point; the maximum magnetic force on a moving positive test charge divided by its charge and its velocity.

Mass A measure of a body's inertia.

Mass defect The difference between the sum of the masses of neutrons and protons forming a nucleus and the mass of that nucleus.

Mass number The total number of protons and neutrons in the nucleus of an atom.

Momentum A vector quantity; mass times velocity.

Node Points where the displacement of a standing wave remains zero at all times.

Normal In optics, the normal is a line drawn perpendicular to the boundary between two media.

Normal force The force that two surfaces in contact exert on each other in a direction perpendicular (normal) to the area of contact.

Nucleon A component of the nucleus, either a proton or neutron.

Pascal's principle The pressure applied to an enclosed fluid is transmitted undiminished to every portion of the fluid and to the walls of the vessel containing the fluid.

Period The time necessary to complete one cycle.

Polarized light Light that has all of its electric field vectors parallel.

Positron Antiparticle of an electron; it has the same mass as an electron and a charge that is equal to the charge of an electron in magnitude but opposite in sign (i.e., positive).

Potential difference The difference in electrical potential between two distinct points; the work needed to move a unit positive charge between two points.

Potential energy The energy that a body has as a result of its position when a conservative force is acting on it.

Power The time-rate at which work is done or energy is transferred.

Pressure Force per unit area.

Quantum A discrete bundle of energy, such as a photon (particle of light).

Radiation The transfer of energy by electromagnetic waves.

Resonance The phenomena in which an oscillatory system absorbs, with extremely high efficiency, the energy transmitted by an external oscillatory force having a frequency equal to one of the system's natural frequencies.

Reflection The change in direction of a wave at the boundary of a medium when the wave remains in the medium.

Refraction The change in direction of a wave as it passes obliquely through a boundary from one medium to another.

Resistance A characteristic property of a conductor, which measures the opposition to current flowing through it; the ratio of the voltage applied to a conductor and the current that results.

Resistivity A measure of the intrinsic resistance of a material independent of its shape or size.

rms current The maximum current divided by the square root of 2; used to measure the current in an AC circuit in lieu of the average current, which is zero.

Rotation The turning of an extended body about an axis or center; change in orientation.

Rotational equilibrium The condition in which the sum of the torques acting on a body is zero; also called the *second condition of equilibrium.*

Scalar A quantity that has a magnitude but not a direction; an ordinary number.

Simple harmonic motion Periodic motion about an equilibrium position resulting from a linear restoring force.

Sound level Ten times the logarithmic ratio of the intensity of a given sound to the intensity of the faintest sound that can be heard by humans.

Specific gravity The ratio of the density of a substance to the density of water.

Specific heat The number of calories needed to raise the temperature of one gram of a substance by 1°C.

Speed A scalar quantity; the instantaneous rate at which distance is being covered by a moving object.

Standing wave A wave with a displacement that appears fixed in space and time. It can be produced when two waves of the same frequency, amplitude, and speed travel in opposite directions.

Superposition principle The resulting displacement of a medium at a point where two or more waves meet is the algebraic sum of the individual displacements of each wave at that point.

Thermal expansion The change in an object's size with a change in temperature. In general, objects expand as the temperature increases.

Torque The magnitude of the force acting on a body times the perpendicular distance between the direction of the force and the point of rotation.

Translation Motion through space without a change in orientation.

Translational equilibrium The condition in which the sum of the forces acting on a body is zero, also called the *first condition of equilibrium.*

Transverse wave A wave in which the oscillation is perpendicular to the direction of propagation.

Vector A quantity that has both magnitude and direction.

Velocity A vector quantity whose magnitude is speed and whose direction is the direction of motion.

Viscosity A fluid's internal resistance to flow.

Wavelength The distance between two corresponding points in successive cycles of a sinusoidal wave; the distance from one crest to the next.

Weight The force of gravity on an object, not to be confused with *mass.*

Work A scalar quantity; the force acting on an object times the distance the object moves times cos θ, where θ is the angle between the force and the direction of motion.

Index